THE EUROPEAN CONVENTION ON HUMAN RIGHTS AND THE EMPLOYMENT RELATION

The accession by the European Union to the European Convention on Human Rights (ECHR) has opened up new possibilities in terms of the constitutional recognition of fundamental rights in the EU. In the field of employment law it heralds a new procedure for workers and trade unions to challenge EU law against the background of the ECHR. In theoretical terms this means that EU law now goes beyond recognition of fundamental rights as mere general principles of EU law, making the ECHR the 'gold standard' for fundamental (social) rights.

This publication of the Transnational Trade Union Rights Working Group focuses on the EU and the interplay between the Strasbourg case law and the case law of the Court of Justice of the European Union (CJEU), analysing the relevance of the ECHR for the protection of workers' rights and for the effective enjoyment of civil and political rights in the employment relation. Each chapter is written by a prominent European human rights expert and analyses the case law of the European Court of Human Rights (ECtHR), and also looks at the equivalent international labour standards within the Council of Europe (in particular the (Revised) European Social Charter), the International Labour Organization (ILO) (in particular the fundamental rights conventions) and the UN Covenants (in particular the International Covenant on Economic, Social and Cultural Rights) and the interpretation of these instruments by competent organs.

The authors also analyse the ways in which the CJEU has acknowledged the respective ECHR articles as 'general principles' of EU law and asks whether the Lisbon Treaty will also warrant a reassessment of the way it has treated conflicts between these 'general principles' and the so-called 'fundamental freedoms'.

The European Convention on Human Rights and the Employment Relation

Edited by

Filip Dorssemont
Klaus Lörcher
and
Isabelle Schömann

etui.

·HART·
PUBLISHING

OXFORD AND PORTLAND, OREGON
2013

Published in the United Kingdom by Hart Publishing Ltd
16C Worcester Place, Oxford, OX1 2JW
Telephone: +44 (0)1865 517530
Fax: +44 (0)1865 510710
E-mail: mail@hartpub.co.uk
Website: http://www.hartpub.co.uk

Published in North America (US and Canada)
by Hart Publishing
c/o International Specialized Book Services
920 NE 58th Avenue, Suite 300
Portland, OR 97213-3786
USA
Tel: +1 503 287 3093 or toll-free: (1) 800 944 6190
Fax: +1 503 280 8832
E-mail: orders@isbs.com
Website: http://www.isbs.com

Hart Publishing is an imprint of Bloomsbury Publishing plc

British Library Cataloguing in Publication Data
Data Available

ISBN: 978-1-84946-338-6

Typeset by Compuscript Ltd, Shannon
Printed and bound in Great Britain by
TJ International Ltd, Padstow

Preface

'All human rights are universal, indivisible and interdependent and interrelated.' This Credo of the Council of Europe, reaffirmed by the Committee of Ministers on the occasion of the 50th Anniversary of the European Social Charter on 12 October 2011, may be considered as the 'leitmotif' of this publication. In particular, the indivisible nature of civil and political rights on the one side and social and cultural rights on the other side can best be expressed by exploring the 'social dimension' of the European Convention on Human Rights (ECHR). Their interdependent and interrelated character can best be demonstrated by the jurisprudence of the European Court of Human Rights (ECtHR), taking into account international and European human rights standards when interpreting the Convention, especially in the social field.

Against this background, 'The European Convention on Human Rights and the Employment Relationship' is the result of a research project directed by the Transnational Trade Union Rights Experts Network (TTUR). Filip Dorssemont, Klaus Lörcher and Isabelle Schömann have coordinated the efforts of the members of the network and the external experts involved. The TTUR network is an independent expert network providing valuable advice to the European Trade Union Institute (ETUI). Founded in 1999 by the late Brian Bercusson, it brings together leading labour law professors from eight Member States with an active interest in the development of EU labour law and ETUI researchers.

At present, the composition of this group is as follows: Niklas Bruun (Stockholm and Helsinki Universities), Klaus Lörcher (former legal secretary at the European Union Civil Service Tribunal), Thomas Blanke (Oldenburg University), Simon Deakin (Cambridge University), Filip Dorssemont (Université Catholique de Louvain), Antoine Jacobs (Tilburg University), Csilla Kollonay-Lehoczky (Central European University, Eötvös Loránd University, Budapest, Hungary), Mélanie Schmitt (University of Strasbourg), Bruno Veneziani (University of Bari) and Isabelle Schömann (ETUI).

On the occasion of this publication, other recognised ECHR specialists have also been invited to contribute. The publication is thus the result of the joint efforts of distinguished and upcoming experts in the fields of labour law and human rights working in a variety of EU Member States.

This book was preceded by two other scientific projects of the TTUR network which gave rise to the following two publications:

B Bercusson, *European Labour Law and the EU Charter of Fundamental Rights* (Baden-Baden, Nomos, 2006).
N Bruun, K Lörcher and I Schömann, *The Lisbon Treaty and Social Europe* (Oxford, Hart Publishing, 2012).

The conceptual approach of these two books, the first two volumes of a trilogy, bears witness to the TTUR's attachment to fundamental rights as a lever for social justice and progress. The present volume, the last of the trilogy, maps the progressive development of human rights within the EU legal order and the increasing relevance of human rights in achieving a more social Europe.

The basic idea behind the book is to highlight the potential of the ECHR when interpreted using the methodology developed in the *Demir and Baykara* unanimous judgment of the Grand Chamber of the ECtHR of late 2008. Alongside looking closely at this approach, the authors were asked not just to analyse ECtHR case law, but also to take account of the equivalent international labour standards within the Council of Europe (in particular the (Revised) European Social Charter), the International Labour Organization (ILO) (in particular the fundamental rights conventions) and the United Nations (UN) (in particular the International Covenant on Economic, Social and Cultural Rights), reviewing how these instruments are interpreted by the competent organs and comparing this with relevant ECtHR case law.

Article 6 of the Treaty on European Union (TEU),[1] as amended by the Lisbon Treaty, articulates the EU's more elaborated human rights architecture. This provision can be unfolded as a triptych. Historically, human rights protection was developed through the case law of the Court of Justice of the European Union (CJEU) referring to the ECHR as a source of the 'general principles' of EU law (*cf* Article 6, § 3 TEU). The classical reference to fundamental rights as mere 'general principles' raises the question whether a reassessment is needed of the way in which the CJEU has treated conflicts between these 'general principles' and the so-called 'fundamental (economic) freedoms'. This provision recognises human rights as a source of *fundamental* principles.

As the second panel of the unfolding triptych, this book gains further momentum from the EU's constitutional obligation (Article 6, § 2 TEU) to accede to the ECHR. But finally and most importantly—and completing the 'triptych'—the TEU sets a minimum level of protection of fundamental rights in recognising that the EU Charter of Fundamental Rights has the same legal value as the Treaties (Article 6 § 1 TEU). This is particularly important with regard to the fundamental social rights enshrined under the 'Solidarity' Title of the Charter. Indeed, the final horizontal provisions of the Charter contain these safeguards by referring twice to the ECHR (*cf* Articles 52(3) and 53 of the Charter).

---

[1] Article 6 TEU:
1. The Union recognises the rights, freedoms and principles set out in the Charter of Fundamental Rights of the European Union of 7 December 2000, as adapted at Strasbourg, on 12 December 2007, which shall have the same legal value as the Treaties.
   The provisions of the Charter shall not extend in any way the competences of the Union as defined in the Treaties.
   The rights, freedoms and principles in the Charter shall be interpreted in accordance with the general provisions in Title VII of the Charter governing its interpretation and application and with due regard to the explanations referred to in the Charter, that set out the sources of those provisions.
2. The Union shall accede to the European Convention for the Protection of Human Rights and Fundamental Freedoms. Such accession shall not affect the Union's competences as defined in the Treaties.
3. Fundamental rights, as guaranteed by the European Convention for the Protection of Human Rights and Fundamental Freedoms and as they result from the constitutional traditions common to the Member States, shall constitute general principles of the Union's law.

The book is the result of two seminars held in Brussels in the winters of 2010 and 2011, where the project itself and its draft chapters were discussed in the presence of external discussants. Both seminars were organised by the *Atelier de Droit social* of the Université Catholique de Louvain on the premises of the Fondation Universitaire of Belgium. They were hosted by Filip Dorssemont with the indispensable assistance of two junior researchers, Auriane Lamine and Marco Rocca. The TTUR network is indebted to the new President of the ECtHR, Judge D Spielmann, for his presence and valuable guidance in the 2010 seminar. The final chapters were submitted in the summer and autumn of 2012. The conclusions were written in the winter of 2012.

The book provides a balanced equilibrium of general chapters elucidating the conceptual background of the research project and chapters providing an in-depth analysis of the *acquis* of Strasbourg case law and the potential of the most relevant provisions of the ECHR with a social dimension. No formal grid was imposed on the authors writing the commentaries, though a common methodology has been respected. The book also contains provisional conclusions relating to the ECHR's impact on individual and collective employment relations. Also elucidating the book's concept, these conclusions can thus be read as an introductory chapter.

The book shows in several ways how the ECHR continues to be a 'living instrument', to be 'interpreted and applied in a manner which renders the guarantees practical and effective and not theoretical and illusory' (to use the ECtHR's standard formulation).

The ETUI would like to thank the authors for their in-depth analysis, which shows how a comprehensive interpretation of fundamental social rights, based on ECtHR case law and underlined by both international standards and the role of the CJEU in upholding the rights enshrined in the ECHR, can contribute to the achievement of a better and more social Europe.

Maria Jepsen
ETUI
Director of the Research Department

Contents

General Part

Analysis of the ECHR

Conclusions

List of Contributors

Niklas Bruun is Professor of Law at Hanken School of Economic in Helsinki. He is also the director of the research program Regulating Markets and Labour (ReMarkLab), Stockholm University, and a member of the Centre of Excellence in the Foundations of European Law and Polity, University of Helsinki.

Olivier De Schutter is Professor of Human Rights Law at the Université catholique de Louvain and at the College of Europe (Natolin). An expert on economic and social rights and economic globalisation, he has since 2008 been the United Nations Special Rapporteur on the right to food.

Filip Dorssemont is Professor of Labour Law at the Centre interdisciplinaire Droit, entreprise et société of the Unversité catholique de Louvain. He teaches as a guest lecturer at the Université Saint-Louis de Bruxelles. He is a member of the ReMarkLab Group.

Frank Hendrickx is Professor of Law at the University of Leuven, the Director of the Institute for Labour Law, and a part-time Chairholder in European labour law at Tilburg University. His research interests include labour and employment law, EU labour law, and sports law. He is the editor in chief of the European Labour Law Journal, and the author of numerous articles and books on Belgian, European, and comparative labour law.

John Hendy QC is a barrister in London specialising in trade union law. He is a visiting professor in the School of Law, Kings College, London; visiting professor in the Faculty of Law, University College, London; President of the International Centre for Trade Union Rights; and Chair of the Institute of Employment Rights.

Patrick Humblet is Professor of Labour Law at the Law Faculty of Ghent University. He teaches as visiting professor at Antwerp Management School and at the Royal Military Academy.

Rick Lawson is Dean of the Law School of Leiden University, the Netherlands, and Professor of European Human Rights Law. His key areas of interest are the case-law and the institutional set-up of the European Court of Human Rights, and the protection of human rights in the EU legal order.

Klaus Lörcher is former Legal Adviser to the European Trade Union Confederation (ETUC) and former Legal Secretary of the Civil Service Tribunal of the European Union.

Virginia Mantouvalou is Reader in Human Rights and Labour Law at University College London (UCL), and Co-Director of the UCL Institute for Human Rights.

Petra Herzfeld Olsson is Associate Professor in Private Law and Senior Lecturer in International Labour Law at the Law Faculty, Uppsala University. She is also member of the ReMarkLab Group.

Aline Van Bever is a research and teaching assistant at the Institute for Labour Law of the University of Leuven. She is writing a PhD concerning the potential role of so-called 'open textured norms', such as good faith, in employment law.

Sébastien Van Drooghenbroeck is Professor of Constitutional Law and Human Rights Law at the Université Saint-Louis de Bruxelles. He is Dean of the Law Faculty and Assessor at the Belgian Council of State.

Isabelle Van Hiel is assistant in the Department of Social Law of the University of Ghent and is currently working on her PhD on freedom of association.

Lucy Vickers is Professor of Law at the School of Law, Oxford Brookes University.

Dirk Voorhoof is Professor of Media Law, Copyright Law and Journalistic Ethics at Ghent University. He teaches European Media Law as a guest lecturer at Copenhagen University. He is a member of the Human Rights Centre and the Centre for Journalism Studies (UGent), focusing on freedom of expression and information, media regulation, human rights and democracy.

Table of Cases

European Court/Commission of Human Rights

Court of Justice of the European Union

Other International Courts/Tribunals

Other International Supervisory Bodies

ILO Freedom of Association Committee

European Committee of Social Rights

National Cases

Belgium

Canada

Denmark

France

Germany

Table of Legislation

Note that, as the entire work concerns the European Convention on Human Rights, only references to specific provisions are included in this Table.

International and European Instruments

National Instruments

Belgium

Canada

Estonia

France

Germany

General Part

1

The New Social Dimension in the Jurisprudence of the European Court of Human Rights (ECtHR): The Demir and Baykara *Judgment, its Methodology and Follow-up*[1]

KLAUS LÖRCHER

Un jour, je l'espère, l'objectif que se rapprochent les droits civils et politiques et les droits économiques et sociaux sera atteint. C'est l'intérêt de tous.
(*Jean Costa*, Former President of the ECtHR, 18 October 2011, on the occasion of the 50th anniversary of the European Social Charter)

IN A GLOBALISED economy rocked by (financial) crises at increasingly short intervals, the problem facing all sections of society with regard to their rights and interests is becoming more and more acute. The European Convention of Human Rights (hereinafter the Convention or the ECHR), until now seen mainly as an instrument for ensuring civil and political rights, has been given an important push by recent European Court of Human Rights (hereinafter the Court or the ECtHR) case law giving it a more socially oriented dimension.

The *Demir and Baykara* judgment of November 2008[2] can be considered as *the* landmark case[3] in this respect. It not only provides freedom of association

---

[1] Certain parts of this contribution are based on N Bruun and K Lörcher, 'Social Innovation: The New ECHR Jurisprudence and its Impact on Fundamental Social Rights in Labour Law' in I Schömann (ed), *Mélanges à la mémoire de Yota Kravaritou: A Trilingual Tribute* (Brussels, ETUI, 2011) 335 ff, though further developed and updated.

[2] ECtHR (Grand Chamber [GC]) (12 November 2008), App No 34503/97, *Demir and Baykara v Turkey* [2008] ECHR 1345. The substantive consequences of this judgment on Article 11 ECHR will be dealt with under Section 4.3.6. However, it should be noted from the outset that a first judgment in this case was handed down by a Chamber of the Second Section (21 November 2006), a judgment against which the Turkish government appealed to the Grand Chamber. For the sake of simplicity, any subsequent mention in this contribution of *Demir and Baykara* will, in the absence of further specification, refer to the Grand Chamber's judgment of November 2008.

[3] See, for example, K Ewing and J Hendy, 'The Dramatic Implications of *Demir and Baykara*' (2010) 39(1) *ILJ* 1; V Wedl, 'Neues aus der Judikatur des EGMR zu gewerkschaftlichen Grundrechten, (2009) *Das Recht der Arbeit* 458 ff; J-P Marguénaud and J Mouly, 'La Cour européenne des droits de l'homme à la conquête du droit de grève—A propos de l'arrêt de Chambre de la Cour européenne des droits de l'homme Enerji Yapi Yol Sen c. Turquie du 21 avril 2009' (2009) *Revue du Droit du Travail* 502 ff;

(Article 11 ECHR) with real content by explicitly recognising the right to bargain collectively (in contrast to its previous jurisprudence),[4] it also opens up the whole ECHR to a more socially oriented interpretation,[5] mainly by referring to international (labour) standards.[6] This chapter aims to look into this methodological approach in greater detail.

1 INTRODUCTION

Methodology in legal matters is a challenging exercise, in particular when it comes to human rights and even more so when the relation to international standards is at stake. It is in this context that the *Demir and Baykara* judgment is placed and has therefore to be analysed.

It might appear strange that this judgment should deserve such attention. Out of the approximately 15,000 judgments handed down by the Court since its establishment

---

K Lörcher, 'Das Menschenrecht auf Kollektivverhandlung und Streik—auch für Beamte (Zu den Urteilen ... *Demir und Baykara* und ... *Enerji Yapi-Yol-Sen*) (2009) *AuR* 299 ff; Comments by *Dorssemont* und *Gerards*, European Human Rights Cases (EHRC) 2009, pp 65 ff; S Van Drooghenbroek, 'Les frontières du droit et le temps juridique: La Cour européenne des droits de l'homme repousse les limites, Cour européenne des droits de l'homme (Grande Chambre), Demir et Baykara c. Turquie, 12 novembre 2008' (2009) *Revue Trimestrielle des Droits de l'Homme* 811 ff. More critical points of view (in particular in relation to the methodology used) are expressed by J-F Cohen-Jonathan and G Flauss, 'La Cour européenne des droits de l'homme et le droit international' (2008) *Annuaire français de droit international* 529; A Seifert, 'Recht auf Kollektivverhandlungen und Streikrecht für Beamte. Anmerkungen zur neuen Rechtsprechung des EGMR zur Vereinigungsfreiheit' (2009) *KritV* 357 ff; ATJM Jacobs and J van Drongelen, 'Nieuwe vleugels voor de vakverenigingsvrijheid van art. 11 EVRM' (2009) 84(36) *Nederlands Juristenblad* 2345 ff. For a more recent general analysis of the interpretation approaches used by the ECtHR, see the special issue of the 'Revue Générale de Droit International Public' ((2011) 115(2) with 'Dossier *Les techniques interprétatives de la norme international*) and H Senden, *Interpretation of Fundamental Rights in a Multilevel Legal System—An Analysis of the European Court of Human Rights and the Court of Justice of the European Union* (Cambridge, Intersentia, 2011).

[4] In a more general perspective, see F Dorssemont, 'The Right to Form and to Join Trade Unions for the Protection of His Interests under Article 11 of the European Convention on Human Rights—An Attempt "to Digest" the Case Law (1975–2009) of the European Court on Human Rights' (2010) 2 *European Labour Law Journal* 185 ff.

[5] The contributions on the substantive articles of the ECHR will deal with this aspect in greater detail. Concerning the Court's increasing case law on social rights and issues, see, eg: R Allen, R Crasnow and A Beale, *Employment Law and Human Rights*, 2nd edn (Oxford, Oxford University Press, 2007); L Caflisch, 'Labour issues before the Strasbourg Court' in ILO (ed), *The Distinguished Scholars Series*, http://www.ilo.org/public/english/bureau/leg/download/series.pdf; J-P Marguénaud and J Mouly, 'Cour Européenne des Droits de l'Homme et droit du travail' presentation, Paris, 21 March 2008; E Palmer, *Judicial Review, Socio-Economic Rights and the Human Rights Act* (Oxford, Hart Publishing, 2007).

[6] See also the former ECtHR's president, Costa, in respect of the Court's references to the European Social Charter: 'D'abord, la Convention a fait des incursions sur le terrain de la Charte sociale (principalement dans le domaine du travail et du droit syndical). Ensuite, notre Cour s'est livrée à une utilisation extensive de l'article 14 de la Convention européenne des droits de l'homme en faveur des droits économiques et sociaux. Enfin, elle cite de plus en plus fréquemment la Charte sociale dans ses arrêts, pour s'en inspirer'. 18 October 2011, speech on the occasion of the 50th anniversary of the European Social Charter, p 2, http://www.coe.int/t/dghl/monitoring/socialcharter/Activities/50anniversary/SpeechCostaCeremony50Ann_en.pdf, 15 ff. For a more general analysis of the Court's case law referring to Council of Europe treaties, see European Court of Human Rights (Research Division) (ed), *The Use of Council of Europe Treaties in the Case Law of the European Court of Human Rights*, Council of Europe, European Court of Human Rights, Strasbourg, June 2011 http://www.echr.coe.int/Documents/Research_report_treaties_CoE_ENG.pdf.

in the late 1950s,[7] it is the one to which most attention is devoted in this chapter. This is due to several factors: it constituted an open reversal of previous jurisprudence (a rare fact in judicial history), it was adopted by the Grand Chamber, the decision was taken unanimously and—in the context of this contribution the most important element—it develops an internationally oriented interpretation methodology with binding ('must') character.

This chapter attempts to analyse the explicit methodological considerations presented by the Court in that judgment, exploring the extent to which the ECHR may indeed be of relevance for (different) social rights by discussing three main questions: first, the main essence of the Court's methodology is clarified (Section 2); second, the criticism raised against this methodology is examined (Section 3); third, the follow-up of this approach is explored—has the Court applied this methodology in its subsequent practice, in particular with regard to social issues or rights (Section 4)?; and, finally, a number of conclusions are provided (Section 5).

2 THE METHODOLOGY: INTERPRETING THE ECHR IN LINE WITH INTERNATIONAL (LABOUR) STANDARDS (THE '*DEMIR AND BAYKARA* APPROACH')

In *Demir and Baykara* the Court adopted a clearly defined attitude to economic and social rights by its explicit and unprecedented use of a consolidated approach to interpreting the Convention by means of systematic reference to international (labour) standards. In the Court's own language, the message could be called 'Interpretation of the Convention in the light of other international instruments'.[8] In her recent in-depth analysis of the Court's interpretation methods and principles, Hanneke Senden also acknowledges the great importance of this judgment in respect of 'comparative' methodology.[9]

2.1 Development of its Approach

How did the Court proceed? On the basis of the description and analysis of previous jurisprudence, it developed a consolidated methodology by way of systematic reference to international (labour) standards and the case law of their respective supervisory bodies.

---

[7] The 'old' Court delivered fewer than 1,000 judgments. The number of judgments delivered by the new Court exceeds 14,000. *European Court of Human Rights*—Annual Report 2011 (Strasbourg, 2012), p 12.

[8] As heading II.A. It appears at least surprising that Cohen-Jonathan and Flauss (n 3) qualify this heading as 'intitulé didactique' (532), thus diminishing if not rejecting its legal value.

[9] 'Only on rare occasions, such as in the Grand Chamber judgment *Demir and Baykara*, does the Court extensively discuss its use of the comparative method': Senden (n 3) 224. Attributing references to international (human rights) standards to a 'comparative' method would, however, appear to be questionable. To answer this (more terminological) question is not the purpose of this contribution and will therefore not be developed further here.

2.1.1 Basic Interpretation Principles

In §§ 65–68 of *Demir and Baykara*, the Court describes the basics of its interpretation approach, ie, the respective general interpretation rules contained in Articles 31–33 of the Vienna Convention on the Law of Treaties (VCLT) (§ 65),[10] the necessity of interpreting ECHR rights in a manner making them 'practical and effective' (§ 66), the consideration of references to international law for interpretation purposes (§ 67) (sometimes called the 'consensus method') and, finally, that the Convention is a 'living' instrument (§ 68). One might assume that these principles are separate and that the third (references to international law in § 67) had no outstanding importance. Though all interlinked, it is this third principle to which the Court now attaches greater importance than in the past, as reflected by the heading of this section of the judgment ('The practice of interpreting Convention provisions in the light of other international texts and instruments') with no further mention of the other principles. However, this becomes obvious when looking at the further reasoning (§§ 69 ff).

2.1.2 Description of the Relevant Case Law in Respect of International Instruments

The starting point in the description of the Court's case law is the term 'Diversity' (of international texts and instruments used for the interpretation of the Convention). This can be seen as confirming the assumption that the Court had no systematic point of view on this element prior to *Demir and Baykara*. Describing first the previous jurisprudence referring to 'General international law' (§§ 69–73) and then highlighting the specific role of 'Council of Europe instruments' (§§ 74 and 75), the Court continues with a more analytical section ('Consideration by the Court'). In § 76 it refers to the 'rules and principles ... accepted by the vast majority of States' and in § 77 to the case law of the supervisory organs of the European Social Charter (ESC).[11] It goes on to clarify that it has 'never distinguished between sources of law according to whether or not they have been signed or ratified by the respondent State' (§ 78) by quoting relevant case law (§§ 79–83).

2.2 Three Elements to which Reference is Made and their Degree of Relevance as 'Conclusions'

Under the heading 'Conclusions', the Court summarises its methodology in §§ 85–86.[12] These two paragraphs are quoted in full on account of their eminent importance. It is

---

[10] In ss 2 and 3, references to §§ without further specification refer to paragraphs in the *Demir and Baykara* judgment.

[11] It is interesting to note that the two cases mentioned here pertain to Article 11 ECHR (*Sigurður A Sigurjónsson v Iceland*, 30 June 1993, § 35, Series A, No 264; and *Sørensen and Rasmussen v Denmark* [GC], App Nos 52562/99 and 52620/99, §§ 72–75, (2006) ECHR 24).

[12] See F Tulkens, 'Introduction to the Seminar Dialogue between Judges 2009' in European Court of Human Rights (ed), *Fifty Years of the European Court of Human Rights viewed by its fellow International Courts* (Strasbourg, 2009) 13.

on the basis of these conclusions that the methodology will be described below (and the criticism examined later):

> 85 The Court, in defining the meaning of terms and notions in the text of the Convention, *can and must take* into account *elements of international law* other than the Convention, the *interpretation* of such elements *by competent organs*, and the *practice of European States* reflecting their common values. The consensus emerging from specialised international instruments and from the practice of Contracting States may constitute a relevant consideration for the Court when it interprets the provisions of the Convention in specific cases.

> 86 In this context, it is *not necessary for the respondent State to have ratified* the entire collection of instruments that are applicable in respect of the precise subject matter of the case concerned. It will be sufficient for the Court that the relevant international instruments denote a continuous evolution in the norms and principles applied in international law or in the domestic law of the majority of member States of the Council of Europe and show, in a precise area, that there is common ground in modern societies ... (Emphasis added)

Accordingly, the ECtHR's methodology involves taking into account three main elements:

(1)   elements of international law;
(2)   the interpretation of such elements by competent organs;
(3)   the practice of Council of Europe Member States.

These elements will now be examined further, before analysing the *Demir and Baykara* judgment with regard to whether the Court (and in the affirmative to which extent) applies these elements in the interpretation of the Convention in its later case law.

2.2.1 Reference to 'Elements of International Law' Irrespective of Ratification

This reference is obviously the most important and far-reaching element of this judgment.

2.2.1.1 'Elements of International Law'

Under this term, the Court not only understands universally applicable (ie, the UN or the International Labour Organization (ILO)) treaties but even non-European ones such as the American Convention on Human Rights (§ 72). Furthermore, it points out that it has also referred to 'intrinsically non-binding instruments of Council of Europe organs' (§ 74), ie, a vast array of instruments.

In the case at hand, the Court takes into account at a universal level ILO Conventions 87,[13] 98[14] and 151,[15] giving them priority over the two UN Covenants

---

[13] See the references to the Freedom of Association and Protection of the Right to Organise Convention 1948 (No 87) in *Demir and Baykara* (n 2) §§ 37, 100, 122 (the reference in §§ 123–25 and 152 are more of a factual nature).
[14] See the references to the Right to Organise and Collective Bargaining Convention 1949 (No 98) in *Demir and Baykara* (n 2) §§ 42, 147, 165, 166.
[15] See the references to the Labour Relations (Public Service) Convention 1978 (No 151) in *Demir and Baykara* (n 2) §§ 44, 148, 165.

on Civil and Political Rights[16] and on Economic, Social and Cultural Rights,[17] and at a European level the European Social Charter.[18] As non-binding instruments, a Council of Europe Recommendation[19] and the EU Charter of Fundamental Rights[20] are mentioned. The Court thus follows in full its own criteria.

2.2.1.2 'Irrespective of Ratification'

Looking at the case law quoted in §§ 79–83, the Court has 'never' made a distinction as to whether a treaty has been ratified or not.[21] Therefore, it is logical that the Court concludes that '(i)t is sufficient for the Court that the relevant international instruments denote a continuous evolution in the norms and principles applied in international law or in the domestic law of the majority of Member States' (§ 86). It is this element which is perhaps the most criticised (see below, 3.2.1.2).

On the basis of the set of arguments put forward in §§ 65 ff and §§ 79–83 in particular, the Turkish government's objection (§§ 54 and 62) on the grounds of Turkey not having accepted either Article 5 or 6 ESC[22] were rejected by the Court.

2.2.2 *Reference to 'the Interpretation of Such Elements by Competent Organs' (Case Law of the Relevant Supervisory Organs)*

It is important to recall that the Court, in interpreting the ECHR, refers not only to the standards as such but also to the case law of the respective supervisory organs established to review the conformity of national situations with respect to international (labour) standards. As justification, the Court refers to previous jurisprudence (§ 77).

Looking at the case at hand, the Court refers to the ILO's Committee of Experts on the Application of Conventions and Recommendations (CEACR)[23] and the Committee on Freedom of Association (CFA),[24] as well as the Council of Europe's European Committee of Social Rights (ECSR).[25]

2.2.3 *Reference to 'the Practice of European States'*

As the third element needing to be taken into account in the Court's interpretation of the Convention, the 'practice of European States reflecting their common values'

---

[16] See the references in *Demir and Baykara* (n 2) §§ 40, 99, 122, 124.

[17] See the references in ibid.

[18] See the references in *Demir and Baykara* (n 2) to Article 5 in §§ 45, 103, 122; and to Article 6 in §§ 49, 149, 165.

[19] See the references in *Demir and Baykara* (n 2) on the status of public officials in Europe in §§ 46 and 104.

[20] See the references in *Demir and Baykara* (n 2) to Article 12(1) in §§ 47, 105, 122; and to Article 28 in §§ 51, 150, 165. At the time of publication of this judgment, the Lisbon Treaty making this Charter legally binding (by virtue of the (new) Article 6(1) TEU) was not yet in force.

[21] The main authority to which the Court refers in § 79 is the *Marckx v Belgium* (GC) judgment. The importance is underlined by the fact that this is the only judgment to which the Court refers in its conclusions on the interpretation methodology (§§ 85 and 86).

[22] See the references in *Demir and Baykara* (n 2) § 149 (concerning Article 6 ESC).

[23] See the references in ibid, §§ 38, 43, 101, 122, 147, 166.

[24] See the references in ibid, §§ 38, 102, 122; see also subsequent (Fifth Section) judgment (30 July 2009), App No 67336/01, *Danilenkov and others v Russia*, § 130.

[25] See the references in *Demir and Baykara* (n 2) §§ 50, 149.

(§ 85) is mentioned. It is first interesting to note that the Court does not quote previous case law to justify this element. Second, the Court would have to examine not only the practice as such but also to which extent it reflects 'their common values'. Third, there is a close link to the acceptance of international instruments by the Council of Europe Member States inasmuch as this is also an element of 'practice' of these States.

Accordingly, in later sections of this judgment, the Court describes in brief the practice in European Council of Europe Member States, including the interpretation and application process.[26]

2.2.4 Degree of Relevance: 'Can and Must Take into Account'

The Court not only mentions the three elements of (internationally oriented) interpretation but also defines their relevance in the process of interpretation. The main message here is that these elements not only 'can' but also 'must' be taken into account. This self-obligation is far-reaching: taking this statement literally—a normal assumption for a judgment—it means that in *all* applications in which it has to interpret the Convention ('defining the meaning of terms and notions in the text of the Convention': § 85), the Court has to search for and find all elements of international law and practice relevant for the specific problem to be solved. This is the first step towards 'taking into account' what follows and consists of carefully examining the contents of these elements and weighing up their relevance.

It will probably be at this stage that the somewhat contradictory wording 'may constitute' will come into play. Indeed, it would appear that the main purpose of the whole examination exercise is to find out whether there is a common denominator ('consensus emerging', 'continuous evolution': § 85).

In any event, in the case at hand the Court not only took account of but also based its whole decision on the elements described. Their relevance for the decision-making process (aimed at reversing previous jurisprudence on Article 11 ECHR) could not be demonstrated better.

2.3 New or Consolidated Approach?

Does this constitute a new approach? One might negate this by pointing out that in its previous case law, as quite extensively demonstrated, the Court had already referred to international (even non-binding) standards and also—to a certain extent—to the case law of relevant bodies.[27] Interestingly enough, such references had been used by the Court even in certain cases pertaining to social rights.[28] This aspect of the methodology may thus be considered as already well established.

---

[26] See the references in ibid, concerning the right to organise in §§ 48 and 106, and the right to bargain collectively in 52, 151 and 165.

[27] See the references to previous case law in *Demir and Baykara* (n 2) §§ 67 ff; see later reference to *Demir and Baykara* in ECtHR (First Section) judgment (15 January 2009), App No 42454/02, *Menchinskaya v Russia*, § 34.

[28] See the references in *Demir and Baykara* (n 2), inter alia § 70 to the ILO Forced Labour Convention (No 29) in the ECtHR (Second Section) judgment (26 July 2005), App No 73316/01, *Siliadin v France* [2005] ECHR 545, § 85.

The innovative aspect, however, is the consolidation of this interpretation approach based on a systematic analysis of the relevant international (labour) standards. Normally, if and when interpretation of the rights granted by the Convention is required, the ECtHR relies on the affirmation that the ECHR is a 'living instrument'[29] and that it must be interpreted 'in a manner which renders its rights practical and effective, not theoretical and illusory', even sometimes expressly referring to the 'principle of effectiveness'.[30] This approach could be characterised as directly Convention-based. Against this 'internal' background, the recognition of a systematic external influence gives the interpretation process a new dimension.

Of course, two generally accepted anchors exist. The first refers to the international framework offered by the Universal Declaration of Human Rights[31] (to which the first recital of the Convention's Preamble explicitly refers) and its Covenants, in particular the International Covenant on Economic, Social and Cultural Rights (ICESCR), together forming what has been described by the UN as the 'International Bill of Rights',[32] as well as the other 'Core International Human Rights Instruments'[33] representing a worldwide minimum of human rights standards specifically related to social issues. The second refers to the regional (European) level in respect of the instruments adopted in the framework of the Council of Europe, in particular the (Revised) European Social Charter.

More generally speaking, in the field of social rights, there is the undeniably groundbreaking standard-setting work conducted within the ILO, which has given rise to nearly 190 Conventions[34] (and even more Recommendations).[35] In this respect, it appears important to stress that the ECtHR explicitly recognises the specific role played by the ILO and its supervisory bodies in relation to interpretations in the area of labour relations.[36]

§§ 85 and 86 summarise the Court's methodological approach to interpreting the Convention. Although (many) elements of reference were to be found in the Court's case law prior to *Demir and Baykara*, the latter combines these different elements, systematically consolidating them (the 'consolidated approach') as an 'internationally friendly interpretation' or an 'interpretation in line with international standards'.

As to the application of this consolidated approach in the *Demir and Baykara* judgment itself, it has been demonstrated that the Court is very much aware of being consistent in applying the developed principles.

---

[29] See 2.1.1 and, in particular, *Demir and Baykara* (n 2) § 68.

[30] See as one more recent Grand Chamber's reference: ECtHR, 10 February 2009, App No 14939/03, *Zolotukhin v Russia*, § 80.

[31] See, eg, the reference to the UDHR in previous case law in *Demir and Baykara* (n 2) § 73; see also judgment of 7 January 2010, App No 25965/04, *Rantsev v Cyprus and Russia*, in § 277.

[32] http://www.ohchr.org/Documents/Publications/FactSheet2Rev.1en.pdf.

[33] For example, the Convention on the Elimination of All Forms of Discrimination Against Women (CEDAW), the Convention on the Rights of the Child (CRC), the International Convention on the Protection of the Rights of All Migrant Workers and Members of their Families (ICRMW) and the Convention on the Rights of Persons with Disabilities (CRPD).

[34] http://www.ilo.org/ilolex/english/convdisp1.htm.

[35] http://www.ilo.org/ilolex/english/recdisp1.htm.

[36] *Demir and Baykara* (n 2) § 147: 'one of the fundamental instruments concerning international labour standards'. See also the fact that the Court, in order to define the permissible restrictions, refers in § 166 to the ILO CEACR's case law.

3 THE CRITICISM ('GOING TOO FAR') AND COUNTER-ARGUMENTS

Although this consolidated approach has been welcomed—in many cases enthusi-astically[37]—it has, however, also been criticised, sometimes in very harsh words. It therefore appears necessary to deal in more detail with the main arguments raised against it.

On a very general level, it could be argued that the ECtHR is going too far[38] in its 'social' interpretation of the Convention, as this would change the ECHR's very nature. As its primary purpose is to protect civil and political human rights, it should not be turned into a social rights instrument.

This argument is not convincing. No restriction whatsoever is to be found in its official title (the 'Convention for the Protection of Human Rights and Fundamental Freedoms'). This is confirmed by the Convention's operative part prohibiting forced labour (Article 4) and protecting freedom of association, in particular with regard to trade unions (Article 11), articles which undoubtedly contain an important social rights element. Furthermore, the Convention's Preamble contains no reference to the Convention being restricted to civil and political rights. On the contrary, its first and second recitals refer to the Universal Declaration of Human Rights, the landmark definition of human rights protecting civil and political but at the same time and to an important extent also social rights[39] in one instrument.[40] More generally, civil and political rights cannot be (fully) enjoyed if social rights are not guaranteed. Finally, the Council of Europe's general concept of the 'indivisibility' of human rights between, on the one hand, civil and political rights and, on the other hand, economic, social and cultural rights cannot be disregarded.

Further general criticism levelled against the Court accuses it of not providing substantive arguments deriving directly from the Convention, but instead having to resort to 'external' argumentation. Again, this argument does not appear convincing. Besides the generally accepted references to international standards in interpreting international treaties (see 2.2.1 and 3.2.1), this argument neglects the substantive character of the relevant international standards and their application. Indeed, the ILO Conventions and the ESC have been elaborated and are applied, taking into account the specifically relevant experience of the competent bodies on which—at least to a certain extent—employers and trade unions often also sit.[41] This allows

---

[37] See, eg, Ewing and Hendy as well as Wedl (n 3).

[38] See, for example, Jacobs in this publication at pp 313–314.

[39] See, eg, the rights to social security (Article 22), individual and collective labour rights (Article 23) to reasonable working time (Article 24) and to social protection (Article 25).

[40] Referring even to the fifth recital ('to take first steps for the enforcement of certain of the rights stated in the Universal Declaration'), there is no direct indication that social rights as such should be excluded.

[41] This is obviously the case in the ILO's tripartite (including representatives from governments, employers and trade unions) standard setting (in particular the International Labour Conference) as well as supervisory bodies (in particular the Committee on Freedom of Association) and the Council of Europe's Committees (with social partners as observers: the so-called 'CHARTE-REL[LANCE]'-Committee for preparing, inter alia, the Revised European Social Charter and the Governmental Committee of the European Social Charter). Other bodies such as the ILO Committee of Experts (CEACR) or the European Committee of Social Rights (ECSR) are composed of independent and highly qualified experts.

the Court to benefit from this specialised knowledge. Moreover, it should not be forgotten that the Court also based its judgment on the government's failure 'to show how the nature of the duties performed by the applicants, as municipal civil servants, requires them to be regarded as "members of the administration of the State" subject to such restrictions' (§ 107).

From a more specific legal point of view, the Court is criticised for not abiding by obligations stemming from the international legal framework.

3.1 The VCLT Interpretation Framework

In general terms, it is argued that (parts of) this new consolidated approach would violate in particular Article 31 VCLT which lays down the rules for interpreting international treaties.

Before going into more detail, it should be recalled that the Vienna Convention is in itself legally binding neither to the Council of Europe in general nor to the ECtHR in particular. As international organisations/institutions, they are not (and cannot be)[42] contracting parties to this Treaty. But even if they were bound, Article 5 VCLT gives priority to internal rules in the case of treaties adopted within international organisations.[43]

Nevertheless, it is generally accepted that many of the principles enshrined in the Vienna Convention represent binding international law, in particular the guidelines governing questions of interpretation. Furthermore, the ECtHR itself refers to the principles of these provisions,[44] albeit employing formulations which make it clear that these principles are not intended to be a direct and totally binding instrument, in particular as regards matters of interpretation. By formulating certain qualifications such as 'guided mainly by the rules'[45] or 'in the light of the rules'[46] of interpretation provided for in Articles 31–33 VCLT or qualifying them as a 'backbone for the interpretation',[47] the Court obviously wants to ensure that some degree of flexibility is retained. It is therefore against this background that the consolidated interpretation approach will have to be analysed.

In assessing the pertinence of these arguments, it should be noted, from the outset, that the Court, at least to a certain extent, was already offered the opportunity to react to the Turkish government's preliminary objection (*ratione materiae*) in

---

[42] See Articles 81 ff VCLT providing for the ratification and accession by States (only).

[43] 'Article 5—Treaties constituting international organizations and treaties adopted within an international organization

The present Convention applies to any treaty which is the constituent instrument of an international organization and to any treaty adopted within an international organization *without prejudice to any relevant rules of the organization*' (emphasis added).

[44] See ECtHR (Grand Chamber) judgment (18 February 2009), App No 55707/00, *Andrejeva v Latvia*, § 18; see also §§ 19–20; ECtHR (Third Section) judgment (15 September 2009), App No 798/05, *Mirojubovs and others v Latvia*, § 62; ECtHR (First Section) judgment (7 January 2010), App No 25965/04, *Rantsev v Cyprus and Russia*, §§ 273–74.

[45] *Demir and Baykara* (n 2) § 65.

[46] ECtHR (Grand Chamber) judgment (23 March 2010), App No 15869/02, *Cudak v Lithuania*, § 56.

[47] ECtHR (Grand Chamber) judgment (18 February 2009), App No 55707/00, *Andrejeva v Latvia*, § 19.

defence of its position before the Grand Chamber.[48] Indeed, the government had argued against any idea of creating new obligations in respect of provisions that it had been neither ratified nor accepted. Together with the further arguments that were developed in the subsequent academic 'review' of the *Demir and Baykara* judgment, they will be examined in more detail.

3.2 Three Elements of Reference and their Degree of Relevance

In principle, all three elements of reference established by the Court are criticised. In relation to all interpretation requirements stemming from the Vienna Convention, it should be recalled that the ECtHR's interpretation is—to some extent at least—justified under the (flexibility) provision of Article 5 VCLT for international organisations.

3.2.1 *Reference to 'Elements of International Law' Irrespective of Ratification*

The critics are not happy with the Court's general reference to international standards. They conclude that Article 31(3)(c) VCLT[49] is violated mainly in two respects.

3.2.1.1 'Elements of International Law'

The first question is the more general question about the extent to which there are 'any relevant rules of international law'.

The critics start by reproaching the Court for its terminology ('elements of international law') and the consequences derived therefrom. In conformity with Article 38(1)(c) of the Statute of the International Court of Justice, the correct term of 'international law' should be understood as 'general principles of law recognized by civilized nations'.[50] Such an understanding would severely restrict possible references to instruments outside the Convention. However, there is no indication in Article 31(3)(c) VCLT of such a limitation.[51] Conversely, it should be noted that the term 'rules' is not limited in itself, being preceded by 'any'.[52] This points to an extensive interpretation. Similarly, the reference to two further authentic language

---

[48] See *Demir and Baykara* (n 2) §§ 54, 56, 61, 78–80 (responding to the arguments raised by the Turkish government in its appeal against the Second Section's judgment in 2006).

[49] Article 31(3): 'There shall be taken into account, together with the context: (a) any subsequent agreement between the parties regarding the interpretation of the treaty or the application of its provisions; (b) any subsequent practice in the application of the treaty which establishes the agreement of the parties regarding its interpretation; (c) any relevant rules of international law applicable in the relations between the parties.'

[50] See Cohen-Jonathan and Flauss (n 3) 534; Van Drooghenbroek (n 3) 823.

[51] It is interesting to note that the CJEU sees human rights included (without explicitly referring to Article 38(1)(c) of the Statute of the ICJ): 'fundamental rights form an integral part of the general principles of law, the observance of which the Court ensures'. See judgment of 3 May 2005 in Joined Cases C-387/02, C-391/02 and C-403/02, *Berlusconi* [2005] ECR I-3565, para 67; and Case C-260/89, *ERT* [1991] ECR I-2925, para 41.

[52] This aspect appears to be neglected by critics, eg, Cohen-Jonathan and Flauss (n 3) 534 (although 'toute' is quoted, this qualification is not taken into account at all).

versions (Article 85 VCLT) permits the conclusion that a strict interpretation is not required ('règle' in French; 'forma' in Spanish).[53]

It is true that there is no hierarchy between the different instruments referred to by the Court in respect of their binding force. There are however several degrees of 'bindingness' which could be taken into account.

Looking at legal texts which are supposed to become legally binding when ratified by Council of Europe Member States, there are already possible degrees of legally binding force. They could be distinguished by the number of ratifications:

— by all Council of Europe Member States;
— by a (large) majority of Council of Europe Member States;
— by the State involved in the case in question.

Besides the last alternative, which will be discussed in more detail below (3.2.1.2), the main choice has to be made between the first two alternatives. One might concede that only the first offers absolute legal certainty and foreseeability. But would such a choice solve the interpretation problem? The solution lies in answering the more fundamental question: what is the ultimate purpose of the references? If the ultimate aim is to explore whether there is a trend, a development, growing common ground, etc, in international law, the first alternative can be excluded as a solution. Indeed, in practice, it would be nigh impossible to find any such trend in 47 such diverse Member States. Therefore, in principle it would have to be the second alternative. At the end of the day, even a completely non-ratified instrument could already point to a trend, since the adoption of an instrument requires strong participation of the respective Member States with at least a majority for adoption (eg, a Council of Europe[54] or ILO Convention[55] would need a two-thirds majority).

From a legal point of view, the borderline between international (hard) 'law' and 'soft law' would be transgressed by giving 'Recommendations' (ILO, Council of Europe, etc), which by definition cannot become legally enforceable, the same legal status as (potentially) legally binding instruments (ie, irrespective of their ratification status).[56] There are however different ways of making the borderline permeable. For example, explicit references in 'hard law' to 'soft law', even international customary law in *status nascendi*[57] or unilaterally binding instruments,[58] would provide sufficient justification for such a reference.

Though it might be difficult to base an international trend (solely) on recommendations, it appears less problematic to add references to a 'soft law' instrument as a supplementary form of 'evidence' supporting already-established trends. The question to be answered in the affirmative would be does reference to 'soft law' provide

---

[53] See n 49 for the English version; 'De toute règle pertinente de droit international applicable dans les relations entre les parties' (French version); 'toda forma pertinente de derecho internacional aplicable en las relaciones entre las partes' (Spanish version).

[54] No I, Statutory Resolution (93) 27 on majorities required for decisions of the Committee of Ministers (adopted by the Committee of Ministers on 14 May 1993, at its 92nd Session).

[55] ILO Constitution, Article 19(2).

[56] For analysing purposes, the element (1) for international standards is accompanied by a point (1a) for the 'soft law' group of Recommendations etc.

[57] Van Drooghenbroeck (n 3) 824.

[58] Cohen-Jonathan and Flauss (n 3) 534, fn 17.

only additional evidence? In the negative (ie, that the references to soft law would be the only or the main source for justification of a new interpretation), this could indeed appear more problematic.

In any event, the *Demir and Baykara* judgment is an example of the solely supplementary character of 'soft law', referring to only one (Council of Europe) Recommendation.[59] Indeed, it was the overwhelming set of ('hard law') international standards to which the Court was able to refer and therefore establish this international trend.

3.2.1.2 'Irrespective of Ratification' (Reference to Non-ratified Instruments)

Probably the strongest criticism[60] is levelled against the Court's statement that 'it is not necessary for the respondent State to have ratified the entire collection of instruments that are applicable in respect of the precise subject matter of the case concerned. It is sufficient for the Court that the relevant international instruments denote a continuous evolution in the norms and principles applied in international law or in the domestic law in the majority of member States' (§ 86).[61]

It should first of all be recalled that this is not a new principle, since the Court had in the past already referred to instruments which were non-binding, had not entered

---

[59] Recommendation R (2000) 6 of the Committee of Ministers of the Council of Europe on the status of public officials in Europe (§ 46) was taken into account in § 104. But this is a different problem, since the Court attributes a specific role which for the Council of Europe's instruments is different from the universal level.

[60] See, eg, Seifert (n 3) 366 ('sprengt klar den Rahmen ... von Art. 31 Abs. 1 lit. c WVK'); Cohen-Cohen-Jonathan and Flauss (n 3) 535 ('proche de ... manipulation normative').

[61] It is interesting to note that in reaffirming the relevance of non-ratified instruments, the Court has recently referred to *Demir and Baykara* (n 2), but (only) to its § 78 (see ECtHR (Fourth Section) judgment, 11 October 2011, App No 53124/09—*Genovese v Malta*, § 44). It is also used in the Concurring opinion of judge Tulkens under ECtHR (Second Section) 31 March 2009, App No 44399/05—*Weller v Hungary*: 'Secondly, if the children's mother had herself lodged an application with the Court, the refusal to award her maternity benefit on the basis of nationality could certainly have been challenged, on the basis of our case law, as being contrary to Article 14 of the Convention taken together with Article 8, construed, inter alia, in the light of Article 12 § 4 of the European Social Charter, which provides that domestic law cannot reserve social-security rights to their own nationals.'2 Footnote 2: 'Admittedly, Hungary, whilst being a party to the Social Charter, has not accepted Article 12 § 4. However, the Court has already had occasion to rely on provisions of the Social Charter which have not been accepted by the respondent State [see *Demir and Baykara v Turkey* (n 2) §§ 45, 46, 49, 50, 86, 103, 129 and 149, regarding Articles 5 and 6 of the Social Charter].' ECtHR (Third Section), 22 February 2011, App No 26036/08—*Lalmahomed v The Netherlands*, Concurring Opinion of judge Ziemele: 'My problem goes back to another case in which the Grand Chamber, when asked to explain the rules of interpretation of the Convention in the light of other rules of international law, arrived at the following conclusions: "The Court, in defining the meaning of terms and notions in the text of the Convention, can and must take into account elements of international law other than the Convention, the interpretation of such elements by competent organs, and the practice of European States reflecting their common values ... In this context, it is not necessary for the respondent State to have ratified the entire collection of instruments that are applicable in respect of the precise subject matter of the case concerned. It will be sufficient for the Court that the relevant international instruments denote a continuous evolution in the norms and principles applied in international law" (*Demir and Baykara v Turkey* (n 2) §§ 85–86)'. It may well be that the *Demir and Baykara* case represents an example of unfortunate drafting and that nothing further beyond the scope of Article 31 § 3 (c) [VCLT] should be read into it. However, if we were to follow the literal meaning of what the Grand Chamber said, it might suggest that in our case, even though the Netherlands has not ratified Protocol No. 7, since it does provide for a leave-to-appeal system of sorts the Chamber should have assessed whether the leave-to-appeal system as such complied with Article 6. After all, the applicant did complain that the domestic law governing this procedure was contrary to the Convention' (paragraphs 26–27).

into force or were even still in the draft phase.[62] Turning more specifically to Article 31(3)(c) VCLT, the critics' arguments relate to the fact that Turkey had not accepted Articles 5 and 6 of the Revised European Social Charter (RESC) and thus was not 'party' to the two articles protecting freedom of association[63] which had nonetheless been taken into account by the ECtHR. It was therefore argued that the condition 'between the parties' in Article 31(3)(c) VCLT was not fulfilled.

Nevertheless, there are important arguments in support of the Court's interpretation. Looking first at the International Law Commission's conclusions concerning the interpretation of Article 31(3)(c) VCLT in the context of (avoiding) fragmentation of international law,[64] it would appear that the Convention is based on a 'concept' that 'has a very general nature or is expressed in such general terms that it must take into account changing circumstances'[65] and is therefore to be considered as conforming with this requirement. Besides this more formal argument, treaties adopted within international organisations and, even more so, human rights treaties require a uniform interpretation, as otherwise the relevant courts would be obliged to accept 'double standards'. Moreover, such acceptance would amount to an indirect reservation inconsistent with the formal requirements of either Article 57 ECHR or Article 2(1)(d) VCLT. In the case at hand, Turkey had already ratified, many years earlier, ILO Convention No 98 on collective bargaining, meaning that it was prevented from relying on a different international instrument guaranteeing the same principles as an instrument (Article 6, § 2 RESC on collective bargaining) which it had not accepted.

3.2.2 Reference to 'Interpretation of Such Elements by Competent Organs' (Case Law of the Relevant Supervisory Bodies)

The next important problem raised is the multiple references to international supervisory bodies' case law.[66] Before going into any detail, it should be clarified that it is not just any sort of supervisory body to which the Court refers. There is the clear link to the instruments previously taken into account.

Generally speaking, this approach may already be justified by the longstanding case law of the Court that clearly takes into account this important international practice, be it in case law before[67] or after[68] the *Demir and Baykara* judgment. In

---

[62] See *Demir and Baykara* (n 2) §§ 68, 74–75; and also ECtHR (First Section) judgment (15 January 2009), App No 42454/02, *Menchinskaya v Russia*, § 34 (referring to *Demir and Baykara*); see also Van Drooghenbroek (n 3) 818 ff.

[63] Based on Article A RESC, Turkey had not accepted Articles 5 and 6 RESC (in continuation of its restrictive approach already demonstrated during the ratification of the (former) ESC where it had also refused to accept these two articles).

[64] 'Conclusions of the work of the Study Group on the Fragmentation of International Law: Difficulties Arising from the Diversification and Expansion of International Law', http://untreaty.un.org/ilc/texts/1_9.htm, §§ 17 ff; see also (for a more pragmatic approach) I Van Damme, 'Treaty Interpretation Revisited, Not Revised', International Labour Organization Distinguished Scholar Series, 30 October 2008.

[65] Ibid, § (23)(c).

[66] See nn 23, 24 and 25.

[67] Van Drooghenbroek (n 3) 811 ff.

[68] In particular in reference to §§ 85–86 of the *Demir and Baykara* judgment (n 2), see ECtHR (GC) judgment (27 April 2010), App No 7/08, *Tănase v Moldova*, § 176; (Third Section) judgment (9 September 2009), App No 33401/02, *Opuz v Turkey*, § 164.

this respect, it appears helpful to mention that the Court reserves a certain margin of appreciation.[69]

But the Court is not very explicit on the legal basis of these references. It would appear that the Court considers it part of its approach to discern trends in international law by also referring to non-ratified and/or non-binding rules under Article 31(3)(c) VCLT.[70] This would be a logical consequence given that there would be no compelling reason to treat references to non-binding rules differently from references to the (possibly also) non-binding case law of supervisory bodies.

Nevertheless, Article 31(3) VCLT provides for a further alternative concerning legal justification. In this case, these references would also be considered as 'subsequent practice', an element mentioned in paragraph (3)(b) as also needing to be taken into account for interpretation purposes.[71] In both the academic field[72] and in judicial practice,[73] it is recognised that this case law is indeed to be taken into consideration. Any systematic approach to the international context would be very much incomplete if the practice of the competent bodies in interpreting and applying the relevant international standards were left aside. Insofar as these bodies have their own case law demonstrating consistency and continuity in interpretation, any reference to it is not incidental but reflects state-of-the-art practice.

In practice, there are several questions needing to be answered. How should we distinguish between reports from international supervisory bodies when they are used for different purposes (interpretation or application)? Indeed, sometimes reports are referred to in respect of establishing facts with regard to a specific country concerned by the application (fact-finding purpose) which would be different when used for interpretation purposes. It would therefore be helpful if these different purposes were clearly separated. How should we deal with reports coming

---

[69] ECtHR (GC) judgment (27 April 2010), App No 7/08, *Tănase v Moldova*, § 176 (here the Court clarifies that: 'It is for the Court to decide which international instruments and reports it considers relevant and how much weight to attribute to them').

[70] See n 49.

[71] 'Any subsequent practice in the application of the treaty which establishes the agreement of the parties regarding its interpretation'; see in this sense, eg, M Weiss and A Seifert, 'Der Streik im Recht der Internationalen Arbeitsorganisation' in Th Dieterich, M Le Friant, L Nogler, K Kezuka and H Pfarr (eds), *Individuelle und kollektive Freiheiten im Arbeitsrecht* (Baden-Baden, Nomos Verlag, 2010) 137 ff.

[72] See, eg, N Ando, 'The Development of the Human Rights Committee's Activities under the ICCPR and its Optional Protocol through My Twenty-Year Experience as a Committee Member' in G Venturini and S Bariatti (eds), *FS Pocar* (Milan, Giuffrè Editore, 2009), 15 (No 6.2) referring to the case of the application of the term 'territory' in respect of the US's report on Guantanamo (outside US 'territory'); to a certain extent also R Gardiner, *Treaty Interpretation* (Oxford, University Press, 2008) 246.

[73] See, eg, Constitutional Court of South Africa, judgment 13 December 2002, CCT 14/02, National Union of Metalworkers of South Africa: '[32] Although none of the ILO Conventions specifically referred to mentions the right to strike, both committees engaged with their supervision have asserted that the right to strike is essential to collective bargaining ... [33] These principles culled from the jurisprudence of the two ILO committees are directly relevant to the interpretation both of the relevant provisions of the Act and of the Constitution'; or Supreme Court of Canada, judgment 8 June 2007, 2007 SCC 27, Health Services and Support—Facilities *Subsector Bargaining Association v British Columbia*, 2007 SCC 27, [2007] 2 SCR 391: '76 ... *Convention No. 87* has been the subject of numerous interpretations by the ILO's Committee on Freedom of Association, Committee of Experts and Commissions of Inquiry. These interpretations have been described as the "cornerstone of the international law on trade union freedom and collective bargaining"'; '79. In summary, international conventions to which Canada is a party recognize the right of the members of unions to engage in collective bargaining, as part of the protection for freedom of association'.

from sources that are not clearly independent? While there is no question mark over supervisory bodies whose members are explicitly chosen on grounds of their independence, are the political bodies included in the supervisory procedures (eg, the ILO Conference Committee on the Application of Standards, the Council of Europe's Governmental Committee on the European Social Charter[74] and indeed its Committee of Ministers) really appropriate to be referred to without further examination? What is the benchmark for including or excluding certain (competent) organs? The Court does not really provide any very clear criteria in this respect.[75]

3.2.3 Reference to 'Practice of European States'

As the third non-Convention element used for interpretation purposes, the Court mentions the 'practice of European States reflecting their common values' (§ 85). One might first ask what the term 'European States' refers to. It would appear self-evident that, given the very close link between the ECHR and the Council of Europe, all 47 Member States (and, indeed, Contracting Parties to the Convention) would be included. This would mean that countries like Belarus or—from an ILO perspective—Israel are not to be taken into account. The Court's general approach would appear to follow this line of reasoning.

Second, it is interesting to note that the Court did not quote any previous case law to justify this element. The reason might be that it would appear self-evident when acknowledging that 'trends' in the Council of Europe's Member States are the main point of reference for interpretation (in particular, in respect of the first element). The UN Study Group 'Treaties over time'[76] recently stated that 'The ECtHR places more emphasis on subsequent practice by referring to the common legal standards among member states of the Council of Europe' by referring inter alia to the *Demir and Baykara* judgment,[77] and continued by saying that 'the ECtHR has frequently employed an evolutionary interpretation that was explicitly guided by subsequent practice'. The legal basis for such an approach would—as pointed out previously (3.2.2)—be Article 31(3)(b) VCLT.

Third, if the Court were to follow its own interpretation principles, it would have to examine not only the practice as such but also to what extent this reflects 'their common values'. In legal terms, it would appear to a certain extent that this formulation can be seen in connection with Article 31(3)(b) VCLT, which requires the establishment of 'the agreement of the parties'. Embedded in this context, it could mean the 'subjective' element which provides the additional justification for such references for interpretation purposes. Even so, the question remains as to what this could mean in practice. Looking at the judgment at hand, it does not appear that the Court needed to separately examine this element. It was sufficient that an

---

[74] Governmental Committee: it has already been referred to by ECtHR (Grand Chamber) in *Sørensen and Rasmussen v Denmark* (n 11) § 72; *Sigurdur A Sigurjónsson v Iceland* (n 11) § 35.

[75] For analysing purposes, the element (2) for supervisory bodies' case law is accompanied by a specific point (2a) for any sort of Report or other 'international material' the Court refers to.

[76] http://untreaty.un.org/ilc/sessions/63/TreatiesOverTimeSGChairReport28Aug2011.pdf.

[77] See n 10. See also, eg, *Demir and Baykara v Turkey* (n 2) §§ 52, 76, 85; *A v UK*, App No 35373/97, § 83, ECHR 2002-X.

'objective' (common) Council of Europe Member States' practice be established in order to see the 'common values' represented. The additional subjective dimension appears to be derived from the establishment of a 'consensus' between the Council of Europe Member States.

Finally, the close link to the acceptance of international instruments by the Council of Europe Member States inasmuch as this is also an element of 'practice' of these States (see 3.2.1) points to a mutual reinforcement of these two elements.

Although not giving many details (sources in particular), the Court does briefly describe the practice in Council of Europe Member States.[78]

3.2.4 Degree of Relevance: 'Can and Must Take into Account'

It is somewhat surprising that less criticism has been raised in respect of the specific problem of the degree of relevance. Referring to *Demir and Baykara*, the Grand Chamber emphasised in its *Tănase v Moldova* judgment: 'It is for the Court to decide which international instruments and reports it considers relevant and how much weight to attribute to them.'[79] Without any clarification as regards the criteria used, such a case-by-case approach might be considered as lacking in transparency.

The *SH and others v Austria* judgment is an example in which the Court had, on the one hand, found 'a clear trend in the legislation of the Contracting States, which reflects an emerging European consensus', but had added, on the other hand, a new criterion under which this consensus was not *'based on settled and long-standing principles established in the law of the member States but rather reflects a stage of development within a particularly dynamic field of law and does not decisively narrow the margin of appreciation of the State'.*[80] This approach was heavily criticised by the dissenting opinion[81] and, indeed, raises severe problems of consistency.

The relationship alone between the two sentences in § 85 of *Demir and Baykara* raises problems. By itself, the first sentence appears fairly clear. But the addition of the second sentence could make the methodology less clear ('take account' versus 'relevant consideration') and even contradictory ('can and must' versus 'may'). One proposal here is to find a solution combining the relevant elements (see 2.2.4).

The relevance could be questioned when references to international standards are used to restrict a human right. Article 53 ECHR mainly protects human rights at national level. Similar provisions exist in international human rights standards. In the social field it is worthwhile highlighting Article 19(8) ILO Constitution[82] and Article

---

[78] See references in n 26.

[79] See § 176 of the *Tănase v Moldova* judgment below, 4.2.1.1, (2).

[80] ECtHR (Grand Chamber), 3 November 2011, App No 57813/00, *SH and others v Austria*, § 96 (for both quotations in this paragraph of the text).

[81] 'The Court thus takes the unprecedented step of conferring a new dimension on the European consensus and applies a particularly low threshold to it, thus potentially extending the States' margin of appreciation beyond limits. The current climate is probably conducive to such a backward step. The differences in the Court's approach to the determinative value of the European consensus and a somewhat lax approach to the objective indicia used to determine consensus¹ are pushed to their limit here, engendering great legal uncertainty': Joint Dissenting Opinion of Judges Tulkens, Hirvelä, Lazarova Trajkovska and Tsotsoria, § 8.

[82] Article 19(8) (Conventions and Recommendations) reads as follows: 'In no case shall the adoption of any Convention or Recommendation by the Conference, or the ratification of any Convention by

H RESC[83] (= Article 32 ESC). In such cases, therefore, the relevance of references to international standards (whether they refer only to the standards as such or also to the supervisory bodies' case law) should be examined very carefully, in order that they are not used to justify a restrictive interpretation of the Convention.

3.3 Further Criticism

Other criticism relates not to the methodology as such, but to elements specific to this case and should therefore be separated from the general elements examined above.

3.3.1 *No Additional Protocol to the ECHR on Social Rights*

Defending its position, the Turkish government also invoked the fact that attempts to adopt a new additional protocol to the Convention explicitly covering social rights had failed. The intention of this argument was to prevent the Court from extending the interpretation of the Convention's rights to include a social dimension. Obviously, this is more a political than a convincing legal argument and is therefore of less importance. In § 84 the Court argued that the absence of an additional protocol in this respect did not preclude the possibility of moving in a direction suggested by the proponents of an additional protocol. On the contrary, the Court rightly observed 'that this attitude [the absence of political support for an additional protocol] of the member States was accompanied ... by a wish to strengthen the mechanism of the Social Charter. The Court regards this as an argument in support of the existence of a consensus among Contracting States to promote economic and social rights. It is not precluded from taking this general wish of Contracting States into consideration when interpreting the provisions of the Convention'.

3.3.2 *No* Ratione Temporis *Limitation*

The final argument used against this jurisprudence deals with the Court's unwillingness to restrict the new jurisprudence to cases not decided upon.[84] In his Separate Opinion, Judge Zagrebelsky[85] discussed the problems arising in this respect. For reasons of foreseeability and legal security, he would 'have preferred it if the Court had stipulated the time from which the right in question "became" (paragraph 154 of the [*Demir and Baykara*] judgment) one of the essential elements of the right set forth in Article 11'.[86] But this is more a debate in respect of the general approach

---

any Member, be deemed to affect any law, award, custom or agreement which ensures more favourable conditions to the workers concerned than those provided for in the Convention or Recommendation.'

[83] 'Article H—Relations between the Charter and domestic law or international agreements
The provisions of this Charter shall not prejudice the provisions of domestic law or of any bilateral or multilateral treaties, conventions or agreements which are already in force, or may come into force, under which more favourable treatment would be accorded to the persons protected.'

[84] Van Drooghenbroek (n 3) 843 ff.

[85] Annexed to the *Demir and Baykara* judgment (n 2).

[86] Ibid, point 8.

taken by the Court and the problems faced by Contracting States in the case of a reversal of jurisprudence than a problem pertaining specifically to the *Demir and Baykara* judgment.[87]

From a more practical point of view, there is no denying that the *Demir and Baykara* judgment's methodology (in respect of fundamental social rights) and in particular its consequences (in respect of Article 11 ECHR, but also of the further articles examined here) are of relevance to all existing and new cases and problems.

3.4 Interim Conclusions

The Court's consolidated approach referring to international standards generally and to their subsequent case law is an important step towards a more systematic and less fragmented consideration of the developments in international law for interpretation purposes. Even if questions have been raised as to whether (certain) references are in full harmony with the wording of the relevant provisions of the Vienna Convention, it would appear that the Court has some degree of flexibility in this respect. In any event, in determining the impact of developments in international labour law—and in particular its human rights dimension—on interpretation of the Convention, no valid case can be made for excluding certain elements such as supervisory bodies' case law.

4 THE FOLLOW-UP: IN THE AFTERMATH OF *DEMIR AND BAYKARA*

This section attempts to clarify whether and to what extent the Court has followed the *Demir and Baykara* methodology in its subsequent practice.[88] This analysis is called for because the Court (Grand Chamber) unanimously stated that it 'can and must' take into account the three elements described above (see 2.2). Since it would be difficult to look at all judgments and since one of the aims of this book is to analyse the consequences of *Demir and Baykara*, this examination will be mainly restricted to the social field[89] and in particular to Article 11 ECHR. Certain path-setting judgments referring to specific articles of the Convention will not appear here, either because they are pre-*Demir and Baykara* judgments or because they do not concern social matters.

4.1 Overview

The focus of this contribution is on the *Demir and Baykara* judgment with its focus on the social dimension. This follow-up analysis therefore concentrates primarily on those judgments in which the Court directly refers to it (Categories

---

[87] Van Drooghenbroek (n 3) 849 ('les temps sont mûrs pour réinvestir le débat du droit transitoire jurisprudentiel').

[88] The analysis of the Court's jurisprudence is limited to the first three years after the *Demir and Baykara* judgment.

[89] For example, the right to (free) education will not be examined; see ECtHR (Fourth Section) judgment (21 June 2011), App No 5335/05, *Anatoliy Ponomaryov and Vitaliy Ponomaryov v Bulgaria*.

(A) and (B)). Nevertheless, other judgments in the social field are also examined (Categories (C) and (D)). The main question is to what extent the Court refers to international standards, the main thrust of the so-called *Demir and Baykara* approach (Categories (A) and (C)), or does not follow this approach in substance (Categories (B) and (D)).

The judgments in Category (A) are (best) examples of a good follow-up, whereas judgments in Category (D) can be considered the most problematic for the *Demir and Baykara* approach.

The following table may clarify the four categories.

ECtHR judgments with	reference to *Demir and Baykara*[90]	*no* reference to *Demir and Baykara*
reference to international standards	(A)	(C)
no reference to international standards	(B)	(D)

The following analysis focuses mainly on judgments in the social field. Due to the quantity of judgments, it is not possible to cover the entirety of the Court's case law in this contribution.

Exceptions are made in respect of explicit references to *Demir and Baykara*. As the number of such judgments is rather low, and even lower when confining the examination to references in the social field, it appears justified to look at all these references (Categories (A) and (B)).

Concerning the other two categories ((C) and (D)), the attempt is made here to include the whole range of ECtHR judgments in the social field.[91] A different presentation is used here, with the analysis concentrating on the different articles of the Convention. The aim here is to see to what extent international references have been used by the Court.

For reasons of quick and easy cross-referencing, the Court's judgments referred to in the following analysis are numbered sequentially. As far as the three elements developed above (2.2) are concerned they are referred to by their number (1) to (3).

4.2 Categories (A) and (B): ECtHR Judgments with References to Demir and Baykara

4.2.1 *Category (A): References to* Demir and Baykara *and International Standards*

Exploring the references to the *Demir and Baykara* approach, two different types of reference are found. The first follow the '*Demir and Baykara* approach', explicitly referring to §§ 85 and/or 86 of the judgment. Since this approach is mainly based

---

[90] Cases are excluded in which *Demir and Baykara* (n 2) is quoted, but this reference is not found in the operative parts of judgments (eg, only in the submission of the parties or in dissenting opinions).

[91] Only those three judgments with direct references to *Demir and Baykara*, albeit within the social field (see below (6), (13) and (16)), are dealt under Categories (A) and (B).

on previous references in the Court's case law, there are also several specific parts of this approach to which the subsequent case law individually refers.

4.2.1.1 Explicit References to § 85 and/or § 86 (the 'Conclusions' of the 'Demir and Baykara Approach')

Only six judgments explicitly take the *Demir and Baykara* approach into account. Most importantly, two of them are Grand Chamber judgments:

(1) ECtHR (Grand Chamber), 7 July 2011, App No 23459/03 *Bayatyan v Armenia* (conscientious objection), reference in § 102 to § 85 of *Demir and Baykara*.

The *Bayatyan v Armenia* judgment could well be compared with *Demir and Baykara* in the sense that developments in international law (§§ 105–07) and in the practice in the Council of Europe's Member States (§§ 103 and 104) were a main consideration for the Grand Chamber to reverse its previous jurisprudence which the Chamber had hitherto followed.[92] The *Demir and Baykara* approach could thus be interpreted as an important tool for (more coherently) justifying further important developments in jurisprudence.

(2) ECtHR (Grand Chamber), 27 April 2010—7/08—*Tănase v Moldova*— (nationals holding other nationalities sitting as members of Parliament), reference in § 176 to §§ 85 and 86 of *Demir and Baykara*.

Although the *Tănase v Moldova* judgment does not imply a reversal of jurisprudence, it appears that the case deals with a highly sensitive problem (in the national context) and probably for this reason requires further justification. Indeed, comparing the references in the reasoning of the Chamber with those in the Grand Chamber's judgment, it appears obvious that the latter is going into far more detail.[93]

(3) ECtHR (First Section), 10 February 2011, App No 4663/05, *Soltysyak v Russia* (freedom of movement), reference in § 51 to § 85 of *Demir and Baykara*.
(4) ECtHR (First Section), 10 March 2011, App No 2700/10 *Kiyutin v Russia* (refusal to enter country on HIV reasons), reference in § 65 to § 85 of *Demir and Baykara*.
(5) ECtHR (Third Section), 9 June 2009, App No 33401/02 *Opuz v Turkey* (right to life), reference in § 164 to §§ 85 and 86 of *Demir and Baykara*.

The First Section Chamber's judgments *Soltysyak v Russia* and *Kiyutin v Russia* highlight 'common standards', whereas the Third Section Chamber's *Opuz v Turkey* judgment emphasises 'consensus and common values'.

---

[92] This situation differs from *Demir and Baykara* in which the Chamber had already established a violation.

[93] Whereas the Chamber attributes only two paragraphs to the Council of Europe's activities (§§ 47 and 48), the Grand Chamber not only expands these references (§§ 83–86) but also includes an extensive analysis of the 'Law and Practice in the Council of Europe Member States' (§§ 87–93). In this context, it might be noted that no international standards (UN, etc) are mentioned. Nonetheless, in its description of the facts, the Court describes in detail the 'International reactions to the electoral reform' (§§ 45–52), including not only Council of Europe reactions (§§ 45–51) but also 'Other international criticism' (§ 52).

(6)   ECtHR (Third Section), 21 April 2009, App No 68959/01 *Enerji Yapi-yol Sen v Turkey* (right to strike), reference in § 16 to §§ 34–52 of *Demir and Baykara*, description of relevant international law, references in § 24 to *Demir and Baykara* in general and in § 31 to §§ 110 and 119 of *Demir and Baykara*.

The *Enerji Yapi-yol Sen v Turkey* case ended with a landmark judgment,[94] with the ECtHR for the first time expressly recognising the right to strike as enshrined in Article 11 ECHR. But it is not very explicit as to the *Demir and Baykara* approach, since it does not mention §§ 85 and 86. Nevertheless, it appears justified to place it in this category for at least two reasons. The Third Section refers in § 16 to the international law as described in *Demir and Baykara* in §§ 34–52. Furthermore, in mentioning ILO Convention No 87, it states (yet without a concrete reference) that the Court has referred to international standards outside the Convention. In doing so, it refers generally to *Demir and Baykara*.[95] In total, the close link to *Demir and Baykara* is underlined by the three references.[96]

A more in-depth analysis would consider the description of international standards as being complete in the *Demir and Baykara* context (the right to organise and collective bargaining). But this is not totally the case in the *Enerji Yapi-Yol Sen* context (the right to strike). With regard to international standards (1) the references to Article 8(1)(d) ICESCR and Article 3 ILO Convention No 87[97] is missing. More importantly, there is a lack of references to the relevant case law (2). Although the judgment states that the ILO supervisory bodies have recognised the right to strike,[98] no case law of any of the Human Rights Committee, the Committee on Economic, Social and Cultural Rights or the European Committee of Social Rights is referred to, even those which, in principle, come to similar conclusions.[99] As regards the Council of Europe Member States' practice (3), the judgment contains no further information.

Since the substantive problem in the two cases is different (*Demir and Baykara*: the right to organise and the right to bargain collectively; *Enerji Yapi-Yol Sen*: the right to strike), additional information on all three elements regarding the specific problem of the right to strike (of civil servants) would have made the reasoning even more convincing and transparent and would have been even more in line with the *Demir and Baykara* methodology.

---

[94] It also served as a point of reference in the *Kaya and Seyhan v Turkey* judgment, § 26 (see below, 4.3.6.3 (54)).

[95] 'Pour la prise en compte par la Cour des éléments de droit international autres que la Convention, voir *Demir et Baykara*, précité', § 24 of the *Enerji Yapi-yol Sen v Turkey* judgment (which only exists in French).

[96] The third reference concerns the positive obligations under Article 11 ECHR (in § 31 to *Demir et Baykara* (n 2) §§ 110 and 119).

[97] The *Demir and Baykara* judgment (n 2) only refers to Article 2 ILO Convention No 87 (§ 38). However, by referring to international standards, the admissibility decision in *Enerji Yapi-Yol Sen* (31 January 2008) (B.4) also mentions the other relevant Articles 3, 8 and 11 of ILO Convention No 87.

[98] Without exactly quoting the ILO's case law, the Court nevertheless makes a correct general statement: 'La Cour note également que le droit de grève est reconnu par les organes de contrôle de l'Organisation internationale du travail (OIT) comme le corollaire indissociable du droit d'association syndicale protégé par la Convention C87 de l'OIT sur la liberté syndicale et la protection du droit syndical' (§ 24).

[99] Lörcher, *Internationale Rechtsgrundlagen des Streikrechts*, in Däubler (ed), *Arbeitskampfrecht* 3rd edn (Baden-Baden, Nomos 2011) § 10, para 76.

4.2.1.2 References to the 'Practice of Interpreting Convention Provisions in the Light of Other International Texts and Instruments' (§§ 65–84.)

Before coming to its conclusions on its methodological approach,[100] the Court—in its *Demir and Baykara* judgment—had further developed its previous jurisprudence in respect of references to international standards (part II.3. of the *Demir and Baykara* judgment). Analysing the references in post-*Demir and Baykara* case law, it is surprising that the Court hardly ever refers to the approach as such (for the rare exceptions, see above, 4.2.1.1), but only to specific elements of its description of the development of pre-*Demir and Baykara* jurisprudence.

(7) ECtHR (Second Section), 14 April 2009, App No 41870/05, *Ferreira Alves v Portugal (No 4)*.
(8) ECtHR (Second Section), 14 April 2009, App No 30381/06, *Ferreira Alves v Portugal (No 5)*.

In this context, two Second Section judgments (*Ferreira Alves v Portugal (Nos 4 and 5)* referring to all four interpretation principles (§§ 65–68) may be mentioned. But these dealt with the Portuguese government's argument to apply the restrictive admissibility criterion included in the 14th Protocol (concerning Article 35, § 3b) of the Convention) which had not yet entered into force (but had already been ratified by a large majority of Member States, including the Defendant State). Since the restrictive elements would in any case not have been fulfilled, the Court saw no necessity to base its decision on the (in)admissibility of the new criterion introduced by this Protocol (using its reference to §§ 65–68 in the *Demir and Baykara* judgment). Because of their non-decisive character, these references in the two judgments should not be over-estimated.

(9) ECtHR (First Section), 7 January 2010, App No 25965/04, *Rantsev v Cyprus and Russia* (human trafficking), reference in § 273 to § 67 of *Demir and Baykara*.

As far as § 67 (references to international law) is concerned, at least a specific relation to international standards is accepted. The *Rantsev v Cyprus and Russia* judgment is an illustrative example in this respect. It concerns the failure to protect a daughter ('artiste') from being trafficked[101] and to conduct an effective investigation. In §§ 137–85 of the judgment, the First Section lists international standards (UN, Council of Europe etc) and refers in § 273 to *Demir and Baykara*, though only to its § 67. It remains unclear why the First Section does not take the consolidated approach as such into account.

(10) ECtHR (Third Section), 15 September 2009, App No 798/05, *Miroļubovs and others v Latvia*, reference in § 62 to § 65 of *Demir and Baykara*.

When a reference to the *Demir and Baykara* judgment is restricted to its § 65 (VCLT), it appears obvious that only the ordinary interpretation principle and

---

[100] II.4; see above, 2.2.
[101] See in general H Askola, *Legal Responses to Trafficking in Women for Sexual Exploitation in the European Union* (Oxford, Hart Publishing, 2007).

not the general consolidated approach is being used. An example of such an argumentation is provided by the Third Section in the *Miroļubovs and others v Latvia* judgment (concerning unwarranted intervention in an internal dispute within the old Orthodox community).

> (11) ECtHR (First Section), 15 January 2009, App No 42454/02, *Menchinskaya v Russia* (infringement of equality of arms in civil proceedings over a claim to unemployment allowances, as the prosecutor had entered the proceedings on the side of the State agency), reference in § 34 to §§ 74 and 75 of *Demir and Baykara*.

Apart from the references to the basic interpretation principles (§§ 65–68), the subsequent practice of the Court also mentions specific parts of its pre-*Demir and Baykara* jurisprudence. In the *Menchinskaya v Russia* case, the First Section refers in § 34 to §§ 74 and 75 of *Demir and Baykara* for the Council of Europe's instruments (in particular the Venice Commission; see §§ 19–20), while neglecting all other elements of the *Demir and Baykara* approach. It is surprising that this in itself is used as an important argument in interpreting and applying Article 6 ECHR in this case and not, eg, European States' practice.[102] Furthermore, in referring (§ 38) to a Parliamentary Assembly of the Council of Europe (PACE) recommendation without specifically indicating its interpretative role, the Court does not contribute much to further methodological clarity.

> (12) ECtHR (Fourth Section), 11 October 2011, App No 53124/09, *Genovese v Malta* (acquisition of citizenship), reference in § 44 to § 78 of *Demir and Baykara*.

To justify the reference to non-binding international standards in its *Genovese v Malta* judgment, the Fourth Section only mentions § 78 of *Demir and Baykara* and—surprisingly—not § 86 as an important element of the consolidated approach. This would have seemed even more obvious since the main elements of the consolidated approach (§ 85) are taken into account in the same paragraph.[103]

---

[102] However, in referring to 'the public's increased sensitivity to the fair administration of justice', one could be tempted to see a reference to the European States' practice (3), since the authority quoted in § 24 ('*Borgers v Belgium*, 30 October 1991, § 24, Series A No 214-B') refers to not less than 10 different Court judgments concerning Austria (3), Belgium (2), Denmark, Malta, Sweden, Switzerland and the UK: (*Sramek v Austria* of 22 October 1984, Series A No 84, p 20, para 42; *Bönisch v Austria* of 6 May 1985, Series A No 92, p 15, para 32; *Brandstetter v Austria* of 28 August 1991, Series A No 211, p 21, para 44; *Piersack v Belgium* of 1 October 1982, Series A, No 53, pp 14–15, para 30; *De Cubber v Belgium* of 26 October 1984, Series A, No 86, p 14, para 26; *Hauschildt v Denmark* of 24 May 1989, Series A, No 154, p 21, para 48; *Demicoli v Malta* of 27 August 1991, Series A, No 210, p 18, para 40; *Langborger v Sweden* of 22 June 1989, Series A, No 155, p 16, para 32; *Belilos v Switzerland* of 29 April 1988, Series A, No 132, p 30, para 67; *Campbell and Fell v UK* of 28 June 1984, Series A, No 80, pp 39–40, para 18). This might—at least to a certain extent—be considered as looking for a sort of Council of Europe Member States' practice. However, no specification is made to the public's attitude in respect of the problem at hand. Therefore, accepting this as an (element of?) analysis of European States' practice would not really lead to further clarity in respect of this element.

[103] 'Thus, it is clear that the domestic law of the member States of the Council of Europe has evolved and is continuing to evolve, in company with the relevant international instruments on the subject.' (§ 44 of the *Genovese* judgment)

4.2.1.3 Further References

One further judgment refers specifically to *Demir and Baykara*, though without being greatly related to interpretation questions.

> (13)   ECtHR (Fifth Section), 30 July 2009, App No 67336/01, *Danilenkov and others v Russia* (trade union activity—discrimination), reference in § 123 to § 144 of *Demir and Baykara*.

In its *Danilenkov and others v Russia* judgment, the Fifth Section established a violation of the Convention since the Russian State authorities had tolerated an employer's discriminatory policies (at least indirectly related to the applicants' participation in a strike) and refused to examine a discrimination complaint. In doing so, the Court referred to international standards and respective case law,[104] and also to the *Demir and Baykara* judgment.[105] But these two references were not directly linked: the latter reference deals with the application of the evolution of ECtHR case law in respect of Article 11 ECHR and not with the *Demir and Baykara* approach as such, to which the former should have been related. This attitude is not very convincing.

Furthermore, a number of references are missing. The international standards should have included, in particular, Articles 2(2) and 8(1)(a) ICESCR. As regards case law, references should have been made not only to the respective CESCR but also to the ILO Committee of Experts on the Application of Conventions and Recommendations (CEACR) (references to the Committee on Freedom Association (CFA) are consistent but not sufficient). Moreover, no analysis of Council of Europe Member States' practice (3) was included. What is striking is that the Court, in its reasoning, only refers to one (though most important) general statement (in its reasoning in § 123 to § 107, where the court quotes three further statements from the CFA Digest) and to one specific case (in its reasoning in § 130 to § 108, CFA case No 2199).[106] This means that the other sources were not really taken into account.

In the end, the Court concentrated its discussion on (nevertheless important) procedural aspects. If it had taken more standards and case law into account, the assessment would probably have gone in the direction of a substantive violation of Article 11. In particular, the question of the strike and its negative consequences are not sufficiently taken into account.

4.2.2 Category (B): References to Demir and Baykara *But Not to International Standards*

> (14)   ECtHR (Grand Chamber), 29 March 2010, App No 3394/03, *Medvedyev and others v France*.

---

[104] ESC in §§ 102–04, ILO in §§ 105–08.

[105] Reference in § 123 to *Demir and Baykara* (n 2) § 144.

[106] Complaint against the Government of the Russian Federation presented by the Russian Labour Confederation (KTR) (Case No 2199, CFA Report No 331).

The references to *Demir and Baykara* without any connection to international standards concern a procedural question in the *Medvedyev and others v France* case (reference in § 71[107] to § 58 of *Demir and Baykara*)
and

>   (15)   ECtHR (Fifth Section), 10 November 2009, App Nos 30190 and 30216/06, *Sedelmayer v Germany*.

the fair balance to be struck in respect either of positive obligations or in terms of an interference in the *Sedelmayer v Germany* decision (reference to § 111 of *Demir and Baykara*).

>   (16)   ECtHR (Third Section), 2 February 2010, App No 42430/05, *Aizpurua Ortiz and others v Spain*.

A reference of a different character is to be found in the *Aizpurua Ortiz and others v Spain* case, in which the Third Section considered that the deprivation of supplementary pension rights on the basis of a collective agreement concluded between parties (not entitled to represent the applicants) was not in violation of Article 1 of the First Protocol (protection of property; see below, 4.3.7). Again, the reference to *Demir and Baykara* concerned not the interpretation approach (and no direct reference to international standards was mentioned), but the Grand Chamber's substantive conclusion concerning Article 11 ECHR and its respective protection of the right to collective bargaining.[108] As a borderline case between Article 1 of the First Protocol (protection of property) and Article 11 (freedom of association), it is even more complicated since the applicants were not members of the trade unions concluding the respective collective agreement.[109]

4.3 Categories (C) and (D): ECtHR Judgments (in the Social Field) with No References to *Demir and Baykara*

The following judgments in principle not referring to *Demir and Baykara*[110] are characterised by their impact in the social field. Analysed in line with the Convention's different articles,[111] they can in theory be categorised as to whether they refer to international standards (Category (C)) or not (Category (D)).

---

[107] 'The Court must examine the question, which goes to its jurisdiction, the extent of which is determined by the Convention itself, in particular by Article 32, and not by the parties' submissions in a particular case'.

[108] Reference in § 49 *Demir and Baykara* (n 2) § 154.

[109] Outside the three-year period examined in this section, it is interesting to note that the Third Section referred again to *Demir and Baykara* (n 2) twice in its judgment: 31 January 2012, App No 2330/09, *Sindicatul Păstorul Cel Bun v Romania*, in respect of the right to organise in churches: § 58 refers to § 110 in *Demir and Baykara* (concerning the State's positive obligation) and §§ 61–120 (prohibition as too radical a measure). Again, this did not involve the interpretation approach. (This judgment is under appeal by the Grand Chamber.)

[110] Although four of the following judgments do refer to the *Demir and Baykara* approach (and would therefore fall within Category (A)), they are nonetheless dealt with here due to their social impact.

[111] The non-discrimination provision (Article 14 ECHR) is not dealt with separately; the respective cases can be found under the 'ambit' of substantive rights (inter alia the other material articles in the Convention or in the respective Protocols).

4.3.1 Article 5 ECHR: Right to Liberty and Security

(17) ECtHR (Grand Chamber), 28 September 2010, App No 12050/04, *Mangouras v Spain*

This case is perhaps not a typical 'social field' case, dealing more with environmental and penal law issues. Indeed, the case relates to the applicant's complaints concerning his pre-trial detention for offences including an offence against natural resources and the environment, and the bail set to ensure that he would attend his trial. But it is closely linked insofar as the employer is at least indirectly involved in respect of the bail.

Concerning the three elements, it should be noted that the description of the international standards ((1): §§ 34, 37, 38, 40–42, 43, 44 and 45, 54) and the supervisory bodies' case law ((2): §§ 46 and 47) contain elements which are not directly linked to these criteria ((1a): § 55 and (2a): §§ 35, 48–51). Furthermore, the assessment of the tendency (§ 86) is not very explicit on the concrete basis leading to this result (there is only a general reference).[112] Nevertheless, the Court explicitly refers to the *Hoshinmaru (Japan v Russian Federation)* judgment of the International Tribunal for the Law of the Sea (ITLOS)[113] (§ 89), while stating that it is 'conscious of the fact that the Tribunal's jurisdiction differs from its own'. Finally, it is surprising that no Council of Europe Member States' practice (3) as such was examined.

4.3.2 Article 6 ECHR: Right to a Fair Trial[114]

Although most of the judgments in the social field concern problems regarding Article 6, they do not generally refer to international standards. The reason might be that there are few international standards setting concrete targets for the solution of procedural problems. Generally speaking, the jurisprudence of the Court can be seen as the most advanced, in particular as regards the length of proceedings and the enforcement of judgments.

In this brief analysis, only those judgments which offer a greater basis for possible international standards involvement will be dealt with in some detail.[115]

(18) ECtHR (Second Section), 31 May 2011, App No 46286/09 etc, *Maggio and others v Italy.*

This case immediately merits mention. It concerns the exclusion by law of migrant workers' pension treatments already liquidated. The law settled retrospectively the terms of the disputes before the ordinary courts. Again, no reference is made to international standards.

---

[112] It is interesting to note that the seven dissenting judges agree on this but come to a different conclusion ('we fully share the view of the majority as to the growing and legitimate concerns, in Europe and more broadly, in relation to environmental damage and the increasing tendency to use the criminal law as a means of enforcing the environmental obligations imposed under international law. However, even if, as the majority argue, these new realities have to be taken into account in interpreting the requirements of Article 5 § 3, the seriousness of the offence of which a person is suspected cannot be the decisive factor justifying the size of the bail', para 8)

[113] ITLOS judgment of 6 August 2007, Case No 14.

[114] See, for more detail, Van Drooghenbroek in this volume pp 159 et seq.

[115] For the ECtHR (First Section) judgment (15 January 2009), App No 42454/02, *Menchinskaya v Russia*, see above 4.2.1.2 (11).

4.3.2.1 State Immunity

Three judgments increasingly restrict governments claiming state immunity in cases where individuals access courts for their labour law or social security claims. In this respect, the Court relies very much on developments in international law.

> (19)   ECtHR (Grand Chamber), 23 March 2010, App No 15869/02, *Cudak v Lithuania*.

The first Grand Chamber's judgment in *Cudak v Lithuania* deals with a secretary and switchboard operator at the Polish Embassy requesting compensation for unlawful dismissal before the Lithuanian courts. It refers to 'international law and practice'. The international instruments (1) are mentioned in §§ 25 and 26, 30, 32 and 33, and the description of the practice (3) is taken from the International Law Commission (§ 29).

> (20)   ECtHR (Grand Chamber), 29 June 2011, App No 34869/05, *Sabeh El Leil v France*.

The second Grand Chamber's judgment in *Sabeh El Leil v France* concerns the access to court by the Head Accountant of the French Embassy in Kuwait concerning his termination of employment before the French courts. The judgment refers to relevant international law instruments ((1): § 18–21, France's signing thereof (§ 22), and reference to *Cudak v Lithuania* ([GC], App No 15869/02, §§ 25 ff in § 23): see above). The question of non-ratification of the relevant instrument does not pose the Court any problem since the relevant provision applies under 'customary international law' (§ 54). It is therefore not deemed necessary to refer to § 86 of the *Demir and Baykara* judgment.

> (21)   ECtHR (First Section), 21 June 2011, App No 5613/04, *Zylkov v Russia*.

Although the First Section's *Zylkov v Russia* judgment on the relevant jurisdiction for a social security claim (to the Russian embassy in Vilnius) for an allowance payable to parents of minor children mentions relevant instruments ((1): §§ 16 and 17: Vienna Convention on Diplomatic Relations and the respective bilateral agreement (the latter might perhaps be more a factual element)), there is no indication regarding the ratification status of this UN Convention. Furthermore, no case law or Council of Europe Member States' practice ((2) and (3)) is mentioned. This might be explained by the fact that the two international standards are only mentioned in respect of the national courts' unjustified argumentation. No legal requirements are formulated on this basis.

> (22)   ECtHR (Second Section), 18 January 2011, App No 2555/03, *Guadagnino v Italy and France*.

It should first be noted that the *Guadagnino v Italy and France* judgment (on Italian courts which should have heard industrial disputes concerning an employee of the French school in Rome) lists the relevant international standards (1)[116] and the

---

[116] The general references to the *Cudak* case (see above, 4.3.2.1 (19)) appear somewhat problematic in the sense of specific information on Lithuania which is not relevant to the case at hand; the information should have been given in respect of Italy.

relevant case law (2). However, the practice of Council of Europe Member States (3) was not examined. Consequently, the elements have only been partially taken into account. Concerning the question of the absence of ratification of the State concerned (Italy), the Court did not refer to *Demir and Baykara* (§ 86), but to the fact that this 2004 Convention is a 'partie intégrante du droit coutumier international' (§ 70) and would therefore be binding on Italy anyhow (regarding the same approach, see above (20)).

4.3.2.2 Tribunal

(23)   ECtHR (Second Section), 31 May 2011, App No 45912/06, *İçen v Turkey.*

In the *İçen v Turkey* judgment, a translator, as a civil servant employed by the Turkish army, was convicted of inter alia disobeying orders and was tried by a military tribunal. One might be tempted to see all three elements taken into account by the reference in § 17 to the *Ergin v Turkey (n° 6)* judgment[117] (§§ 20–25), but it appears to be more an additional argument than a decisive element.

4.3.2.3 Length of Proceedings

Seven interesting cases concern the problem of length of proceedings. Since they do not refer to international standards, they are only briefly mentioned.

(24)   ECtHR (Second Section), 27 September 2011, App No 10971/05, *Erciyas v Turkey* (dismissal).

(25)   ECtHR (Second Section), 21 May 2011, App No 29672/02, *Cingil v Turkey* (compensation for work-related illness).

(26)   ECtHR (First Section), 10 March 2011, App No 25966/04, *Titarenko v Russia* (employment dispute).[118]

(27)   ECtHR (Fourth Section), 23 November 2010, App No 7908/07, *Zarembová v Slovakia* (dismissal).

(28)   ECtHR (Fifth Section), 21 October 2010, App No 46881/06, *Ivanov and Dimitrov v The Former Yugoslav Republic of Macedonia* (wages).

(29)   ECtHR (Fifth Section), 14 October 2010, App No 31508/07, *Veriter v France* (period of military service in respect of promotion and pension entitlements).[119]

(30)   ECtHR (First Section), 23 September 2010, App No 34784/02, *Vasilchenko v Russia* (reinstatement, etc).

4.3.2.4 Diverging Jurisprudence

Although the most recent Grand Chamber's judgment on this issue but outside the social field (20 October 2011, App No 13279/05, *Nejdet Şahin and Perihan Şahin v Turkey*) refers to 'comparative law' (§§ 33 and 34), it is interesting to note that the

---

[117] ECtHR No 47533/99, CEDH 2006-VI.
[118] This judgment does not appear in the HUDOC data basis.
[119] The references to the 'Droit européen' (§§ 44–46) are related to the factual assessment of the complexity of the case (§ 67).

following two Chamber judgments do not contain any references to international standards or States' practice:

(31)   ECtHR (Third Section), 2 November 2010, App No 38155/02, *Stefanica and others v Romania* (dismissal).

(32)   ECtHR (Second Section), 13 September 2011, App No 37204/08, *Zivic v Serbia* (salary).

4.3.2.5 Enforcement

Also in respect of the enforcement cases, no references to international standards have been used:

(33)   ECtHR (Second Section), 31 May 2011, App No 1789/07, *Rašković and Milunović v Serbia* (final judgments on several employment rights).

(34)   ECtHR (First Section), 5 April 2011, App No 39272/04, *Kravtsov v Russia* (allowances).

(35)   ECtHR (Second Section), 12 October 2010, App No 29608/05 etc, *Liman-Is Sendikasi v Turkey* (final decisions cancelling calls for tenders for the privatisation of ports).

4.3.3 Article 8 ECHR: Right to Respect for Private and Family Life[120]

Article 8 ECHR has come to play an important part in individual human rights protection, as witnessed inter alia by developments regarding the environment. Yet developments concerning labour issues are only now beginning to gain relevance, underlining the role of the *Demir and Baykara* approach.

4.3.3.1 Private Life and Employment

(36)   ECtHR (Third Section), 3 May 2011, App No 26125/04, *Sipoş v Romania*.

In the *Sipoş v Romania* case, a journalist claimed that a press release had damaged her reputation. Again, this is a Category (D) judgment. Even acknowledging that international standards in the legal sense might not exist, it appears difficult to see that no relevant international material would be available.

(37)   ECtHR (Second Section), 19 October 2010, App No 20999/04, *Özpinar v Turkey* (professional life—judge).

In the *Özpinar v Turkey* case, the dismissal of a judge for reasons related to her private life led the Second Section seeing a violation of Article 8. Since this is a very specific case (Category (D)) with individual circumstances, one might see

---

[120] See for more detail, Hendrick and Van Bever in this volume pp 183 et seq.

justification for not referring to international standards. Nevertheless, it could prove helpful to analyse practice in Council of Europe Member States (3).[121]

> (38)   ECtHR (Fifth Section), 5 October 2010, App No 420/07, *Köpke v Germany*.

In the *Köpke v Germany* case (concerning video surveillance of a supermarket cashier), there is no reference to any of the three elements. This appears a major problem, given that video surveillance in workplace premises is not only becoming increasingly prevalent but also that it is an area that has been taken up in European law.[122]

> (39)   ECtHR (Fifth Section), 23 September 2010, App No 1620/03, *Schüth v Germany*.

There are two cases concerning church employees and their private life: *Schüth v Germany* and *Obst v Germany* (see below (40)). In the former case, a church employee was dismissed for adultery. The Fifth Section's reference to an EU Directive (2000/78,[123] § 27 and § 40, transposed into national legislation) is perhaps not a real reference to international standards (1), though the initiation of an infringement procedure against Germany (also mentioned in § 40) concerning the incorrect transposition of this Directive could perhaps be seen more as case law (2), since the European Commission is the guardian of the Treaties (Article 17(1), third sentence TEU). However, there is no description (let alone analysis) of Council of Europe Member States' practice (3).

As to reliance on international standards, there is a sort of additional argumentation based on the EU Directive and the initial steps of an infringement procedure. These two elements do not thus appear to be the main aspects of the interpretation. In any event, there is a general lack of reference to international standards concerning protection against unfair dismissal (see *Heinisch v Germany*, Section 4.3.5.1 below (46)) and general anti-discrimination norms.

> (40)   ECtHR (Fifth Section), 23 September 2010, App No 425/03, *Obst v Germany*.

The parallel *Obst v Germany* judgment also refers to EU Directive 2000/78 (1), though without any reference to case law (2) or European States' practice (3).

---

[121] In its most recent judgment (9 January 2013, App No 21722/11, *Oleksandr Volkov v Ukraine*) concerning the dismissal of a Supreme Court judge, the Former Fifth Section not only referred to the *Özpinar v Turkey* judgment (§ 165) and thus confirmed the scope of Article 8 in respect of protection against dismissal but also to Council of Europe material (§§ 78–80) and a comparative law research report entitled 'Judicial Independence in Transition' which was completed in 2012 by the Max Planck Institute for Comparative Public Law and International Law (§§ 81 and 82), thus giving an example of element (3) in a Chamber case.

[122] The Court took into account Directive 95/46/EC. But it would have been worthwhile also to consider the Venice Commission to which it attributes so much importance (Opinion on Video Surveillance by Private Operators in the Public and Private Spheres and by Public Authorities in the Private Sphere and Human Rights Protection—Adopted by the Venice Commission at its 71st Plenary Session (Venice, 1–2 June 2007): '18. For the purposes of this study, the private sphere will also include workplaces and the use of video surveillance in workplace premises, which raises legal issues concerning the employees' privacy rights.'

[123] Directive 2000/78/EC of 27 November 2000 establishing a general framework for equal treatment in employment and occupation.

In its reasoning, this judgment refers even less to international standards, only marginally mentioning the EU Directive (§ 51). The deficits noted in respect of the *Schüth* judgment (see above (39)) are at least equally valid here.

4.3.3.2 Private Life and Discrimination (Article 14)

There are two main areas in which social questions have been brought to the Court. The first concerns access to employment, while the second covers social security issues in a wider sense.[124]

> (41)   ECtHR (Second Section), 7 April 2009, App No 26652/02, *Žičkus v Lithuania.*

Looking at the *Žičkus v Lithuania* judgment, a case belonging to Category (D) (no reference either to *Demir and Baykara* or to any international instrument), it should be recalled that relevant international instruments on employment discrimination exist which should be taken into account (eg, Articles 2(2) and 6 ICESCR, ILO Convention No 111, Article 1(2) RESC, together with the relevant case law). By applying the *Demir and Baykara* approach, more convincing arguments establishing a violation could probably have been used.[125]

> (42)   ECtHR (First Section), 28 October 2010, App No 40080/07, *Fawsie v Greece.*

In the *Fawsie v Greece* case, the authorities (the family allowance section of a farmer's social security organisation) had refused to grant social security benefits to political refugees. As an international standard (1), the First Section takes into account solely Article 23 of the 1951 Geneva Convention (in § 38 of the judgment). Yet there are further standards, in particular the scope of the RESC[126] and the respective case law concerning its Article 12, § 4(2),[127] which go unmentioned. Further references to the practice in European States (3) would also be required.

> (43)   ECtHR (First Section), 28 October 2010, App No 40083/07, *Saidoun v Greece.*

---

[124] For the other cases directly related to social security, see below, 4.3.7.2. The ECtHR (Fourth Section) judgment (28 September 2011), App No 37060/06, *JM v UK* is not included in the analysis because it deals with child maintenance obligations (more related to family law).

[125] The narrow 4:3 majority for a violation could thus perhaps have been increased.

[126] 'Appendix to the European Social Charter (Revised) Scope of the Revised European Social Charter in terms of persons protected ...

2. Each Party will grant to refugees as defined in the Convention relating to the Status of Refugees, signed in Geneva on 28 July 1951 and in the Protocol of 31 January 1967, and lawfully staying in its territory, treatment as favourable as possible, and in any case not less favourable than under the obligations accepted by the Party under the said convention and under any other existing international instruments applicable to those refugees.'

[127] ECSR, Digest 2008: 'The scope of Article 12 § 4 extends to refugees and stateless persons', p 93; 'This exception does not simply confirm parties' obligations under these conventions regarding equal treatment for refugees and stateless persons but also invites states to go further by offering them treatment as favourable as possible', p 182.

In the parallel *Saidoun v Greece* case, the same references and argumentation apply as in the *Fawsie v Greece* judgment (see above (42)).

(44)   ECtHR(First Section), 7 October 2010, App No 30078/06, *Konstantin Markin v Russia*.

The core issue in the *Konstantin Markin v Russia* case is the refusal to grant parental leave. By referring to ILO reports (§§ 26–27), this judgment attempts to provide relevant information on the first two elements. However, this does not appear to be sufficient: with regard to international standards (1), no reference is made to Article 27(2) RESC and Article 33(2) CFREU. The lack of any reference to Article 27(2) RESC is even less understandable since the Russian Federation has accepted this provision. Concerning the relevant case law (2), the European Committee of Social Rights dealt with this issue in respect of the Contracting Parties accepting this provision. Nevertheless, the Court adds a comparative analysis (3) in respect of parental leave (§§ 28–30).

The general argument for a lack of further references to international standards might be that the case concerned mainly the discrimination aspect and not the right to parental leave as such. In such a situation and taking the *Demir and Baykara* approach seriously, it would be all the more important to take the whole set of international standards and relevant case law into account, as seen by the recent Grand Chamber judgment.[128]

4.3.4 *Article 9 ECHR: Freedom of Thought, Conscience and Religion*[129]

(45)   ECtHR (Fifth Section), 3 February 2011, App No 18136/02, *Siebenhaar v Germany*.

The close relationship between Articles 8 and 9 ECHR is shown in the *Siebenhaar v Germany* (on the dismissal of a kindergarten teacher by a church for active commitment to another religious community), in which the Fifth Section's judgment refers to the *Schüth* and *Obst* judgments. The same evaluation would therefore apply (see above 4.3.3.1 (39) and (40)).

---

[128] Outside the reference period of this analysis, this case has been decided by the Grand Chamber (judgment 22 March 2012). On the one hand, the references to international standards have been significantly improved. Besides general references to non-discrimination, we find references to provisions in international law which provide for parental leave; see the references to Articles 5 and 16 CEDAW (§§ 49 and 50) and the relevant case law (§ 51). Similarly, the relevant ILO standards (Article 1 Convention 111; Article 3 Convention 156 and Article 22 of the respective Recommendation No 165) are mentioned (§§ 52–54). Concerning the Council of Europe, the references include Article 27(2) RESC as well as several Resolutions and Recommendations of the Parliamentary Assembly and the Committee of Ministers (§§ 55–62). Finally, in respect of the EU, the relevant provisions of Directives 96/34/EC and 2010/18/EU as well as the relevant jurisprudence of the CJEU are mentioned (§§ 63–70). On the other hand, all these references have not brought the Grand Chamber to recognise a right to parental leave under Article 8 ECHR (§ 130; see, conversely, the Partly Concurring Opinion of Judge Pinto De Albuquerque, who explicitly states: 'The right to parental leave is a Convention right'). From an equally disappointing methodological point of view, the Grand Chamber, in analysing the developments in international and comparative law materials (§ 140), lays its main emphasis on the latter ('legal changes to the domestic laws of Contracting States').

[129] See for more detail, Vickers in this volume.

4.3.5 Article 10 ECHR: Freedom of Expression[130]

4.3.5.1 Related to Individual Labour Rights

> (46) ECtHR (Fifth Section), 21 July 2011, App No 28274/08, *Heinisch v Germany*.

The *Heinisch v Germany* judgment (on the dismissal of an employee for having lodged a criminal complaint against the employer) refers to international standards (1),[131] but in its reasoning, only CoE Recommendation (1a) is mentioned as an additional argument (in § 73)[132] and only concerning a minor question (whether the applicant had alternative channels for making the disclosure). Furthermore, the references to the ILO and the RESC are not accompanied by any case law and the Court does not examine the Council of Europe Member States' practices. The reason for the former could be that there is not much specific case law available in this field, whereas the reason for the latter might be that it is difficult to obtain.

> (47) ECtHR (First Section), 30 September 2010, App No 28369/07, *Balenović v Croatia*.

In the *Balenović v Croatia* case, an employee was dismissed for having informed the public about inter alia alleged fraud of his employer (whistleblowing). The decision of the First Section (inadmissibility on ground of being manifestly ill-founded) did not refer to any of the *Demir and Baykara* approach elements. Compared to the *Heinisch* judgment (see above (46)),[133] one can see certain advantages in taking into account at least some of the relevant elements.

> (48) ECtHR (Fourth Section), 17 September 2009, App No 13936/02, *Manole and others v Moldova*.

In the *Manole and others v Moldova* case, the applicants, who were all employed or formerly employed as journalists at Teleradio-Moldova ('TRM'), alleged that they were victims of a practice of undue political influence over editorial policy,

---

[130] See for more detail, Voorhoof and Humblet in this volume pp 237 et seq.

[131] § 37: Resolution 1729 (2010) of the Parliamentary Assembly on 'The protection of "whistle-blowers" and related Recommendation 1916 (2010); § 38: Article 24 of the Revised European Social Charter; § 39: Termination of Employment Convention of the International Labour Organisation (ILO Convention No 158 of 22 June 1982). In the *Sosinowska v Poland* case (judgment 18 October 2011, App No 14277/04) (not dealing directly with labour law issues but with disciplinary proceedings brought against the applicant) in which the medical courts had found that the applicant had discredited another doctor, in breach of the *Code of Medical Ethics*, and had given her a reprimand, the Fourth Section did not refer to any international (labour) standards. This may be explained merely by the fact that the case did not primarily deal with labour law issues (separate labour court proceedings had been initiated by the applicant in this respect).

[132] 'The Court further notes that similar reasoning is reflected in the Parliamentary Assembly's guiding principles on the protection of whistle-blowers [see 'Relevant international law and practice' above] stipulating that where internal channels could not reasonably be expected to function properly, external whistle-blowing should be protected.'

[133] Perhaps the most striking difference to the *Heinisch* case (dealing even with a criminal complaint against the employer) is: 'With regard to the first factor, the Court notes that the applicant was not a journalist—whose role is to inform and alert the public and impart information and ideas on matters of public concern—but an employee, who owes her employer a duty of loyalty, reserve and discretion' (under 'The Law' B.2 (b)(ii)).

in breach of Article 10 ECHR. According to the new law on the privatisation of TRM, the staff of the old State Company TRM had to pass an examination in order to be employed at the new Public Company. Only some were (re-)employed, the others being made redundant.[134] Although there are references to CoE materials (§§ 51–52, 61), elements (1)–(3) do not appear in this case in a strict sense. With regard to element (1), no legally binding international standard was referred to; consequently, no relevant case law (2) is to be found. Moreover, there is no reference to European States' practice (3). However, CoE Recommendation 1a is quoted and in two paragraphs the Court states that 'standards relating to public service broadcasting which have been agreed by the Contracting States through the Committee of Ministers of the Council of Europe provide guidance as to the approach which should be taken to interpreting Article 10 in this field' (§§ 102 and 107).

> (49) ECtHR (First Section), 26 February 2009, App No 29492/05, *Kudeshkina v Russia.*

The *Kudeshkina v Russia* case concerned the dismissal of a judge from the judiciary because of a public accusation of higher judicial officials (in particular, the President of the Moscow City Court) of having put pressure on her. In its judgment, the First Section does not refer to any of the three elements, although several international standards in respect of dismissals are in force (ILO Convention No 158, Article 24 RESC and Article 30 CFREU).[135]

4.3.5.2 Related to Collective Labour Rights

In this section, the general question is whether the respective problems are more connected to Article 10 or Article 11 ECHR. In the following judgments, the Court tends more towards Article 10, whereas, in principle, any trade union activity should be considered under Article 11[136] (see in this sense below, 4.3.6.2 (52)).

> (50) ECtHR (Grand Chamber), 12 September 2011, App Nos 28955/06, 28957/06, 28959/06 and 28964/06, *Palomo Sánchez and others v Spain.*

The Grand Chamber's *Palomo Sánchez and others v Spain* judgment (concerning the dismissal of a group of trade unionists after the union's newsletter had published a cartoon and articles considered to be insulting to two other employees and a manager) could at first glance be considered as exemplary in respect of references to international standards. It covers all the three relevant elements and is even more detailed in respect of Council of Europe Member States' practice. However, there are still several problems to which the dissenting opinions explicitly refer. Furthermore, reference to ILO case law in order to restrict interpretation of the Convention might well conflict with the relevant provision.[137]

---

[134] The background of the case is a protest strike against political influence (in particular § 33); sanctions followed (§§ 37 ff).

[135] Had these been taken into account, the narrow 4:3 majority for a violation could perhaps have been increased.

[136] See in this sense (Article 11 *lex specialis* in relation to Article 10) ECtHR (Second Section) Admissibility decision (1 February 2011), App No 2344/02, *Dritsas and others v Italy.*

[137] See n 82.

(51)   ECtHR (Fifth Section), 6 October 2011, App No 32820/09, *Vellutini and Michel v France*.

In the *Vellutini and Michel v France* judgment (concerning the conviction of the president and the general secretary of a union for public defamation of a mayor, on the basis of statements made in their capacity as union officials), the Fifth Section does not refer to any elements of the *Demir and Baykara* approach. Even the reference to the Grand Chamber's *Palomo Sánchez and others v Spain* judgment, with its nigh-exemplary references to international standards, is only related to an '*a contrario*' argumentation (in § 39 to *Palomo Sánchez and others v Spain*; see above (50), § 67).

4.3.6 Article 11 ECHR: Freedom of Assembly and Association

This article is examined in some more detail, given the fact that it is the most 'social rights'-oriented provision in the Convention. For this reason, admissibility decisions (in the post-*Demir and Baykara* period) are also covered. Of the several decisions looked at,[138] it appears that one of them could raise substantive problems under Article 11 insofar as the legal argument developed by the applicant's trade union had not been shared by the domestic courts;[139] this more procedural problem could, however, be considered as relating more to Article 6 than to Article 11.

It is interesting to note that there is an admissibility decision concerning an employer's case involving the freedom of association as a human right,[140] in which the Court refers to international standards (1) and respective case law (2).

---

[138] The following decisions were not examined: (Second Section) Committee Decision (14 September 2010), App No 46749/06, *Pešić v Serbia*: the description of the facts does not reveal to what extent Article 11 was involved (which the Court denies). (Fourth Section) Decision 27 April 2010, App No 36748/05—*Bogatu v Moldova*: the applicant did not complain about labour rights (many journalists who had protested earlier against censorship were not selected), but about a sanction for participation in an 'unauthorised demonstration'. (Third Section) Decision 19 January 2010, App No 35812/02 *Vodà v Romania*: the applicant had originally complained under Article 11 of the Convention of interference with his right to participate in a trade union by dismissal from his job, but later declared that he was abandoning his complaints under Articles 8 and 11 of the Convention. In four cases in which the applicants had complained on grounds of having been dismissed for absence from work due to their participation at a properly organised strike, a friendly settlement was reached: (Fifth Section) Decisions (2 December 2008), App No 21080/06, *Iljeva and others*; No 30350/06, *Stojanovski*; No 10278/06, *Maruskov and others*; No 19667/06, *Zekir v the former Yugoslav Republic of Macedonia*. The facts will most probably be similar to those described in the ECtHR (Fourth Section) judgment (17 September 2009), App No 13936/02, *Manole and others v Moldova*, in particular §§ 33 and 34 (see below 4.3.4 (49)).

[139] (Second Section) Decision (12 May 2009), App No 22433/05 *Davitashvili v Georgia*: 'Under Article 11 of the Convention, the applicant complained that the domestic courts had not shared the arguments of the labour union of which she was a member. ... However, in the light of all the material in its possession, and in so far as the matters complained of are within its competence, the Court finds that they do not disclose any appearance of a violation of the rights and freedoms set out in the Convention or its Protocols.'

[140] ECtHR (Fourth Section) Decision (2 December 2008) which led afterwards to the Judgment (27 April 2010), App No 20161/06, *Vörður Ólafsson v Iceland* (referring in substance to the same quotations concerning the ESC in § 22, and the ILO in §§ 23 ff): imposition of an obligation by law to pay an industry charge.

4.3.6.1 Right Not to Be Discriminated Against

As regards the protection of trade union(ists) against discrimination based on their respective activities, reference is made to the previously examined *Danilenkov and others v Russia* case (see above, 4.2.1.3 (13)).

4.3.6.2 Right to Trade Union Activity

(52) ECtHR (Second Section), 27 September 2011, App No 1305/05, *Şişman and others v Turkey.*

Closely linked to freedom of expression but examined under Article 11 ECHR,[141] the *Şişman and others v Turkey* judgment concerned trade union posters encouraging participation in the annual 1 May demonstration on office walls rather than on the notice board set aside for that purpose. No reference was made to any of the three elements. This is all the more surprising since the Grand Chamber judgment (see above, 4.3.5.2 (50)) given two weeks before extensively referred to the relevant international standards in a somewhat similar context.

4.3.6.3 Right to Strike[142]

(53) ECtHR (Fifth Section), 5 March 2009, App No 31684/05, *Barraco v France*

The *Barraco v France* case (concerning a lorry driver who participated in a traffic-slowing operation with complete blockage of motorway traffic organised as part of a national day of protest by a joint trade union committee representing hauliers and who had subsequently faced criminal charges) refers neither to *Demir and Baykara* nor to any international standards. This appears surprising as the core of the case was a collective action.[143] But the Court implicitly neglected this dimension and reduced it to the question of a 'peaceful assembly' (with strong links to Article 10; see § 27). Taking the core of the case seriously, an enormous quantity and quality of international standards, case law, etc would have had to have been referred to in an even more extensive manner than in *Enerji Yapi-yol Sen c Turquie* (see above, 4.2.1.1 (6)), which for the first time expressly recognised the right to strike as enshrined in Article 11 ECHR.

(54) ECtHR (Second Section), 15 September 2009, App No 30946/04, *Kaya and Seyhan v Turkey.*

In continuation of the *Karaçay* case (27 March 2007, App No 6615/03, *Karaçay c Turquie*),[144] but in several places referring to the *Enerji Yapi-yol Sen c Turquie*

---

[141] 'Ils invoquent la violation des articles 10, 11 et 14 de la Convention. Eu égard à la formulation des griefs, la Cour décide de les examiner uniquement sous l'angle de l'article 11' (§ 16).

[142] See for more detail, see Dorssemont in this volume pp 333 et seq.

[143] 'Day of protest by a joint trade-union committee' (press release by the Registrar 176, 5 March 2009); 'déposer un préavis de grève' (§ 7).

[144] 'Quant au fond, la Cour rappelle qu'elle a déjà eu l'occasion d'examiner de tels griefs dans l'arrêt *Karaçay* précité (§§ 14–17) et a conclu à la violation des articles 11 et 13 de la Convention. Elle ne voit aucune raison en l'espèce de s'écarter de cette jurisprudence.'

judgment (see above, 4.2.1.1 (6)), the Second Section, in its *Kaya and Seyhan v Turkey* judgment (dealing with teachers and trade union members taking part in collective action organised by the trade union and as a result having received warnings) has strengthened Article 11 ECHR by prohibiting discrimination based on participation in strike action (national action days). Although it does not directly refer to international standards, there is, however, an indirect link: in § 29, the judgment refers to the *Enerji Yapi-Yol Sen* judgment (§ 32),[145] which is itself based on the *Demir and Baykara* judgment (see above, 4.2.1.1 (6)).

> (55)   ECtHR (Second Section), 15 September 2009, App No 22943/04, *Saime Özcan v Turkey*.
>
> (56)   ECtHR (Second Section), 13 July 2010, App No 33322/07, *Çerikci v Turkey*.

In contrast to these indirect links to the *Demir and Baykara* approach, the other two Second Section judgments, ie, *Saime Özcan v Turkey* (teachers and members of the trade union taking part in national days of strike action organised by the trade union and consequently facing criminal charges) and *Çerikci v Turkey* (civil servant sanctioned for having taken part in a strike action in the context of a national action day) do not contain references to any of the elements of this approach.

> (57)   ECtHR (Fifth Section), 28 October 2010, App No 4241/03, *Trofimchuk v Ukraine*.

In the *Trofimchuk v Ukraine* judgment (concerning the dismissal of an employee for systematic breach of her employment duties on 10 March 1999, which was one week after she had participated in a picket to express concerns over past unpaid wages and the management of the company she worked for), no references to elements (1)–(3) are to be found. This is even less acceptable, since most of the relevant instruments are mentioned in the *Demir and Baykara* judgment itself. In addition, all instruments providing protection against discrimination on account of trade union activity (eg, ILO Conventions Nos 98 and 158, Article 24 RESC with annex) should have been referred to. In particular, picketing is a normal trade union (strike) activity recognised by the ILO supervisory bodies in particular.[146]

4.3.7 Additional Protocol[147] 1, Article 1: Protection of Property (also in Conjunction with Article 14 ECHR: Prohibition of Discrimination)

Protection of property rights is to a large extent recognised in international standards. In respect of social matters, it is interesting to explore practice in Council of Europe Member States (in particular concerning constitutional protection). The

---

[145] In § 32 of the *Enerji Yapi-Yol Sen* judgment, no direct reference to *Demir and Baykara* is to be found. However, the same reasoning is indirectly applied in respect of taking international standards into account.

[146] CEACR: Individual Observation concerning Freedom of Association and Protection of the Right to Organise Convention, 1948 (No 87) Turkey (ratification: 1993) published: 2009; CFA Digest 2006, §§ 648 ff.

[147] The official title is 'Protocol to the Convention for the Protection of Human Rights and Fundamental Freedoms' (Paris, 20 March 1952) with no reference to its character as 'first' (Additional) Protocol.

connection of this right to social issues is described below in greater detail.[148] In the following section, only the respective Court's judgments in the aftermath of *Demir and Baykara* are briefly looked at.

4.3.7.1 Labour Law Rights

Two cases have already been mentioned: *Aizpurua Ortiz et autres c Espagne* (see above, 4.2.2 (16)) and *Rašković and Milunović v Serbia* (see above 4.3.2.5 (33)). As in these cases, the following judgments similarly do not contain any reference to the *Demir and Baykara* approach.

(58) ECtHR (First Section), 20 May 2010, App No 55555/08, *Lelas v Croatia*.
(59) ECtHR (First Section), 18 October 2011, App Nos 38767/07, etc, *Šarić and others v Croatia*.

Both cases deal with the employer's (the state) refusal to pay special allowances for demining work.

4.3.7.2 Social Security Rights

The Court has always seemed cautious in respect of a general recognition of the (fundamental) right to social security, although there are several international instruments or provisions that include this right.[149]

Apart from this general observation, a number of judgments concerning social security issues which have already been mentioned may be recalled. One is the Second Section's *Cingil v Turkey* judgment (see above 4.3.2.3 (25)), this time concerning the amount of compensation for work-related illness and the level of statutory interest in relation to the rate of inflation. Again, the Court does not use the *Demir and Baykara* approach in whatever form. The same applies to the *Maggio and others v Italy* case (see above 4.3.2 (18)), this time concerning the 'readjustment' of migrants workers' pension rights where, again, no reference is made to international standards.[150]

(60) ECtHR (Grand Chamber), 7 July 2011, App No 37452/02, *Stummer v Austria*.

In the *Stummer v Austria* case concerning a former prisoner's complaint of his non-affiliation to the old-age pension system for work performed in prison and his consequent inability to receive pension benefits under that scheme, the Grand Chamber mentioned all three elements. However, it is surprising that this decision only refers to the CoE Prison Rules and practice of the Council of Europe Member States (negatively), but does not refer in its reasoning to the trends in international law, although they are mentioned to quite some extent in the description of the facts.

---

[148] See Herzfeld Olsson's contribution in this volume pp 381 et seq.
[149] See below inter alia (63).
[150] In contrast to some other judgments, the (international law) Italo-Swiss Convention on Social Security is described in §§ 27–30 under the heading 'Relevant Domestic Law and Practice'.

(61)   ECtHR (Grand Chamber), 16 March 2010, App No 42184/05, *Carson and others v UK*.

In the *Carson and others v UK* case concerning the failure to up-rate the applicants' pensions in line with inflation, the Grand Chamber refers to international standards (1), but not to case law (2) or Council of Europe Member States' practice (3). International standards are taken into account, but more to reject a positive interpretation.[151] This again could raise problems, at least in respect of Article 19(8) ILO Constitution.[152]

(62)   ECtHR (Grand Chamber), 18 February 2009, App No 55707/00, *Andrejeva v Latvia*.

The Grand Chamber's judgment in the *Andrejeva v Latvia* case concerns the application of transitional provisions of the relevant State Pensions Act leading to the deprivation of pension entitlements in respect of many years of employment. It only mentions (in §§ 44 ff) bilateral agreements (1), but not any case law (2) or Council of Europe Member States' practice (3). Moreover, this reference is only used to answer the government's argument of an absence of binding force of the bilateral agreements by referring to the relevant obligations deriving from Article 14 ECHR (§ 90) and therefore rejecting this argument. Interestingly enough, the dissenting opinion by Judge Ziemele refers to *Demir and Baykara* in two respects. First, she does not refer to the summary (§ 85), but only to the description of the case law in respect of references to international standards (§ 67). Second, this reference is not used in respect of the bilateral agreement(s), but instead applies to international law on the succession of states.

(63)   ECtHR (Fifth Section), 4 November 2010, App Nos 14480/08 and 47916/08, *Tarkoev and others v Estonia*.

In the *Tarkoev and others v Estonia* judgment concerning the failure of the Estonian authorities to pay the applicants pensions, one could perhaps acknowledge that international standards (1) were referred to (this could be challenged since this is more a bilateral (and thus factual) level of the case). However, it should be noted that no other international standards on social security (pensions) are mentioned (eg, Article 9 ICESCR, ILO Conventions 102, Article 12 RESC, etc). Case law (2) and Council of Europe Member States' practice (3) are also missing. The reason is probably linked to the Court's reluctance to interpret Article 1 of Protocol No 1 in the sense of covering social security or pensions 'as such' and should therefore possibly be reconsidered.

(64)   ECtHR (First Section), 3 March 2011, App No 57028/00, *Klein v Austria*.

The *Klein v Austria* case is probably not the 'typical' workers' case insofar as it concerns a (self-employed) lawyer whose claim to a lawyer's old-age pension (the Chamber of Lawyers Pension Fund) was refused after he lost his right to practice.

---

[151] But the dissenters do not refer to this aspect.
[152] See n 82.

The First Section refers neither to *Demir and Baykara* nor to any international standards, whereas they do exist even in respect of liberal professions (see, eg, Article 12§4 RESC).[153] As in the *Tarkoev and others v Estonia* case (see above (63)), the very general problem (of interpretation) of Article 1, First Protocol remains, insofar as—according to the Court's case law—it does not cover pensions 'as such': taking into account all international instruments, case law and European States' practice, it would probably have to be reconsidered.

(65) ECtHR (Fourth Section), 26 July 2011, App No 30614/06, *Iwaszkiewicz v Poland*.

The *Iwaszkiewicz v Poland* case concerns the withdrawal of a veteran's disability pension. The Fourth Section does not refer to any international standards. Even if ILO Convention 102 would not appear to apply to this branch of social security as regards Poland,[154] it should be recalled that the Court did not attribute significance to the fact of whether the country concerned had ratified (or accepted) the relevant part of an international instrument (see above, 3.2.1.2). Moreover, Poland has accepted all provisions on social security contained in Article 12 ESC.[155]

(66) ECtHR (Fifth Section), 17 February 2011, App No 6268/08, *Andrle v Czech Republic*.

In the *Andrle v Czech Republic* case concerning the discrimination against a man in respect of pension age, the Fifth Section refers twice (§ 49)[156] to the developments in European States by referring to previous judgments (although it does not mention them in the description of the facts). Other international standards are not mentioned.

(67) ECtHR (Fifth Section), 10 March 2011, App No 10972/05, *Suk v Ukraine*.

The Fifth Chamber made an important statement in the *Suk v Ukraine* case concerning the refusal to pay benefits (subsistence payment) for budgetary reasons: 'the Court does not accept the Government's budgetary argument, as it is not open to a State authority to cite a lack of funds as an excuse for not honouring its obligations' (§ 24). However, this is again not based on or related to any element of the *Demir and Baykara* approach.

(68) ECtHR (Fourth Section), 25 October 2011, App No 2033/04, *Valkov and others v Bulgaria*.

---

[153] ECSR, Digest 2008, 93: 'The scope of Article 12 §4 extends to refugees and stateless persons. Self-employed workers are also covered' (see also respective notes 389 and 390 with the authorities).

[154] In its ratification, Poland did not accept Part IX (Invalidity Benefits) of the ILO Social Security (Minimum Standards) Convention 1952 (No 102).

[155] See, eg, Article 12(3) ESC obliging Contracting Parties 'to endeavor to raise progressively the system of social security to a higher level'.

[156] 'one of the relevant factors may be the existence or non-existence of common ground between the laws of the Contracting States (see *Rasmussen v Denmark*, 28 November 1984, § 40, Series A no. 87) ... efforts for advancement of the equality of the sexes which is today a major goal in the member States of the Council of Europe (see *Konstantin Markin v Russia*, App No 30078/06, § 47, 7 October 2010 (not final, subject to Article 44 § 2 of the Convention [see now Grand Chamber's judgment 22 March 2012, n 128]), and *Ünal Tekeli*, cited above, § 59).'

The *Valkov and others v Bulgaria* case concerning pension caps appears problematic since the Fourth Section refers, under the heading of 'Relevant Comparative Material', to World Bank and OECD studies without taking into account information from other sources like the ILO[157] or the European Committee of Social Rights assessments in respect of Article 12 RESC. Furthermore, any international standard in this respect is neglected.

4.4 Interim Conclusions

Looking at the Court's follow-up of the *Demir and Baykara* judgment in the three following years is all the more relevant, given that the Court's Grand Chamber established a guideline for interpreting the Convention, stating that it 'can and must take into account' international standards (see above, 2.2). Therefore, one could perhaps assume that this approach would be found in a large number of judgments, even taking into account that many judgments apply principles (and therefore do not interpret the Convention) and that in several cases international standards are not available.[158]

Only 16 judgments of this three-year period of ECtHR jurisprudence directly quote *Demir and Baykara*. Of these, only six refer to and apply the consolidated approach (though not always in a comprehensive manner), whereby two of these are Grand Chamber judgments. The other 10 judgments (including one decision) refer only to certain aspects of this approach or even to other elements not directly linked to the approach.

In quantitative terms, the total of 16 judgments with references to *Demir and Baykara,* in relation to a total of about 4,500 judgments during this period,[159] represents less than half of one per cent. Were this analysis to stop there, the quantitative result would be that the Court in practice ignored its own guidelines. However, the picture can be somewhat improved by comparing (only) the respective Grand Chamber's judgments. As already pointed out, two of them directly quote the consolidated approach and one further judgment refers to a different point in the *Demir and Baykara* judgment. In relation to about 50 Grand Chamber judgments,[160] the percentage now rises to six per cent, though this is still quite a low rate.

Against this background, it is worthwhile conducting a first qualitative analysis. In doing so, the quantity of judgments is a problem for such an analysis. Bearing in mind that some 4,500 judgments would have to be examined, such an attempt does not appear feasible. In the context of this publication, it therefore seemed logical

---

[157] See, eg, ILO (ed), *Social Security for Social Justice and a Fair Globalization* (Report VI, International Labour Conference, 100th Session, 2011), (Geneva, International Labour Office, 2011).

[158] Including the practice of Council of Europe Members States in the term 'international standards', it would be surprising not to find any European practice in most of those cases. Following its own guidelines, in such a scenario, the Court should at least include an analysis of such practice.

[159] For reasons of simplicity, the three years 2008–10 are taken instead of the period December 2008–November 2011: 2008: 1,534, 2009: 1,625; 2010: 1,499 (4,658). Since the 2011 figure until the end of September stands at 1,047 judgments, the level of 2010 might not be reached. Therefore, the very rough figure of about 4,500 judgments is used.

[160] 2008: 16, 2009: 17, 2010: 18 (see n 162).

to restrict exploration to judgments dealing with social questions including mainly labour and social security[161] issues as well as the respective procedural problems.

Besides this restriction, it is necessary to define what is meant by 'qualitative analysis'. It should first be recalled that Categories (C) and (D) only deal with judgments not directly referring to *Demir and Baykara*. In order to be related to the *Demir and Baykara* approach, it would, in principle, be necessary for them to follow—at least in substance—the *Demir and Baykara* approach (see above, 2.2). Yet, in the follow-up, there are, if any, only a few judgments fully applying it. A large 'grey area' therefore exists which could end once any of the three elements is referred to. In such a case, the *Demir and Baykara* approach as such would not have applied; instead, it would represent a simple repetition of pre-*Demir and Baykara* references to international standards. But even in those cases, one can imagine that *Demir and Baykara* might have contributed (at least to a certain extent) to references to international standards. In any event and for reasons of simplicity, it appears justifiable that all judgments referring in some way to international standards are taken into account in Category (C).

The second group of judgments in the social field refers neither to the *Demir and Baykara* approach nor to any sort of international standards (Category (D)). These cases need to be looked at carefully, as they can raise very substantial questions as to the interpretation of the Convention. Here the more fundamental question is: why does the Court not apply its own methodology?

Against this background, this analysis lists some 50 judgments dealing with social questions during this period.[162] At first glance, such a low number might seem surprising. As an initial explanation, it should be recalled that the Court has only recently started interpreting civil and political rights as also containing a social dimension. It will therefore take time for more 'social' cases to be dealt with by the Court.

Out of these 50 judgments, about two-fifths refer (at least to a certain extent) to international standards and can thus be considered to have at least in substance followed the main thrust of the *Demir and Baykara* approach. In the other set of cases (about three-fifths of the total number), international standards are ignored. One possible explanation might be their absence. But even in the social field, such absence is becoming increasingly improbable in the light of such legal instruments as the RESC and the EU's primary (including the CFREU) and secondary social legislation. Moreover, even in such a case, it is hardly conceivable that no practice exists in Council of Europe Member States representing the third element in the *Demir and Baykara* approach. Another probable explanation is a lack of knowledge and a very limited framework, not allowing for in-depth studies in all cases. But this is exactly what is required to make the *Demir and Baykara* approach fully effective. In general, one might even assume a Court's reluctance to openly discuss interpretation questions and a preference for a 'low-profile' approach allowing for pure references to previous judgments (often on a somewhat selective and not totally coherent

---

[161] Although 'social security' is in general terms not covered by the publication's heading ('employment relationship'), it appears useful for this methodological analysis (in particular in respect of gaining more opportunities for comparison).

[162] If a judgment deals with more than one article, it is only counted once.

basis). This is all the more deplorable since *Demir and Baykara* literally requires a consistent and friendly approach towards international standards ('can and must take into account': § 85).

5 CONCLUSIONS

The Court has established a consolidated methodology which may be called the '*Demir and Baykara* approach'. The main idea is to take international standards, case law and Council of Europe Member States' practice into account when interpreting the Convention. This is particularly relevant in the social field to which the Court is increasingly paying attention on account of the plethora of international standards and associated case law coming mainly from the UN, the ILO, the CoE itself and the EU.

However, this approach has been (sometimes severely) criticised. This contribution has attempted to defuse the arguments put forward, implying that the Court should follow its own approach.

Analysing the Court's subsequent jurisprudence, it seems impossible to demonstrate consistent use of the *Demir and Baykara* approach. Conversely, the meagre number of references to this approach or even to international standards only demonstrates how important it is to increase awareness in respect of this approach. In the social field in particular, there is a need to apply this approach in a consistent manner in order to avoid contradicting judgments and, more generally, legal uncertainty. In doing so, social rights can be expected to fully attain the status of human rights.

Summing up, the Court's 'consolidated' approach referring to international standards in general and to the associated case law is an important step forward towards a more systematic and less fragmented consideration of developments in international law for interpretational purposes, underlining the importance of the principles of the indivisibility of human rights. It remains to be applied in future cases far more, in particular in the social field, and requires detailed litigation strategies.

2

A Twenty-First-Century Procession of Echternach: The Accession of the EU to the European Convention on Human Rights

RICK LAWSON

1 INTRODUCTION

THE PROCESSION OF Echternach is an annual dancing procession held in the medieval town centre of Echternach, the oldest city of Luxembourg. Traditionally its participants take three steps forward and two steps back—thus taking five steps in order to advance one. This is not unlike the process that is supposed to result, eventually, in the EU's accession to the European Convention on Human Rights (ECHR).

Already in the 1960s, academic writing had addressed the question of whether human rights were sufficiently protected in the emerging legal order of the European Communities; several authors argued that, one way or another, the Communities ought to be bound by the ECHR.[1] Nothing much happened until some 10 years later, in 1979, the Commission issued a memorandum proposing that the Communities accede to the ECHR.[2] This prompted another lively debate,[3] but no concrete steps followed.

---

[1] See, for instance, M Waelbroeck, 'La Convention européenne des Droits de l'Homme lie-t-elle les Communautés européennes?' in *Droit communautaire et droit national* (Bruges, College d'Europe, 1965) 306–33; HG Schermers, 'De binding van internationale organisaties aan regelingen tot bescherming van mensenrechten' in Van Boven and others, *Rechten van de mens in perspectief* (Deventer, Kluwer, 1968) 121–37; P Pescatore, 'Les droits de l'homme et l'integration européenne' (1968) 4 *Cahiers droit europeen* 629–73; J Kropholler, 'Die europäischen Gemeinschaften und der Grundrechtsschutz' (1969) 4 *Europarecht* 128–46; M Sørensen, 'The Enlargement of the European Communities and the Protection of Human Rights' (1971) 19 *Annales d'études européennes* 3–22; M Zuleeg, 'Fundamental Rights and the Law of the European Communities' (1971) 8 *Common Market Law Review* 446–61.
[2] Bull EC, Suppl 2/79.
[3] See, for instance, CD Ehlermann and E Noël, ‚Die Beitritt der EG zum EMRK: Schwierigkeiten—Rechtfertigung' in Bieber and Nickel (eds), *Das Europa der zweiten Generation* dl. II (Baden-Baden, Nomos 1981), pp 685–701; F Capotorti, 'A propos de l'adhésion éventuelle des Communautés à la Convention européenne des droits de l'homme', in ibid, 703–26; G Cohen-Jonathan, 'La problématique de l'adhésion des communautés européennes à la Convention européenne des Droits de L'Homme', in Manin and others (ed), *Études de droit des Communautés européennes* (Paris, A Pedone 1984) 81–108; J Iliopoulos-Strangas (ed), *Grundrechtsschutz im europäischen Raum—Der Beitritt der Europäischen Gemeinschaften zur Europäischen Menschenrechtskonvention* (Frankfurt am Main, Lang 1993); R Bontempi, 'L'adhésion de la Communauté à la Convention européenne des droits de l'homme' in Bieber and others (ed), *Au nom des peuples européens* (Baden-Baden, Nomos 1996) 68–82.

More than a decade later, the Commission launched a second attempt. In 1990, it requested the Council to provide it with a mandate to open formal negotiations about the Community's accession to the ECHR.[4] No agreement was reached, however, within the Council.

After several years of fruitless talks, a compromise was found: the Court of Justice of the European Union (CJEU) was asked to give an opinion on the question of whether the Community would be competent at all to accede to the Convention. In 1996, the Court answered that question in the negative.[5] It observed that the Treaties establishing the Communities did not provide for an express legal basis for accession. Yet such a basis was needed, given the broad institutional implications and constitutional significance of such a step.

Coincidentally, the CJEU issued its opinion on 28 March 1996, in the middle of the negotiations that would eventually lead to the Treaty of Amsterdam. Thus, there was ample opportunity for the Member States to take up the invitation and insert an express legal basis for accession in the Treaty. However, they did not.

So, in three decades, the debate on EU accession resembled the procession of Echternach: there were some steps forward and about as many steps back. The main difference would seem to be that there were protracted periods during which no steps were taken at all.

It was only in the late 1990s that a real impetus was given. The then German Foreign Minister Joschka Fischer proposed the adoption of a 'bill of rights' for the European citizen. This initiative—which culminated in the adoption of the EU Charter of Fundamental Rights in 2000—also led to the rediscovery of an old idea: the accession of the EU to the ECHR.

The idea was still alive when, in December 2001, the Laeken European Council took the initiative for a new debate on the future of Europe and the drafting of a European Constitution. The first drafts, of February 2003, provided in Article 5 that 'the Union may accede' to the ECHR.[6] The wording may appear somewhat lukewarm, but at least it did provide the legal basis that was considered necessary in Opinion 2/94. Be that as it may, half a year later, a new draft with a stronger formulation saw the light of day: the Union 'shall seek' accession.[7] But the drafters were still not satisfied: apparently, they wanted to give an even stronger signal that accession must take place. As a result, the final version of the Constitutional Treaty provided, in Article I-7, the rather confident assertion that the Union 'shall accede' to the ECHR.

Now that we are in the archives anyway, it is perhaps useful to insert a small footnote. The way in which Article I-7 was formulated might give rise to *a contrario* arguments: the Union has the competence (and indeed the clear wish) to accede to the ECHR, but *because* the Convention is singled out, the EU does not have the power to accede to *other* human rights treaties. Whatever the merits of such a line of reasoning in general, it is useful to note that this has never been the intention of the drafters of the Constitution. In the official explanation of the draft text of

---

[4] SEC(90)2087 def of 19 November 1990; see *Bull EC* 10-1990, p 76 (1.3.218) and 11-1990, p 72 (1.3.203).
[5] CJEU, Opinion 2/94 [1996] ECR I-1759.
[6] See doc CONV 528/03, 6 February 2003.
[7] See doc CONV 850/03, 18 July 2003.

26 May 2003, it was emphasised that there are no reasons at all for such a restrictive interpretation.[8] It may be useful to remember that the drafters of the Constitution never meant to close the door for EU accession to *other* human rights treaties.

At any rate, an express legal basis for EU accession to the ECHR was a fact. But the big step forward was followed—fully in line with the Echternach tradition—by a big step back. The Constitutional Treaty was rejected in 2005, following referenda in France and the Netherlands. This necessitated fresh negotiations. It was only in December 2009 that the Lisbon Treaty entered into force. Article I-7 of the Constitutional Treaty had survived this episode, miraculously perhaps, and re-emerged as Article 6 TEU.

2 PREPARING THE GROUND FOR ACCESSION

2.1 The Legal Basis

So Article 6(2) TEU now provides an unequivocal legal basis for accession:

> The Union shall accede to the European Convention for the Protection of Human Rights and Fundamental Freedoms. Such accession shall not affect the Union's competences as defined in the Treaties.

This strong formulation ('The Union *shall* accede', 'L'Union adhère' in French, 'Die Union tritt ... bei' in German and 'L-Unjoni għandha taderixxi' in Maltese) conveniently ignores the fact that accession will require a number of steps. To begin with, Article 218(8) TFEU stipulates that a rather heavy ratification procedure must be followed: the consent of the European Parliament is needed, as well as unanimity in the Council, and then approval by Member States in accordance with constitutional requirements.

And there is the other side as well: the Council of Europe and its 47 Member States. Obviously, their consent will be needed too. Admittedly, the Council of Europe has repeatedly indicated that it would welcome EU accession, and it has carried out fairly detailed studies on the technical aspects of accession.[9] Protocol 14 to the ECHR—which entered into force in 2010—added a new Article 59(2) to the Convention: 'The European Union may accede to the Convention.' The explanatory memorandum, however, warns us that this does not settle the matter:

> It should be emphasised that further modifications to the Convention will be necessary in order to make such accession possible from a legal and technical point of view ... At the

---

[8] CONV 724/03, annex 2, p 58: 'This paragraph may ask that the Union *seek* accession only in the specific case of the ECHR; however this particular formula is not in any way intended to rule out the *possibility* of accession to other conventions. As the Praesidium has already pointed out, only the European Convention on Human Rights is mentioned in this paragraph because of the fact that a Court of Justice opinion in 1996 had rejected Community competence to accede to that Convention on the basis of considerations specific to it.' The opinion referred to is of course Opinion 2/94. The Praesidium referred to is the Praesidium of the 'Convention' that drafted the Constitutional Treaty.

[9] For instance, in 2002, the Steering Committee on Human Rights (CDDH) had already adopted a report identifying the modifications to the ECHR which would be necessary in order to make accession by the EU possible from a legal and a technical point of view (document DG-II(2002)006, available at: www.coe.int).

time of drafting of this protocol, it was not yet possible to enter into negotiations—and even less to conclude an agreement—with the European Union on the terms of the latter's possible accession to the Convention, simply because the European Union still lacked the competence to do so. This made it impossible to include in this protocol the other modifications to the Convention necessary to permit such accession. As a consequence, a second ratification procedure will be necessary in respect of those further modifications, whether they be included in a new amending protocol or in an accession treaty.[10]

It remains to be seen how this 'second ratification procedure', involving 47 Member States (including the Russian Federation and Turkey to name a few), will proceed.

In addition, more details about the accession are set out in Protocol No 8 to the Treaty of Lisbon. Article 1 stipulates that the accession agreement:

[S]hall make provision for preserving the specific characteristics of the Union and Union law, in particular with regard to:

(a)   the specific arrangements for the Union's possible participation in the control bodies of the European Convention;
(b)   the mechanisms necessary to ensure that ... individual applications are correctly addressed to Member States and/or the Union as appropriate.

Paragraph (b) refers to what has become known as the 'co-respondent mechanism'. Since applicants are free in deciding against which High Contracting Party they address their complaints, mistakes can easily (or deliberately) be made. A complaint that concerns in reality the EU may be addressed against one of its Member States, and vice versa. As such, there is need for a clever mechanism to ensure that the 'right' respondents are involved in cases before the court. This is a delicate area, since the determination of the 'right' respondent may also depend on the proper interpretation of EU law. And the interpretation of EU law is a matter that should be left to the EU itself, notably the CJEU. Should it then be left to the EU to decide when it is appropriate to appear in cases before the Strasbourg Court? That would not be acceptable either, as it would enable the EU to decide unilaterally when it wants to be held accountable.

Article 2 of the Protocol first repeats—just to avoid any possible misunderstanding, it seems—what is already stated in Article 6 TEU: the accession agreement 'shall not affect the competences of the Union or the powers of its institutions'. It then adds that the accession should not affect the position of Member States in relation to the European Convention either: whether they are bound by specific protocols or not, the EU's accession to the Convention will not change that position. The same applies to reservations that Member States may have made when becoming a party to the Convention.

Finally, Article 3 of the Protocol contains a somewhat enigmatic message: the accession agreement shall not affect Article 344 of the Treaty on the Functioning of the EU.[11] The message appears to be that the EU Member States should not submit

---

[10] Protocol 14 to the Convention for the Protection of Human Rights and Fundamental Freedoms, amending the control system of the Convention (CETS No 194, adopted 13 May 2004), Explanatory Memorandum, paras 101–02, available at: http://conventions.coe.int.

[11] Article 344 Treaty on the Functioning of the EU (the former Article 292 Treaty establishing the European Community) provides that the Member States undertake not to submit a dispute concerning the interpretation or application of the Treaties to any method of settlement other than those provided for therein.

any internal disputes concerning the interpretation or application of EU law to the European Court of Human Rights, which makes sense: the task of the Strasbourg Court is merely to ensure that the ECHR is complied with.

In order to complete the picture, mention should be made of the declarations annexed to the Final Act of the Intergovernmental Conference which adopted the Treaty of Lisbon. One declaration specifically addresses Article 6(2) TEU:

> The Conference agrees that the Union's accession to the European Convention for the Protection of Human Rights and Fundamental Freedoms should be arranged in such a way as to preserve the specific features of Union law. In this connection, the Conference notes the existence of a regular dialogue between the Court of Justice of the European Union and the European Court of Human Rights; such dialogue could be reinforced when the Union accedes to that Convention.

Although it could be asked why it was necessary to repeat verbatim the language of Protocol No 8, the message is clear. The relationship between the CJEU and the Strasbourg Court is an issue that merits special attention. Accession should not result in a hierarchy, with one court being elevated above the other.

2.2 The Negotiations: First Phase

Shortly after the Lisbon Treaty entered into force on 17 March 2010, the Commission issued a proposal for negotiation directives. Thus, the accession process was set on track very rapidly, probably in an attempt to use the post-Lisbon momentum. A press release, issued on this occasion, quoted President José Manuel Barroso:

> Accession to the ECHR has political, legal and symbolic importance. The EU's accession to the European Convention on Human Rights will provide a coherent system of fundamental rights protection throughout the continent. It will complete the level of protection introduced by the Lisbon Treaty through the legally binding Charter of Fundamental Rights.[12]

The press release continued to point out, in a nutshell, what was at stake:

> The EU's accession to the ECHR will introduce an additional judicial control in the field of the protection of fundamental rights in the EU. It will make the European Court of Human Rights in Strasbourg competent to review acts of the EU institutions, bodies and agencies, including rulings by the European Court of Justice, for respect of the European Convention on Human Rights. Accession will also provide a new possibility of remedies for individuals. They will be able to bring complaints—after they have exhausted domestic remedies—about the infringement of fundamental rights by the EU before the European Court of Human Rights. Accession will also:
>
> — Help develop a common culture of fundamental rights in the EU.
> — Reinforce the credibility of the EU's human rights' system and EU external policy.
> — Show that the EU puts its weight behind the Strasbourg system of fundamental rights protection.
> — Ensure that there is a harmonious development of the case law of the European Court of Justice and the European Court of Human Rights.

---

[12] See press release IP/10/291 of 17 March 2010, available at: http://europa.eu/rapid.

The text of the Commission proposal itself was confidential, but it was partly declassified in February 2011.[13] For one, the Commission proposed that it would represent the EU in the negotiations. Other elements of the proposal remain to be made public, but logic dictates that certain issues must have been addressed. Should the EU accede to all or some of the protocols, in addition to the Convention proper? Should there be an additional Strasbourg judge in respect of the EU—and who should elect him or her? And what about the representation of the EU in the Committee of Ministers when voting on the execution of judgments? What about the so-called 'co-respondent mechanism', referred to in Article 1(b) of Protocol No 8?

Discussions in France focused on another question: should the Common Foreign and Security Policy (CFSP) be excluded from the scope of the Union's accession (the so-called 'carve out'), given that the CJEU itself has very limited competences in this policy area?

A last issue was highlighted first by Judge Timmermans, a senior member of the CJEU, at a hearing organised by the European Parliament[14] and a few weeks later by the CJEU itself. In a fully fledged 'discussion document'—to the best of my knowledge the very first document of this nature—the CJEU observed:

> [I]n order to observe the principle of subsidiarity which is inherent in the Convention and at the same time to ensure the proper functioning of the judicial system of the Union, a mechanism must be available which is capable of ensuring that the question of the validity of a Union act can be brought effectively before the Court of Justice before the European Court of Human Rights rules on the compatibility of that act with the Convention.[15]

What is at stake here has become known in the meantime as the *prior involvement procedure*. The concern is that the European Court of Human Rights could be called upon to adjudicate situations that have not yet been considered by the CJEU. This situation could arise if a case against an EU Member State, concerning a matter that involves the application of EU law, is brought before the Strasbourg Court. Normally, if the validity of EU law is challenged, for instance, because it is considered to be in breach of fundamental rights, the domestic courts would refer the matter to the CJEU for a preliminary ruling. In that scenario, the CJEU would be in a position to review all arguments and, if need be, rule that the impugned EU act or measure is invalid. If, however, the domestic court refrains from making a reference to the CJEU—a scenario that is not, apparently, hypothetical—then the CJEU would be deprived of the opportunity to review the case. That scenario, the CJEU argues, is incompatible with the principle of subsidiarity on which the Convention system is based. Thus, there is need to devise a separate mechanism that would ensure, one way or anther, the so-called 'prior involvement' of the CJEU. After a complaint has been lodged in Strasbourg, the CJEU should be seized and express its views before the European Court of Human Rights rules on the case.

---

[13] See Council of the EU, 25 February 2011, doc 7668/10 EXT 2 (FREMP 5, JAI 227, COHOM 74), available at: http://register.consilium.europa.eu.

[14] 18 March 2010.

[15] See *Accession of the European Union to the European Convention for the Protection of Human Rights and Fundamental Freedoms*, Luxembourg, 5 May 2010. The CJEU even went to so far as to create a special 'button' on its website for discussion documents (plural) in order to publish the present memorandum: see http://curia.europa.eu/jcms/jcms/P_64268.

One could raise the question of how the introduction of this new mechanism could be reconciled with Article 6(2) TEU, which stipulates that accession shall not affect the Union's competences. The reply might be, perhaps, that the new mechanism is a new 'procedure' and not a new 'competence' of the CJEU. But from the perspective of the domestic courts, the landscape does change. Imagine the situation where the supreme court in an EU Member State decides not refer a case to the CJEU for a preliminary ruling, for instance, because it finds that there is an *acte clair*: there is no doubt about the interpretation of the relevant rules of EU law. After the case is decided at the domestic level, one of the parties lodges a complaint in Strasbourg—thus triggering a 'postliminary' procedure before the CJEU. Arguably, this scenario affects the existing balance between the CJEU and the judiciary in the Member States.

The next step was made on 4 June 2010. After lengthy internal debates, the EU Justice Ministers gave the Commission the mandate to conduct the negotiations on their behalf.[16] Within the Commission, it was the *équipe institutions* of the Legal Service that was made responsible for the negotiations.

Meanwhile, on 26 May 2010, the Committee of Ministers of the Council of Europe gave an ad hoc mandate to its Steering Committee for Human Rights (CDDH) to elaborate, with the EU, the necessary legal instrument for the EU's accession to the ECHR. The CDDH in turn entrusted this task to an informal group, called the CDDH-UE, consisting of 14 members. These members had a somewhat ambiguous status: they were chosen on the basis of their expertise, but at the same time, care was taken to ensure that seven members came from EU Member States and seven others from non-EU Member States.

Official talks on the EU's accession to the ECHR finally started on 7 July 2010 in the presence of Thorbjørn Jagland, the Secretary General of the Council of Europe, and Viviane Reding, Vice-President of the European Commission. Between July 2010 and June 2011, eight meetings took place. It was agreed to divide the talks into five chapters: general issues, technical amendments, procedure before the Strasbourg Court, institutional and financial issues, and final matters. In the context of these meetings, two exchanges of views with representatives of civil society were held.

The negotiators also received help from an unexpected quarter. In January 2011, the Presidents of the European Court of Human Rights and the CJEU issued a joint statement about the accession. They expressed their support for the idea to introduce a 'prior involvement' procedure:

> [A] procedure should be put in place, in connection with the accession of the EU to the Convention, which is flexible and would ensure that the CJEU may carry out an internal review before the ECHR carries out external review.[17]

Perhaps it is unusual that courts play such a visible role in political discussions that pertain to their own competences—according to some constitutional traditions, this

---

[16] See 10630/1/10 REV 1, press release of the 3018th Council meeting Justice and Home Affairs, Luxembourg, 3–4 June 2010, available at: www.consilium.europa.eu.

[17] See *Joint communication from the Presidents of the European Court of Human Rights and the Court of Justice of the European Union, further to the meeting between the two courts in January 2011*, available at the CJEU website (http://curia.europa.eu), under the heading 'discussion documents'.

is a matter that falls within the realm of the legislator. But the negotiators seemed to appreciate the joint intervention of the two courts, stating that it made the talks easier.[18] At the same time, it may well be that this polite response is inspired by the prospect that the CJEU will be asked to deliver an opinion on the association agreement.

Meanwhile, the parliamentarians of the Council of Europe and the EU also reached agreement. In June 2011, it was agreed by representatives of both institutions that, following accession, the European Parliament would be entitled to participate in the sittings of the Parliamentary Assembly of the Council of Europe and its relevant bodies when the latter exercises its functions related to the election of judges to the European Court of Human Rights under Article 22 of the Convention.[19]

3 AN AGREEMENT!

Within a year after the start of the negotiations, on 24 June 2011, a draft accession agreement was adopted.[20] In fact, it was a complex package, consisting of several 'layers': a number of formal amendments to the ECHR (as included in the Accession Agreement), remaining text of the Accession Agreement and an Explanatory Report. In addition, there was a set of draft rules to be added to the Rules of the Committee of Ministers for supervision of execution of judgments. Finally, a reference was made to the need to draft 'internal' EU rules. These latter rules govern, for instance, the division of labour between the Member States and the EU in specific cases before the Strasbourg Court.

Article 1 of the Accession Agreement determines the scope of the EU's accession. It provides that the EU will accede to the ECHR proper, as well as to Protocols 1 and 6. It contains a caveat that sounds familiar as it reflects the wording of the Lisbon Treaty:

> [A]ccession shall impose on the EU obligations with regard only to acts, measures or omissions of its institutions, bodies, offices or agencies, or of persons acting on their behalf. Nothing in the [ECHR] shall require the EU to perform an act or adopt a measure for which it has no competence under EU law.

Article 1 also makes clear what seems fairly obvious: where terms 'State', 'State Party', 'national security' and so on appear, they shall be understood as referring

---

[18] See the *Explanatory Report to the draft Accession Agreement*, para 18: 'The Joint Declaration by the Presidents of the two courts resuming the results of the discussion provided, in this respect, valuable reference and guidance for the negotiation on one of the most delicate aspects of the accession' (doc DDH-UE(2011)05, Strasbourg, 25 February 2011).

[19] See PACE—EP Joint Informal Body, *Synopsis of the Meeting Held in Paris on 15 June 2011* (Doc PACE ref: AS/Bur/AH EP PACE (2011) 04; EP ref: 467.248 v01-00—CM 871223 EN).

[20] See doc CDDH-EU(2011)16, available at: www.coe.int. For a more detailed analysis, see X Groussot, T Lock and L Pech, *EU Accession to the ECHR: A Legal Assessment of the Draft Accession Agreement of 14 October 2011*, Robert Schuman Foundation Policy Paper (European issues, No 218, 7 November 2011). See also N O'Meara, '"A More Secure Europe of Rights?" The European Court of Human Rights, the Court of Justice of the European Union and EU Accession to the ECHR' (2011) 12 *German Law Journal* 1813–32.

also to the EU. In a similar vein, Article 4 of the Agreement provides that the term 'Inter-State cases' (Article 33 ECHR) shall be replaced by 'Inter-Party cases'.

Article 2 sets out that the EU may make reservations, just like States can do, in accordance with Article 57 ECHR, when becoming a party to the Convention.

Article 3 is more complex, as it deals with the so-called co-respondent mechanism and with the prior involvement procedure. The principle is clear: 'a co-respondent is a party to a case'. There are two possibilities: the Court may 'invite' the EU or (one of) its Member States to become co-respondent (it being understood that 'the EU or its Member States could not be compelled against their will to become a co-respondent'), or a party becomes a co-respondent at its own request. In the latter case, the Court decides on the admission of the co-respondent to the proceedings and informs the parties to the case as well as the co-respondent of its decision. 'It is expected that such requests will normally be granted', according to the Explanatory Report. Article 3 is silent on the consequences (eg, allocation of liability). The Explanatory Report explains why the mechanism is necessary and then adds:

> The co-respondent mechanism is thus no procedural privilege for the EU or its member States, but a means to avoid gaps in participation, accountability and enforceability under the Convention system. This corresponds to the very purpose of EU accession and serves the proper administration of justice.[21]

The co-respondent mechanism is not meant to change the current practice under which the Strasbourg Court makes a preliminary assessment of an application, with the result that many manifestly ill-founded or otherwise inadmissible applications are not communicated. Therefore, the co-respondent mechanism should only be applied to cases which have been notified to a High Contracting Party. In those cases, the procedure initially follows the information indicated by the applicant in the application form.

As to the prior involvement procedure, Article 3 sets out that in proceedings to which the EU is a co-respondent, if the CJEU has not yet assessed the compatibility with the Convention right at issue of the provision of EU law, 'then sufficient time shall be allowed to the CJEU to make such an assessment'. The Explanatory Report indicates that the CJEU would perform this task within six to eight months by using the accelerated procedure. The legal basis for this procedure is left implicit, but that, of course, is more a matter of *cuisine interne* of the EU. At the same time, one may wonder what the legal effect of the CJEU's ruling will be, to what extent the various parties will be involved (the applicant in the Strasbourg procedure, but possibly also other parties in the domestic procedure), whether legal aid will be available and so on.

A minor technical clarification is laid down in Article 5. Of far greater interest is the election of judges. There will be a special judge elected in respect of the EU. Perhaps it would have been conceivable that the EU would only have a say in the election of this particular judge, but a more generous approach has been agreed upon: a delegation of the European Parliament will fully participate, with the right to vote, in all stages of the election procedure of each of the judges, which is the

---

[21] *Explanatory Report to the draft Accession Agreement*, para 37 (doc DDH-UE(2011)05, Strasbourg, 25 February 2011).

responsibility of the Parliamentary Assembly of the Council of Europe (see Article 22 ECHR).

A more thorny issue is the participation of the EU in the Committee of Ministers of the Council of Europe and more particularly when it exercises supervision of the execution of judgments of the Strasbourg Court (Article 46 § 2 ECHR). This issue is covered by Article 7 of the Association Agreement. The essence of the problem is that the EU expects its Member States to coordinate their votes, whereas the non-EU Member States are concerned that they will be systematically outvoted as a result. Currently, the EU Member States already count for 27 of the 47 Council of Europe Member States; after the accession of Croatia to the EU (2013), there would be a bloc of 28; and after the accession of the EU to the ECHR, there would even be a bloc of 29 out 48 parties. The compromise reached in Article 7 is as follows. If the Committee of Ministers is to supervise the execution of a judgment that is addressed to the EU, then the EU and its Member States will coordinate their votes. If the case concerns an EU Member State, then the EU will not vote. And if the case involves a non-EU Member State, there is no obligation to coordinate the votes.

A less controversial issue, also covered by Article 7, is the adoption of Protocols to the Convention. In that case, the EU shall be entitled to participate in the Committee of Ministers, with the right to vote.

Finally, Article 8 addresses the issue of expenditure, whereas Articles 9–12 deal with technical matters.

4 ONE STEP BACK ...

Given the extremely long and winding road that led to the agreement of June 2011, it would be naive to expect that the story ends here. And, indeed, within a few weeks, it became apparent that there were still difficulties—notably from within the EU.

At an extraordinary meeting of the CDDH on 12–14 October 2011—which was called to endorse the draft agreement and submit it to the Committee of Ministers—no less than six EU Member States expressed their discontent with various aspects of the draft.[22] This must have been a somewhat embarrassing situation for the negotiators of CDDH-EU, especially those coming from the EU Member States. Later, the impression was created that the first round of negotiations only had a limited ambition: it had produced a text with technical solutions and it had identified the 'tricky issues'. Now the time had come for a discussion at the political level.

Be that as it may, the CDDH had no option other than to note that no agreement had been reached: 'given the political implications of some of the pending problems, they could not be solved at this stage by the CDDH itself nor by the CDDH-EU'. For this reason, the CDDH 'considered it had done all it could ... and agreed to transmit the present report and the draft instruments to the Committee

---

[22] See doc CDDH(2011)009.

of Ministers for consideration and further guidance'.[23] This was the beginning of another impasse.

The EU Member States engaged in a round of talks among themselves—in the so-called Working Party on Fundamental Rights, Citizens Rights and Free Movement of Persons (FREMP). According to a (very short) note from the Council Presidency of December 2011, the discussions in the FREMP were 'very intense'. The note continued: 'However, given the importance of the issues at stake, further reflection will be necessary in order to obtain the desired outcome.'[24] This does not bring us much further.

Given the confidential nature of these discussions, one can only speculate what the problems were. Part of them may be political—the electronic daily *The European Voice* reported in January 2012 that France and the UK were among the main opponents.[25] France was said to object to the possibility that the Strasbourg Court would be competent to hear cases about the CFSP, since the CJEU itself is not competent in that area either. The UK, which at the time held the presidency of the Committee of Ministers of the Council of Europe, was engaged in a rather public confrontation with the European Court of Human Rights; it is conceivable that the British government simply did not want to make any progress with an agreement that could be seen as strengthening the Strasbourg Court. Some observers believe that the UK will continue to delay the formal adoption of the agreement until after the next UK general elections, scheduled in 2015 ...

Be that as it may, the Brighton Declaration of 20 April 2012 was quite positive on the issue of accession:

> The accession of the European Union to the Convention will enhance the coherent application of human rights in Europe. The Conference therefore notes with satisfaction progress on the preparation of the draft accession agreement, and calls for a swift and successful conclusion to this work.[26]

And, indeed, in June 2012 the negotiations resumed.

5 ... AND ONE STEP FORWARD ...

The second round of negotiations took a different format. Whereas the Council of Europe was represented in the first phase by an informal group of 14 members chosen on the basis of their expertise (CDDH-UE), this time all 47 Member States were present. Technically, a series of meetings between an 'ad hoc negotiation group' of the CDDH and the European Commission—known as 47 + 1—was agreed upon.

---

[23] Ibid, paras 14–15. This document (CDDH(2011)009 of 14 October 2011) contains a consolidated version of the draft legal instruments so far. This collection has been used as reference afterwards.

[24] Presidency, Council of the European Union, *Accession of the EU to the ECHR—State of Play*, para 9, doc 18117/11 (FREMP 112, JAI 918, COHOM 284, COSCE 22, of 6 December 2011), available at: http://register.consilium.europa.eu.

[25] C Brand, 'Human Rights Convention Deal blocked', *European Voice* (26 January 2012), available at: www.europeanvoice.com.

[26] High Level Conference on the Future of the European Court of Human Rights, Brighton, 19–20 April 2012, Final Declaration, para 36.

The first meeting took place on 21 June 2012, the second on 17–19 September and the third on 7–9 November.

The fresh round of talks did not have an easy start. Several non-EU Member States were annoyed by the delays caused by the EU and its Member States. In June 2012, the representative of the Russian Federation made the following statement:

> It was difficult to reach consensus on all these basic elements, but we would like to say that it had been reached, and that all sides made compromises to reach it. For the Russian Federation, certain elements were very difficult, but we decided to agree to them.
>
> Now, because of the internal problems of the EU, we have received amendments from our European Union colleagues. We are going to study them with great care. But the fact is these amendments reopen the agreed draft. Therefore, we will look at the EU proposals having in mind that we will also have the right to present our own amendments to the draft that was agreed by the CDDH Working Group, as well as to the documents circulated by the EU. We assume that our possible proposals will have the same status as the draft amendments proposed by the EU. We hope as well that future negotiations will really be negotiations between 47 individual member States and the European Commission and not between a 'European Union block' and those who are not members of the European Union.[27]

As a result, the negotiators have both proposals for amendments from the EU and other proposals on the table. So far, little progress seems to have been reached. During the second meeting, virtually every proposal tabled by the EU met with reservations and doubts. Leaving through the meeting reports, the outsider finds it difficult to remain optimistic:

> Many delegations have also underlined that the drafting proposed was excessively detailed and that it was not appropriate to have it included in the text of the Convention. ... Many delegations of States which are not members of the EU expressed reservations on various aspects of this proposal, underlining notably the extreme complexity of the panel procedure, questioning its necessity and also raising doubts.[28]

The most recent development at the time of writing is the third meeting, which started with an exchange of views with representatives of civil society.[29] They stressed, inter alia, the need for transparency and participation of civil society throughout the negotiation process and issued comments on the various texts. When the negotiations resumed, it became clear that very diverging views among the various parties remained.

The overall picture is that very detailed mechanisms are being developed that are meant to apply in situations that may very rarely occur in practice. Very little is left to the wisdom of the European Court of Human Rights. For instance, considerable time is spent on a proposal to amend the co-respondent mechanism (Article 3 of the draft Accession Agreement), in order to ensure that the EU could become

---

[27] Doc 47+1(2012)002, Strasbourg, 4 July 2012, available at: www.coe.int.
[28] Doc 47+1(2012)R02, Strasbourg, 19 September 2012, available at: www.coe.int.
[29] Doc 47+1(2012)R03, Strasbourg, 19 November 2012, available at: www.coe.int. The NGOs involved are the AIRE Centre, Amnesty International, the European Trade Union Confederation (ETUC), the International Commission of Jurists, the European Group of National Human Rights Institutions and the Conference of International Non-Governmental Organisations of the Council of Europe.

a co-respondent not only when an application is directed against an EU Member State, but also when it is directed against a State which is not a member of the EU, and an application puts into question the compatibility with the Convention of an international agreement between that State and the EU. How big is the problem that is being solved and does it have be solved at treaty level? And the more detailed the proposals become, the more resistance is encountered. Thus, when it comes to voting in the Committee of Ministers, the EU has now proposed a 'panel procedure' that should be followed in certain circumstances. This leads to objections:

> [A] large majority of delegations of States which are not members of the EU who took the floor reiterated their strong opposition to the proposal as it stands, underlining again its complexity, the erosion of the Committee of Ministers' prerogatives, and the fact that it did not preclude the possibility, for the EU and its member States, to eventually disregard the conclusions of the panel and use their block of votes in a decisive manner …

> The Chair concluded the discussion on this issue stressing that neither the 'panel procedure', as it stands, nor the solution presented by the '7 + 7' group, which would not be acceptable for the EU and its member States, represented valid options for the negotiation.[30]

To be continued, that is the only thing we know at this stage. New meetings have been scheduled for January and April 2013.

6 CONCLUDING REMARKS

In its written submission for the 47 + 1 group, of 7 November 2012, the European Trade Union Confederation (ETUC) made the following observation:

> Enshrined in Article 6(2) TEU the obligation for the European Union to adhere to the Convention exists since 1 December 2009, [the] date of the entry into force of the Lisbon Treaty. Nearly three years have elapsed since and no text has been adopted yet (by the Committee of Ministers) or even drafted as final version.[31]

As we have seen in this overview, the situation is actually even worse. With only a bit of exaggeration, it could be said that the call for accession to the ECHR is now 50 years old. In a series of conferences, proposals, negotiations, opinions and treaty amendments, a pattern has emerged that somehow resembles the procession of Echternach: three steps forward, two steps back. Progress has been extremely slow. But one should remain optimistic: there has been progress after all.

In 2010, the procession of Echternach was inscribed on the *UNESCO Representative List of the Intangible Cultural Heritage of Humanity*.[32] Let us hope that the current negotiations will result in a tangible contribution to the heritage of mankind.

---

[30] Doc 47 + 1(2012)R03, paras 18–19.
[31] Submission by the ETUC to the CDDH Ad-hoc Negotiation Group and the European Commission on the Accession of the European Union to the European Convention on Human Rights for the consultation on 7 November 2012 (Third Negotiation meeting), available at: www.coe.int.
[32] See www.unesco.org/culture/ich/index.php?lg=en&pg=00011&RL=00392.

3

Procedure in the European Court of Human Rights (with a Particular Focus on Cases Concerning Trade Union Rights)

JOHN HENDY QC

1 INTRODUCTION

THERE ARE MANY useful books which explain the procedure of the European Court of Human Rights (ECtHR).[1] The ECtHR has *Rules of Court*[2] (and publishes *Practice Directions* from time to time), which set out how it deals with applications alleging breach of the European Convention on Human Rights and Fundamental Freedoms (ECHR). Any lawyer instructed by an applicant to take a case to the ECtHR will need to be familiar with this material. This chapter is not intended to duplicate or summarise either the Court's procedural guidance or the academic commentary thereon. But it is hoped that it will identify a few of the particular issues in applications to the ECtHR that are of significance to the lawyer concerned with cases alleging breach of trade union rights. Those rights are very diverse and it would be impossible to identify, still less to deal with, all the procedural issues that can arise in relation to them. In general terms, however, the procedure discussed below is equally relevant to those seeking to bring an employment case to the Court.

The procedure of the ECtHR is continuously evolving, as, no doubt, are the procedures of national courts. But such has been the success of the ECtHR in upholding

---

[1] Eg, K Reid, *A Practitioner's Guide to the European Convention on Human Rights*, 4th edn (London, Sweet & Maxwell, 2011); P Leach, *Taking a Case to the European Court of Human Rights*, 3rd edn (Oxford, Oxford University Press, 2011); F Jacobs et al, *The European Convention on Human Rights*, 5th edn (Oxford, Oxford University Press, 2010); R Clayton and H Tomlinson, *The Law of Human Rights*, 2nd edn (Oxford, Oxford University Press, 2009); DJ Harris et al, *The Law of the European Convention on Human Rights*, 2nd edn (Oxford, Oxford University Press, 2009); EL Abdelgawad, *The Execution of Judgments of the European Court of Human Rights*, 2nd edn (Council of Europe Press, 2008); P van Dijk, *Theory and Practice of the European Convention on Human Rights*, 4th edn (Intersentia, 2006).

[2] Available from the ECtHR website and the latest edition of which is dated 1 February 2012. Each reference below to a 'Rule' is to one of these *Rules of Court*. The ECtHR has a useful flowchart at http://www.echr.coe.int/NR/rdonlyres/DD9DE91F-2494-4347-B9B6-C5B9F89BAC32/0/ENG_SCHEMA.pdf.

human rights against Member States that it is not surprising that some States have been pressing the Council of Ministers to make changes to confine the jurisdiction, hamper the procedure and restrict applications to the ECtHR. This pressure may result in changes to the Court's procedure. The recent compromise reached in the Brighton Declaration of April 2012 is evidence of the battle behind the scenes.[3]

2 THE APPLICATION FORM

The application form to the ECtHR constitutes a convenient preliminary agenda for the discussion to follow.

The application form (as part of a pack which includes with the *Rules of Court* and other fundamental documents) can be downloaded from the ECtHR website.[4]

It should be noted that there is a procedure by which application can be made to to the ECtHR for urgent 'interim measures' to be ordered.[5] The essential requirement is to show that the applicant faces a real risk of serious, irreversible harm if the measure is not applied. This condition is unlikely to be fulfilled in many cases involving trade union issues.

2.1 The Applicant

The form begins with the necessary identification of the parties. First is the Applicant and his/her/its representative. The representative must additionally submit with the application form the standard form of authority required.[6]

Notwithstanding the academic discussion as to whether certain rights are individual or collective in nature (or whether, like Article 1, Protocol 1, they can be enjoyed by non-human persons), the ECtHR expressly permits 'applications by any person, non-governmental organisation or group of persons'.[7] Thus, applications are receivable from individual workers or union members, and from trade unions— whether or not the union has corporate status, is registered or is merely an ad hoc

---

[3] The Brighton Declaration of April 2012 (www.coe.int/en/20120419-brighton-declaration). Note the prior contentious draft by the British government (Draft Brighton Declaration presented on 23 February 2012) compared to the sophisticated position of the ECtHR itself in the Preliminary Opinion of the Court in preparation for the Brighton Conference, 20 February 2012 (www.echr.coe.int/NR/rdonlyres/BF069E9B-8EE5-4FA8-877E-2DFAA4C167BD/0/2012_Avis_Cour_Conférence_de_Brighton_1820_avril_2012_EN.pdf) and the speech of the President, Sir Nicolas Bratza (www.echr.coe.int/NR/rdonlyres/8D587AC3-7723-4DB2-B86F-01F32C7CBC24/0/2012_BRIGHTON_Discours_Bratza_EN.pdf).

[4] www.echr.coe.int/NR/rdonlyres/850CEB0E-3DC8-4E92-9F5D-7E6910C81A47/0/EnglishP0pack.pdf (for the English-language version).There are accompanying notes which should be referred to; see also Rule 47. There is a *Practice Direction* on the institution of proceedings of 1 November 2003, amended on 22 September 2008 and 24 June 2009. See also the *Practice Direction* on written pleadings of 10 December 2007.

[5] Rule 39 and Practice Direction on interim measures of 5 March 2003, amended 16 October 2009 and 7 July 2011.

[6] Rule 36. The form of authority is standard and is in the downloadable pack.

[7] Article 34. See I Van Hiel in chapter 11 on the individual right to organise.

grouping of workers.[8] Artificial persons such as corporations are included.[9] In cases concerning trade union rights, there are many examples in the jurisprudence of the ECtHR of successful applications brought solely by individuals, solely by unions and jointly by individuals and unions.[10]

2.1.1 Victim

A critical condition of the right to be an applicant is that he, she or it must be 'a victim of a violation' within the meaning of that term used by the ECtHR.[11] The victim must be directly affected by the impugned act or omission, though actual prejudice or detriment need not be shown where a risk of such can be demonstrated.[12] Even where the applicant has exercised the ECHR right in question, notwithstanding that the exercise of it was contrary to national law and notwithstanding too, that the prohibition on it has subsequently been quashed by the national court, it may still be possible to establish that the applicant is a victim. This may occur because of the chilling effect of the fact that the action was, at least at the time, prohibited. In *Bączkowski and others v Poland*[13] a march of some 3,000 people took place to draw attention to discrimination against homosexuals in spite of a ban on its taking place. The ban was subsequently quashed in domestic proceedings, but the fact that there had been a ban was in breach of Article 11:

> The applicants took a risk in holding [static assemblies of some 3,000 persons] given the official ban in force at that time. The assemblies were held without a presumption of

---

[8] In the UK, a trade union (which is essentially defined as an organisation of workers which has the purpose of regulating relations with employers) has negligible legal status beyond being an unincorporated association to which certain legal attributes and duties are attached and which may or may not be registered as a trade union: Trade Union and Labour Relations (Consolidation) Act 1992, pt I. In the case of *Syndicatul Păstorul Cel Bun v Rumania*, App No 2330/09, 9 July 2013, the Grand Chamber reversed the Section at first instance and found no breach of Article 11 in the nullification of the registration of a small union of clergy (*cf Gorzelik v Poland* (2004) 38 EHRR 1, where the refusal to register a national minority organisation was permissible since registration could have been obtained by slightly changing the name and making one amendment to its constitution).

[9] As to which latter, see M Emberland, *The Human Rights of Companies* (Oxford, Oxford University Press, 2006). Some human rights cannot be exercised by a non-human body, eg, the right not to suffer inhuman treatment: *Verein Kontakt Information Therapie and Hagan v Austria* (1988) 57 DR 81.

[10] As examples, see *Demir and Baykara v Turkey*, App No 34503/97, 12 November 2008, (2009) 48 EHRR 54, [2009] IRLR 766; *Associated Society of Locomotive Engineers and Firemen (ASLEF) v UK*, App No 1002/05, 27 February 2007, (2007) 45 EHRR 33, [2007] IRLR 361; *Wilson, National Union of Journalists v UK*, App No 30668/96, *Palmer, Wyeth, National Union of Rail, Maritime and Transport Workers v UK*, App No 30671/96 and *Doolan, Farrugia, Jenkins, Jones, Parry, Parry, Pine, Webber v UK*, App No 30678/96, all dealt with in the single judgment of 2 July 2002, (2002) 35 EHRR 20, [2002] IRLR 568 and hereinafter referred to as '*Wilson and Palmer*'. Just as the Article 11 right to freedom of assembly can be invoked both by the organisers and by the participants (*Djavit An v Turkey*, App No 20652/92, (2005) 40 EHRR 45, para 56; and *Christians against Racism and Fascism v UK* (1980) 21 DR 138, para 93), so can the right to strike (*Karaçay v Turkey*, App No 6615/03, 27 March 2007, definitive version of the judgment on 27 June 2007, only in French, brought by a member of Yapi Yol Sen; and *Enerji Yapi-Yol Sen v Turkey*, App No 68959/01, 21 April 2009, brought by a section of that union) and the right to protection against anti-union discrimination (see *Wilson and Palmer*, where the applicants were individuals and their unions).

[11] Article 34 and see also Article 35(3)(b). There is a discussion on the nature of victimhood in *Klass v Germany* (1978) 2 EHRR 214. The concept must be interpreted in the light of present-day conditions: *Loizidou v Turkey (Preliminary Objections)* (1995) 20 EHRR 99, paras 71–72.

[12] Eg, *Campbell and Cosans v UK* (1982) 4 EHRR 293; *Bowman v UK* (1998) 26 EHRR 1.

[13] *Bączkowski and others v Poland*, App No 1543/06, 24 September 2007.

legality, such a presumption constituting a vital aspect of effective and unhindered exercise of freedom of assembly and freedom of expression. The Court observes that the refusals to give authorisation could have had a chilling effect on the applicants and other participants in the assemblies. It could also have discouraged other persons from participating ...[14]

Likewise, the fact that the interference with a right may be trivial may not prevent the applicant being a victim if the interference is nonetheless dissuasive of the exercise of the right in question. In *Karaçay v Turkey*[15] and *Çerikçi v Turkey*,[16] both in 2007, and in *Kaya and Seyhan v Turkey*[17] in 2009, public servants, in the first case allegedly leaving work without permission to participate in a demonstration, in the second leaving work to participate in a national day of action to celebrate Workers' Day (1 May 2007), and in the third case admittedly leaving work without permission to participate in a protest strike day, were all subjected to disciplinary inquiries (a process governed, in the public service, by law) and each was disciplined for leaving their workplaces without authority. Each was given the written warning provided for in the disciplinary regime: 'to be more attentive to the accomplishment of his/her functions and in his/her behaviour'.[18] On application to the ECtHR, the applicants were held to be 'victims'.[19] This penalty was held to constitute an attenuation of their right of freedom of association under Article 11(1),[20] the ECtHR holding:

> Or, la sanction incriminée, si minime qu'elle ait été, est de nature à dissuader les membres de syndicats de participer légitimement à des journées de grève ou à des actions pour défendre les intérêts de leurs affiliés.[21]

It is possible to be a victim by not receiving a benefit given to others. In *Wilson and Palmer v UK*,[22] the individual workers were victims by reason of the fact that they were not given pay rises awarded to colleagues who had agreed to surrender entitlement to trade union representation.

Thus, establishing victimhood is rarely a problem for an individual in a case alleging breach of trade union rights. The requirement can be a little more problematic for unions. A trade union claiming an incursion into the rights of its members but not directly of itself will not be a victim.[23] On the other hand, where the infringement of

---

[14] Ibid, para 67. See also (in relation to much heavier penalties quashed by the domestic courts) *Urcan v Turkey*, App No 23018/04, etc, 17 October 2008; and *Saime Özcan v Turkey*, App No 22943/04, 15 September 2009.

[15] *Karaçay v Turkey* (n 10).

[16] *Çerikçi v Turkey*, App 33322/07, 13 October 2010, only in French.

[17] *Kaya and Seyhan v Turkey*, App No 30946/04, 15 September 2009, only in French.

[18] *Karaçay v Turkey* (n 10) paras 11 and 15; *Kaya and Seyhan v Turkey* (n 17) para 12. (The judgment in *Çerikçi v Turkey* simply referred to that in *Karaçay v Turkey* without repeating the reasoning.)

[19] *Karaçay v Turkey* (n 10) para 27; *Kaya and Seyhan v Turkey* (n 17) para 22.

[20] *Karaçay v Turkey* (n 10) para 28; *Kaya and Seyhan v Turkey* (n 17) para 24.

[21] *Karaçay v Turkey* (n 10) para 37; *Kaya and Seyhan v Turkey* (n 17) para 30. I translate this as: 'the impugned sanction, minimal as it was, was of a kind to dissuade union members from participating lawfully in strike days or other actions to defend the interests of the membership'.

[22] See n 10 above.

[23] Eg, *X Union v France* (1983) 32 DR 261 (restriction on location of teachers' homes placed on teachers alone); *Purcell v Ireland* (1991) 70 DR 262 (broadcasting restrictions placed on union members, but not on the union); *Ahmed v UK* (2000) 29 EHRR 1 (political restrictions on local government employees, but not on the union).

an ECHR right impinges directly on the trade union, it will be a victim.[24] Often, as in the case of complaints about abridgements of collective rights, both the union and the individual members will be victims in reciprocal ways, the member because he or she is deprived of the right to be heard through the union and the union because it is deprived of the right to be heard on behalf of the members.[25]

This double-bladed feature in many collective trade union issues is both an important and a useful attribute of ECtHR applications. It is important because the right of individual application distinguishes the jurisdiction of the ECtHR over the other *fora* familiar in the field of trade union rights where there is no right of individual complaint, in particular: the International Labour Organisation (ILO) Committee on Freedom of Association (CFA), and to the European Committee of Social Rights (ECSR) of the European Social Charter (ESC).[26] It is also useful for quite another reason.

2.1.2 'Another Procedure of International Investigation'—Article 35(2)(b)

It is well known that the ECtHR pays significant regard to the jurisprudence of other international law bodies—see below. In consequence, trade union legal strategists have advocated applications to the ILO to 'lay the ground', so to speak, for potential applications to the ECtHR. The ECSR also pays much regard to the decisions of the ILO, so that an application to the ILO might provide a means of the same issue being raised in advance of the ECSR. The hope would be that, by the time an application comes to be dealt with in the ECtHR, the ground might be firmed up by a supportive decision by the ILO CFA (or, better still, by the CEACR)[27]

---

[24] Eg, *ASLEF v UK* (n 10): right of union to decide for itself who its members would be.

[25] *Wilson and Palmer* (n 10) is the classic case. In the following cases, the applications were brought by unions alone, but there appears to have been no reason not to have joined individual members complaining of their loss of protection by their unions: *Council of Civil Service Unions v UK* (1987) 50 DR 228; *National Association of Teachers in Further and Higher Education v UK* (1998) EHRR CD 122; *UNISON v UK*, App No 53574/99, 10 January 2002, [2002] IRLR 497; and *Federation of Offshore Workers Trade Unions ('OFS') v Norway*, App No 381/97, (2002) ECHR 2002-VI, 301.

[26] The ILO Constitution (Article 24) permits applications 'by an industrial association of employers or of workers that any of the Members has failed to secure in any respect the effective observance within its jurisdiction of any Convention to which it is a party'. This permits complaints by national and international trade union bodies. Complaints may also be made by delegates of Member States (Article 26 of the Constitution). In addition, complaints may be made by the UN and by certain NGOs which have consultative status with the ILO; see *Special Procedures for the examination by the ILO of complaints alleging violations of Freedom of Association* (Annex 1 of the *Digest of Decisions and Principles of the Freedom of Association Committee of the Governing Body of the ILO* (see n 83 below), para 31. Since 1951, complaints of breach of freedom of association have gone to the Committee on Freedom of Association. So far as the European Social Charter is concerned, the ECSR is cannot entertain complaints by anyone, save in relation to States which have ratified the Collective Complaints Protocol of 1995. In those cases, complaints may be lodged by international trade union federations and by accredited NGOs. In Member States which have not ratified the Protocol, unions are confined to sending in comments on the Reports cyclically provided to the ECSR by the government concerned. It is understood that such comments are considered by the ECSR, though are never referred to in their Conclusions. Neither the ILO nor the ECSR makes provision for individual complaints under any circumstances. I will not describe the procedure for the Court of Justice of the European Union or the International Committee on Economic, Social and Cultural Rights under the International Covenant on Economic, Social and Cultural Rights 1966, though both are *fora* with which the European trade union lawyer must be familiar.

[27] Though note the challenge at the International Labour Conference in 2012 by the Employers Group on the jurisdiction of the CEACR to consider any aspect of the right to strike on the spurious ground that

and, perhaps, by the ECSR. This strategy is of course attractive to the trade union lawyer, since both the ILO and its Conventions and the ECSR and ESC are naturally regarded as an appropriate—indeed, sympathetic—to the kind of trade union rights applications that unions might wish to make.

The strategy also has logistical benefits, since applications to the ILO CFA are usually dealt with much more quickly than under the ECtHR procedure.[28] Of course, the ECtHR has a six-month time limit from the alleged violation, which in some cases make this strategy impossible, but applications can be made simultaneously in the expectation that the ILO CFA decision would pre-date and hence influence the subsequent ECtHR judgment.[29]

The relevance of all this to the fact that individuals as well as trade unions can be applicants to the ECtHR is that the identity of the applicants may provide some protection against the danger that the application is declared inadmissible by reason of Article 35(2)(b). This provides that an application is inadmissible in the ECtHR if it:

> [I]s substantially the same as a matter that has already been examined by the Court or has already been submitted to another procedure of international investigation or settlement and contains no relevant new information.

Note that merely submitting a case to a relevant forum is sufficient, even if no decision has yet been pronounced.

Article 35(2)(b) is a real danger, as the recent cases of *Fédération Hellénique des Syndicats des Employés du Secteur Bancaire (OTOE) v la Grèce* and *Professional Trades Union for Prison, Correctional and Secure Psychiatric Workers and Others (POA), Bates and Watts v UK* show.[30] In both cases the union had made two applications to the ILO CFA which had been heard and decided in favour of the union, and the respective governments were asked to take steps to ameliorate the

---

the ILO Convention does not expressly refer to the right to strike (note the criticism of this by the outgoing Secretary General of the ILO, Mr Somavia, in the Provisional Record, 6 June 2012, www.ilo.org/wcmsp5/groups/public/---ed_norm/---relconf/documents/meetingdocument/wcms_182727.pdf and the comprehensive rebuttal by the CEACR itself at www.ilo.org/public/libdoc/ilo/P/09661/09661%282012-101-1B%29.pdf, pp 46 ff). In fact, the tripartite CFA have, since 1952 (2nd Report, Case No 28, para 68), held that the right to strike was 'an essential [element] of trade union rights' and the CEACR first endorsed the right to strike in 1959 (*General Survey*, 1959, paras 68, 148). Both Committees have applied that right to assess compliance (the CEACR) and for the determination of complaints (the CFA) ever since—without apparent challenge until recently. The right to strike derives from Convention 87, Article 3(1) (*General Survey*, 1994, paras 136–41) and from Convention 98 as inherent in the right to collective bargaining. Both Committees have developed extensive jurisprudence to determine the legitimate limits on the right to strike. Presumably this issue will not be resolved until the International Labour Conference in June 2013.

[28] *Wilson and Palmer* (n 10) took a little under seven years from application to judgment; *ASLEF v UK* (n 10) took two years. See the subsequently introduced prioritisation procedure introduced in the ECtHR referred to later in this chapter.

[29] Article 35(1). In some cases where the national law is clear and poses a continuous restriction on rights, the incident said to constitute the violation might to some extent be 'chosen' from amongst repeated violations to enable an application to be within time.

[30] *Fédération Hellénique des Syndicats des Employés du Secteur Bancaire (OTOE) v la Grèce*, App No 72808/10, 6 December 2011. I am grateful to Dr V Mantouvalou for drawing this case to my attention. *Professional Trades Union for Prison, Correctional and Secure Psychiatric Workers and Others (POA), Bates and Watts v UK*, App No 59253/11, 21 May 2013.

situation. *Cereceda Martin et al v Spain* had already established that the ILO CFA was 'another procedure of international investigation' notwithstanding the absence of any court-like procedure, such as the chance for the applicant to see and comment upon the governmental response to the application, the absence of any possibility of oral hearing and the lack of any effective enforcement mechanism (so that many governments simply ignore findings they do not like).[31] In both the *Fédération Hellénique* and the *POA* cases, the ECtHR held that the prior CFA proceedings had the effect of excluding the jurisdiction of the ECtHR. In so concluding, it took into account (in the cases brought in the two different jurisdictions) the identity of the parties, the legal arguments on which the cases were based, the nature of the complaints and the remedies sought.[32] It was concluded that the proceedings before the ILO CFA were essentially the same as those before the ECtHR, notwithstanding that in the *POA* case there were individual applicants to the ECtHR who had not been involved in the application to the ILO CFA.[33]

As the *POA* case shows, the mere addition of individual parties to proceedings addressed to the ECtHR will not in every case avoid inadmissibility under Article 35(2)(b) where the union has been the complainant on the same dispute on the same grounds to the ILO CFA. But additional parties certainly would help to distinguish the two sets of proceedings, especially where the interest of the individual(s) is not identical to (even if it is the reciprocal of) the union's interest, thus raising different arguments. This would be fortified if the individual could point to additional facts not considered by the ILO CFA, especially facts subsequent to the decision of the ILO CFA.[34]

With this in mind, trade unions might consider that it would be a wiser strategy, where possible, in relation to a specific trade union rights issue which on its face would appear to fall within the jurisdictions of both the ILO CFA and the ECtHR, to couch any complaint to the ILO in terms of an attack on a general rule with the specific incident as one of several examples of the application of the general rule. This would make it easier for individual applicants to take the case to the ECtHR complaining of the specific injury to them (with, or even without, their union).

The position could be further strengthened by complaints to the ILO CFA being brought by union federations (at national or at European level), leaving the ECtHR applications to the specific union and individual members; the union federation could always apply to join in the ECtHR proceedings later (see below).

---

[31] *Cereceda Martin et al v Spain* (1992) 73 DR 120. In *Fédération Hellénique* (n 30), the ECtHR explained (at para 37) that the CFA was composed of members chosen for their independence and expertise and (reflecting the composition of the ILO) in equal numbers of government, employer and worker representatives who did not represent any country or specific organisation. It adopted a quasi-judicial procedure by the application of objective (labour) standards imposing obligations on States through ratified Conventions. The CFA had an adversarial procedure and decisions were taken unanimously. Governments could be invited to indicate the measures taken in consequence.

[32] *Fédération Hellénique*, n 30 paras 39 and 44; *POA*, n 30, paras 27–32; both citing the previous jurisprudence of the ECtHR on the point.

[33] In truth, Article 35(2)(b) is a crude device to reduce the caseload of the ECtHR. Other international complaints procedures such as that to the ECSR or to the ILO CFA do not contain any such barring mechanism.

[34] See *X v UK*, 28 November 1994; *Patera v Czech Republic*, 10 January 2006.

The breadth of wording of Article 35(2)(b) is striking. It is not clear if it could extend to disqualify an ECtHR application if the Applicant had submitted an observation to the ILO Committee on the Application of Conventions and Recommendations (CEACR) with the intention of causing the CEACR annual report to find that the Member State in question had acted incompatibly with a Convention in relation to some particular matter. Of course, the CEACR does not entertain 'applications'; there is no such procedure. But it does consider submissions made by unions made in response to a Member State's annual account of its compliance with ratified Conventions. Such a submission should be made (pursuant to Art 24 of the ILO Constitution) to the CEACR (with a copy to the government) via the Director-General. This should be done by August if it is to have any chance of being considered in the November annual meeting of the CEACR leading to the publication of its report (as part of the director General's Report to the International Labour Conference the following June). There does not appear to be any ECtHR decision on whether such a submission by a union could amount to 'a matter that has already been ... submitted to another procedure'. It might be best therefore to act with an abundance of caution and select parties as for the ILO CFA.

2.2 The State Respondent

The application form, of course, requires identification of the Member State (the 'High Contracting Party') against which the application is brought. There is usually no difficulty here. But potential applicants will bear in mind that the injustice of which they complain need not have been directly at the hands of the State. The ECHR imposes both positive and negative obligations so that an application may be made against the State in respect of a deficiency in its legal regime which has permitted a private employer to invade rights which the State should have protected. There are many examples of this in the cases. In *Bączkowski and others v Poland*, the ECtHR held that:

> Genuine and effective respect for freedom of association and assembly cannot be reduced to a mere duty on the part of the State not to interfere; a purely negative conception would not be compatible with the purpose of Article 11 nor with that of the Convention in general. There may thus be positive obligations to secure the effective enjoyment of the freedoms.[35]

So, in *Wilson and Palmer*, the ECtHR held:

> 46 It is the role of the State to ensure that trade union members are not prevented or restrained from using their union to represent them in attempts to regulate their relations with their employers.

---

[35] *Bączkowski and others v Poland* (n 13) para 64, *Wilson and Palmer* (n 10) and *Ouranio Toxo v Greece*, App No 74989/01, 20 October 2005 were relied upon in this connection. In *Nurettin Aldemir and others v Turkey*, App Nos 32124/02, 32126/02, 32129/02, 32132/02, 32133/02 32137/02 and 32138/02; 2 June 2008, at para 41; and *Saya and others v Turkey*, App No 4327/02, 7 January 2009, at para 44, it was held that: 'States must not only safeguard freedom of peaceful assembly, but must also refrain from applying unreasonable indirect restrictions on that right.'

47 United Kingdom law permitted employers to treat less favourably employees who were not prepared to renounce a freedom that was an essential feature of union membership. Such conduct constituted a disincentive or restraint on the use by employees of union membership to protect their interests ...

48 Under United Kingdom law at the relevant time it was, therefore, possible for an employer effectively to undermine or frustrate a trade union's ability to strive for the protection of its members' interests ... The Court ... considers that, by permitting employers to use financial incentives to induce employees to surrender important union rights, the respondent State failed in its positive obligation to secure the enjoyment of the rights under Article 11 of the Convention. This failure amounted to a violation of Article 11, as regards both the applicant unions and the individual applicants.

As an employer itself, the Member State is equally bound by Article 11 so that in *Tüm Haber Sen and Çınar v Turkey*[36] the ECtHR held that there was

no distinction between the functions of a contracting state as holder of public power and its responsibilities as employer. ... Article 11 is accordingly binding upon the State as employer', whether the latter's relations with its employees are governed by public or private law.

2.3 Statement of Facts

The application requires 'an exposition of the facts'. This will be the summary both of the facts said to constitute the violation of right (with sufficient factual context) and, in the usual case, of the legal proceedings which led to the adverse decision under challenge. The facts will usually be uncontroversial in the sense that they will usually be contained one or more judgments of a national court. The dispute for the ECtHR will be whether the law applied by the national court was in conformity with the ECHR or not. All relevant court decisions and legislation will be required to be appended to the application.

Other core documents should be appended to illustrate the facts, but it is necessary to be ruthlessly discriminating. Certainly, the ECtHR will not wish to see the entire documentation examined by the national court. However, key documents such as the union's rulebook and any official certification of status would be desirable where the union is an applicant. Obviously, documents evidencing the impugned act or omission will be required.

Occasionally, a situation arises where the facts are not set out in a national court decision. This may be because the law is regarded by the applicant as so clear that legal challenge in the domestic courts was pointless. In such a situation, the applicant should support the summary of the facts with witness statements, relevant documents and an opinion by a lawyer that the law is so clear that a legal challenge to the situation would have been futile.

Should the facts be disputed, the ECtHR has powers (rarely used) to investigate them.[37]

---

[36] *Tüm Haber Sen and Çınar v Turkey*, App No 28602/95, (2008) 46 EHRR 19, para 29.
[37] Annex to the Rules: Rules A1–A8.

2.3.1 Exhaustion of Domestic Remedies

Where application to the domestic courts would be pointless, the applicant is excused the usual (and fundamental) requirement that domestic remedies must be exhausted.[38] But it should be noted that doubts about the prospects of success in the national courts are not enough; there must be *no* reasonable prospects of success.[39]

Likewise, where national law provides no effective remedy, it is not necessary to exhaust that route.[40] The application will not be debarred either if the applicant has in fact exhausted it and taken the benefit of the ineffective remedy.[41]

2.3.2 National Law

It is to be observed that judgments of the ECtHR customarily have a heading 'Relevant Non-Convention Material' and that this begins with an exposition of the relevant national law. It is therefore incumbent on the draftsperson to provide a succinct and accurate exposition of the relevant domestic legal material. As is usual, every proposition of law should be made good by reference to constitutional provision, statute or case law, and these will need to be reproduced in the Appendices. There is no reason not to refer to academic analysis, but, again, this must be referenced and copied. The materials available to the judges and the non-judicial rapporteurs at Strasbourg are substantial but not exhaustive, and to make the argument and its bases accessible is part of the art of the advocate.

Where the focus of the attack of the application is directed (as it usually is) at some provision of national law, the Statement of Facts is a reasonable place to set out the relevant legal regime (and, where necessary, its history). It is not necessary to place this analysis in this part of the application form and it may be more logical to put it, in an appropriate case, after the exposition of ECHR law. But generally, since national law is the target, it is most logical to draw it, and its deficiencies, to the attention of the ECtHR before turning to ECHR law.

2.4 Statement of Alleged Violations

The third heading in the application form requires the applicant to identify the violations of the ECHR or its protocols which he or she alleges the facts show. This requires a concise analysis of the relevant Articles and their associated ECtHR jurisprudence in relation to the alleged facts.

It goes without saying that expertise in the relevant jurisprudence is a pre-requisite for the draftsperson, since the actual text of the Convention rights on which

---

[38] Article 35(1).

[39] *Whiteside v UK* (1994) 76-A DR 80; *Akdivar v Turkey* (1997) 23 EHRR 143, paras 66–67; *Aksoy v Turkey* (1996) 23 EHRR 553, para 52; *Terem Ltd et al v Ukraine*, App No 70297/01, 18 October 2005, paras 37–38; *D v Ireland* (2006) 43 EHRR SE16, para 89.

[40] *Montion v France* (1987) 52 DR 227; *Devlin v UK*, 11 April 2002; *Agee v UK* (1976) 7 DR 164; *B v UK* (1993) 15 EHRR CD 100.

[41] *Armonienè v Lithuania* (2009) 48 EHRR 53 (violation of privacy by a major newspaper—compensation capped at a 'derisory' €2,896).

trade union applications depend is concise to the extent of being uncommunicative of the specific rights which lie beneath.

2.4.1 Relevant Articles of the ECHR

The subject matter of potential violations in the field of trade union rights is examined in the relevant substantive chapters of this book. These rights principally derive from Article 11 of the ECHR, though other articles are, of course, relevant. Article 14 (against discrimination) may be engaged in cases where union members have suffered detriment because of union membership or activity.[42] Articles 6 and 8 may be relevant to loss of employment amounting to loss of the right to a profession or to prejudice some aspects of working life by reason of trade union activity or membership.[43] Article 10 may be relevant to trade union leafleting and picketing.[44]

Article 11 is, of course, in two parts, protecting both freedom of assembly and freedom of association. The latter freedom contains within it the specific express freedom to be a member of a trade union for the protection of one's interests. Picketing is an aspect of freedom of assembly, a provision which is obviously relevant to aspects of trade union action.[45] The right to freedom of assembly does not have attached to it the rider of being 'for the protection of his interests', as does freedom of association.[46] The cases show, unsurprisingly, that demonstrations, marches and picketing (and industrial action to take part in them) are all regarded as protected by Article 11(1).[47]

---

[42] Eg, *Danilenkov and others v Russia*, App No 67336/01, 10 December 2009. See N Bruun, ch 14 in this volume.

[43] *Le Compte, Van Leuven and de Meyere v Belgium* [1982] 4 EHRR 1; *Werner v Poland*, 15 November 2001, paras 12, 22, 31 and 33; *Pfeifer v Austria* (2009) 48 EHRR 8, paras 34–35; *Niemitz v Germany* (1993) 16 EHRR 97, para 37; *Sidabaras v Lithuania* [2006] 42 EHRR 6, paras 29, 47 and 48; *Volkov v Ukraine* (2013) 57 EHRR 1, [2013] IRLR 480, para 165. Although none of these involved trade union membership or activity, the principles could be relevant. See S Van Drooghenbroeck, ch 7, this volume and F Hendrickx-Leuven, ch 8.

[44] In relation to union publications, see the duo of recent cases: *Palomo Sánchez v Spain*, Nos 28955/06, 28957/06, 28959/06 and 28964/06, 12 September 2011, (2012) 54 EHRR 24, [2011] IRLR 934; and *Vellutini and Michel v France*, App No 32820/09, 6 October 2011. In relation to picketing, though there is no ECtHR case in point, there is no reason why the latter should not follow the reasoning of the the Canadian Supreme Court in *Pepsi-Cola Canada Beverages (West) Ltd RWDSU v Local 558* 2002 SCC 8, where it was held that there was nothing illegal or unlawful about picketing (indeed, secondary picketing in that case) and that to find otherwise would have been contrary to the freedom of expression guaranteed by the Canadian Charter. In a recent case, *United Food and Commercial Workers, Local 401 v Alberta (Attorney General)*, 2012 ABCA 130, the Alberta Court of Appeal held that data processing legislation which caused a union to be liable by reason of the threat to publish photos of workers crossing picket lines was unconstitutional since it infringed the union's freedom of expression. D Voorhoof and P Humblet consider Article 10 in ch 10 of this volume.

[45] Picketing in a non-industrial context in which workers do not appear to have been called upon to desist from work was protected in *Kuznetsov v Russia*, App No 10877/04, 23 January 2009. There appears to be no reason of law or logic why peaceful picketing in an industrial context and with the purpose of peacefully dissuading workers from working should not equally be protected by Article 11 (or Article 10—see n 44 in relation to Canada). Picketing was regarded as an aspect of the right to strike in *Trofimchuk v Ukraine*, App No 4241/03, 28 January 2011.

[46] Interestingly, freedom of association seems to have been used as a proxy for the right to strike to some extent, eg, *Karaçay v Turkey* (n 15); *Çerikçi v Turkey* (n 16); *Urcan v Turkey* (n 14); *Enerji Yapi-Yol Sen v Turkey* (n 10); *Saime Özcan v Turkey* (n 14); *Kaya and Seyhan v Turkey* (n 17).

[47] *Saya* (n 35) involved a trade union-organised May Day march; and *Nurettin Aldemir* (n 35) involved a demonstration against a proposed bill on trade unions. *Bączkowski and others v Poland* (n 13)

Notwithstanding the exposition of the Convention rights in other chapters of this book, there are some further points to be made in relation to the substantive law in this chapter.

2.4.2 *Living Instrument*

It is worth reiterating that the ECtHR regards the ECHR as a 'living instrument'.[48] Thus, for example, in the landmark case of *Demir and Baykara v Turkey*[49] (the repercussions of that decision have been discussed in other chapters of this book and elsewhere),[50] it was held that the list of essential elements of freedom of association:

> is subject to evolution depending on particular developments in labour relations. In this connection it is appropriate to remember that the Convention is a living instrument which must be interpreted in the light of present-day conditions, and in accordance with developments in international law, so as to reflect the increasingly high standard being required in the area of the protection of human rights, thus necessitating greater firmness in assessing breaches of the fundamental values of democratic societies.[51]

In consequence, the ECtHR 'reconsidered' its earlier judgments in *Swedish Engine Drivers' Union v Sweden*[52] and *Schmidt and Dahlström v Sweden*[53] effectively reversing the *ratio decidendi* in those cases that collective bargaining was merely one of a set of optional rights from which Member States, within their margin of appreciation, could choose as a means of allowing unions to be heard on behalf of their members.[54] This was 'so as to take account of the perceptible evolution in such matters, in both international law and domestic legal systems' and to maintain 'a dynamic and evolutive approach'.[55]

Because of this approach and the willingness of the ECtHR, in appropriate cases, to decline to follow its previous case law, it is necessary to carefully consider the

involved a march to draw attention to discrimination against homosexuals; *Alekseyev v Russia*, App Nos 4916/07; 25924/08; 14599/09; 21 October 2010 involved an annual Gay Pride March; *Patyi v Hungary*, App No 5529/05, 7 January 2009 involved a demonstration in front of the Prime Minister's residence to seek compensation for the creditors of an insolvent private company; *Christians against Racism and Fascism v UK* (n 10) para 93 involved a march against fascists. And see D Mead, 'The Right to Peaceful Protest under the European Convention on Human Rights—A Content Study of Strasbourg Case Law' [1997] EHRLR 345. A prospective order preventing an assembly or the imposition of damages or other punishment after the event will both be regarded as restrictions on the exercise of the right of freedom of assembly: *Ezelin v France* (1992) 14 EHRR 362, para 39.

[48] The doctrine has been applied by the ECtHR since *Tyrer v UK*, 25 April 1978, (1979–80) 2 EHRR 1, para 31. It is to be noted that the ECtHR applies Articles 31–33 of the Vienna Convention on the Law of Treaties of 23 May 1969: *Golder v UK*, 21 February 1975, 1 EHRR 524, para 29; reaffirmed in *Banković v Belgium* (2007) 44 EHRR SE 5.

[49] *Demir and Baykara v Turkey* (n 10). The Grand Chamber unanimously upheld the unanimous judgment of the Second Chamber (see paras 98–101, 147–51). Since there was only one judge in common, it can be said that, in *Demir and Baykara*, 23 judges of the ECtHR came to similar conclusions.

[50] KD Ewing and J Hendy, 'The Dramatic Implications of *Demir and Baykara*' (2010) 39 ILJ 2.

[51] *Demir and Baykara* (n 10) para 146.

[52] *Swedish Engine Drivers' Union v Sweden* (1979–80) 1 EHRR 617.

[53] *Schmidt and Dahlström v Sweden* (1976) 1 EHRR 632.

[54] For a discussion of the pre-*Demir and Baykara* law, see M Forde, 'The European Convention on Human Rights and Labor Law' (1983) 31 *American Journal of Comparative Law* 301. As to the freedom of collective bargaining and as to the right to be heard, see T Jacobs in ch 12 of this volume.

[55] *Demir and Baykara* (n 10) para 154.

validity of propositions derived from earlier ECtHR judgments (and especially decisions of the now-defunct European Commission on Human Rights) in the light of
more recent decisions.[56]

Furthermore, it is necessary to note the detailed and valuable research by
K Lörcher in Chapter 1 in which he demonstrates remarkable inconsistencies in
the extent to which principles established in one case are applied in other cases,
in particular, stark omissions to refer to applicable international law provisions,
notwithstanding the importance attached to such references by the Grand Chamber
in *Demir and Baykara* and, indeed, remarkable failures to reference *Demir and
Baykara* itself in relevant subsequent cases, notwithstanding its pre-eminent status.

The practitioner should therefore conclude that previous cases in the jurisprudence
of the ECtHR which fail to take proper account of principles which it has recently
held to be of importance should be given lesser significance in his or her submission
on violations than those which establish or apply the modern principles.

2.4.3 Trade Union Rights

It has been noted elsewhere in this book that in its groundbreaking decision in
Demir and Baykara, the Grand Chamber established that:

> [T]he right to bargain collectively with the employer has, in principle, become one of the
> essential elements of the 'right to form and to join trade unions for the protection of [one's]
> interests' set forth in Article 11 of the Convention.[57]

The Court identified other 'essential elements' of the right to join a trade union 'for
the protection of his interests' in Article 11:[58]

> [T]he right to form and join a trade union (see, as a recent authority, *Tüm Haber Sen
> and Çınar*),[59] the prohibition of closed-shop agreements (see, for example, *Sørensen and
> Rasmussen*)[60] and the right for a trade union to seek to persuade the employer to hear what
> it has to say on behalf of its members (*Wilson and Palmer*).[61]

---

[56] It also means that there is considerable danger and, indeed, futility in the construction of an all-
embracing statement of a general rule on a particular aspect of Convention law which attempts to
integrate all the ECtHR's case law on the subject matter regardless of changes in direction and emphasis.
This point is highlighted by K Lörcher's observations (referred to below) as to the lack of coherence of
the ECtHR jurisprudence after *Demir and Baykara*. The evolutive approach of the Court to the ECHR
as a living instrument led Professor Ewing and myself to suggest that, for example, *UNISON v UK*
(n 25) can no longer be regarded as authoritative, at least insofar as it held that the restrictions on the
right to strike in that case were justifiable by reference to Article 11(2): KD Ewing and J Hendy, *Days
of Action: The Legality of Protest Strikes against Government Cuts* (Liverpool, Institute of Employment
Rights, 2011), 26–30. See also J Hendy, 'Caught in a Fork' (2000) 29 *ILJ* 5; B Simpson, 'Trade Disputes
and Industrial Action Ballots in the Twenty-First Century' (2002) 31 *ILJ* 270; T Novitz, *International
and European Protection of the Right to Strike* (Oxford, Oxford University Press, 2003), 231–32. By
way of further example, *National Association of Teachers in Further and Higher Education v UK* (n 25),
in which the Commission held that a statutory obligation to disclose the names of intended strikers to
the employer as a condition of lawfulness of the strike was not a breach of Article 11, seems inconsistent
with the Court's modern jurisprudence.

[57] *Demir and Baykara* (n 10), para 154.

[58] *Demir and Baykara* (n 10), para 144.

[59] *Tüm Haber Sen and Çınar v Turkey*, (n 36).

[60] *Sørensen and Rasmussen v Denmark*, App No 52562/99, 52620/99, (2008) 46 EHRR 29.

[61] See n 10 above.

The ECtHR in *Demir and Baykara* pointed out that the list is not finite,[62] though it omitted to mention decisions clearly establishing other essential elements, such as: the right to draw up and enforce union constitutions (*Cheall v UK*,[63] *Johansson v Sweden*[64] and *ASLEF v UK*);[65] the right to appropriate facilities for workers' representatives to enable them to carry out their trade union functions effectively (*Sanchez Navajas v Spain*);[66] and the negative right to dissociate (*Young, James and Webster v UK*,[67] confirmed in *Sigurjonsson v Iceland*;[68] see also *Sibson v UK*).[69]

As to the right to strike, like Professor Dorssemont in chapter 13, Professor Ewing and I have sought to show (elsewhere) that the ECtHR has recognised that the right to strike is inherent in Article 11(1).[70] In every recent case involving consideration of strikes, the ECtHR has accepted that the impugned restriction on the right to strike is in breach of Article 11(1).[71] In no recent case has the Court held that a restriction on the right to strike was not, prima facie, within the protection of Article 11(1). In every recent case in which it has held that the strike was not protected by the Article as a whole, it was because the restrictions on the right to strike could be justified by reference to Article 11(2).[72]

We also sought to make the point which Professor Dorssemont makes in his chapter, which is that there is no logical basis for confining the right to strike under Article 11 to collective bargaining matters.[73] Recent cases in the ECtHR are supportive of this thesis.[74]

Thus, the identification of the apposite trade union rights deriving from the modern jurisprudence of the ECtHR is the first task of the draftsperson alleging violations in Part III of the form.

---

[62] Ibid, para 146.
[63] *Cheall v UK* (1985) 42 DR 178, 185.
[64] *Johansson v Sweden* (1990) 65 DR 202, 205.
[65] *ASLEF v UK* (n 10).
[66] *Sanchez Navajas v Spain*, App No 57442/00, 21 June 2001.
[67] *Young, James and Webster v UK* [1981] IRLR 408.
[68] *Sigurjonsson v Iceland* (1993) 16 EHRR 462.
[69] *Sibson v UK* (1993) ECHR Series A 258-A.
[70] I use the 'right to strike' to mean the right to take and/or to organise industrial action (in any form): KD Ewing and J Hendy, 'The Dramatic Implications of *Demir and Baykara*' (n 50), 13–19; Ewing and Hendy (n 55) 19–20. See also F Dorssement, 'The Right to Form and Join Trade Unions for the Protection of His Interests under Article 11 of the ECHR' (2010) 1 *European Labour Law Journal* 185. The scepticism expressed by the English Court of Appeal in *Metrobus v UNITE the Union* [2009] IRLR 851, para 35 is unwarranted.
[71] *Federation of Offshore Workers Trade Unions (OFS) v Norway* (n 25); *UNISON v UK* (n 25); *Wilson and Palmer* (n 10), in which the existence of the right to organise (or take) industrial action was crucial to the Article 11 reasoning (see paras 45 and 46)—though the case was not about industrial action; *Karaçay v Turkey* (n 15); *Çerikçi v Turkey* (n 16); *Dilek et al v Turkey*, App Nos 74611/02, 26876/02 and 27628/02, 30 January 2008; *Urcan v Turkey* (n 14); *Enerji Yapi-Yol Sen v Turkey* (n 10); *Danilenkov and others v Russia* (n 41); *Saime Özcan v Turkey* (n 14); *Kaya and Seyhan v Turkey* (n 17); and *Trofimchuk v Ukraine* (n 44).
[72] *OFS, UNISON* and *Trofimchuk*, all mentioned in the previous note.
[73] 'The ambit of the employment contract', as F Dorssemont puts it, p 354. Ewing and Hendy (n 56) 19–21.
[74] Eg, *Karaçay v Turkey* (n 15), where the object of a national day of strike action was to defend the purchasing power of public servants; *Çerikçi v Turkey* (n 16) where the activity was participation in a May Day rally; *Kaya and Seyhan v Turkey* (n 17), where the national day of strike action was to protest against a proposed law on the organisation of the public service then before Parliament.

But this may be only the beginning of the task, since the right contended for may not be evident on the face of the relevant article and there may not be, in the extant jurisprudence of the ECtHR, an unequivocal statement of it—at least not in the form that the draftsperson seeks to say it should be applied.

It is here that, as K Lörcher emphasises, that reliance on the approach of the ECtHR invoking international law (so fully explained in *Demir and Baykara*) must be prayed in aid.

2.4.4 Non-Convention Material

The ECtHR in *Demir and Baykara* stated that in determining the existence of an essential element amongst the bundle of rights contained in Article 11(1), the Court:

> takes into account the international law background to the legal question before it. Being made up of a set of rules and principles that are accepted by the vast majority of States, the common international or domestic law standards of European States reflect a reality that the Court cannot disregard when it is called upon to clarify the scope of a Convention provision that more conventional means of interpretation have not enabled it to establish with a sufficient degree of certainty ...[75]

> The Court, in defining the meaning of terms and notions in the text of the Convention, can and must take into account elements of international law other than the Convention, the interpretation of such elements by competent organs, and the practice of European States reflecting their common values. The consensus emerging from specialised international instruments and from the practice of contracting States may constitute a relevant consideration for the Court when it interprets the provisions of the Convention in specific cases.[76]

This approach is, to some extent, also supported by Article 60 of the Convention, which states that nothing in the Convention shall be construed as limiting or derogating from any of the human rights and fundamental freedoms which may be ensured by other treaties to which a Contracting State is a party.[77]

In *Demir and Baykara*, there was extensive consideration of international labour standards, including relevant provisions of: the ILO Conventions;[78] the Council of Europe's Social Charter of 1961;[79] the Charter of Fundamental Rights of the European Union of 2000;[80] and the International Covenant on Economic, Social and Cultural Rights 1966.[81]

---

[75] *Demir and Baykara* (n 10) para 76.

[76] Ibid, para 85.

[77] Indeed, the Ministerial Conference in Rome on 5 November 1990 called for the recognition of 'the indivisible nature of all human rights, be they civil, political, social or cultural'. In *Tănase v Moldova*, App No 33401/02, judgment of 27 April 2010 (GC) at para 176, the ECtHR made the point that it was for it to decide which international instruments and reports it considers relevant and how much weight to attribute to them.

[78] *Demir and Baykara* (n 10) paras 37–39, 42–44, 147–48; and see paras 100–02.

[79] Ibid, paras 49–50, 74, 77, 149; and see paras 46, 103–04.

[80] Ibid, paras 51, 150; and see para 80. The Charter of Fundamental Rights of the European Union was adopted in Nice in 2000 and is recognised as having equal value to the Treaties by Article 6 of the Treaty on European Union. Article 12 (on trade union rights) of the Charter is referred to in *Demir and Baykara* (n 10) para 47.

[81] Ibid, para 41; para 40 also refers to the International Covenant on Civil and Political Rights.

Not merely did the ECtHR make reference to these instruments, it relied on the elaboration and application of those standards in the jurisprudence of their supervisory bodies. In treating the ECHR as a living instrument, the Strasbourg court also acknowledged that these other treaties are living instruments as well, so that in considering their scope and content, it is necessary to have regard not only to the text of the treaties but also to the elaboration and development of the rights thereunder in the case law of the supervisory bodies.[82]

In the case of the ILO, the Grand Chamber in *Demir and Baykara* did not confine its attention to ILO findings in relation to Turkey specifically, but also referred to the body of principles drawn from earlier decisions of the CFA and the CEACR. These were taken from, respectively, the *Digest of Decisions and Principles of the Freedom of Association Committee of the Governing Body of the ILO*[83] and the *General Survey*, properly entitled *Freedom of Association and Collective Bargaining: General Survey by the Committee of Experts on the Application of Conventions and Recommendations*.[84]

The Grand Chamber had similar regard to the jurisprudence of the ESC established by decisions of the ECSR[85] and of the Committee of Ministers of the Council of Europe.[86] The body of decisions of the ECSR is found in the Annual 'Conclusions' of the ECSR, summarised in its *Digest of the Case Law of the European Committee of Social Rights*.[87]

These various sources are therefore fundamental tools in the fashioning of the applicant's application to the ECtHR.

From its publication in 2012, the CEACR's magisterial *General Survey on the Fundamental Conventions Concerning Rights at Work in the Light of the ILO Declaration on Social Justice for a Fair Globalization, 2008* will become an equally essential part of the trade union lawyer's toolkit and will, no doubt, soon take its place in the jurisprudence of the ECtHR.[88]

The Grand Chamber in *Demir and Baykara* further held that it was immaterial that the respondent State had not ratified any otherwise apposite international treaty provision:

> In this context, it is not necessary for the respondent State to have ratified the entire collection of instruments that are applicable in respect of the precise subject matter of the case

---

[82] Reference to these instruments and their jurisprudence had been made in earlier cases and in particular *Sigurjonsson v Iceland* (1993) 16 EHRR 462, para 35; *Wilson and Palmer* (n 10) paras 30, 35, 36, 37; *ASLEF v UK* (n 10) paras 22 and 25; and since: *Vördur Ólafsson v Iceland*, App No 20161/06, 27 July 2010.

[83] Published by the ILO, latest edition is the 5th, 2006.

[84] Published by the ILO, the *General Survey* has not been updated since 1994. But see now the CEACR's *General Survey on the Fundamental Conventions Concerning Rights at Work in the Light of the ILO Declaration on Social Justice for a Fair Globalization, 2008*, below.

[85] Referred to in para 149. In *Wilson and Palmer* (n 10), the references to the ESRC were yet more extensive; see paras 30–33 of that judgment.

[86] *Demir and Baykara* (n 10), para 104.

[87] Published by the Council of Europe; the latest edition was published on 1 September 2008.

[88] Report III (part 1B) of the Report of the CEACR to the International Labour Conference, 2012, available at www.ilo.org/public/libdoc/ilo/P/09661/09661%282012-101-1B%29.pdf. Note the Employers' Group denial of ILO jurisdiction over the right to strike (and the CEACR rebuttal of it) at pp 46–50. Since then the Employers' Group (and some governments) have sought to denigrate the status of the CEACR.

concerned. It will be sufficient for the Court that the relevant international instruments denote a continuous evolution in the norms and principles applied in international law or in the domestic law of the majority of Member States of the Council of Europe and show, in a precise area, that there is common ground in modern societies.[89]

In consequence of the reliance placed on these international treaties, the relevant jurisprudence of the ILO, the ESC and the International Covenant on Economic, Social and Cultural Rights (ICESCR) (and other international treaties) is essential material to deploy to the extent that it supports an applicant's argument that a relevant provision of the ECHR should be similarly construed so as to protect the alleged violated right. The importance of this cannot be underestimated and the review of this international treaty material in the applicant's application form may need to be more extensive than his or her exposition of ECtHR law. This is, in particular, because it is reasonable to assume that the judges of the ECtHR and their non-judicial rapporteurs will not be as familiar with this international material as they will with the Court's own case law.

In identifying the scope of the Convention right in question, *Demir and Baykara* also referred to the law and practice of 'European countries which are like-minded and have a common heritage of political traditions, ideals, freedom and the rule of law'.[90] Although there was little discussion of 'the practice of European States' in the Court's judgment,[91] it is plain that the ECtHR, being composed of judges from Member States, will bring their own knowledge of the law and practice of, at least, their own State to judicial discussions.[92] In drafting the applicant's form, the lawyer will, as noted above, have set out the law and practice of the respondent State, inevitably exposing

---

[89] *Demir and Baykara* (n 10) para 86, citing *Marckx v Belgium*, 13 June 1979, Series A, No 31, para 41 (and see also para 20). The ILO has always considered that its fundamental conventions apply to states irrespective of their ratification of them (eg, to the Republic of South Africa in the apartheid era) and the very fact of membership of the ILO carries with it a constitutional obligation to respect the fundamental principles. Indeed, some authors regard the fundamental principles as having arguably become part of customary international law: ILO, *The Trade Union Situation in Chile*, Report of the Fact-Finding and Conciliation Commission on Freedom of Association (ILO, 1975), para 466; CW Jenks, *The International Protection of Trade Union Freedom* (London, Stevens & Sons, 1957), 561–2; P O'Higgins, 'International Standards and British Labour Law' in R Lewis (ed), *Labour Law in Britain* (Oxford, Basil Blackwell, 1986), 577. The logic adopted by the ECtHR in resting on international law standards is consistent with the common law principle of legality explained by Lord Hoffmann in *R v Secretary of State for the Home Department, ex p Simms* [2000] 2 AC 115 at 131; followed by Gleeson CJ in *Electrolux etc v Australian Workers Union* (2004) 221 CLR 309 at 329.

[90] *Demir and Baykara* (n 10) paras 165–66; Preamble to the Convention, 4 November 1950.

[91] Though see *Demir and Baykara* (n 10) paras 52, 151 and 165. In *Stummer v Austria*, App No 37452/02, 7 July 2011, after due consideration it was found that there was insufficient convergence in the law and practice of European States to hold that prisoners had a right not to be excluded from old-age pensions. In *Palomo Sánchez v Spain*, (n 44), paras 27–32, 75, the Grand Chamber (hearing a case referred by the applicants from the Court's Third Section (*sub nom: Jimenez v Spain*) made reference to comparative law research apparently undertaken (presumably by the ECtHR, though this is not clear) in relation to 35 Council of Europe Member States, though no examples were given. The conclusion was shortly stated as demonstrating convergence. The court held (at para 75) that: 'The homogeneity of European legal systems in this area is a relevant factor in balancing the various rights and interests at stake in the present case.' The case involved the dismissal of union activists for publishing a cartoon derogatory of management and both the Third Section and the Grand Chamber held there was no breach of Article 10 or 11 (*cf Vellutini and Michel v France*, App No 32820/09, 6 October 2011). In the pre-*Demir* case of *UNISON v UK* (n 25), the extensive comparative material submitted by counsel for the applicant and designed to show that the challenged restriction had no parallel elsewhere in Europe was simply ignored by the ECtHR.

[92] As will the non-judicial rapporteurs drawn from different Member States.

it to criticism in relation to the alleged violation. It may be that the comparative law of other European States will not so readily be to hand, though there is now a considerable body of comparative labour law material published and available. Contact by the union with the European Trade Union Confederation (ETUC) and its NETLEX network of lawyers or contact by the lawyer with other networks of sympathetic lawyers such as European Lawyers for Workers or the International Centre for Trade Union Rights may be of assistance in identifying colleagues. The relevant union's own European level trade union federation covering the industry from which the application originates might be able to provide some comparative material.

But the value of comparative law to ECtHR applications does not stop at the borders of the Council of Europe. In *Jehovah's Witnesses of Moscow v Russia*,[93] the ECtHR found support for its reasoning not merely from a judgment of the Constitutional Court of Spain[94] and one by the UK Court of Appeal,[95] but it also cited judgments from the Supreme Court of the Tatarstan Republic,[96] the Ontario Supreme Court,[97] the Court of Appeals of New York,[98] the South African Supreme Court,[99] the Supreme Court of Argentina[100] and one from the Supreme Court of Japan.[101] In *Palomo Sánchez v Spain*, the Grand Chamber cited an Advisory Opinion of the Inter-American Court of Human Rights.[102]

The applicant's lawyer, in drafting the submission in support of the alleged violation of an ECHR right, should therefore seek to draw on this global jurisprudence where he or she can access it—and where it is consistent and supportive. It is to be noted, for example, that the applicants' submissions in *Demir and Baykara* itself could have been fortified, had timing permitted it, by reliance on a judgment of the Supreme Court of Canada in the previous year based on near-identical reasoning to that adopted by the ECtHR.[103]

2.4.5 Permissible Restrictions: Article 11(2)

Many of the rights guaranteed by the ECHR are qualified. Thus, to take the primary provision in relation to trade union law, Article 11(2) sets out the only permissible

---

[93] *Jehovah's Witnesses of Moscow v Russia* (2011) 53 EHRR 4, App No 302/02, 10 June 2010, para 85.
[94] Ibid, para 88.
[95] Ibid, paras 86 and 138.
[96] Ibid, para 84.
[97] Ibid, para 85.
[98] Ibid, para 87.
[99] Ibid, para 88.
[100] Ibid, para 88.
[101] Ibid, para 88.
[102] *Palomo Sánchez v Spain*, *App* (n 44) in relation to Article 8 ('trade union rights') of the San Salvador Protocol (17 November 1988, effective 16 November 1999) to the American Convention on Human Rights (22 November 1969, effective 18 July 1978).
[103] *Health Services and Support-Facilities Subsector Bargaining Association v British Columbia*, 2007 SCC 27, [2007] 2 SCR 391. See J Fudge, 'The Supreme Court of Canada and the Right to Bargain Collectively' (2008) 37 *ILJ* 25. This case has been followed but slightly diminished by *Attorney General of Ontario v Fraser*, 2011 SCC 20, discussed in J Fudge, 'Constitutional Rights, Collective Bargaining and the Supreme Court of Canada: Retreat and Reversal in the *Fraser* Case' (2012) 41 *ILJ* 1; and KD Ewing and J Hendy, 'Giving Life to the ILO: Two Cheers for the SCC' in F Faraday, J Fudge and E Tucker (eds), *Constitutional Labour Rights in Canada: Farm Workers and the Fraser Case* (Toronto, Irwin Law, 2012).

basis for restricting the rights contained in Article 11(1). Other Articles have similar qualifications and it is on this aspect of the case that the forensic battle in the
ECtHR will usually be fought. The drafter of the application form must therefore
deploy the necessary arguments to defeat the government's predictable reliance on
Article 11(2) in its response to the application, though tactically it may be best (in
some cases) to await the government response in order to see to what extent and
how Article 11(2) is deployed. Article 11(2) provides that:

> No restrictions shall be placed on the exercise of these rights other than such as are pre-
> scribed by law and are necessary in a democratic society in the interests of national security
> or public safety, for the prevention of disorder or crime, for the protection of health or
> morals or for the protection of the rights and freedoms of others. This Article shall not
> prevent the imposition of lawful restrictions on the exercise of these rights by members of
> the armed forces, of the police or of the administration of the State.

The first point to highlight is that such restrictions are to be strictly construed:
Sunday Times v UK[104] and *Demir and Baykara*.[105] In *Tüm Haber Sen and Çinar v
Turkey*, the ECtHR held:

> The exceptions set out in Article 11 are to be construed strictly; only convincing and com-
> pelling reasons can justify restrictions on such parties' freedom of association.[106]

It is worth briefly mentioning some of these permissible restrictions on Convention
rights in the context of the allegation that the applicant's rights have been violated.

2.4.6 Permissible Restrictions—Prescribed by Law

The first condition of Article 11(2) (as in other Articles) is that the restriction be
prescribed by (national) law, although fulfilment of that condition is not, of course,
determinative of whether the impugned restriction is permissible. But the fact that
the law is subsequently held by the domestic courts to be unwarranted or invalid
will not mean that the restriction, whilst it applied, did not fulfil the requirement of
being prescribed by law.[107]

However, the fact that the legal restriction was subsequently held to be invalid in
national law may, in some circumstances, be evidence that it was not 'necessary in a
democratic society'. Thus, the retrospective imposition of a penalty imposed by law,
even a trivial one, though satisfying the legal prescription requirement, may well fail

---

[104] *Sunday Times v UK* (1977) 28 ECHR B 64, paras 194–95.

[105] *Demir and Baykara* (n 10) para 146. The ECtHR there referred to: *Refah Partisi (the Welfare Party) v Turkey* (GC), App Nos 41340/98, 41342/98, 41343/98 and 41344/98, ECHR 2003-II; and *Selmouni v France* (GC), App No 25803/94, ECHR 1999-V.

[106] *Tüm Haber Sen and Çinar v Turkey* (n 36) para 35.

[107] In *Bączkowski and others v Poland* (n 13) a march of some 3,000 people took place to draw attention to discrimination against homosexuals in spite of a ban on its taking place. The ban was subsequently
quashed in domestic proceedings, but the fact that there had been a ban was in breach of Article 11:
'The applicants took a risk in holding [static assemblies of some 3,000 persons] given the official ban
in force at that time. The assemblies were held without a presumption of legality, such a presumption
constituting a vital aspect of effective and unhindered exercise of freedom of assembly and freedom of
expression. The Court observes that the refusals to give authorisation could have had a chilling effect
on the applicants and other participants in the assemblies. It could also have discouraged other persons
from participating' (at para 67). See also (in relation to heavy penalties quashed by the domestic courts)
Urcan v Turkey (n 14); *Saime Özcan v Turkey* (n 14).

other aspects of Article 11(2).[108] So minimal disciplinary warnings to be more attentive to duties as punishment for necessarily unauthorised absence from work whilst participating in a strike were, as we have seen, held to be in breach of Article 11(1) and could not fulfil the test of necessity in a democratic society.[109]

2.4.7 Permissible Restrictions: Legitimate Aim

Legitimacy of objective is not often a difficulty for States seeking to justify restrictions on Article 11 rights by domestic law. But even so:

> it is important for the public authorities to show a certain degree of tolerance towards [in that particular case] peaceful gatherings if the freedom of assembly guaranteed by Article 11 of the Convention is not to be deprived of all substance.[110]

Even a non-violent sit-in which unlawfully blocked a public road may demand the tolerance of the authorities under Article 11(2).[111] But there is a limit to tolerance and it has been held to be permissible under Article 11(2) to ban demonstrations to prevent reasonably anticipated disorder,[112] excessive noise[113] or excessive disruption to passers-by.[114]

The legitimate aim asserted by the State should not be accepted at face value and should be carefully scrutinised since the ECtHR may not accept the legitimacy of the government's asserted objective.[115]

2.4.8 Permitted Restrictions: Necessity in a Democratic Society

The condition that the restriction must be 'necessary in a democratic society' is of the greatest significance in pleading a violation of trade union rights. 'Pluralism,

---

[108] In *Kuznetsov v Russia* (n 45), 10 days' notice for a picket was required by law and the organisers gave only eight days. This breach of the law led to a fine equivalent to some €35. The restriction was thus prescribed by law (and fulfilled the legitimate aim of preventing disorder and protecting the rights of others). But it failed the ultimate requirement of Article 11(2), necessity in a democratic society, because the ECtHR held that the breach of the legal time limit in this case 'was neither relevant nor a sufficient reason for imposing administrative liability on the applicant. In this connection the Court emphasises that the freedom to take part in a peaceful assembly is of such importance that a person cannot be subjected to a sanction—even one at the lower end of the scale of disciplinary penalties—for participation in a demonstration which has not been prohibited, so long as this person does not himself commit any reprehensible act on such an occasion' (at para 43).

[109] *Karaçay v Turkey* (n 15) para 37; *Çerikçi v Turkey* (n 16); and *Kaya and Seyhan v Turkey* (n 17) para 30.

[110] *Kuznetsov v Russia* (n 45) para 44, citing: *Galstyan v Armenia*, App No 26986/03, 15 November 2007; *Bukta and others v Hungary*, App No 25691/04, ECHR 2007-IX, 17 October 2007; *Oya Ataman v Turkey*, App No 74552/01, 5 December 2006.

[111] *G v Germany* (1989) 60 DR 256 (ECHR).

[112] *Christians against Racism and Fascism v UK* (n 10); *Cisse v France*, 9 April 2002.

[113] *S v Austria*, 13 December 1990.

[114] *Friedl v Austria*, 30 November 1992. In *Barraco v France*, App No 31684/05, 5 June 2009, a three-lane cortège of lorries driven along a busy motorway on a Monday morning at less than 10 kph ('opération escargot') with frequent stops had been tolerated for several hours by the authorities. But they intervened when the road became completely blocked and arrested the drivers, who were subsequently convicted and sentenced to a three-month suspended sentence of imprisonment and a fine of €1,500. The ECtHR held that this was lawful, legitimate and proportionate under Article 11.

[115] Eg, in a strike case, *Kaya and Seyhan v Turkey* (n 17): 'La Cour doute que l'ingérence dans la présente affaire poursuivît un but légitime au sens de l'article 11 § 2 de la Convention.'

tolerance and broadmindedness are the hallmarks of a "democratic society"'.[116] It is here that the non-Convention material, so decisive in *Demir and Baykara* and so extensive in *Jehovah's Witnesses v Russia*, really comes into its own. For *Demir and Baykara* made clear that the relevance of the international material was not confined to identifying the rights protected (in that case) by Article 11(1), the international material was also relevant to determining the standard of necessity in a democratic society pursuant to Article 11(2).[117] It is therefore incumbent on the drafter of an application to be familiar with, and apply where supportive, the jurisprudence of the supervisory bodies of the international treaties discussed earlier, both generally and in relation to the particular State against which the allegation is brought.

A restriction which is 'necessary in a democratic society' must be shown to fulfil a 'pressing social need' which is proportionate and which relates to one or more of the legitimate aims identified in the text of Article 11(2), based on an acceptable assessment of the relevant facts in the circumstances prevailing in the given country at the time.[118] 'Necessary in this context does not have the flexibility of such expressions as "useful" or "desirable"'.[119] 'Exceptions to the rule of freedom of association are to be construed strictly and only convincing and compelling reasons can justify restrictions on that freedom.'[120] Necessity must be 'convincingly established'.[121] *Demir and Baykara* reiterated established jurisprudence in holding that:

> In determining in such cases whether a 'necessity'—and therefore a 'pressing social need'—within the meaning of Article 11 § 2 exists, States have only a limited margin of appreciation, which goes hand in hand with rigorous European supervision embracing both the law and the decisions applying it, including those given by independent courts.[122]

As to proportionality, the task of the ECtHR:

> is not to substitute its own view for that of the relevant national authorities but rather to review the decisions they delivered in the exercise of their discretion. This does not mean that it has to confine itself to ascertaining whether the respondent State exercised its discretion reasonably, carefully and in good faith; it must look at the interference complained of in the light of the case as a whole and determine whether it was 'proportionate to the legitimate aim pursued' and whether the reason adduced by the national authorities to justify it are 'relevant and sufficient'. In so doing, the Court has to satisfy itself that the national authorities applied standards which were in conformity with the principles embodied in the

---

[116] *Young, James and Webster v UK* (n 67) para 105.

[117] *Demir and Baykara* (n 10) paras 165–66.

[118] *Sunday Times v UK* (n 104) paras 59 and 62; *Olsson v Sweden* (1988) 11 EHRR 259; *The Observer and The Guardian v UK* (1991) ECHRR (Series A) 216; *Lingens v Austria* (1986) ECHRR (Series A) 103, para 43; *Ezelin v France* (1991) ECHRR (Series A) 202, para 51; *Oberschlick v Austria* (1991) ECHRR (Series A) 204, para 60; *Demir and Baykara* (n 10) para 164.

[119] *Young, James and Webster v UK* (n 67) para 104; *Jehovah's Witnesses of Moscow v Russia* (n 93) para 100, citing *Gorzelik v Poland* (2005) 40 EHRR 633, at paras 94 and 95 with further references.

[120] *Jehovah's Witnesses of Moscow* (n 93) para 100.

[121] *Autronic AG v Switzerland* (1990) ECHRR (Series A) 178 para 61; *Weber v Switzerland* (1990) ECHRR (Series A) 177, para 47; *Barthold v Germany* (1985) ECHRR (Series A) 90, para 58.

[122] At para 119. The Court referred in that passage to *Sidiropoulos v Greece*, 10 July 1998 para 40, Reports 1998-IV. This principle had been stated in *Tüm Haber Sen and Çınar v Turkey* (n 36) para 35 and was more recently restated in *Patyi v Hungary* (n 47) paras 38–39; and *Jehovah's Witnesses of Moscow v Russia* (n 93) para 108.

appropriate provision of the Convention and, moreover, that they based their decisions on an acceptable assessment of the relevant facts.[123]

It goes without saying that 'the nature and severity of the sanction are factors to be taken into account when assessing the proportionality of the interference'.[124]

Necessity in a democratic society cannot, of itself, justify a restriction of an Article 11(1) right. The restriction must be imposed for one of the very limited reasons identified in Article 11(2); only if it is can necessity in a democratic society sustain the impugned restriction. If the government cannot establish one of those reasons, then the fact that it is arguable that the restriction is necessary in a democratic society will be irrelevant. The Article 11(2) bases for invoking necessity in a democratic society are exhaustive: there is no residual category. Those bases include justification by reference to 'interests of national security or public safety, for the prevention of disorder or crime, [and] for the protection of health or morals'. These categories are elaborated in the textbooks and do not require further consideration here, save to point out that government invocation of such grounds should be carefully scrutinised and may well be open to challenge.

The possible justification of necessity in a democratic society for the 'protection of the rights and freedoms of others', together with Article 1 of the First Protocol, which provides the right to peaceful enjoyment of property, does warrant a brief word, however, especially in relation to the right to strike.

Every form of industrial action interferes with the rights and freedoms of others and, in particular, those of the targeted employer(s). The whole rationale of industrial action is to impact adversely on those against whom it is directed in order to bring pressure to bear to achieve the objective of those taking the action. But if the mere fact of interference with the rights of employers was sufficient in itself to justify restricting the right to strike, there would be no right to strike in Europe so that the express acknowledgement of the right to strike in the European Social Charter (both in the 1961 and 1996 versions), in other international treaties and in the constitutions and laws of almost every Contracting State[125] would be inexplicable. The

---

[123] *Jehovah's Witnesses of Moscow v Russia* (n 93) para 108, citing *Utd Communist Party of Turkey v Turkey* (1998) 26 EHRR 121 T, para 47; and *Partidul Comunistilor (Neperceristi)* (2007) 44 EHRR 17, para 49. The last sentence is a reiteration of *Demir and Baykara* (n 10) para 119, which cited *Yazar v Turkey*, App No 22723/93, etc, ECHR 2002-II, also recently restated in *Patyi v Hungary* (n 47) para 40.

[124] *Jehovah's Witnesses of Moscow v Russia* (n 93) para 154, citing *Refah Partisi (Welfare Party) v Turkey* (2003) 37 EHRR 1 para 133.

[125] Note the list of examples of States having the right to strike in their constitutions referred to by the CEACR *General Survey* of 2012 (see n 88) at 50. They are: Albania, Algeria, Angola, Argentina, Armenia, Azerbaijan, Belarus, Benin, the Plurinational State of Bolivia, Bosnia and Herzegovina, Brazil, Bulgaria, Burkina Faso, Burundi, Cambodia, Cameroon, Cape Verde, Central African Republic, Chad, Chile, Colombia, Congo, the Czech Republic, the Democratic Republic of the Congo, Costa Rica, Côte d'Ivoire, Croatia, Cyprus, Djibouti, the Dominican Republic, Ecuador, El Salvador, Estonia, Ethiopia, France, Georgia, Greece, Guatemala, Guinea, Guinea-Bissau, Guyana, Haiti, Honduras, Hungary, Italy, Kazakhstan, Kenya, Republic of Korea, Kyrgyzstan, Latvia, Lithuania, Luxembourg, the Former Yugoslav Republic of Macedonia, Madagascar, the Republic of the Maldives, Mali, Mauritania, Mexico, the Republic of Moldova, Montenegro, Morocco, Mozambique, Nicaragua, Niger, Panama, Paraguay, Peru, the Philippines, Poland, Portugal, Romania, the Russian Federation, Rwanda, San Marino, Sao Tome and Principe, Senegal, Serbia, the Seychelles, Slovakia, Slovenia, South Africa, Spain, Suriname, Sweden, Switzerland, Timor-Leste, Togo, Turkey, Ukraine, Uruguay, the USA and the Bolivarian Republic of

economic interests of employers cannot by itself trump the human rights of workers and their unions. To that extent, it appears that the decision in *UNISON v UK*[126] is, respectfully, wrong and inconsistent with the subsequent jurisprudence of the ECtHR.[127] In that case, a statutory prohibition on the right to strike was held to be justified by reference to Article 11(2) as necessary in a democratic society for the protection of the economic interests of the current employer against the strike.[128] Significantly, the ECSR (after the ECtHR decision) held that the prohibition was not compatible with Article 6(4) of the European Social Charter.[129] Had that decision preceded that in the ECtHR, it might have been influential.

It is only if the damage inflicted is intended to ruin the business that the jurisprudence of some Contracting States permit that factor to outweigh the right to strike.[130] On that basis, the decision in *OFS v Norway*[131] is unexceptional, since the ECtHR accepted that the consequences to the national economy of a strike in the offshore oil industry would have been so catastrophic that the State was justified in ordering it to cease.

The ECSR has rejected the proposition that there is any principle of proportionality between the damage caused by, and the object of, industrial action.[132] Likewise, the ILO:

[H]as never included the need to assess the proportionality of interests ... The Committee has only suggested that, in certain cases, the notion of a negotiated minimum service in order to avoid damages which are irreversible or out of all proportion to third parties, may be considered and if agreement is not possible the issue should be referred to an independent body.[133]

After *Demir and Baykara*, of course, these are significant decisions.

Venezuela. To this could have been added States where the highest courts have held that the right to strike is implicit in their Constitutions, eg, Ireland (*Education Co v Fitzpatrick* [1961] IR 294 at 397) and Canada (*Health Services etc*—see n 103 above).

[126] See n 25 above.

[127] See n 56 above.

[128] *UNISON v UK* (n 25), paras 42–43. The strike was intended to pressure the employer to ensure particular terms and conditions of work after the transfer of the business to one of several tenderers. The English court held that the strike lost statutory protection because the dispute was as to terms and conditions payable by a future employer and because it would benefit not just the existing workforce but also workers yet to be employed.

[129] See ECSR, *Conclusions C XVII-1*, at 516–19; ECSR, *Conclusions XVIII-1*, 819–22; and see *Conclusions XIX-3*. There was no suggestion that the breach of Article 6(4) could be justified under Article 31 of the Social Charter, which permits restrictions on Charter rights (including Article 6(4)) similar in terms to those to be found in Article 11(2) of the Convention.

[130] See A Stewart and M Bell (eds), *The Right to Strike: A Comparative Perspective; a Study of National Law in 6 EU States* (Liverpool, Institute of Employment Rights, 2008).

[131] *OFS v Norway* (2002) ECHR 2002-VI 301.

[132] ECSR, *Conclusions XVI-1* (Belgium).

[133] 2010 Report of the CEACR rejecting the arguments in *VikingLine ABp v ITWF* [2008] IRLR 14, Case C-438/05, judgment of CJEU, 11 December 2007; and *Laval un Partneri Ltd v Svenska Byggnadsarbetareföbundet* [2008] IRLR 160, Case C-346/06, judgment of CJEU, 18 December 2007, in its decision on an application brought by BALPA. On the BALPA case, see KD Ewing and J Hendy, 'The CJEU Decisions and Trade Union Freedom: Lessons from the United Kingdom' in KD Ewing and J Hendy (eds), *The New Spectre Haunting Europe—The ECJ, Trade Union Rights, and the British Government* (Liverpool, Institute of Employment Rights, 2009).

Any review of recent cases concerning the right to strike in the ECtHR shows that State governments' attempts to invoke Article 11(2) to justify restrictions have generally not met with success. This might be suggested to reflect, in many cases, the grossness of the violation in the cases which have been brought,[134] but analysis of the principles shows that there are formidable obstacles for governments to overcome.

2.5 Time limits

The next heading in the application form requires the applicant to deal with Article 35(1), which requires that the application be lodged within six months of the date of the final decision in the process of exhaustion of domestic remedies. So far as it is necessary for this chapter, the requirement of the exhaustion of remedies has been considered briefly above.

As to the time limit for the service of the application, the time runs from the date of the final decision.[135] In the absence of a domestic remedy, time runs from the date when the applicant was directly affected by or became aware that he or she was directly affected by the impugned act (or omission).[136] There is no mechanism for extension of the time limit, whether by agreement of the parties or by decision of the ECtHR.

Where the alleged violation consists of a continuing act, the time limit will not operate. In *Dudgeon v UK* (1982) 4 EHRR 149[137] the existence of statutory provisions which had been in effect since 1861 and 1885 criminalising homosexual acts did not prevent the Applicant from succeeding in an application in 1976 for breach (amongst others) of Article 8 since those laws posed a continuing 'threat hanging over him [which] was real' (para 41). In *Hilton v UK*:

> The Commission further observes that the six months rule does not apply to that part of the applicant's complaint under Articles 8 and 10 of the Convention which relates to the continued retention of personal information about the applicant since such a complaint concerns a continuing situation.[138]

However, it has been noticed that the ECtHR has ignored this principle in a recent case and held that the application (in respect of a continuing failure to provide protection in UK law against sanctions short of dismissal imposed by a private

---

[134] Though the minimal warning cases of *Karaçay*, *Çerikçi* and *Kaya and Seyhan* (nn 15–17 above) do not fit this thesis.

[135] Article 35(1). Or the date the applicant was informed of the decision if the decision was not publicly made: *K, C, M v The Netherlands* (1995) 80-A DR87, 88. Or the date when reasons were given for the decision if such reasons were required in order to make the application: *Monory v Hungary and Romania*, 17 February 2004.

[136] *Hilton v UK* (1988) 57 DR 108, 113; *Gongadze v Ukraine*, 8 November 2005, para 155.

[137] *Dudgeon v UK* (1982) 4 EHRR 149.

[138] *Hilton v UK* (1988) 57 DR 108 at 113. See also *Almeida Garett v Portugal* (29813/96 and 30229/96; 11 Jan 2000) where the applicant succeeded in an application in 1996 for breach of Article 1 of Protocol No 1 in respect of land which had been expropriated from him in 1975. Though any claim in respect of the expropriation was out of time, the continuing failure to pay compensation for the expropriation meant that the time limit did not apply to the claim for failure to pay it (see para 43). In *Roche v UK* (32555/96; 23 May 2002) an application made in 1996 was admissible under Articles 8 and 10 in respect of a continuing refusal to provide information concerning the applicant's test exposures to chemical weapons in the 1960s (see para 2).

employer for taking lawful industrial action) was out of time notwithstanding that the sanction (withdrawal of travel benefits) was a continuing one and the State's violation in failing to provide protection was equally continuing. Since a decision on inadmissibility is not a 'judgment' (see below), there was no possibility of appeal by way of taking the case to the Grand Chamber.[139]

2.6 Remedies

No doubt many applications to the ECtHR are made to establish a principle and it will be enough that the principle will be set out in the judgment of the Court. However, if there is also a claim for some other remedy, such as an injunction and/ or compensation the form requires a 'Statement of the Object of the Application'. This is the place to explain what is sought and why. If compensation is sought, then a claim for 'just satisfaction' must be made and it is essential that the basis for the claim (losses incurred, future losses, injury to feelings, damage to reputation, etc) must be fully laid out and all documentation evidencing every aspect of the claim must be appended.[140] Such a claim for compensation can include the legal costs in the national courts which failed to remedy the violation and in the ECtHR (although the scale of costs in the latter appears, in English eyes, low, and well below the accepted levels of reasonable charges that English lawyers make). Without the supporting documentation, a claim for just satisfaction has little prospect of success.[141]

2.7 Statement Concerning Other International Proceedings

This section of the application form bearing this heading requires the applicant to state whether and, if so, what proceedings have been or are intended to be launched in other international fora. No comment is needed, save to observe the relevance of this provision to Article 35(2)(b) discussed above.

2.8 List of Documents

It has already been noted that any judgment, decision, statute, treaty, witness statement or other document referred to must be appended to the application. This is the place to list this material in some logical order (eg, chronological in sections such as ECtHR judgments, national judgments and statutes, ILO material, ESC material, witness statements, etc). It is not necessary to copy the ECHR or parts of it (though

---

[139] *Roffey and others v UK* App No 1278/11, 21 May 2013. Significantly, this objection was not raised by the Court when the application was first submitted, nor in the Statement of Facts and Questions for the Parties, nor was it raised by the Government. The applicants were taken wholly by surprise and given no opportunity to seek to rebut the argument that time ran from a fixed point of time. This appears to be a negation of their rights under Article 6.

[140] Article 41, Rule 75 and *Practice Direction* of 28 March 2007 on just satisfaction claims.

[141] See, eg, *Wilson and Palmer* (n 10) paras 65 ff, especially at paras 68–69.

it is usual to set out the text of the relevant Article(s) at the appropriate point in the exposition of the alleged violation), but copies of the judgments of the ECtHR should be appended for ease of reference by the judges and non-judicial rapporteurs. Original material should not be appended; only photocopies should be used.

The material should be printed single-sided and filed in an openable ring binder since it (and the application form) will need to be copied in the Registry.

3 FILING THE APPLICATION FORM AND THEREAFTER

The application form and its appendices should be served by post or courier on the Registrar of the European Court of Human Rights, Council of Europe, F-67075, France.[142] Though service by fax is possible, in the cases dealt with in this book, the material is likely to be far too bulky to be faxed.[143]

Once the application has been lodged, the next step is to wait for the ECtHR Registry to notify that it has been received and given a Court number (and sometimes a barcode) which must be used in all further communications with the Court.

3.1 Statement of Facts and Questions for the Parties

Thereafter, the ECtHR will examine the application against its admissibility criteria.[144] If it is considered that the application appears to be admissible, then notice of it is given to the respondent State and simultaneously to the applicant through his/her/its representative. The Court sends to both a 'Statement of Facts and Questions to the Parties'. The State is invited to submit observations on the application, ie, to provide its defence to the claim of violation of a protected right.[145] It has 12 weeks to notify its intention to do so.[146]

3.2 Third Parties[147]

It is at the stage (communication of the application to the government concerned) that the question of involvement of third parties arises, though thought should have been given to this aspect at the outset.

The value to the ECtHR of allowing third parties to make submissions is to receive an independent insight into the issues (or some of them) from a viewpoint

---

[142] Note the full provisions of the *Practice Direction* on institution of proceedings of 1 November 2003, amended on 22 September 2008 and 24 June 2009.

[143] It is only after an application is filed that application can be made for the limited scheme of Legal Aid available from the ECtHR: Rules 100–05.

[144] Article 35. Usually by a single judge pursuant to Article 26 and Rule 27A. There is a procedure for a contested hearing on admissibility: Rule 54A.

[145] Rule 54(2)(b).

[146] Rule 44 (1)(b).

[147] I am indebted to K Lörcher for his help with this section of the chapter. Any errors, however, are mine.

other than those of the parties. The criterion is that the President of the Chamber must find that granting leave would be in the 'interests of the proper administration of justice'. The third party may be able to supply (from national and/or international experience) further facts or experience about the issues arising in the case or a greater insight into the legal aspects. It is not unusual for States to seek to be joined as third parties, no doubt often at the instigation of the respondent State. But sometimes States seek to intervene to express a view conflicting with that of the respondent State.

The benefit for the applicant is usually to add the weight of a third party with gravitas and eminence, yet which independently makes a submission supportive of the applicant. In particular, the third party may advance other reasons to reach the same conclusion. Or it may be able to present evidence that the restriction on the right in question has a wider and more adverse effect than might otherwise appear on the facts of a particular case. Or it might be able to present evidence that the restriction is not one imposed in other democratic societies of which the third party has particular knowledge and experience.

In a case involving trade union rights, the obvious third parties are other national unions, the national trade union centre, the ETUC or European trade union federations of the relevant sector,[148] or from respected NGOs.[149]

As third parties, trade unions will of course be interested in supporting applications which might achieve future protection for their members. But there is a reputational advantage too in that the more trade union organisations show their interest in defending (social) human rights, the more they will be considered and respected as defenders of human rights.[150]

Any litigation strategy requires the potential damage if the case is lost to be weighed against the potential benefits if the case is won. For the applicant, the consequence of losing may be disappointing but otherwise tolerable. From the perspective of a trade union, a national trade union centre and, especially, an international confederation, the equation may look very different indeed. It is therefore vital for the applicant to involve potential trade union or union confederation third parties at the earliest stage.

Procedurally, the initiative to become a third party might come from the applicant or from the potential third party, or from the Court itself. If the initiative is

---

[148] Cases in which a third intervention of trade unions has been accepted by the ECtHR: LO Denmark in *Sørensen and Rasmussen v Denmark*, (n 60) paras 49 ff; International Transport Workers' Federation (ITF) in *Mangouras v Spain*, (2012) 54 EHRR 25,—App No 12050/04, 28 September 2010,) para 11; United Services Union, Germany (Vereinte Dienstleistungsgewerkschaft—ver.di) in *Heinisch v Germany*), (judgment 21 July 2011, App No 28274/08) paras 5 and 61; European Trade Union Confederation (ETUC) and Trade Union Congress (TUC) in *POA v UK* (n 30).

[149] A labour law case coming to the ECtHR will be constituted as a complaint against a State for alleged failures in their legal systems, though in reality many will originate as a dispute between workers and unions on the one side and a private employer on the other. So far, States have not sought to enrol the private employer (or employers' association) as a third party. Should employers or their associations seek to be heard as third parties, the importance for applicants of bringing in third parties to support them will be increased.

[150] In the context of the 'indivisibility' of human rights—a principle to which the Council of Europe attaches great importance—such a recognition helps to show that fundamental social rights should be safeguarded as effectively as civil and political rights.

that of the applicant or the potential third party, application must be made to the President of the Chamber to which the case has been allocated[151] within 12 weeks of the notice having been sent to the respondent State.[152] It must be made in a 'duly reasoned' form in one of the official languages (with exceptions)[153] and it must ask the President to invite the proposed third party to submit written comments or, in exceptional cases, to be invited to take part in the hearing.[154]

If the application is to be supported, a tactical question is whether a national and European trade union federation should make a joint intervention or whether they would prefer to have separate submissions. Arguments for the latter are that they would have double the number of pages available and that they might better divide the arguments related to the national level and to the European level, and thus show their specific field of knowledge and competence. On the other hand, a joint submission might be thought to carry more weight. The answer, as always, will depend on the circumstances.

The 'duly reasoned' request should probably not exceed two pages. Though there is no particular format, it would be usual to begin by describing the characteristics of the trade union body, its membership, the sector(s) in which it operates, its record as a human rights defender, and its specific competence, knowledge and experience about the issues raised in the application on which it wishes to make submissions.[155] Thereafter, the request should not really go into the substance of the case, but should identify the issues on which the potential third party believes it could contribute in order to assist the Court in the 'interests of the proper administration of justice'. Appropriate emphasis should be given to the questions the Court has put to the parties in the 'Statement of Facts and Questions to the Parties'.[156]

Experience suggests that relevant trade union bodies, both national and international, are usually granted third-party status and are invited to make a submission, subject to a time limit and the maximum number of pages (normally 10–15).[157] The President invariably directs that no comments on the facts or merits of the case should be made and that the third party addresses only those aspects of the case which concern the third party's particular interest in the matter and/or the general principles involved in the solution of the case.

The full submission must observe these points. A national trade union body may wish to emphasise evidence that the restriction on the right in question has a wider and

---

[151] See the relevant 'Statement of Facts and Questions to the Parties' (in the 'Facts and Complaints Collection', http://cmiskp.echr.coe.int/tkp197/search.asp?skin=hudoc-cc-en) at the beginning of which the relevant Section is indicated.

[152] At the beginning of each week, a list of newly communicated cases is published by the Court in the 'Communicated Cases Collection' (http://cmiskp.echr.coe.int/tkp197/search.asp?skin=hudoc-cc-en). On this basis, it is still not easy to identify the most important cases which might be appropriate for a trade union request for a third-party intervention, though each 'Statement of Facts' referred to in this list must be examined separately.

[153] Rule 34(4) (use of languages).

[154] Rule 44(3) and Article 36. Another time limit may be fixed by the President of the Chamber for exceptional reasons.

[155] If the applicant were a member of the requesting union, this should be indicated in order to be fully transparent vis-a-vis the Court.

[156] Which might include questions of admissibility such as whether the applicant has 'victim' status: see above.

[157] Rule 44(5).

more adverse effect than might otherwise be evident and, on analysis, lacks national justification. It may be able to show that what appears to be protection of the rights in question is not, in the national circumstances, effective. Indeed, it may wish to show that fundamental labour rights more broadly are not respected in the particular State. It may be able to show why, because of other factors, the protection of the right in question is of special importance to the class of workers concerned. An international trade union body may be able to show (using comparative labour law or research amongst its affiliates) that the restriction is not one imposed in other democratic societies and it may be in a better position than the applicant or a national trade union to give an exposition of the jurisprudence of relevant international and European standards supporting a conclusion that the ECHR should provide similar protection.

Third parties' submissions will be forwarded by the Registrar to the parties to the case, who are entitled to file written observations in reply.

There is no doubt that such interventions can be influential with the Court, particularly if they go beyond the applicant's arguments in showing that the restriction on the right in question has a profound impact or that the restriction is not one imposed in other democratic societies of which the third party has particular knowledge and experience.[158]

3.3 Reply

Once the State's response is to hand, the applicant will be given a stipulated time period in which to make a response to it (and to any third party submissions), which again should be cogently argued and with all documents appended.[159]

3.4 Friendly Settlement

Negotiated settlement is encouraged by the ECtHR and negotiations to that end between the applicant and the State are confidential. The Court approves settlements reached, which must be on the basis of respect for human rights. Applicants should be wary of settlement offers by governments which do not effectively recognise the violated right. Nowadays, the Court itself is more proactive in encouraging negotiations with a view to friendly settlement.

3.5 The Hearing, if any

Assuming the case is admissible, in the usual case the application will be adjudicated by the ECtHR without the need for an oral hearing. If, in the exceptional case

---

[158] Even if there is no direct reference in the Court's subsequent judgment, the (at least indirect) impact should not be underestimated. If the intervention provides reliable, relevant and additional information, the Court will surely be able to base its judgment on a more complete description of the situation and the consequences of the impugned restriction.

[159] Reference should be made to the *Practice Direction* of 10 December 2007 on written pleadings.

(where, for example, the case is seen to be important), a date will be given for an oral hearing by the Court. The length of time between application and hearing is unpredictable but long (seven years in *Wilson and Palmer*, though that was exceptional). This is because the Court evaluates the importance and urgency of cases for the purposes of listing them to be dealt with.[160] It is also because there are over 120,000 outstanding cases (at the beginning of 2013).[161] As noted, most cases are dealt with without an oral hearing on the basis of the papers alone. There is a test case procedure for hearing a lead case (or cases) where several cases raise a similar issue, but this 'pilot judgment procedure' is mainly devoted to cases of a 'structural or systemic problem or other similar dysfunction'.[162]

The ECtHR divides itself into Chambers, to which judges are allocated by the President. Each Section has seven judges, save for the Grand Chamber, which sits with 17.[163] A Sectional Chamber may refer a case to the Grand Chamber in certain circumstances—the nearest the Court gets to an appeal procedure—see below.[164]

The hearing by the Court is usually no more than half a day (9.30–11.30 or 14.30–16.30), with counsel for the applicant being allowed no more than a strictly enforced 30 minutes to make his or her presentation, 30 minutes for the respondent State's response, followed by questions by the Court, then a 15–20 minute break for the Court to consider the oral submissions and then 10 minutes each for reply. This is the norm, which illustrates the very great significance given to the written submissions (in contrast, for example, to the British courts, which are much more heavily reliant on oral submissions). There is no doubt that the procedure is daunting for the advocate, not least because there is barely time to settle himself or herself. The need to speak slowly and clearly to assist the translators is obvious. In dealing with questions from the Court, the advocate who has some familiarity with the language of the questioning judge is in the quandary of whether to trust or attempt to ignore his or her own translation and rely on the delayed translation of the translator, whilst at the same time attempting to arrange his or her thoughts for an answer. The Court continues its deliberations after the parties have withdrawn.

3.6 Judgment and Appeal

There may be many weeks before judgment is pronounced. The judgments follow a standard form.[165] There is no right of appeal (though there is a limited right to request revision of a judgment by the Chamber which heard the case),[166] but where

---

[160] Rule 41 reflects the (undated) *Priority Policy* adopted by the ECtHR.

[161] The number of applications decided by judgment during 2012 was 1,678, compared to 1,511 in the previous year. Overall, the Court decided almost 88,000 applications, which is an increase of 68% in relation to 2011. The number of pending applications stood at 151,600 at the beginning of 2012—by the end of the year it was 128,100, a decrease of 16%; see the speech of President Dean Spielmann on the occasion of the opening of the Judicial Year on 25 January 2013, http://www.echr.coe.int/Documents/Speech_20130125_Spielmann_JY_PC_ENG.pdf.

[162] Rule 61(1) and Registrar's Information Note, *The Pilot-Judgment Procedure* (undated).

[163] Article 26.

[164] Article 30 and Rule 72.

[165] Rule 74.

[166] Rule 80.

a judgment has been given by a Chamber, any party may in exceptional cases and on limited grounds, request that the case be referred to the Grand Chamber for a full rehearing.[167] The time limit is three months. Note that this procedure is not available in relation to 'decisions' (such as on admissibility) as opposed to 'judgments'. It is only after this possibility has been exhausted that the judgment becomes final. Supervision of judgments is a matter for the Council of Ministers.

4 CONCLUSION

The significance of an ECtHR judgment to the hundreds of millions of citizens of the States of the Council of Europe cannot be underestimated. Therefore, the significance of an adverse decision is horrifying. It thus behoves the lawyer taking a trade union case to consult widely amongst colleagues in the trade union movement at all levels and in as many countries as possible in order to ensure that the potential benefits of taking a case significantly outweigh the risks. Ultimately, it must be for the trade unions themselves to make such decisions in the light of the best legal advice possible, since the only justification for taking a trade union case to the ECtHR can be that it has a reasonable prospect of achieving a result which will improve or defend the ability of trade unions to protect the interests of the working class.

---

[167] Article 43 and Rule 73.

CONCLUSION

4

The Future of the European Court of Human Rights in the Light of the Brighton Declaration

KLAUS LÖRCHER

1 INTRODUCTION

EFFECTIVE PROTECTION OF human rights in Europe depends on many factors at both the national and the European level. The most prominent European institution in this field is undoubtedly the European Court of Human Rights (hereinafter the ECtHR or the Court). Its capacity to work effectively and efficiently is indispensable to the full enjoyment of human rights.

It is therefore important to see this institution embedded in a more general framework, especially in the light of the growing reluctance to accept the further-ance of human rights, and not only at a European level. Looking for instance at the International Labour Organization (ILO), a bulwark of the supervisory machinery, the (mandate of the) Committee of Experts on the Application on Conventions and Recommendations (CEACR) is under attack from the Employers Group.[1] And even at the UN level, a number of states are pushing for a reform of treaty bodies, criticising that the latter are overstepping their mandates and engaging in activities (general comments, follow-up reports, inquiry procedures) from which they should abstain.[2]

Against this background, it is well known that the Court is under pressure. However, the most evident problem arises from the Court's workload, which increased dramatically until 2011. The 11th and 14th Protocols to the European Convention on Human Rights (hereinafter the Convention) have contributed to

---

[1] ILO, Governing Body, 316th Session, Geneva, 1–16 November 2012, Follow-up to the decision adopted by the International Labour Conference on certain matters arising out of the report of the Committee on the Application of Standards, in particular concerning the employers' position, para 8: www.ilo.org/wcmsp5/groups/public/---ed_norm/---relconf/documents/meetingdocument/wcms_192468.pdf.

[2] See, eg, the draft resolution prepared by 13 States (including Belarus, China, Iran, the Russian Federation and Zimbabwe) A/66/L.37 (16 February 2012), which led to the General Assembly's Resolution 66/254 and more particularly the Russian Federation's follow-up position (Letter of 21 September 2012 from the Permanent Representative of the Russian Federation to the United Nations addressed to the Secretary-General—A/67/390—para 34: 'The observations and recommendations should be realistic and pragmatic and should also take into account the actual capacities and needs of States parties').

important progress through providing the Court with new instruments to adapt to these challenges.

However, it is obvious that much remains to be done in order to enable the Court to decide on individual applications within 'reasonable time'. In procedural terms, this is crucial because it is exactly what the Court requires from national judicial systems. And it is well known that a large number of cases take more than five years for the Court to arrive at a decision—and thus do not meet this requirement.

During its chairmanship of the Council of Europe (November 2011–May 2012),[3] the UK's top priority was to empower the Court to cope with this challenge. In this priority context, the 'High Level Conference on the Future of the European Court of Human Rights'[4] was held in Brighton to define the political framework for the necessary future developments. In many areas, compromises had to be found between the sometimes very divergent views of the 47 Council of Europe Member States, all of which are Contracting Parties to the Convention. On the basis of previous preparation and taking into account a 'Preliminary opinion' of the Court,[5] the Conference adopted a political instrument, known as the 'Brighton Declaration'.[6] As the most recent political decision, in all probability it marks the last leg of a political debate covering two similar conferences basically dealing with the same problem—in Interlaken (2010)[7] and Izmir (2011).[8]

The Brighton Conference was preceded by intensive discussions, greatly fuelled by a draft declaration prepared by the UK Chairmanship and leaked in late February 2012[9] which highlighted the dangers inherent to a certain extent in any initiative regarding the 'future' or 'reform' of the Court. Further documents, including

---

[3] CM/Inf(2011)41, 27 October 2011—Priorities of the United Kingdom Chairmanship of the Committee of Ministers of the Council of Europe (7 November 2011–14 May 2012) ('a. reforming the European Court of Human Rights and strengthening implementation of the European Convention on Human Rights').

[4] Council of Europe, Directorate General of Human Rights and Rule of Law (ed), *The Future of the European Court of Human Rights*, Proceedings (Strasbourg, 2012).

[5] Preliminary opinion of the Court in preparation for the Brighton Conference (adopted by the Plenary Court on 20 February 2012).

[6] High Level Conference on the Future of the European Court of Human Rights—Brighton Declaration: www.echr.coe.int/NR/rdonlyres/8AC14EA9-A92B-4875-A76A-4E21A8B3AC5A/0/ENG_20120418_ BRIGHTON_DECLARATION_FINALE.pdf. See also NP Engel, *Stablisierungsperspektive für den Europäischen Gerichtshof für Menschenrechte (EGMR)*, (2012) Europäische Grundrechte-Zeitschrift, 264 f.; C Tomuschat, 'Die Erklärung von Brighton' (2012) 2 Schweizerische Zeitschrift für internationales und europäisches Recht, 191 ff.; N Hervieu, Bilan contrasté pour la périlleuse conférence de Brighton sur l'avenir de la Cour européenne des droits de l'homme: http://combatsdroitshomme.blog.lemonde. fr/2012/04/23/avenir-de-la-cour-europeenne-des-droits-de-lhomme-une-bataille-de-brighton-cruciale-mais-aucune-paix-sur-le-front-europeen.

[7] 'Interkalen Declaration—19 February 2010', www.coe.int/t/dghl/cooperation/capacitybuilding/ Source/interlaken_declaration_en.pdf. See for example H Keller, A Fischer, D Kühne, 'Debating the Future of the European Court of Human Rights after the Interlaken Conference: Two Innovative Proposals' (2010) 21 *EJIL* 1025 ff.

[8] 'Izmir Declaration—27 April 2011', www.coe.int/t/dghl/standardsetting/conferenceizmir/ Declaration%20Izmir%20E.pdf.

[9] 'Draft Brighton Declaration on the Future of the European Court of Human Rights: A Leaked Draft of the UK's Proposals for the Reform of the Strasbourg Court', www.guardian.co.uk/law/ interactive/2012/feb/28/echr-reform-uk-draft.

a Joint NGO Statement[10] and a European Trade Union Confederation (ETUC) submission,[11] addressed the problem of a lack of transparency and participation.

This reform debate is also of importance for the Court's recent developments in respect of employment relationships. In fact, any further development might easily be considered as departing from established case law. Moreover, any new provision restricting access to the Court might have a (further) dissuasive effect on workers or trade unions filing an application to the Court.

2 THE BRIGHTON DECLARATION AND ITS FOLLOW-UP

In 39 paragraphs the Brighton Declaration deals with a wide range of problems, naming the institutions and bodies responsible for solving them and addressing the respective measures. On this basis, the Committee of Ministers has instructed the Steering Committee for Human Rights (CDDH) to prepare all relevant documents allowing the Committee of Ministers to decide within the timeframe set by the Declaration.

In principle, two different sets of action are envisaged. The first concerns the text of the Convention itself, where two Protocols to the Convention are to be added. The second relates to all other measures of legal, political, financial or other nature at the respective levels (the Court, the Council of Europe and Member States). Nevertheless, all measures decided are supposed to be based on certain reconfirmed principles.

2.1 Basic Principles: Strengthening the Convention System and the Responsibility of the States Parties

The Brighton Declaration starts by reconfirming basic principles of human rights protection in Europe, stating that the States Parties 'reaffirm their deep and abiding commitment to the Convention, and to the fulfilment of their obligation under the Convention to secure to everyone within their jurisdiction the rights and freedoms defined in the Convention' (1 BD).[12] This is further developed by referring to responsibility (shared between the States Parties and the Court) for 'effective implementation' (3 BD) and for 'ensuring the viability of the Convention mechanism' (4 BD).

---

[10] 'Reform of the European Court of Human Rights: Open Letter to All Member States of the Council of Europe—Consideration of the Drafts of the Brighton Declaration Must Include Civil Society', www.amnesty.org/en/library/asset/IOR61/004/2012/en/43258555-7591-4e84-80f4-f8004005b1e3/ior610042012en.pdf; see also www.opensocietyfoundations.org/press-releases/joint-statement-strengthening-protection-human-rights-europe-0.

[11] Submission by the European Trade Union Confederation (ETUC) to the High Level Conference on the Future of the European Court of Human Rights Brighton, United Kingdom, 18–20 April 2012 ('Brighton Conference'), (11 April 2012).

[12] Numbers in parentheses followed by 'BD' refer to the respective paragraphs in the 'Brighton Declaration'; see n 6.

As another basic principle, the States Parties 'reaffirm their attachment to the right of individual application to the European Court of Human Rights ("the Court") as a cornerstone of the system' (2 BD). In other words, all individuals (after having exhausted domestic remedies) must have the right to apply to the Court.

2.2 Envisaged Changes to the Convention Text

2.2.1 *(Amending) Protocol No 15: Changes in the Convention Text*

For quite a long time, different approaches have been discussed, in particular concerning access to the Court. In the run-up to the Brighton Declaration, several of these approaches[13] were already abandoned and others were altered. However, the most important issue—the references to the principle of subsidiarity and the margin of appreciation doctrine—remained on the agenda.

In the meantime and on the basis of all previous work having been done by the CDDH and its respective subgroups the Committee of Ministers has adopted Protocol No 15 (Council of Europe Treaty Series (CETS) No 213) and opened it for signature. Indeed, by 30 June 2013 20 Council of Europe Member States had signed it. However, as an amending protocol it will only enter into force following the ratification of all 47 Council of Europe Member States.

2.2.1.1 Reference to the Principle of Subsidiarity and the Doctrine
of the Margin of Appreciation

These two principles developed in the Court's case law apply to all human rights. In respect of social rights, they have perhaps an even more specific impact as the Court might in particular tend to accept a (wider) margin of appreciation for States when dealing with social rights.

The Brighton Declaration 'welcomes' the Court's case law in this respect and at the same time 'encourages the Court to give great prominence' to these principles (12 a BD).[14] It subsequently concludes that these principles should be included in the Preamble to the Convention (12 b BD). On the basis of its draft,[15] it is not surprising that the UK wanted an even stronger impact. In its view, a binding operative provision in the Convention would have been appropriate. This was however unacceptable for a number of States and for all NGOs which had submitted observations to the Conference.[16] The inclusion of these references in the Preamble to the Convention represented the compromise.

---

[13] www.coe.int/t/dgi/brighton-conference/Documents/CDDH-amendment-measures-report_en.pdf.

[14] 'Welcomes the development by the Court in its case law of principles such as subsidiarity and the margin of appreciation, and encourages the Court to give great prominence to and apply consistently these principles in its judgments.' (12a BD).

[15] See n 9.

[16] See also Tomuschat (n 6) 194, criticising the unequal importance attributed to these two principles in respect of all the other (interpretation) principles the Court takes (or has to take) into account.

However, the subsequent discussion on the wording of this new recital shows that the divergent views continued to exist. The main bone of contention was to what extent the Court's power to define both elements is expressly recognised:

Brighton Declaration	GT-GDR-B[17](2012)R1[18]	GT-GDR-B(2012) R2	DH-GDR[20](2012) R2	Protocol No 15 (CETS 213) Article 1
	Addendum	Addendum I[19]	Addendum III	
20 April 2012	14 September 2012	15 October 2012	31 October 2012	24 June 2013
12 b) Concludes that, for reasons of transparency and accessibility, a reference to the principle of subsidiarity and the doctrine of the margin of appreciation as *developed in the Court's case law* should be included in the Preamble to the Convention and invites the Committee of Ministers to adopt the necessary amending instrument by the end of 2013, while recalling the States Parties' commitment to give full effect to their obligation to secure the rights and freedoms defined in the Convention;[21]	['Affirming that in accordance with the principle of subsidiarity, the Contracting Parties have the primary responsibility to secure the rights and freedoms laid down in the Convention, *under the supervision of the Court established by this Convention* and within the margin of appreciation the Court defines.']	'Affirming that the High Contracting Parties [, {in accordance with/based on} the principle of subsidiarity and *subject to the supervisory jurisdiction of the Court,*] have the primary responsibility to secure the rights and freedoms defined in this Convention and the Protocols thereto, and in doing so [enjoy] / [have] a margin of appreciation [that the Court defines].'[1]	'Affirming that the High Contracting Parties, in accordance with the principle of subsidiarity, have the primary responsibility to secure the rights and freedoms defined in this Convention and the Protocols thereto, and in doing so enjoy a margin of appreciation, *subject to the supervisory jurisdiction of the European Court of Human Rights established by this Convention.*'	'Affirming that the High Contracting Parties, in accordance with the principle of subsidiarity, have the primary responsibility to secure the rights and freedoms defined in this Convention and the Protocols thereto, and *that* in doing so *they* enjoy a margin of appreciation, subject to the supervisory jurisdiction of the European Court of Human Rights established by this Convention,'

[1] Alternative proposal: 'Affirming that the High Contracting Parties have the primary responsibility to secure the rights and freedoms defined in this Convention and the Protocols thereto, and in doing so [enjoy/have] a margin of appreciation [that the Court defines] and that therefore the Convention system is subsidiary to the safeguarding of human rights at national level.'

[17] The GT-GDR Committee of Experts on the Reform of the Court (established as a subgroup of the CDDH) is working on proposals for possible further reform of the ECHR control system, notably in the light of the Conclusions of the Interlaken and Izmir Conferences as well as the Brighton Declaration.
[18] These are the document numbers referring to the Meeting Reports of the GT-GDR (R1, R2, etc), see n 17.
[19] See nn 17 and 18.
[20] See n 8; the following wording has been approved by the CDDH. See CDDH(2012)R76_Addendum III. However, it has been slightly amended by the Committee of Ministers itself (see next column).
[21] All emphasis in this table concerning the role and scope of the Court has been added.

The different proposals indicate that one (if not the most) crucial point is the supervisory role of the Court and whether the scope thereof applies only to the margin of appreciation or also to the principle of subsidiarity. At the end of the day—and probably irrespective of the specific wording—it will be the Court which decides how to interpret this new recital. Generally speaking, it would appear very unlikely that the Court will change its actual (case-by-case) approach. If it really were to give these two elements a more prominent role, it would probably not be the wording but the general (legal-political) framework which would lead the Court to more judicial 'self-restraint'.

2.2.1.2 Changes in Admissibility Criteria, etc

The Brighton Declaration expresses firm hopes that the Court will apply consistently and strictly already-existing *admissibility criteria* (14, 15 b and d BD). As regards new criteria, two (out of several)[22] suggestions have been retained and will lead to amendments of Article 35 ECHR.

The first and probably most problematic is the reduction of the time limit for an application from six to four months. However, it was the Court itself which suggested that 'the time has perhaps come to consider whether this period, which was entirely reasonable 50 years ago, remains the appropriate' by referring to 'today's digital society with swift communication tools'.[23] This reduction continues to attract criticism, in particular in respect of those remote areas in Europe where such communication technology is not available to applicants,[24] as well as in respect of the lower quality of applications leading to a greater Court workload.[25] However, the draft foresees a six-month[26] transition period once the Protocol enters into force 'in order to allow potential applicants to become fully aware of the new deadline'.[27]

Intended to give greater effect to the maxim *de minimis non curat praetor*,[28] the other element is the deletion of the words 'and provided that no case may be rejected on this ground which has not been duly considered by a domestic tribunal' (in Article 35 § 3 (b) ECHR). Newly introduced by the 14th Protocol, this element was aimed at balancing the restrictive 'significant disadvantage' criteria. Based on an initial assessment, in which the Court (only) found four cases where this element

[22] See n 13.
[23] See n 5, para 37.
[24] Joint preliminary comments on the drafting of Protocols 15 and 16 to the European Convention for the Protection of Human Rights and Fundamental Freedoms (August 2012): www.londonmet. ac.uk/fms/MRSite/Research/HRSJ/EHRAC/Advocacy/Joint%20NGO%20submission%20-%20 Protocols%2015%20and%2016%20to%20the%20ECHR%20-%20August%202012.pdf, p 2 (A.2).
[25] 'Die *Kürzung der Beschwerdefirst* von 6 auf 4 Monate wird nicht zu weniger, sondern zu schlechteren Beschwerden führen, deren Bearbeitung den EGMR blockiert': www.forausblog.ch/reform-des-egmr-der-europarat-auf-abwegen.
[26] Originally the GT-GDR-B had opted for a one-year transitional period (GT-GDR-B(2012)R2 Addendum I). This was reduced to six months by the DH-GDR (see Explanatory Report in CDDH(2012) R76 Addendum IV, para 22).
[27] GT-GDR-B(2012)R2 Addendum II, para 19.
[28] 'The Court is not concerned by trivial matters': GT-GDR-B(2012)R2 Addendum II, para 20.

had played an important role,[29] it is hoped that the effect of this amendment will turn out not to be as serious as had been envisaged.

What might at first sight appear a minor element ('In Article 30 of the Convention, the words "unless one of the parties to the case objects" shall be deleted') actually relates to a more fundamental issue: a Chamber's *relinquishment of jurisdiction* in favour of the Grand Chamber. In fact, the Court itself had indicated that it intended to modify its Rules of Court (Rule 72) so as to make it obligatory for a Chamber to relinquish jurisdiction where it envisaged departing from settled case law.[30] Put in concrete terms, this means that Chambers will be prevented from modifying 'settled case law' themselves. Intended to contribute to greater consistency in the Court's future case law,[31] such relinquishment as a procedural means is intended to empower the Grand Chamber as the sole guarantor of consistent case law. In this perspective, it is only consequent to prohibit government 'vetoes'.

It should however also be noted that in the past, Chambers have relinquished their jurisdiction in favour of the Grand Chamber—at least to some extent—in potential cases of divergent jurisprudence. From this perspective, one might conclude that existing practice will be and in fact has been made binding by the amendment of Rule 72 of the 'Rules of the Court' even without reference to 'settled' case law, but still subject to a 'duly reasoned objection' (Rule 72(4)).

On the other hand, strategies to avoid openly departing from settled case law are well known in other jurisdictions faced with a similar problem. In certain cases, Chambers might be tempted to demonstrate that there is no 'settled case law' or that the case at hand differs from those considered as representing 'settled case law' in order to avoid relinquishment.[32] Therefore, the real impact will have to be considered at a later stage when the effect of the amended Rule 72 can be evaluated.

The question of the definition of the admission *age of judges*, now fixed at 65 years (instead of the termination of office at 70 years; see Article 23(§ 2) ECHR), appears to have been resolved by opting for a 'date sufficiently certain at which the age of 65 must be determined'.[33] However, with a judge's (non-renewable) term of office set at nine years, this still means that judges may stay in office much longer than nowadays. It remains to be seen whether the Court and its efficiency will really benefit that much from this new provision.

---

[29] 'However, with the exception of these four cases, the second safeguard clause has not been a major obstacle in the application of the new criterion.' European Court of Human Rights (ed), *The New Admissibility Criterion under Article 35 § 3 (b) of the Convention: Case Law Principles Two Years On—Research Report—*(Strasbourg 2012), para 29.

[30] GT-GDR-B(2012)R2 Addendum II, para 13.

[31] Ibid.

[32] However, it should be recalled that governments (as the applicants) are always free to ask for a referral to the Grand Chamber, in particular in a case in which they are of the opinion that there is divergent jurisprudence.

[33] Explanatory report to Protocol No 15, para 13, on the basis of DH-GDR(2012)R2 Addendum IV, para 13; the new Article 21(§ 2) of the Convention shall read: 'Candidates shall be less than 65 years of age at the date by which the list of three candidates has been requested by the Parliamentary Assembly further to Article 22' (Article 2(1) of Protocol No 15 CETS No 213).

2.2.2 *(Additional) Protocol No 16: Extension of the Court's Competence to Give Advisory Opinions*

In the extension of the existing Convention, Articles 47–49 on advisory opinions (at the request of the Committee of Ministers) and to a certain extent parallel to the Court of Justice of the European Union (CJEU) procedure of preliminary rulings, a new dimension is envisaged allowing the (highest) national courts to ask the Court for an advisory opinion.[34] After some controversy, the Brighton Declaration now contains an open formulation on possible advisory opinions of the Court (12 d BD).[35] This new element (in respect of national courts) is in principle aimed at clarifying important issues in the national context and thus contributing to a reduction of the Court's workload (at least in the medium term). Under it, the highest national courts will be allowed to address the Court 'on questions of principle relating to the interpretation or application of the rights and freedoms defined in the Convention or the Protocols thereto'.[36]

Even if this new element appears similar to Article 267 Treaty on the Functioning of the European Union (TFEU), there are very important differences. Besides the question of first and second instance courts which will not be given this opportunity, the expressly non-binding nature contrasts with the idea behind Article 267 TFEU. What is the sense of a new interpretation procedure if its outcome is not binding in the case at hand? If not binding,[37] uncertainties will remain. And finally, in the case of the 'highest court' departing from the Court's opinions, this would mean that (once domestic remedies have been exhausted) an application to the Court would be the normal consequence. The danger is that this new procedure could thus contribute to further lengthening proceedings—something to be avoided as much as possible.

What would be the consequences for States not ratifying such an Additional Protocol? If the opinions are not even binding for the referring court or tribunal, the effect on non-ratifying States and possibly similar cases is even less obvious and might even contribute to new applications (in contrast to the original aim of this new procedure).

However, as an Additional Protocol, it has the great advantage of entering into force relatively quickly and therefore having an impact in the short term. Ratification will undoubtedly be based on the assumption that the (highest) national courts will take the ECHR into account in a more efficient way than they possibly do now. This could be of particular relevance for States in which social rights in general and trade union rights in particular are not complied with.

---

[34] ECtHR, 'Reflection Paper on the Proposal to Extend the Court's Advisory Jurisdiction', www.coe.int/t/dgi/brighton-conference/Documents/Court-Advisory-opinions_en.pdf.

[35] '12 d) Notes that the interaction between the Court and national authorities could be strengthened by the introduction into the Convention of a further power of the Court, which States Parties could optionally accept, to deliver advisory opinions upon request on the interpretation of the Convention in the context of a specific case at domestic level, without prejudice to the non-binding character of the opinions for the other States Parties; invites the Committee of Ministers to draft the text of an optional protocol to the Convention with this effect by the end of 2013; and further invites the Committee of Ministers thereafter to decide whether to adopt it.'

[36] Draft Protocol No 16 to the Convention—GT-GDR-B(2012)R2—Addendum III—of 15 September 2012, Article 1(1) of the Draft, confirmed by the CDDH; see CDDH(2012)R76_Addendum V.

[37] It would appear from the Court's 'Reflection Paper' (n 34) that a majority of judges were in favour of a non-binding character. 'A number of judges, however, pleaded in favour of a binding nature of advisory opinions.'

2.3 Envisaged Developments in the Convention System

It should always be remembered that the most relevant factor for the effective protection of human rights is the Contracting Parties' will to take the rights and freedoms enshrined in the ECHR seriously and to effectively refrain from any violations. This would in itself drastically reduce the workload of the Court. Indeed, the Brighton Declaration lists a large number of concrete measures which the States Parties should implement. Further measures are also envisaged for the Court and the Council of Europe.

2.3.1 At the Court Level

In respect of coping with its increasing workload, much depends on the Court itself. A clear indication of the relevant fields of action can be found in its 'Preliminary Opinion'.[38] In line with its prioritisation policy,[39] the Court lists seven different categories of cases,[40] for each of which it indicates the measures already implemented (and to be further developed). Concerning 'inadmissible cases' (VI and VII), the single-judge procedure and stricter application of the six-month rule are foreseen (para 20). As regards 'repetitive cases' (V), the Court envisages referring a list of such cases 'directly to the Government to be settled in an appropriate way'. Failure to provide redress within a fixed period of time would lead to a 'default judgment' awarding compensation to the applicant (para 21).[41] Turning to 'non-repetitive, non-priority cases' (IV) (eg, freedom of association), the Court states that many of them can be dealt with under a summary Committee procedure; where a case falls to be determined in this way because it is in reality manifestly well founded, respondent States could be expected to offer friendly settlements or, where appropriate, unilateral declarations under a simplified or 'light' communication process (23). Finally, certain priority cases (I–III) may be deemed suitable for committee adjudication (para 24).

The Brighton Declaration several times explicitly signals appreciation of these measures,[42] while at the same time expressing the expectation that the Court will do more in such areas as (the stricter application of) admissibility criteria (14, 15 b, d, g BD), amending the Rules of Court (15 f, 25 e BD),[43] intensifying dialogue (12 c BD) and consultation (20 f and g BD), and enhancing the high quality of judgments (25 f BD).

---

[38] See n 5.

[39] The Court's Priority Policy: www.echr.coe.int/NR/rdonlyres/DB6EDF5E-6661-4EF6-992E-F8C4ACC62F31/0/Priority_policyPublic_communication_EN.pdf.

[40] In the following list, the categories appear in Roman numerals, while the paragraph numbers in brackets refer to the 'Preliminary Opinion'.

[41] The idea of 'default judgments' was still included in the UK draft (see n 9, para 28 d), but was not retained in the Brighton Declaration.

[42] For example: 'Notes with appreciation the Court's assessment that it could dispose of the outstanding clearly inadmissible applications pending before it by 2015' (20 b BD).

[43] The Court is invited 'to consider whether the composition of the Grand Chamber would be enhanced by the ex officio inclusion of the Vice Presidents of each Section'.

However, the question of appropriate resources lacks appropriate responses. The Brighton Declaration would like to set a benchmark of one year for communicating a case and an additional two years for its adjudication.[44] As a pre-requisite, it sees the possible future necessity of appointing additional judges.[45] It was obvious, however, that the Member States were unwilling to increase the Council of Europe's budget.

2.3.2 At the Council of Europe Level

The Brighton Declaration contains several demands under which the Council of Europe's institutions can and indeed should contribute to a better implementation of the Convention. The first concerns (a better framework for) technical assistance (9 g BD). A second one involves improving the procedure for supervising the execution of judgments (29 c–e BD). The Committee of Ministers is invited to give full effect to the Brighton Declaration and to determine which measures should be introduced in a long-term perspective (35 and 39 BD).

2.3.3 At the National Level

The cornerstone is the correct implementation of the Convention and in particular human rights at national level, ie, at the level of the Contracting Parties (the Council of Europe Member States). In para 9, the Brighton Declaration sets forth an impressive list of exhortations and concrete measures expected to be implemented by all parties involved. It is deemed appropriate to quote them:

> 9. The Conference ...
> a) Affirms the strong commitment of the States Parties to fulfil their primary responsibility to implement the Convention at national level;
> b) Strongly encourages the States Parties to continue to take full account of the recommendations of the Committee of Ministers on the implementation of the Convention at national level in their development of legislation, policies and practices to give effect to the Convention;
> c) In particular, expresses the determination of the States Parties to ensure effective implementation of the Convention at national level by taking the following specific measures, so far as relevant:
> > i)   Considering the establishment, if they have not already done so, of an independent National Human Rights Institution;
> > ii) Implementing practical measures to ensure that policies and legislation comply fully with the Convention, including by offering to national parliaments information on the compatibility with the Convention of draft primary legislation proposed by the Government;

---

[44] The Conference 'envisages that the full implementation of these measures with appropriate resources should in principle enable the Court to decide whether to communicate a case within one year, and thereafter to make all communicated cases the subject of a decision or judgment within two years of communication' (20 h BD).

[45] The Conference notes 'that, to enable the Court to decide in a reasonable time the applications pending before its Chambers, it may be necessary in the future to appoint additional judges to the Court' (20 e BD).

iii)   Considering the introduction if necessary of new domestic legal remedies, whether of a specific or general nature, for alleged violations of the rights and freedoms under the Convention;

iv)   Enabling and encouraging national courts and tribunals to take into account the relevant principles of the Convention, having regard to the case law of the Court, in conducting proceedings and formulating judgments; and in particular enabling litigants, within the appropriate parameters of national judicial procedure but without unnecessary impediments, to draw to the attention of national courts and tribunals any relevant provisions of the Convention and jurisprudence of the Court;

v)   Providing public officials with relevant information about the obligations under the Convention; and in particular training officials working in the justice system, responsible for law enforcement, or responsible for the deprivation of a person's liberty in how to fulfil obligations under the Convention;

vi)   Providing appropriate information and training about the Convention in the study, training and professional development of judges, lawyers and prosecutors; and

vii)   Providing information on the Convention to potential applicants, particularly about the scope and limits of its protection, the jurisdiction of the Court and the admissibility criteria.

The subsequent measures include the necessity to have significant judgments and the 'Admissibility Guide' translated into national languages (9 d BD). Specific measures are also required in respect of the better execution of judgments (29 a BD).

As impressive as these measures might appear and even if they were to be effectively implemented, it could turn out that they are not sufficient to fully address all problems. In particular, the way in which ECtHR judgments are taken into account by Contracting Parties not party to the Court's proceedings (and which therefore are not directly bound by the obligations arising from Article 46 ECHR) needs to be improved. For example, the ETUC has proposed the creation of a focal point responsible for dealing with all consequences of a judgment (even if it is not directly linked to the country concerned).[46]

3 CONCLUSION

There are two separate dimensions addressed in this document: (i) the Court's workload; and (ii) (indirect) criticism of the Court's '(over-)activism'. Looking first at the Court's workload, the Court proposes a number of initiatives describing concrete and deep-going ways of reducing it. In particular, Member States need to do (much) more to align their laws and practice with Convention requirements. Moreover, many practical measures are addressed to the respective institutions. However, little is said about according the Court the necessary resources.

---

[46] See n 11.

[47] It is also interesting to note that the new President recently stated that it would appear to him that the Court was strengthened by the Brighton Conference ('Je pense pouvoir dire que la Cour sort renforcée de cette conférence'. 'Remarques introductives par le Président Spielmann'—Réunion avec les ONG et les représentants des requérants, Strasbourg, le 15 novembre 2012; these observations contain the latest information on current developments).

Nevertheless, a positive trend can be noted, at least in the short term,[47] with the latest figures pointing for the first time to a significant decrease in the number of cases pending. Although (new) allocated applications have increased by one per cent (from 64,400 in 2011 to 65,150 in 2012), the number of pending applications has decreased enormously in the same period by a much higher 16 per cent (from 151,600 in 2011 to 128,100 in 2012). This was due to a very significant increase of applications decided by 68 per cent during the same period (11 per cent for judgments and 70 per cent for decisions (inadmissible or struck-out cases)).[48] There is great hope that this development, based mainly on the outcomes of the 14th Protocol as well as of the Interlaken, Izmir and perhaps even the Brighton Conferences will continue (albeit not at the expense of a thorough examination of each application). However, the possibility of a new wave of applications should not be underestimated, as demonstrated, for example, by the influx of about 8,000 applications against Hungary concerning the reduction of pension benefits.[49] Such increasing influxes could rapidly send the Court 'back to square one', with the number of pending cases again rising. At the end of the day, all measures envisaged (also by the Brighton Declaration) might only lead to maintaining the current (unacceptable) 'status quo' and not to a situation where the Court is in a position to deal with cases within a 'reasonable time'.

The second dimension relates to the (indirect) criticism of the Court's '(over)activism'. In this respect, sometimes very divergent views existed (and continue to exist) which needed to be reconciled. It is possible to conclude that the dangers associated with directly encroaching on the Court's independence have been avoided. However, many (indirect) measures are clearly intended to put pressure on the Court to exercise greater self-restraint. One of the main indications here is the envisaged new recital in the Preamble of the Convention referring to the principles of subsidiarity and the doctrine of the margin of appreciation. It will very much depend on the Court itself as regards the extent to which it can continue to hand down rulings fully independent of government pressures. This aspect is of crucial importance for ensuring that the Court continues to uphold the Convention's 'social dimension'.

---

[48] European Court of Human Rights, 'Analysis of Statistics 2012', Strasbourg, January 2013: www.echr.coe.int/NR/rdonlyres/9113BE4E-6682-41D4-9F8B-0B29950C8BD4/0/Analysis_Statistics_2012_ENG.pdf, p 6.

[49] Press release ECHR 009 (2011), 11 January 2012: 'European Court Registrar Calls for Special Measures to Deal with Influx of Hungarian Pension Cases'. (Concerning the new legislation in Hungary on private pension funds, see the (inadmissibility) decision of 15 January 2013, App No 34929/11, *EB v Hungary*.)

5

Human Rights in Employment Relationships: Contracts as Power

OLIVIER DE SCHUTTER

1 INTRODUCTION

HUMAN RIGHTS TRANSFORM the relationship between the State and the market in ways that are now well understood. States are required to protect human rights by regulating the conduct of private actors, such as employers, in order to ensure that these actors do not adopt conduct that could lead to human rights violations. This obligation to protect is an obligation of means: it is understood as a duty to adopt all reasonable measures that, in the circumstances, a State could be expected to take in order to ensure that what it cannot do directly, it does not allow to happen indirectly. In situations where an employer does infringe the rights of its employee, any responsibility of the State would be of a derivative kind: if we leave aside the exceptional cases where the said employer may be considered to act as a de facto agent of the State, such State responsibility may only stem not from the conduct of the employer itself, which cannot be imputed to the State, but from the failure of the State to adopt the measures that would have been appropriate to avoid the violation from occurring. This failure is sometimes described as a failure to exercise due diligence, by which we mean that the duty of the State is to control conduct adopted by another, using various instruments at its disposal, including (albeit not limited to) regulation.

The theory is now well accepted and broadly agreed to.[1] Under the European Convention on Human Rights (ECHR), it may be said to have emerged, in the context of employment relationships, in the famous 1981 case of *Young, James and Webster v UK*. There, the European Court of Human Rights (ECtHR), sitting in plenary, concluded that the UK could not seek refuge behind the fact that the 'closed-shop' agreement that the applicants were denouncing had been concluded between

---

[1] See, eg, EA Alkema, 'The Third-Party Applicability or "*Drittwirkung*" of the European Convention on Human Rights' in F Matscher, H Petzold, and GJ Wiarda (eds), *Protecting Human Rights: The European Dimension* (Cologne, Carl Heymans Verlag, 1988) 35; A Clapham, *Human Rights in the Private Sphere* (Oxford, Clarendon Press, 1993); A Drzemczewski, 'The European Human Rights Convention and Relations between Private Parties' (1979) 2 *Netherlands International Law Review* 168; AR Mowbray, *The Development of Positive Obligations under the European Convention on Human Rights by the European Court of Human Rights* (Oxford, Hart Publishing, 2004); O De Schutter, *International Human Rights Law* (Cambridge, Cambridge University Press, 2010) ch 4.

the British Rail and three unions. The view of the British government was that, as a collective agreement, the measure challenged by the applicants was in essence a private agreement between two non-State actors (a company and unions), for which the State could bear no responsibility. The agreement provided that employment within British Rail would be reserved to the members of those unions, forcing all current or prospective employees to join one of the unions in question: the Court noted that, while it had been concluded between British Rail and the unions, 'it was the domestic law in force at the relevant time that made lawful the treatment of which the applicants complained'.[2] The judgment condemned the UK for not having sufficiently protected workers from a collective agreement affecting the substance of their freedom of association under Article 11 of the Convention.

There is little doubt that the finding of violation must have pleased, in fact, the government concerned: by the time the case was litigated before the Court, the Conservative Thatcher government had removed the Labour Party from power, and it does not require a stretch of the imagination to think that it may have been relieved that the 1974 Trade Union and Labour Relations Act, which had lifted the prohibition on closed shops, which the Thatcher government had intended to abolish anyway, would now have to be revised because of the mandate from the European Court of Human Rights. What matters to us, however, is that an important principle had now been affirmed: under the ECHR, States Parties must protect human rights in employment relationships, even if this requires interfering in agreements concluded between the employers and the workers, and whether or not the workers are acting through their unions.

The *Young, James and Webster* case left a number of questions open, however, many of which are still not fully answered today. Two difficulties in particular emerge. First, it has become common for States to discharge their duty to protect human rights in private (or inter-individual) relationships by simply applying the rules of international human rights law to those relationships directly, without adopting further implementation measures. Through the doctrine of direct application of human rights treaties (or, less frequently, by incorporating the rules contained in such treaties into domestic constitutions or legislation), national courts are then empowered to impose on private actors, including employers, rules that were initially designed in the international legal order to apply to States and that were to regulate the relationships between the State organs and individuals under their jurisdiction. But this process of transposition creates a number of difficulties.[3] The position of the employer cannot be simply equated to that of the State, and courts may face obstacles in trying to address the employer–worker relationship on the basis of rules that were framed for other purposes.

The second question concerns the significance that should be recognised to the choice of the individual right-holder, when the alleged violation has its source in a contractual relationship between the employer and the worker. Is that choice

---

[2] ECtHR (plen), *Young, James and Webster v UK*, judgment of 13 August 1981, Series A, No 44, para 49.

[3] Some of these are addressed, at a theoretical level, in the contribution of Steven R Ratner, 'Corporations and Human Rights: A Theory of Legal Responsibility' (2001) 111 *Yale LJ* 443.

real and must it be respected as the manifestation of the self-determination of the individual? Or is that choice necessarily—and fatally—tainted by coercion, in a context in which the employment relationship is bound to be unequal? The latter was the position famously adopted by Engels in his 1844 book *Condition of the Working Class in England*, at a time when the issue that was debated was whether the legislator should be allowed to intervene to limit to 10 hours per day the maximum working time.[4] But even supposing the worker gives her genuine consent to certain conditions attached to the employment, how determinative should that fact be? May the worker dispose of her freedom as if it were a mere property right? If A is recognised a right X, does that imply that A may choose to sell X off, or to barter the right X away against an advantage to which A attaches greater value? The question of waiver is both narrower and broader than the previous one. It is narrower in the sense that it may be seen as a sub-question that is raised in the process of moving from the duties of the State towards the citizen to the duties of private actors towards other private actors, referred to above; indeed, one of the most important differences between the power exercised by the State over the individual and the power exercised by the employer over the worker is that, in principle at least, the worker is free (in the formal sense) to accept the terms of employment offered or to reject them. But the questions of consent and coercion, and of the possibility of one worker waiving his rights in the employment context, is at the same time broader: it concerns the role of basic rights in the employment relationship, regardless of the source of that basic right—whether the right is found in an international human rights treaty, in a domestic constitution or in legislation.

In order to address these questions, this chapter proceeds in three steps. The next section examines the relationship between the *procedural* rights to form and join unions, to resort to collective action and to enter into collective bargaining processes, and the *substantive* rights of workers vis-a-vis employers, such as their freedom of expression or their right to respect for private and family life.[5] It addresses the question whether the two sets of rights are in some sense a substitute for one another; in other words, whether strengthening procedural rights (and the role of unions as representatives of workers' interests) might justify adopting a weaker degree of scrutiny of measures that might affect the substantive rights of workers. Section 3 then describes the first (procedural) route, examining how the ECtHR has protected the right of workers to form and join unions and to resort to collective action in order to defend their rights. Section 4 moves to the other (substantive) route. It looks at how the substantive rights of workers (such as freedom of expression or the right to respect for private and family life) are in fact protected in the implementation of the ECHR: it attempts to summarise the difficulties we face when we transpose rights and duties designed to regulate the 'vertical' relationships between the State and the individual to the 'horizontal' relationships between the employer and the worker. Section 5 discusses in greater detail one specific question that arises in this process of transposition, which concerns the possibility for the worker to waive her rights—to

---

[4] F Engels, *The Condition of the Working Class in England* (St Albans, [1844] 1974).
[5] It is acknowledged that freedom of expression may be used as a procedural right against employers when exercised to challenge certain working conditions, for instance.

sacrifice them against the promise of certain advantages which she may value more highly. Finally, Section 6 provides a brief summary of the conclusions reached.

2 TWO APPROACHES TO PROTECTING HUMAN RIGHTS IN EMPLOYMENT RELATIONSHIPS

2.1 The Emergence of the Duty to Protect Workers' Rights

Though it may have been predictable, the extension of human rights to private relationships, as was foreshadowed in *Young, James and Webster*, was not inevitable in any logical sense. In theory, one could imagine a regime in which the human rights of the individual can only be invoked against the State, without any positive duty to protect being imposed upon the State. In such a regime, human rights would be simply irrelevant to the relationships between private employers and workers. Beyond perhaps an elementary duty to protect the parties entering into a contractual relationship of employment from physical assault,[6] the State would have no other obligation to intervene in such relationships, imbalanced though as they may be. In the sphere of the market, individual freedoms would be clashing with one another, and the outcome of the clash would be determined solely by the ability of each party to force the other into a certain agreement—a truce in the battle they wage against each other—based on the bargaining power each party would be able to exercise. Courts would have no choice but to enforce the agreement, whatever the conditions under which it was concluded (excluding situations of duress or coercion) and whatever the consequences for the rights of the individual. Private parties would have 'freedoms' and they would be allowed to exercise such freedoms, in particular, by seeking to push other private parties into the conclusion of agreements on terms that are most favourable to them. But they would have no 'rights' to oppose other private parties, in the sense that no private actor would be duty-bound to abstain from certain forms of conduct that could threaten any other private actor's enjoyment of his rights.

Such a regime, however, would not ensure that the human rights of the individual are 'practical and effective', rather than 'theoretical and illusory', as famously expressed by the ECtHR.[7] It would expose job-seekers, and all those involved in

---

[6] As has been remarked by Matthew H Kramer, 'in almost every situation outside the Hobbesian state of nature, conduct in accordance with a liberty will receive at least a modicum of protection', particularly through the role of the State in guaranteeing the physical security of the person (in MH Kramer, NE Simmonds and H Steiner, *A Debate Over Rights. Philosophical Enquiries* (Oxford, Oxford University Press, 1998, reprinted 2000) 11–12).

[7] Eur Ct HR, *Airey v Ireland*, judgment of 9 October 1979, Series A, No 32, 2 EHRR 305, para 24; ECtHR (GC), *Demir and Baykara v Turkey* (App No 34503/97), judgment of 12 November 2008, para 66 ('Since the Convention is first and foremost a system for the protection of human rights, the Court must interpret and apply it in a manner which renders its rights practical and effective, not theoretical and illusory'). For another example of where this requirement of effectiveness led the European Court of Human Rights to conclude that the rights of the Convention imposed positive obligations on States Parties (in particular, allowing an interpretation of Article 4 ECHR on the prohibition of slavery to also apply to private action), see ECtHR (2nd sect), *Siliadin v France* (App No 73316/01), judgment of 26 July 2005, ECHR 2005-VII, para 89 (where the Court takes the view that limiting the question of compliance with Article 4 of the Convention only to direct action by the State authorities would be

an employment relationship, to various forms of abuse, the result of their generally weak bargaining position. And while it would still not be allowable for States to directly interfere with the basic rights of the individual, the result for the individual, for all practical purposes, would be the same: the passivity of the State—its failure to react to violations committed by the private employer—would allow violations of the rights of the individual to continue unabated, as the private actors responsible would benefit from a complete impunity. There may be no logical necessity under the Convention in imposing on the State a duty to protect individuals from the infringements of human rights that occur in private relationships, but the political necessity does seem inescapable.

2.2 Two Routes Towards Protecting Workers' Rights

The State therefore must rescue the individual from the impacts of entering into employment relationships in which, due to her weak bargaining position, she may not be able to resist certain sacrifices that have far-reaching consequences on the enjoyment of her basic rights. But there are in principle two routes through which the State could discharge this duty. One route is to simply equalise the bargaining positions of both sides to the employment contract in order to ensure that no imbalance between the parties emerges such that one can impose its will upon the other. 'Equalising' means, in general, strengthening the position of workers by allowing them to form unions, and then forcing employers to negotiate with the unions as representatives of the workers' interests. Adam Smith made perfectly clear more than two centuries ago why that may be required: the wages paid for labour, he wrote in *The Wealth of Nations*, depend on the terms of the contract negotiated between the worker and the employer. But the interests of both parties are 'by no means the same. The workmen desire to get as much, the masters to give as little as possible. The former are disposed to combine in order to raise, the latter in order to lower the wages of labour'. And Smith noted lucidly that it would be naive to simply equate the result of the negotiation between the two parties with the just price of labour because of the imbalance between them:

> It is not ... difficult to foresee which of the two parties must, upon all ordinary occasions, have the advantage in the dispute, and force the other into a compliance with their terms. The masters, being fewer in number, can combine much more easily; and the law, besides, authorizes, or at least does not prohibit their combinations, while it prohibits those of the workmen. We have not acts of parliament against combining to lower the price of work; but many against combining to raise it. In all such disputes the masters can hold out much longer. A landlord, a farmer, a master manufacturer, or merchant, though they did not employ a single workman, could generally live a year or two upon the stocks which they have already acquired. Many workmen could not subsist a week, few could subsist a

inconsistent with the international instruments specifically concerned with this issue, including the ILO Forced Labour Convention, the Supplementary Convention on the Abolition of Slavery, the Slave Trade, and Institutions and Practices Similar to Slavery and the International Convention on the Rights of the Child, and would amount to rendering it ineffective).

month, and scarce any a year without employment. In the long run the workman may be as necessary to his master as his master is to him; but the necessity is not so immediate.[8]

In remarking that employers more frequently combine between themselves to lower the price of labour than workers are able to conspire for the opposite purpose, and that workers generally, because they have no property, are compelled to find work and cannot afford to remain idle, Smith was in fact building a powerful argument in favour of the freedom to form unions and to force the employer to set wage through collective bargaining processes. In this, he was clearly ahead of his times. More than a century later, we would still find the legal profession in the US grappling with this issue: progressives on the Supreme Court such as Oliver Wendell Holmes or Louis D Brandeis were still compelled at that point in time to painstakingly explain to their colleagues why 'yellow dog' contracts, through which employers gave work on the condition that the workers would refrain from joining a union while in the company's employment, could be challenged by strikes or other forms of collective action. They made the argument that such a clash of freedoms, each party seeking to coerce the other into making certain concessions (the unions seeking to force the employer to abandon the practice of 'yellow dog' contracts and the employer seeking to force prospective workers to accept such clauses), was simply one manifestation of the 'struggle for life' characteristic of market relationships in general. In fact, even these progressives would not have gone so far as to say that the legislator had a positive duty to prohibit 'yellow dog' contracts altogether.[9]

These debates remain strikingly relevant to our contemporary situation. The following section examines how far has the ECtHR travelled along this procedural route, one that seeks to ensure that the rights of workers are protected by strengthening their ability to rely on collective action and by empowering unions. The Court has built a strong jurisprudence protecting the procedural rights of workers, thus equalising the otherwise generally imbalanced relationship between the employer and the individual worker. However, this jurisprudence has been forced to navigate between the protection of the rights of individual workers, including the right not to join a union, and the protection of the rights of unions as such, whose ability to act effectively may justify restrictions on individual workers' rights. It is the search for a balance between these two imperatives that explains how the case law has developed, and why it has been doing so with so much hesitation.

3 THE PROCEDURAL ROUTE: THE UNION RIGHTS OF WORKERS UNDER THE ECHR

3.1 Workers' Rights and Unions' Rights in European Human Rights Law

The position of the ECtHR in the area of union rights may be conceptualised as having shifted along a spectrum of solutions. At one end of that spectrum (the

---

[8] Adam Smith, *An Inquiry into the Nature and Causes of the Wealth of Nations* (London, 1776), Book I, ch viii.

[9] *Hitchman Coal & Coke Co v Mitchell et al*, 245 US 229, 263 (1917) (Brandeis J dissenting, with Holmes and Clark JJ concurring with the dissent).

individualistic end), *individual workers' rights* would be paramount, and any form of collective action or any possibility for unions to force employers to agree to collective bargaining would depend on whether they manage to mobilise individual workers into exercising pressure—and the employer, reciprocally, could use any incentives he might choose to avoid workers from coalescing and to refuse to enter into dialogue with unions. At the other end of the spectrum (the collectivist end), the rights of workers would be seen to require for their effective protection that *unions' rights* be strengthened, as it is only through collective representation at all levels, including at the level of the undertaking, that workers can improve their bargaining position. In this alternative logic, the individual rights of workers (including their right not to join unions and their right to opt out from the regimes established through collective bargaining) could be sacrificed in order to allow the unions' prerogatives to be maximised.

The Court has chosen a middle route in its interpretation of Article 11 ECHR, which guarantees the right to form and join unions. On the one hand, departing from the original intent of the drafters of the Convention, it has gradually espoused the view that their right to organise implied a right for workers *not* to join a union. This resulted in excluding closed-shop agreements. The Court was moved to such a solution largely on the basis of the European Social Charter and the case law of its supervisory organs, as well as by reference to other European or universal instruments, which demonstrate an emerging consensus at the international level on the need to protect the negative aspect of the freedom of association. This was a gradual shift that began with *Young, James and Webster* in 1981 and was confirmed in judgments of the 1990s.[10]

On the other hand, however, the Court did recognise the limits of a purely individualistic logic. In its extreme form, such a logic essentially would cause the relationships between employers and unions to resemble a 'struggle for life'—a brute clash of competing forces seeking to coerce each other into making certain concessions.[11] Some cases suggest that the Court is relatively tolerant when such a

---

[10] See *Sibson v UK*, judgment of 20 April 1993, Series A, No 258-A, para 27; *Sigurður A. Sigurjónsson v Iceland*, judgment of 30 June 1993, Series A, No 264, para 35; and ECtHR (GC), *Sørensen and Rasmussen v Denmark* (App Nos 52562/99 and 52620/99), judgment of 11 January 2006, paras 72–75 (finding that the fact that the applicants had been compelled to join a particular trade union struck at 'the very substance of the right to freedom of association guaranteed by Article 11', the Court found that Denmark had not protected the negative right to freedom of association, noting that 'there is little support in the Contracting States for the maintenance of closed-shop agreements' and that several European instruments 'clearly indicate that their use in the labour market is not an indispensable tool for the effective enjoyment of trade union freedoms' (para 75).

[11] That was, in substance, the position advocated by Justice Brandeis in the *Hitchman Coal & Coke Co* case, where he defended the view that unions should not be prohibited from exercising pressure on an employer to abandon his practice of imposing non-unionisation as a condition for employment. He saw the confrontation between the employer and the union as one in which two freedoms were exercised, aiming at opposite objectives, and without any one of the parties having any duty towards the other. In exercising collective action in order to force the employer to open his company to unionised workers, Brandeis noted, the unions were not 'coercing' the employer in a legal sense, for 'coercion' in that sense 'is not exerted when a union merely endeavours to induce employees to join a union with the intention thereafter to order a strike unless the employer consents to unionize his shop. Such pressure is not coercion in the legal sense. The employer is free either to accept the agreement or the disadvantage. Indeed, the [company's] whole case is rested upon agreements [ie, employment contracts including a 'non-unionization' clause] secured under similar pressure of economic necessity or disadvantage. If it is

struggle turns in favour of the workers. In the 1996 case of *Gustafsson v Sweden*, for instance, where a restaurant owner was finally obliged to close his business because of a union boycott against him to force him to join a collective agreement, the Court acknowledged that 'although compulsion to join a particular trade union may not always be contrary to the Convention, a form of such compulsion which, in the circumstances of the case, strikes at the very substance of the freedom of association guaranteed by Article 11 will constitute an interference with that freedom' and that therefore 'national authorities may, in certain circumstances, be obliged to intervene in the relationships between private individuals by taking reasonable and appropriate measures to secure the effective enjoyment of the negative right to freedom of association'.[12] However, since the restaurant owner in this case was being pressured by industrial action not to join an association, but rather to conclude a collective agreement (that could be tailored to the specific conditions of his business), the Court considered that the State had not exceeded its margin of appreciation by refusing to prohibit the blockade and boycott against the restaurant, and thus protecting the alleged right of the restaurant owner to conclude only individual contracts of employment with his (seasonally recruited) employees: strictly speaking, the right of the restaurant owner not to be forced to become a member of an association was entirely preserved.[13]

The individualistic logic meets its limit once it leads to what might be called the commodification of the right of the individual worker to be represented by a union or to resort to collective action. While the Court recognises in principle that the worker should have a right to choose whether or not to join a union, it does require State authorities to intervene in situations where an employer aims to discourage workers from unionisation by using financial incentives: the promise of financial rewards is seen as an unacceptable way to seek to influence the worker's choice, which should be untainted by such incentives. In the 2002 case of *Wilson, National Union of Journalists and Others v UK*, the workers were offered by their employers to sign a personal contract and lose union rights or accept a lower pay rise; in other words, an employer could under British law offer higher wages to workers in order to encourage them to not join the union and not be represented by the

coercion to threaten to strike unless the plaintiff consents to a union shop, it is also coercion to threaten not to give one employment unless the applicant will consent to a closed non-union shop. The employer may sign the union agreement for fear that *labor* may not be otherwise obtainable; the workman may sign the individual agreement for fear that *employment* may not be otherwise obtainable. But such fear does not imply coercion in the legal sense' (*Hitchman Coal & Coke Co* (n 9) 263 (Brandeis J dissenting, with Holmes and Clark JJ concurring with the dissent)).

[12] ECtHR, *Gustafsson v Sweden* (App No 15573/89), judgment of 25 April 1996, para 45. Rights other than freedom of association may also call for the adoption of measures of protection by the State in the employment relationship: see, eg, ECtHR (GC), *Palomo Sánchez and others v Spain* (App Nos 28955/06, 28957/06, 28959/06 and 28964/06), judgment of 12 September 2011 (freedom of expression).

[13] The Court noted that States Parties to the Convention have a wide margin of appreciation in this regard. See *Gustafsson v Sweden* (n 12) para 45: 'In view of the sensitive character of the social and political issues involved in achieving a proper balance between the competing interests and, in particular, in assessing the appropriateness of State intervention to restrict union action aimed at extending a system of collective bargaining, and the wide degree of divergence between the domestic systems in the particular area under consideration, the Contracting States should enjoy a wide margin of appreciation in their choice of the means to be employed.'

union in collective bargaining schemes. This was in effect undermining the ability for the unions to represent the workers effectively. The Court noted that 'it is of the essence of the right to join a trade union for the protection of their interests that employees should be free to instruct or permit the union to make representations to their employer or to take action in support of their interests on their behalf. If workers are prevented from so doing, their freedom to belong to a trade union, for the protection of their interests, becomes illusory. It is the role of the State to ensure that trade union members are not prevented or restrained from using their union to represent them in attempts to regulate their relations with their employers'.[14] It concluded that Article 11 ECHR had been violated since:

[I]t was open to the employers to seek to pre-empt any protest on the part of the unions or their members against the imposition of limits on voluntary collective bargaining, by offering those employees who acquiesced in the termination of collective bargaining substantial pay rises, which were not provided to those who refused to sign contracts accepting the end of union representation. The corollary of this was that United Kingdom law permitted employers to treat less favourably employees who were not prepared to renounce a freedom that was an essential feature of union membership. Such conduct constituted a disincentive or restraint on the use by employees of union membership to protect their interests. However ... domestic law did not prohibit the employer from offering an inducement to employees who relinquished the right to union representation, even if the aim and outcome of the exercise was to bring an end to collective bargaining and thus substantially to reduce the authority of the union, as long as the employer did not act with the purpose of preventing or deterring the individual employee simply from being a member of a trade union.[15]

In other words, although workers have a freedom not to join a union, which excludes closed-shop agreements, the employer must be enjoined from pressuring how that freedom is exercised by inducing workers through financial means to prefer the negotiation of individual contracts of employment to collective representation through the union. Indeed, allowing the employer to use such means would destroy the ability for unions to exercise their core function—ie, to represent the collective views of the workers who seek, by joining the union, to strengthen their bargaining position vis-a-vis the employer. When, in 2008, the Court for the first time recognised the right to collective bargaining under the ECHR in the case of *Demir and Baykara*—a right it had been reluctant to accept in the past[16]—this position of the Court, being opposed to the commodification of union rights, was implicitly further

---

[14] ECtHR (2nd sect), *Wilson, National Union of Journalists and others v UK* (App Nos 30668/96, 30671/96 and 30678/96), judgment of 2 July 2002, para 46.

[15] Ibid, para 47.

[16] See, for instance, *National Union of Belgian Police v Belgium*, 27 October 1975, Series A, No 19, para 39; *Schmidt and Dahlström v Sweden*, judgment of 6 February 1976, Series A, No 21, paras 34–35; *Swedish Engine Drivers' Union v Sweden*, judgment of 6 February 1976, Series A, No 20, 15–16, paras 39–40 (noting that 'While the concluding of collective agreements is one of these means, there are others. What the Convention requires is that under national law trade unions should be enabled, in conditions not at variance with Article 11, to strive for the protection of their members' interests'); or, more recently, *Francesco Schettini and others v Italy* (dec) (App No 29529/95), 9 November 2000; and *UNISON v UK* (dec) (App No 53574/99), ECHR 2002-I; and in the *Wilson, National Union of Journalists and others v UK*, judgment of 2 July 2002 (App Nos 30668/96, 30671/96 and 30678/96), para 44.

confirmed.[17] For how would a union be able to effectively persuade an employer to enter into collective bargaining if the employer could simply bribe workers to opt for individual contracts of employment instead?

In sum, the trajectory of the Court's case law has been to move from an approach that initially allowed for the unions to protect the rights of workers by obtaining 'closed-shop' agreements (the reverse, in a way, of 'yellow dog' contracts imposed by the employer on prospective workers) to an approach that now ensures that unions can defend the interests of workers by collective bargaining, but leaving it free to workers to choose whether or not to join the unions purporting to represent them. The Court has never situated itself at the 'collectivist' end, in which only the positive freedom to join unions would be recognised and in which collective bargaining would be guaranteed, both benefiting unions even at the expense of workers' freedom to choose, but the 'individualist' parenthesis that was opened in the early 1990s was closed in 2002 with *Wilson and others* and in 2008 with *Demir and Baykara*. This evolution may be summarised as follows.

	A. No right to collective bargaining	B. Right to collective bargaining
1. Freedom to form and join unions, but no 'negative' freedom not to join unions	A1 Initial position of the court (phase 1, until recognition of the negative freedom of association in the 1980s)	B1 'Collectivist' approach to the protection of workers' rights: solution encouraging representation of these rights through the unions
2. Freedom both to form and join unions, and 'negative' freedom not to join unions	A2 'Individualist' approach to workers' rights: both employers and unions seek to gain workers' loyalty, using various incentives at their disposal— position adopted by the Court in the 1990s, until *Wilson and others* confirmed limits to the possibility for employers to resort to financial incentives (phase 2)	B2 Current position of the Court (phase 3)

---

[17] ECtHR (GC), *Demir and Baykara v Turkey* (App No 34503/97), judgment of 12 November 2008, para 154 ('the Court considers that, having regard to the developments in labour law, both international and national, and to the practice of Contracting States in such matters, the right to bargain collectively with the employer has, in principle, become one of the essential elements of the "right to form and to join trade unions for the protection of [one's] interests" set forth in Article 11 of the Convention, it being understood that States remain free to organise their system so as, if appropriate, to grant special status to representative trade unions').

These procedural safeguards have evolved over time. But they do guarantee the right of workers to act through unions; and they recognise certain rights to the unions themselves. But should such safeguards be seen as a substitute for the protection of the substantive rights of workers, restricting the ability for employers to impose certain restrictions on the rights of workers in the employment relationship? We may in principle imagine a situation in which, without prejudging the outcome, the State simply discharges its duty to protect fundamental rights in the employment relationship by ensuring that the workers may form unions, and unions resort to collective action, in order to compensate for the imbalance between the employer and the individual worker in the negotiation of the said contract. An interesting question would be whether, following this procedural approach, the recognition by the Court of a fully 'collectivist' solution—tolerant of 'closed-shop' agreements where the unions manage to obtain such agreements and recognising the fact that the right to collective bargaining is an essential component of the freedom to form and join unions for the defence of workers' interests (B1)—would suffice to justify a 'hands-off' attitude of the Court with respect to the substantive rights of workers that could be affected in the employment relationship. In other words, to which extent would the ability of the worker to be represented by unions in the negotiation of working conditions lead the Court to trust the result of that bargaining process without assessing in substantive terms the compatibility of the agreement reached? Is it enough to strengthen the bargaining position of workers without also assessing the outcomes of the negotiation concerning the conditions of employment?

That question must remain, for the moment, a theoretical one. The Court has remained shy from moving to B1 (the fully 'collectivist' solution). It has instead sought to achieve a balance between the individual rights of workers and the rights of unions as their representatives. Unions are guaranteed certain rights under the Convention and workers are therefore not unable to organise and to pursue the defence of their rights collectively, including by resorting to industrial action and by entering into collective bargaining. By recognising these rights and by protecting workers from measures adopted by employers that would negate them (as illustrated by the case of *Wilson and others*), the States Parties are providing certain means to the workers to defend their interests. At the same time, however, each individual worker has the right not to join a union and thus may choose not to be represented by the union in the negotiation of working conditions; provided that choice is not distorted by financial incentives, it is a choice that must be respected. It is in this sense that the position of the Court is an intermediate one, which cannot be seen as a substitute for assessing whether the substantive rights of the workers are respected in the employment relationship.

3.2 The Strength of Unions in Contemporary Europe

The procedural route in any case may be insufficient. That is not only because 'closed-shop' agreements granting the unions, in effect, a monopoly in the representation of workers, are seen as an interference with the (negative) freedom of association of employees, thus denying unions a monopoly in the representation of workers' interests. It is also because employment contracts are increasingly individualised, leading to a myriad of kinds of employment, with highly variable levels of security, being proposed to the worker;[18] in the context of increasingly flexibilised and casualised forms of employment, collective action through unions is an option that cannot be seen as a substitute for the protection of the basic rights of the worker in the employment relationship.

Indeed, the strength of social dialogue, and thus the ability for collective bargaining to effectively protect the worker from the imposition of conditions of employment that might lead to a sacrifice of her fundamental rights, vary significantly from country to country. In the EU-27, for instance, about two-thirds of the workers are covered by collective agreements, but the coverage rate is much higher in Austria, Belgium, Finland, France, Slovenia and Sweden, all countries where 90 per cent or more of workers are covered by a collective agreement, than in the Baltic States, where this applies only to a quarter of all employees or less.[19] The Member States having acceded to the EU in 2004 have generally much lower collective bargaining coverage rates than the 'older' Member States: with the exception of Slovenia and Romania, all of the 'new' Member States have collective bargaining coverage rates of around 50 per cent or less. The following graph illustrates these discrepancies.

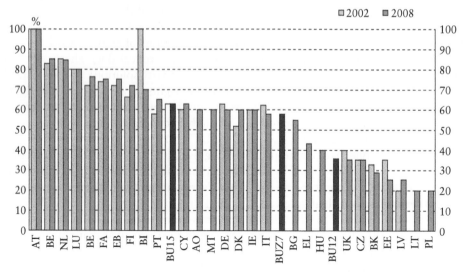

Figure 1: Bargaining coverage rates by country, 1997/1999 and 2007/2009

Source: European Commission, *Industrial Relations in Europe 2010*, Report, MEMO/11/134 of 3.3.2011 (chart prepared on the basis of J Visser, ICTWSS database 3.0, 2010)

---

[18] On this evolution, see in particular Robert Castel, *La montée des incertitudes. Travail, protections, statut de l'individu* (Paris, Seuil, 2009); and Robert Castel, *Les métamorphoses de la question sociale. Une chronique du salariat* (Paris, Fayard, 1995) (especially the conclusions, where he discusses the current evolution of waged employment as 'negative individualism' that is the result of the individual worker being 'substracted' from his membership into groups).

[19] European Commission, *Industrial Relations in Europe 2010* Report, MEMO/11/134 of 3 March 2011.

The insufficiency of a purely procedural approach to the protection of the fundamental rights of workers—which would protect rights to form and join unions and,
for unions, to enter into collective bargaining—also results from the relatively weak
rate of unionisation in some EU Member States. This provides a further indicator
of the individualisation of the employment contract and of the relative inability
of unions to effectively intervene on behalf of the workers whom they purport to
represent.

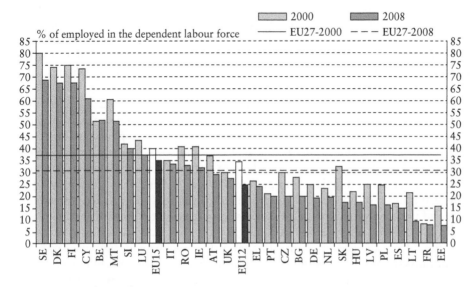

Figure 2: Union density by country, 2000–08

Source: European Commission, *Industrial Relations in Europe 2010*, Report, MEMO/11/134
of 3 March 2011 (chart prepared on the basis of J Visser, ICTWSS database 3.0, 2010)

These figures concerning the degree of unionisation or the coverage of collective agreements in EU Member States provide another demonstration that, taken
alone, the procedural route would be insufficient to adequately protect the rights
of workers: unions, in short, are often not in a position that is sufficiently strong
to justify a court using only a low level of scrutiny of the restrictions on the fundamental rights of workers. For these rights to be effectively protected, something
more is required: an understanding of how the rights of the Convention other than
the freedom to form and join unions can be invoked in the context of employment relationships. Indeed, the other route through which the fundamental rights
of workers could be protected in the employment relationship is to regulate that
relationship directly in order to ensure that the human rights of workers are fully
preserved, and that the employer does not abuse his dominant position by imposing restrictions on these rights that go beyond what the nature of the employment
requires. It is to this second route—substantive, rather than procedural—that we
now turn.

4 THE SUBSTANTIVE ROUTE: TRANSPOSING HUMAN RIGHTS FROM THE STATE TO THE EMPLOYER

How should the rights and freedoms guaranteed in the ECHR be applied to the employment relationship? By which techniques should provisions, designed to be invoked in the context of the 'vertical' relationships between the State and the citizen, by transposed into 'horizontal' relationships between private parties? One obvious possibility—by now the most commonly adopted by the Member States of the Council of Europe[20]—is to apply directly the rights and freedoms of the ECHR to the inter-individual relationships, that is, to empower domestic courts to adjudicate private law disputes on the basis of the substantive guarantees of the Convention. This is the option sometimes referred to as 'direct third-party applicability' of human rights, by reference to the theory of 'unmittelbare Drittwirkung' originally developed in Germany to justify the reliance, especially in labour disputes, of the fundamental rights of the German Basic Law.[21]

But such a transposition is not necessarily easy to effectuate. In part, this is because national courts receive relatively little guidance from the ECtHR in this regard, as the role of a regional jurisdiction ensuring the compliance of States with their human rights obligations in the international legal order are quite different from the role of domestic courts in seeking to achieve a balance between conflicting rights or interests of individuals in private disputes.[22] But this is not simply a problem of framing—of how issues are presented to the judge in private law adjudication and in the international legal process respectively. It is, more fundamentally, a problem at a substantive level. Human rights were originally designed to protect the individual from the power of the State, and their regime is deeply marked by that initial purpose. With the exception of some rights, of marginal significance for the employment relationship, restrictions on rights are allowable, provided the limitations imposed comply with certain conditions; that is the case, for instance, under the ECHR, for the right to respect for private and family life, freedom of religion,

---

[20] See, for studies comparing the status of the European Convention on Human Rights in different national legal orders, Robert Blackburn and Jörg Polakiewicz (eds), *Fundamental Rights in Europe. The ECHR and its Member States, 1950–2000* (Oxford, Oxford University Press, 2001); Helen Keller and Alec Stone Sweet (eds), *A Europe of Rights: The Impact of the ECHR on National Legal Systems* (Oxford, Oxford University Press, 2008).

[21] See HC Nipperdey, *Allgemeiner Teil des bürgerlichen Rechts, I* (Tübingen, Mohr Siebeck, 1952) 53 ff; W Leisner, *Grundrechte und Privatrecht* (Munich/Berlin, Ch Beck'sche Verlagsbuchhandlung, 1960); and, for an examination of how the German courts have applied this approach, KM Lewan, 'The Significance of Constitutional Rights for Private Law: Theory and Practice in West Germany' (1968) 17 *International and Comparative Law Quarterly* 571; Ted Oliver Ganten, *Die Drittwirkung der Grundfreiheiten* (Berlin, Duncker & Humblot, 2000) 26–28.

[22] For this reason, Andrew Clapham has taken the view that 'Drittwirkung is not helpful at the international level. The European Court of Human Rights is not seeking to harmonise constitutional traditions but to ensure international protection for the rights contained in the Convention. Key questions in Drittwirkung doctrine are the weight to be given to different rights such as: the right to free development of the personality, the right to work, the right to strike, the right to property, freedom of conscience, the right to equality, the right to free enterprise, and the right to freedom of contract. Drittwirkung theories which are based on the presence of social power or the sanctity of freedom of contract (protected under Article 2 of the German Basic Law) cannot really help to solve the international protection of the rights found in the European Convention on Human Rights' (Andrew Clapham, *Human Rights in the Private Sphere* (Oxford, Clarendon Press, 1993) 181–82).

freedom of expression or the freedom to form and join unions. But those conditions are defined with the regulatory and executive powers of the State in mind, and the regime applicable to the 'vertical' relationship between the individual and the State may therefore not always be easily transposable, mutatis mutandis, to the 'horizontal' relationship between private individuals.

4.1 A Legitimate Aim

Consider first the condition of legitimacy, which imposes on the State that it always ground the restrictive measures it adopts on a legitimate objective. It is of course the duty of the State to act in the public interest, and it is the duty of courts to ensure that, in imposing restrictions on human rights, the public authorities remains faithful to what the public interest requires. In contrast, individuals pursue a variety of aims and it would violate an elementary principle of moral pluralism to impose on all individuals that they only act in accordance to some pre-defined notion of what serves the common good. Hence, the condition according to which restrictions on the rights of the individual may only be justified if they are based on the pursuit of a legitimate aim is generally of little use in relationships between private parties.

However, the employment context deserves a specific comment in this regard. In principle, employers acting in the context of the employment relationship should have in mind their fiduciary duty to the shareholders, and they should therefore aim at maximising profits and minimising costs. Whether or not a particular employer acts according to such 'business necessity' should be ascertainable by the judge, and only exceptionally should it be allowable for the employer to put forward other objectives to justify imposing restrictions on the rights of workers. Thus, the sphere of employment, just like market relationships in general,[23] may in principle

---

[23] Indeed, in market relationships, the roles of each individual (and thus the conditions that such an individual may force another party to accept in their mutual relationships) are in principle defined by the nature of the transaction between them. As noted by Hüseyin Özel, this explains the 'de-humanizing' aspect of the market: 'since an "individual in the market" must behave only on the basis of the hope of gain or fear of hunger (or pain and pleasure for that matter), he is forced to be reduced to an individual who lacks "depth", as we ordinarily use this metaphor for people'; we must behave in the market, that is, as 'shallow Utilitarians', 'by identifying hunger and profit as the only two motives that guide our lives' (H Özel, 'Reclaiming Humanity: The Social Theory of Karl Polanyi' (PhD dissertation, University of Utah, 1997) 54–55). It is this characteristic of market relationships that explains why the anti-discrimination law can generally apply to such relationships, when it would be more difficult (and highly contestable with regard to the exigencies of the right to respect for private life) to apply the prohibition of discrimination, for instance, to the choice of friends whom X invites for a party at home, or to whom Y chooses to become a member of a private association. Thus, when the question was asked, in the context of the negotiation of Protocol No 12 to the European Convention on Human Rights, of the scope of application of the principle of non-discrimination that States Parties were committed to enforce under the protocol, the answer was that 'any positive obligation in the area of relations between private persons would concern, at the most, relations in the public sphere normally regulated by law, for which the state has a certain responsibility (for example, arbitrary denial of access to work, access to restaurants, or to services which private persons may make available to the public such as medical care or utilities such as water and electricity, etc)' (Explanatory Report to Protocol No 12 to the Convention for the Protection of Human Rights and Fundamental Freedoms, opened for signature in Rome on 4 November 2000, para 28). These are domains where private preferences should not be allowed to matter: they are 'semi-public' rather than just 'private'.

be seen to occupy an intermediate position between the public sphere (in which the State seeks to fulfil the public interest) and the private sphere (in which individuals are free to make choices that correspond to their beliefs and convictions, whether or not these are aligned with those of the majority): the nature and scope of the restrictions that the employer may impose on the individual worker should depend not on the subjective preferences or 'tastes' of the employer, but on the necessities of the undertaking.

But that apparently simple criterion—'business necessity'—may be difficult to apply in practice. First, the conduct of an employer based exclusively on what is objectively in the interests of the business enterprise may lead to defer to the 'tastes' of the public, which may be tainted by social norms and discriminatory attitudes.[24] It would not be acceptable for an employer, or for any other market actor, to adopt decisions on the basis of such illegitimate motives, for instance, by refusing to recruit an employee who would be in contact with the clientèle from which hostile reactions are feared, or who may not be made welcome by her colleagues.[25] This was one of the issues at stake in the case of *Feryn* presented to the European Court of Justice under the EU's Race Equality Directive.[26] A representative of the Feryn NV company had publicly asserted that his firm would not recruit persons of Moroccan origin, and the Court of Justice was asked whether this constituted a form of discrimination prohibited by the Directive. One of the arguments of the company was that, since the recruitment was for fitters to install up-and-over doors at the customers' houses, the distaste customers had for Moroccans could be a factor in recruitment decisions. In response, Advocate General Poiares Maduro noted that:

> The contention made by Mr Feryn that customers would be unfavourably disposed towards employees of a certain ethnic origin is wholly irrelevant to the question whether the Directive applies. Even if that contention were true, it would only illustrate that 'markets will not cure discrimination' and that regulatory intervention is essential. Moreover, the adoption of regulatory measures at Community level helps to solve a collective action problem for employers by preventing the distortion of competition that—precisely because of that market failure—could arise if different standards of protection against discrimination existed at national level.[27]

---

[24] See, eg, Cass Sunstein, 'Why Markets Won't Stop Discrimination' (1992) 8 *Social Philosophy and Policy* 21 (reproduced in *Free Markets and Social Justice* (Oxford, Oxford University Press, 1997)).

[25] See, per analogy, concerning homophobia in the armed forces of the UK, that the British government was invoking as a justification for excluding homosexuals from the army, the position of the European Court of Human Rights according to which: 'these attitudes, even if sincerely felt by those who expressed them, ranged from stereotypical expressions of hostility to those of homosexual orientation, to vague expressions of unease about the presence of homosexual colleagues. To the extent that they represent a predisposed bias on the part of a heterosexual majority against a homosexual minority, these negative attitudes cannot, of themselves, be considered by the Court to amount to sufficient justification for the interferences with the applicants' rights outlined above any more than similar negative attitudes towards those of a different race, origin or colour' (ECtHR (3rd sect), *Smith and Grady v UK*, judgment of 27 September 1999, para 97).

[26] Council Directive 2000/43/EC of 29 June 2000 implementing the principle of equal treatment between persons irrespective of racial or ethnic origin ([2000] OJ L 180, 22).

[27] Case C-54/07, *Centrum voor gelijkheid van kansen en voor racismebestrijding v Firma Feryn NV* [2008] ECR I-5187. In his opinion, AG Poiares Maduro cites the work of Cass Sunstein referred to above.

The Court apparently agreed, finding the answer too obvious to deserve an explicit discussion of the argument.[28]

The *Feryn* case illustrates that we cannot trust the market to ensure that irrational behavior, tainted by prejudice, shall be 'filtered out' simply through competitive pressure, as in the fantasised world of some neo-classical economists or law and economics scholars.[29] Rather, the market registers preferences: it functions as a receptacle for social norms and tastes. It would therefore not be consistent with the requirements of human rights in employment that 'business necessity' should always provide the baseline from which to assess the acceptability of certain restrictions on workers' rights. The duty of courts, rather, is to screen out those motives: they must ensure that the motives invoked by business actors are not tainted by social norms or result in arrangements that lead to the exclusion of certain individuals because of certain characteristics they present, unless such characteristics are strictly related to the requirements of the post.

Indeed, even that may not be sufficient. There exists a right to work in international human rights law, variously described as imposing on States a duty to formulate and implement an employment policy with a view to 'stimulating economic growth and development, raising levels of living, meeting manpower requirements and overcoming unemployment and underemployment',[30] or to adopt 'effective measures to increase the resources allocated to reducing the unemployment rate, in particular among women, the disadvantaged and marginalized'.[31] A core obligation of States in this regard—one that States must comply with even if they face important resource constraints—is to ensure non-discrimination and equal protection of employment, and thus in particular to ensure 'the right of access to employment, especially for disadvantaged and marginalized individuals and groups, permitting them to live a life of dignity'.[32] It follows again that 'business necessity' alone is not sufficient if that leads to take as given certain routine ways of organising the workplace, of recruiting the workforce or of defining the tasks of the individual workers that result in excluding certain categories of workers (or potential workers) and prohibiting them from acceding to employment or from realising their full potential within the organisation.

Indeed, it is this that the notion of 'reasonable accommodation' seeks to convey. At the EU level, the notion has been codified in the 2000 Employment Equality Directive as a means of favouring equality of treatment of persons with disabilities.[33] At the

---

[28] For comments, see Rüdiger Krause (2000) 47(3) *Common Market Law Review* 917–31; or Laetitia Driguez, 'Lutte contre les discriminations à l'embauche fondées sur la race ou l'origine ethnique' (2008) *Europe*, comm n° 321, 27–28.

[29] See, in particular, Gary Becker, *The Economics of Discrimination*, 2nd edn (Chicago, Chicago, University Press, 1971); or Richard A Epstein, *Forbidden Grounds: The Case Against Employment Discrimination Laws* (Cambridge, MA, Harvard University Press, 1992).

[30] ILO Convention (No 122) concerning Employment Policy, 1964 (entered into force on 15 July 1966), Article 1, para 1.

[31] Committee on Economic, Social and Cultural Rights, General Comment No 18: The Right to Work (Article 6 of the International Covenant on Economic, Social and Cultural Rights) (2005) UN Doc E/C.12/GC/18 (6 February 2006), para 26.

[32] Ibid, para 31.

[33] See Council Directive 2000/78/EC of 27 November 2000 establishing a general framework for equal treatment in employment and occupation, OJ L 303 of 2 December 2000, 16 (reasonable

international level, 'reasonable accommodation' is referred to in the Convention on the rights of persons with disabilities, where it is defined as 'necessary and appropriate modification and adjustments not imposing a disproportionate or undue burden, where needed in a particular case, to ensure to persons with disabilities the enjoyment or exercise on an equal basis with others of all human rights and fundamental freedoms'.[34] As a legal requirement, reasonable accommodation has its source in attempts to reconcile freedom of religion and the requirement of equal treatment of persons with disabilities, on the one hand, with occupational requirements, on the other hand. Its defining feature is that it requires that laws, regulations or practices that may lead to indirect discrimination against certain groups, or that may create obstacles to certain individuals having access to certain jobs or exercising certain responsibilities, be reassessed in order to eliminate that impact wherever possible without imposing on the employer an 'undue burden'.[35] The 'constraints' of the employer are not fixed or immutable—they are plastic, and it is this plasticity that the employee, or the prospective employee, may insist on, in requesting that her rights be accommodated within the organisation of the workplace. That is not to say that the positive duty of the employer to rearrange the policies of the enterprise is without limits—it must be understood reasonably, and in particular it should not impose on the employer costs that would be disproportionate to the need to ensure an inclusive working environment.[36] However, despite this limitation, the notion is a promising

accommodation 'means that employers shall take appropriate measures, where needed in a particular case, to enable a person with a disability to have access to, participate in, or advance in employment, or to undergo training, unless such measures would impose a disproportionate burden on the employer').

[34] Convention on the Rights of Persons with Disabilities (adopted by the UN General Assembly in A/RES/61/106 on 13 December 2006, entered into force on 3 May 2008), 2515 UNTS 3. Article 5(3) of the Convention includes the duty to provide reasonable accommodation as included in the prohibition of discrimination: 'In order to promote equality and eliminate discrimination, States Parties shall take all appropriate steps to ensure that reasonable accommodation is provided.'

[35] The leading case was *Eldridge v British Columbia* (1997) 3 SCR 624, decided by the Supreme Court of Canada. The appellants in that case were born deaf and their preferred means of communication was sign language. They argued that it followed from the requirement of equality that they should be provided sign language interpreters as an insured benefit under the Medical Services Plan. They relied on s 15(1) of the Canadian Charter of Rights and Freedoms, which provides that: 'Every individual is equal before and under the law and has the right to the equal protection and equal benefit of the law without discrimination and, in particular, without discrimination based on race, national or ethnic origin, colour, religion, sex, age or mental or physical disability'. Having failed to obtain a declaration to that effect in the Supreme Court of British Columbia, they then appealed to the Supreme Court of Canada, contending that the absence of interpreters impaired their ability to communicate with their doctors and other healthcare providers, and thus increased the risk of misdiagnosis and ineffective treatment. The Canadian Supreme Court agreed, noting: 'The principle that discrimination can accrue from a failure to take positive steps to ensure that disadvantaged groups benefit equally from services offered to the general public is widely accepted in the human rights field ... It is also a cornerstone of human rights jurisprudence, of course, that the duty to take positive action to ensure that members of disadvantaged groups benefit equally from services offered to the general public is subject to the principle of reasonable accommodation. The obligation to make reasonable accommodation for those adversely affected by a facially neutral policy or rule extends only to the point of "undue hardship"' (paras 78–79). For an example concerning freedom of religion, see also *Multani v Commission scolaire Marguerite-Bourgeoys* (2006) 1 SCR 256.

[36] In the US, Title VII of the Civil Rights Act of 1964 provides that an employer must *reasonably accommodate* an employee's religious beliefs and practices unless doing so would cause 'undue hardship on the conduct of the employer's business'. The notion of 'undue hardship' that appears under this legislation has been interpreted in a way that is particularly generous to the employer, as illustrated by the leading case of *Trans World Airlines, Inc. v Hardison*, 432 US 63 (1977), in which the Supreme Court

one. It could be made to serve not only to promote the integration of persons with disabilities but also, more broadly, to ensure that the 'right to work' becomes a reality for all those who—whether or not as a consequence of a disability or a religious belief—present certain 'differences' that may create obstacles to their employment.[37] Indeed, even notions that are apparently beyond reproach—such as 'merit', 'qualifications' or 'ability to perform the job'—can in fact turn out to be highly contestable once it is realised that their definitions depend on certain preconceived ways of organising the workplace or of performing the job.

Finally, there is a third reason why the question of which objectives the undertaking may legitimately pursue—allowing it to impose certain restrictions on the rights of its employees—may be difficult to answer. Some organisations pursue objectives that go beyond or are distinct from profit-making, and they may insist on the fact that the message they wish to convey to the public would be blurred if they were forced to include within their workforce workers whose conduct could be seen as contradicting their advocacy. That is the specific situation of churches or other organisations whose ethics is based on religion or on (non-religious) convictions, or of advocacy organisations such as political parties, trade unions or media that promote a certain political message.

In agreement in this regard with the EU legislator,[38] the ECtHR has recognised that employees of such organisations may be subject to particular restrictions in

---

ruled that an employer need not incur more than minimal costs in order to accommodate an employee's religious practices. According to the Equal Employment Opportunity Commission (EEOC), an employer can deny a requested accommodation if it can demonstrate that it causes it an undue hardship where accommodating an employee's religious practices would require anything more than ordinary administrative costs, would diminish the efficiency in other jobs, would infringe on other employees' rights or benefits, would impair workplace safety, would cause co-workers to carry the accommodated employee's share of potentially hazardous or burdensome work, or if the proposed accommodation conflicts with another law or regulation. That is a particular restrictive reading of the duties of the employer to provide reasonable accommodation of the employee's religious beliefs.

[37] The scope of the requirement to provide reasonable accommodation and, in particular, its meaning in the context of alleged religious discrimination in the workplace, was central to the *Eweida, Chaplin, Ladele and McFarlane v UK* cases on which the European Court of Human Rights delivered judgment on 15 January 2013 (Joined App Nos 48420/10, 59842/10, 51671/10 and 36516/10 (4th section, not final at the time of writing)). The Court appears to consider that the expression of religious belief, for instance by visibly wearing a crucifix on a neck-chain when in uniform at work, should be accommodated in the absence of 'evidence of any real encroachment on the interests of other' (para 95): the Court notes for instance, in the case of *Eweida* that concerned the wearing of a crucifix by an employee of British Airways, that 'There was no evidence that the wearing of other, previously authorised, items of religious clothing, such as turbans and hijabs, by other employees, had any negative impact on British Airways' brand or image' (para 94). This seems to confirm that the Court is prepared to recognise a duty of reasonable accommodation of expressions of religious belief. For the decisions adopted by the domestic courts in these cases, see *London Borough of Islington v Ladele* (2009) EWCA Civ 1357 (Court of Appeal, 15 December 2009); *McFarlane v Relate Avon Ltd* (2010) EWCA Civ B1 (Court of Appeal, 29 April 2010); *Eweida v British Airways plc* (2010) EWCA Civ 80 (Court of Appeal, 12 February 2010); and *Chaplin v Royal Devon & Exeter Hospital NHS Foundation Trust* (2010) ET 1702886/2009 (Employment Tribunal, 21 April 2010).

[38] See Council Directive 2000/78/EC (n 33) Article 4, § 2 (providing that the EU Member States may provide that 'in the case of occupational activities within churches and other public or private organisations the ethos of which is based on religion or belief, a difference of treatment based on a person's religion or belief shall not constitute discrimination where, by reason of the nature of these activities or of the context in which they are carried out, a person's religion or belief constitute a genuine, legitimate and justified occupational requirement, having regard to the organisation's ethos': such organisations

order to ensure that their responsibilities within the organisation shall not put in jeopardy the possibility for such organisations to disseminate their message. The leading judgment adopted on 4 June 1985 by the German Federal Constitutional Court (*BundesVerfassungsGericht*) provided the model for this doctrine. There, the German Federal Constitutional Court was asked to decide whether a doctor employed by a Catholic hospital who has publicly expressed views favourable to the freedom to seek abortion and an employee of a youth club established by a Catholic monastic order who had left the Catholic Church could be laid off by the churches by which they were employed. Overruling the labour courts, the Federal Constitutional Court considered that they could.[39] It based its judgments on the right recognised to the churches under Article 137, § 3 of the 1919 Weimar Constitution to freely regulate matters pertaining to their internal functioning—what the Court called their right to self-determination, or *Selbstbestimmungsrecht*—a freedom that, in the Court's view, also extends to the conclusion of employment contracts. While this did not entirely remove the employment relationship between the Church and its employees from the protection of labour law when churches exercise their contractual freedom (*Privatautonomie*), and while it did not allow the Church to impose on its employees arbitrary and disproportionate restrictions on their constitutionally protected freedoms, or conditions contrary to good morals and public policy, it did imply the right for the churches to impose on its employees certain conditions of loyalty that the Court saw as a condition of credibility for the Church.[40]

Following those judgments, the European Commission on Human Rights approved the position of the German Federal Constitutional Court concerning the case of the doctor employed in a Catholic hospital. It referred in that regard to the need to respect the freedom of expression of the Church under Article 10 of the ECHR, essentially ensuring that such freedom of expression would guarantee churches the same freedom as that recognised under the *Selbstbestimmungsrecht* guaranteed under the German Constitution.[41] The recent case law of the ECtHR appears to confirm that approach. In *Obst v Germany*, for instance, the Court agreed with the German courts that an employee of the Mormon Church in charge of public relations, who had confessed to his superiors to having committed adultery and had sought their help in this regard, could be dismissed because adultery is considered by the Mormon faith to be among the worst sins. The Court noted that the rights of the Mormon Church under Articles 9 and 11 ECHR (respectively guaranteeing freedom of religion and freedom of association) should be balanced against the right of the employee to respect for his private life (under Article 8 of the

---

therefore may be authorised to require individuals working for them 'to act in good faith and with loyalty to the organisation's ethos').

[39] Case Nos 2 *BvR* 1703/83, 1718/83 and 856/84, *BVergG*, vol 70, pp 138–73.

[40] Churches may in that regard rely on Article 2, § 1 of the German Basic Law (*Grundgesetz*, initially promulgated on 23 May 1949), which stipulates that: 'Every person shall have the right to free development of his personality insofar as he does not violate the rights of others or offend against the constitutional order or the moral law.' In the case of churches, this right to self-determination is defined by Article 137, § 3 of the Weimar Constitution, to which Article 140 of the 1949 Basic Law refers (by stating that the articles of the Weimar Constitution relating to religious societies (*Kirchernartikel*) remain valid).

[41] Eur Comm HR, *M. Rommelfanger v Federal Republic of Germany* (App No 12242/96), decision of 6 September 1989, *DR*, vol 62, p 151, 171.

Convention), and that in the case in question, the German courts may not be said to have acted unreasonably.[42]

At the same time, it is important to insist on the limits of this case law. First, the Court does not abandon the requirement of proportionality between the objective that the Church seeks to achieve by imposing a requirement of 'loyalty' on its employees, and the degree of the restrictions imposed on the employee's rights; instead, the Court links the acceptability of such restrictions to the fact that an employee openly adopts a behaviour that would run counter to the message of the Church and might damage its credibility.[43]

Second, in contrast to the views expressed by the European Commission on Human Rights in the *Rommelfanger* case, the Court does not rely on the freedom of expression of the employer to convey a message to the general public, based on Article 10 of the Convention. Instead, the Court explicitly notes in *Obst* that it takes into account the specific nature of the occupational requirements imposed by an employer whose ethos is based on religion or convictions. And it cites in this regard the provisions of the Convention that protect freedom of religion and freedom of association (Articles 9 and 11, respectively), as well as Article 4 of the EU Employment Equality Directive, which is limited to churches or organisations whose ethos is based on a religion or on (non-religious, philosophical) convictions.[44] Therefore, the judgment of the Court should not be interpreted as automatically extending to employers who want to convey a message, for instance, opposed to extra-marital relationships or in favour of tolerance towards migrants that would justify them in excluding employees who commit adultery or who express intolerant views, outside the specific situation where the employer is an organisation whose ethos is based on religion or convictions.[45]

That is not to say that, under the ECHR, there is no place for what the US courts call the 'expressive freedom of association',[46] recognised by (non-religious) organisations

---

[42] ECtHR (5th sect), *Obst v Germany* (App No 425/03), judgment of 23 September 2010, paras 51–52. See also, for instance, ECtHR (5th sect), *Siebenhaar v Germany* (App No 18136/02), judgment of 3 February 2011, para 46 (concerning the dismissal of the applicant from her job as educator in a kindergarten set up by the Protestant Church after her employer learned about her activities within the Universal Church, to which the applicant had vowed obedience: 'La Cour note que la nature particulière des exigences professionnelles imposées à la requérante résulte du fait qu'elles ont été établies par un employeur dont l'éthique est fondée sur la religion ou les convictions ... A cet égard, elle estime que les juridictions du travail ont suffisamment démontré que les obligations de loyauté étaient acceptables en ce qu'elles avaient pour but de préserver la crédibilité de l'Eglise protestante à l'égard du public et des parents des enfants du jardin d'enfants').

[43] On the condition of proportionality, see the following section below.

[44] See above, n 37.

[45] See also *Palomo Sánchez and others v Spain* (n 12) para 76 ('the requirement to act in good faith in the context of an employment contract does not imply an absolute duty of loyalty towards the employer or a duty of discretion to the point of subjecting the worker to the employer's interests').

[46] See *Roberts v United States Jaycees*, 468 US 609, 622 (1984) (noting that 'implicit in the right to engage in activities protected by the First Amendment' is 'a corresponding right to associate with others in pursuit of a wide variety of political, social, economic, educational, religious, and cultural ends', and thus to be protected from regulation compelling an association to accept certain members that it does not desire and that could impede the ability of the association to express its views). In *Boy Scouts of America and Monmouth Council, et al. v Dale*, 530 US 640 (2000), the membership in the Boy Scouts of James Dale had been revoked when the Boy Scouts learned that he was an avowed homosexual and gay rights activist. The New Jersey Supreme Court considered that the Boy Scouts had violated New Jersey's public accommodations law and that the Boy Scouts were required to admit Dale (160 NJ 562,

who wish to convey certain messages or values that may justify them in choosing whom to employ on the basis of criteria that may otherwise be suspect.[47] Employers may invoke the freedom of expression recognised under Article 10 of the Convention where they are political parties, media, non-governmental organisations or unions—what the German doctrine refers to as *Tendenzbetriebe* or advocacy-based organisations,[48] or what, in her concurring opinion to *Roberts v Jaycees*, Justice O'Connor called 'expressive associations'.[49]

The 2007 case of *Associated Society of Locomotive Engineers & Firemen (ASLEF) v UK* provides an illustration of this. In this case, the Court found a violation of Article 11 ECHR due to the inability of a trade union to expel one of its members who belonged to an extreme right-wing political party which advocated views inimical to its own. The Court noted on this occasion that:

> Article 11 cannot be interpreted as imposing an obligation on associations or organisations to admit whosoever wishes to join. Where associations are formed by people, who, espousing particular values or ideals, intend to pursue common goals, it would run counter to the very effectiveness of the freedom at stake if they had no control over their membership. By way of example, it is uncontroversial that religious bodies and political parties can generally regulate their membership to include only those who share their beliefs and ideals. Similarly, the right to join a union 'for the protection of his interests' cannot be interpreted as conferring a general right to join the union of one s choice irrespective of the rules of

---

734 A 2d 1196 (1999)). The Supreme Court, in a 5:4 decision with the opinion delivered for the majority by Justice Rehnquist, considered that this requirement violated the Boy Scouts' 'expressive associational right' grounded in the First Amendment, a right that benefits not only advocacy groups, but also all groups that 'engage in some form of expression, whether it be public or private'. On the impact of the *Dale* judgment on employment anti-discrimination law, see, inter alia, Dale Carpenter, 'Expressive Association and Anti-Discrimination Law after *Dale*: A Tripartite Approach' (2001) 85 *Minnesota Law Review* 1515 (proposing a typology distinguishing commercial organisations, expressive organisations and quasi-expressive organisations, the latter being organisations that both engage in expression and participate in the commercial marketplace); Richard A Epstein, 'The Constitutional Perils of Moderation: The Case of the Boy Scouts' (2000) 74 *Southern California Law Review* 119 (approving *Dale* and noting that the pluralism and diversity of organisations are in the long term more conducive to individual freedom than imposed uniformity); and Karen Lim, 'Freedom to Exclude after *Boy Scouts of America v Dale*: Do Private Schools Have a Right to Discriminate Against Homosexual Teachers?' (2003) 71 *Fordham Law Review* 2599.

[47] In the case law of the (now abolished) European Commission on Human Rights, see *Van der Heijden v The Netherlands* (App No 11002/84), decision of 8 March 1985, DR, 41, p 264), in which the Commission accepts as compatible with the ECHR the dismissal of the applicant from the Limburg Foundation for immigration, an organisation aiming at defending the rights of migrants, after his membership of an extreme-right political party was disclosed.

[48] As defined in Germany under § 118 of the Works Constitution Act (BetrVG) (which describes such undertakings or organisations as 'Unternehmen und Betriebe, die unmittelbar und überwiegend 1. politischen, koalitionspolitischen, konfessionellen, karitativen, erzieherischen, wissenschaftlichen oder künstlerischen Bestimmungen oder 2. Zwecken der Berichterstattung oder Meinungsäußerung, auf die Artikel 5 Abs. 1 Satz 2 des Grundgesetzes Anwendung findet'). See also, inter alia, Dominique Laszlot-Fenouillet, *La conscience* (Paris, LGDJ, 1993) 357.

[49] See *Roberts v United States Jaycees* (n 46) 633–34 (contrasting the situation of an organisation 'engaged in commercial activity', which 'enjoys only minimal constitutional protection of its recruitment, training, and solicitation activities', with the situation of 'an association engaged exclusively in protected expression enjoys First Amendment protection of both the content of its message and the choice of its members', and noting that in the latter case 'Protection of the message itself is judged by the same standards as protection of speech by an individual. Protection of the association's right to define its membership derives from the recognition that the formation of an expressive association is the creation of a voice, and the selection of members is the definition of that voice').

the union: in the exercise of their rights under Article 11 § 1 unions must remain free to decide, in accordance with union rules, questions concerning admission to and expulsion from the union.[50]

It related this to the fact that unions are not quasi-public bodies simply set up to perform certain functions in the interests of workers, by delegation from the State. Instead, said the Court, 'historically, trade unions in the United Kingdom, and elsewhere in Europe, were, and though perhaps to a lesser extent today are, commonly affiliated to political parties or movements, particularly those on the left. They are not bodies solely devoted to politically-neutral aspects of the well-being of their members, but are often ideological, with strongly held views on social and political issues'.[51]

The freedom of expression of employees or members of advocacy-based organisations may thus be limited in order to ensure that the organisation shall be able to convey its message to the public without this mission being interfered with, or being made more difficult, by the individual opinions expressed by its employees or members.[52] But the doctrine must be treated with great caution. It certainly would not extend to situations where an employer wishes to impose a certain 'culture' or project an 'image' towards the outside world, and would seek to rely on that objective to justify otherwise inadmissible restrictions on the rights of its employees.

4.2 A Predictable Legal Framework

Once it is agreed in principle that human rights designed to apply to the relationships between the State and individuals under its jurisdiction are applicable, mutatis mutandis, to relationships between the employer and the employees, we must confront a second question. Restrictions to human rights traditionally may only be imposed when 'in accordance with the law'. The requirement is that the domestic law be sufficiently clear in its terms, or in the interpretation it has been given by the courts, to provide the right-holders with adequate indications as to the circumstances in which public authorities are empowered to interfere with their freedoms, and the conditions that the authorities must comply with in doing so, thus allowing the citizens to anticipate the consequences of their conduct.[53] But how is this condition of legality to be understood when the interference is the result of conduct by a private party, the employer, rather than by a State agent?

In contrast to a wide range of other situations in which human rights are applied to relationships between private parties, the answer to this question is relatively straightforward in the context of employment. The reason for this is simple. The

---

[50] ECtHR (4th sect), *Case of Associated Society of Locomotive Engineers & Firemen (ASLEF) v UK* (App No 11002/05), judgment of 27 February 2007, para 39.

[51] Ibid, para 50.

[52] See, however, Evert Verhulp, *Vrijheid van meningsuiting van werknemers en ambtenaren* (The Hague, Sdu, 1996) 104–05 (according to whom employees of such organisations should be recognised as having a freedom to express views critical of the orientation of the organisation).

[53] See, for instance, *Leander v Sweden*, judgment of 26 March 1987, Series A, No 116, p 23, paras 50–51; *Malone v UK*, judgment of 2 August 1984, Series A, No 82, p 30, para 67.

employer and the worker are not just individuals who interact in the marketplace, whose mutual relationships can be understood as two freedoms that may occasionally clash when they seek to gain access to the same advantages for which they compete; instead, these relationships are *regulated*, and it is this regulatory framework that must comply with this requirement of legality.

We may express this in Hohfeldian terms.[54] Most relationships in the market sphere are relationships that are not mediated by rights and obligations, so that to the liberty (or 'privilege') of A (to adopt a certain course of action), there corresponds merely the absence of a right of B (to object to that course of action being chosen). Actions are taken and losses may be incurred by others as a result, without any such losses having to be compensated. That, after all, is what the struggle for life—or 'competition'—is all about. This is not so, however, in the employment relationship. Once a worker and the employer are linked through a contract, their relationships are regulated by the statutes applicable to that relationship, as well as by the contract itself within the limits set by law. Indeed, regulations also apply prior to the conclusion of the contract, in the course of the negotiation of its terms or in the process of matching the demand for skills expressed by the employer and the supply of labour by the candidate-worker. Although at this stage, the role of power relationships remains important—the respective bargaining power of the parties may matter considerably in setting the terms of the contract—the negotiation thus does not take place in a void.

It is therefore not particularly difficult to require from the various sets of rules that apply to the employment relationship both prior to the conclusion of the employment contract and afterwards that such rules present the qualities (particularly in terms of their clarity, allowing their application to be relatively predictable) that are otherwise required from State regulation when it is the public authorities rather than private actors that impose restrictions to human rights. Whether the rules defining the conditions according to which restrictions may be imposed are stipulated in laws[55] or regulations (or in the case law providing them with an authoritative interpretation), in statutes adopted by professional associations,[56] in collective agreements,[57] in the staff regulations adopted by the employer or in the individual contract of employment itself should not make any difference: what

---

[54] WN Hohfeld, 'Some Fundamental Legal Conceptions as Applied in Judicial Reasoning' (1913) 23 *Yale LJ* 16; WN Hohfeld, 'Fundamental Legal Conceptions as Applied in Judicial Reasoning' (1917) 26 *Yale LJ* 710. These essays are reproduced in WN Hohfeld, *Fundamental Legal Conceptions as Applied in Judicial Reasoning*, WW Cook (ed) (New Haven, Yale University Press, 1964, reprinted by Greenwood Press, 1978).

[55] See, eg, ECtHR (4th sect), *Fuentes Bobo v Spain* (App No 39293/98), judgment of 29 February 2000 (in which restrictions to the freedom of expression of the applicant, who had been laid off after he insulted the management of the Spanish television—his employer—were said to be based on the Statute of Workers and on Law No 4/80 of 10 January 1980 on the status of radiodiffusion and television: the dismissal was finally found to constitute a disproportionate sanction and thus a violation of freedom of expression); or *Palomo Sánchez and others v Spain* (n 12) (in which the dismissal of the employees on disciplinary grounds was based on the Labour Regulations, approved by Royal Legislative Decree No 1/1995 of 24 March 1995, which provided that 'verbal or physical attacks on the employer or persons working in the company' could constitute grounds for dismissal).

[56] ECtHR, *Casado Coca v Spain* (App No 15450/89), judgment of 19 February 1993, Series A, No 285-A, paras 41–43.

[57] ECtHR (plen), *Young, James and Webster v UK*, judgment of 13 August 1981, Series A, No 44.

matters is that the powers of the employer to impose certain restrictions on the employees' rights, for instance in the exercise of the supervision of the work performed in the undertaking, are circumscribed by a legal or regulatory framework sufficiently precise and detailed to avoid the risk of arbitrariness or discrimination, and to ensure that the worker shall not refrain from exercising the freedom he or she should be accorded simply because of uncertainty about the consequences that might result from such an exercise.

4.3 Restrictions that are Proportionate

The third condition that restrictions on rights or freedoms protected under the Convention must comply with is that such restrictions must be proportionate, ie, that they should not go beyond what is 'necessary in a democratic society'. In practice, it is this condition that is generally decisive. Yet, it is one where the transposition from vertical relationships between the State and the individual under its jurisdiction to the horizontal relationships between private parties, for instance between the employer and the worker, may be the source of particular difficulties. The reason for this is that, whereas the imbalance between the State and the individual justifies us in requiring from the State that it refrains from imposing restrictions on the individual's right that go beyond what is necessary for the fulfilment of the public interest, we are not presented with the same imbalance in the relationships between two private parties. Particularly when a private actor infringes upon the human right of another by exercising a basic freedom—for instance, when freedom of expression impacts on the right to respect for private life, or when the freedom of association exercised by the union in adopting its internal regulations affect the 'negative' freedom of association of its members—it cannot be expected from a private actor X that it only adopts a conduct that brings about a minimal impairment to the right of other private actors with whom X interacts.[58]

This does not imply, however, that the condition of proportionality is inappropriate in such situations. In the case of *Palomo Sánchez and others v Spain,* for instance, the applicants had been dismissed following what their employer considered to be an abusive exercise of their freedom of speech. The ECtHR had to decide whether the restriction imposed on the freedom of expression of the applicants satisfied the test of proportionality. The Court had no difficulty in applying the test to private relationships, concluding from its comparative law analysis that 'the domestic legislation seeks to reconcile the employee's right to freedom of expression with the employer's rights and prerogatives, requiring in particular that a dismissal measure be proportionate to the conduct of the employee against whom it is taken' and that 'even if the requirement to act in good faith in the context of an employment contract does not imply an absolute duty of loyalty towards the employer or a duty of discretion to the point of subjecting the worker to the employer's interests,

---

[58] See in particular on this difficulty O De Schutter and F Tulkens, 'The European Court of Human Rights as a Pragmatic Institution' in E Brems (ed), *Conflicts Between Fundamental Rights*, (Oxford, Intersentia, 2008) 169–216.

certain manifestations of the right to freedom of expression that may be legitimate in other contexts are not legitimate in that of labour relations'.[59]

That the transposition of the 'proportionality' test from 'vertical' (State-individual) to 'horizontal' relationships (between private actors) is possible in principle does not mean that it is always easy to effectuate in practice. All too often, the case law of the ECtHR provides little guidance to domestic authorities, including judicial authorities, as to how to achieve this. Indeed, since the protection of the 'rights of others' may constitute a legitimate aim justifying that restrictions be imposed on the rights and freedoms of the Convention, it is tempting for the Court to consider that, where rights of private parties are in tension with one another, the conflict between, on the one hand, the right asserted by the alleged victim before the Court (such as the right of the worker aggrieved by a measure adopted by the employer) and, on the other hand, the right which the national authorities have sought to protect by the adoption of measures (such as the right of the employer imposing the restriction) should be resolved through the classical application of the necessity test. According to this test, only where the protection of the rights of others by the Legislator or by the Executive—or, indeed, by the courts—strictly requires that a limitation be brought to rights and freedoms guaranteed under the Convention, should such limitations be allowed. This, in practice, has been the preferred way to solve situations of conflict. It is, moreover, a practice clearly encouraged by the reference, in the 'limitation clauses' contained in the second paragraphs of Articles 8–11 of the Convention or in paragraph 3 of Article 2 of Protocol No 4 ECHR, to the 'rights and freedoms of others' among the legitimate aims which may justify certain restrictions being brought to the rights concerned. And it presents two significant advantages: it dispenses the Court from explicitly acknowledging the existence of a conflict between rights; and it ensures that the conflict will be addressed by reliance on a well-established technique which both the Court and the commentators are familiar with.

Obvious as it may seem, however, this solution is problematic. It distorts the reality of the conflict between competing rights or interests. Such a distortion may influence the outcome in two different directions. On the one hand, by its very structure, the 'necessity' test is based on the idea that the right is the rule, and the measure interfering with the right the exception: thus, far from ensuring that both rights be effectively balanced against one another, it may result in one right being recognised a priority over the other simply because it has been invoked by the applicant before the Court, when the competing right is invoked by the government in defence of the measure which is alleged to constitute a violation of the Convention.[60] On the

---

[59] *Palomo Sánchez and others v Spain* (n 12) paras 75–76.

[60] As noted by Eva Brems, the result is that: 'Although both human rights are equally fundamental and a priori carry equal weight, they do not come before the judge in an equal manner. The right that is invoked by the applicant receives most attention, because the question to be answered by the judge is whether or not this right was violated. The arguments of the defendant may advance the theory that granting the applicant's claim would violate an additional human right. Through these arguments, the protection of that secondary right may find its way to the judge's reasoning, but it is not among the legal questions to be directly addressed.' See E Brems, 'Conflicting Human Rights: An Exploration in the Context of the Right to a Fair Trial in the European Convention for the Protection of Human Rights and Fundamental Freedoms' (2005) 27 *Human Rights Quarterly* 305.

other hand, however, the very opposite bias may be interfering with the judgment of the ECtHR in such situations: because the situation presented to the Court is one in which the State must refute an allegation of violation presented by an individual right-holder, the stakes may be biased against the individual and in favour of the State which is presumed to embody the interest of the collectivity. This is the danger which Ch Fried and L Frantz first pointed to when, in 1959, the balancing test first made its appearance in the First Amendment case law of the US Supreme Court.[61] Roscoe Pound had already anticipated this danger in 1921, noting that: 'If [in weighing two competing interests] we put one as an individual interest and the other as a social interest we may decide the question in advance of our very way of putting it'.[62] This danger, clearly implicated by the 'balancing' metaphor, is of course especially real where the conflict between two fundamental rights occurs—as is always the case before the ECtHR—in a procedural setting in which one of the rights in conflict is endorsed by an entity such as the State, who is presumed to embody a broad collective interest whose weight, in comparison to that of the individual right-holder, will necessarily appear considerable, at least until we realise that this individual might well be representative, in his claims, of far wider societal interests, to which the State may have paid insufficient consideration.[63]

None of this is to suggest that the requirement of proportionality has no role to play in assessing the acceptability of the restrictions that the employer seeks to impose on workers' fundamental rights, or that judges face insuperable obstacles in relying on such a test. Rather, what these difficulties show is that there are risks involved in simply equating the relationship that may exist between the employer and the worker to the relationship that exists between the State and the individual under its jurisdiction. This explains, in part, why the case law of the ECtHR may be an imperfect guide for domestic jurisdictions confronted to such situations.[64]

---

[61] *Barenblatt v United States*, 360 US 109, 126 (1959): 'Whether First Amendment rights are asserted to bar governmental interrogation resolution of the issue always involves a balancing by the courts of the competing private and public interests at stake in the particular circumstances shown'. See Ch Fried, 'Two Concepts of Interests: Some Reflections on the Supreme Court's Balancing Test' (1963) 76 *Harvard Law Review* 755 ff; L Frantz, 'Is the First Amendment Law? A Reply to Professor Mendelson' (1963) 51 *California Law Review* 729 ff, 747–49.

[62] R Pound, 'A Survey of Social Interests' (1943) 57 *Harvard Law Review* 2 (study initially written in 1921). The full citation is the following: 'When it comes to weighing or valuing claims or demands, we must be careful to compare them on the same plane. If we put one as an individual interest and the other as a social interest we may decide the question in advance of our very way of putting it.'

[63] See, for other examples, O De Schutter, 'La souveraineté de l'Etat et les droits de la personne immigrée' (1995) 84 *Revue du droit des étrangers* 261–70.

[64] The direct application in private relationships of human rights recognised in domestic constitutions creates similar difficulties: as noted by Aharon Barak, the President of the Supreme Court of Israel (although writing here in his non-judicial capacity), 'where constitutional provisions do not contain limitations clauses regarding the restriction of one person's right arising from the right of another, the obvious result is that judges will have to create judicial limitation clauses. Thus, judges will acquire enormous constitutional power without any concomitant constitutional guidance': A Barak, 'Constitutional Human Rights and Private law' in D Friedmann and D Barak-Erez (eds), *Human Rights in Private Law* (Oxford, Hart Publishing, 2001) 17.

5 THE QUESTION OF WAIVER: CONTRACTING
OUT OF HUMAN RIGHTS

A perhaps even more delicate question is whether, by entering freely into the employment relationship, the worker may be considered to have waived certain fundamental rights, either because certain limitations to such rights are inherent in the nature of the employment concerned or because the worker agreed explicitly to certain limitations. In a number of instances, including in the recent past, the ECtHR has recognised that certain restrictions on the rights of employees could be deemed acceptable where such restrictions had been consented to and because of such consent. In that sense, the waiver of rights is not unconditionally prohibited under the ECHR.[65] Yet, whether such a consent given by the employee provides a sufficient and adequate justification for the restriction shall depend on the scope of the restriction and on the seriousness of the consequences to the individual: the more wide-ranging and important the restriction, the more difficult it will be to save it by invoking the individual's consent. Thus, in a judgment delivered on 7 October 2010 in a case concerning Russia, where a serviceman was denied a parental leave in violation, allegedly, of the right not to be discriminated against on grounds of sex, the ECtHR considered that the argument that a serviceman was free to resign from the army if he wished to take personal care of his children was particularly questionable, given the difficulty in directly transferring essentially military qualifications and experience to civilian life.[66] A similar reasoning had already been held by the Court in the 1995 case of *Vogt v Germany*, where the Court found that Mrs Vogt, a secondary school teacher who had been a permanent civil servant but who had been suspended and dismissed on account of her membership and activities with the German Communist Party (Deutsche Kommunistische Partei: DKP), was a victim of a violation of freedom of expression because of the impossibility for her, in pratice, to find employment as a schoolteacher outside the public sector.[67]

The consent of the individual to certain restrictions on her rights is thus *one* factor that the Court may take into account, but it is never the *sole* factor determining the outcome; it is only in combination with other factors that it may play a role. This is confirmed in the *Eweida and others v UK* judgment delivered by the European Court of Human Rights on 15 January 2013, where the Court explicitly states that where an individual complains of a restriction on freedom of religion

---

[65] See, for instance, ECtHR, *Kalaç v Turkey* (App No 20704/92), judgment of 1 July 1997, para 28; *Obst v Germany* (n 42) para 50; ECtHR (5th sect), *Siebenhaar v Germany* (App No 18136/02), judgment of 3 February 2011, para 46.

[66] ECtHR, *Konstantin Markin v Federation of Russia* (App No 30078/06), judgment of 7 October 2010.

[67] ECtHR, *Vogt v Germany* (App No 17851/91), judgment of 26 September 1995, para 44 (where the Court notes that there were several reasons for considering dismissal of a teacher to be a very severe sanction: the effect on the reputation of the person concerned, the loss of livelihood and the virtual impossibility in Germany of finding an equivalent post). Compare this with ECtHR, *Otto v Germany* (App No 27574/02), decision of 24 November 2005 (concerning a police officer denied a promotion to the position of a chief inspector, because of his membership and activities for a political party, Die Republikaner: the Court concluded that the application alleging a violation of the freedom of expression guaranteed under Article 10 ECHR was manifestly ill-founded, in particular since 'Unlike Mrs Vogt, the applicant was not threatened with losing his livelihood by not receiving further promotion').

in the workplace, the mere possibility for that individual of changing job cannot, per se, exclude the existence of a violation, as this 'would negate any interference with the right': instead, says the Court, 'the better approach would be to weigh that possibility in the overall balance when considering whether or not the restriction was proportionate'.[68] The fact that an individual has voluntarily and knowingly chosen to enter into an employment relationship that would imply a restriction to his freedom to manifest his religious beliefs is not irrelevant.[69] However, the Court 'does not consider that an individual's decision to enter into a contract of employment and to undertake responsibilities which he knows will have an impact on his freedom to manifest his religious belief is determinative of the question whether or not there been an interference with Article 9 rights, this is a matter to be weighed in the balance when assessing whether a fair balance was struck'.[70]

In past decisions, the Court has set forth a number of conditions which the 'consent' of the individual to the sacrifice of his or her rights must satisfy in order to be taken into consideration. By setting out such conditions, the Court seeks to ensure that, to the extent that such consent plays a role at all in defining the scope of the obligation to protect, it will not be abused.

The leading judgment in this regard was delivered on 13 November 2007 by the Grand Chamber of the ECtHR in the case of *DH and others v Czech Republic*. There, in response to the complaint of their parents that Roma children were placed in special schools for children with learning difficulties considered unable to follow the ordinary school curriculum, the Czech Republic had expressed the view that the parents had in fact consented to the placement: 'it follows', the government argued, 'that any such consent would signify an acceptance of the difference in treatment, even if discriminatory, in other words a waiver of the right not to be discriminated against'. The Court disagreed. It noted that 'the waiver of a right guaranteed by the Convention—in so far as such a waiver is permissible—must be established in an unequivocal manner, and be given in full knowledge of the facts, that is to say on the basis of informed consent ... and without constraint'.[71] The Court found that these conditions were not satisfied in the case it was presented with. In particular, it doubted whether 'the parents of the Roma children, who were members of a disadvantaged community and often poorly educated, were capable of weighing up all the aspects of the situation and the consequences of giving their consent', especially in the absence of adequate information provided by the authorities.[72]

---

[68] ECtHR (4th sect), *Eweida, Chaplin, Ladele and McFarlane v UK* (Joined App Nos 48420/10, 59842/10, 51671/10 and 36516/10), judgment of 15 January 2013 (not final at the time of writing).

[69] § 106, in the case of Ms Ladele, who was employed by a local municipality but refused to agree to be designated a registrar of civil partnerships because of her religious convictions.

[70] § 109, concerning the case of McFarlane, who was employed by a private company with a policy of requiring employees to provide services equally to heterosexual and homosexual couples, but faced disciplinary proceedings after he had refused to commit himself to providing psycho-sexual counselling to same-sex couples, because his religious convictions led him to oppose same-sex relationships.

[71] ECtHR (GC), *DH and others v Czech Republic* (App No 57325/00), judgment of 13 November 2007, para 202 (referring to *Pfeifer and Plankl v Austria*, judgment of 25 February 1992, Series A, No 227, paras 37–38 (on the requirement of informed consent) and to *Deweer v Belgium*, judgment of 27 February 1980, Series A, No 35, para 51 (on the absence of constraint)).

[72] *DH and others v Czech Republic* (n 71) para 203.

The approach of *DH* is in principle transposable to employment relationships, as acknowledged by subsequent judgments of the European Court.[73] However, in order to understand the full range of the implications, it must first be observed that, notwithstanding the insistence of the Court on the need for the waiver to be expressed univocally—in other words, the individual alleged to have renounced a right must have done so explicitly rather than implicitly—in practice, the consent may be deemed to be real, if implicit, where it follows from the very nature of the employment concerned. Indeed, certain restrictions on the exercise of fundamental rights that would otherwise not be acceptable may be justified in the particular context of the employment relationship, as the Court has repeatedly stated.[74] Such restrictions may be considered admissible, even in the absence of an explicit consent of the individual; in other words, by taking up the employment, the individual must be presumed to have agreed to the restrictions that follow unavoidably from the nature of the occupation concerned.

In listing when it may be acceptable to justify restrictions on certain rights and freedoms by the waiver of the individual, the Court alluded to two other conditions that deserve a particular comment in the context of the employment relationship. First, the Court explicitly required that the waiver be authentically free—at a minimum, not tainted by coercion. This of course does not merely exclude physical coercion; it also excludes other, more subtle forms of pressure. Indeed, it is meant to reach even beyond duress as it appears in contract law. In fact, the reference to the 1980 case of *Deweer v Belgium* suggests that the Court had in mind any situation in which, *either because of the fear of negative consequences or because of the irresistible attractiveness of the advantages offered*, the (prospective) worker cannot realistically be expected to refuse to consent to a particular limitation to her right.

The reference to the *Deweer v Belgium* judgment is indeed remarkable, because that judgment acknowledged with a particular clarity the dangers associated with presenting an individual with an alternative where the benefits associated with one branch so clearly outweigh the benefits associated with the other that the 'freedom to choose' of the right-holder becomes purely formal, or even fictitious. The case concerned a retail butcher in Louvain, Belgium, who was facing prosecution for having violated certain price regulations. In addition to imprisonment of a period

---

[73] See, for instance, ECtHR (GC), *Konstantin Markin v Federation of Russia* (App No 30078/06), judgment of 22 March 2012, para 150 (applying the doctrine of *DH v Czech Republic* to the situation of a man serving in the army and denied the parental leave that he would have been granted had he been a servicewoman: citing *DH*, the Court rejected the government's argument that by signing a military contract, the applicant had waived his right not to be discriminated against on grounds of sex).

[74] See *Palomo Sanchez and others v Spain* (n 12). Freedom of expression provides a typical example. The Court considers that, in principle, employees owe their employer a duty of loyalty and discretion, which implies in particular that their freedom of expression may be interpreted more narrowly than if they were simply members of the general public: see, for instance, *Vogt v Germany* (n 67) para 53; ECtHR (1st sect), *De Diego Nafría v Spain* (App No 46833/99), judgment of 14 March 2002, para 37; ECtHR (GC), *Guja v Moldova* (App No 14277/04), judgment of 12 February 2008, para 70 ('Article 10 applies also to the workplace, and ... civil servants ... enjoy the right to freedom of expression. At the same time, the Court is mindful that employees owe to their employer a duty of loyalty, reserve and discretion. This is particularly so in the case of civil servants since the very nature of civil service requires that a civil servant is bound by a duty of loyalty and discretion'); ECtHR (5th sect), *Marchenko v Ukraine* (App No 4063/04), judgment of 19 February 2009, para 45 (referring to the 'duty of loyalty, reserve and discretion' owed to the employer).

from one month to five years and a fine of 3,000–30,000,000 BF (a significant sum at the time), Deweer was liable to various criminal and administrative sanctions, including the closure of the offender's business. However, the prosecuting authorities suggested that he pay a sum of 10,000 BF by way of friendly settlement, which would also allow him to avoid having his business provisionally closed, pending the outcome of proceedings before a criminal court. As one might expect, Deweer paid the transactory fee and he thus escaped prosecution. But he then filed an application against Belgium, alleging that he had been coerced into waiving his right to have his case decided by an independent tribunal. The Court agreed. It rejected the argument that the compromise proposed to Deweer was particularly favourable to him. Indeed, said the Court, it precisely therein—in the '"flagrant disproportion" between the two alternatives facing the applicant'—that the problem lies: 'The "relative moderation" of the sum demanded ... *added to the pressure* brought to bear by the closure order. The moderation rendered the pressure *so compelling* that it is not surprising that Mr. Deweer yielded'.[75]

The *Deweer* judgment, approvingly quoted by the Court in the 2007 case of *DH v Czech Republic*, stands as a reminder that coercion may take two forms: it may consist in the threat of sanctions imposed on those who refuse to comply, but it may also consist in the promise of certain advantages to those who will yield. The prohibition of coercion thus appears as a bulwark against the subjection of rights to market relationships. Once a particular human right may be bartered away, or exchanged against a monetary reward, it becomes a mere commodity: those with the highest bargaining power will be in a position to obtain from others that they sacrifice their rights, and those who have less will be highly vulnerable to pressure.[76] It is precisely the same reasoning which led the Court, in the 2002 case of *Wilson and others* referred to above, to conclude that the UK had been acting in violation of the ECHR by allowing a private employer to offer financial rewards to the employees who would conclude individual contracts of employment rather than be represented by the unions. What the Court says, in substance, is that a wider range of opportunities—the choice whether or not to trade the right against another advantage, that the right-holder values more highly—does not necessarily result in more freedom in the substantive sense. It may instead be a source of vulnerability and allow forms of pressure to be exercised that otherwise would not be allowable.[77]

By assimilating the promise of financial rewards to coercion, the Court also draws the attention to the fact that, in having to choose whether or not to accept the offer, the individual is *alone*—and that, should he reject the offer, others might in turn accept it, thereby increasing the costs to the individual of his choice. The last condition identified by the Court in *DH v Czech Republic* among the conditions that might make waiver acceptable relates to precisely that issue. The Court

---

[75] ECtHR, *Deweer v Belgium*, judgment of 27 February 1980, para 52 (emphasis added).
[76] On this, see in greater detail Olivier De Schutter, 'Waiver of Rights and State Paternalism under the European Convention on Human Rights' (2000) 51(3) *Northern Ireland Legal Quarterly* 481–508.
[77] Robert Lee Hale was one of the most insightful writers on this apparent paradox. See generally Robert L Hale, 'Coercion and Distribution in a Supposedly Non-coercive State' (1923) 38 *Political Science Quarterly* 470. For an excellent comment from an institutionalist economist's perspective, see Warren J Samuels, 'The Economy as a System of Power and its Legal Bases: The Legal Economics of Robert Lee Hale' (1973) 27 *University of Miami Law Review* 261.

stated there that, even if the Roma parents had consented to their children being placed in special schools meant for children with learning disabilities, this could not be construed as a choice in favour of segregated education. This was because the choice of an integrated system was not really open to these parents; indeed, since each Roma family had to make that choice *alone, without knowing what the others might choose*, their 'choice' may have been motivated primarily by a desire not to place their children in a hostile environment in which they would feel isolated and ostracised.[78] This situation may be described as a simple prisoner's dilemma, in which the solution that appears optimal from the *individual*'s point of view (to remain in the 'special school' in order not to have to fear plunging the child into the hostile environment of the regular school) does not correspond to what would be considered optimal from the point of view of all individuals in the same situation if they were able to act *jointly* through collective action:

| | | Choice for parents of B | |
		Send child B to the regular school	Send child B to the 'special' (predominantly Roma) school
Choice for parents of A	Send child A to the regular school	A:3, B:3 collectively optimal	A:-3, B:0 A is plunged into a hostile environment in the regular school as other Roma children remain in the 'special' school
	Send child A to the 'special' (predominantly Roma) school	A:0, B:-3 B is plunged into a hostile environment in the regular school as other Roma children remain in the 'special' school	A:0, B:0 individually optimal

It hardly deserves emphasis that it is such a collective action problem that workers face when asked on an individual basis to consent certain sacrifices against the promise of financial or other rewards. While such rewards, if obtained by unions representing workers, might be welcome and perhaps worth the sacrifices involved, where the same is proposed to individual workers acting in isolation, acceptance may reflect a fear that others might accept (so that the worker rejecting a proposal will end up in a worse situation) more than a genuine agreement to the terms

---

[78] In the words of the Court: 'the Roma parents were faced with a dilemma: a choice between ordinary schools that were ill-equipped to cater for their children's social and cultural differences and in which their children risked isolation and ostracism and special schools where the majority of the pupils were Roma' (*DH and others v Czech Republic* (n 71) para 203).

offered. Where the choices are interdependent, true consent requires the possibility of collective action.

In sum, while not irrelevant, the choice of the individual worker to waive her rights in order to obtain an employment or certain rewards from the employer is to be treated with caution. It is not a substitute for assessing whether the restriction to her rights complies with the conditions outlined above, including the condition of proportionality: only the restrictions that pursue a legitimate aim, are adequately regulated, and are necessary for the pursuance of the objectives of the organisation will in principle be acceptable. At most, the consent of the individual may lead the judge to be more lenient in applying the proportionality test.

And such caution is entirely justified. Of course, the kind of compulsion on the right-holder that a private actor may exercise in contractual relationships differs from that which the State may exercise. As noted by Heilbroner:

> [T]here is a qualitative difference between the power of an institution to wield the knout, to brand, mutilate, deport, chain, imprison, or execute those who defy its will, and the power of an institution to withdraw its support, no matter how life-giving that support may be. Even if we imagined that all capital was directed by a single capitalist, the sentence of starvation that could be passed by his refusal to sell his commodities or to buy labor power differs from the sentence of the king who casts his opponents into a dungeon to starve, because the capitalist has no legal right to forbid his victims from moving elsewhere, or from appealing to the state or other authorities against himself.[79]

But that difference between the police State and the capitalist monopolising economic power relates to the means through which compulsion may be exercised, or to its nature, rather than to the reality of compulsion itself. For in fact, private compulsion may exercise an equally powerful constraint on the free will of the individual right-holder. In situations where the right-holder is in a situation of need and where she faces few alternatives (or none at all, as in situations of monopoly or monopsony), in particular, the possibility for the private actor with whom the right-holder interacts to withhold certain goods or services (such as a waged employment) may in fact lead to a form of coercion equivalent to that at the disposal of the State.

Particularly since the rise of large-scale private organisations in the early twentieth century, it is understood that the liberty of the individual whether or not to submit to certain conditions which another actor seeks to impose on him is not always more present in inter-individual (or 'horizontal') relationships, particularly in market relationships, than in the ('vertical') relationships between the State and the individual. It is therefore fitting that human rights courts have generally considered with suspicion the argument that the State should be allowed not to intervene in private contractual relationships out of respect for the 'free will' embodied in such contracts. On the contrary, they have generally adopted the view that, while the consent of the individual may be *necessary* to justify certain restrictions on his rights, such a consent, as expressed in contractual clauses, should never be considered, as such, a *sufficient* justification. It is significant, for instance, that, in a number of cases concerning restrictions on the right to respect for the private life of

---

[79] Robert L Heilbroner, *The Nature and Logic of Capitalism* (New York, WW Norton & Co, 1985) 39–40.

employees, the ECtHR did not satisfy itself with the consideration that the employees concerned must be presumed to have consented to such restrictions as a condition for their employment, but instead examined whether the said restrictions were justified as 'necessary, in a democratic society' (as required under para 2 of Article 8 ECHR) to the achievement of the legitimate aims put forward—for instance, public safety on a vessel or on a nuclear plant,[80] or respect for the rights of the Church, the employer, under Articles 9 and 11 of the Convention.[81]

6 CONCLUSION

This chapter has sought to address how the rights of workers in the employment relationship are protected under the ECHR. Three conclusions emerge. First, although the ECtHR protects, to a certain extent, not only the right to form and join unions (as explicitly guaranteed in the Convention) but also the right to collective action and to collective bargaining, the exercise of such procedural rights is not seen as a substitute for the protection of the substantive rights of workers. In part, this can be explained by the fact that in its interpretation of Article 11 of the Convention, the Court adopts an intermediate position that accepts neither the monopolisation of the power to represent workers in the hands of unions (as would be the case under 'closed-shop' systems) nor the possibility for the employer to buy the loyalty of individual workers by promising financial rewards to those who choose not to be represented through a union. If the power of unions were even stronger, it might be seen as representing a sufficient safeguard against the risk of workers' rights being abused, and the Court may have felt that it was dispensated

---

[80] ECtHR (1st sect), decision of 7 November 2002, *Madsen v Denmark* (App No 58341/00) (inadmissibility); and ECtHR (4th sect), decision of 9 March 2004, *Wretlund v Sweden* (App No 46210/99) (inadmissibility).

[81] See ECtHR (5th sect), *Schüth v Germany*, judgment of 23 September 2010, paras 53–75. In this case, the Court concluded that the applicant's right to respect for private and family life had been violated after he was dismissed by the Catholic Church, which was employing him as a chief organicist in a non-ecclesiastical function. The Court noted in this regard that since the dismissal was based on elements that related to the private life (the separation of the application from his spouse and his cohabitation with another women from whom he was expecting a child), the German labour courts should have exercised a stricter degree of scrutiny, adequately balancing the rights of the Church as employer with those of the applicant. According to the Court, the duty of loyalty agreed to by the applicant upon signing his contract of employment could not be interpreted as depriving him from the protection of the Convention rights in this regard: 'La Cour admet que le requérant, en signant son contrat de travail, a accepté un devoir de loyauté envers l'Eglise catholique qui limitait jusqu'à un certain degré son droit au respect de sa vie privée. De telles limitations contractuelles sont autorisées par la Convention si elles sont librement acceptées. La Cour considère cependant que l'on ne saurait interpréter la signature apposée par le requérant sur ce contrat comme un engagement personnel sans équivoque de vivre dans l'abstinence en cas de séparation ou de divorce. Une telle interprétation affecterait le cœur même du droit au respect de la vie privée de l'intéressé, d'autant que, comme les juridictions du travail l'ont constaté, le requérant n'était pas soumis à des obligations de loyauté accrues' (para 71). It is noteworthy that this judgment was delivered by a Chamber of the Court established within the same section that, on the same day, delivered the *Obst* judgment referred to above (n 42), where the Court took the view, *a contrario*, that an employee of the Mormon Church, having confessed to adultery, could be dismissed, considering that the Mormon Church is a faith-based organisation. In neither of these cases was the consent of the individual, expressed by agreeing to the terms of employment, the decisive factor: even where such a consent is established, the courts are still under a duty to examine whether the restriction imposed on the rights of the individual comply with the substantive conditions imposed under the Convention.

from being diligent in ensuring that such abuses do not take place. But the Court, wisely, has not opted for that approach; the measures adopted by the employer are no more to be trusted because unions could in principle protest them than measures adopted through democratic procedures should be immune from scrutiny because the political opposition can make itself heard.

But if courts are to protect human rights in employment relationships, then how should they do so? A range of difficulties emerge from the fact that the rights and freedoms listed in the ECHR were designed, and drafted, in order to address State power and not the private power exercised by organisations on their employees. The guidance that the ECtHR may provide remains limited, in part because the geometry of the cases it is presented with presents strong differences in comparison to the kind of private law litigation that develops before domestic courts. The implication is not necessarily that human rights, as they appear stipulated in international treaties as obligations imposed on the State, cannot be relied upon by domestic courts in order to impose obligations on private parties. But in applying these rights to private relationships, courts may have to be inventive, and the criteria developed by international monitoring bodies may not always provide them with well-suited answers. There are also other options available to States than the direct application of internationally recognised human rights to inter-individual relationships. Domestic courts may interpret notions of domestic law (such as the notions of 'fault' or 'negligence' in civil liability cases, or 'good faith' or 'abuse of rights' in employment relationships) in order to ensure that these notions embody the requirements of international human rights.[82]

Finally, there is the question of waiver. The single most important difference between the power yielded by the State in its regulatory capacity and the power exercised by the employer (including the State as employer) on its employee is that the employer may only exercise such power because of the consent of the individual towards whom it is addressed. This factor alone, however, is not to be treated as decisive. The ECtHR adopts a realistic view about the respective bargaining position of parties in the employment relationship and, more importantly, it refuses to treat all human rights as following the model of the right to property. Even where the individual values a particular advantage, for instance, a higher wage, more than the ability to exercise the right which he agrees to sacrifice, this will not end the inquiry. Rights are not mere commodities, nor are they just bargaining chips in a negotiation that the individual right-holder may choose to barter away—the fact that they are enjoyed and protected matters not to that individual alone, but to all society. It is here, in the recognition of the status of human rights as public goods, the preservation of which matters to all, that the ECtHR provides us with its most important lesson: where the rights of one individual can be taken away by an unscrupulous employer abusing his position, it is the rights of all that are under threat of being revoked.

---

[82] This is a technique sometimes referred to as '*mittelbare Drittwirkung*': see, eg, Barak (n 64) 21–24; S Gardbaum, 'The "Horizontal Effect" of Constitutional Rights' (2003) 102 *Michigan Law Review* 401 ff). The 1958 *Lüth* decision of the German Federal Constitutional Court provides the classic illustration: in this case, the Constitutional Court took into account the freedom of expression of Lüth in order to find that the boycott he had initiated against a film produced by a former collaborator with the Nazis should not be treated as the kind of intentionally caused damage that may give rise to an obligation to compensate, under s 826 of the German Civil Code (BGB) (7 BverfGE (1958)).

Analysis of the ECHR

6

The Prohibition of Slavery, Servitude and Forced and Compulsory Labour under Article 4 ECHR

VIRGINIA MANTOUVALOU

1 INTRODUCTION

HAVING BEEN ADOPTED as a bulwark to totalitarian regimes, the European Convention on Human Rights (hereinafter the ECHR or the Convention) was drafted to address a set of circumstances very different from today's world. Article 4 of the ECHR, which prohibits slavery, servitude, forced and compulsory labour, is paradigmatic of this. Even though a few years ago it seemed like an obsolete provision, case law in recent years has shown that it is relevant to today's world and is an essential guarantee against labour exploitation. The prohibition contains a very important moral norm that can capture the gravest abuses of labour rights in present-day Europe. What is the threshold for the provision to be applicable? And are there any exceptions to the prohibition that at first glance appears to be absolute?

This chapter presents and discusses the principles that emerge from key case law of the European Court of Human Rights (hereinafter the ECtHR or the Court). First, the piece examines jurisprudence involving the absolute prohibition of slavery and servitude. It finds that the Court is open to an interpretation of the ECHR, which addresses grave violations of labour rights in today's world. Second, the chapter turns to the prohibition of forced and compulsory labour. It explores the definition of these terms by the Court, before turning to the existing exceptions to the prohibition of Article 4 and the interpretive difficulties that these create. This part of the piece suggests that the Court often relies on these permissible exceptions to reach decisions that are not always justified. The final part of the chapter turns to the interplay of the ECHR with other international law materials, such as those of the International Labour Organization (ILO), and the background debate of labour rights as human rights that has attracted much interest in recent years.[1] It

---

[1] See, for instance, T Novitz and Collin Fenwick (eds), *Human Rights at Work: Perspectives on Law and Regulation* (Oxford, Hart Publishing, 2010); VA Leary, 'The Paradox of Workers' Rights as Human Rights' in *Human Rights, Labor Rights and International Trade* (Pittsburg, University of Pennsylvania Press, 2003) 22; P Alston (ed), *Labour Rights as Human Rights* (Oxford, Oxford University Press, 2005);

draws some conclusions in light of Article 4 of the ECHR case law. What emerges from this chapter is that a traditional civil and political rights instrument, like the Convention, has the potential to protect some fundamental labour rights, which are recognised as basic human rights, and to empower individuals who are faced with labour exploitation.

2 THE STRUCTURE OF ARTICLE 4

Article 4 of the Convention prohibits slavery, servitude and forced and compulsory labour. Its first two paragraphs provide as follows:

1. No one shall be held in slavery or servitude.
2. No one shall be required to perform forced or compulsory labour.

The prohibition of these paragraphs of the provision appears to be absolute. This is similar to Article 3 ECHR, which prohibits torture, inhuman and degrading treatment. An absolute provision reflects a value of fundamental importance that does not permit limitations. This is unlike other provisions such as the right to private life in Article 8, which permits limitations for the protection of collective goods, like national security, health or morals, insofar as the restrictions of the right are proportionate to the legitimate aims pursued. In the case of Article 4, even if the government pursues a legitimate aim, like economic efficiency goals or some other public interest, there can be no limitation to the ban. The prohibition of slavery and servitude in particular is also a non-derogable obligation under Article 15 of the Convention. States cannot opt out from it in times of war or other public emergency that threatens the life of the nation.

The third paragraph of Article 4, though, shows that when it comes to the prohibition of forced and compulsory labour, the prohibition is not as clear-cut. The provision contains exceptions:

3. For the purpose of this article the term forced or compulsory labour shall not include:
   (a) any work required to be done in the ordinary course of detention imposed according to the provisions of Article 5 of this Convention or during conditional release from such detention;
   (b) any service of a military character or, in case of conscientious objectors in countries where they are recognized, service exacted instead of compulsory military service;
   (c) any service exacted in case of an emergency or calamity threatening the life or well-being of the community;
   (d) any work or service which forms part of normal civic obligations.

The interpretation of the provision has given rise to three types of questions. First, the Court has had to define slavery and servitude so as to examine whether they

---

H Collins, 'Theories of Rights as Justifications for Labour Law' in G Davidov and B Langille (eds), *The Idea of Labour Law* (Oxford, Oxford University Press, 2011) 137; V Mantouvalou, 'Are Labour Rights Human Rights?', (2012) 2 *European Labour Law Journal* 151; V Mantouvalou, 'Human Rights for Precarious Workers: The Legislative Precariousness of Domestic Labor' (2012) 34 *Comparative Labor Law and Policy Journal* 133.

are relevant in contemporary Europe. Second, it has had to distinguish forced and compulsory labour from slavery and servitude so as to assess whether restrictions are permitted. Third, it has had to explore the scope of the permitted exceptions. These tasks have generated controversy both within judicial decision making and in academic literature.

3 SLAVERY AND SERVITUDE

Looking at the concept of 'slavery', the Court has ruled that it ought to be interpreted narrowly, according to the 1927 United Nations Slavery Convention, which provides that 'slavery is the status or condition of a person over whom any or all of the powers attaching to the right of ownership are exercised'.[2] Only if a person is owned by another, being treated as an object that can be bought and sold, is the prohibition of slavery of Article 4 applicable.

The concept of 'servitude', on the other hand, is somewhat more general and broad. When examining servitude, the Court has stated that it prohibits a 'particularly serious form of denial of freedom'.[3] It includes an obligation to provide certain services for someone, an obligation to live in another person's property and the impossibility of changing this condition.[4] Servitude requires a person to provide services with the threat of coercion. Are there instances of slavery and servitude in the 47 Member States of the Council of Europe?

3.1 Domestic Work as Servitude, Forced and Compulsory Labour

For a few decades, it appeared that the prohibition of slavery and servitude had no contemporary relevance in Europe. It was not until 2005 that the Court ruled for the first time in its history that there was a breach of Article 4 of the Convention. The case in question was *Siliadin v France*,[5] which involved the living and working conditions of a migrant domestic worker. Its facts illustrate the gravity of the social problem. The applicant was a Togolese national who was brought to France to work and be educated, but was instead kept at home as a domestic worker. She had to clean the house and the employer's office, as well as look after three children; she slept on the floor in their room; she rarely had a day off; and she was almost never paid. When she escaped from her employers, she was faced with the fact that French law did not criminalise the employers' conduct.

The Court explained that Siliadin's situation is not 'slavery', because the employer did not exercise a right of legal ownership over the worker. Slavery and legal ownership go hand in hand, according to this judgment. Yet the ECtHR classified

---

[2] *Siliadin v France*, App No 73316/01, Judgment of 26 July 2005, para 122.

[3] *Van Droogenbroeck v Belgium*, Commission's report of 9 July 1980, Series B, No 44, p 30, paras 78–80.

[4] *Van Droogenbroeck v Belgium*, App No 7906/77, Commission decision of 5 July 1979, DR 17, p 59.

[5] *Siliadin* (n 2). For analysis, see V Mantouvalou, 'Servitude and Forced Labour in the 21st Century: The Human Rights of Domestic Workers' (2006) 35 *Industrial Law Journal* 395.

it as 'servitude', which is still within the scope of Article 4. On servitude, it said that 'what is prohibited is a "particularly serious form of denial of freedom" ... It includes, "in addition to the obligation to perform certain services for others ... the obligation for the 'serf' to live on another person's property and the impossibility of altering his condition"'.[6] Being a minor at the time, Siliadin had to work almost 15 hours a day, seven days per week. She had not chosen to work for her employers, had no resources, was isolated, had no money to move elsewhere and 'was entirely at [the employers'] mercy, since her papers had been confiscated and she had been promised that her immigration status would be regularised, which had never occurred'.[7] The restriction of her freedom was such that the Court was prepared to classify it as servitude.

Importantly, *Siliadin* also established that Article 4 is not only applicable to situations that state authorities keep individuals in conditions of slavery, servitude and forced labour. As the employment relation is most of the time a private relation, it is not primarily regulated by human rights law, unless the latter has horizontal application. The Court has a long-established jurisprudence on positive obligations[8] and *Siliadin* showed that, like other provisions, Article 4 does not only involve vertical relationships; it is relevant to private relations and imposes a duty on the authorities to criminalise non-state conduct that falls short of human rights standards.[9] Given that most instances of forced labour occur in the private economy,[10] the decision of the Court to extend human rights principles in the private sphere is crucial.

The *Siliadin* judgment recognised that a most vulnerable worker—a minor, migrant or live-in domestic worker—must be protected against grave abuse.[11] It is therefore of great importance for this reason. However, the decision is significant not only for giving a voice to the individual domestic worker whose labour rights were breached. It is also important because it attracted attention and raised awareness of the vulnerability of domestic workers more generally, beyond this individual case, and the need for special regulation that has become an issue of concern in numerous national and supranational fora.[12] To give a few examples of the judgment's impact, in a line of developments, it was heavily relied upon in non-governmental organisation (NGO)

---

[6] *Siliadin* (n 2) para 123.

[7] Ibid, para 126.

[8] See A Mowbray, *The Development of Positive Obligations under the European Convention on Human Rights by the European Court of Human Rights* (Oxford, Hart Publishing, 2004).

[9] See H Cullen, '*Siliadin v France*: Positive Obligations under Article 4 of the European Convention on Human Rights' (2006) 6 *Human Rights Law Review* 585.

[10] See ILO, 'The Cost of Coercion', International Labour Conference, 98th Session 2009, Report I(B).

[11] For further analysis of the vulnerability of domestic workers, see B Anderson, *Doing the Dirty Work? The Global Politics of Domestic Labour* (London, Zed Books, 2000); V Mantouvalou, 'Human Rights for Precarious Workers: The Legislative Precariousness of Domestic Labour' (2012) 34 *Comparative Labor Law and Policy Journal* 101.

[12] For discussion of the case in documents of international organisations, see *Forced Labour and Human Trafficking: Casebook of Court Decisions* (Geneva, International Labour Organization, 2009). See also MF Perrez Solla, 'Slavery and Human Trafficking: International Law and the Role of the World Bank', Social Protection and Labour Paper No 0904 of 2009, p 52. For discussion of the judgment by NGOs, see Human Rights Watch Report, 'As If I Am Not Human', 7 July 2008, Chapter V. For references to the case in parliamentary documents and debates, see UK HL Debs, 5 November 2009, col 400. See also the 2008 Report of the Victorian Equal Opportunity and Human Rights Commission in Australia, entitled 'The Victorian Charter of Human Rights and Responsibilities', p 8.

submissions and parliamentary debates, leading to the enactment of legislation in the UK criminalising 'modern slavery';[13] it was referred to as 'groundbreaking' and 'landmark' in the ILO Report that was drafted before the adoption of ILO Convention No 189 on Domestic Workers;[14] and it was discussed in a Report of the EU Fundamental Rights Agency, which opened up by referring to *Siliadin* as a case that 'highlighted the extent to which a person in an irregular situation can be deprived of her most fundamental rights'.[15]

3.2 Sex Trafficking as Slavery, Servitude, Forced and Compulsory Labour

The definition of slavery and servitude under Article 4 was revisited in another landmark case involving cross-border human trafficking for sexual exploitation. The problem of human trafficking both in Europe and worldwide has been the subject of analysis in recent years, and the law in the area is evolving.[16] Even though not explicitly prohibited by Article 4, the Grand Chamber judgment had to address it in *Rantsev v Cyprus and Russia*.[17] This case involved a young woman from Russia who was trafficked to Cyprus under an 'artiste visa' regime. An 'artiste' was defined in the legislation as 'any alien who wishes to enter Cyprus in order to work in a cabaret, musical-dancing place or other night entertainment place and has attained the age of 18 years'.[18] Under this scheme, Ms Rantseva received a temporary work and residence permit. Having worked at a cabaret for three days, she escaped, only to be captured soon after and taken to the police. Since her immigration status was not irregular, the police returned her to her employer, who took her to the flat of another male employee. Later that night she was found dead on the street below the flat. The case was taken to the ECtHR by the victim's father, who claimed that Russia and Cyprus had breached Article 4 of the Convention (among other provisions).

The Court examined whether human trafficking for sexual exploitation is another area covered by Article 4 of the Convention. On this issue, it ruled that 'trafficking in human beings, by its very nature and aim of exploitation, is based on the exercise of powers attaching to the right of ownership. It treats human beings as commodities to be bought and sold and put to forced labour, often for little or no payment, usually in the sex industry but also elsewhere ... It implies close surveillance of

---

[13] Section 71 of the Coroners and Justice Act 2009, noted in V Mantouvalou, 'Modern Slavery: The UK Response', (2010) 39 *Industrial Law Journal* 431.

[14] ILO Report IV(1), 'Decent Work for Domestic Workers', pp 7 and 66. For an analysis of the Convention, see E Albin and V Mantouvalou, 'The ILO Convention on Domestic Workers: From the Shadows to the Light' (2012) 41 *Industrial Law Journal* 67.

[15] Report of the European Union Fundamental Rights Agency, 'Migrants in an Irregular Situation Employed in Domestic Work: Fundamental Rights Challenges for the European Union and its Member States', Publications Office of the European Union, 2011, p 3.

[16] See, for instance, H Askola, *Legal Responses to Trafficking in Women for Sexual Exploitation in the European Union* (Oxford, Hart Publishing, 2007); AT Gallagher, *The International Law of Human Trafficking* (Cambridge, Cambridge University Press, 2010); S Scarpa, *Trafficking in Human Beings—Modern Slavery* (Oxford, Oxford University Press, 2008).

[17] *Rantsev v Cyprus and Russia*, App No 25965/04, Judgment of 7 January 2010.

[18] Ibid, para 113.

the activities of victims, whose movements are often circumscribed ... It involves the use of violence and threats against victims, who live and work under poor conditions'.[19]

Without distinguishing between the four concepts of Article 4, the Court was prepared to rule that trafficking falls within its ambit for the reason that it is incompatible with human dignity and other underlying values of the Convention. Interpreting the ECHR as a living instrument,[20] the ECtHR was satisfied that the ban on labour exploitation, which supports Article 4, covers human trafficking too, even though such behaviour was probably not a priority at the time of the drafting of the Convention.

In terms of general principles on positive obligations, *Rantsev* took these a step further than *Siliadin*. The Court in the *Rantsev* judgment found that these include, first, an obligation to legislate to protect individuals from abusive conduct; second, a duty to take positive operational measures in order to protect victims or potential victims when the authorities were aware or ought to have been aware of circumstances of actual trafficking, or of a risk of trafficking; third, a duty to investigate situations of potential trafficking, which should not depend on a formal complaint being lodged; and, fourth, because trafficking is a cross-border crime, a duty to cooperate with authorities of states of origin, transit and destination, which may be involved, in the investigation of acts that took place in their territories.[21]

Even though Cypriot law had satisfactory anti-trafficking provisions, the immigration policy framework was found to be in breach of Article 4. Of particular concern was the fact that cabaret managers made an application for an entry permit for the artiste in a way that rendered the migrant dependent on her employer or agent. This artiste visa scheme made individuals vulnerable to traffickers, as both the Council of Europe Human Rights Commissioner and the Cypriot Ombudsman had previously stressed.[22] In addition, the Court found that the obligation of the employers to inform the authorities if an artiste leaves her employment is a legitimate means to the end of monitoring compliance with immigration law. However, it is only the authorities that should take steps for non-compliance. Monitoring compliance cannot be the duty of the manager. This is why the Court was particularly troubled by the practice of asking cabaret owners and managers to lodge a bank guarantee to be used to cover artistes that they employed. A visa regime, then, which is very restrictive and creates strong ties between the worker and the employer, creating the opportunity to exercise control over her, may violate the Convention.

Similarly, the Court ruled that the authorities failed to take protective measures, even though they were aware for many years that women were being trafficked from abroad (mainly the former USSR) to Cyprus for the purpose of sexual exploitation. The failure to investigate Rantseva's situation when she was found at the police

---

[19] Ibid, para 281.
[20] Ibid, para 277. On the interpretation of the Convention as a living instrument, see G Letsas, 'The ECHR as a Living Instrument: Its Meaning and its Legitimacy', in G Ulfstein, A Follesdal and B Schlutter (eds), *The European Court of Human Rights in a National, European and Global Context* (Cambridge, Cambridge University Press, 2012).
[21] *Rantsev* (n 17) paras 283–289.
[22] Ibid, paras 89, 91, 94, 100.

station, even though the police had indications that she may have been a victim of trafficking, was also problematic. The fact that the police did not question her, did not investigate the issue or release her, and did not take any further measures to protect her was contrary to positive duties imposed by Article 4 ECHR. Finally, the Court ruled that Russia was also in breach of Article 4 of the Convention for the reason that its authorities did not investigate how Rantseva was recruited when she was there.

The *Rantsev* judgment brought human trafficking for sexual exploitation in the scope of the Convention and has therefore been applauded.[23] The problem of 'modern slavery' that has attracted much interest among international organisations, national governments and academic scholars was captured by the Convention, was explored and will no doubt continue to be explored by the Court in the context of Article 4 ECHR. The decision has also been criticised for not contributing to conceptual clarity in the interpretation of slavery and servitude, complicating the definition of the concepts and also narrowing down the definition of human trafficking.[24] The potential for problems that arose in the different definitions employed in *Rantsev* and *Siliadin* was emphasised in a recent criminal law case in the UK.[25] *R v SK* involved the trafficking of a domestic worker from Africa into the UK. The complainant had been convicted of the offence of trafficking for exploitation.[26] However, the Court of Appeal quashed the conviction and ordered a retrial. The reason for this was that the judge did not adequately elaborate on what form of exploitation was at stake in the instant case, having only said that exploitation for the present purposes means treating someone 'more like property than a person' and 'more like an object'. The limited analysis of the key concepts meant that the conviction could not stand.

Even though it is true that the precise definition of what constitutes a crime is crucial in law, the stance of the Court in *Rantsev*, which did not require the element of legal ownership as an essential component of slavery, is in line with the approach of the International Criminal Tribunal for the former Yugoslavia. The *Kunarac* decision explained that elements that can constitute slavery include the 'control of someone's movement, control of physical environment, psychological control, measures taken to prevent or deter escape, force, threat of force or coercion, duration, assertion of exclusivity, subjection to cruel treatment and abuse, control of sexuality and forced labour'[27] and concluded that it is impossible to have a comprehensive list of all elements of modern slavery.

At this point, it should also be said that leading work in sociology has suggested that it is a mistake to define slavery (even in its traditional form) by making reference to legal ownership.[28] Orlando Patterson claimed that other characteristics are

---

[23] See, for instance, S Farrior, 'Human Trafficking Violates Anti-Slavery Provision: Introductory Note to *Rantsev v Cyprus and Russia*' (2010) 49 *International Legal Materials* 415.

[24] J Allain, 'The European Court of Human Rights and Trafficking as Slavery' (2010) 10 *Human Rights Law Review* 546.

[25] *R v SK*, Court of Appeal (Criminal Division) [2011] England and Wales Court of Appeal (Criminal Division) 1691.

[26] Sections 4(1) and 5 of the Asylum and Immigration (Treatment of Claimants) Act 2004.

[27] ICTY, *Prosecutor v Kunarac, Vukovic and Kovac*, 12 June 2002, para 119.

[28] O Patterson, *Slavery and Social Death* (Cambridge, MA, Harvard University Press, 1982) 21 ff.

key, such as the victim's natal alienation and dishonour.[29] On this analysis, legal ownership is not a sufficient element for the definition of slavery because it does not go to the heart of what is problematic about it. This point becomes evident when thinking about an instance where people are owned today, in the sense that they can be bought and sold as objects. This is the case for professional athletes. Patterson explained that it is absurd to call them 'slaves' because there are other key features of slavery, which are more fundamental than ownership rights and which are missing in their case.[30] Key features of slavery, which do not characterize the position of athletes, are the power of the parties in the relationship, the origins of the power and the alienation that slaves suffer.

In legal scholarship, on the other hand, James Penner has argued that the inclusion of 'ownership' in the 1926 Slavery Convention to which the ECtHR has repeatedly referred is not necessarily problematic for the definition of slavery today. Building on Patterson's idea of social death as a key element of slavery, Penner claimed that in examples of modern slavery, like the situation in *Siliadin*, we have in fact a relationship that falls within the scope of the Convention definition to which the ECtHR made reference.[31] This is because in situations like these, we are faced with immediate, exclusive, corporeal possession and de facto slavery: the transfer of the worker from one person to another and the acceptance of her as a gift constitute exercise of powers attaching to ownership. This reality, coupled with the person's social isolation, lead to the conclusion that modern forms of slavery can satisfy the criterion of ownership—not de jure but de facto. In this way, Penner suggests that the definition found in the 1926 Convention, which was accepted by the ECtHR in *Siliadin*, can capture instances of modern slavery. To this analysis, it can fairly be added that legislation does have a role to play in the situation of exploitation faced by migrant workers, so we might be able to talk about de jure slavery too. This is not due to the exercise of a right of legal ownership, which the 1926 Convention requires, but due to immigration legislation, which may gravely restrict the worker's freedom by offering the employer a power to control the worker.[32]

To conclude, the prohibition of slavery and servitude is far from obsolete in present-day Europe. On the contrary, the Convention provision is interpreted in a manner that captures instances of 'modern slavery' that are conceptualised more like a problem of objectification and commodification of the person, which is due not only to a legal right of property but also to restrictive immigration rules that generate a significant power to control the worker. In such instances, the Court has decided that the state authorities have a wide range of positive obligations to legislate and take positive operational measures to enforce the law in order to comply with Article 4 of the ECHR.

---

[29] Ibid, 1–14.

[30] Ibid, 24–25.

[31] J Penner, 'The Concept of Property and the Concept of Slavery' in J Allain (ed), *The Legal Understanding of Slavery: From the Historical to the Contemporary* (Oxford, Oxford University Press, 2012). For further analysis of the definition of slavery, see the contributions in the special issue on 'Slavery Today' (2012) 14 *Global Dialogue*.

[32] On the effects of immigration legislation in the creation of precarious work, see B Anderson, 'Migration, Immigration Controls and the Fashioning of Precarious Workers' (2010) 24 *Work, Employment and Society* 300.

4 FORCED AND COMPULSORY LABOUR: SCOPE AND EXCEPTIONS

How does forced and compulsory labour differ from slavery and servitude? First, with respect to their definition, which this section examines; and, second, because the Convention permits certain exceptions in their prohibition, which the section that follows addresses. In one of the old cases under Article 4, *Van der Mussele v Belgium*,[33] the applicant complained that the obligation of pupil advocates to represent clients without pay during the period of their pupillage was forced and compulsory labour. The Court noted that the wording of Article 4 of the Convention has striking similarities to the ILO Convention No 29 and interpreted 'forced and compulsory labour' to encompass 'all work or service which is exacted from any person and under the menace of any penalty and for which the said person has not offered himself voluntarily'.[34] There are two key elements, in other words: first, the fear of a penalty; and, second, the contrary will of the person. The situation of Siliadin, for instance, who was living and working with the fear of deportation (menace of penalty), and performed the job against her will (as she was offered no other option), was ruled to be forced and compulsory labour.[35]

Yet in all other cases where the Court had to examine the compatibility of state conduct with Article 4(2), the claims were rejected. The ECtHR consistently ruled that the relevant state conduct fell within the scope of one of the exceptions of Article 4(3), 'which is not intended to "limit" the exercise of the right guaranteed by paragraph 2, but to "delimit" the very content of that right, for it forms a whole with paragraph 2 and indicates what "the term 'forced and compulsory labour' shall not include" ... This being so, paragraph 3 serves as an aid to the interpretation of paragraph 2'.[36]

4.1 Civic Duties and Military Service

In examining the scope of the exceptions in Article 4, the Court has found that they are governed by the following principles: 'notwithstanding their diversity, [they] are grounded on the governing ideas of the general interest, social solidarity and what is in the normal or ordinary course of affairs'.[37] In *Van der Mussele*, for instance, the Court pointed out that the applicant gained advantages from his work, such as the experience that he gained for a job that he freely chose, with the knowledge, at the time that he accepted it, that he would be under an obligation to work pro bono. It is interesting to note that the Court applied a test of proportionality,[38] stating that the means employed were not disproportionate to the legitimate aim pursued (that of social solidarity). It ruled that Van der Mussele's obligation was not in breach of Article 4 of the Convention. Such a test of proportionality is made possible when it comes to the obligation of Article 4(2) precisely because of the exceptions. The

---

[33] *Van der Mussele v Belgium*, App No 1989/80, Judgment of 23 November 1983.
[34] Ibid, para 32.
[35] *Siliadin* (n 2) paras 118–20.
[36] *Karlheinz Schmidt v Germany*, App No 13580/88, Judgment of 18 July 1994, para 22.
[37] *Van der Mussele* (n 33) para 38.
[38] Ibid, para 39.

prohibition of slavery and servitude, in contrast, is absolute and would not have permitted a test of proportionality.

The Court has applied the same principle in a line of cases looking at the duty imposed on dentists to work for up to two years for a public dental service,[39] the requirement imposed on barristers to represent poor clients under the threat of punishment and without adequate compensation,[40] the obligation to seek and take a suitable job as a pre-requisite to unemployment benefits,[41] the obligation for compulsory jury service[42] or the costs incurred by an enforcement judicial officer in the process of enforcing a court decision.[43] All these have been ruled by the ECtHR to be part of a person's normal civic duties, compatible with Article 4 ECHR. Similarly, military service has been found to be in accordance with Article 4.[44] The applicants in *W, X, Y and Z v UK* enlisted in the navy voluntarily for nine years when they were 15 and 16 years old. Their requests to be discharged early from the military for personal reasons that each one of them had were rejected. The Commission ruled that their treatment was not contrary to Article 4, as it was covered by the exception of the third paragraph of the provision.

This aspect of Article 4 of the Convention has become topical again in recent years, at times of high levels of unemployment, when governments adopt welfare to work schemes, also known as activation policies.[45] According to these policies, welfare benefits, such as unemployment benefits, are made conditional upon undertaking unpaid work. To give an example from a national jurisdiction, the UK High Court of Justice addressed this issue under Article 4 ECHR in a recent case[46] and found that it cannot be differentiated from *Van der Mussele*. The Court said that the categorisation of such schemes as slavery or forced labour is both far from the views of the drafters of the Convention who wished to ban colonial labour exploitation and from contemporary thinking.[47]

4.2 Prison Labour

Prison labour ought to be distinguished from the above discussion, because as the ILO said several decades ago, 'whenever human labour is performed in conditions of subordination, dangers arise; and with prison labour these conditions and the resulting dangers are pushed to the extreme'.[48] The case law of the ECtHR has not

---

[39] *Iverson v Norway*, App No 1468/62, Admissibility Decision of 17 December 1963, Yearbook, Vol VII, p 278.

[40] *X v Germany*, App No 4673/70, Admissibility Decision of 1 April 1974.

[41] *Talmon v Netherlands*, App No 30300/96, Admissibility Decision of 26 February 1997.

[42] *Zarb Adami v Malta*, App No 17209/02, Judgment of 20 June 2006.

[43] *Karol Mihal v Slovakia*, App No 23360/08, Admissibility Decision of 28 July 2011.

[44] *W, X, Y and Z v UK*, App Nos 3435–3438/67, Admissibility Decision of 19 July 1968.

[45] On this issue, see A Paz Fuchs, *Welfare to Work—Conditional Rights in Social Policy* (Oxford, Oxford University Press, 2008).

[46] *Reilly and Wilson v Secretary of State for Work and Pensions* [2012] EWHC 2292 (Admin), 6 August 2012.

[47] Ibid, para 174.

[48] ILO, 'Prison Labour: I' (1932) 25 *International Labour Review* 311 at 312. For further analysis with a focus on privately run prisons, see C Fenwick, 'Private Use of Prisoners' Labor: Paradoxes of International Human Rights Law' (2005) 27 *Human Rights Quarterly* 249.

been sufficiently sensitive to this reality. Early on, the Court accepted that work that one has to perform while in prison and which aims at rehabilitation falls within the scope of Article 4(3)(a) and does not constitute a breach of the Convention.[49] In *Van Droogenbroeck*,[50] the applicant was a recidivist prisoner who had been convicted for theft. His release was conditional upon gathering a certain amount of savings and he complained that work that he had to do while in detention was in violation of Article 4. The Commission rejected the claim that this situation could be classified as servitude because the notion of servitude demands a serious form of denial of freedom and includes an obligation for the person to live in the property, as well as the inability to change this situation.[51] As to forced and compulsory labour, the Court was satisfied without much hesitation that the duty imposed on the applicant was covered by the exception in the provision. Work while in detention has a legitimate aim, on the view of the Court, namely the reintegration of the applicant into society, and did not reach beyond what was ordinary in other Member States of the Council of Europe.[52] Similarly, in another case, it was ruled that societal reintegration justified a duty to work for very low pay under the Belgian vagrancy legislation.[53]

The question of prison labour was explored afresh in the Grand Chamber judgment in *Stummer v Austria*.[54] This case examined the exclusion of the applicant from the Austrian pension system, despite the fact that he had worked in the prison kitchen and bakery for long periods of time during his 28-year period of imprisonment. Before the ECtHR, he argued that the fact that he was not affiliated to a pension system while he performed work in prison amounted to a breach of Article 4. The Court rejected the argument that this situation amounted to forced labour, mainly because there was insufficient consensus between Member States that prison labour has to be linked to an old-age pension system. The argument of the applicant that the ECHR should be interpreted as a 'living instrument', and that the Court should therefore be open to his claim even though it had in the past rejected a similar case,[55] was not upheld. No consensus was established on the affiliation of prisoners to an old-age pension system, so the applicant's situation was covered by the exception under Article 4(3)(a).

The *Stummer* judgment is an unfortunate development in the evolution of the case law under Article 4 and in the interpretation of the Convention more generally. The Court did not approach the Convention as a living instrument, but sought to establish majorities' consensus. This is contrary to the purpose of any human rights document, the role of which is to protect individuals and minorities

---

[49] *De Wilde, Ooms and Versyp v Belgium*, App Nos 2832/66, 2835/66, 2899/66, Judgment of 18 June 1971, para 90.
[50] *Van Droogenbroeck* (n 4) Admissibility Decision of 5 July 1979, 12.
[51] Ibid, 30. This principle was reiterated in *Siliadin*.
[52] *Van Droogenbroeck* (n 4) Judgment of 24 June 1982, paras 58–59.
[53] *De Wilde, Ooms and Versyp (Vagrancy Cases) v Belgium*, App Nos 2832/66, 2835/66, 2899/66, Judgment of 18 June 1971, paras 89–90.
[54] *Stummer v Austria*, App No 37452/02, Grand Chamber Judgment of 7 July 2011.
[55] See the *Twenty-one Detained Persons v Germany*, App Nos 3134/67, 3172/67, 3188–3206/67, Admissibility Decision of 6 April 1968.

from majoritarian preferences.[56] It is exactly the nature of the ECHR as a living instrument, and the role of the Court in the protection of individuals (particularly the most vulnerable), that has led to the adoption of landmark decisions like *Siliadin* and *Rantsev*. These decisions have constituted a driving force for legislative change and have led to increased awareness on sex trafficking and exploitation of domestic workers at a global level.

It should not come as a surprise that in a forceful and convincing dissenting opinion in *Stummer*, Judge Tulkens disagreed with the view of the majority on the question of forced labour, saying that today 'prisons have gradually opened up to fundamental rights'.[57] Judge Tulkens emphasised that in Austria prisoners have a duty to work under the menace of a penalty (that of solitary confinement), which falls within the meaning of forced and compulsory labour of ILO Convention No 29. 'Nowadays', she went on to stress, 'work without adequate social cover can no longer be regarded as normal work'[58] and is therefore in breach of Article 4 too, as it does not fall within the exemption of work performed in the ordinary course of detention (Article 4 (3)). Prison work without affiliation to an old-age pension scheme is not ordinary work, as Judge Tulkens argued, challenging the argument of the majority of the Court that was founded on consensus. The decision of the majority placed older prisoners at a particular disadvantage and left a very wide margin of appreciation to the States.

5 THE INTERPLAY BETWEEN LABOUR RIGHTS AND HUMAN RIGHTS

More generally, even though the case law of the ECtHR under Article 4 is limited, it contributes significantly to academic debates on labour rights as human rights, as the introduction of this chapter indicated. Labour law scholars have traditionally been sceptical about the impact of human rights on their field, because on a commonly held view, human rights law undermines the interests of labour.[59] As the ECHR is primarily a civil and political rights document, while labour rights are mainly classified as social rights, the danger would be that Convention rights would be irrelevant to the interests of workers.

However, in the case law of the Court that has been explored in this chapter, it can be observed that there is a constant interplay between the norms of human rights law that are included in the Convention and the norms of international labour law, which are mainly found in ILO Conventions and other international law documents of the United Nations and the Council of Europe. In the Article 4 decisions, from

---

[56] See G Letsas, *A Theory of Interpretation of the European Convention on Human Rights* (Oxford, Oxford University Press, 2007) ch 5.

[57] *Stummer* (n 54), Judge Tulkens, dissenting opinion, para 7.

[58] Ibid, para 8.

[59] See K Ewing, 'The Human Rights Act and Labour Law' (1998) 27 *Industrial Law Journal* 275; K Kolben, 'Labor Rights as Human Rights?' (2010) 50 *Virginia Journal of International Law* 449; Lord Wedderburn, 'Freedom of Association or Right to Organise? The Common Law and International Sources' in B Wedderburn (ed), *Employment Rights in Britain and Europe* (London, Lawrence & Wishart, 1991) 138; J Youngdahl, 'Solidarity First: Labor Rights Are Not the Same as Human Rights' (2009) 18 *New Labor Forum* 31.

early on in the case law described above, the Court noted the similarities between the ECHR and other materials, which it constantly used as a source of inspiration. In *Van der Mussele*, it relied on the ILO Convention No 29 (1930) on Forced Labour, stressing the similarities of its Article 2, paragraph 2 with Article 4(3) of the Convention, and made further reference to a General Survey of the Committee of Experts on the Application of Conventions and Recommendations.[60] In *Siliadin*, the 1930 ILO Convention was used to support the imposition of a state duty to suppress forced labour in private relationships,[61] and in *Stummer* both this Convention and other ILO materials on prison labour were referred to in the judgment and in the dissent of Judge Tulkens. In *Rantsev* too, the Court took note of international conventions on human trafficking, such as the Protocol to Prevent, Suppress and Punish Trafficking in Persons, especially Women and Children ('the Palermo Protocol'), supplementing the United Nations Convention against Transnational Organised Crime and the Council of Europe Convention on Action against Trafficking in Human Beings ('the Anti-Trafficking Convention') in support of its decision that the principles underlying Article 4 are similar to the prohibition of human trafficking.

This interplay between Convention norms and international labour law materials, which is not limited to Article 4 of the Convention, has come to be known as an 'integrated approach' to interpretation[62] because it integrates certain social and labour rights in a civil rights document. Exploring this trend and looking at the Convention system in particular, Judge Rozakis suggested that it is 'in constant dialogue with other legal systems':[63] namely, the European legal order, the international legal order and other national legal orders.[64] The ECtHR and its judges 'do not operate in the splendid isolation of an ivory tower built with materials originating solely from the ECHR's interpretative inventions or those of the States party to the Convention'. Materials of other bodies have gained weight in the case law and 'this is a good sign for the founders of a court of law protecting values which by their nature are inherently indivisible and global'.[65]

This adoption of an integrated approach to the interpretation of the ECHR has built the confidence of labour law scholars in human rights law.[66] In 2010, Ewing and Hendy, who are leading proponents of trade union rights and had been critical of human rights law in the past,[67] celebrated the *Demir and Baykara v Turkey*

---

[60] *Van der Mussele* (n 33) paras 33 ff.

[61] *Siliadin* (n 2) 85.

[62] V Mantouvalou, 'Work and Private Life: *Sidabras and Dziautas v Lithuania*' (2005) *European Law Review* 575.

[63] C Rozakis, 'The European Judge as a Comparatist' (2005) 80 *Tulane Law Review* 257 at 268.

[64] Ibid, 269–70.

[65] Ibid, 278–79.

[66] On the right to organise under Article 11 of the ECHR, see F Dorssemont, 'The Right to Form and to Join Trade Unions for the Protection of His Interests under Article 11 ECHR' (2010) 1 *European Labour Law Journal* 185; K Ewing, 'The Implications of *Wilson and Palmer*' (2003) 32 *Industrial Law Journal* 1; and K Ewing and J Hendy, 'The Dramatic Implications of *Demir and Baykara*' (2010) 39 *Industrial Law Journal* 2. On the right to private life and the right to work, see Mantouvalou (n 62).

[67] See, for example, K Ewing, 'The Unbalanced Constitution', in T Campbell, K Ewing and A Tomkins (eds), *Sceptical Essays on Human Rights* (Oxford, Oxford University Press, 2001) 103.

judgment,[68] which recognised a right to collective bargaining as a component of the right to form and join a trade union. They said that in this decision, 'human rights have established their superiority over economic irrationalism and "competitiveness" in the battle for the soul of labour law, and in which public law has triumphed over private law and public lawyers over private lawyers'.[69]

The positive effects of the interplay between the ECHR and other international labour law bodies are several. First, this interpretive technique gives indirect legal effect to international treaties, which would otherwise not be justiciable, in the context of individual petitions before the ECtHR. Second, it emphasises the nature of the ECHR as a 'living instrument', which must be interpreted in the light of present-day conditions. Neither the problems related to domestic labour nor the issue of human trafficking are raised in the text of the Convention itself. Yet, thanks to analysis of other international law materials, the scope of the Convention opens up to contemporary problems. Third, by using this interpretive method, the effectiveness of the relevant treaties is increased.[70] Fourth, by adopting an integrated approach to interpretation, the ECtHR develops its case law in line with other international bodies that are expert in the field, and gains legitimacy when dealing with issues that are controversial for social or political reasons. The interplay between human rights and labour rights norms, then, has much to offer to the discussions of labour rights as human rights, for it shows that the two bodies of norms are not antithetical by definition. They can lend support to each other in a way that is mutually beneficial.

It is interesting to note at this point that this integration does not only take place in one direction (labour rights materials used in the interpretation of civil rights). It occurs in the other direction too: in a manner similar to the Court, the European Committee of Social Rights (ECSR), which is the counterpart of the ECHR in the area of social and labour rights, takes note of materials of the ECHR in the interpretation of the European Social Charter (ESC). Significantly, for the present purposes, the *Siliadin* judgment was specifically mentioned by the ECSR, which stressed that the ban on forced labour under Article 2 of the ESC also covers domestic servitude.[71] The ECtHR's judgment was also mentioned in the Committee's Conclusions on the UK that examined the compatibility with the right to safe and healthy working conditions of the exclusion of domestic workers from health and safety inspections.[72] The importance of the *Siliadin* judgment was highlighted despite the fact that, in reality, someone like Siliadin, found in a condition of modern slavery, would be excluded from the protection of the ESC because of her migration status.[73] The interplay between the Convention and labour standards, then, shows that, instrumentally, labour rights can be protected as human rights in judicial decision

[68] *Demir and Baykara v Turkey*, App No 34503/97, Grand Chamber Judgment of 12 November 2008.

[69] Ewing and Hendy (n 66) 47–48.

[70] L Helfer and A-M Slaughter, 'Toward a Theory of Effective Supranational Adjudication' (1997–98) 107 *Yale Law Journal* 273 at 323.

[71] Conclusions, 2008, Vol I, p 314, France.

[72] Conclusions XIX-2, 2009, p 487, United Kingdom.

[73] See the Appendix of the ESC.

making. It is therefore a mistake to say that labour rights cannot be protected as human rights.

The interplay between labour rights and human rights in Article 4 of the Convention also shows that labour rights and human rights have much to share at a normative level.[74] A key characteristic of human rights as moral standards is that they are claims that prohibit grave moral wrongs,[75] but scholars have sometimes questioned the character of labour rights as rights that prohibit such wrongs.[76] The examples discussed in this chapter show that certain labour rights are as compelling as other human rights, such as torture, covered by an absolute ban. Article 4 of the Convention, in other words, which is interpreted in light of labour rights materials, exemplifies both how human rights law can be instrumentally valuable to labour lawyers and how the two bodies of principles have shared foundations at a theoretical, normative level.

6 CONCLUSION

Article 4 of the ECHR is a provision of fundamental importance in present-day Europe. The threshold for the provision to be applicable is set high by the ECtHR, which requires that a worker be treated as an object by the employer for the absolute prohibition of slavery and servitude to become applicable. Yet exactly because of the severity of the restrictions of freedom that migrant domestic workers and victims of sex trafficking suffer, the Court has not hesitated to rule that the provision applies to their situation. On forced and compulsory labour, and particularly when considering prison labour, the threshold is too high, as Judge Tulkens forcefully and convincingly argued in *Stummer*. The wide interpretation of the permissible exceptions to the prohibition of Article 4 may, at times, be justified when dealing with duties that all citizens have (such as jury duty). But not all exceptions are legitimate, as the example of prison labour discussed earlier on suggests. It is to be hoped that the Court will keep on exploring the potential of Article 4 by making reference to materials of social and labour rights bodies, and that it will continue to explore the shared underlying values of labour rights and human rights, instead of relying on authorities' consensus—a majoritarian ideal, which a human rights court should guard against.[77]

---

[74] For further analysis of the instrumental and the normative approach to the question of labour rights as human rights, see V Mantouvalou, 'Are Labour Rights Human Rights?' (n 1).

[75] J Tasioulas, 'On the Nature of Human Rights' in G Ernst and J-C Heilinger (eds), *The Philosophy of Human Rights* (Berlin, de Gruyter, 2011) at 22.

[76] See Collins (n 1) 140–44.

[77] See Letsas (n 56).

7

Labour Law Litigation and Fair Trial under Article 6 ECHR

SÉBASTIEN VAN DROOGHENBROECK*

1 INTRODUCTION

According to Article 6 of the European Convention on Human Rights (ECHR):

1. In the determination of his civil rights and obligations or of any criminal charge against him, everyone is entitled to a fair and public hearing within a reasonable time by an independent and impartial tribunal established by law. Judgment shall be pronounced publicly but the press and public may be excluded from all or part of the trial in the interests of morals, public order or national security in a democratic society, where the interests of juveniles or the protection of the private life of the parties so require, or to the extent strictly necessary in the opinion of the court in special circumstances where publicity would prejudice the interests of justice.
2. Everyone charged with a criminal offence shall be presumed innocent until proved guilty according to law.
3. Everyone charged with a criminal offence has the following minimum rights:
    (a) to be informed promptly, in a language which he understands and in detail, of the nature and cause of the accusation against him;
    (b) to have adequate time and facilities for the preparation of his defence;
    (c) to defend himself in person or through legal assistance of his own choosing or, if he has not sufficient means to pay for legal assistance, to be given it free when the interests of justice so require;
    (d) to examine or have examined witnesses against him and to obtain the attendance and examination of witnesses on his behalf under the same conditions as witnesses against him;
    (e) to have the free assistance of an interpreter if he cannot understand or speak the language used in court.

This chapter does not aim to provide a complete overview of the case law regarding the application of this provision to litigation arising within the context of labour relations. Such an enterprise would not only be disproportionate—Article 6 being the Convention guarantee creating by far the most litigation before the judges in Strasbourg—but it would also be of limited interest since most of these decisions involve the mechanical and not very original reproduction of rules or general principles of fair trial.

* The author is very grateful to Jérémie Van Meerbeeck for helping him to translate this chapter into English.

More modestly, we are going to try to identify in the extensive case law currently available on the theme of 'fair trial' in labour litigation the more or less explicit traces of the paradigm, which, according to the works of classic scholars, governs all of Strasbourg's output: the search for a balance between unity and diversity.[1]

The promotion of unity results in bringing, inter alia and through an extensive and evolutive interpretation, as many legal situations as possible under the Law of the European Convention and the control of its judges. Applied to the discussion at hand, this trend creates a phenomenon of increased 'conventionalisation' of labour law litigation (See section 2 below). Respect for diversity leads to an admission of the need to adapt standards and rules that are a priori common so that they can accommodate historical or cultural traditions within a specific subject matter, or do justice to the specific situation of parties in a determined legal relationship. This process leads to what could be called a *labourisation of the fair trial's standards* (See section 3 below).

2 THE 'CONVENTIONALISATION' OF LABOUR LAW LITIGATION

'Justice cannot stop at the prison gate.' This famous dictum from the *Campbell and Fell*[2] case represents, in the most explicit way possible, the expansionist policy which has always been adopted by the European Court of Human Rights when it has had to sketch in the boundaries of fair trial.

While some areas of litigation continue to escape from the ambit of Article 6, their perimeter and number tend to shrink. Moreover, their very existence is being increasingly challenged.[3]

This expansionist policy can be found in labour law litigation.[4] Not only does justice make its way past the prison gates, but it also goes beyond the doors of administrations (See section 2.1 below), Parliament (See section 2.2 below), international organisations (See section 2.3 below) and embassies, consulates or other foreign public institutions (See section 2.4 below).

---

[1] On this paradigm, see E Kastanas, *Unité et diversité. Notions autonomes et marges d'appréciation des États dans la jurisprudence de la Cour européenne des droits de l'Homme* (Brussels, Bruylant, 1996).

[2] *Campbell and Fell*, App No 7819/77; 7878/77, Judgment of 28 June 1984, Series A, vol 80, at para 69.

[3] See, in support of the application of Article 6 to all types of litigation, S Van Drooghenbroeck, 'Vingt-cinq ans après *Benthem*: sens et non-sens d'une applicabilité limitée de l'Article 6 de la Convention européenne des droits de l'Homme dans le contentieux de droit public', in *Liège, Strasbourg, Bruxelles: parcours des droits de l'Homme. Liber amicorum M. Melchior* (Anthemis, Louvain-La Neuve, 2010) 691 ff; W Verrijdt, 'Is er nog plaats voor politieke rechten in het toepassingsgebied van Art. 6, § 1er EVRM na het Arrest-Vilho Eskelinen?' in A Alen and J Van Nieuwenhove (eds), *Leuvense Staatsrechtelijke Standpunten* (Bruges, La Charte, 2008) 239 ff; P van Dijk, 'Het EHRM zet weer een stap, maar gaat het ver genoeg?', noot onder EHRM, 19 April 2007, Vilho Eskelinen, (2007) *NJCM-Bulletin*, at 697–706.

[4] It was long and uncontroversially admitted that the employment relationship between private employers and employees could generate 'disputes over civil rights and obligations' in the sense of Article 6. See *Obermeier v Austria*, App No 11761/85, Judgment of 28 June 1990, Series A, vol 179, at para 67.

2.1 Administrations

Early case law from Strasbourg dedicated to the issue[5] states that 'disputes relating to the recruitment, careers and termination of service of civil servants are as a general rule outside the scope of Article 6 § 1'.[6] Exceptions to this general inapplicability were admitted when the object of the litigation was 'purely economic'[7] or 'essentially economic',[8] in such a way that this litigation did not generally call into question 'the authorities' discretionary powers'.[9]

At the end of the last century, the European Court of Human Rights realised that the application of such principles led to erratic case law, which was unable to guarantee the required legal certainty. This realisation resulted in a spectacular overruling of the early jurisprudence with the *Pellegrin v France* judgment of 8 December 1999.[10] In this case, the Court opted for a 'functional criterion based on the nature of the employee's duties and responsibilities' and in doing so set new boundaries for the application of Article 6 to litigation (contractual or statutory) involving the civil service:

> The only disputes excluded from the scope of Article 6 § 1 of the Convention are those which are raised by public servants whose duties typify the specific activities of the public service in so far as the latter is acting as the depositary of public authority responsible for protecting the general interests of the State or other public authorities. The armed forces and the police provide a manifest example of such activities. In practice, the Court will ascertain, in each case, whether the applicant's post entails—in the light of the nature of the duties and responsibilities appertaining to it—direct or indirect participation in the exercise of powers conferred by public law and duties designed to safeguard the general interests of the State or of other public authorities. In so doing, the Court will have regard, for guidance, to the categories of activities and posts listed by the European Commission in its communication of 18 March 1988 and by the Court of Justice of the European Communities ...

> Accordingly, no disputes between administrative authorities and employees who occupy posts involving participation in the exercise of powers conferred by public law attract the application of Article 6 § 1 since the Court intends to establish a functional criterion ... Disputes concerning pensions all come within the ambit of Article 6 § 1 because on retirement employees break the special bond between themselves and the authorities; they, and a fortiori those entitled through them, then find themselves in a situation exactly comparable to that of employees under private law in that the special relationship of trust and loyalty binding them to the State has ceased to exist and the employee can no longer wield a portion of the State's sovereign power.[11]

---

[5] For a synthesis of the previous case law, see D Yernault, 'Procession d'Echernacht à Strasbourg? Le droit des fonctionnaires à un procès équitable et l'exercice de la puissance publique' (1998) *Revue Trimestrielle des Droits de l'Homme* 307 ff.

[6] See, eg *Le Calvez v France*, App No 25554/94, Judgment of 29 July 1998, *Reports* 1998-V, para 28.

[7] *De Santa v Italy*, App No 25574/94, *Lapalorcia v Italy*, App No 25586/94 and *Abenavoli v Italy*, App No 25587/94, Judgments of 2 September 1997, Reports 1997-V, respectively paras 18, 21 and 16.

[8] *Nicodemo v Italy*, App No 25839/94, Judgment of 2 September 1997, *Reports* 1997-V, para 18.

[9] *Benkessiouer v France*, App No 26106/95, Judgment of 24 August 1998, *Reports* 1998-V, paras 29–30; *Couez v France*, App No 24271/94, Judgment of 24 August 1998, *Reports* 1998-V, para 25.

[10] *Pellegrin v France*, App No 28541/95, Judgment of 8 December 1999.

[11] Ibid, paras 66–67.

However, this change of direction did not have the expected stabilising effect, as the Court bitterly realised eight years later with the *Vilho Eskelinen* case.[12] It therefore decided to change its approach again by formulating new principles that remain unchanged to this day:

> In order for the respondent State to be able to rely before the Court on the applicant's status as a civil servant in excluding the protection embodied in Article 6, two conditions must be fulfilled. Firstly, the State in its national law must have expressly excluded access to a court for the post or category of staff in question. Secondly, the exclusion must be justified on objective grounds in the State's interest. The mere fact that the applicant is in a sector or department which participates in the exercise of power conferred by public law is not in itself decisive. In order for the exclusion to be justified, it is not enough for the State to establish that the civil servant in question participates in the exercise of public power or that there exists, to use the words of the Court in the Pellegrin judgment, a 'special bond of trust and loyalty' between the civil servant and the State, as employer. It is also for the State to show that the subject matter of the dispute in issue is related to the exercise of State power or that it has called into question the special bond. Thus, there can in principle be no justification for the exclusion from the guarantees of Article 6 of ordinary labour disputes, such as those relating to salaries, allowances or similar entitlements, on the basis of the special nature of [*sic*] relationship between the particular civil servant and the State in question. There will, in effect, be a presumption that Article 6 applies. It will be for the respondent Government to demonstrate, first, that a civil-servant applicant does not have a right of access to a court under national law and, second, that the exclusion of the rights under Article 6 for the civil servant is justified.[13]

The first condition clearly sets out the principle of subsidiarity underlined in Article 53 of the Convention: a State could not validly invoke the inapplicability of Article 6 to a litigation that it already decided to 'judicialise' in internal law.[14] The applicability of Article 6 is, under this first condition, completely disconnected from any 'autonomous' interpretative process regarding the 'civil' qualification. This disconnexion has been criticised by a significant minority of Strasbourg judges:

> As to the argument based on the existence of access to a domestic court, we are not convinced by it. As Article 53 of the Convention rightly points out, nothing prevents a High Contracting Party from recognising in its law freedoms or guarantees which go further than those set forth in the Convention; in addition, as legal systems vary from one State to another, the reasoning in the instant judgment is likely to have the effect of making the applicability of Article 6 § 1 to disputes between the State and its agents dependent on

---

[12] *Vilho Eskelinen v Finland*, App No 63235/00, Judgment of 19 April 2007.
[13] Ibid, para 62.
[14] Such a position had already been advocated, in a visionary way, by P Lemmens, *Geschillen over burgerlijke rechten en verplichtingen* (Anvers, Kluwer, 1989) 264 ff, especially at 268. See also the dissenting opinion of judges Tulkens and others in the *Pellegrin* case (pt 6): 'The main reason for the exclusion of civil service disputes from the scope of Article 6, which was to a large extent prompted by a State-centred outlook, was to preserve the public authorities' ius imperii, which was supposedly in danger of being undermined by judicialisation of related disputes. But that justification has now largely lost its significance. Of their own accord most member States have "judicialised" civil service disputes, if not entirely then at least for the most part. To avoid discrimination between the subjects of law the procedural safeguards afforded on that account to civil servants must logically be the same as those applicable to other types of dispute, which incontestably fall within the scope of Article 6. Since the Convention acts as a benchmark, it would be surprising if the institutions charged with its supervision afforded fewer safeguards than the domestic courts.'

there existing access to a court with jurisdiction to decide them within the domestic legal system. To sum up, instead of the 'autonomous interpretation' (by the Court) that the latter considered it important to establish for the purposes of Article 6 § 1 ... the instant judgment encourages a dependent and variable, not to say uncertain, interpretation, in other words an arbitrary one. In our opinion, this is an inappropriate step back.[15]

A 'step back'? With the benefit of hindsight, one sees that this dark prediction has not materialised. It is indeed hard to imagine that a State would decide, with the sole purpose of avoiding the application of Article 6 to a specific case, to remove the judicial guarantee that it had previously and spontaneously granted to civil servants. A kind of *standstill* is being established, if not de jure, then at least de facto. Furthermore, a State that adopts such an attitude should also prove that this 'dejudicialisation' fulfils the second condition set out in *Vilho Eskelinen*. In other words, the State would have to convince the European Court of Human Rights that 'the subject matter of the dispute in issue is related to the exercise of State power or that it has called into question the special bond'. However, in light of subsequent judgments, it has become apparent that such a demonstration is far from easy to make. An example of a successful demonstration can be found in the case where the Court decided that Article 6 was inapplicable to a dispute involving the dismissal of a public prosecutor for reasons of forgery and bribery committed during the performance of his duties.[16] The same happened in the case of the dismissal, on disciplinary grounds, of an army officer.[17] Having said that, it is enough to establish that the internal legal system has provided for such disputes to be brought before a 'tribunal'—even if atypical (see the *Savino* case below)—for Article 6 to be applicable under the first criterion of *Vilho Eskelinen*.[18] This is precisely the conclusion reached by the Court in the vast majority of cases brought before it between 2007 and 2011. No 'step back' is to be observed here; indeed, quite the opposite.

---

[15] Joint dissenting opinions of Judges Costa, Wildhaber, Turmen, Borrego Borrego and Jociene. This criticism was echoed by scholars. See M Melchior, 'Quant à l'applicabilité de l'article 6, § 1er, de la Convention européenne des droits de l'Homme au contentieux de la fonction publique—Evolution de la jurisprudence de Strasbourg' in Pintens, Alen, Senaeve and Dirix (eds), *Vigilantibus Jus Scriptum. Feestbundel voor Hugo Vandenberghe,* (Bruges, La Charte, 2007) 206; J van Compernolle, 'De revirement en revirement: à la recherche d'un critère d'applicabilité de l'article 6, § 1er, de la Convention européenne des droits de l'Homme au contentieux des agents publics' (2008) *Revue Trimestrielle des Droits de l'Homme* 1134–35.

[16] *Hakkı Nazsiz and Melis Merve Nazsiz v Turkey*, App No 22412/05, decision of 26 May 2009. See also *Serdal Apay v Turkey*, App No 3964/05, decision of 11 December 2007.

[17] See *Osman Sukut v Turkey*, App No 59773/00, decision of 11 September 2007.

[18] See, in a very significant way, *Majski v Croatie (No 2)*, App No 16924/08, Judgment of 19 July 2011, paras 54–55: 'Following the *Vilho Eskelinen* case, the Court found Article 6 to be inapplicable to proceedings concerning recruitment (see *Apay v Turkey*, App No 3964/05, 11 December 2007) and (disciplinary) proceedings concerning the termination of employment of public prosecutors (see *Nazsiz v Turkey*, App No 22412/05 26 May 2009) but only because the domestic law expressly excluded access to court. However, turning to the circumstances of the present case, the Court first notes that section 66 of the Administrative Disputes Act provides for "a request for the protection of a constitutionally guaranteed right", a judicial remedy open to anyone who considers that his or her rights or freedoms guaranteed by the Constitution have been violated by a decision of a public authority in a situation where no other judicial remedy is available ... It further notes that in the present case the applicant was entitled to contest the impugned decision of the State Attorneys Council of 11 January 2005 before the Administrative Court by lodging such a request in so far as that decision was contrary to his constitutional right to equal access to the public service ... In the light of the foregoing, the Court finds that Article 6 of the Convention under its civil head is applicable to the present case.'

2.2 The Parliament

K Muylle recalls that parliamentary autonomy is one of the cardinal principles of parliamentary law.[19] In most classic theories of public law, this autonomy implies and justifies the exclusion of any intervention or interference from the other State's authorities—including the judiciary—in the internal organisation of the Parliament. This also concerns the relations between the institution and its own personnel. Disputes which are likely to arise within these relations are then, in many States,[20] more or less taken away from the competence of 'external' judges and will raise strictly internal proceedings.

The question of compatibility of such institutional arrangements with the right to judicial protection has been raised in a few States, including Belgium.[21] The same question, raised in the context of a violation of Article 6 of the Convention, was at the core of *Savino and others v Italy*.[22]

The facts of the case can be summarised as follows. The two first applicants, a surveyor (Savino) and an architect (Persichetti), were employees of the Italian Chamber of Deputies. They applied to their administration for a special project allowance and the first applicant (Savino) also requested the reimbursement of insurance contributions. The case was brought before the Judicial Committee for Officials of the Chamber of Deputies. This Committee is made up of six MPs chosen randomly from a list established by the President of the Chamber, the Secretary General and trade union organisations. In decisions of February 2004, the Committee partly upheld the applicants' claims and granted the first applicant's specific request. The administration appealed to the Judicial Section of the Bureau of the Chamber of Deputies and requested a stay of execution on the decisions. In decisions of October 2004, the Judicial Section of the Bureau of the Chamber of Deputies, while finding the requests for a stay of execution inadmissible as they were out of time, upheld the administration's appeals on the merits and set aside the Committee's decisions.

The other applicants (Borgo, Carbonara, Colasanti, Fantoni and Giordani) were selected and invited to sit a written examination organised by the Chamber of Deputies, but were not included in the shortlist of candidates who passed the written examination. They appealed to the Judicial Committee for Officials of the Chamber of Deputies, complaining about the organisation of the examination and the criteria adopted for assessment of the papers. They sought the annulment of the administration's decision not to include them on the shortlist of candidates invited to the oral

---

[19] K Muylle, 'L'autonomie parlementaire à l'abri des droits de l'Homme ?' (2010) *Revue Trimestrielle des Droits de l'Homme* 705.

[20] For a synthetic approach, see M Veys, 'Analyse des réponses données par les correspondants CERDP sur le thème du *contrôle juridictionnel des actes accomplis par le parlement en dehors de la sphère d'exercice des fonctions parlementaires essentielles*' in N Igot, A Rezsohazy and M Van der Hulst (eds), *Parlement & Pouvoir judiciaire* (Brussels, Service juridique de la Chambre des représentants de Belgique et Service des Affaires juridiques du Sénat de Belgique, 2008) at 246–49.

[21] For a synthetic presentation of the Belgian Constitutional Court's case law regarding the matter and of the legislative changes it brought about, see K Muylle, 'Rechterlijke controle op niet-wetgevende handelingen van een wetgevende vergadering: democratie versus rechtsstaat, of toch maar scheiding der machten?' in Alen and Van Nieuwenhove (n 3) 148–51.

[22] *Savino and others v Italy*, App Nos 17214/05, 42113/04 and 20329/05, Judgment of 28 April 2009.

examination and, at the same time, a stay of execution on that decision. In decisions of May 2002, the Committee upheld the applicants' appeals. The administration of the Chamber of Deputies appealed to the Judicial Section of the Bureau of the Chamber of Deputies and also requested a stay of execution on the Committee's decisions. The Section upheld the administration's appeals. The applicants appealed to the Court of Cassation, which declared their appeal against the decisions of the Chamber of Deputies' internal judicial bodies inadmissible.

In all these cases the applicants complained that they had not had access to a 'tribunal' within the meaning of Article 6, § 1 of the Convention for the adjudication of their claims. They argued that the Judicial Committee and Judicial Section for Officials of the Chamber of Deputies were not tribunals established by law and were not independent and impartial as required by the Convention.

The first question addressed by the Court in its judgment of 28 April 2009 was to know whether, by application of the *Vilho Eskelinen* case law, such disputes fell within the scope of Article 6 of the Convention. The judgment answered this question in the affirmative. The Court noted that the judicial bodies to which the applicants had appealed had considered their cases on their merits and had not deemed it necessary to dismiss them as being ill founded. Furthermore, domestic law afforded judicial protection to the applicants, since the Judicial Committee and Judicial Section of the Chamber of Deputies were competent to determine any dispute against the Chamber's administration and, in the Court's opinion, performed a judicial function. Through a constructive application of the first *Vilho Eskelinen* criterion, it could be concluded, on that ground alone, that the disputes at issue fell within the ambit of Article 6.[23] Echoing the second *Vilho Eskelinen* criterion, the Court added, without having to do so, that there was no special bond of trust between the State and the applicants such as to justify excluding them from the rights safeguarded by the Convention.

On the merits, the Court considered that the regulations of the Italian Parliament establishing the appellate bodies (the Judicial Committee and the Judicial Section of the Bureau) could come under the remit of the 'law' as required by Article 6 (*tribunal established 'by law'*). According to the Court, the Chamber's secondary regulations establishing these bodies derived from its rule-making powers under the Constitution and were designed to preserve the legislature from any outside interference, including by the executive.

The last question concerned the independence and impartiality of the appellate bodies. Regarding the Judicial Committee, the Court identified no violation of Article 6.[24] It reached a different conclusion[25] on the Judicial Section of the Bureau of the Chamber of Deputies: this appellate body, whose decisions were final, was

---

[23] Ibid, paras 71–79.

[24] Paragraph 104: 'the mere fact that two members of judicial bodies of the Chamber of Deputies are chosen from among the MPs of the House should not cast doubt on the independence of the courts' (Author's translation).

[25] Paras §§ 104–05: '[La Cour] ne saurait ignorer le fait que la Section, organe d'appel statuant à titre définitif, est entièrement composée de membres du Bureau, c'est-à-dire de l'organe de la Chambre des députés compétent pour régler les principales questions administratives de la Chambre, y compris celles concernant la comptabilité et l'organisation des concours pour le recrutement du personnel ... En particulier, le protocole additionnel au règlement comptable de la Chambre des députés ainsi que le règlement

entirely made up of members of the Bureau, ie, the Chamber's competent body for ruling on its main administrative matters. In the *Savino* case, the administrative decisions complained of had been indeed adopted by the Bureau in accordance with its rule-making powers. According to the Court, this factual situation was sufficient to give rise to doubts as to the objective impartiality of the appellate body. The Court further noted the close connection between the subject of the judicial proceedings before the Section and the decisions taken by the Bureau. Therefore, there had been a violation of Article 6, § 1 on that account.

According to some scholars, the position of the Court in this case appears to be rather lenient.[26] The Court does not condemn the principle of a justice rendered 'in house' by the members of the Parliament themselves (*Autodichia*, according to Italian terminology) and the correlate exclusion of any intervention of an external judge in disputes between the Parliament and its employees. However, the following fact remains: the Court has no intention to leave Article 6 at the doors of the Parliament, unlike the Italian government, which radically contended that derogation from Article 6 of the Convention's principles was an essential condition to allow the House of Representatives to have a privileged space of autonomy and independence.[27]

2.3 The International Organisations

In its principled judgments in *Waite and Kennedy v Germany*[28] and *Beer and Regan v Germany*,[29] the European Court of Human Rights acknowledged that the immunity from jurisdiction that an international organisation enjoys can validly prevent a national judge from deciding a dispute between that organisation and one of its employees. According to the Court:

> The attribution of privileges and immunities to international organisations is an essential means of ensuring the proper functioning of such organisations free from unilateral interference by individual governments.

> The immunity from jurisdiction commonly accorded by States to international organisations under the organisations' constituent instruments or supplementary agreements is a long-standing practice established in the interest of the good working of these organisations.

---

des concours pour le recrutement du personnel, objets des litiges respectifs des requérants ... sont des actes adoptés par le Bureau dans le cadre de ses prérogatives normatives.

En outre, la Chambre des députés est représentée devant la Section par le Secrétaire général, nommé lui aussi par le Bureau.

Dans ces conditions, la Cour comprend les craintes des requérants quant à l'impartialité de la Section. De l'avis de la Cour, le fait que l'organe administratif ayant des compétences telles que celles du Bureau soit le même que l'organe juridictionnel compétent pour trancher tout contentieux administratif peut suffire à inspirer des doutes quant à l'impartialité de la juridiction ainsi formée.'

[26] See K Muylle (n 19) 716–17.

[27] *Savino and others v Italy* (n 22) para 55.

[28] *Waite and Kennedy v Germany*, App No 26083/94, Judgment of 18 February 1999, *Reports* 1999-I.

[29] *Beer and Regan v Germany*, App No 28934/95, Judgment of 18 February 1999, *Reports* 1999-I.

The importance of this practice is enhanced by a trend towards extending and strengthening international cooperation in all domains of modern society.[30]

Even with a legitimate aim, the limitation on the right to a fair trial could only be declared compatible with Article 6, § 1 if there was a reasonable relationship of proportionality between the means employed and this aim:

> Where States establish international organisations in order to pursue or strengthen their cooperation in certain fields of activities, and where they attribute to these organisations certain competences and accord them immunities, there may be implications as to the protection of fundamental rights. It would be incompatible with the purpose and object of the Convention, however, if the Contracting States were thereby absolved from their responsibility under the Convention in relation to the field of activity covered by such attribution. It should be recalled that the Convention is intended to guarantee not theoretical or illusory rights, but rights that are practical and effective. This is particularly true for the right of access to the courts in view of the prominent place held in a democratic society by the right to a fair trial ...

> For the Court, a material factor in determining whether granting [the organisation] immunity from [national] jurisdiction is permissible under the Convention is whether the applicants had available to them reasonable alternative means to protect effectively their rights under the Convention.[31]

Scholars have debated the exact meaning of the 'reasonable alternative means to protect' requirement.[32] Does 'alternative means' necessarily relate to a type of dispute brought before a body fulfilling the definition of a 'tribunal' as mentioned in Article 6 and interpreted by the European Court?[33] If so, and according to well-established case law, that body should, without necessarily adopting the characteristics of a 'classic' (typical) jurisdiction, at least present the basic guarantees of

---

[30] *Waite and Kennedy v Germany* (n 28) para 63.

[31] Ibid, para 67.

[32] See F Sudre, 'La jurisprudence de la Cour européenne des droits de l'Homme' in Pingel (ed), *Droit des immunités et exigences du procès équitable* (Paris, Pedone, 2004) 27; I Pingel-Lenuzza, 'Autonomie juridictionnelle et employeur privilégié: concilier les contraires' (2000) *Revue Générale de Droit International Public*. 458; H Trigoudja, 'L'immunité de juridiction des organisations internationales et le droit d'accès à un tribunal' (2000) *Revue Trimestrielle des Droits de l'Homme* 102; N Angelet and A Weerts, 'Les immunités des organisations internationales face à l'article 6 de la Convention européenne des droits de l'homme' (2007) *Journal de Droit International* 3–28; A Reinish, 'The Immunity of International Organization and the Jurisdiction of their Administrative Tribunals' (2008) 7(2) *Chinese Journal of International Law* 292.

[33] According to the 'classic' definition of the *Belilos* case, 'a "tribunal" is characterised in the substantive sense of the term by its judicial function, that is to say determining matters within its competence on the basis of rules of law and after proceedings conducted in a prescribed manner ... It must also satisfy a series of further requirements—independence, in particular of the executive; impartiality; duration of its members' terms of office; guarantees afforded by its procedure—several of which appear in the text of Article 6 § 1 itself'. See also App Nos 17214/05, 42113/04 and 20329/05, Judgment of 28 April 2009, para 73: '[La jurisprudence de la Cour] n'entend pas nécessairement, par le terme "tribunal", une juridiction de type classique, intégrée aux structures judiciaires ordinaires du pays ... Aux fins de la Convention, une autorité peut s'analyser en un "tribunal", au sens matériel du terme, lorsqu'il lui appartient de trancher, sur la base de normes de droit, avec plénitude de juridiction et à l'issue d'une procédure organisée, toute question relevant de sa compétence ... En effet, un "tribunal" se distingue par son pouvoir de réformer en tous points, en fait comme en droit, la décision rendue par une autorité administrative ... Enfin, le pouvoir de rendre une décision obligatoire ne pouvant être modifiée par une autorité non judiciaire au détriment d'une partie est inhérent à la notion même de "tribunal".'

independence. It should also be able to issue, at the end of organised and adversarial proceedings, obligatory decisions based on rules of law.

It is not certain, in light of the *Waite and Kennedy* judgment[34] and subsequent case law applying that notion of 'reasonable alternative means',[35] that the Court meant to set such a high standard.[36] This is precisely why this case law attracted sometimes vehement criticism from certain scholars.[37] When faced with the issue of immunity from jurisdiction of international organisations, the Court would content itself with a 'light' due process, instead of a fair trial 'full options'.

This conclusion is certainly not yet definitive. However, we can already observe that a number of national judges have decided to give a relatively exacting interpretation to the *Waite and Kennedy* doctrine.[38]

The Court of Appeal of Brussels,[39] in its historic judgment in a labour law dispute, discussed the compatibility of the immunity invoked by the Secretariat of the African, Caribbean and Pacific Group of States with Article 6 of the Convention. The Secretariat argued that there were 'reasonable alternative means' in accordance with *Waite and Kennedy*. It held the role of the 'Council of the ACP Secretariat' to be that of an appellate body which could judge disputes. In its judgment of 4 March 2003, the Brussels Court rejected this argument, considering that 'the Secretariat brings ... no real evidence establishing either the *judicial role* of that Council, or that it would present if needed *all the conditions and guarantees required by the right of access to a judge*'.[40] The Court of Appeal concluded that Article 6 of the Convention had primacy over the immunity of execution of the ACP Secretariat. The appeal brought against that judgment to the Belgian Court of Cassation was rejected by a judgment of 21 December 2009.[41]

In a judgment delivered on the same day[42] involving disputes between the Union of Western Europe and a member of its personnel, the Belgian Court of Cassation appeared to be particularly demanding on the level of impartiality and independence expected from the internal body competent to examine the appeal proceedings. It is not enough for this independence to be stated in a general and abstract way by

---

[34] *Waite and Kennedy v Germany* (n 28). See, *a contrario*, Trigoudja (n 32) 102.

[35] See notably *A v UK*, App No 35373/97, Judgment of 17 December 2002, para 86 (regarding immunity of liability of an MP).

[36] N Angelet and A Weerts (n 32) 3–28.

[37] See the studies of F Sudre and H Trigoudja quoted above. See also L Milano, *Le droit à un tribunal au sens de la Convention européenne des droits de l'Homme* (Paris, Dalloz, 2006), at 304–05 and the references quoted therein.

[38] For a complete overview of the impact and the reception of the *Waite and Kennedy* case law in the case law of the different European national jurisdictions, see A Reinish (n 32) 294 ff.

[39] Court of Appeal of Brussels, 4 March 2003 (2003) *Journal des Tribunaux* 684.

[40] Emphasis added. 'Le Secrétariat n'apporte ... aucun élément probant démontrant *le rôle juridictionnel* de ce Conseil, ni le fait qu'il présente le cas échéant *toutes les conditions et garanties que suppose le droit d'accès à un juge*.'

[41] Cour de cassation (b), 21 December 2009, C.03.0328.F, available at: www.cass.be; (2010) *Journal des Tribunaux* 129 ff with a comment by E David.

[42] Cour de cassation (b), 21 December 2009, S.04.0129.F, available at: www.cass.be, with the conclusions of Advocate General Genicot. See also J Wouters, 'Case Note: Western European Union v Siedler; General Secretariat of the ACP Group v Lutchmaya; General Secretariat of the ACP Group v B.D.' (2003) 105(3) *American Journal of International Law* 560–67.

a standardised formula of the founding act of the international organisation;[43] it must be checked, *in concreto*, through an examination of the exact status of the people sitting on that body. The same severity can be found in a judgment of the social chamber of the French Court of Cassation dating from 25 January 2005.[44] This case held that: 'The African Bank of development cannot invoke the immunity from jurisdiction in a dispute with the employee that it fired given that at the time of the facts, it had not set up internally a *tribunal* with competence to decide such cases'.[45]

The above-quoted national jurisdictions clearly adopted a *maximalist* interpretation of the *Waite and Kennedy* case law, going even further than the European Court itself.[46] According to them, Article 6 does not stop at the door of international organisations; on the contrary, it penetrates them and brings with it the full range of its protection. It cannot be excluded that, conscious of the evolution of the 'European consensus' on the issue, the European Court will some day draw inspiration from this innovative national case law to harden its own position.[47]

2.4 The Embassies

The immunity of the jurisdiction of States can legitimately end up in the non-justiciability of disputes between States acting outside their respective borders and members of the personnel of their embassies, consulates or other public establishments. Such is the lesson drawn from a Strasbourg case decided at the beginning of the current millennium. However, his jurisprudence is not set in stone, as can be seen from the stream of the subsequent cases: *Fogarty*,[48] *Cudak*,[49] *Guadagnino*[50] and *Sabeh El Leil*.[51]

Mary Fogarty was an Irish national. On 8 November 1993, she started working as an administrative assistant at the US Embassy in London. After being dismissed in February 1995, she issued proceedings against the US government before a labour court. She claimed that her dismissal had been the result of sex discrimination,

---

[43] Ibid: 'Lorsque, pour déterminer si l'immunité de juridiction invoquée par une organisation internationale est admissible au regard de l'article 6, § 1er, de la Convention de sauvegarde des droits de l'homme et des libertés fondamentales, le juge saisi de la contestation constate que la personne à laquelle cette immunité est opposée dispose de la possibilité de soumettre le litige à une commission de recours, il ne peut se limiter à prendre acte que les instruments qui instituent cette commission la qualifient d'indépendante.'

[44] Cour de cassation (f) (Soc), 25 January 2005 (2005) *Journal des Tribunaux* 454 ff with a comment by E David; (2005) *Journal de droit international* 1142 ff, with a comment by L Corbion.

[45] Emphasis added. 'La Banque africaine de développement ne peut se prévaloir de l'immunité de juridiction dans le litige l'opposant au salarié qu'elle a licencié dès lors qu'à l'époque des faits elle n'avait pas institué en son sein un *tribunal* ayant compétence pour statuer sur des litiges de cette nature.'

[46] See, for a criticism of the Belgian case law on this matter, M Vidal, 'Case Note: Ms Siedler v Western European union, Brussels Labour Court of Appeal, 17th September 2003' (2006) *Oxford Law Reports*. (electronic publication)

[47] See L Milano, 'Les immunités issues du droit international dans la jurisprudence européenne' (2008) *Revue Trimestrielle des Droits de l'Homme* 1089–92.

[48] *Fogarty v UK*, App No 37112/97, Judgment of 21 November 2001.

[49] *Cudak v Lithuania*, App No 15869/02, Judgment of 23 March 2010.

[50] *Guadagnino v France and Italy*, App No 2555/03, Judgment of 18 January 2011.

[51] *Sabeh El Leil v France*, App No34869/05, Judgment of 29 June 2011.

contrary to the Sex Discrimination Act 1975, alleging that she had suffered persistent sexual harassment from her supervisor and that their working relationship had broken down in consequence. On 13 May 1996, the tribunal upheld her complaint and she was paid £12,000 in compensation.

In June 1996 and August 1996, Fogarty applied unsuccessfully for two posts at the US Embassy. On 15 September 1996, she issued a second application before a labour court, claiming that the embassy had refused to re-employ her as a consequence of her previous successful sex discrimination claim, which constituted victimisation and discrimination under the 1975 Act. On 6 February 1997, she was advised that the US government was entitled to claim immunity under the 1978 Act, which grants immunity from suit in relation to administrative and technical staff of a diplomatic mission seeking to bring proceedings concerning their contract of employment.

By a decision of 21 November 2001, the European Court of Human Rights decided that the legitimacy of the aim pursued by this limitation to the right of access to the courts could not be disputed:

> Sovereign immunity is a concept of international law, developed out of the principle *par in parem non habet imperium*, by virtue of which one State shall not be subject to the jurisdiction of another State. The Court considers that the grant of sovereign immunity to a State in civil proceedings pursues the legitimate aim of complying with international law to promote comity and good relations between States through the respect of another State's sovereignty.[52]

And the Court added:

> Measures taken by a High Contracting Party which reflect generally recognised rules of public international law on State immunity cannot in principle be regarded as imposing a disproportionate restriction on the right of access to court as embodied in Article 6 § 1. Just as the right of access to court is an inherent part of the fair trial guarantee in that Article, so some restrictions on access must likewise be regarded as inherent, an example being those limitations generally accepted by the community of nations as part of the doctrine of State immunity.[53]

The legitimate restriction on the right of access to the courts was also said to be proportionate. To support this conclusion, the judgment of 21 November 2001 made the following reflections:

> There appears to be a trend in international and comparative law towards limiting State immunity in respect of employment-related disputes. However, where the proceedings relate to employment in a foreign mission or embassy, international practice is divided on the question whether State immunity continues to apply and, if it does so apply, whether it covers disputes relating to the contracts of all staff or only more senior members of the mission. Certainly, it cannot be said that the United Kingdom is alone in holding that immunity attaches to suits by employees at diplomatic missions or that, in affording such immunity, the United Kingdom falls outside any currently accepted international standards.

---

[52] *Fogarty v UK* (n 48) para 34.
[53] Ibid, para 36.

The Court further observes that the proceedings which the applicant wished to bring did not concern the contractual rights of a current embassy employee, but instead related to alleged discrimination in the recruitment process. Questions relating to the recruitment of staff to missions and embassies may by their very nature involve sensitive and confidential issues, related, inter alia, to the diplomatic and organisational policy of a foreign State. The Court is not aware of any trend in international law towards a relaxation of the rule of State immunity as regards issues of recruitment to foreign missions. In this respect, the Court notes that it appears clearly from the materials referred[54] ... that the International Law Commission did not intend to exclude the application of State immunity where the subject of proceedings was recruitment, including recruitment to a diplomatic mission.[55]

This initial standpoint of the Court raised both internal[56] and external[57] criticisms. However, it presented two 'openings' which offered the possibility of future evolution. On the one hand, the Court acknowledged, in a general way, the evolving and non-definitive character of the position of international law on the issue. On the other hand, the judgment emphasised the fact that the case brought by Ms Fogarty related to her recruitment by the foreign embassy and not to the 'contractual rights of a current embassy employee'. The possibility of *distinguishing* was hence preserved.

This double opening was exploited, nine years later, in *Cudak v Lithuania*.[58] In 1997, Ms Čudak was hired as a secretary and switchboard operator by the Embassy of the Republic of Poland in Vilnius. In 1999, she complained to the Lithuanian Equal Opportunities Ombudsperson that she was being sexually harassed by one of her male colleagues, as a result of which she had fallen ill. The Ombudsperson recognised that she was indeed a victim of sexual harassment.

Put on sick leave for two months, Ms Čudak was not allowed to enter the building upon her return on 29 October 1999, and on two other occasions in the weeks that followed. She complained in writing to the ambassador and a few days later, on 2 December 1999, was informed that she had been dismissed for her failure to come to work during the last week of November 1999. She brought an action for unfair dismissal before the civil courts, which declined jurisdiction on the basis of the doctrine of State immunity from jurisdiction. The Lithuanian Supreme Court found in particular that Ms Čudak had exercised a public-service function during her employment with the Polish Embassy and established that, merely from the title of her position, it could be concluded that her duties facilitated the exercise by the Republic of Poland of its sovereign functions and therefore justified the application of the State immunity rule.

In its judgment of 23 March 2010, the Grand Chamber of the European Court concluded, unanimously, that Article 6 of the Convention had been violated. In support of this conclusion, the Court referred to the emergence in international law of new customary rules that in labour law disputes limit, in accordance with well-determined conditions, the legitimate evocation of immunity from jurisdiction. This case deserves to be quoted extensively insofar as it relates to this issue:[59]

> The Court found, already in the Fogarty judgment, that there was a trend in international and comparative law towards limiting State immunity in respect of employment-related disputes, with the exception, however, of those concerning the recruitment of staff in embassies ...
>
> In this connection, the Court notes that the application of absolute State immunity has, for many years, clearly been eroded. In 1979 the International Law Commission was given the task of codifying and gradually developing international law in the area of jurisdictional immunities of States and their property. It produced a number of drafts that were submitted to States for comment. The Draft Articles it adopted in 1991 included one—Article 11—on contracts of employment.[60] In 2004 the United Nations General Assembly adopted the Convention on Jurisdictional Immunities of States and their Property.[61]

---

[59] Ibid, paras 63–67.

[60] This article reads as follows:

'1. Unless otherwise agreed between the States concerned, a State cannot invoke immunity from jurisdiction before a court of another State which is otherwise competent in a proceeding which relates to a contract of employment between the State and an individual for work performed or to be performed, in whole or in part, in the territory of that other State.

2. Paragraph 1 does not apply if:
  (a) the employee has been recruited to perform functions closely related to the exercise of governmental authority;
  (b) the subject of the proceeding is the recruitment, renewal of employment or reinstatement of an individual;
  (c) the employee was neither a national nor a habitual resident of the State of the forum at the time when the contract of employment was concluded;
  (d) the employee is a national of the employer State at the time when the proceeding is instituted; or
  (e) the employer State and the employee have otherwise agreed in writing, subject to any considerations of public policy conferring on the courts of the State of the forum exclusive jurisdiction by reason of the subject-matter of the proceeding.'

[61] Article 11 of this Convention reads as follows:

'1. Unless otherwise agreed between the States concerned, a State cannot invoke immunity from jurisdiction before a court of another State which is otherwise competent in a proceeding which relates to a contract of employment between the State and an individual for work performed or to be performed, in whole or in part, in the territory of that other State.

2. Paragraph 1 does not apply if:
  (a) the employee has been recruited to perform particular functions in the exercise of governmental authority;
  (b) the employee is:
      (i) a diplomatic agent, as defined in the Vienna Convention on Diplomatic Relations of 1961;
      (ii) a consular officer, as defined in the Vienna Convention on Consular Relations of 1963;
      (iii) a member of the diplomatic staff of a permanent mission to an international organization or of a special mission, or is recruited to represent a State at an international conference; or
      (iv) any other person enjoying diplomatic immunity;
  (c) the subject-matter of the proceeding is the recruitment, renewal of employment or reinstatement of an individual;
  (d) the subject-matter of the proceeding is the dismissal or termination of employment of an individual and, as determined by the head of State, the head of Government or the Minister for Foreign Affairs of the employer State, such a proceeding would interfere with the security interests of that State;
  (e) the employee is a national of the employer State at the time when the proceeding is instituted, unless this person has the permanent residence in the State of the forum; or

The 1991 Draft Articles, on which the 2004 Convention (and Article 11 in particular) was based, created a significant exception in matters of State immunity by, in principle, removing from the application of the immunity rule a State's employment contracts with the staff of its diplomatic missions abroad. However, that exception was itself subject to exceptions whereby, in substance, immunity still applied to diplomatic and consular staff in cases where: the subject of the dispute was the recruitment, renewal of employment or reinstatement of an individual; the employee was a national of the employer State; or, lastly, the employer State and the employee had otherwise agreed in writing.

The report appended to the 1991 Draft Articles stated that the rules formulated in Article 11 appeared to be consistent with the emerging trend in the legislative and treaty practice of a growing number of States (ILC Yearbook, 1991, Vol. II, Part 2, p. 44, § 14). This must also hold true for the 2004 Convention. Furthermore, it is a well-established principle of international law that, even if a State has not ratified a treaty, it may be bound by one of its provisions in so far as that provision reflects customary international law, either 'codifying' it or forming a new customary rule (see the North Sea Continental Shelf cases, ICJ Reports 1969, p. 41, § 71). Moreover, there were no particular objections by States to the wording of Article 11 of the International Law Commission's Draft Articles, at least not by the respondent State. As to the 2004 Convention, Lithuania has admittedly not ratified it but did not vote against its adoption either.

Consequently, it is possible to affirm that Article 11 of the International Law Commission's 1991 Draft Articles, on which the 2004 Convention was based, applies to the respondent State under customary international law.

In concreto, the Court decided that none of the exceptions regarding the exclusion of immunity, as considered by the International Law Commission's 1991 Draft Articles and the 2004 Convention, were applicable in the case: 'Ms Cudak did not perform any particular functions closely related to the exercise of governmental authority. In addition, she was not a diplomatic agent or consular officer, nor was she a national of the employer State. Lastly, the subject matter of the dispute was linked to the applicant's dismissal.'[62]

The new line of reasoning thereby established was subsequently confirmed in *Sabeh el Leil*[63]—which concerned an accountant expert of French nationality who was fired for economic reasons by the Embassy of Koweït—and in *Guadagnino v France and Italy*[64]—which concerned a dispute over the reconstitution of the career and dismissal of an employee from the 'École française' of Rome.

* * *

To varying degrees and through more or less innovative creations, the most recent Strasbourg case law shows an incontestable trend to reduce the amount of labour law disputes that fall outside the scope of Article 6. This jurisprudential tendency illustrates, in many ways, the process of an interpretative enrichment that the Court has been engaged in over the past number of years and which came out in

---

(f) the employer State and the employee have otherwise agreed in writing, subject to any considerations of public policy conferring on the courts of the State of the forum exclusive jurisdiction by reason of the subject-matter of the proceeding.'

[62] *Cudak v Lithuania* (n 49) para 69.
[63] *Sabeh El Leil v France* (n 51).
[64] *Guadagnino v France and Italy* (n 50).

its famous *Demir and Baykara* judgment of 12 November 2008.[65] In interpreting the Convention, the European Court can draw inspiration from 'external sources'— whatever their respective legal status—when they disclose the emergence of a consensus on one issue or another. This enrichment is particularly obvious in the *Vilho Eskelinen* judgment, where the Court supported its spectacular overruling by reference to the 'universal' fair trial of Article 47 of the Charter of Fundamental Rights of the European Union, and to the case law of the European Court of Justice dedicated to the right to judicial protection.[66] No less spectacular is the *Cudak* judgment, where the Court read between the lines of the work of the International Law Commission and of a not yet internationally in force treaty,[67] the expression of an international custom limiting the extent to which the immunity from the jurisdiction of States can be invoked within labour law litigation.

3 THE 'LABOURISATION' OF THE FAIR TRIAL STANDARDS

The analysed extension of the scope of Article 6 given above does not lead to the emergence of an absolutely uniform body of rules and principles, and even less to the setting up of a single and fixed model of fair trial that would be applicable to all kinds of litigation in every Member State. In the construction of a European 'fair trial', the European Court of Human Rights proved itself to be tolerant as regards what characterises the incontestable specificity of labour law litigation: the possibly representative character of jurisdictions called on to intervene (See section 3.1 below) and the special attention paid to problems encountered by the worker-litigant (See section 3.2 below).

3.1 'Partisane mais paritaire, donc impartiale' (Partisan But Equal, Therefore Impartial)[68]

Some Member States of the Council of Europe have a long tradition of a collaborative court model with lay adjudicators (employers and employees) sitting and deliberating alongside professional judges ('échevinage') in labour law litigation.

[65] *Demir and Baykara v Turkey*, App No 34503/97, Judgment of 12 November 2008. See S Van Drooghenbroeck, 'Les frontières du droit et le temps juridique: la Cour européenne des droits de l'Homme repousse les limites. Cour européenne des droits de l'Homme, *Demir et Baykara c. Turquie*, 12 novembre 2008' (2009) *Revue Trimestrielle des Droits de l'Homme* 815–34. See also T Barkhuysen and ML van Emmerik, 'Ongebonden binding: verwijzing naar Soft-Law-Standaarden in uitspraak van het EHRM' (2010) 7 *Nederlands Juristen Comité voor de Mensenrechten-Bulletin* 827 ff; F Tulkens, S Van Drooghenbroeck and F Krenc, 'Le *Soft Law* et la Cour européenne des droits de l'Homme. Questions de méthode et de légitimité', (2012) *Revue trimestrielle des Droits de l'Homme* 433 ff.
[66] *Vilho Eskelinen v Finland*, App No 63235/00, Judgment of 19 April 2007, §§ 29–30 and 60.
[67] Because it was not sufficiently ratified: in accordance with its Article 30, the United Nations Convention on Jurisdictional Immunities of States and Their Property *'shall enter into force on the thirtieth day following the date of deposit of the thirtieth instrument of ratification, acceptance, approval or accession with the Secretary-General of the United Nations'*. On 6 September 2011, the Convention had been signed by 28 States and ratified by 12. The defending States in the *Cudak* (Lithuania) and *Guadagnino* (Italy) cases were not part of them. France ratified the Convention on 12 August 2011, so after the *Sabeh El Leil* judgment.
[68] To quote P Morvan ('Partisane mais paritaire, donc impartiale : la juridiction prud'homale', JCP G 2004, Actualité, no 7).

Belgium is one such State.[69] According to Articles 199 and 216 of the Judicial Code, the labour courts of first instance ('tribunaux du travail') and the labour courts of appeal ('cours du travail') are respectively composed of lay judges ('juges sociaux') and lay counsellors ('conseillers sociaux'), sitting alongside professional judges. They are appointed by the king after being presented by the representative organisations of employers, workers, employees and self-employed workers. Their mandate, a term of five years, is renewable upon being presented again by their organisations. According to Article 300 of the Code on civil procedure (*Code judiciaire*), the position of 'juge social' or 'conseiller social' is not incompatible with the parallel exercise of a function within an organisation representing workers or employers.

The French system goes one step further with this logic of parity and representativeness.[70] The Labour Court ('Conseil des Prud'Hommes') is composed of lay judges—the 'Labour Counsellors' ('conseillers prud'homaux')—elected for a five-year term and representing, in equal numbers, employers and employees. The counsellors representing employers and employees decide on a case with equal voice. However, in the event of a deadlock, the Labour Court gathers again, under the chairmanship of a judge of the court of first instance (*Tribunal d'instance*)— the Judge 'départiteur': this new hearing makes it possible for the judge to decide between the counsellors.

There was a time[71] when scholars were suspicious of the very special status of these lay judges with regard to the impartiality of the courts where they were called to serve. For Belgium, it is enough to mention the particularly harsh words of G Potvin: 'I still believe that it is not only possible but also desirable to avoid the equal representation ... it is an illusion to see it as a guarantee of good justice for the world of the workers ... Establishing, without practical effect, a court where only one of the three judges is neutral, the other two being known for their sympathies to each of the respective litigants creates bad conditions for judging ... One cannot emphasize enough that the proper functioning of a court is determined by the independence and objectivity of its members.'[72]

Over time, critics and doubts from scholars have been gradually silenced.[73]

---

[69] For an overview of this tradition, see J Petit, *Arbeidsgerechten en sociaal procesrecht*, Algemene Praktische Rechtsverzameling (Ghent/Leuven, Story Scientia, 1980) 12 ff.

[70] J Villebrun and G-F Quétant, *Traité de la juridiction prud'homale* (Paris, LGDJ, 1998) 846; J Pélissier, A Supiot and A Jeammeaud, *Droit du travail* (Paris, Dalloz, 2008) 159–92.

[71] The question of the maintaining and of the modalities of the lay jurisdictions in labour law gave rise in Belgium to passionate scholar and parliamentarian debates at the end of the 1950s. See e. a X Kleinermann de Lance, 'La justice paritaire est-elle un mythe ?' (1959) *Journal des Tribunaux* 183; FJ de Weert, 'Het probleem der arbeidsgerechten' (1956–57) *Rechtskundig Weekblad* 330 ff; R Henrion, 'L'unité de juridiction' (1959) *Journal des Tribunaux* 233 ff; M Taquet, 'Les Cours et Tribunaux du travail' (1955) *Journal des Tribunaux* 38 ff.

[72] 'Je persiste à croire qu'il est non seulement possible, mais encore souhaitable d'éviter la représentation paritaire ... c'est une illusion d'y voir une garantie de bonne justice pour le monde des travailleurs ... Constituer, sans effet utile, un tribunal dont un seul des trois juges est neutre, les deux autres étant connus pour leurs sympathies respectives envers chacun des deux plaideurs, c'est créer de mauvaises conditions de jugement ... L'on ne saurait assez souligner combien le bon fonctionnement d'une juridiction est conditionné par l'indépendance et l'objectivité des membres qui la composent' (G Potvin, 'À propos des projets de réforme du contentieux social' (1959) *Journal des Tribunaux* 487 ff).

[73] See, however, P Lemmens, 'The Independence of the Judiciary in Belgium' in *Effectiveness of Judicial Protection and the Constitutional Order. Belgian Report at the Second International Congress of Procedural Law* (Dordrecht, Kluwer, 1983) 57–58.

Occasionally, the question of the structural impartiality of these atypical jurisdictions has reappeared in court. Each time, however, the issue has been resolved in the affirmative.

In Belgium, we can refer to the judgment of 16 April 2004 in which the Labour Court of Nivelles[74] said:

> In general, the principle of impartiality is assured by the neutrality of the judge who has to decide the case. In the system of collaborative justice (*Échevinage*), the principle of the right to an impartial judge cannot be assessed solely with regard to the character of one of the social judges. Impartiality is guaranteed by the balance resulting from the presence of an 'employer' judge, a 'worker' judge and a professional judge. It is achieved by the debate that takes place between people from organisations (whose views and sensitivities are, in principle, different) and the professional judge.[75]

And the judgment of 16 April 2004 added that: 'In a democratic judicial system, it must be admitted that justice is done by professional judges, assisted by lay judges from organisations defending opposing interests and who collectively, try to give a solution to a dispute in accordance with law and adapted to the reality.'[76]

The Belgian Supreme Court stated in a judgment of 2 June 2008,[77] that the system described above 'is not ... against conditions of impartiality imposed in particular by the European Convention on Human Rights and Fundamental Freedoms, considered from an organic and objective point of view, as long as the person concerned, like all professional judges, sits in his personal capacity. In exercising his judicial function, a labour counsellor cannot be considered as representing one of the trade union organisations involved'.[78]

The French system[79] was the subject of a direct but unsuccessful attack before the Supreme Court (Cour de cassation). In a judgment dated 19 December 2003,

---

[74] See, however, Labour Tribunal of Nivelles, 16 June 2004: (2004) *Journal des Tribunaux* 557.

[75] 'En règle générale, le principe d'impartialité est assuré par la neutralité du juge amené à statuer. Dans le système de "l'échevinage", le principe du droit à un juge impartial ne peut s'apprécier uniquement en fonction de la personnalité d'un des juges sociaux. L'impartialité est garantie par l'équilibre résultant de la présence d'un juge "employeur", d'un juge "travailleur" et d'un magistrat professionnel. Elle se réalise par le débat qui s'instaure entre personnes issues d'organisations dont les points de vue et les sensibilités sont, en principe, différents et avec le magistrat professionnel.'

[76] 'Dans un système judiciaire démocratique, il doit être admis que la justice soit rendue par des juges professionnels, assistés de juges non professionnels, issus d'organisations défendant des intérêts opposés et qui, collégialement, s'efforcent de donner à un litige une solution conforme au droit et adaptée aux réalités .'

[77] Cour de cassation (b), 2 June 2008, C.08.0215.N. See also, later and in the same dispute, Cour de cassation (b), 8 July 2008, C.08.0285.N. These two judgments are available at: www.cass.be. On the case, see W Vandeput, 'Arbeidshof bevestigt principiële onpartijdigheid rechters in sociale zaken' (2008) *Juristenkrant*, n°170, 1. See also I Van Hiel, 'Waarom alleen representatieve werknemersorganisaties kandidaten bij de sociale verkiezingen mogen voordragen' (2009) 5 *Orientatie* 129–32.

[78] 'Ne va pas ... à l'encontre des conditions d'impartialité imposées en particulier par la Convention de sauvegarde des droits de l'homme et des libertés fondamentales, examinées d'un point de vue organique et objectif, dès lors que la personne concernée, comme tous les magistrats professionnels, siège en son nom propre. Dans l'exercice de sa fonction juridictionnelle, un conseiller social ne peut pas être considéré comme étant le représentant d'une des organisations syndicales concernées.'

[79] See the synthesis realised by J Normand, 'L'impartialité du juge en droit judiciaire privé français' in J van Compernolle and G Tarzia (eds), *L'impartialité du juge et de l'arbitre. Étude de droit comparé* (Brussels, Bruylant, 2006) 86. See also the conclusions of the Advocate General M Collomb before the Cour de cassation (f) (Soc), 19 December 2003 (2 judgments), available at: www.courdecassation.fr.

this Court decided that 'respect for the impartiality requirement, as imposed both by the rules of internal law and by Article 6 para.1 of the European Convention for the Protection of Human Rights and Fundamental Freedoms is guaranteed, in labour matters, by the very composition of labour tribunals which include an equal number of elected employees and employers, by the public order prohibition of any imperative mandate, the option of using an external judge and the opportunity, when needed, to appeal to Court of appeal or to the Supreme Court ... it follows that the fact that one or more members of a Labour Court belong to the same union as one of the parties to the dispute is unlikely to affect the balance of interests inherent in the functioning of the labour court or to question the impartiality of its members'.[80]

The Belgian and French courts lean on a 'collective' conception of impartiality. The impartiality of the collegial court would be sought not in the absence of pre-conceptions from individual members,[81] but in the neutralisation of these potential individual biases within a group that, being equally composed, ensures a balance of opposite interests. To take over the inspiring words from P Morvan: 'The labour court justice is unlike any other: parity creates impartiality by the clash of potential preconceptions.'[82]

Such an approach is not contrary to the European Court of Human Rights case law.[83] On the contrary, the idea of collegial impartiality 'by balance of interests' has been accepted many times regarding lay jurisdictions in rental,[84] insurance[85] or land[86] litigation.

[80] 'Le respect de l'exigence d'impartialité, imposé tant par les règles de droit interne que par l'article 6-1 de la Convention européenne de sauvegarde des droits de l'Homme et des libertés fondamentales, est assuré, en matière prud'homale, par la composition même des conseils de prud'hommes, qui comprennent un nombre égal de salariés et d'employeurs élus, par la prohibition d'ordre public de tout mandat impératif, par la faculté de recourir à un juge départiteur extérieur aux membres élus et par la possibilité, selon le cas, d'interjeter appel ou de former un pourvoi en cassation ... il en résulte que la circonstance qu'un ou plusieurs membres d'un conseil de prud'hommes appartiennent à la même organisation syndicale que l'une des parties au procès n'est pas de nature à affecter l'équilibre d'intérêts inhérent au fonctionnement de la juridiction prud'homale ou à mettre en cause l'impartialité de ses membres.'

[81] Some lay judges sometimes openly claim the 'partisan' character of their mission. See B Augier, 'Une juridiction paritaire à conserver et à défendre, une institution démocratique, une institution d'avenir' (2000) 149(51) *Gazette du Palais* 2–3.

[82] 'La justice prud'homale est à nulle autre semblable: la parité y engendre l'impartialité par l'entrechoc des éventuels parti-pris' (P Morvan (n 68) 269).

[83] See F Tulkens and S Van Drooghenbroeck, 'La double vie du juge est-elle compatible avec son impartialité?' in *L'humanisme dans la résolution des conflits. Utopie ou réalité ? Liber amicorum P. Martens* (Brussels, Larcier, 2007) 502–05.

[84] *Langborger v Sweden*, App No 11179/84, Judgment of 22 June 1989, Series A, vol 155, para 35.

[85] Regarding jurisdictions in charge of applying the medical price lists agreed by collective negociations, see *Thaler v Austria*, App No 58141/00, Judgment of 3 February 2005, para 33. See also, more recently, *Puchstein v Austria*, App No 20089/06, Judgment of 28 January 2010.

[86] See European Commission of Human Rights, *Ferdinand and Maria-Theresa Kholer v Austria*, App No 18991/91, decision of 13 October 1993.

It is no different in litigation in the field of labour and social security.[87] In the *AB Kurt Kellermann* judgment,[88] the Court decided that: 'Lay assessors sitting on the Labour Court, who take the judicial oath, have special knowledge and experience of the labour market. They therefore contribute to the court's understanding of issues relating to the labour market and appear in principle to be highly qualified to participate in the adjudication of labour disputes. It should also be noted that the inclusion of lay assessors as members of various specialised courts is a common feature in many countries.' Similar considerations were recently reiterated and extended in the *Luka v Romania*[89] judgment: 'the existence of a college with a mixed composition including judges, public officials or representatives of interest groups does not in itself amount to an evidence of a partiality ... The Court cannot deny the advantage of collegiate courts with mixed composition, having professional and lay judges to hear disputes in areas where their experience is needed to address specific issues that may arise ... These legal systems based on the principle of collaborative justice, in particular as regards the labour courts, exist in a number of States which are party to the Convention'.[90]

However, the patent of impartiality and independence so awarded by the Court to these special courts has two limitations.

The first limitation stems from the *concrete*, as opposed to purely *abstract*, aspect of the Court's evaluation of the 'balance of interests' when reaching a conclusion on the structural impartiality of the jurisdiction at issue. This assessment is done on a case-by-case basis, depending on the object and the issue at stake of particular disputes brought before it and not solely based on organic laws governing the composition of jurisdictions. As the Court decided in *AB Kurt Kellermann*, in the line of the precedent *Langborger*, 'with respect to the objective impartiality of the lay assessors in the present case ... the decisive issue is whether the balance of interests in the composition of the Labour Court was upset and, if so, whether any such lack of balance would result in the court failing to satisfy the requirement of impartiality in the determination of the particular dispute before it'.[91] The impartiality of the

---

[87] The question, before being brought before the ECHR, had already been the subject of quite precise case law from the European Commission of Human Rights. See European Commission of Human Rights, *Stallarholmens Platslageri o Ventilation Handelsbolag and others v Sweden*, App No 12733/87, decision of 7 September 1990; European Commission of Human Rights, *Siglfirdingur ehf v Iceland*, App No 34142/96, decision of 7 September 1999; European Commission of Human Rights, *Smeeton-Wilkinson v Sweden*, App No 24601/94, decision of 28 February 1996.

[88] *AB Kurt Kellermann v Sweden*, App No 41579/98, Judgment of 26 October 2004, para 60. On this judgment, see the observations of J-P Marguénaud and C Mouly (2005) *Droit social* 863.

[89] *Luka v Romania*, App No 34197/02, Judgment of 21 June 2009, paras 41–42.

[90] 'L'existence d'un collège à composition mixte comprenant des magistrats, des fonctionnaires publics ou des représentants de groupements d'intérêt ne constitue pas en soi une preuve de partialité ... La Cour ne saurait nier l'avantage que des juridictions collégiales à composition mixte, juges professionnels et non professionnels connaissent des litiges dans des domaines ou l'expérience de ces derniers est nécessaire à régler des questions spécifiques pouvant s'y poser ... Ces systèmes judiciaires fondés sur le principe de l'échevinage, en particulier les juridictions de travail, existent dans un certain nombre d'États parties à la Convention.'

[91] *AB Kurt Kellermann v Sweden* (n 88) para 63. According to the same judgment, the tribunal would be lacking the required impartiality 'either if the lay assessors had a common interest contrary to those of the applicant or if their interests, although not common, were such that they were nevertheless opposed to those of the applicant (see *Stallarholmens Plåtslageri o Ventilation Handelsbolag and Others v Sweden*, No 12733/87, Commission decision of 7 September 1990, Decisions and Reports 66, p 111, at p 118)'.

court is lacking when the issue is the very validity of a collective agreement between the interest groups that appointed the lay judges,[92] or the possibility to make an exception to such an agreement.[93] The fact that the lay judges had not been personally involved in negotiating the collective agreement at issue is in this context irrelevant. According to the Court, 'situations falling short of the direct involvement of a member of a tribunal in the subject matter to be decided may give rise to legitimate doubts as regards that tribunal's independence and impartiality'.[94] In contrast, according to *AB Kurt Kellermann*, a violation of Article 6 does not come from the sole fact that one party to the dispute, in contrast to the other, is not affiliated with a trade union having designated one of the lay judges that is deciding the case.[95] To take up the reasoning of that case, 'to accept that [this situation of asymmetrical affiliation] gives rise to doubts as to the Labour Court's impartiality would, in the Court's opinion, be tantamount to considering that, in cases where lay assessors have been nominated by any labour market organisation, the Labour Court would fail to meet the requirement of being an "impartial tribunal" in all disputes where one of the parties is not affiliated to such an organisation'.[96]

The second limitation is highlighted by the *Luka v Romania* case mentioned above: the status of lay judges should be sufficiently protected to ensure the real independence of the latter—and, as a result, the jurisdiction in which they sit—vis-a-vis the pressures from outside and, particularly, from the Executive. On this point, and thereby following the soft law directives of the Council of Europe,[97] the Court does not appear to be less demanding on the status of lay judges than it is regarding the status of professional judges.[98] According to the *Luka* judgment, there is no requirement that a lay judge must have a lifetime appointment—a fixed term is consistent with the notion of independence.[99] This independence is, however, questionable when, as part of this mandate, the Executive can remove the lay judge[100] without the law determining a priori the criteria or circumstances in which this can

---

[92] *Thaler v Austria* (n 85) § 35: 'As regards the first set of proceedings the Court considers that, for the reasons set out in *Hortolomei*, the mere fact that the two bodies which had concluded the impugned general agreement appointed the assessors to the Regional Appeals Commission is sufficient to justify the applicant's fears as regards the Commission's lack of independence and impartiality. The case relied on by the Government (*Siglfirðingur ehf*, cited above) cannot lead to another finding, since the assessors in the labour courts at issue in that case were representatives of conflicting spheres of interest but, unlike the present case, there were no circumstances liable to upset the balance inherent in such a system.'

[93] *Langborger v Sweden* (n 84) para 35.

[94] *Thaler v Austria* (n 85) para 33.

[95] *AB Kurt Kellermann v Sweden* (n 88) para 68.

[96] Ibid, para 68.

[97] See Chapter I, Articles 1 and 2 of the annex to Recommendation CM/Rec(2010)12 of the Committee of Ministers to Member States on judges: independence, efficiency and responsibilities (17 november 2010): 'This recommendation is applicable to all persons exercising judicial functions, including those dealing with constitutional matters. The provisions laid down in this recommendation also apply to non-professional judges, except where it is clear from the context that they only apply to professional judges.'

[98] *Luka v Romania* (n 89) para 42.

[99] *Luka v Romania* (n 89).

[100] 'Appointment of judges by the executive is permissible, provided that appointees are free from influence or pressure when carrying out their adjudicatory role' (*Henryk Urban and Ryszard Urban v Poland*, App No 23614/08, Judgment of 30 November 2010, para 49).

take place.[101] To find a violation of Article 6, the same judgment also contended that the Romanian law on lay judges did not foresee that they served 'in their own name'[102] and did not prohibit 'the exercise of other functions and mandates assigned by the organisation on behalf of which they were elected'.[103]

3.2 Article 6 and the Particular Vulnerability of Parties to Labour Law Disputes

Disputes brought before the labour courts can be characterised by a significant asymmetry as regards the situation of the parties or by the very specific vulnerability of one of them. One can think, for example, of disputes relating to dismissal or financial compensation for an accident.

The European Court of Human Rights is clearly not insensitive to these vulnerabilities, and the rules and standards of fair trial that it shapes therefore present the practical flexibility that allows them to consider such situations on a case-by-case basis. This arises, for example, in the field of legal costs. It is commonly accepted, since the *Kreuz v Poland* judgment, 'that the interests of the fair administration of justice may justify imposing a financial restriction on the individual's access to a court' and that 'neither an unqualified right to obtain free legal aid from the State in a civil dispute, nor a right to free proceedings in civil matters can be inferred from that provision'.[104]

The fact remains that, in special circumstances and under the principle of proportionality, a financial barrier to access to court may result in a violation of Article 6. Everything will be assessed on a case-by-case basis: 'the amount of the fees assessed in the light of the particular circumstances of a given case, including the applicant's ability to pay them, and the phase of the proceedings at which that restriction has been imposed are factors which are material in determining whether or not a person enjoyed his right of access'.[105]

In *Ulger v Turkey*,[106] a worker was unable to enforce the order obtained by him against his employer (amounting to €10,000) due to his failure to obtain a copy of the order. The issuance of this copy was subject to the payment of all legal costs (the amount not yet paid: €598), which was normally borne by the losing party.[107] Given the specific circumstances of the case, the Court found a violation of Article 6:

> [T]he fulfilment of the obligation to secure effective rights under Article 6 § 1 of the Convention does not only mean the absence of an interference but may also require positive

---

[101] *Luka v Romania* (n 89) para 44. In a decision of 25 November 1996 (*Hans-Jürgen Stieringer v Germany*, App No 28899/95), the Commission seems to have considered that the 'independence defect' connected to the revocation power of the Executive could be corrected if there was a *judicial review* of the revocation decisions. See also *Henryk Urban and Ryszard Urban v Poland* (n 100) para 53.

[102] *Luka v Romania* (n 89) para 43.

[103] Ibid, para 44.

[104] *Kreuz v Poland*, App No 28249/95, Judgment of 29 June 2001, para 59.

[105] *Urbanek v Austria*, App No 35123/05, Judgment of 9 December 2010, para 51.

[106] *Ulger v Turkey*, App No 25321/02, Judgment of 26 June 2007.

[107] The applicant, although apparently willing to pay the charges in order to obtain what he was owed, no longer had sufficient means to do so (ibid, para 43).

action on the part of the State ... [The Court] considers that by shifting to the applicant the full responsibility to meet the court costs, the State avoided its positive obligation to organise a system for the enforcement of judgments which is effective both in law and in practice ... Thus, some consideration should also have been given in the present case to the reasonable relationship of proportionality ... between the amount and payment of the court costs, the applicant's ability to pay them and the work required for the task in hand, i.e. merely providing him with a copy of the judgment.[108]

In the above-mentioned case, the solicitude of the Court and of Article 6 vis-a-vis the worker is based on a punctual, practical approach, which is justified by the circumstances of the case. In some areas of litigation relating to Article 6, however, this solicitude exists a priori and relies on a more 'structural' axiom. Such is the case about the guarantee of 'reasonable time' of the procedure. According to traditional case law of the Court, 'the reasonableness of the length of proceedings must be assessed in the light of the circumstances of the case and with reference to the following criteria: the complexity of the case, the conduct of the applicants and the relevant authorities and what was at stake for the applicants in the dispute'.[109] Regarding the last criterion of appreciation, consistent case law from the Court[110] states that 'an employee who considers that he or she has been wrongly suspended or dismissed by his or her employer has an important personal interest in securing a judicial decision on the lawfulness of that measure promptly, since employment disputes by their nature call for expeditious decision, in view of what is at stake for the person concerned, who through dismissal loses his or her means of subsistence'.[111]

This one-off or systematic 'sollicitude' of the Court towards workers is, however, not borne out by each and every decision or judgment handed down in Strasbourg. A good example of the 'non-labourisation' of Article 6 can be found in the very recent decision delivered in *Tripon v Romania*.[112] On 21 September 2001, the applicant, a customs officer at a border post, was placed in pre-trial detention on suspicion that he had committed an offence of abuse of office to the detriment of the State's interests. The court extended his detention until 1 December 2001, when he was released. In the meantime, on 28 November 2001, Mr Tripon had been dismissed on the basis of Article 130(j) of the Labour Code, which made it possible to dismiss an employee if he or she was placed in pre-trial detention for more than 60 days, on whatever grounds.

Before the Court, Mr Tripon argued that his dismissal was contrary to his right to be presumed innocent, which was guaranteed by Article 6, § 2 of the Convention. However, this complaint was declared manifestly ill-founded on the basis of the following reasons.

The Court noted first that the right, under Article 130(j) of the Labour Code, to dismiss an employee placed in pre-trial detention for more than 60 days was based

---

[108] Ibid, para 44.
[109] *Gjonbocari and others v Albania*, App No 10508/02, Judgment of 23 October 2007, para 61.
[110] *Frydlender v France*, App No 30979/96, Judgment of 27 June 2000, *Reports* 2000-VII, para 45 and further references. For an application, see *Delgado v France*, App No 38437/97, Judgment of 14 November 2000. See also Adde, J-P Marguénaud and C Mouly, 'Convention européenne des droits de l'Homme et droit du travail' (2008) 123(7) *Les Petites Affiches* 6–7.
[111] *Mishgjoni v Albania*, App No 18381/05, Judgment of 7 December 2010, para 59.
[112] *Tripon v Romania*, App No 27062/04, Judgment of 6 March 2012.

on an objective factor, namely the extended absence of the employee from his or her work, and not on any other grounds. By enacting that provision, the national legislature had sought to protect employers against the possibly damaging consequences of the prolonged absence of an employee who consequently did not fulfil his or her contractual obligations. The Court also observed that the Romanian legislation at the relevant time had provided sufficient safeguards against arbitrary or abusive treatment of employees who were absent from work because they were in custody. Further, the Court stated that no representative of the State, whether a judge, court or other public authority, had made any explicit statements reflecting an opinion that Mr Tripon was guilty of an offence before his guilt had been established by the competent criminal court.

According to the applicant, there existed a 'less restrictive alternative' capable of achieving a better balance between the interests of the employer and the rights of the workers in a situation of pre-trial detention of the latter: the mere suspension of their contracts until the criminal court concerned had given a final decision determining their guilt. The Court's reply to this line of argument is, however, quite weak and—frankly speaking—inadequate: 'It is true that, had the criminal proceedings resulted in the applicant's acquittal, the law would not have required the applicant's former employer to reinstate him. It would nevertheless have then been possible for the applicant to bring an action for damages against the State in order to obtain compensation for the judicial error made in his case.'[113]

---

[113] 'Il est vrai que, si à l'issue de la procédure pénale, le requérant avait été acquitté, la loi n'obligeait pas pour autant son ancien employeur à le réintégrer sur son ancien poste. Néanmoins, il aurait alors été possible au requérant d'introduire une action en réparation contre l'Etat, en vue d'obtenir des dédommagements pour l'erreur judiciaire dont il aurait fait l'objet.'

8

Article 8 ECHR: Judicial Patterns of Employment Privacy Protection

FRANK HENDRICKX AND ALINE VAN BEVER

1 INTRODUCTION

THIS CONTRIBUTION EXAMINES Article 8 of the European Convention on Human Rights (ECHR), which guarantees the right to privacy.[1] The issue of privacy in the employment context, referred to in short as employment privacy, has gained importance in the labour law discourse over the last few decades. There are a couple of reasons for this. First, privacy has gained relevance in the daily functioning of employment relations. Employee privacy covers a broad range of issues, including personnel information processing, medical screening, psychological testing, surveillance and monitoring of workers through the Internet and email. There is a growing interest in information about an employee's personal life style or conduct that is often made available through new social media. Second, the right to privacy is protected as a fundamental right. The introduction of a fundamental rights discourse in labour law and the constitutionalisation of the workplace have enabled privacy rights to develop. Third, there is the growing relevance of information technology and data protection legislation. Both the Council of Europe and the European Union (EU) have been using rule-setting power and relatively detailed techniques to protect the personal data of citizens, including employees.

This contribution researches the scope and functioning of Article 8 ECHR in an employment context, looking at the judicial patterns of employment privacy protection before the European Court of Human Rights (ECtHR). What is meant by privacy in an employment relationship and how is it recognised by the ECtHR? How does Article 8 ECHR allow a balancing of an employee's reasonable privacy expectations with the employer's managerial interests? What guarantees does ECtHR judicial review provide for the employee's right to respect for his private life? These questions will be considered against the background of a number of specific research interests.

---

[1] According to Article 8 § 1 ECHR, everyone has the right to respect for his private and family life, his home and his correspondence. Article 8 § 2 ECHR continues that there shall be no interference by a public authority with the exercise of this right except such as is in accordance with the law and is necessary in a democratic society in the interests of national security, public safety or the economic well-being of the country, for the prevention of disorder or crime, for the protection of health or morals, or for the protection of the rights and freedoms of others.

First of all, the protection afforded by Article 8 ECHR needs to be put into the context of employment law. Employment privacy cases imply a balancing of the rights and interests of employers and employees, arguably a function performed through employment case law as well. The question is how this interest-balancing is influenced by an approach involving Article 8 ECHR. Does it imply an advance towards a more progressive, ie, a more protective, view on employee privacy?

Second, the use of the ECHR framework could be seen as a tool for the pro-motion of social rights. This idea seems to have been permitted in the *Demir and Baykara*[2] case law. The potential cross-fertilisation of civil rights (such as privacy) and social rights will therefore be examined. The analysis will, in this context, also raise the question as to what extent the case law related to the right to privacy contributes to a so-called 'integrative approach', according to which the enjoyment of civil rights (eg, the right to privacy) is considered in the light of associated social rights (eg, the right to work).[3]

Third, the relationship of the ECHR protection to other international or European instruments is a matter of concern. The ECtHR case of *Demir and Baykara*[4] is seen as providing an explicitly consolidated approach in the interpretation of the rights laid down in the Convention by implying the need for systematic reference to other international standards. In this light, not only is the recognition of the right to pri-vacy in the EU Charter on Fundamental Rights relevant, but so is the existence of specific (employee) data protection instruments provided by the Council of Europe, the EU as well as the International Labour Organization (ILO). The question is whether cross-referencing, in this context, would help raise the level of protection offered by the ECHR framework. If not, the alternative question would be whether the ECHR is more progressive and thus capable of exercising a positive influence when the EU accedes to the Convention.

This contribution is divided into three sections. The first section discusses the right to privacy in the specific context of the employment relationship and has a double objective. First, this section is concerned with Article 8 § 1 ECHR. In this respect, the notion of reasonable privacy expectations is considered to be important, given the fact that, although these expectations are only one criterion to determine whether there is an interference with the employee's right to privacy, the absence of such expectation may lead to the conclusion that there is no interference with Article 8 § 1 ECHR. After this conceptual clarification, a range of cases in which an interference with the employee's right to privacy is found are looked at, thereby examining the scope of privacy protection under Article 8 § 1 ECHR, which involves various stages in the employment relationship. Second, this section aims to explore, in the ECtHR's case law, the extent to which privacy rights are considered in the light of related social rights such as the right to work.

Once the scope of application of Article 8 ECHR to employment privacy issues has been determined in Section 1, the second section focuses on the test of Article 8 § 2

---

[2] ECtHR (Grand Chamber) judgment of 12 November 2008, App No 34503/97, *Demir and Baykara v Turkey*.

[3] *Cf* V Mantouvalou, 'Work and Private Life: *Sidabras and Dziautas v Lithaunia*' (2005) 30 *EL Rev* 573.

[4] *Demir and Baykara v Turkey* (n 2).

ECHR, considering under which circumstances an interference to the right to privacy can be justified. Attention will be paid to the balance of interests under Article 8 § 2 ECHR in light of the doctrine of horizontal effect and that of the margin of appreciation.

Finally, Section 3 looks at the value of the protection mechanism underlying Article 8 ECHR in comparison with the protection afforded by specific data protection instruments. Attention is paid to instruments of the Council of Europe, the EU and the ILO.

2 THE SCOPE OF EMPLOYMENT PRIVACY

Article 8 § 1 ECHR guarantees everyone the right to respect for his private and family life, his home and correspondence. In short, everyone has a right to privacy. The fact that 'everyone' enjoys the right to privacy is relevant. To what extent does this imply that employers need to respect the right to privacy of employees or job applicants?

2.1 The Specific Context of the Employment Relationship

When studying employee privacy, attention must be paid to the employment environment. An employment relationship implies, as a general rule, a subordinate relationship. This means that the employer is contractually allowed to exercise authority over his employees. In other words, being an employee implies that one's freedom is partly impaired in the sense that the employer can control personal behaviour. The employee's right to privacy is therefore qualified by the employment relationship,[5] which is based in particular on the opposition or reconciliation of rights and interests in the employment context. Indeed, it must be recognised that the right to privacy is not absolute. As the European Commission of Human Rights observed in the past, 'the claim to respect for private life is automatically reduced to the extent that the individual himself brings his private life into contact with public life or into close connection with other protected interests'.[6] Because of the authority relationship binding the employee to his employer, the employee's reasonable privacy expectations are reduced. Moreover, apart from managerial prerogatives, the employment relationship implies the co-existence of rights and interests of other employees (colleagues) and third parties (customers, society at large).[7] These different rights and interests can also limit the right to privacy of the individual employee.

A similar reasoning holds in recruitment procedures. Although (as yet) no authority relationship exists between a job applicant and a recruiting employer, in such a prospective employment relationship, the latter needs to be able to rely on certain rights and legitimate interests. Indeed, from his freedom of recruitment (freedom

---

[5] F Hendrickx, *Privacy en arbeidsrecht* (Bruges, die Keure, 1999) 47 and 51.
[6] *Brüggeman and Scheuten v Germany* (1981) 3 EHRR 244, § 56 (Commission Decision).
[7] *Madsen v Denmark*, App No 58341/00, 7 November 2002.

of contract), his legitimate business interests and the *intuitu personae* nature of the employment contract, the recruiting employer derives the right to inform himself about the candidate.[8] He must, however, exercise that right with respect to the right to privacy of the job applicant. Nevertheless, the latter's reasonable privacy expectations are also in this case reduced because of the specific context.

The fact that the employment relationship (or the relationship between the job applicant and the recruiting employer) implies restrictions on the exercise of the right to privacy can be seen as reducing the (candidate) employee's reasonable privacy expectations, which, in turn, makes it more difficult for the employee to prove an interference with his right to privacy. This, however, does not automatically imply that he cannot raise any privacy claim against the (recruiting) employer. The (candidate) employee is *only* subject to the employer's authority insofar as this authority is embodied in their (prospective) relationship. The specificity of their relationship is, nevertheless, sufficiently relevant to examine the employee's reasonable privacy expectations.

2.2 Reasonable Expectations of Privacy

In an (employment) privacy discourse, privacy expectations have to be taken into consideration in order to determine whether there is an interference with one's right to privacy and, if so, whether or not the right to privacy is violated. An important caveat, however, has to be made in light of the concept of 'reasonable expectations of privacy'. This concept finds its origin in the US legal system. While the ECtHR applies a rather similar concept of reasonable privacy expectations, the role that it plays is nevertheless different.

2.2.1 Reasonable Privacy Expectation in the US

In the US, the notion of reasonable privacy expectations came up under the Fourth Amendment.[9] In the reference case of *Katz v US*,[10] the US Supreme Court made privacy protection dependent on the requirement of the existence of reasonable privacy expectations. The Court specified that there are two kinds of expectations. If an individual actually believes that a situation or location is private—which varies from person to person—then his privacy expectation is subjective. Objective privacy expectations, on the other hand, are those generally recognised by society. Hence, it has been accepted that private places, such as a person's home, belong to the private sphere, whereas public areas and things held to the public, such as garbage on the street or a car parked outside[11]—in short, 'anything in open fields'—do not imply

---

[8] Hendrickx (n 5) 112.
[9] S Nouwt and BR de Vries, 'Introduction' in S Nouwt, BR de Vries and C Prins (eds), *Reasonable Expectations of Privacy?* (The Hague, TMC Asser Press, 2005) 3. The Fourth Amendment to the Constitution protects US citizens against unreasonable seizures and searches by requiring a judicially sanctioned warrant and a probable cause. This specific context may have an influence on the way in which the right to privacy and privacy expectations are considered.
[10] *Katz v US*, 389 US 347 (1967).
[11] *Miller v US*, 425 US 435 (1976).

an objective expectation of privacy.[12] An exception is made for public places which are specifically provided for private aims.[13] For example, cameras pointed at a public thoroughfare do not in general interfere with one's right to privacy,[14] but phone calls made in a telephone booth are protected against any 'uninvited ear'.[15]

In the US, the existence of (objective) privacy expectations seems to depend on the reasonable care taken by an individual: 'what a person knowingly exposes to the public, even in their home or office, is not subject to a Fourth Amendment protection'.[16] The idea of reasonable privacy expectations is thus used to determine the scope of the right to privacy. As a consequence, the absence of reasonable privacy expectations may cause a range of issues to fall outside the private sphere, so that the right to privacy is not involved. The US approach may lead to the finding that employees, while under the authority of the employer, cannot automatically claim reasonable privacy expectations. For this reason, in the US employee privacy seems to be approached somewhat differently than in Europe. It has been concluded that the US approach 'fails to conceive of the possibility of "private space", literally or metaphorically, while at work'.[17] The European approach by contrast appears to conceive privacy expectations from a different starting point.

2.2.2 Reasonable Privacy Expectations in the ECHR

Contrary to the US, the ECtHR seems to accept as a matter of principle that privacy rights are also guaranteed in the public space. In the case of *PG and JH v UK*, the Court accepted that there is 'a zone of interaction of a person with others, even in a public context, which may fall within the scope of "private life"'.[18] With respect to the employment context, the ECtHR adopted the view (in the case of *Niemietz v Germany*) that:

> [T]here appears ... to be no reason of principle why this understanding of the notion of 'private life' should be taken to exclude activities of a professional or business nature since it is, after all, in the course of their working lives that the majority of people have a significant, if not the greatest, opportunity of developing relationships with the outside world.[19]

The ECtHR nevertheless recognises the notion of reasonable privacy expectations as a way to determine the reach of the protection afforded by the right to privacy: if it is less reasonable to expect that one's right to privacy can be guaranteed, the claim to respect for private life is automatically 'reduced'. This idea of reduced privacy expectations is explicitly present in the cases of the European Commission of Human Rights. In *Brüggeman and Scheuten*, for example, the Commission ruled

---

[12] P Bergman and SJ Berman-Barrett, *The Criminal Law Handbook: Know Your Rights, Survive the System* (Berkeley, Nolo, 2007) 62.

[13] *Katz v US* (n 10) 361.

[14] *Knotts v US* 460 US 276 (1983).

[15] *Katz v US* (n 10)352.

[16] Ibid, 351; eg, garbage that has been left on the street, as in *California v Greenwood*, 486 US 35 (1988).

[17] MW Finkin, *Privacy in Employment Law*, 2nd edn (Washington DC, BNA Books, 2003) xxix.

[18] *PG and JH v UK* (44787/98) [2001] ECHR 546 (25 September 2001), § 56.

[19] *Niemietz v Germany*, 16 December 1992, Series A, No 251-B § 29.

that 'the claim to respect for private life is automatically reduced to the extent that the individual himself brings his private life into contact with public life or into close connection with other protected interests' and hence conceived this reduction as a logical consequence of the presence of interfering and competing rights'.[20] The Court itself seems to accept this idea, introducing the idea of reasonable privacy expectations in the case of *Lüdi v Switzerland*[21] by stating that persons involving in criminal activities, eg, drug trafficking, must accept a lesser privacy expectation. As Lüdi was prepared to sell (the undercover agent) two kilograms of cocaine, he must have known that he was engaging in a criminal activity and therefore running the risk of encountering an undercover agent, whose task would in fact be to expose him.[22] The Court hence accepted that the implication of the undercover agent did not affect Lüdi's right to privacy, as guaranteed by Article 8 § 1 ECHR.

Nevertheless, the ECtHR has also emphasised that a person's reasonable privacy expectations are not the only criterion used in determining whether or not Article 8 § 1 ECHR applies. Indeed, in *PG and JH v UK*,[23] the ECtHR moderated its earlier conclusion in the *Lüdi* case by stating that in order to know whether a person's privacy is protected by Article 8 § 1 ECHR, privacy expectations are a significant but not necessarily conclusive factor.[24] The Court reasoned that:

> [T]here are a number of elements relevant to a consideration of whether a person's private life is concerned by measures effected outside a person's home or private premises. Since there are occasions when people knowingly or intentionally involve themselves in activities which are or may be recorded or reported in a public manner, a person's reasonable expectations as to privacy may be a significant, although not necessarily conclusive, factor. A person who walks down the street will, inevitably, be visible to any member of the public who is also present. Monitoring by technological means of the same public scene (for example, a security guard viewing through closed-circuit television) is of a similar character. Private-life considerations may arise, however, once any systematic or permanent record comes into existence of such material from the public domain.[25]

The ECtHR seems to advance the concept of privacy expectations from an opposite departure point. In principle, the scope of privacy protection includes activities of a professional or business nature. Therefore, the ECtHR seems to accept that an employee has reasonable privacy expectations at work, but in a way that avoids that such privacy expectations would exclude too many forms of intrusions from the protective reach of Article 8 § 1 ECHR. In other words, most cases would still require States to justify their actions under Article 8 § 2 ECHR. This approach allows a stronger, more inclusive protection of the right to privacy. Nevertheless, despite this, privacy expectations can be reduced in the balancing of rights and interests under Article 8 § 2 ECHR. In sum, in the ECtHR's case law, reasonable privacy expectations only marginally affect the scope of the privacy right

---

[20] *Brüggeman and Scheuten v Germany* (1981) 3 EHRR 244, § 56 (Commission Decision).
[21] *Lüdi v Switzerland*, Series A, No 238 (1992) 15 EHRR 173, § 40.
[22] C Gorman, *Is Society More Reasonable than You? The Reasonable Expectation of Privacy as a Criterion for Privacy Protection* (Tilburg, University of Tilburg Press, 2011) 28.
[23] *PG and JH v UK* [2001] ECHR 546, § 57.
[24] Confirmed in *Peck v UK* (2003) 36 EHRR 41, § 58 and *Perry v UK* [2003] ECHR 375, § 37.
[25] *PG and JH v UK* (n 23) § 57.

(*cf* Article 8 § 1 ECHR) and rather take effect in the assessment of the reasonableness of the interference with this right (*cf* Article 8 § 2 ECHR).

2.2.3 *An Employee's Reasonable Privacy Expectations*

The case of *Halford v UK*[26] provides an illustration of the way in which the ECtHR assesses the reasonableness of an employee's privacy expectations. Indeed, since there was no evidence that Ms Halford was given any warning that office calls made on the internal telecommunications system would be liable to interception, the ECtHR concluded that she could have a reasonable expectation of privacy as regards such calls. This conclusion was further reinforced by the fact that, as Assistant Chief Constable, Ms Halford had sole use of her office where there were two telephones—one of which was specifically designated for her private use. Furthermore, the fact that Ms Halford had been authorised to use her office phone to attend, while on duty, to the sex discrimination case in which she was involved supported the reasonableness of her expectations.

To determine the reasonableness of privacy expectations in an employment context, the ECtHR seems to depart from the concrete context and the relevant facts.[27] The reasonableness of these expectations thus depends, amongst other things, on the question whether the employee was informed about the fact that an interference with his right to privacy was possible, on the presence of specific indications of the possibility of such interference or on the (permanent) nature and the impact of the interference.

2.3 Employment Privacy in Different Stages of the Employment Relationship

Employees enjoy a right to privacy in different stages of the employment relationship. The ECtHR's case law concerning employment privacy is not limited to the stage in which the employee and employer actually perform their contract, but extends both to the hiring phase and to cases in which that contract has been terminated on the basis of private facts or information. In order to get a clear view of the protective reach of Article 8 ECHR, this sub-section provides an overview of different cases in which the right to privacy has been raised. The focus is on the question whether there is an interference with the right to respect for private life in application of Article 8 § 1 ECHR, rather than whether that interference could be justified under Article 8 § 2 ECHR. The latter question will be dealt with further below.

Another aspect of the analysis of the case law is the search for links between privacy rights and social rights. In the case of *Niemietz v Germany*[28] referred to above, the ECtHR explicitly rejected a narrow interpretation of Article 8 § 1 ECHR,

---

[26] *Halford v UK* (1998) 24 EHRR 523.
[27] F Raepsaet, 'Les attentes raisonnables en matière de vie privée' (2011) 10 *Journal des tribunaux du travail* 145, 147 and 153.
[28] *Niemietz v Germany*, 16 December 1992, Series A, No 251-B § 29.

holding that since the notion of private life must include the right to establish relationships with others, there is no reason of principle why that notion should be taken to exclude activities of a professional or business nature. After all, it is in the course of their working lives that most people have a significant opportunity of developing relationships with the outside world.[29] The relevance of *Niemietz* is clear when the connection between the right to privacy and social rights is considered. Moreover, as discussed hereafter, the Court's case law allows finding more—and perhaps stronger—forms of integration between privacy and social rights. The cases seem to support the view that civil rights, such as the right to privacy, only have real meaning if they are integrated with social rights.[30]

2.3.1 Recruitment and Selection

Job applicants enjoy the protection of the right to privacy. This implies privacy protection in the context of job access and pre-employment screening. In this context, a connection between the right to privacy and social rights may occur.

A clear illustration is the case of *Sidabras and Dziautas v Lithuania*,[31] in which the ECtHR not only considered the right to privacy as such, but linked it to the dignity of the (candidate) employee. The Court concluded that the Lithuanian Act, which temporary prohibited former KGB officers from working as public officials or civil servants, or from performing a job requiring the carrying of a weapon—as a consequence of which they were unable to find a job in various branches of the private sector—amounted to a violation of the right to privacy. Indeed, although Article 8 ECHR does not encompass a right of access to the civil service, the ECtHR considered that 'having regard in particular to the notions currently prevailing in democratic states ... a far-reaching ban on taking up private-sector employment does affect private life'.[32] Moreover, the Court justified its broad interpretation of 'private life' by associating it with the right to work, as protected by Article 1 of the European Social Charter (ESC) and with the principle of non-discrimination referred to in ILO Convention No 111.[33] It thus emphasised the close connection between the (civil) right to privacy and the (social) right to work. By thus interpreting the right to privacy in a holistic manner, the ECtHR delivered an integrative approach, in line with the so-called theory of the indivisibility and interdependence of fundamental rights.[34] The Court recalled that 'there is no watertight division separating the sphere of social and economic rights from the field covered by the

---

[29] Ibid, § 29.
[30] *Cf* Mantouvalou (n 3).
[31] *Sidabras and Dziautas v Lithuania*, ECHR 2004-VIII (2004) 42 EHRR 104.
[32] Ibid, § 47.
[33] Ibid, §§ 31–32.
[34] *Cf* the *Limburg Principles on the Implementation of the International Covenant on Economic, Social and Cultural Rights* (UN Doc E/CNA/1987/17; (1987) 9 *Human Rights Quarterly* 122–35) and the *Maastricht Guidelines on Violations of Economic, Social and Cultural Rights* ((1998) 20 *Human Rights Quarterly* 691); V Leary, 'Lessons from the Experience of the International Labour Organisation' in P Alston (ed), *The United Nations and Human Rights: A Critical Reappraisal* (Oxford, Oxford University Press, 1992) 580, 590; Mantouvalou (n 3) 574.

Convention'.[35] The right to work and the right to respect for one's private and family life are thus closely intertwined.

The case of *Leander v Sweden*[36] is also interesting in light of the so-called integrative approach of the ECtHR, although the Court's conclusion is less far-reaching. In this case, the ECtHR had to judge whether the rejection to grant a permanent position to Mr Leander, who worked as a temporary replacement at the Naval Museum at Karlskrona, was compatible with Article 8 ECHR. The rejection was justified by reasons of national security and based on personal data that were secretly kept in a police register and which allegedly made him a security risk. With respect to the applicability of Article 8 § 1 ECHR, the ECtHR ruled that both the storage and the release of Mr Leander's personal data, coupled with the refusal to allow him the chance to refute it, amounted to an interference with his right to respect for private life. The interference was, however, considered to be justified and proportional, given its valid basis in domestic law, namely the Personnel Control Ordinance, and its purpose to protect national security. Accordingly, there had been no breach of Article 8 ECHR. In the ECtHR's view, the Swedish authorities had stayed within their margin of appreciation, even if that adversely affected Mr Leander's possibilities of accessing certain sensitive posts within the civil service. The Court reasoned that the right of access to a civil service was not as such enshrined in the ECHR.[37]

2.3.2 Control and Surveillance

Another question with respect to employment privacy is the extent to which the employer's managerial power to exercise control over his employees is limited by Article 8 ECHR. In this field of application, the Court seems to give a wide scope of application to Article 8 § 1 ECHR, although the employer's legitimate interests also remain widely recognised.

The first major case in the area of employee surveillance is the case of *Halford v UK*,[38] in which Article 8 ECHR was invoked in the context of discrimination proceedings before the Industrial Tribunal. Ms Halford claimed to be discriminated against in her attempts to be promoted to the rank of Deputy Chief Constable within the Police Department. She invoked a breach of her right to privacy, as guaranteed by Article 8 ECHR, based on evidence that her employer, the police, had intercepted her home and office telephone calls with the aim of gathering information to be used in its defence against the discrimination claim. With respect to the calls that *Halford* had held on her office telephone,[39] the Court ruled that these fell within the scope of her private life. Consequently, Article 8 § 1 ECHR was applicable. Moreover, the interception of those office calls infringed her right to privacy, as there was no

---

[35] Ibid, § 47.

[36] *Leander v Sweden*, Series A, No 116 (1987) 9 EHRR 433.

[37] Ibid, § 59. See also *Kosiek v Germany*, Series A, No 105 (1986) 9 EHRR 328.

[38] *Halford v UK* (n 26).

[39] Telephone calls made from business premises as well as from the home may be covered by the notions of 'private life' and 'correspondence' within the meaning of Article 8(1) ECHR (*cf Klass and others v Germany*, Series A, No 28 (1979–80) 2 EHRR 214, § 41; *Malone v UK*, Series A, No 82 (1984) 7 EHRR 14, § 64). In this case, however, the ECtHR found no interference with *Halford*'s right to privacy in relation to her home telephone.

domestic regulation of interceptions of calls made on telecommunications systems outside the public network.

Another example is the case of *Madsen v Denmark*,[40] in which it was questioned whether the introduction of a random mandatory alcohol and drug test, requiring the employees of a Danish shipping company to provide a urine sample when on duty onboard a ship, amounted to an unjustified interference with their right to privacy. According to the company's policy, the employees could expect to undergo such a test without notice at least once a year, and the disrespect of the regulations regarding the use or possession of alcohol and drugs onboard would constitute a considerable breach of their employment conditions, justifying summary dismissal. After having to take the test himself, Mr Madsen, a passenger assistant, contested the policy not only because the test itself would interfere with his right to privacy, but also because the test would reveal which activities he had been involved in during his free time. The Court of Arbitration, to which the case was brought at the national level, rejected his claim, emphasising the right of management to issue rules justified by operational considerations, including control measures that had a reasonable purpose and did not offend employees' dignity or cause them any loss or appreciable inconvenience. Moreover, the Court underlined that an employer is entitled to demand that an employee coming to work is capable of performing his duties, even if this entails some limits on the latter's free time before coming to work. Having regard to the fact that the consumption of alcohol and use of drugs, unless taken on a regularly basis, did not leave traces for more than one or two days, it concluded that the random test did not infringe Mr Madsen's right to privacy in such a way that it should be excluded. The case was taken to the ECtHR, which simply assumed there had been an interference by a public authority and did not elaborate on the applicability of Article 8 § 1 ECHR. Accordingly, the ECtHR examined whether the interference could be justified under Article 8 § 2 ECHR. In general, it found that the test could be justified as 'necessary in a democratic society' for the protection of public safety and the rights of others. It was indeed essential that crew members belonging—when onboard—to the safety crew were at all times able to perform functions related to the safety onboard in a fully adequate way, implying that their mental or physical functioning was not negatively influenced by the consumption of alcohol or the use of drugs. As a result, Mr Madsen's application was rejected as being manifestly ill-founded and was thus declared inadmissible.

The case of *Madsen v Denmark* illustrates that employees may be compelled—under penalty of dismissal—to accept certain requirements or to undergo certain tests that might interfere with their privacy. However, it seems logical that the issue did not raise a concern about the applicability of Article 8 § 1 ECHR, but required a discussion on the justification of an interference with the employee's right to privacy under Article 8 § 2 ECHR. By focusing on the employer's right to manage the workforce, including the right to submit his employees to testing, the ECtHR engaged in the question of the 'necessity' of the assumed interference. This appears as the better way for the Court to assure the employee a high level of protection. A more problematic route for the Court might have been to deny the application of

---

[40] *Madsen v Denmark* (n 7).

Article 8 § 1 ECHR, although it would be hard to see how drug testing would not raise a privacy issue.

Similarly, in *Köpke v Germany*,[41] the ECtHR declared the employee's application manifestly ill-founded and inadmissible. Here, however, the Court also considered the applicability of Article 8 ECHR. Ms Köpke, a cashier and shop assistant, complained that the covert video surveillance by her employer and the recording and uncontrolled processing of the personal data violated her right to respect for her private life, as guaranteed by Article 8 § 1 ECHR.[42] The employer had carried out the covert video surveillance with the help of a detective agency after having noticed irregularities concerning the accounts in the supermarket's drinks department. On the basis of the data collected, the employer accused Ms Köpke of having manipulated the accounts and of having taken money from the tills, and dismissed her without notice. In considering the applicability of Article 8 § 1 ECHR, the ECtHR recalled that it is relevant to consider whether an individual is targeted by monitoring,[43] and how personal data were obtained, further processed and used.[44] It noted that the video recording was organised without prior notice. Moreover, the data were processed and examined by several persons and used in public court proceedings. In view of this, the Court seemed to accept that Ms Köpke could have a reasonable privacy expectation and consequently recognised that the video surveillance interfered with her private life. The next question was whether that interference was justified under Article 8 § 2 ECHR—a question which the Court answered affirmatively.[45]

A last example of the influence of the right to privacy on the employer's managerial power to exercise control over his employees is the case of *Copland v UK*,[46] which can be seen as a follow-up case to *Halford*. It concerns the monitoring, collection and storage of personal information relating to the employee's telephone, email and Internet usage at the workplace. The ECtHR considered that Ms Copland, who worked as a personal assistant at a public school,[47] had been given no warning that her calls, made from her work telephone, were liable to be monitored. She nevertheless

---

[41] *Köpke v Germany*, App No 420/07, 5 October 2010 (Commission Decision).

[42] Although Ms Köpke's complaint did not concern surveillance measures taken by State agents—the video surveillance was carried out by her (private) employer—she was able to bring her case before the ECtHR by questioning whether there was adequate State protection of her private life in connection with the video surveillance at her workplace. According to her, the domestic labour courts had failed to strike a fair balance between her right to respect for her private life and both her employer's interest in the protection of its property rights and the public interest in the proper administration of justice.

[43] Cf *Rotaru v Romania*, ECHR 2000-V, §§ 43–44; *Peck v UK* (2003) 36 EHRR 41, § 59; *Perry v UK* (2004) 39 EHRR 76, § 38.

[44] Cf *Perry v UK* (m 43) §§ 40–41; *I v Finland* [2008] ECHR 20511, § 35.

[45] Taking into account that the video surveillance was only carried out after irregularities had been discovered, raising an arguable suspicion of theft committed by Ms Köpke, that the surveillance measure was limited in time and restricted in respect of the area it covered, and finally that the visual data obtained were processed by only a limited number of persons and used only for the purposes of the termination of Ms Köpke's employment contract, the German Court had struck a fair balance between *her* right to privacy, her employer's property right and the public interest in the proper administration of justice.

[46] *Copland v UK* [2007] ECHR 253.

[47] The case of *Copland v UK* is thus one concerning a direct violation of Article 8 ECHR by a public authority, here the public school, acting as *Copland*'s (public) employer.

had a reasonable privacy expectation with regard to these calls,[48] as well as with regard to her email and Internet usage. Moreover, recalling the case of *Malone v UK*,[49] the Court regarded the information relating to the data and length of telephone conversations and the numbers dialled to be an 'integral element of the communications made by telephone', falling within the protective scope of Article 8 § 1 ECHR, so that the storage and use thereof amounted to an interference with Ms Copland's right to respect for her private life and correspondence, irrespective of the question whether these data were disclosed or used against her in disciplinary or other proceedings.[50] Once again, the Court opted for a broad interpretation of the notion 'privacy' in favour of the employee's protection, as the applicability of Article 8 § 1 ECHR urges the employer to justify the monitoring of Copland's telephone and Internet usage under the different principles set by Article 8 § 2 ECHR.

2.3.3 Discipline and Employment Termination

Privacy questions also arise in the final stage of the employment relationship in cases in which the contract of employment is terminated for reasons related to the employee's private life. Here as well, links emerge between privacy rights and social rights.

The cases of *Lustig-Praen and Beckett v UK*[51] and *Smith and Grady v UK*[52] are instructive in this respect. Both cases concern the administrative discharge of the applicants from the armed forces on the sole ground of their homosexual orientation. This discharge was in line with the Ministry of Defence policy, which excluded homosexuals from service in the armed forces, arguing that homosexuality was incompatible with service in the armed forces 'not only because of the close physical conditions in which personnel often have to live and work, but also because homosexual behaviour can cause offence, polarise relationships, induce ill-discipline and, as a consequence, damage morale and unit effectiveness'. It was argued that allowing homosexuals would have a detrimental effect on the morale amongst service personnel and, consequently, would negatively affect the armed forces' operational effectiveness. After having exhausted domestic remedies, the applicants lodged a claim with the ECtHR, invoking their right to respect for private life.[53] The Court accepted that the investigations by the military into the applicants' homosexuality, together

---

[48] See also *Halford v UK* (n 26) § 45.

[49] *Malone v UK* (n 39) § 84. See also *Amann v Switzerland*, ECHR 2000-II [2000] ECHR 87, § 65.

[50] As there was no domestic law regulating the monitoring of information relating to an employee's telephone, email and Internet usage at the relevant time, the ECtHR concluded that this interference was not 'in accordance with the law' as required by Article 8(2) ECHR, so that Ms Copland's right to privacy had been violated.

[51] *Lustig-Prean and Beckett v UK* [1999] ECHR 71; (2001) 31 EHRR 23.

[52] *Smith and Grady v UK* [1999] ECHR 72; (2000) 29 EHRR 493; (2000) 31 EHRR 24.

[53] The applicants also argued that they were being discriminated against on the ground of their sexual orientation. For that reason, they not only claimed a violation of Article 8 ECHR, taken alone, but also of Article 8 taken in conjunction with Article 14 ECHR. Moreover, the applicants complained that the policy of excluding homosexuals from the armed forces and the consequent investigations and discharges amounted to degrading treatment according to the meaning of Article 3 ECHR, and that it violated their right to give expression to their sexual identity under Article 10 (taken alone and in conjunction with Article 14 ECHR). Finally, they argued that the judicial review proceedings did not constitute an effective domestic remedy within the meaning of Article 13 ECHR.

with the preparation of a final report for the armed forces on these investigations, constituted a direct interference with their privacy, as these investigations included detailed interviews with each of them and with third parties on matters relating to their sexual orientation and practices. The subsequent administrative discharge also amounted to an interference with Article 8 § 1 ECHR.[54] The Court thus had to determine whether that interference could be justified under Article 8 § 2 ECHR. Surprisingly, referring to the sensitivity of the matter and the specific military context, the Court ruled that the national government, acting as an employer, enjoyed a wide margin of appreciation in this case. The policy against homosexuals in the armed forces could therefore be justified on the basis of legitimate reasons. Nevertheless, the interviews and discharges amounted to such an exceptional intrusion into the applicants' private life that, in light of their intended purpose, they could not be deemed to be 'necessary in a democratic society'. Article 8 ECHR was thus violated.

In two recent cases, the Court had to decide whether a summary dismissal for engaging in and maintaining an extramarital relationship amounted to a violation of Article 8 ECHR.[55] Both concerned complaints against the refusal of the national court to overturn the dismissal.[56] In *Obst v Germany*, the employee, who grew up in the Mormon faith and married in accordance with Mormon rites, held a position as a European public relations officer within the Mormon Church. According to a clause in his employment contract related to his conduct and behaviour in and outside the workplace, the employee was supposed to know the essential principles of the Mormon Church and had to refrain from communication and from behaviour likely to injure the Church's reputation under penalty of dismissal without notice. In a conversation with his spiritual superior, the employee confided that he was sexually involved with another woman. Moreover, on advice of the latter, the employee confessed the adultery to his hierarchical supervisor, who did not show any understanding of the employee's marital situation and thereupon dismissed him without notice.

In *Schüth v Germany*, the employee, an organist and choirmaster in a Catholic parish, was similarly dismissed for engaging in an extramarital relationship and expecting a child with another woman, thereby violating his obligations of loyalty under the basic Catholic rules for the ecclesiastical service. Yet, the issue was whether or not an extramarital affair really sufficed to justify a summary dismissal and whether (the acceptance of) such dismissal interfered with the employee's right to respect for privacy. Indeed, according to the Court, being a broad term,

---

[54] See also *Dudgeon v UK*, Series A, No 45 (1981) 4 EHRR 149, § 41.

[55] *Obst v Germany*, App No 425/03, 23 September 2010; *Schüth v Germany*, App No 1620/03, 23 September 2010.

[56] In both cases, the employee did not complaint of a direct violation of Article 8 ECHR by Germany, but reproached the German labour courts for failing to protect his right to respect for his family life against an interference by his employer, the Mormon and the Catholic Church respectively, which itself has no prerogative of public power, despite its status as a public corporation under German law (see also *Rommelfanger v Germany*, App No 12242/86, 6 September 1989 (Commission Decision)). The ECtHR accepts this complaint, recalling that although Article 8 ECHR is essentially to protect the individual against arbitrary interference by public authorities, it does not merely compel the State to abstain from such interference (see also *Fuentes Bobo v Spain* (2001) 31 EHRR 50, § 38; *Evans v UK* (2006) 43 EHRR 210, §§ 75–76).

not susceptible to exhaustive definition, the notion of 'privacy' must include some aspects of an individual's physical and social identity, such as the right to establish and develop relations with others, the right to personal development or the right to self-determination.[57] Consequently, items such as sexual orientation and sexual life also fall within the personal sphere that is protected by Article 8 ECHR.[58] The ECtHR thus had to determine whether the German labour courts, by not overturning the dismissal for maintaining an extramarital relationship, had struck a fair balance between the different interests involved, taking into account Germany's margin of appreciation.[59] In *Obst v Germany*, the ECtHR found that the German labour courts had properly weighed the competing interests and came to the conclusion that Mr Obst's summary dismissal did not violate Article 8 ECHR for various reasons. Not only had the Church only acted after Mr Obst had voluntarily confessed his adultery, but Mr Obst's visible and important role in the Church was also not compatible with his behaviour. Finally, given his young age and his profession, Mr Obst was expected to find another position quickly. Yet, in *Schüth v Germany*, the Court ruled to the contrary. Although also in this case the Catholic Church had argued that it had had no choice but to dismiss Mr Schüth in order to preserve its own credibility, his dismissal amounted to a violation of his right to privacy. Indeed, contrary to Mr Obst, Mr Schüth had always kept his extramarital affair quiet, had never criticised the Catholic Church's rules and, as an organist and choirmaster, had only very few other job opportunities, so that the damage caused by his summary dismissal was not in proportion to the protection of the Church's reputation. Precisely by taking into account Mr Obst's and Mr Schüth s job opportunities after dismissal for the evaluation of the proportionality of their dismissal, and by thus linking the right to privacy to the right to work, both cases provide another illustration of the Court's integrative approach.

In light of this integrative approach, another relevant reference is *Pay v UK*.[60] The applicant, a probation officer who treated sex offenders, but also maintained BDSM activities in his leisure time, was subject to disciplinary action as his behaviour was seen by the supervising authorities as incompatible with his role as a probation officer and the reputation of the service. The ECtHR held that 'the dismissal of the applicant from his employment for engaging in such activities may be said to amount to an interference with his rights' under Article 8 ECHR. This interpretation only leaves a thin line between the (civil) right to privacy and the (social) right not to be unfairly dismissed.

---

[57] Ibid, § 53.

[58] See also *EB v France* (2008) 47 EHRR 21, § 43.

[59] In both cases, the ECtHR examined the balance made by the German labour courts of the employee's right to respect for his private life (Article 8 ECHR) with the Churches' right to freedom of thought, conscience and religion (Article 9 ECHR), and their right to freedom of assembly and association (Article 11 ECHR) in order to determine whether the protection offered to the employee by the domestic courts achieved a sufficient degree of balance.

[60] *Pay v UK* (2009) 48 EHRR SE2; [2009] *IRLR* 139. Although this case concerns a decision on admissibility, it remains relevant for its principles.

3 ARTICLE 8 ECHR AND FUNDAMENTAL RIGHTS PROTECTION MECHANISMS

The question remains to what extent Article 8 ECHR is relevant and of additional value in matters of employment privacy. After all, employment privacy issues are concerned with the balancing of rights and interests of employers and employees, an exercise which would arguably be a core focus of employment protection laws.

3.1 The Value of Article 8 ECHR in an Employment Law Context

The value of Article 8 ECHR in an employment law context seems to be found in the introduction of the fundamental rights protection mechanism in the employment context. The perspective of Article 8 ECHR leads to the adoption of the Convention's fundamental rights-based principles such as legality, finality and proportionality. This is different from an employment law approach.

Indeed, a traditional feature of an employment law approach is the use of concepts related to the system of private law when recognising employee privacy rights. To the extent that no specific privacy legislation is applicable, (labour) courts may use norms with an open texture, such as 'reasonableness' or 'good faith', to imply or recognise privacy rights in balancing the employer's and employee's interests.[61] In this manner, a constitutional or fundamental rights-based approach to privacy is less prominent, with pragmatism possibly governing judicial decision making.[62]

Article 8 ECHR influences the balance of rights and interests to be struck in employment cases in a particular way. It suggests that such a balance must necessarily be organised along the lines of Article 8 § 2 ECH.

This would, in the first place, lead to the application of the principle of 'finality', expressing that the right to privacy is of such a fundamental nature that it may only be interfered with for the protection of other legitimate purposes or interests, enumerated in Article 8 § 2 ECHR. The recognition of 'rights and freedoms of others' obviously suggests that employers may have legitimate interests that interfere with the privacy of employees.

Perhaps more protective is the principle of proportionality, requiring any interference with Article 8 § 1 ECHR to be 'necessary in a democratic society'.[63] 'Necessary' means 'proportionate to the legitimate aim pursued'.[64] It is believed that although this is not a requirement of being 'indispensable', it is nevertheless stronger than

---

[61] *Cf* MAC de Wit, *Het goedwerkgeverschap als intermediair van normen in het arbeidsrecht* (Deventer, Kluwer, 1999) 161–64.

[62] F Hendrickx, 'Privacy and data protection in the workplace: The Netherlands' in Nouwt, de Vries and Prins (eds) (n 9) 163–64.

[63] M-A Eissen, 'The Principle of Proportionality in the Case-Law of the European Court of Human Rights' in RStJ MacDonald, F Matscher and H Petzold (eds), *The European System for the Protection of Human Rights* (Dordrecht, Nijhoff, 1993) 125–46.

[64] *Handyside v UK*, Series A, No 24 (1976) 1 EHRR 737; *Dudgeon v UK* (n 54).

being merely 'acceptable' or 'reasonable',[65] for it guarantees that the employee's right to privacy will not easily be set aside.

The cases of *Obst v Germany* and *Schüth v Germany*[66] illustrate how the courts may engage in proportionality. In *Obst*, the German labour court was seen to have organised a careful balancing exercise with regard to the interests involved. The dismissal was viewed as a necessary measure aimed at preserving the Church's credibility, having regard in particular to the nature of the applicant's function. The German court also explained why the Church had not been obliged to impose a less severe penalty, such as a warning, and it underlined the fact that the injury suffered by the applicant as a result of his dismissal was limited, taking into account, among other things, his relatively young age. In *Schüth*, however, the German courts were found not to have balanced the full range of interests properly. Contrary to the *Obst* case, Mr Schüth had always kept his extramarital affair quiet, had never criticised the Catholic Church's rules and, as an organist and choirmaster, had only very few other job opportunities, so that the damage caused by his summary dismissal was not in proportion to the protection of the Church's reputation.[67]

Finally, there is a requirement of 'legality' or transparency. Article 8 § 2 ECHR provides that 'there shall be no interference by a public authority with the exercise of this right except such as is in accordance with the law'. In *Malone v UK*,[68] the ECtHR explained this requirement as delivering a measure of legal protection against arbitrary interference with the right laid down in Article 8 ECHR, especially where a certain power is exercised and the risk of arbitrariness is evident. Moreover, in *Sunday Times v UK*,[69] the purpose of this legality requirement was explained as being designed 'to enable the citizen to regulate his conduct: that person must be able—if need be with appropriate advice—to foresee, up to a reasonable degree—given the circumstances, the consequences which a certain action may entail'.

The meaning of the legality could thus be that any interference with the employee's right to privacy should be in accordance with a clear and accessible norm. In both *Halford* and *Copland*, violations of the right to privacy were found due to the absence of pre-existing policy rules clarifying the worker's privacy expectations with regard to monitoring and surveillance. Furthermore, the ECtHR made it clear that the requirement of legality can be fulfilled through collective bargaining agreements and/or case law. In *Wretlund v Sweden*,[70] the employee's obligation to submit to drug testing did not follow from legislation, but the Court observed that labour market issues are, according to a long-standing tradition in Sweden, mainly regulated by the parties on the labour market.

The implications of introducing Article 8 ECHR into an employment dispute can also be illustrated by examples in national case law. In a French case, an employee, hired as a sales representative, was obliged to move his family home to a new

---

[65] M Delmas-Marty and C Chodkiewicz (eds), *The European Convention for the Protection of Human Rights: International Protection Versus National Restrictions* (Dordrecht, Nijhoff, 1992) 326.

[66] *Obst v Germany* (n 55); *Schüth v Germany* (n 55).

[67] *Schüth v Germany* (n 55) § 73: 'le fait qu'un employé licencié par un employeur ecclésial ait des possibilités limitées de trouver un nouvel emploi revêt une importance particulière'.

[68] *Malone v UK* (n 39).

[69] *Sunday Times v UK*, Series A, No 30 (1979) 2 EHRR 245.

[70] *Wretlund v Sweden*, App No 46210/99, 9 March 2004.

working area where his employer was established. However, the employee arranged accommodation for himself during the week in his new area of work, but refused to move his family home. He was subsequently dismissed by his employer. While the lower courts referred to the terms of the employment contract and ruled in favour of the employer, the French Cour de Cassation revised the judgment by applying Article 8 ECHR directly and stating that everybody has the right to choose his personal and family home.[71] Restrictions on the employee's right to privacy, according to the French Cour de Cassation, must be necessary to protect the company's legitimate interests and must be proportionate, taking into account regard to the employee's position and function.[72] In this case, the test of proportionality would thus stand in the way of the employer's residence policy. It appears that it provides a stronger protection of the employee's privacy. Indeed, when the right to privacy and the employer's rights would be weighed out in a more vague interest balancing, it might be easier to tilt the balance in favour of the employer.[73] Another example is the *Nikon* case,[74] in which the French Cour de Cassation went quite far in protecting the employee's right to privacy. In applying Article 8 ECHR, the court held that an employer may be liable for violation of the right to privacy when searching an employee's files stored on a professional computer, even if the employer's policy expressly prohibited the use of the company's equipment for private purposes. In this case, the court seemed to concentrate on the procedural aspects of the monitoring undertaken by the employer in light of the employee's privacy.[75]

Nevertheless, the application of Article 8 ECHR does not necessarily lead per se to employee-friendly case law. This is illustrated by a case put before the Belgian Cour de Cassation in which an employer secretly filmed an employee in order to obtain evidence of the employee's theft. The Belgian Cour de Cassation decided that the right to privacy, as guaranteed in Article 8 ECHR, was applicable, but also that it is not an absolute right. According to the court, it does not preclude an employer, where there is a legitimate suspicion of a worker's involvement in criminal activities, taking appropriate measures, including the use of secret camera surveillance in his own business premises. The court followed by stating that such camera surveillance, conducted for the purpose of filing a complaint with the police department, could be considered as sufficient, appropriate and not excessive, and did not constitute an unlawful interference in light of Article 8 § 2 ECHR.[76]

---

[71] Cass Soc 12 January 1999 (*Spileers v SARL Omni Pac*) D 1999, 635.
[72] D Oliver and J Fedtke (eds), *Human Rights and the Private Sphere: A Comparative Study* (Abingdon, Routledge, 2007) 106–07.
[73] A Belgian labour court also reasoned on the basis of privacy (and in favour of the employee's right to choose his dwelling): Labour Tribunal of Bruges, 13 December 1993, *Sociaalrechtelijke kronieken/ Chroniques de droit social* 1994, 79. For a critical appraisal of the fundamental rights approach in the case of residence clauses, see P Humblet, 'De woonplaatsclausule: een (on)geldig beding?' (note under Labour Tribunal of Bruges, 13 December 1993), *Sociaalrechtelijke kronieken/Chroniques de droit social* 1994, 81.
[74] Cass Soc, 2 October 2001 (*Nikon France v Onof*), No 4164.
[75] Oliver and Fedtke (n 72) 118.
[76] Cass 27 February 2001, *RW* 2001–02, note P Humblet 1171; see discussion in F Hendrickx, 'Verwelkoming van Big Brother op de werkvloer?' (2001) 5 *Personeelszaken* 41–45.

3.2 Horizontal Application of the Right to Privacy

Reliance on the protection mechanism provided by Article 8 § 2 ECHR in an employment relationship raises the question of the horizontal application of the ECHR.

The origin of the concept of the horizontal application of fundamental rights can be found in the German notion of *Drittwirkung*.[77] It means that fundamental rights can be applied by individuals versus other individuals or private parties. This is opposed to vertical application, which refers to the traditional operation of fundamental rights in the relationship between the State and its citizens.

Under the ECHR system, horizontal effect may arise as a concern in the ECtHR's assessment of a State's respect for the right to privacy through positive interventions, such as government action, legislation or case law.[78] However, real horizontal application of Article 8 ECHR takes place before national courts under their respective national jurisdiction.

With regard to horizontal effect in national case law, the distinction between the direct and indirect horizontal application of fundamental rights is relevant.[79] *Direct* horizontal application refers to the ability to directly rely on the (constitutional or international) provisions guaranteeing fundamental rights. This would allow applicants to directly invoke Article 8 ECHR in a private law dispute. *Indirect* horizontal application refers to the respect of fundamental rights through the interpretation of general clauses or terms of reasonableness and fairness (eg, 'good faith') in private law. This is in line with the above-mentioned employment law approach.

National courts seem to prefer the route of indirect horizontal application. This may be due to the fact that constitutional documents themselves do not provide for specific remedies, so that references to private law instruments still need to take place in order to arrange remedies for violations of fundamental rights in a horizontal relationship. Moreover, hesitation about the direct horizontal application of the right to privacy may be due to the existence of a dualistic view in national legal systems with regard to the relationship between international and national

---

[77] A Drzemczewski, *The European Human Rights Convention in Domestic Law* (Oxford, Clarendon Press, 1983) 199; A Gatto, *Multinational Enterprises and Human Rights: Obligations under EU Law and International Law* (Cheltenham, Edward Elgar, 2011) 68. This notion has received equivalent terms, such as 'third applicability' (EA Alkema, 'The Third-Party Applicability or "Drittwirkung" of the European Convention on Human Rights' in F Matscher and H Petzold (eds), *Protecting Human Rights: The European Dimension. Studies in Honour of Gérard J. Wiarda*, (Cologne, Carl Heymanns Verlag, 1988) 45) and 'effets à l'égard des tiers' (MA Eissen, 'La Convention européenne des droits de l'homme et les obligations de l'individu: une mise à jour' in International Institute of Human Rights (ed), *René Cassin Liber Amicorum Disciplinorumque*, III, *Protection des droits de l'homme dans les rapports entre personnes privées* (Paris, Pedone, 1971) 151).

[78] In the case of *X and Y v The Netherlands*, the ECtHR held that the obligations arising from Article 8 ECHR 'may involve the adoption of measures designed to secure respect for private life even in the sphere of the relations of individuals between themselves' (*X and Y v The Netherlands*, Series A, No 32 (1985) § 23) When examining the protection of employment privacy, it is important to note that the cases brought before the ECtHR concern alleged violations of Article 8(1) ECHR by a State Party. According to Article 34 ECHR, the Court can only receive applications in response to alleged violations by one of the 'High Contracting Parties'. Claims against individuals for non-respect of the ECHR or the Protocols are inadmissible.

[79] *Cf* 'unmittelbare' (direct) and 'mittelbare' (indirect) *Drittwirkung*; *cf* Drzemczewski (n 77) 200.

law.[80] However, the practical difference between the direct and indirect horizontal application of the right to privacy remains limited, as long as the protection mechanism underlying a fundamental right is applied.

The horizontal application of the right to privacy in an employment context needs to be nuanced. First, an employment law approach that is based on well-organised interest-balancing may deliver results similar to those achieved in the horizontal application of the right to privacy. Furthermore, the benchmark of Article 8 § 2 ECHR also incorporates a degree of flexibility, as it refers to 'the protection of the rights and freedoms of others'. This may be seen as an open-ended ground for justifying interferences with the right to privacy in the interest of private parties.[81] For example, the reputation of an organisation or institution could be referred to for limiting the right to privacy.[82] Nevertheless, Article 8 § 2 ECHR does not endorse any reference to (a company's) purely commercial or financial interests. In *Hatton and others v UK*,[83] for example, a mere reference to economic interests, which could be a standard employer defence, was considered to be an insufficient justification for interfering with the right to private life. Employers, as a consequence, might need to come up with more specific counterbalancing interests. A good example in this respect is the *Madsen v Denmark* case,[84] in which the ECtHR found that the mandatory alcohol and drug test could be justified as necessary in a democratic society for the protection of the public safety and for the rights of others. In this case, the public safety interest could be seen as similar to or, at least, concurring with the (public) employer's interest. It was indeed essential that crew members who were— when onboard—part of a safety crew were at all times able to perform functions related to the safety onboard in a fully adequate way, implying that their mental or physical functioning was not negatively influenced by the consumption of alcohol or by the use of drugs. Moreover, in *Halford* and *Copland*, the Court did not seem to have excluded the idea that the monitoring of an employee's use of telephone, email or Internet at the place of work may be considered 'necessary in a democratic society' in certain situations in pursuit of legitimate aims.

It remains, however, rather unclear as to how wide or limited the employer's legitimate aims should be seen. The case of *Wretlund v Sweden*,[85] for example, seems to show that the employer's entitlement to exercise managerial authority may be protected as a legitimate aim under Article 8 § 2 ECHR. The case concerned an office cleaner at a nuclear plant who challenged the company's drug policy programme, involving the taking of urine samples from employees. The aim of the tests was to detect the use of both drugs and alcohol, but the drug part of the tests concerned only the presence of cannabis. The ECtHR stated that 'the employer's

---

[80] Direct effect of Article 8 ECHR would be a condition for direct horizontal effect; *cf* D Harris, M O'Boyle and C Warbrick (eds), *Law of the European Convention on Human Rights*, 2nd edn (Oxford, Oxford University Press, 2009), 24.

[81] RCA White and C Overy, *The European Convention on Human Rights* (Oxford, Oxford University Press, 2010), 323.

[82] *Schmidt v Austria*, App No 513/05, 17 July 2008 (concerning the reputation of the Vienna Food Inspection Agency).

[83] *Hatton and others v UK*, App No 3602/77, 2 April 2007.

[84] *Madsen v Denmark* (n 7).

[85] *Wretlund v Sweden* (n 70).

right to manage and organise the work ... constitutes a general legal principle' and that 'according to the Labour Court's case-law, the employer may have a right to carry out control measures as part of the right to manage and organise the work'. Here, the ECtHR clearly distinguished between the rights of the employer and the requirements of public safety. It considered that 'the measure in question pursued legitimate aims under Article 8, § 2, including "public safety" and "the protection of the rights and freedoms of others"'.

The case of *Pay v UK*[86] may be seen to engage further in an employment law style of reasoning, while still using a fundamental rights approach. With regard to the dismissal of a probation officer who had responsibility over sex offenders, but who also maintained BDSM activities in his leisure time, the ECtHR stated that it 'is mindful that an employee owes to his employer a duty of loyalty, reserve and discretion'. It continued in finding that:

> [T]he applicant's job involved, inter alia, working closely with convicted sex offenders who had been released from prison, to ensure that they complied with the conditions of release and did not re-offend. As such, it was important that he maintained the respect of the offenders placed under his supervision and also the confidence of the public in general and victims of sex crime in particular.

It may thus be concluded that the protection system of Article 8 ECHR does not preclude that rights and interests which are specific in an employment context can be taken into account. To a certain extent, the fundamental rights approach and an employment law approach may be seen, at least partly, to be convergent.

3.3 The Role of the Margin of Appreciation

Notwithstanding the strengths of a fundamental rights approach to employee privacy, the doctrine of the margin of appreciation puts the guarantee of strong privacy protection into perspective. According to this doctrine, states enjoy a margin of appreciation by which they can judge for themselves whether their actions adhere to the conditions of legality, finality and proportionality in case they would interfere with the ECHR. This affects the ECtHR's degree of judicial review.

The doctrine is connected with the principle of subsidiarity, according to which a state should itself decide democratically what is appropriate for itself.[87] Hence, in the case of *Handyside v UK*, the ECtHR held—with regard to Article 10 § 2 ECHR—that, by reason of their direct and continuous contact with the vital forces of their countries, state authorities are in principle in a better position than the international judge to give an opinion on the exact content of the requirements of legality and finality, as well as to make the initial assessment of the reality of the pressing social need implied by the notion of 'necessity'.[88] After all, the ECtHR is called not to replace the discretion and independent evaluation exercised by national

---

[86] *Pay v UK*, App No 32792/05, Decision on admissibility of 16 December 2008.
[87] R Clayton and H Tomlinson, *The Law of Human Rights* (Oxford, Oxford University Press, 2000) 285.
[88] *Handyside v UK* (n 64) § 48.

authorities.[89] Indeed, it is clearly not an appeal court providing for a new and full review of the case that was brought before the national court.[90]

The relevance of the doctrine of the margin of appreciation seems to become very apparent in cases in which different rights and interests are to be balanced.[91] What seems more remarkable is that the doctrine of the margin of appreciation might be transposed, although implicitly, to the interest-balancing in employment cases. Indeed, a similar margin of discretion (or appreciation) may be applied in order to grant employers some leeway in cases where the exercise of managerial authority competes with employee privacy. In this context, it is interesting to refer back to the case of *Pay v UK*,[92] where a degree of discretion was granted to the local authorities, acting as employer, judging over the dismissal of the applicant. In relation to the right to free off-duty conduct at issue (BDSM activities), the ECtHR examined not only the way in which a society perceives such activities, reasoning that a '"democratic society" includes pluralism, tolerance and broadmindedness', but also continued by stating that 'given the sensitive nature of the applicant's work with sex offenders, the Court did not consider that the national authorities exceeded the margin of appreciation available to them in adopting a cautious approach as regards the extent to which public knowledge of the applicant's sexual activities could impair his ability effectively to carry out his duties.' Furthermore, the Court went into the question of whether the supervising authorities, acting as employer, had alternatives for the dismissal, noting that 'it might have been open to the [service] to take less severe measures, short of dismissal, to limit the risk of adverse publicity caused by the applicant's activities'. The ECtHR can therefore be seen to respect a margin of appreciation of the local authority acting in its quality as supervising employer. This employer-related margin of discretion can be seen to apply in the shadow of the wider margin of appreciation doctrine.

The cases of *Lustig-Praen and Beckett v UK*[93] and *Smith and Grady v UK*[94] were even more explicit in this respect. Here, the Court also recognised a margin of appreciation for the national authority acting in its capacity of employer in legitimising policies on homosexuality in the armed forces.

The role of the margin of appreciation doctrine seems thus inevitable in employment cases. But the degree of discretion allowed to states seems to vary according to the competing interests at stake. More discretion may be given if a state's public policy is at stake, such as public security or public morals, or if a fundamental right needs to be balanced with another fundamental right. The margin of appreciation would be narrower if particular private interests are at stake.[95] Employer-related

---

[89] *Ireland v UK* (1978) 2 EHRR 25, §§ 91–92.

[90] Y Shany, 'Toward a General Margin of Appreciation Doctrine in International Law?' (2006) 16 *European Journal of International Law* 907, 926.

[91] Cf O Bakircioglu, 'The Application of the Margin of Appreciation Doctrine in Freedom of Expression and Public Morality Cases' (2007) 8 *German Law Review* 711, 721.

[92] *Pay v UK*, App No 32792/05, Decision on admissibility of 16 December 2008.

[93] *Lustig-Prean and Beckett v UK* (n 51).

[94] *Smith and Grady v UK* (n 52).

[95] Cf DJ Harris, M O'Boyle, EP Bates and CM Buckley, *Law of the European Convention on Human Rights*, 2nd edn (Oxford, Oxford University Press, 2009) 13.

interests and concerns are nevertheless accorded a fair degree of recognition, as is shown in the case of *Pay*.

4 ARTICLE 8 ECHR AND DATA PROTECTION MECHANISMS

The relationship between ECHR protection and other international or European instruments is a matter of concern. As indicated above, the case of *Demir and Baykara*[96] is seen as promoting a consolidated approach in the interpretation of the rights laid down in the Convention, implying a need for systematic references to other international standards.

The Council of Europe has had a Data Protection Convention since 1981.[97] At a later stage, the EU adopted a Data Protection Directive in 1995.[98] These two data protection instruments apply to the employment context. However, the desirability of adapting these data protection rules to the particular requirements of the employment sector has become apparent over time. This desire to establish sector-specific rules led to the adoption, on 18 January 1989, of Council of Europe Recommendation No R(89)2 on the Protection of Personal Data Used for Employment Purposes.[99] Likewise, under the European Data Protection Directive, the European 'Working Party'[100] adopted Opinion 8/2001 of 13 September 2001 on the processing of personal data in the employment context.[101] There are even more detailed instruments, such as the EU Working Document of 29 May 2002 on workplace communications.[102] In other words, similar concerns have led to parallel initiatives from the two European organisations. Furthermore, the need for more specific guidance also triggered the attention of the ILO, which adopted a code of practice on worker data protection in 1996.[103] In a later stage, the EU Charter of Fundamental Rights incorporated not only the right to privacy (Article 7) but also the right to personal data protection (Article 8).

As is clear from the ECtHR's case law, Article 8 ECHR is open for interpretation and, as a result, employment privacy protection evolves on a case-by-case basis. Due to the open nature of Article 8 ECHR, the ECtHR might be willing to refer to the

---

[96] *Demir and Baykara v Turkey* (n 2).

[97] Convention for the Protection of Individuals with Regard to Automatic Processing of Personal Data, Strasbourg, 28 January 1981, ETS no 108.

[98] Directive 95/46/EC of the European Parliament and of the Council of 24 October 1995 on the protection of individuals with regard to the processing of personal data and on the free movement of such data, OJ 23 November 1995, L281/31.

[99] Recommendation no R (89) 2 of the Committee of Ministers to Member States on the protection of personal data used for employment purposes, adopted by the Committee of Ministers on 18 January 1989 at the 423rd meeting of the Ministers' Deputies (available at www.coe.int).

[100] The Working Party is an advisory group composed by representatives of the data protection authorities of the Member States, which acts independently and has the task, inter alia, of examining any question covering the application of the national measures adopted under the Data Protection Directive in order to contribute to the uniform application of such measures.

[101] Opinion 8/2001 of 13 September 2001 on the processing of personal data in the employment context, 5062/01/EN/Final, WP 48, 28 pages.

[102] Data Protection Working Party, Working Document on the Surveillance of Electronic Communications in the Workplace, 29 May 2002, 5401/01/EN/final, 35 pages.

[103] ILO, *Protection of Workers' Personal Data. An ILO Code of Practice* (Geneva, ILO, 1997) 47.

more specific instruments in its case law under the Convention. However, the Court has not really explored this potential so far.

Obviously, cross-references to employee data protection instruments should be useful. In this context, three issues can be mentioned.

First, there is the issue of coherence. The degree to which the data protection initiatives have been coordinated in the past remains a question. It may well be considered that the ECtHR should attach more importance to the Council of Europe's own framework, such as the 1981 Convention, though the EU or ILO instruments also have their referential value. The Council of Europe's data protection revision round explicitly promotes the objective to 'ensure for coherence and compatibility with the legal framework of the European Union',[104] though it also expresses the desire to search for internal consistency in the Council of Europe's system itself by aligning the concepts of the Data Protection Convention with the case law of the ECtHR.[105]

A second issue is the dynamic context of data protection rules. Specific instruments on data protection do not have the flexibility of the Article 8 ECHR framework and become, sooner or later, outdated in light of new technological realities. It is no coincidence that both the Council of Europe and the EU are in a process of revising their data protection instruments.[106]

The third, and perhaps most important, issue concerns the degree of protection. The question is whether cross-referencing to the specific data protection instruments would help raise the level of protection of Article 8 ECHR, as would be the suggested effect of following the method of *Demir and Baykara*, referred to above. On the one hand, the additional value of cross-referencing seems to be only relative. Indeed, strong parallels can be found in the mechanisms of protection in the ECHR and data protection frameworks. For example, EU Working Party Opinion 8/2001 establishes the principles of finality, proportionality and transparency in line with the principles of protection expressed in Article 8 § 2 ECHR and discussed above.[107] On the other hand, the data protection instruments offer a more secure level of protection when conceived at their level of detail. For example, the EU Working Document of 29 May 2002 regarding employee monitoring in the field of communication[108] accepts the employer's right to determine the professional and/or private use of ICT facilities at work, but considers a 'blanket ban' on the personal use of the Internet by employees not to be reasonable and failing to reflect the degree to

---

[104] The Consultative Committee of the Convention for the protection of individuals with regard to automatic processing of personal data [ETS No 108], Modernisation of Convention 108: new proposals, (T-PD-BUR(2012)01Rev2_en), Strasbourg, 27 April 2012, 2.

[105] Ibid, 4. With regard to Article 5 on the legitimacy of data processing and quality of data, it is stated that 'this article is foreseen to expressly incorporate the principle of proportionality. The proposed wording takes the case-law of the European Court of Human Rights into account, which requires a fair balance between the competing public and private interests'.

[106] For the EU Data Protection Directive revision, see Commission Communication, 'Safeguarding Privacy in a Connected World A European Data Protection Framework for the 21st Century', Brussels, 25 January 2012, COM(2012) 9 final, 13 pages.

[107] Opinion 8/2001 of 13 September 2001 on the processing of personal data in the employment context, 5062/01/EN/Final, WP 48, 3.

[108] Data Protection Working Party, Working Document on the Surveillance of Electronic Communications in the Workplace, 29 May 2002, 5401/01/EN/final, 35 pages.

which the Internet can assist employees in their daily lives.[109] In cases like *Halford* and *Copland* referred to above, such principles may constitute useful guidance for the ECtHR in determining the legitimate privacy expectations of employees and therefore may affect the assessment of the scope of protection of Article 8 ECHR.

There is thus room for interaction between, on the one hand, Article 8 ECHR and, on the other hand, the Council of Europe's own legislative route (the 1981 Convention and the 1989 Recommendation) and the EU legislative framework (the 1995 EU Data Protection Directive). The reverse form of interaction is, however, also likely. The Charter of Fundamental Rights of the European Union incorporates two articles regarding privacy (Article 7) and data protection (Article 8). Not only does the EU Charter recognise the link between private life and personal data protection, it also suggests the way in which cross-referencing must be done. Indeed, as far as overlapping rights with the ECHR are concerned, they arguably need to be interpreted in accordance with the ECHR.[110] Existing case law of the Court of Justice of the European Union (CJEU) shows that this cross-referencing is useful. In a case involving HIV testing, the CJEU applied Article 8 ECHR as a fundamental right protected by the EU legal order.[111]

5 CONCLUSIONS

ECtHR case law shows that Article 8 ECHR, protecting the right to privacy, is highly relevant and covers a broad range of issues in the employment relationship.

However, the employee's right to privacy, as protected under Article 8 ECHR, is qualified by the employment relationship. The context of the employment relationship affects the employee's reasonable privacy expectations. Nevertheless, the Court has established, since *Niemietz*, that the scope of privacy protection includes activities of a professional or business nature, such as work relations. The ECtHR also seems to avoid privacy expectations excluding too many forms of intrusions from the protective reach of Article 8 § 1 ECHR. Therefore, most cases would still require States—also when acting as employers—to justify their actions under Article 8 § 2 ECHR.

The principle of the *Niemietz* case law is also relevant in establishing a connection between the right to privacy and social rights. The Court's case law shows forms of integration between the right to privacy and social rights, such as the right to work. The ECtHR seems to accept that measures that affect the employment opportunities of an employee (eg, disciplinary action) may amount to an interference with the employee's rights under Article 8 ECHR. For example, according to the ECtHR's case law in *Sidabras* and *Pay*, the ability to engage in work is considered to constitute an important part of one's privacy. The right to privacy and the right to work would seem to go hand in hand. In *Sidabras*, the ECtHR explicitly accepted that 'there is no watertight division separating the sphere of social and economic rights

---

[109] Data Protection Working Party, Working Document on the Surveillance of Electronic Communications in the Workplace, 29 May 2002, 5401/01/EN/final, 2.

[110] Article 52 of the Charter of Fundamental Rights of the European Union of 7 December 2000.

[111] *X v Commission*, Judgment of the Court of 5 October 1994, C-404/92, ECR 1994, I-4737.

from the field covered by the Convention' (§ 47). The right to work and the right to respect for one's private and family life are thus closely intertwined.

In certain instances where the link with social rights is made, the ECtHR has referred to the European Social Charter—including the interpretations of the European Committee on Social Rights—and the ILO. However, systematic cross-referencing does not characterise employment privacy case law. In this context, therefore, the *Demir and Baykara* method has not yet taken full effect. Nevertheless, it seems that there is a certain potential for further integrating privacy with social rights, such as the right to work. Also conceivable is further integration with such social rights as the right to equal treatment, the right to protection against unfair dismissal, or the right to fair and decent working conditions. This is likely to have the effect of increasing the level of employee privacy protection. But how far case law should develop on this remains a question.[112] The ECtHR might value the objective of internal consistency in the ECHR system as much as external consistency. Furthermore, the potential of cross-fertilisation between directly effective civil rights (eg, the right to privacy) and aspirational social rights (eg, the right to work) may include limits.

The ECtHR's case law shows the value of Article 8 ECHR for privacy in the employment context. Recognition under Article 8 ECHR leads to the adoption of a fundamental rights-based approach to employment-related cases and necessitates the application of the Convention's protection principles. Article 8 ECHR thus influences the balance of rights and interests to be struck in employment cases, suggesting that such a balance must necessarily be organised along the lines of Article 8 § 2 ECHR and implying that interferences with the employee's privacy should be assessed on the basis of the principles of legality, finality and proportionality.

Employees can, in this context, raise a privacy claim against their employer on a stronger basis compared to general employment law-related interest-balancing. However, the fundamental rights approach and the employment law approach may be seen, at least partly, as convergent. Well-organised interest-balancing may allow (national) courts to properly recognise the mutual interests at stake and therefore recognise privacy at a similar level of protection. However, it would still demand national courts to provide horizontal effect of the right to privacy if the standard of Article 8 ECHR is to be reached.

The relevance of the doctrine of the margin of appreciation is quite inevitable in employment cases. But the degree of discretion allowed to states seems to vary according to the competing interests at stake (eg, public policy versus private interests). However, employer-related interests and concerns are accorded a fair degree of recognition. Moreover, it seems that the doctrine of the margin appreciation might be transposed, although implicitly, to the interest-balancing in employment cases. In other words, the ECtHR respects a certain margin of appreciation of the local authority acting in its capacity as the supervising employer. This employer-related

---

[112] Bruun and Lörcher are of the opinion that 'article 8 ECHR will have to be opened up to encompass new dimensions of concrete fundamental social rights in the field of labour law'. See N Bruun and K Lörcher, 'Social innovation: the new ECHR jurisprudence and its impact on fundamental social rights in labour law' in I Schomann (ed), *Mélanges à la mémoire de Yota Kravaritou: a trilingual tribute* (Brussels, European Trade Union Institute, 2010) 372.

margin of discretion can be seen to apply in the shadow of the wider margin of appreciation doctrine.

Finally, from the perspective of the *Demir and Baykara* approach, the ECtHR has not yet created any specific link between employment privacy protection cases and specific international or European instruments (Council of Europe, EU and ILO) on data protection. There is nevertheless room for such interaction, which is likely to contribute to improved privacy protection of employees. The reverse conclusion may also be found. The EU's accession to the ECHR has the potential to reinforce the level of protection of privacy and data protection in the employment context. In short, a more consolidated approach in the European fundamental rights framework is possible and this may imply an advance towards a more progressive (ie, more protective) view on employee privacy.

9

Freedom of Religion and Belief, Article 9 ECHR and the EU Equality Directive

LUCY VICKERS

T HE RIGHT TO freedom of religion is recognised in most international human rights documents as a fundamental human right.[1] It is often accompanied by a right not to be discriminated against on grounds of religion.[2] This chapter explores the ways in which Article 9 ECHR protection for the right to freedom of religion and belief interacts with the EU law on equality on grounds of religion and belief. It starts with an overview of the two legal regimes in Europe which engage with religion, beginning with the Article 9 protection and then considering the protection under EU Equality Directive 2000/78. It then considers some of ways in which religious freedom and non-discrimination both work towards common goals, as well as potentially conflicting with each other. The chapter then examines a number of cases in detail to assess what each of the different legal frameworks adds to the understanding of the other when engaging with religion and belief.

1 PROTECTION OF RELIGION AND BELIEF UNDER THE EUROPEAN CONVENTION ON HUMAN RIGHTS

Article 9

1. Everyone has the right to freedom of thought, conscience and religion; this right includes freedom to change his religion or belief, and freedom, either alone or in community with others and in public or private, to manifest his religion or belief, in worship, teaching, practice and observance.

2. Freedom to manifest one's religion or beliefs shall be subject only to such limitations as are prescribed by law and are necessary in a democratic society in the interests of public safety, for the protection of public order, health or morals, or the protection of the rights and freedoms of others.

---

[1] For example, Article 18 Universal Declaration on Human Rights, Article 18 ICCPR, Article 9 ECHR.

[2] For example, Article 14 ECHR, Article 13 Treaty of Rome, Article 21 EU Charter of Fundamental Rights and also the constitutions of South Africa, Canada, the US and India.

Freedom of religion, thought and conscience is protected as one of the foundations of a democratic society, and as one of the 'most vital elements that go to make up the identity of believers and their conception of life'.[3] Article 9 recognises that freedom of religion has both an individual and a collective dimension: the right is to manifest religion 'either alone or in community with others', so that the right applies to religious groups as well as to religious individuals.

The right to freedom of thought, conscience and religion (the *forum internum*) is an absolute right under the Convention and refers to the right to have inner thoughts and beliefs. To the extent that these matters are usually intangible, the *forum internum* raises few difficulties in relation to the employment relation: it is instead focused on preventing state interference with a person's thought and conscience, state indoctrination and forcible attempts to change a person's religion or beliefs.[4] Instead, cases involving freedom of religion at work have involved the qualified right to manifest religion (*forum externum*). Common examples of the manifestation of religion in the workplace include work uniforms which interfere with a right to manifest a religion, requests for time off for religious observance, special dietary needs and requests to be excused from work tasks due to religion-based objections. Moreover, religion can interact with the employment relationship where employers themselves have a religious ethos and require staff to share that religion. This can interfere with the religious freedom of potential job applicants, but equally restrictions on the freedom of religious organisations to choose their employees can be seen as an interference with the freedom to manifest religion 'in community with others'.

The right to manifest religion and belief is a qualified right, and so interferences can be justified where they comply with the restrictions set out in Article 9(2). Demonstrating that the right to manifest religion or belief has been restricted involves first showing that the activity in question is, indeed, a manifestation of religion or belief and second that any restriction does not come within the restrictions provided in Article 9(2).

Before considering these elements of Article 9 protection, however, there is a prior concern regarding the application of Article 9 in the work context. This concern arises because 'Article 9 does not necessarily imply that one can back out of one's obligations consented to or contracted freely'.[5] This has led to the argument that staff who enter employment have freely contracted to limit their religious freedom and that their freedom is retained via the right to resign from employment.

1.1 Application to Employment

Early cases relating to other Convention rights suggested that dismissal does not interfere with human rights because the Convention does not cover access to work,

---

[3] *Kokkinakis v Greece*, Series A, No 260-A [1993] 17 EHRR 397, para 31.
[4] P van Dijk and G van Hoof, *Theory and Practice of the European Convention on Human Rights*, 2nd edn (The Hague, Kluwer, 1990) 541 ff.
[5] P van Dijk and G van Hoof, *Theory and Practice of the ECHR*, 4th edn (Antwerp and Oxford, Insentia, 2006) 766.

and so is not covered by the Convention.[6] The reasoning suggested that dismissal from employment involves no prima facie interference with Convention rights, because the rights do not apply at work. This reasoning was followed in several cases involving Article 9. In *Ahmad v UK*,[7] a teacher claimed that Article 9 was breached when he was refused permission to change his working hours to enable him to attend the local Mosque for prayer on Friday lunchtimes. His claim was ruled inadmissible: his right to freedom of religion was not infringed as he was free to resign. Again, in *Stedman v UK*,[8] involving a dismissal for refusing to work on Sundays, the Commission took the view that there was no breach of Article 9, as the employee was free to resign. In *Thlimmenos v Greece*,[9] the Court also pointed out that the Convention does not protect the right to choose a particular profession.[10]

However, other cases involving different Convention rights[11] allowed for fundamental rights to apply at work. For example, in some Article 8 and Article 10 cases, the court has allowed for privacy and freedom of speech to apply at work. In *Vogt v Germany*,[12] the European Court of Human Rights (ECtHR) decided that dismissal of a teacher for her political activity amounted to an interference with her freedom of expression, and in *Niemietz v Germany*[13] and *Sidabras v Lithuania*,[14] the ECtHR considered the concept of privacy and the private sphere could be extended to cover the workplace.

In some Article 9 cases too, the ECtHR had been receptive to the idea that sanctions imposed at work can amount to an interference with the Convention right. In *Saniewski v Poland*,[15] the Court implied that there is an interference with the right to freedom of religion where an employment related penalty was suffered for its exercise and in *Pitkevich v Russia*,[16] the Court found that the dismissal of a judge for the expression of her religious views involved a prima facie interference with her rights under Article 9 (although on the facts, discussed below, the dismissal was found to be proportionate and in pursuit of a legitimate aim).

Finally, in the most recent case of *Eweida and Others v UK*[17] the Chamber of the ECtHR followed the approach in *Vogt* to find that the right to religious freedom does operate within the workplace. The Court held that 'where an individual complains of a restriction on freedom of religion in the workplace, rather than holding that the possibility of changing job would negate any interference with the right, the better approach would be to weigh that possibility in the overall balance when

---

[6] The cases relate to Article 10. See *Kosiek v Germany*, Series A, No 105 (1986) 9 EHRR 328; *Glasenapp v Germany*, Series A, No 104 (1987) 9 EHRR 25. See also *Leander v Sweden*, Series A, No 116 (1987) 9 EHRR 433.
[7] *Ahmad v UK* (1981) 4 EHRR 126.
[8] *Stedman v UK* (1997) 23 EHRR CD 168.
[9] ECHR 2000-IV, (2001) 31 EHRR 15.
[10] Ibid, para 41.
[11] This point is covered elsewhere in this volume in more detail.
[12] *Vogt v Germany*, Series A, No 323 (1996) 21 EHRR 205.
[13] *Niemietz v Germany*, Series A, No 251-B (1992) 16 EHRR 7.
[14] *Sidabras v Lithuania*, App Nos 55480/00 and 59330/00, ECHR 2004-VIII.
[15] *Saniewski v Poland*, App No 40319/98, decision of 26 June 2001.
[16] *Pitkevich v Russia* App No 47936/99, decision of 8 February 2001.
[17] App Nos 48420/10, 59842/10, 51671/10 and 36516/10, judgment 15 January 2013.

considering whether or not the restriction was proportionate'.[18] It would seem, then, that the Court has now accepted, in the context of Article 9, that workbased restrictions on a person's exercise of religious freedom can amount to a prima facie infringement of the right. Nonetheless, even if the prima facie case may be made out, claimants will still need to show that any interference with Article 9 is the result of a manifestation of religion, and that it cannot be justified as proportionate and for a legitimate aim. These two further aspects of Article 9 are discussed below.

1.2 Manifestation of Religion

A distinction is drawn in ECHR case law between religious manifestations and activity which is merely 'religiously motivated'. Where an activity is identified as only motivated by religion, it is not protected under Article 9 and so employers will be under no obligation to accommodate it. Much therefore turns on the scope of the term 'manifest ... in worship, teaching, practice and observance'. The case law on the issue has been fairly restrictive. In *Arrowsmith v UK*,[19] a committed pacifist was prevented from distributing pacifist leaflets to soldiers. The Court's view was that distributing leaflets was not a manifestation of her beliefs and so her right to manifest religion or belief was not infringed. Similarly, in *Pichon and Sajous v France*,[20] where two pharmacists refused to sell contraceptives as a result of a religious objection, the court held that the term religious 'practice' in Article 9 does not 'denote each and every act or form of behaviour motivated or inspired by a religion or a belief' and that only acts 'forming part of the practice of a religion or belief in a generally accepted form' are protected.[21] In the work context, this approach has meant that if behaviour is not required by religion as part of religious observance, it can be restricted by an employer without engaging Article 9. The effect has been that protection from Article 9 is significantly restricted, as many of the accommodations of religion requested by religious staff are for religiously inspired behaviour rather than for pure religious observance. However, in *Eweida et al v UK*[22] the Court took a more flexible approach to the issue of manifestation of religion. Although it reiterated that 'the act in question must be intimately linked to the religion or belief' and gave the act of worship as an example, it went on to say that 'the manifestation of religion or belief is not limited to such acts; the existence of a sufficiently close and direct nexus between the act and the underlying belief must be determined on the facts of each case. In particular, there is no requirement on the applicant to establish that he or she acted in fulfilment of a duty mandated by the religion in question'.[23] After *Eweida* it now seems clear that many of the accommodations sought by employees, such as the meeting of dietary requirements, time off for religious observance, and uniform codes, can be viewed as manifestations of religion and thus potentially be protected by Article 9.

---

[18] *Eweida*, ibid, at para 83.
[19] *Arrowsmith v UK* [1978] 3 EHRR 218.
[20] *Pichon and Sajous v France*, App No 49853/99, admissibility decision of 2 October 2001.
[21] Ibid.
[22] Note 17.
[23] Ibid, para 82.

1.3 Article 9(2)

Where an employer's actions have interfered with the manifestation of religion at work, the next issue under Article 9 is to consider whether interference can be justified in accordance with Article 9(2). An interference with religious freedom will not breach the Convention if the limitations imposed are prescribed by law and are necessary in a democratic society in the interests of public safety, for the protection of public order, health or morals, or for the protection of the rights and freedoms of others.

1.3.1 Legitimate Aims in Article 9(2)

The most obvious legitimate aim for restrictions on the manifestation of religion at work is the protection of the rights and freedoms of others. Freedom of religion may interfere with other Convention rights, such as the right to privacy (a matter discussed elsewhere in this volume)[24] and the right to freedom of association.[25] Religious rights may also conflict with others' equality rights, such as rights to gender and sexual orientation equality.[26] This aspect of the rights of others is explored more fully below, as equality rights are directly protected in EU law. Other rights that religion may interfere with are less formally recognised, such as the freedom of the employer to manage the business as he or she sees fit. A somewhat vague 'right' that has been recognised by the European Commission of Human Rights in the work context was the right of the employer 'to protect its own proper functioning and carrying out of its duties on behalf of the public', which was infringed by a male employee who wished to wear what are conventionally considered female clothes.[27] Another right which has been identified by the Court is the right not to be put under pressure by another's observance: thus, in *Sahin v Turkey*,[28] the Court noted that the wearing of a headscarf may put other students under pressure to adopt more fundamentalist approaches to their faith. Of course, in the light of the decision in *Lautsi v Italy*,[29] discussed briefly below, the operation of this right may be called into question, as the court there seemed unconcerned about the potential for a different religious symbol, the crucifix, to influence pupils as it was displayed 'passively'.

1.3.2 Necessity in a Democratic Society and the Margin of Appreciation

The standard of review by the ECHR under this heading is high: for any restriction to be necessary, it must be proportionate to the legitimate aim pursued.[30] However, the ECtHR has also recognised that States need a certain flexibility in their observance

---

[24] See chapter 8 by Hendrickx and Van Bever.
[25] *Sindicatul Păstorull cel Bun v Romania*, App No 2330/09, decision of 31 January 2012.
[26] *Dahlab v Switzerland*, App No 42393/98, decision of 15 February 2001; *Eweida* (n 17).
[27] See *Kara v UK*, App No 36528/97, decision of 22 October 1998.
[28] *Sahin v Turkey*, App No 44774/98, judgment of 10 November 2005.
[29] *Lautsi v Italy*, App No 30814/06, judgment of 18 March 2011.
[30] *Handyside v UK*, Series A, No 24 (1981) 1 EHRR 737, para 48.

of the Convention, and so a 'margin of appreciation' is allowed to States in setting the parameters of their domestic law. The margin of appreciation has particular significance in respect of religious cases and a fairly wide margin operates, reflecting the lack of consensus across Europe about how religion should be treated.[31] The issue of how to treat the wearing of religious apparel, such as the hijab or turban, serves as a good illustration of the huge variation in approach to the public manifestation of religion within Europe. The Islamic headscarf and Sikh turban are routinely worn in the UK, in public and private sector employment, even among the police and judiciary. In France and Belgium, not only would such apparel not be allowed to be worn in public sector workplaces, but face coverings are even banned in public spaces. In the cases of *Sahin and Karaduman v Turkey*,[32] the Grand Chamber recognised the strength of argument both in favour and against a ban on headscarves, as well as the range of treatment given to the issue across Europe, and took the view that where opinion in a democratic society can reasonably differ widely, the issue is best left for local determination.[33] The wide margin of appreciation applicable in Article 9 cases was confirmed again in the decision in *Eweida et al v UK*,[34] particularly where States practice is still evolving across Europe.[35]

Guidance can be found from case law to help assess when a restriction on religious freedom is proportionate to the legitimate aim pursued. For example, the ECtHR has recognised that some jobs will involve a greater restriction on religious freedom than others. Thus, in *Pitkevich v Russia*,[36] where a judge was dismissed for a series of religious actions, such as praying publicly during hearings and promising favourable outcomes to those who agreed to join her church, the Court held that in the context of work as a judge, it was particularly necessary to uphold the impartiality and authority of the judiciary, and so her dismissal was proportionate. Similarly, in *Kalaç v Turkey*,[37] it was accepted that greater restrictions on religious freedom may be proportionate in the armed services, and in *Dahlab v Switzerland*[38] that greater restrictions may be acceptable for teachers.

An additional factor in determining proportionality is the identity of the employer. Where the employer is the state, the ECtHR has recognised the desire of the state to be religiously neutral. Thus, in *Dahlab v Switzerland*,[39] a factor in deciding that the prohibition on the teacher wearing a headscarf was proportionate as she was a 'representative of the state'.

The nature of the employer may also be relevant where the employer is religious in nature. The ECHR case law gives particularly clear protection to religious

---

[31] C Evans, *Freedom of Religion under the ECHR* (Oxford, Oxford University Press, 2001) 143–44.

[32] *Karaduman v Turkey*, App No 16278/90.

[33] There is great variety of practice with regard to the acceptance of the wearing of headscarves across Europe. See M Mahlmann, 'Religious Tolerance, Pluralist Society and the Neutrality of the State: The Federal Constitutional Court's Decision in the Headscarf Case' (2003) 4(11) *German Law Journal* (available at http://www.germanlawjournal.com/article.php?id=331); D McGoldrick, *Human Rights and Religion: The Islamic Headscarf Debate in Europe* (Oxford, Hart Publishing, 2006).

[34] Note 17.

[35] Such as on issues of legal protection for same-sex couples see *Eweida* (n 17) para 105.

[36] App No 47936/99, decision of 8 February 2001.

[37] Case No 61/1996/680/870, 1 July 1997.

[38] App No 42393/98 decision of 15 February 2001.

[39] Ibid.

communities in choosing their own leaders.[40] For example, *Hasan and Chaush v Bulgaria*[41] involved a dispute over the leadership of the Muslim religious community in Bulgaria. As a result of the process of registration of religious denominations, the State had been involved in the dispute. Hasan and Chaush claimed that the State had interefered with their freedom to organise their religion. The ECtHR confirmed that the 'personality of the religious ministers is undoubtedly of importance to every member of the community'[42] and that Article 9 covers participation in the life of the community. Moreover, 'where the organisation of the religious community is at issue, Article 9 of the Convention must be interpreted in the light of Article 11, which safeguards associative life against unjustified State interference'.[43] In effect, this means that the Court will be very careful before allowing inteferences with the freedom of religious groups to appoint their own religous leaders. Where a religious body acts as an employer, then, the proportionality of any restrictions on employees will reflect the religious community's religious interests. Thus, if an employee of a religious organisation does not comply with the teaching of the organisation, his rights to remain in the organisation will not be protected. For example, the dismissal of a minister of the established Church in Norway for revoking his oath of loyalty did not breach Article 9.[44]

The ECHR also provides support for religious ethos organisations, such as religious hospitals, to run their organisations along religious lines. For example, in *Rommelfanger v FDR*,[45] a doctor who worked for a Roman Catholic hospital was dismissed for publicly disapproving of the Church's attitude to abortion. He was unsuccessful in his complaint that the dismissal breached his freedom of expression, and the Commission was very clear that the employer was able to set requirements on staff that they comply with the employer's religious ethos. Although the case involved Article 10 rather than Article 9, it does suggest that religious organisations are granted extensive freedom to determine their activities within the Convention jurisprudence.

A final issue of importance in assessing the proportionality of any restriction on religion is the Court's jurisprudence suggesting that it is acceptable to put a 'cost' on religious observance, although this will need to be proportionate. For example, in *Konttinen v Finland*,[46] an applicant asked to change his working hours to enable him to observe the Seventh Day Adventist Sabbath. The European Commission on Human Rights found that it was unreasonable to expect the employer to accommodate the rules of different denominations at work and that it may impose an unfair burden on employer and other employees. It did not find the refusal to accommodate the request to be a disproportionate burden on religious freedom.

In sum, then, Article 9 effectively provides qualified protection for religious freedom at work, as the absolute rights of the *forum internum* are rarely engaged in the

---

[40] *Hasan and Chaush v Bulgaria* (2002) 34 EHRR 55, para 62; see also *Serif v Greece* (2001) 31 EHRR 20.
[41] (2002) 34 EHRR 55.
[42] Ibid, para 62.
[43] Ibid, para 68.
[44] *Knudsen v Norway*, App No 11045/84 (1985) 42 D&R 247.
[45] *Rommelfanger v FDR* (1989) 62 D&R 151.
[46] *Konttinen v Finland* (1996) 87 D&R 68.

work context. Instead, applicants claiming that their religious freedom is infringed in the work context will need to show that the religious activity in question involves a manifestation of religion and that the restriction is not a proportionate means to meet a legitimate aim, for example, that it is not necessary to safeguard the rights of others. The protection also covers religious groups who act as employers.

Given this range of hurdles in front of any particular claimant, the ECHR protection for religion in the work context is clearly heavily qualified. The right is qualified further by the margin of appreciation that the ECtHR allows to States in setting the parameters of their domestic law. This gives flexibility to States in their interpretation of the Convention, while subjecting them at all times to European supervision, in order to ensure that levels of protection do not fall below an acceptable minimum.[47] This allows the Court to reflect the lack of consensus across Europe about how religion should be treated.

2 PROTECTION OF RELIGION AND BELIEF IN EU EQUALITY LAW: DIRECTIVE 2000/78

The way in which the Equality Directive 2000/78 applies in the work context is clearly much more straightforward than Article 9 ECHR, as the Directive was designed to operate in the workplace. The EU Equality Directive protects against direct and indirect discrimination, harassment and victimisation on the grounds of religion or belief.

Direct discrimination occurs where a person is treated less favourably on the grounds of religion and belief. Examples will include situations where employers refuse to employ religious staff altogether, employ some religious staff but refuse employment to those of a particular religion, or employ those of one religion on more favourable terms than those of a different religion.

Direct discrimination cannot be justified. However, there is a defence to a direct discrimination claim where, because of the nature of the occupation or the context in which the work is carried out, a religion or belief constitutes a genuine occupational requirement for the job in question, and it is proportionate to impose that requirement.[48] For example, requiring that a priest be Catholic or that a teacher of Islam be Muslim would not involve unlawful direct discrimination. A slightly wider exception exists where the employer is an organisation with a religious ethos, such as religious hospitals or schools. In these cases, the religious ethos employer can require that members of staff are loyal to that ethos.[49] This is the case even though sharing a religious belief may not be an essential requirement for carrying out the core duties of the job. Any such requirement must not entail discrimination on any

---

[47] See HC Yourow, *The Margin of Appreciation Doctrine in the Dynamics of European Human Rights Jurisprudence* (Dordrecht, Martinus Nijhoff Publishers, 1996); T O'Donnell, 'The Margin of Appreciation Doctrine: Standard in the Jurisprudence of the European Court of Human Rights' [1982] *Human Rights Quarterly* 474; TH Jones, 'The Devaluation of Human Rights Under the European Convention' [1995] *PL* 430.

[48] Article 4 Equality Directive 2000/78.

[49] Ibid, Article 4(2).

other ground.[50] In this way, the Directive recognises the collective dimension to religious rights by allowing, where proportionate, religious groups to create religious ethos workplaces. This preserves freedom for the religious schools, hospitals and other religious foundations that are fairly common across parts of the EU[51] to continue to require loyalty from their staff towards the religion. However, as is discussed below, not all Member States have fully implemented this provision.

Indirect discrimination occurs where an apparently neutral requirement would put persons of a particular religion or belief at a particular disadvantage compared with other persons. It can be justified where there is a legitimate aim for the requirement and the means of achieving the aim are appropriate and necessary.[52] Examples include situations where the employer imposes requirements in terms of uniforms or hours of work with which it is difficult for those of particular religions to comply. For example, bans on headscarves or requests to be exempt from workplace tasks (such as performing civil partnerships) would all be dealt with as examples of indirect discrimination: they disadvantage the religious individual in comparision with others, and the focus then moves to whether the rules can be justified. The need for employers' requirements which have an adverse impact on religious individual to be justified should ensure that job requirements are appropriate to the job in question and should prevent the imposition of unnecessary requirements that have a disproportionate impact on those of any particular religion.

The question of justification is left to domestic courts, and it is not yet clear what factors the courts will accept as justifying indirect religious discrimination. A number of factors will need to be considered in determining whether any indirect discrimination is justified. Factors may include whether the requirement will have the effect of limiting religious freedom, the type of business and the nature of the accommodation required. For example, the Danish Supreme Court[53] allowed an employer to justify clothing guidelines in order to create a religiously neutral workplace, but it is unclear whether such an interpretation is consistent with the Directive. A second example of justified religious indirect discrimination can be found in the UK case of *Azmi v Kirkless Metropolitan Council*,[54] in which a classroom teaching assistant was dismissed for refusing her employer's request to remove her niqab when assisting in class. Her claim for indirect discrimination was unsuccessful. The restriction on Azmi's religious practice was proportionate because her communication with the children was better when they could see her face; thus, the limit on her wearing the niqab during her teaching time upheld the interests of the children in having the best possible education.

The Directive also prohibits harassment, where there is unwanted conduct related to religion and belief with the purpose or effect of violating the dignity of a person and of creating an intimidating, hostile, degrading, humiliating or offensive

---

[50] Article 4(2). Any requirement as to religion or belief must constitute a genuine, legitimate and justified occupational requirement, having regard to the organisation's ethos. Note that, unlike the general exception in Article 4(1), the requirement does not have to be 'determining'.
[51] Eg, faith schools in the UK and religious hospitals in Germany.
[52] Article 2(2)(b).
[53] Decision of 21 January 2005, 22/2004.
[54] *Azmi v Kirkless Metropolitan Council* [2007] ICR 1154.

environment. Victimisation provisions protect against adverse treatment taken as a reaction by the employer to the bringing of a complaint or enforcing of the religion and belief protection contained in the Directive.

The Directive has been implemented in Member States, although there has been some dispute about the scope of the genuine occupational requirement exceptions in Article 4, and the transposition of Article 4 into implementing legislation has not been uniform. Although some have transposed directly, several States introduced exceptions that were either wider or narrower than that allowed by Article 4.[55] These inconsistencies in transposition are of significance in the context of debate over the interaction of EU equality law and ECHR law on religious freedom, as the exceptions to the EU equality law are generally sought in order to uphold the religious freedom of religious groups, rights which are protected by the ECHR.

Some States, including the Czech Republic, Estonia, France, Lithuania, Portugal and Sweden did not include the Article 4(2) religious ethos exception in their incorporating legislation at all. In some of these States (the Czech Republic, Estonia and Lithuania), this was coupled with an exemption of disputes regarding clergy from domestic courts.[56] On the one hand, in cases where clergy are exempt from labour courts' review, the exception applied to all clergy is technically broader than that provided by Article 4(2), as there is no requirement for proportionality. On the other hand, it would be difficult to imagine it not being proportionate to impose a requirement relating to religion upon the appointment of religious leaders. Certainly, in the light of ECHR case law on Article 9, it is clear that freedom of religion encompasses the right to choose religious leaders.[57]

In States where clergy disputes are not exempt from court review, the failure to implement the religious ethos exception means that the more general genuine occupational requirement exception based on Article 4(1) applies instead. This means that the requirement of proportionality and necessity is stricter. Whilst this creates greater protection from religion and belief discrimination for individuals, the result is that the degree of religious freedom for religious groups is reduced, as they are unable to impose religious requirements on staff unless they are absolutely essential to the job. It might be questioned whether such restrictions conflict with the right to collective religious freedom that should be enjoyed by religious groups.

Whilst some Member States, then, have stopped short of transposing Article 4(2) fully, other Member States have transposed Article 4(2) in terms that go beyond the Directive, so that religious ethos organisations are allowed to discriminate more than is allowed for under the Directive. For example, in Ireland, there is an exception to the non-discrimination principle for the purposes of maintaining the religious ethos of an institution.[58] This is broader than is allowed for in the Directive,

---

[55] See L Vickers, *Religion and Belief in Employment—The EU Law* (European Commission, 2007).

[56] Eg, the Czech Constitutional Court has held that labour disputes involving clerics are inadmissible in the civil courts and that labour law does not apply at all in labour relationships involving clerics: Country Report Czech Republic, European Network of Legal Experts in the non-discrimination field (hec, MPG, 2006). In Estonia and Lithuania too, employment laws do not apply to the employment of priests. See Article 7 Law on Employment Contracts in 1992 in Estonia. Country Reports, Estonia and Lithuania, European Network of Legal Experts in the non-discrimination field (hec, MPG, 2006).

[57] *Hasan and Chaush v Bulgaria* (n 37) para 62; see also *Serif v Greece* (n 37).

[58] Section 37(1) Employment Equality Act 1998–2004.

as it does not provide that religion or belief must be relevant to the particular job in question; nor does it limit the exception to discrimination based on the grounds of religion or belief to prevent it from being used to justify discrimination on another ground. Therefore, it may be the case in these States that the equality rights that should be protected by the Directive are not fully enjoyed.

Even where correctly transposed, Article 4(1) and (2) gives rise to some difficulty in terms of determining when an exception to the non-discrimination principle will be proportionate. There seems to be consensus among EU Member States on the need to respect the religious freedom and autonomy of churches and religious groups by allowing them to choose their own staff to teach the religion and lead or participate in religious observance. Discriminatory requirements such as requirements for priests and other equivalent church leaders to be male are therefore likely to be proportionate genuine occupational requirements, as long as they are necessary for the maintenance of religious freedom. However, in the case of Article 4(2), occupational requirements do not need to be *determining*, and so it can be acceptable to impose religious requirements even where the work is not religious in nature, and it is the boundaries of this broader exception which are more difficult to determine, and about which there is room for significant difference of opinion.

The effect of the genuine occupational requirements in the Directive is that religious employers can create workplaces which are homogeneous in religious terms, even where the work is not religious in nature. However, if discrimination on other grounds such as sex or sexual orientation results, such a practice will be in breach of the Directive, as it will amount to discrimination on the other ground. An exception may arise where the work itself is religious in nature. In such a case, the religious requirement, which is indirectly discriminatory on other grounds, may be justified as proportionate because of the need to uphold religious freedom. In some cases, the 'other ground' discrimination may be direct discrimination (the requirement that a Catholic priest be male, for example), but even here, the standard genuine occupational requirements exception would presumably apply and a court is likely to find that, given the nature of the job and its context, the requirement is proportionate.

However, where work is not strictly religious in nature, religious requirements on staff that discriminate on other grounds will be unlawful under the Directive. Thus, for example, a requirement on doctors in religious hospitals to be orthodox Muslim or Christian could entail less favourable treatment of homosexual Muslim or Christian doctors and will be unlawful under the Directive. Some might argue that this position amounts to a limitation on the religious freedom of the religious foundations running schools and hospitals, amounting to a breach of Article 9; however, the counter-position is that any other treatment of the situation undermines the equality rights protected by Equality Directive 2000/78. How this potential conflict between the two sets of rights might be resolved is the subject of discussion below.

Having outlined the ways in which the different frameworks for protection apply to the workplace, it is next necessary to consider further some problem areas where tension between equality and religious freedom could arise in order to explore how the different frameworks might approach a resolution. First, some broader tensions between religious freedom as protected by Article 9 ECHR and religious equality as protected by Equality Directive 2000/78 will be considered. Then a small number of case studies will be examined to reflect in more detail upon how the different legal regimes may treat similar cases.

3 THE INTERACTION OF PROTECTION OF RELIGION AND BELIEF UNDER ECHR AND EU LAW

The various frameworks of protection for fundamental rights that operate at a European level all offer degrees of protection for religious rights, but in slightly differing ways.[59] The focus of Article 9 ECHR is on religious freedom. The focus of Directive 2000/78 is on equality and non-discrimination. In terms of the formal interaction of these different legal frameworks, there now exist a number of different legal bases for the proposition that the EU Equality Directive will need to be interpreted in order to comply with the human rights norms of the ECHR and vice versa. These will not be described in detail, as they have been discussed elsewhere in this volume, but in outline they are as follows: first, there is the acceptance in EU law of the principle of equality as a fundamental principle of EU law, as seen in *Kucukdeveci v Swedex*;[60] second, under the Lisbon Treaty, the EU accedes to the ECHR, meaning that its law will be subject to that of the Convention. Equally, and conversely, the decision in *Demir and Baykarai* shows that the Convention should be interpreted in the light of elements of international law other than the Convention, including the practice of contracting states. This suggests that the ECHR needs to be interpreted in the light of the equality norms of the EU Directive, as implemented in Member States, as well as the norms of the International Labour Organization (ILO), the International Covenant on Civil and Political Rights (ICCPR), the European Charter of Fundamental Rights and other international human rights instruments.[61]

The interaction between the two sets of European legal protection thus seems to be reciprocal. Before considering how this might look in practice in the case studies explored below, it is worth exploring briefly how the different sets of interests in religious equality and religious freedom interact at a more abstract level, because although both freedom of religion and religious equality engage with the protection of matters related to religion and belief, the different forms and forums of legal protection can be seen to be both complementary in their operation and yet at times in tension. The protection offered by Article 9 ECHR (and Article 10 of the Charter of Fundamental Rights of the EU) is viewed as protection for fundamental human rights, and the protection extends to all areas of public life. In contrast, the protection under the EU Directive applies only to employment and occupation and covers non-discrimination; thus, it can be viewed more as a negative 'right' rather than as imposing any positive obligations on actors. To an extent, then, one might

---

[59] For more general discussion of the role of religion and belief in the EU, see R McCrea, *Religion and the Public Order of the European Union* (Oxford, Oxford University Press, 2010).

[60] *Kucukdeveci v Swedex*, judgment of 19 January 2010, Case C-555/07 at para 20.

[61] Religious freedom and non-discrimination are protected under these instruments, but the case law is not extensive and does not add in substance to the case law already developed under the ECHR.

view the protection offered by Article 9 as operating in a different sphere from the EU Equality Directive, despite relating to the same issue of religion and belief.

However, the right to freedom of religion and the right not to be discriminated against on the grounds of religion in employment and occupation are, at the same time, intimately related. Both are founded on the concepts of dignity autonomy and equality.[62] Moreover, equality and religious freedom are also closely linked, since to allow the exercise of religious freedom to result in unjustified differences in life prospects infringes individual equality. From this it can be argued that religious discrimination should be prohibited, as full enjoyment of autonomy, equality and dignity cannot exist where individuals can be discriminated against because of their religon. Full religious freedom therefore requires protection for both freedom from religious discrimination and freedom of religion.

One consequence of a recognition of the links between human rights protection for religion under the ECHR and the non-discrimination norms of the Equality Directive is the recognition from human rights law that religion and belief have a group dimension. Freedom of religion under Article 9 extends to a right to manifest religion alone *or in community* with others. As part of this respect for group religious rights, it is arguable that religious groups should be able to enter employment relationships in order to better organise or facilitate religious activity. Restrictions on the freedom of religious groups—for example, to appoint a teacher or a religious official—may interfere with the religious freedom of the group. Similarly, restrictions on the freedom of religious individuals to work with others as part of manifesting their religious commitment may also infringe their religious freedom. Thus, the link between non-discrimination on grounds of religion and belief in employment interacts with, and will be informed by, the communal aspect of the right to freedom of religion and belief.

Despite this clear complementary relationship between religious freedom and non-discrimination rights, the two types of religious interest can also at times be in tension with each other. First, many religions do not recognise fundamental rights and freedoms of others, such as rights not to be discriminated against on grounds of birth, status, gender, religion (other than their own), sexual orientation or other grounds. It is therefore arguable that a society that values equality and dignity should not protect or accommodate those who do not share those fundamental values. Second, clashes can arise between various human rights where religious interests are concerned. For example, once religious harassment is prohibited at work, there is a possible clash between individual freedom of speech and non-harassment rights (members of staff are not free to speak to colleagues where that speech would cause offence or create a hostile environment) and between non-harassment and religious claims to proselytise.[63] Similar clashes will be found between religious freedom and

---

[62] For more detail, see L Vickers, *Religious Freedom, Religious Discrimination and the Workplace* (Oxford, Hart Publishing, 2008).

[63] For more detail of the debate on freedom of speech and harassment, see E Volokh 'Freedom of Speech and Workplace Harassment' (1992) 39 *UCLA L Rev* 1791. See also KR Browne, 'Title VII as Censorship: Hostile Environment Harassment and the First Amendment' (1991) 52 *Ohio State LJ* 481. For the discussion in the context of religion, see T Dworkin and E Peirce, 'Is Religious Harassment "More Equal"?' (1995) 26 *Seton Hall Law Review* 44; and L Vickers, 'Is All Harassment Equal? The Case of Religious Harassment' (2006) 65(3) *CLJ* 579–605.

privacy if employers impose requirements on staff regarding the morality of their private lifestyles. Third, at times, tension can arise from the fact that religious freedom also extends to freedom from religion, raising questions about how to manage claims relating to the display of religious symbols in workplaces and the extent to which this may be seen to interfere with the rights of those with no religion.

These difficulties and tensions between religious freedom and non-discrimination are particularly pronounced in relation to employment by the State, where it may be felt that tolerance of religious symbols implies State endorsement of religion, and, moreover, where the promotion of a broader equalities agenda may mean public sector employers are reluctant to accommodate those with beliefs that may conflict with that agenda. For example, it might be seen to be at odds with a general equalities agenda for an employer to accommodate a religious practice which itself demonstrates a negative approach to equality, such as a request to be exempt from carrying out civil partnerships or a request to be excused from shaking hands with women.[64] Equally, and balanced against this, is the fact that the interest of the State in promoting multiculturalism and pluralism may support the employment of a diverse workforce, reflecting the make-up of the state's population, giving reason to employ those with views which others might find unpalatable.

In sum, then, the relationship between freedom of religion and belief, and equality on grounds of religion and belief is complex, in some ways strengthening and complementing each other, while in other ways undermining or at least existing in tension with each other.

Perhaps in response to these inherent tensions and conflicts, both the ECHR and the Equality Directive recognise in their different formulations that religious interests do not need to be enjoyed in an absolute sense, but are qualified in nature. With regard to human rights claims, this is reflected in the fact that although religion, belief and conscience are protected absolutely (*the forum internum*), the manifestation of religion and belief (*the forum externum*) can be limited where justified. With regard to discrimination claims, this can be seen in the fact that while direct discrimination cannot be justified, exceptions are allowed where religious employers impose justified and proportionate genuine occupational requirements, and indirect discrimination can be justified where proportionate. Thus, even though the employment protection provided by the EU Equality Directive for religious discrimination should be interpreted to comply with human rights norms, there is no expectation that this will create absolute rights for religious interests to be accommodated.

Similarly, and more generally, both EU and ECHR jurisprudence recognise that there needs to be a level of flexibility and adaptability in the interpretation of the law across different domestic jurisdictions in order to enable local traditions and sensitivities to be respected, despite the transnational nature of the legal regimes. Thus, with respect to the ECHR, the Court allows a 'margin of appreciation' to States in setting the parameters of their domestic law, which gives flexibility to States in their interpretation of the Convention. Although flexible, this margin still requires that States remain subject to European supervision to ensure that levels of

---

[64] See the Dutch case on the issue: ETC opinions 2006-220 and 221, and Rechtbank Utrecht 30 autstus 2007, LJN BB2648; CrvB 7 mei 2009, LJL BI2240.

protection do not fall below an acceptable minimum. Of course, if the concept is used too extensively, it has the potential to undermine the protection afforded by the Convention, but the concept also allows the Court to reflect the lack of consensus across Europe about how religion should be treated.

With regard to EU protection, some flexibility can also be allowed at times, in terms of a 'margin of discretion'. This can be seen in *Schmidberger v Austria*[65] and was confirmed in the *Omega* case,[66] where the CJEU accepted that EU law must be interpreted in the light of fundamental human rights principles. It accepted that there is a margin of discretion in reaching a fair balance between competing economic and social interests, and that it is not necessary that States all agree on a shared conception of how to protect the interests in question. These cases show that, again, as long as the standard of protection provided does not fall below a minimum standard, there is room for different standards of protection for fundamental rights to be accepted as legitimate within the EU Member States so as to reflect different national contexts and traditions.

Thus, it would seem that EU law, like the ECHR framework, provides for a level of flexiblity when setting standards of protection for religion and belief. However, set against this reasonably flexible approach, and partially in tension with it, are clear signals in terms of EU equality law that equality is a fundamental principle of EU law and that there should be no hierarchy as between the different grounds.[67] In the context of the application of equality law on the grounds of gender, it seems inconceivable that the Court would allow a Member State to argue that local custom and practice should be allowed to explain and justify sex or race discrimination in employment. Indeed, it is precisely because these are seen to be fundamental rights that they are not seen as areas of 'reasonable disagreement, that is areas where a variety of States' practice can be respected within a margin of discretion. Thus, viewing the matter through the lens of EU equality law may give rise to tensions between religious equaltiy and religious freedom which are not readily resolved by resort to concepts such as a margin of appreciation or a margin of discretion. This problem can be reduced if it is accepted that the protected ground of religion is different from other protected grounds, such as race and sex. However, this would require an acceptance of a hierarchy as between equality rights, an outcome that is likely to be contested.[68]

Subject to this caveat, then, regarding the extent to which religious equality should be viewed as on a par with other equality grounds such as sex and race, it remains the case that our understanding of EU non-discrimination laws should be enriched by viewing them as connected with the right to freedom of religion and

---

[65] Case C-112/00, *Schmidberger Internationale Transporte Planzüge v Republik Österreich* (2003) ECR I-5659.

[66] Case C-36/02, *Omega v Oberburgermeisterin der Bundesstadt Bonn* [2004] ECR I-9609.

[67] The CJEU has suggested that there should be uniform application of the various equality provisions across the EU: see Case C-13/05, *Chacón Navas v Eurest Colectividades SA* [2006] ECR I-6467, para 40, a case involving the definition of disability.

[68] M Bell and L Waddington, 'Reflecting on Inequalities in European Equality Law' (2003) *European Law Review* 28; M Bell and L Waddington, 'More Equal than Others: Distinguishing European Equality Directives' (2001) *Common Market Law Review* 38; D Schiek, 'A New Framework on Equal Treatment of Persons in EC Law?' (2002) *European Law Journal* 8.

other human rights. This should mean that the jurisprudence of the ECtHR can be used to help determine the parameters of the Directive's protection. Equally, viewing the right to protect freedom of religion as requiring interpretation in the light of the requirements in EU law for equality may also help develop our understanding of what can properly be required of the Article 9 protection, particularly in the work context. In both cases, this interaction is most likely to be played out in the development of the jurisprudence on the standard of 'justification' for any exceptions to the qualified right to manifest religion, and the concept of 'proportionality' for the qualified indirect discrimination right and the genuine occupational requirement exception.

4 APPLYING THE LEGAL FRAMEWORKS TO CASES

Having outlined the ways in which the different legal frameworks for protection of religion and belief apply to the workplace, this section will consider some problem areas where tensions between equality and religious freedom have arisen, in order to explore how the different frameworks approach the issues. Three of the examples are based on UK cases, which were brought under the legal provisions which implement the EU Directive. The first two cases have now been decided by a chamber of the European Court of Human Rights, where it was argued that the UK decisions (applying legislation based on the Directive) resulted in an interference with the applicants' religious freedom (protected under Article 9).[69] The discussion here focuses on issues relating to the interpretation of the Directive-derived equality legislation which were raised by the domestic decisions, although reference is made to the later findings of the ECtHR. The other examples are drawn from other European States.

4.1 Interpreting the EU Directive in the Light of the ECHR

4.1.1 Eweida v British Airways: *Indirect Discrimination and Group Disadvantage*[70]

Eweida was a member of the check-in staff for British Airways (BA) who was refused permission to wear a cross over her uniform, as this was in breach of the company's uniform policy.[71] Her claims of direct and indirect discrimination were

---

[69] This of itself raises some interesting questions about the interaction of the EC and ECHR jurisprudence. It will be interesting to see whether the problems identified in the cases are treated differently according to the different legal frameworks. If this is the case, 'forum shopping' as between the different jurisdictions is likely to occur. However, it ought to be the case that the accession of the EU to the ECHR makes 'forum shopping' redundant, given that both sets of laws should be being interpreted on a reciprocal basis.

[70] [2010] EWCA Civ 80. See the comment on the EAT decision by L Vickers: [2009] *Ecclesiastical Law Journal* 197. The case was appealed to the ECHR. *Eweida and Chaplin v UK*, App Nos 48420/10 and 59842/10.

[71] BA did allow Muslim women to wear the hijab and Sikh men to wear turbans because the items were required by the particular religions and they could not be concealed under the uniform.

unsuccessful. The rejection of her direct discrimination claim was unsurprising: she was not dismissed because of her Christianity, but because of her wearing of the cross. Her claim for indirect discrimination was also unsuccessful in the UK courts and the basis for this is perhaps more surprising. It had already been accepted in another case[72] that a restriction on religious dress at work amounts to indirect religious discrimination, which needs to be justified. However, in Eweida's case, the court did not get as far as considering whether the employer could justify refusing her request to be allowed to wear the cross. Instead, the case was lost at an earlier stage of the argument: the Court held that the refusal to accommodate the request of a single believer was not covered by the indirect discrimination protection, as the Regulations require that a neutral requirement is imposed which puts, or would put, persons of the same religion at a particular disadvantage. It held that this meant that more than one person must hold the belief. As Eweida was the only person identified who held the particular belief, there could be no indirect discrimination.

Read in the light of the protection for religion found in Article 9, this ruling seems surprising, because individual beliefs are protected under Article 9 ECHR. Thus, if the Directive-derived UK legislation is read in the light of the ECHR case law, it could be interpreted more broadly to cover not just persons with the same views, but also individuals.[73] Instead, an interpretation of the Regulations in the absence of reference to the ECHR has resulted in excluding indirect discrimination claims from sole believers, meaning that such believers are not protected when they manifest their beliefs.

In the chamber decision of the ECtHR, Eweida was successful. The Court accepted that her religious rights were engaged, and the restriction therefore had to be justified by the employer. Here the employer argued that its rights to project a particular corporate image were interfered with by Eweida's wish to wear the cross. The Court held that the right of the employer to project a certain image was insufficient to outweigh the employee's right to manifest religion.

The case thus serves as a good example of the benefit to religious individuals that can be achieved by reading the EU law in the light of Article 9 protection. It is worth noting, however, that the ECtHR case does not allow for a right to wear religious symbols in all cases. In the case of the second applicant, Chaplin, the interests of the employer in maintaining health and safety standards outweighed the employee's interest in manifesting her religion at work. As with the approach to religious symbols based on indirect discrimination, then, Article 9 allows for the competing interests of the parties to be balanced against each other. Where the employer has good reason to restrict the display of religious symbols at work, such as those based on health and safety concerns, such a restriction will be justified. This will be the

---

[72] *Azmi v Kirklees Metropolitan Borough Council* [2007] ICR 1154.

[73] Although the Regulations use the term 'persons' in the plural, they also include the word 'puts or would put' persons of the same belief at a disadvantage. The inclusion of the conditional 'would put' persons at a disadvantage could mean 'would also put persons of the same view, were there to be any, at a disadvantage'. Thus, it is possible to interpret the UK law to comply with the ECHR standards. The parent directive is worded solely in the conditional, suggesting again that it may cover individual disadvantage. See N Bamforth, M Malik and C O'Cinneide (eds), *Discrimination Law, Theory and Context* (London, Sweet & Maxwell, 2008) 307–08.

case whether it is viewed as a justification for indirect discrimination or a legitimate restriction on religious freedom.

4.1.2 Ladele v Islington Borough Council: *Refusal of Work Tasks for Religious Reasons and 'Clashes' of Rights*[74]

Ladele worked as a registrar of Births, Deaths and Marriages for a number of years, before being designated a Civil Partnership Registrar under the Civil Partnership Act 2004, qualifying her to carry out civil partnerships for same-sex couples. This caused her difficulties as she believed that participation in registering civil partnerships would be contrary to her religious beliefs, since it would involve promoting an activity which she believed to be sinful. She sought to be excused from carrying out civil partnerships on this basis, but permission was refused. The Council insisted that under its 'Dignity for All' policy, all registrars should be able to carry out all types of ceremony. Ladele was eventually disciplined and threatened with dismissal for refusing to carry out this part of her job. The legal case turned on the question of justification. The Court held that the refusal to accommodate Ladele's request to be exempt from carrying out civil partnerships was justified as the employer was entitled to rely on the dignity for all policy, needed to offer a service to all service users regardless of sexual orientation and Ladele's views on marriage were not a core part of her religious beliefs.

The *Ladele* case can be compared with a similar decision reached by the Dutch Equal Treatment Commission in its finding that civil servants cannot refuse to officiate civil marriages between same-sex couples based on their religious beliefs.[75] However, it is worth noting that the Dutch Equal Treatment Commission has not always been consistent in its approach, which suggests that even within Member States, there can be different approaches to the same issue. For example, the Equal Treatment Commission has accepted in other cases that civil servants might be able to invoke religious objections against carrying out marriages of same-sex couples.[76] Similarly, although in the Dutch case involving the dismissal of a female Muslim teacher for refusing to shake hands on religious grounds, the Equal Treatment Commission found this not to be justified and so indirectly discriminatory,[77] this reasoning was not followed by the District and higher administrative courts.[78] Equally, in *Ladele*, the Court of Appeal expressly refused to rule out the idea that other local councils that had decided to deal with those with objections such as Ladele's by allowing them to swap duties were acting lawfully.[79] These cases illustrate the lack of consensus even within Member States on how to deal with clashes between equality rights of this type.

---

[74] *Ladele v Islington Borough Council* [2009] EWCA Civ 1357.
[75] Opinion 2008/40 by the ETC.
[76] Opinions 2002/25 and 2002/26.
[77] ETC Opinions 2006-220 and 221.
[78] Rechtbank Utrecht 30 autstus 2007, LJN BB2648; CrvB 7 mei 2009, LJL BI2240.
[79] For example, [2009] EWCA Civ 1357, para 75, where Lord Neuberger stated that 'such decisions may well be lawful'.

The case of *Ladele* and the similar case of *McFarlane* were brought under the Directive-derived legislation, but it seems that even considered in the light of the ECHR jurisprudence the same outcome can be expected. In *Ladele*, Article 9 was considered by the Court of Appeal and the conclusion reached was that Article 9 'does not always guarantee the right to behave in the public sphere in a way which is dictated by such a belief'.[80] Thus, the UK court relied on the fact that Article 9 does not guarantee rights at work. However, although when the case was heard by the chamber of the ECtHR, the Court held that religious rights can be claimed at work, they still concluded that the employer was able to restrict the employee's manifestation of religion when it interfered with other equality rights. The Court did this by relying on the wide margin of appreciation allowed to states when dealing with issues over which there is a lack of consensus in Europe. It is interesting to note, therefore, that, as with the domestic court, the ECtHR did not rule that concern for sexual orientation equality would dictate that workers' beliefs on sexual orientation should never be accommodated by employers. The decision was merely that the employer's response to Ladele's request was within the margin of appreciation allowed to states in balancing competing rights.

Thus, the original issue in *Ladele* was based on equality laws, but even if considered under Article 9, the same conclusion was reached. The protection of Article 9 rarely extends to the manifestation of religion where it conflicts with the rights of others; in the gay marriage cases, these include the right of gay and lesbian people to equality, and the rights of the employer to determine is own equality policy. The qualified nature of the protection of the manifestation of religion in Article 9 means that where there are clashes between religious freedom and other equality rights, the equality rights may well prevail. Again the balancing approach of Article 9 comes to similar conclusions to the parallel balancing exercise undertaken with respect to indirect discrimination.

4.1.3 Reaney v Hereford Diocesan Board of Finance: *Occupational Requirements that Discriminate on Other Grounds*[81]

Although the case of *Reaney v Hereford Diocesan Board of Finance* is only a first-level employment tribunal case from the UK, it raises an interesting point relating to the treatment of religious organisations and how clashes between different equality grounds are treated in this context. As discussed above, there have been a number of questions raised as to whether Article 4 was correctly transposed into national legislation in a number of States, and the UK provisions applied in *Reaney* have been subject to a 'reasoned opinion' sent by the European Commission to the UK government, questioning whether the exceptions to the principle of non-discrimination on the basis of sexual orientation for religious employers were broader than that permitted by the Directive.

As referred to above, the Directive allows for genuine occupational requirements to be applied by religious ethos organisations, as long as they are proportionate, in

---

[80] Ibid, para 57.
[81] *Reaney v Hereford Diocesan Board of Finance*, Case No 1602844/2006.

order to maintain the religious ethos of the organisation. This allows religious bodies to create religiously homogeneous workplaces, but only as long as the requirement is proportionate. However, this special provision for religion does not include a right to discriminate on other grounds, because the non-discrimination provisions relating to religion and belief have to be read alongside other non-discrimination prohibitions in the EU Directive. For example, a religious employer that denies employment to a gay applicant on religious grounds will be liable for direct discrimination on grounds of sexual orientation. Even if the employer's rules are more subtle, for example, setting religious observance as a preference in making an appointment in order to maintain the religious ethos of the organisation, this may indirectly discriminate on grounds of sexual orientation if the religion in question is hostile to homosexuality.

Where the discrimination on grounds of sex or sexual orientation is indirect, the employer could try to justify it as proportionate to a legitimate aim, for example, the aim of maintaining religious freedom and autonomy. However, apart from very specialised circumstances, this will be difficult to show, given the strength of the competing interest in gender and sexual orientation equality. One example, however, where it may well be proportionate, particularly if this is viewed from the human rights and ECHR perspective, is where the employment is for religious personnel such as priests. Here, it would seem that the proportionality judgment could take into account the strong ECHR case law upholding collective religious autonomy, and this could lead to a finding that it is proportionate to restrict the employment of clergy to particular genders.

It is suggested, then, that the Directive ensures that exceptions to sex and sexual orientation discrimination are very limited, but yet contains the potential for religious freedom for groups to appoint and choose their own priests or celebrants. To this extent, the provisions of the Directive seem to accord with the ECHR. However, in the UK Equality Act 2010, which contains the transposed provisions in the UK, an additional provision is included to cover the issue of clergy and other similar personnel by providing explicitly that where employment is for the purposes of an organised religion, discrimination on grounds of sex or sexual orientation will be lawful if it is required to comply with religious doctrine, without recourse to the proportionality requirement.[82] The exception only applies to those employed for the purposes of an organised religion; it is not broad enough to cover discrimination in order to maintain the 'religious ethos' of generally religious organisations.

Perhaps unsurprisingly, given that it provides for an express case of direct sex or sexual orientation discrimination, the provision has been narrowly interpreted in the case law. In *Amicus*,[83] it was confirmed that it only applies to the appointment of religious leaders and teachers such as priests and imams and their equivalents. In *Reaney v Hereford*, a Christian youth worker was denied employment as a

---

[82] Given that religious doctrine for some groups is undecided, the provisions are slightly wider than this and cover requirements related to sexual orientation imposed so as to comply with the doctrines of the religion, or so as to avoid conflicting with the strongly held religious convictions of a significant number of the religion's followers: Equality Act 2010, sch 9, para 2.

[83] *R (on the application of Amicus—MSF and others) v Secretary of State for Trade and Industry and others* [2004] EWHC 860 (Admin).

diocesan youth officer because the Bishop did not believe his lifestyle would remain compatible with the church's teachings on homosexuality.[84] In accordance with the beliefs of a significant number of Christians about the appropriate lifestyle for a gay Christian, the Diocese required that the youth officer comply with a requirement to be celibate for the duration of the post. The applicant's work was to involve some 'face-to-face' youth work, and the case confirmed that the sexual orientation exception could be applied in this context. However, the church lost the case, because the tribunal held that the Bishop was unreasonable in his belief that the applicant would not meet the requirement to remain celibate whilst in the post.

Although there may be some questions about whether the removal, in the UK provisions, of the requirement for proportionality to be assessed in the context of clergy and equivalent religious personnel accords with the terms of the EU Directive, it would seem that the rule as applied in practice in the case of *Reaney* accords with the ECHR case law on Article 9. ECHR case law is clear that where an employee is playing a key role in the group's manifestation of religion (for example, carrying out religious rites), the autonomy of the religious group should be accorded great weight when set against other interests.[85] This suggests that a requirement relating to sex or sexual orientation which is applied by a religious group in order to comply with religious doctrine[86] would probably be judged to be proportionate if the EU Directive is to be interpreted to accord with the provisions of the ECHR.

Added to this is the fact that at the EU level, the transposition of these provisions has been varied, as referred to above. This may be viewed as evidence of a lack of consensus in Europe on the issue of how far religious groups should enjoy the freedom to choose their own teachers and leaders, even where to do so offends other equality norms. Where there is a lack of consensus at a European level on how to deal with an issue, the ECtHR has tended to accord a broader margin of appreciation in determining compliance with its provisions. Interpreting the EU Directive to comply with ECHR standards is therefore likely to involve according a reasonably broad margin of discretion to Member States in their interpretation of concepts such as the proportionality of any religious measures which indirectly impact on equality norms.

However, this analysis of the EU Directive also suggests that the special exception contained in the UK legislation, with its removal of the proportionality control, was unnecessary, as the matter would be covered in any event by the standard genuine occupational requirement for which proportionality is required. Where such a gender or sexuality requirement is applied to the role of the clergy, it is likely to proportionate in EU law, particularly if read in the light of ECHR law which gives deference to autonomy for religious groups to appoint their own personnel in accordance with religious doctrine. Nonetheless, and despite the EU 'reasoned opinion', the special exception remains in the UK legislation.

---

[84] *Reaney v Hereford Diocesan Board of Finance* (n 81).

[85] See, for example, *Hasan and Chaush v Bulgaria* (n 37) para 62; and *Serif v Greece* (n 37).

[86] Or to avoid conflicting with the strongly held religious convictions of a significant number of the religion's followers.

4.2 Interpreting the ECHR in the Light of the EU Equality Directive

4.2.1 Obst and Schüth v Germany and Siebenhaar v Germany; Fernandez Martinez v Spain: *Failure to Comply with Religious Teaching*[87]

These cases are the converse of the previous cases, in that they were brought under the ECHR and so raise the question of whether an equality-based approach might have led to a different outcome had they arisen in the context of a case based on the Directive. Although *Obst* , *Schüth* and *Fernández Martínez v Spain* arose in the context of Article 8 claims, rather than Article 9, the facts of the cases are immersed in a religious context, and so they are considered here.

In both *Obst* and *Schüth*, churches wished to dismiss staff for failing to comply with religious teaching. In both cases, the members of staff had been involved in extramarital relationships, in *Schüth* a Catholic Church organist and in *Obst* the Director of European Public Relations for the Mormon Church. The cases were brought under Article 8 (privacy and family life) rather than Article 9 (religion and belief). The ECtHR came down on different sides in the cases, with the claim of the Catholic organist upheld and the claim of the Mormon Public Relations Director rejected, but the reasoning related to a procedural question about the extent to which privacy rights had been considered by the decision makers in each case.

In *Fernández Martínez v Spain* a decision was taken not to renew the contract of employment of a priest, who was married and had five children. He had been given dispensation to marry by the Vatican, and was employed in a school to teach Catholic religion and morals. The decision not to renew his contract followed the publication of an article in which his membership of the 'Movement for Optional Celibacy' was disclosed. In his original appeal against dismissal it was found that he had been discriminated against on grounds of his civil status and his membership of the organisation, but this finding was then overturned on further appeal. At the ECHR he argued, as had *Obst* and *Schüth*, that the dismissal interfered with Article 8 rights to privacy and family life. Again, the ECHR relied on procedural questions to find that the Spanish courts had reached a fair balance between interests of privacy, freedom of religion and freedom of association, and that therefore there had been no violation of Article 8.

In *Siebenhaar*, a member of the Universal Church/Brotherhood of Humanity was dismissed from her post as a teacher in a church kindergarten. The Chamber of the ECtHR found there to be no violation of Article 9 as the German Labour Court had undertaken an appropriate balancing exercise of the relevant interests in reaching its decision that the dismissal was fair.

What is clear from all three cases is that the ECtHR gave significant weight to the fact that national courts had undertaken a careful balance of the competing interests at stake in the cases. The Court thus seems to be tacitly accepting that clear standards are difficult to identify in these cases and that appropriate protection may be best achieved by ensuring that national courts undertake proper balancing

---

[87] *Obst v Germany*, App No 425/03, decision of 23 September 2010; *Schüth v Germany*, App No 1620/03, decision of 23 September 2010; *Siebenhaar v Germany*, App No 18136/02, decision of 3 February 2011; *Fernandez Martinez v Spain* App No 56030/07, decision of 15 May 2012.

exercises, taking account of the correct factors in doing so. Only where it can be shown that the balancing exercise was defective will the ECtHR intervene. Thus, in *Schüth*, the Court upheld the applicant's claim because the balancing exercise undertaken by the national court was defective on the basis that it had failed to include the privacy rights of the applicant and his family in the balancing scales. Where the correct factors have been identified and put into the scales (as in *Obst, Fernández Martínez* and *Siebenhaar*), the ECtHR seems unlikely to intervene. In terms of the general approach, the cases referred to the need to give national courts a degree of discretion in deciding these cases, given that there is no common practice across Member States, and since the issues involved religion and tradition. The cases are good examples of the way in which the margin of appreciation operates in assessing whether Article 9 (or Article 8) has been breached.

In terms of whether the outcome would have been any different if approached under EU Equality Directive 2000/78, it is not clear. In both *Obst* and *Fernández Martínez*, the ECtHR cited the Directive, noting that it allows for exceptions where the employer has a religious ethos and religion is a genuine occupational requirement of the job. This suggests that the outcome could have been the same even if brought under the Directive: under Article 4(2), an employer such as a church, which clearly has a religious ethos, would be allowed to discriminate on the basis of religion in order to uphold its religious ethos.

However, the genuine occupational requirement exception in EU law is subject to a requirement of proportionality, and it is interesting to speculate whether a court would find dismissal to be proportionate in any of the cases, but perhaps most particularly in the fourth ECHR case, *Siebenhaar*. Under the EU Directive, the question on the facts of *Siebenhaar* would be, having regard to the nature of the job or the context of the work, was the requirement not to be a member of the Universal Church a genuine and determining occupational requirement, did it have a legitimate objective and was it proportionate to require it?[88] On the one hand, it is arguable that the fact that the employee was an active member of the Universal Church, and teaching very young children, who might potentially be more readily influenced, might still mean that the interests of the employer in maintaining its religious ethos would prevail and the restriction could be held to be proportionate. Given the tensions and complexity that surround the issue of discrimination and religious employment, it is possible that the CJEU would give full weight to religious freedom issues, allowing a flexible response to the approach taken by local courts when assessing the proportionality of the exception to the non-discrimination rules.

On the other hand, there was no evidence of the applicant using her position to influence the children and so it is arguable that it was not proportionate to dismiss her. Moreover, where the CJEU has determined the proportionality of discriminatory action in contexts such as sex discrimination, the standard of review has been very strict: any requirement must have a legitimate aim, the means chosen for achieving that objective must correspond to a real need on the part of the undertaking, must be appropriate with a view to achieving the objective in

---

[88] Article 4 Directive 2000/78.

question and must be necessary to that end.[89] If such a strict approach were to be taken to proportionality in the *Siebenhaar* case, it is possible that a court could find the decision to dismiss was not proportionate, given that, for example, the employee's behaviour took place outside of the workplace, was not connected to her performance at work and there was no evidence before the court that she had in fact sought to influence the children in her care.

Moreover, and perhaps more controversially, it may be interesting to speculate on how the court might have responded had the applicants failed to comply with religious teaching in ways which might raise other equality issues, such as because they were part of a same-sex relationship. Here an employer may claim that it is not sexual orientation per se that caused the treatment, but the failure to accord with religious lifestyle requirements. Even if this were to be accepted, the treatment would be indirectly discriminatory on the grounds of religion and would need to be justified. Whilst the court may allow for such indirect discrimination to be justified in the case of clergy or equivalent religious personnel, it is unlikely that it would be justified in cases of work which is not religious in nature or content. Thus, if applied to school or kindergarten teachers, or public relations managers, the court would be unlikely to find any indirect gender or sexual orientation discrimination to be justified.

Thus, in some cases, particularly if the strict standard of review established for other grounds of equality is applied, it could be that using the EU law to inform the implementation of the ECHR will lead to greater protection for individuals, as the freedom of religious groups to determine who to employ is tempered with equality requirements. As such, reading the ECHR to accord with the EU Equality Directive may result in a corresponding limitation on the freedom of religious groups. However, as was argued above, the EU law also has to be interperted to comply with ECHR group rights, and so in limited areas, such as the appointment of clergy and other staff intimately involved in the life of the religious group, collective religious rights are likely still to prevail.

4.2.2 Dahlab v Switzerland: *Religious Symbols*[90]

Dahlab v Switzerland is an older case and one that is well known in Article 9 jurisprudence. Here the applicant was a Muslim teacher of young children who wished to wear a headscarf to work. The ECHR decided that a restriction on the headscarf was proportionate in relation to teaching of young children, where the teacher had influence on the intellectual and emotional development of children. The reasoning in *Dahlab* has been strongly contested,[91] with questions asked about how much influence dress codes really have on others. This is particularly the case since the Grand Chamber decision in *Lautsi v Italy*,[92] in which the Court held that the symbol of the crucifix was a 'passive symbol'[93] and so could remain displayed

---

[89] Case C-170/84, *Bilka-Kaufhaus v Weber von Hartz* [1986] ECR 1607.
[90] *Dahlab v Switzerland* (n 25).
[91] Mahlmann (n 33); McGoldrick (n 33).
[92] App No 30814/06 judgment of 18 March 2011.
[93] Ibid, para 72.

in schools. It is difficult to sustain a meaningful distinction between headscarves as having a proseltysing effect and crucifixes which are said to have merely a 'passive' effect. However, despite these strong criticisms of the ECtHR approach to the issue of religious symbols, the question here is whether the case would be treated any differently if viewed from the perspective of the EU Equality Directive.

A refusal to allow the employee to wear a headscarf would be treated as indirect discrimination. The question would be whether the restriction was justified. In the UK, it would seem to be clear that the justification of a restiction on wearing a headscarf would be difficult. In the case of *Azmi*,[94] a refusal to allow a complete face covering (the niqab) was justified because of communication difficulties, but it is clear that the headscarf (hijab) would have been acceptable, and a ban would be difficult to justify. This is especially the case when the strict standard of justification is used as developed in other equality cases: there must be a legitimate aim for any restriction, and the means chosen for achieving that aim must correspond to a real need, must be appropriate with a view to achieving the objective in question and must be necessary to that end.[95] It is possible that justifications based on national practice and local tradition may be acceptable, taking into account the margin of discretion allowed for in EU law. To this extent, then, it is possible that the courts applying the EU Directive may take an approach to the issue of headscarves equivalent to that taken by the ECtHR, with special reference to the lack of consensus across Europe, echoing the ECHR's margin of appreciation approach.

Equally, however, it may be counter-argued that concepts of substantive equality,[96] reflected in the EU case law on indirect discrimination and established in the context of other equality strands such as gender equality, mean that it will be hard to justify bans on religious symbols at work. This is particularly the case when the issue is viewed from an equality perspective, as it then becomes relevant that neutral rules about head coverings at work can have a much greater impact on Muslim women than other groups. Bans on head coverings at work have a much greater impact on minority religions such as Islam and Sikhism, and must therefore be justified as proportionate and having a legitimate aim.

The equality perspective can, however, be complex and contradictory.[97] One argument is that the adverse impact on a religious minority may be hard to justify without clear and objective reasons, particularly because the ban can mean that some women are effectively barred from work, as they will not conform to the ban. A counter-argument is that the headscarf is understood by many to be illustrative of the subjection of women to the power of men, and so as antithetical to the interests of women. Counter to this counter-argument is the view that a ban may not result in more Muslim women entering the workforce and improving their substantive equality. It could, instead, result in fewer such women working, entrenching their disadvantage and inequality. The equality arguments are thus far from conclusive.

This is clearly a highly contested and sensitive subject, and the experience of the ECtHR is varied: whilst bans on religious symbols at work do not automatically

---

[94] *Azmi v Kirklees Metropolitan Borough Council* (n 69).
[95] *Bilka-Kaufhaus v Weber von Hartz* (n 89).
[96] See C Barnard and B Hepple, 'Substantive Equality' (2000) 59 *CLJ* 562.
[97] Mahlmann (n 33).

breach human rights norms, equally, human rights law does not require such bans in order to ensure religious neutrality. It is therefore difficult to predict whether the interpretation of the ECHR would vary if it is to be interpreted in the light of the equality provisions of the EU Equality Directive. It seems clear that bans on head-scarves and other head coverings will be indirectly discriminatory in religious terms, and thus will need justification. The proportionality requirement in the EU Directive allows for a wide range of factors to be taken into account in making this assessment, including the status of the employer (public or private sector), the freedom of religion of other staff and customers, and interests in political or religious neutrality for the employer. A further major factor will be the equality interests, both in relation to religious equality and gender equality. This focus on equality interests, particularly gender equality rather than purely religious interests, may mean that courts will be more ready to overturn headscarf bans.

An additional factor which also supports this position is the fact that it might be hard, from an equality-based perspective, to accept a wide 'margin of discretion' in cases involving religious equality, especially where they may also raise related issues of gender equality. Even though there is a clear lack of consensus on the issue, courts may be wary of allowing national tradition and practice to justify a broad margin of discretion in such cases. After all, EU gender equality law would not have developed very far if national tradition and practice had been allowed to justify continued discrimination; indeed, the very fact that gender discrimination was entrenched in national tradition was a reason for EU action to eradicate it. Thus, unless the Court is prepared to allow the different equality strands to be treated differently, it may be wary of allowing too wide a variation in standards of protection in religion cases in order to retain some parity with the EU treatment of other equality grounds.

Nonetheless, this can only be a very tentative conclusion as the issue remains highly politically sensitive and contested. There is a wide range of conflicting interests at stake in the cases, and thus far EU Member States have taken varied approaches on the issue in cases brought under their equality and constitutional provisions.[98]

5 CONCLUSION

The analysis of cases relating to religious freedom within the workplace brought under the ECHR and under the EU Equality Directive shows up very clearly the tensions and struggles that are likely to arise in any attempt to interpret EU law and ECHR law in conjuction with each other. In many cases, such as those illustrated by the *Eweida* case, the two frameworks do not seem to conflict, and the two systems of law appear to interact relatively harmoniously, providing additional and complementary strength to each other in the search for a principled approach to providing appropriate protection for religion in the workplace.

However, the other cases discussed demonstrate the ways in which the two approaches may be in tension. Both systems have within them a degree of flexibility

[98] See Vickers (n 55).

which may enable them to be interpreted in ways which are mutually compatible, in order to achieve appropriate protection for religious freedom and equality. However, as has been seen, there remain significant areas of tension between the two approaches, with full religious freedom that is at times seemingly incompatible with full equality. It is to be hoped that the increased openness of both systems to interpretation with reference to the other will help to reach practical resolutions to these tensions. For example, limits on gender equality in the context of clergy appointments may be viewed as proportionate, taking into account the ECHR standards on religious autonomy in the appointment of religious leaders. Equally, freedom of religion claims under Article 9 relating to the appointment of religious staff by religious ethos organisations may need to be tempered by reference to the equality norms of the EU Directive, whereby religious requirements on staff must be necessary to the job in question.

It is clear that there is great variance in the practical treatment of religion in the different EU Member States, from established churches to *laïcité*, bans on head-scarves to hijab-wearing teachers and police officers. To add to this rich mix is the fact that there are two separate legal systems which deal with religious issues. It is therefore unsurprising that many commentators[99] have anticipated clashes between ECHR and EC law on religious issues. However, if chaos is to be avoided, it will be necessary for both legal systems to be reflexive in the way in which they apply the law, and open to the insights of the other. In this way, step by step, it may be possible to reach a form of equilibrium between the rights of workers to equality and the rights of religious groups to religious freedom and autonomy.

---

[99] See W Weiss, 'Human Rights in the EU: Rethinking the Role of the European Convention on Human Rights after Lisbon' (2011) 7 *European Constitutional Law Review* 64; S Morano-Foadi and S Andreadakis, 'The convergence of the European Legal System in the Treatment of Third Country Nationals in Europe: The ECJ and ECtHR' (2011) 22(4) *European Journal of International Law* 1; J Callewaert, 'The European Convention on Human Rights and European Union Law: A Long Way to Harmony' [2009] *European Human Rights Law Review* 768.

10

The Right to Freedom of Expression in the Workplace under Article 10 ECHR

DIRK VOORHOOF AND PATRICK HUMBLET[1]

Article 10 ECHR

1. Everyone has the right to freedom of expression. This right shall include freedom to hold opinions and to receive and impart information and ideas without interference by public authority and regardless of frontiers. This article shall not prevent States from requiring the licensing of broadcasting, television or cinema enterprises.
2. The exercise of these freedoms, since it carries with it duties and responsibilities, may be subject to such formalities, conditions, restrictions or penalties as are prescribed by law and are necessary in a democratic society, in the interests of national security, territorial integrity or public safety, for the prevention of disorder or crime, for the protection of health or morals, for the protection of the reputation or the rights of others, for preventing the disclosure of information received in confidence, or for maintaining the authority and impartiality of the judiciary.

1 INTRODUCTION

In the 1930s the French philosopher Simone Weil worked in a factory for some time. It was not so much the heavy and monotonous work that that troubled her, but the fact that she had been completely silenced.[2]

Meanwhile, social relations and labour law have evolved, and it has been recognised that employees enjoy fundamental rights in the workplace, including the right to freedom of expression.[3] Since the European Court of Human Rights (ECtHR) made clear 'that Article 10 applies also to the workplace, and that civil servants ... enjoy the right to freedom of expression',[4] the application of Article 10 ECHR to employees, civil servants included, can no longer be disputed.

---

[1] Ghent, 10 October 2012. The authors wish to express their gratitude to Rónán Ó Fathaigh, PhD researcher at Ghent University, for his valuable assistance with some final editing of the text.
[2] S Weil, 'Expérience de la vie d'usine. Lettre ouverte à Jules Romains' in Œuvres complètes, II, Ecrits historiques et politiques. Vol 2 (Paris, Gallimard, 1991) 292.
[3] T Novitz and C Fenwick, 'The Application of Human Rights Discourse to Labour Relations: Translation of Theory into Practice' in C Fenwick and T Novitz (eds), Human Rights at Work (Oxford, Hart Publishing, 2010).
[4] Vogt v Germany, Series A, No 323 (1996) at para 53; Fuentes Bobo v Spain, App No 39293/98, 29 February 2000; and Kudeshkina v Russia, App No 29492/05, 26 February 2011 at para 85. See also

1.1 From the Workplace to Twitter and Facebook

More recently, new developments are influencing the employment relationship and the application of the employee's right to freedom of expression. As a result of the low threshold of the digital media, employees can express themselves through Twitter, Facebook and other social media. Sometimes this occurs in ways which the employer considers to be inappropriate and which may even lead to dismissal of the employee for breach of the duty of loyalty. Furthermore, opinions expressed by employees may be unlawful or liable to punishment, thus provoking or justifying a reaction by the employer.

The relevance of an analysis of the rights and limits of freedom of expression in the employer–employee relationship is obvious, given some recent developments in the employment relation and in labour law, considering the increased access and use of social media and the Internet offering quasi-unlimited (technical) possibilities for free speech to anyone, at any time and at any place. As these developments went together with the recognition of the applicability of the fundamental rights in private relations ('horizontal effect'), the right of freedom of expression has had an ever-increasing impact on a virtual conflict zone within the relationship between the employee and the employer.

In the following chapter, we will examine the characteristics and boundaries of the right to freedom of expression in the workplace. Article 10 ECHR is a crucial provision in this matter, but it is not the only relevant provision of international human rights law that ensures the employee's right of free speech. Article 19 International Covenant on Civil and Political Rights (ICCPR) and Article 11 Charter of Fundamental Rights of the European Union also guarantee a right of freedom of expression, although (so far) these provisions have played a less important role in practice. The Conventions of the International Labour Organization (ILO) will also be discussed because of the interaction between freedom of expression and trade union freedom. The case law of the Court of Justice of the European Union (CJEU) will be referred to as well.[5]

Peev v Bulgaria, App No 64209/01, 26 July 2007; *Heinisch v Germany*, App No 28274/08, 21 July 2008; and *Palomo Sánchez and others v Spain*, App Nos 28955/06, 28957/06, 28959/06 and 28964/06, 12 September 2011.

[5] European civil servants can indeed also invoke Article 10 ECHR: Case T-82/99, *Michael Cwik v Commission of the European Communities* [2000] ECR II-713 at paras 50 and 51. See FB Ronkes, *Zie ik dat goed? EU-ambtenaren en hun vrijheid van meningsuiting* (Leiden, Meijers Instituut, 2003). However, until the effective EU accession to the ECHR (Article 6(2) EU Treaty), only the EU institutions are authorised to judge the application of the fundamental rights of the ECHR for EU officials: *Bernard Connolly v Germany, Austria, Belgium, Denmark, Finland, France, Greece, Ireland, Italy, Luxembourg, the Netherlands, Portugal, the United Kingdom and Sweden*, App No 73274/01, decision of 9 December 2008: 'La Cour note que seuls les organes communautaires (...) ont eu à connaître du contentieux opposant le requérant à la Commission européenne. Elle constate qu'à aucun moment l'un ou l'autre des Etats mis en cause n'est intervenu, directement ou indirectement, dans ce litige, et ne relève en l'espèce aucune action ou omission de ces Etats ou de leurs autorités qui serait de nature à engager leur responsabilité au regard de la Convention. On ne saurait donc dire que le requérant, en l'espèce, relève de la « juridiction » des Etats défendeurs au sens de l'article 1 de la Convention. La Cour estime qu'en conséquence les violations alléguées de la Convention ne sauraient être imputées aux Etats mis en cause dans la présente affaire. Quant à une responsabilité éventuelle de l'Union européenne, elle rappelle que cette organisation internationale n'a pas adhéré à la Convention et qu'elle ne peut donc voir sa

1.2 In der Beschränkung zeigt sich erst der Meister

Some authors take a broad view regarding freedom of expression and connect it with the right to personal development.[6] We will not elaborate on this aspect separately, if only because all too often, this approach gets tied up with freedom of religion. Indeed, most of the discussions related to personal development centre around religious symbols (headscarves, yarmulkes, etc), while this aspect is analysed in the previous chapter of this book from the perspective of Article 9 ECHR (the right to freedom of thought and religion)[7] and to some extent as well in relation to Article 8 ECHR (the right to privacy).[8] However, some aspects relating to the personal development of individuals are incorporated in the analysis of the right to freedom of expression of an individual in his or her capacity as an employee. The ECtHR has repeatedly held that 'freedom of expression constitutes one of the essential foundations of a democratic society and one of the basic conditions for its progress and for each individual's self-fulfilment', hence explicitly referring to the aspect of the individual's personal development. In addition, there is also the connection between the employee's right to freedom of expression (Article 10 ECHR) and right to freedom of association and peaceful assembly (Article 11 ECHR).[9] As this latter aspect (including collective action, demonstrations, picketing, etc) will be

---

responsabilité engagée au titre de celle-ci.' See also Case C-274/99 P, *Bernard Connolly v Commission of the European Communities* [2001] ECR I-638.

[6] See, eg, M Minne and S Allemand, *Siffler en travaillant. Les droits de l'homme au travail: un état des lieux* (Paris, Le Cavalier Bleu, 2006) 77 ff.

[7] For an illustration of the connection between Articles 9 and 10 ECHR, see *Lombardi Vallauri v Italy*, App No 39128/05, 20 October 2009 at paras 25–43.

[8] See, eg, *Fernández Martínez v Spain*, App No 56030/07, 15 May 2012, at paras 78–80. See also *Predota v Austria*, App No 28962/95, decision of 18 January 2000; and *Laurence Pay v UK*, App No 32792/05, decision of 16 September 2008.

[9] In the ECtHR's case law, the link between Article 10 and Article 11 ECHR is manifest. The Court has repeatedly pointed out that 'one of the aims of freedom of assembly is to secure a forum for public debate and the open expression of protest. The protection of the expression of personal opinions, secured by Article 10, is one of the objectives of the freedom of peaceful assembly enshrined in Article 11 *Galstyan v Armenia*, App No 26986/03, 15 November 2007; *Ashughyan v Armenia*, App No 33268/0, 17 July 2008; and *Éva Molnár v Hungary*, App No 10346/05, 7 October 2008. See also *Nilsen and Johnsen v Norway*, App No 23118/93, 25 November 1999 at para 44; and *Palomo Sánchez and others v Spain* (n 4) at paras 52 and 58–62; *Austin and others v UK*, App Nos 39692/09, 40713/09 and 41008/09, 15 March 2012 at para 68; and *Tatár and Fáber v Hungary*, App Nos 26005/08 and 26160/08, 12 June 2012. General Comment No 34 of the UN Human Rights Committee (CCPR/G/GC/34, 12 September 2011) also emphasises this relationship: 'Among the other articles that contain guarantees for freedom of opinion and/or expression, are articles 18, 17, 25 and 27. The freedoms of opinion and expression form a basis for the full enjoyment of a wide range of other human rights. For instance, freedom of expression is integral to the enjoyment of the rights to freedom of assembly and association.' For a recent example in Belgium, see the dismissal of a university researcher, Barbara Van Dyck, as a consequence of her participation in a demonstration against a GMO experiment at Ghent University, her later statements during a TV interview and her refusal to comply with the request of her employer, the Catholic University of Leuven, to distance herself explicitly from the partial destruction of the scientific experiment: see www.jadaliyya.com/pages/index/1789/petition-against-firing-of-barbara-van-dyck http://sciencescitoyennes.org/contre-le-licenciement-de-la-chercheuse-et-activiste-barbara-van-dyck and http://threerottenpotatoes.wordpress.com. Forcing employees to distance themselves explicitly from certain points of view or opinions is a form of interference with the right of freedom of expression that is very hard to justify: *Kazakov v Russia*, App No 1758/02, 18 December 2008 at para 29: 'to make someone retract his or her own opinion by acknowledging his or her own wrongness is a doubtful form of redress and does not appear to be "necessary"'.

analysed in the next chapter of this book, our focus will be on the right to freedom of expression of the employee.[10]

1.3 We the People

We could have gone about this contribution in a classical way, ie, starting from the definition of the freedom of expression and the *format* of Article 10 ECHR. But others have already done this excellently.[11] Therefore, we decided to use a different method and to write this contribution from a 'subaltern' point of view.[12] In order to understand the manner in which employers 'interfere'[13] with the employee's freedom of expression, we have chosen the perspective of the workers. This means that we look at the issue through the eyes of those to whom the right applies and on whom the limitations regarding freedom of speech are imposed.[14]

---

[10] Note that the relationship between an employee's freedom of expression and his or her intellectual property rights based on Article 1 of the First Protocol to the ECHR will not be dealt with because this issue is too specific. See I Van Puyvelde, *Intellectuele rechten van werknemers* (Antwerp, Intersentia, 2012); J Griffiths and U Suthersanen (eds), *Copyright and Free Speech: Comparative and International Analyses* (Oxford, Oxford University Press, 2008); S Carnelori, 'La création salariée dans l'univers numérique' (2001) *Auteurs & Media* 53 ff; and I Vanderreken and H Van Hoogenbemt, 'Werknemers en intellectuele rechten' (1996) *Chroniques de Droit Social* 209 ff.

[11] See L Vickers, *Freedom of Speech and Employment* (Oxford, Oxford University Press, 2001).

[12] See also P Humblet, 'Moeten werknemers hun mond houden? Bedenkingen bij de (on) vrijheid van meningsuiting in de onderneming' in W Debeuckelaere, J Meeusen and H Willekens (eds), *Met rede ontleed, de rede ontkleed. Opstellen aangeboden aan Fons Heyvaert ter gelegenheid van zijn vijfenzestigste verjaardag* (Ghent, Mys & Breesch, 2002) 263 ff; and P Humblet, 'De la liberté d'expression des travailleurs salariés' (2003) *Chroniques de Droit Social* 157 ff.

[13] Interference with the employee's freedom of expression can take place in different forms, such as searches and seizures in the employee's office (*Peev v Bulgaria* (n 4) at para 59), restrictions on or refusal of promotion (*D Otto v Germany*, App No 27547/02, decision of 24 November 2005), premature termination of employment (*T Lahr v Germany*, App No 16912/05, decision of 1 July 2008), no longer being enlisted as a reservist (*E Erdel v Germany*, App No 30067/04, decision of 13 February 2007), openly threatening not to reappoint a civil servant or judge (*Wille v Liechtenstein*, App No 28396/95, 28 October 1999) or all kinds of disciplinary measures, non-renewal of an appointment, termination of an employment contract or dismissal (*Vogt v Germany* (n 4); *Fuentes Bobo v Spain* (n 4); *Kudeshkina v Russia* (n 4); *Palomo Sánchez and others v Spain* (n 4); and *Heinisch v Germany* (n 4)); see below.

[14] We knowingly disregard the employer's right to freedom of expression because, obviously, companies and corporations also have certain fundamental rights: see P de Fontbressin, *L'entreprise et la Convention européenne des droits de l'homme* (Brussels, Bruylant, 2008). The ECtHR has made clear that legal persons, including commercial companies, can invoke the freedom of expression and information guaranteed by Article 10 ECHR: see, eg, *Markt Intern Verlag GmbH and Klaus Beermann v Germany*, Series A, No 165 (1990); *Groppera Radio AG and others v Switzerland*, Series A, No 173 (1990); *Informationsverein Lentia and others v Austria*, Series A, No 276 (1994); *News Verlags GmbH & CoKG v Austria*, App No 31457/96, 11 January 2000; *Krone Verlag GmbH & CoKG (No 1) v Austria*, App No 34315/96, 26 February 2002; *Plon (Société) v France*, App No 58148/00, 18 May 2004; *Ukrainian Media Group v Ukraine*, App No 72713/01, 29 March 2005; *Independent News and Media and Independent Newspapers Ireland v Ireland*, App No 55120/00, 16 June 2005; *Wirtschafts-Trend Zeitschriften-Verlagsgesellschaft MBH (No 3) v Austria*, App No 66298/01 and 15653/02, 13 December 2005; *Leempoel and SA Ciné Revue v Belgium*, App No 64772/01, 9 November 2006; *Österreichischer Rundfunk v Austria*, App No 35841/02, 7 December 2006; *Standard Verlagsgesellschaft (No 2) v Austria*, App No 37464/02, 22 February 2007; *Hachette Filipacchi Associés v France*, App No 71111/01, 14 June 2007; *Glas Nadezhda Eood & Elenkov v Bulgaria*, App No 14134/02, 11 October 2007; *Meltex Ltd and Mesrup Mousesyan v Armenia*, App No 32283/04, 17 June 2008; *TV Vest AS & Rogaland Pensjonistparti v Norway*, App No 21132/05, 11 December 2008; *Société de Conception de Presse et d'Edition and Ponson v France*, App No 26935/05, 5 March 2009; *Hachette Filipacchi Presse*

The focus is on the employee's right of freedom of expression: his or her freedom of speech in connection with the professional sphere. The right to receive information[15] and ideas or the right of access to certain information or documents,[16] albeit undoubtedly important aspects of Article 10 ECHR and Article 19 ICCPR,[17] will not be analysed separately from the perspective of the employee–employer relationship.

2 FREEDOM OF EXPRESSION IN THE WORKPLACE: NOT SELF-EVIDENT

Article 10 ECHR was, *ab initio*, written with regard to the relationship between citizens and public authorities. It sets out the right to freedom of expression 'without interference by public authority'. Meanwhile, the ECtHR has made it clear that Article 10 ECHR can also be applied in private legal relationships and has repeatedly assessed interferences by private persons in the light of Article 10, § 2 ECHR.[18] In some cases this effectively led to the finding of a violation of Article 10 ECHR. The case law of the ECtHR shows that freedom of speech pursuant to Article 10 ECHR applies both to civil servants, as employees of public authorities, and to employees in the private sector.[19] In *Heinisch v Germany* the Court stated: 'The Court recalls ... that in a number of cases involving freedom of expression of civil or public servants, it has held that Article 10 applied to the workplace in general ... It

---

Automobile and Dupuy v France, App No 13353/05, 5 March 2009; *Hachette Filipacchi Associes ('Ici Paris') v France*, App No 12268/03, 23 July 2009; *Financial Times Ltd and others v UK*, App No 821/03, 15 December 2009; *Nur Radyo Ve Televizyon Yayıncılığı AŞ v Turkey*, App No 42284/05, 12 October 2010; *Sigma Radio Television Ltd v Cyprus*, App Nos 32181/04, 35122/05, 21 July 2011; *Ringier Axel Springer Slovakia, AS v Slovakia*, App No 41262/05, 26 July 2011; *Axel Springer AG v Germany*, App No 39954/08, 7 February 2012; and *Centro Europa 7 Srl and Di Stefano v Italy*, App No 38433/09, 7 June 2012.

[15] See, eg, Directive 2002/14/EC of the European Parliament and of the Council of 11 March 2002 establishing a general framework for informing and consulting employees in the European Community.

[16] *Sdruženi Jihočeské Matky v Tsjech Republic*, App No 19101/03, decision of 10 July 2006; *Társaság a Szabadságjogokért v Hungary*, App No 37374/05, 14 April 2009; *Kenedi v Hungary*, App No 31475/05, 26 May 2009; *Gillberg v Sweden*, App No 41723/06, 3 April 2012. See also W Hins and D Voorhoof, 'Access to State-held Information as a Fundamental Right under the European Convention on Human Rights' (2007) 1 *European Constitutional Law Review* 114–49.

[17] General Comment No 34, UN Human Rights Committee (2011), Nos 18 and 19.

[18] However, each time this is referred to as a matter of indirect horizontal effect because the challenged interference with the freedom of expression and information by a national public authority or judicial body was maintained. See, eg: *Fuentes Bobo v Spain* (n 4); *Özgür Gündem v Turkey*, App No 23144/99, 16 March 2000; *Appleby and others v UK*, App No 44306/98, 6 May 2003; *Verein gegen Tierfabriken VGT v Switzerland*, App No 24699/94, 28 June 2001; *De Diego Nafria v Spain*, App No 46833/99, 14 March 2002; *Verein gegen Tierfabriken VGT (No 2) v Switzerland*, App No 32772/02, 4 October 2007; *Verein gegen Tierfabriken Schweiz (VGT) (No 2) v Switzerland*, App No 32772/02, 30 June 2009; *Khursid Mustafa and Tarzibachi v Sweden*, App No 23883/06, 16 December 2008; *Wojtas-Kaleta v Poland*, App No 20436/02, 16 July 2009; *Heinisch v Germany* (n 4); *Palomo Sánchez and others v Spain* (n 4); and *Vellutini and Michel v France*, App No 32820/09, 6 October 2011.

[19] See D Voorhoof and J Englebert, 'La liberté d'expression syndicale mise à mal par la Cour européenne des droits de l'homme' (2010) *Revue trimestrielle de droits de l'homme* 735 ff. For a confirmation of the recognition of the employee's right to free expression of opinion with regard to interferences by (private) employers, see *Heinisch v Germany* (n 4). See also F Dorssement, 'Vrijheid van meningsuiting op de werkplek in twee maten en gewichten. De werknemer mag blaffen, de "watchdog" wordt gemuilkorfd' (2011) 3 *Arbeidsrechtelijke Annotaties* 66–93.

has further found that Article 10 of the Convention also applies when the relations between employer and employee are governed, as in the case at hand, by private law and that the State has a positive obligation to protect the right to freedom of expression even in the sphere of relations between individuals.'[20]

2.1 Private Sector/Public Sector

Some fundamental rights can be exercised in the same way in the private and public sectors. Thus, it would be difficult to justify a different regulation of the right to privacy. For freedom of expression, on the other hand, a different approach would seem to be possible. For instance, in the interests of the state, civil servants can be subject to a strict duty of discretion (eg, State Security departments), while this is less obvious for workers in a factory. Conversely, *whistle-blowing* is accepted when civil servants denounce wrongdoings, but is not taken for granted if private sector employees resort to this. What is legitimate in one relationship is not necessarily so in another one.

Cliteur even regrets the fact that civil servants have a right of freedom of expression:[21] a civil servant should not be allowed to express himself or herself openly about matters concerning government policy or public affairs, since the civil servant's freedom of speech could force politics into a defensive position. In Cliteur's view, this could result in democracy having to retreat in favour of a bureaucratic oligarchy. As food for thought, one could sympathise somewhat with this point of view, but actually it is outdated, perhaps even reactionary, reflecting an outmoded view of public services. *Ex absurdo*: if one were to apply this line of reasoning, mutatis mutandis, to the right to strike, this would imply that civil servants cannot go on strike (because until late in the twentieth century this was considered to be proof of a lack of loyalty).

Meanwhile the ECtHR has made it clear that civil servants do have the right to freedom of expression as an individual and that they have the right to participate in public discussions, precisely because through their involvement or expertise, they can make an important contribution to the debate in society on matters of public interest.[22] At the same time, civil servants can be subjected to far-reaching limitations on their freedom of expression, notably when, because of the nature of their office or position, they handle secret, confidential or sensitive information. A civil servant working at the Ministry of Defence or a soldier leaking or revealing secret military information will find it hard to invoke his or her right to freedom of expression.[23] Judges are also subject to special restrictions[24] due to the necessity

---

[20] *Heinisch v Germany* (n 4) at para 44.

[21] PB Cliteur, 'EHRM 29 februari 2000, Requête nr. 39293/98 (Fuentes Bobo/Spanje)' (2001) 1 *Arbeidsrechtelijke Annotaties* 82.

[22] *Wojtas-Kaleta v Poland* (n 18); *Vellutini and Michel v France* (n 18); *Wille v Liechtenstein* (n 13); *Michael Cwik v Commission of the European Communities* (n 5); and *Bernard Connolly v Commission of the European Communities* (n 5).

[23] *Hadjianastassiou v Greece*, App No 12945/87, 16 December 1992; and *Pasko v Russia*, App No 69519/01, 22 October 2009 at paras 86–88.

[24] See *Wille v Liechtenstein* (n 13) at para 64; and *Kudeshkina v Russia* (n 4) at para 86. The ECtHR emphasised that 'it [is] incumbent on public officials serving in the judiciary that they should show restraint in exercising their freedom of expression in all cases where the authority and impartiality of the judiciary are likely to be called into question'.

of maintaining public confidence in the judiciary and upholding the perception of impartiality. A journalist working for a public broadcasting company will also have to show reserve when participating in the public debate in order not to encumber the obligation of impartiality or neutrality expected of or imposed on a 'public service' broadcaster.[25] However, the case law of the ECtHR demonstrates that even in those cases, the restrictions or sanctions have to be relevant and proportionate, and that restrictions, disciplinary measures or other sanctions can indeed be considered to be an unlawful infringement of the right to freedom of expression of military personnel, civil servants, judges or journalists of a public broadcasting company.[26] In the words of the ECtHR itself, it is required 'en tenant compte des circonstances de chaque affaire, de rechercher si un juste équilibre a été respecté entre le droit fondamental de l'individu à la liberté d'expression et l'intérêt légitime d'un Etat démocratique à veiller à ce que sa fonction publique œuvre aux fins énoncées à l'article 10 § 2'.[27]

2.2 Mutation of Fundamental Rights, 'Contextualising' and New Media

Some fundamental rights remain in full force within and outside the workplace. The authorities are not allowed to tap citizens' telephone conversations; a fortiori, an employer is not allowed to do so. The fact that the employee is under the authority or supervision of the employer does not mean as a consequence that the fundamental right is sidelined. However, within the context of a working environment, some fundamental rights may 'mutate' or, as Brecher puts it, 'Die Grundrechte sind im Betrieb modifiziert—"mutiert"—durch Aufgabe, Sinn und Zweck eines Betriebes'.[28]

This is obviously the case when it concerns freedom of expression. Employers cannot allow their employees to make political speeches on the company premises because this would disrupt the production process.[29] An employer may also take exception to an employee who launches racist, insulting or sexist messages through Facebook or Twitter, in a newspaper's readers' letters forum, on a weblog or by fax.[30] A striking example is that of the French journalist Pierre Salviac, who, one

---

[25] See also D Voorhoof, *Actuele vraagstukken van mediarecht. Doctrine en jurisprudentie*, (Antwerp, Kluwer rechtswetenschappen, 1992) 565–78; Council of State, 21 September 1984, *Buyle v BRT*; Council of State, 13 January 1988, *François v RTBF*; and Council of State 4 December 1990, *Buyle v BRT*.

[26] *Vereinigung Demokratischer Soldaten Österreichs and Gubi v Austria*, App No 15153/89, 19 December 1994; *Wille v Liechtenstein* (n 13); *Fuentes Bobo v Spain* (n 4); and *Wojtas-Kaleta v Poland* (n 18).

[27] *Jacques Seurot v France*, App No 57383/00, decision of 18 May 2004.

[28] F Brecher, 'Grundrechte im Betrieb' in *Festschrift für Hans Carl Nipperdey zum 70. Geburtstag*, vol II (Munich, Beck, 1965) 44.

[29] See O De Tissot, 'La liberté d'expression des opinions politiques d'un salarié' (1994) *Droit Social* 353–58.

[30] See, eg, Antwerp Labour Court of Appeal, 17 March 2010, AR 2003/AA/353, www. diversiteit.be/?hide_form=1&action=zoek_advanced&search[woord]=arrest&page=11; and Namur Labour Tribunal, 10 January 2011, (2011) 1112 *Journal des Tribunaux du Travail* 462 and (2012) 46 *Revue du Droit des Technologies de l'Information* 79.

day after the French presidential elections on 6 May 2012, lost his job at RTL after posting an insulting and sexist tweet about female journalists.[31]

In Belgium an employee was fired because on the public part of his Facebook page he systematically criticised the state of affairs in the listed company where he worked as a business development manager.[32] The Leuven Labour Tribunal pointed out 'that if an employee uses a social website and identifies himself as a staff member of his employer ... he has to refrain from acts and statements that are disloyal to or harmful for the company'. To determine whether or not public statements by an employee can be designated as unacceptable from the employer's perspective, it is necessary to look at 'the content and style of the public statements'. In this case the tribunal held that the employee's critical comments, given his position, the nature and tone of the criticism and the frequency thereof, could qualify as an offence against the 'elementary loyalty which rendered any further cooperation impossible'. Therefore, the dismissal for serious misconduct because of the critical statements on Facebook was justified.[33] In this case the court took the following specific characteristics into account: first, it concerned a listed company with a strict communication strategy which the employee had to comply with; second, the employee's position as a business development manager included important commercial responsibilities; and, third, the timing of the employee's critical comments on Facebook was crucial, occurring at the moment when the company's CEO tried to reassure the financial markets a few hours after the presentation of the biannual results.

In the Netherlands too, an employee's statements on a Facebook page resulted in dismissal, transposed into termination of the employment contract by the Arnhem Court. In this case the employer took exception to the insulting and discriminating character of some of the statements directed at another employee and to complaints about the management. The court stated that the employee had acted 'in a very reprehensible way' by expressing himself 'in a very negative and discriminating manner' about a colleague. But, as such, these statements were not deemed to justify

---

[31] On the occasion of the election of François Hollande as President, Salviac twittered 'Á toutes mes consœurs je dis: baisez utile vous avez une chance de vous retrouver première Dame de France', making an allusion to the fact that political journalist Valérie Trierweiler as Hollande's partner was going to be the new First Lady of France: '*Le journaliste Pierre Salviac licencié après un tweet injurieux sur Valérie Tierweiler*', *Le Monde* (9 May 2012).

[32] Leuven Labour Tribunal, 17 November 2011, (2012) 46 *Revue du Droit des Technologies de l'Information* 79.

[33] Leuven Labour Tribunal 17 November 2011, (2012) 46 *Revue du Droit des Technologies de l'Information* 79. It should be noted that in this case the employee (apparently) did not invoke his freedom of expression on the basis of Article 10 ECHR, but chiefly wanted to invoke the protection of Article 8 ECHR. However, rightly so, the tribunal judged that the employer's reading of the employee's comments on the public part of a Facebook page did not amount to a breach of the right to privacy. See also K Rosier, 'Réflexions sur le droit au respect de la vie privée et la liberté d'expression sur Facebook dans le cadre des relations de travail' (2012) 46 *Revue du Droit des Technologies de l'Information* 90–99, www.fundp.ac.be/recherche/publications/page_view/74079; K Rosier and S Gilson, 'La vie privée du travailleur face aux nouvelles technologies de communication et à l'influence des réseaux sociaux: l'employeur est-il l'ami du travailleur sur Facebook?' in P Joassart and M Verdussen (eds), *La vie privée au travail* (Louvain-la-neuve, Anthemis, 2011) 59–113, www.fundp.ac.be/universite/personnes/page_view/01004976/cv.html; C Preumont, 'Les médias sociaux à l'épreuve du droit du travail' (2011) 1106 *Journal des Tribunaux du Travail* 355–56; and M Picq, 'Facebook et les salariés: Vie privée, liberté d'expression et humour' (2011) 11 *Revue des droits et des libertés fondamentaux* Chron No 11, http://webu2.upmf-grenoble.fr/rdlf/?p= 927.

dismissal for serious misconduct, in particular because no prior warning had been given. According to the court there had not been any similar complaints before and it could not be assumed that the statements on Facebook 'were the proverbial last straw'. The judge could understand that the employer no longer wanted to employ the employee, but considered immediate dismissal for serious misconduct to be premature. This is the reason why the court ruled for termination of the employ- ment contract with a severance allowance for the employee.[34] Another case in the Netherlands also led to the termination of the employment contract, in this instance without any severance pay. The judge held that the message that the employee had placed on Facebook had insulted the employer 'in a very rude manner'. The judg- ment stated firmly: 'This message has nothing whatever to do with freedom of expression. As a matter of fact this freedom is limited by the principles of due care which the employee has to observe towards [the employer]. As a good employee the employee should not have posted this message. It has been rightfully argued ... that the employee acted in contravention of the obligation to behave as a good employee under Article 7:611 Civil Code.' Apologies after the event cannot dispel the reason for the dismissal for misconduct. The fact that the employee took steps to remove the insulting comments from his Facebook page after receiving notice from his employer to the effect that the insulting message on Facebook was unacceptable and that measures would be taken to end the employee's employment contract 'is of no avail to the employee. It is too little, too late to be of any use'. Furthermore, the fact that the employer had warned the employee beforehand that similar insulting statements on Facebook could be considered as a justified reason for terminating the employment contract was explicitly taken into account.[35]

Another remarkable example on an 'expression of opinion' by an employee that led to a breach with the employer is the dismissal of the Russian journalist and news anchor of REN TV, Tatyana Limanova, in November 2011. As she was reading a news item in which the US President Barack Obama was mentioned, she put up a stiff middle finger, thus apparently making a negative statement with regard to the US President. This was considered to be a disapproving expression of opinion by a newsreader which (obviously) could not be tolerated by the television company's management. She was fired straight away.[36]

A dismissal of a special kind was that of a social worker who was responsible for coaching sexual offenders during their probation (case of *Laurence Pay v UK*). The dismissal followed after the employer had found out, through information and photographs on a website, that the employee was active within BDSM (Bondage, Domination and Sadomasochism) circles. The website contained photographs of the employee in the presence of half-naked women and advertised BDSM events. Even though these practices in themselves were not liable to punishment, the employer considered it inappropriate that, given the specific nature of the employ- ee's job, the employee was involved in practices of this kind and publicised these through a website. The British courts and later the ECtHR acknowledged that the

---

[34] Arnhem Court, 11 April 2012, *JK Vloerverwarming BV v X*, LJN BW2006, www.rechtspraak.nl.

[35] Arnhem Court, 19 March 2012, *Blokker BV v X*, LJN BV9483, www.rechtspraak.nl.

[36] Although the journalist argued that it had not been her intention to show any disapproval toward Mr Obama or the US. See www.standaard.be/artikel/detail.aspx?artikelid=DMF20111123_193.

employee could indeed invoke the freedom of expression guaranteed by Article 10 ECHR, but held the view that in this case the dismissal did not imply a breach of the employee's freedom of expression. The Court highlighted 'the sensitive nature of the applicant's work with sex offenders' and the fact that public knowledge of the rather particular sexual activities of the applicant 'could impair his ability to carry out his duties effectively'.[37]

But sometimes the employer's reaction has insufficient regard for the employee's freedom of expression, particularly when critical comments fit in with a public debate on matters of interest for society. In France a professional football player was dismissed after he had given a few critical interviews in the press in which he had criticised both the coach and the management of his team. However, the French courts, and ultimately also the Cour de Cassation, emphasised that 'sauf abus, le salarié jouit, dans l'entreprise et en dehors de celle-ci, de sa liberté d'expression, à laquelle seules des restrictions justifiées par la nature de la tâche à accomplir et proportionnées au but recherché peuvent être apportées'. The Court pointed out that the persons concerned had already had a heated discussion ('une polémique médiatique') in the press, which meant that the employee had not abused his freedom of expression. The employer for his part did argue that 'un joueur de football professionnel est tenu d'une obligation particulière de loyauté lui interdisant d'adopter un comportement de nature à discréditer l'autorité de l'entraîneur sur le groupe professionnel et, par suite, à déstabiliser ce dernier', but this argument was not decisive for the Court because it ignored in essence the employee's freedom of expression. According to the Cour de Cassation, the Court of Appeal had rightfully decided 'que le salarié n'avait pas abusé de sa liberté d'expression'.[38]

Yet another context is the one in which employees active in a trade union or trade union leaders are held responsible for harsh or offensive criticism towards the employer or management.[39] Over the last few years, the ECtHR has had the opportunity to set out the basic outline for the scope, characteristics and limitations of the freedom of expression of trade unionist employees.[40]

The moral of the story is that the contours of the right to freedom of expression differ according to the context in which this right is exercised. Actually, the influence of the context in determining the boundaries or limits of freedom of expression has turned out to be a basic characteristic of the manner in which, within the framework of the ECHR, the necessity or non-necessity of interferences with the freedom of expression and information is appraised.[41] In assessing the legitimacy

---

[37] *Laurence Pay v UK* (n 8).

[38] Cour de Cassation, 28 April 2011, *ESTAC v Juan-Luis Montero*, www.juritravail.com/dossiers/liberte-d-expression-injures. See also in Belgium the case of Stijn Stijnen, the goalkeeper of the national football team who was given the push by his team (Club Brugge) in February 2011 after a 'smear campaign' through an Internet forum on which both a number of his teammates and the team management were heavily criticised: www.standaard.be/artikel/detail.aspx?artikelid=P236JNOT. Compare Cour de Cassation (France), 28 April 1988, (1988) *Droit Social* 428 and Cour de Cassation (France), 30 October 2002, (2003) *Droit Social* 136.

[39] *R Predota v Austria*, App No 28962/95, decision of 18 January 2000.

[40] *Heinisch v Germany* (n 4); *Palomo Sánchez et al v Spain* (n 4); and *Vellutini and Michel v France* (n 18); see below.

[41] D Voorhoof, 'Freedom of Expression under the European Human Rights System' (2009) 1(2) *Inter-American and European Human Rights Journal* 15–17.

of the employer's interference with an employee's freedom of expression, the recent judgments briefly introduced above demonstrate that a set of contextual elements will have to be taken into account. Relevant criteria are, for instance, the content of the statement or publication, the medium, the social context, the timing, the nature of the employee's position, previous statements by the employee—sometimes in response to statements by the employer—the manner in which the criticism was formulated, whether or not the information was confidential, the employee's intentions, the impact of the statement or publication on the relationship with the employer or on the company's reputation, the possible 'chilling effect' ensuing from an employer's interference with an employee's freedom of expression and finally (and importantly) the nature of the interference or sanction.[42]

The emergence of social media like Facebook and Twitter, blogs and websites has undoubtedly enlarged the possibilities for employees to express, divulge or impart their opinions and ideas, usually quite spontaneously. This increases the risk of emotional, rash language which tends to acquire a much more offensive bearing outside the context of the social media. It also increases the likelihood of the employer being informed about the opinions expressed by the employees. However, the employers and quite often the courts as well appear to have little regard for this specific context of social media and spontaneous language.[43]

3 INTERLUDE: LIMITATIONS TO THE FREEDOM OF EXPRESSION—*SUPPOSÉ CONNU*

In the EU Member States the freedom of expression is, among other things, limited by anti-discrimination directives. For instance, Directive 2000/43/EC prohibits discrimination on the grounds of race or ethnic origins. On the basis of the *Feryn* judgment, the national legislature has the obligation to ensure that statements inciting racism, xenophobia or discrimination on the grounds of (so-called) race, nationality or origin are also forbidden in the workplace and in corporate communications.[44] Mutatis mutandis, this also applies to the discrimination grounds of Directive 2000/78: religion or conviction, disability, age or sexual inclination.

---

[42] These criteria will be further developed and explained in the analysis of the case law of the ECtHR that follows. See also D Voorhoof, 'Het Europese "First Amendment". De Straatsburgse jurisprudentie over artikel 10 EVRM: 2004–2009' Part 1 (2010) 4 *Mediaforum* 106–16 and Part 2 (2010) 6 *Mediaforum* 189.

[43] See, eg, Picq (n 11): 'Plus que sur tout autre support écrit, l'auteur de messages sur Facebook a la sensation de l'éphémère, attaché à l'oral alors même que l'écrit en assure la pérennité. Est donc née la sensation que ce qui est écrit n'est pas gravé dans le marbre et ne peut finalement n'avoir que peu d'échos ou de portée. De ce fait, est implicitement autorisée une liberté de ton, souvent ornée de signes pour indiquer notamment l'absence de sérieux dans les propos. C'est cette spécificité du langage par internet que les juges refusent de reconnaitre. C'est finalement méconnaître cette modalité émergente de discussion'; and Rosier (n 33) 98–99: 'Les réseaux sociaux offrent un outil de communication plus spontané, dans l'utilisation duquel l'on fera peut-être preuve de moins de retenue dans ses propos. Cela n'est pas pris en compte dans les décisions commentées.'

[44] Case C-54/07, *Centrum voor gelijkheid van kansen en racismebestrijding v Feryn* [2008] ECR I-5187.

Article 2(d) Directive 2006/54/EC explicitly refers to unwanted verbal conduct of a sexual nature.[45]

Some directives set out a duty of confidentiality. This implies that certain forms of information may not be revealed. Article 8 Directive 94/45/EC regarding the establishment of a European Works Council, for instance, stipulates that members of the Special Negotiating Body and the experts assisting them (with a view to the establishment of a European Works Council) may not divulge certain data to third parties.

This and other legislation restricting the right to freedom of expression[46] constitute the basis on which interferences with the employee's right to freedom of expression are possible. Considering Article 10 ECHR, however, this does not suffice to restrain the employee's freedom of speech. Although Article 10, § 2 ECHR offers the possibility of interferences, restrictions or sanctions following the exercise of the freedom of expression to which 'duties and responsibilities' are attached, this is only allowed under the conditions of the so-called *triple test,* which substantially reduces the possibility of interference with the right to express, impart and receive information and ideas. Interferences by public authorities or by private persons with the right to freedom of expression and information are only allowed under the strict conditions that any restriction or sanction must be 'prescribed by law', must have a 'legitimate aim' and, finally and most decisively, must be 'necessary in a democratic society'.[47]

Both the case law of the ECtHR concerning Article 10 ECHR[48] and the case law of the United Nations Human Rights Council (UNHRC) and General Comment No 34 with regard to Article 19 ICCPR[49] show that the concept of freedom of expression

---

[45] In practice it is hard to invoke freedom of expression in the event of out-of-bounds verbal conduct because the statements are so rude, insulting or discriminating that claims of freedom of expression are either dismissed or are particularly problematic: see, eg, Case T-333/99, *X v ECB* [2001] (concerning the dissemination of pornographic material and extremist ideas). See also G Zorbas and A Zorbas, *Le harcèlement. Droits européen, belge, français et luxembourgeois* (Brussels, Larcier, 2010) 296 ff. Regarding the withdrawal of protection of the freedom of expression on the basis of the so-called 'abuse clause' of Article 17 ECHR, see H Cannie and D Voorhoof, 'The Abuse Clause and Freedom of Expression under the European Human Rights Convention: An Added Value for Democracy and Human Rights Protection?' (2011) 27 *Netherlands Quarterly of Human Rights* 54–83.

[46] Such as the employee's duty of loyalty; the duty to keep confidential information secret; restrictions and prohibitions regarding the processing of (sensitive) personal data; civil law provisions for the protection of rights relating to the personality; penalties regarding slander, defamation and insults; and anti-racism and anti-discrimination legislation.

[47] Voorhoof (n 41) 5–6. Note that in cases concerning freedom of expression in the employer–employee relationship, there are hardly any problems with regard to the first two conditions: the national courts and the ECtHR always assume that a contested interference by the employer has its basis in a national labour law provision, in employment contract legislation or staff regulations for civil servants or in additional regulations, statutes or contractual provisions ('prescribed by law'). The condition of the legitimate aim does not produce any problems either since the interference always refers to one of the legitimate grounds listed in Article 10, § 2 ('the legitimate aim pursued'). However, the assessment of being 'necessary in a democratic society' is crucial and decisive. Only in *Peev v Bulgaria* (n 4) could the Court confine itself to the observation that the interference with the employee's freedom of expression which led to his dismissal was not provided for by law (at para 62). Compare *Karademirci and others v Turkey*, App Nos 37096/97 and 37101/97, 25 January 2005.

[48] Voorhoof (n 41) 3–49.

[49] General Comment No 34 of the UN Human Rights Committee (CCPR/G/GC/34, 12 September 2011), Nos 11–12.

should be interpreted very broadly: it concerns the freedom to express, impart and receive or seek all kinds of ideas or information, irrespective of frontiers. This means that 'this right includes the expression and receipt of communications of every form of idea and opinion capable of transmission to others ... It includes political discourse, commentary on one's own and on public affairs, canvassing, discussion of human rights, journalism, cultural and artistic expression, teaching, and religious discourse'. In principle, shocking, offending and disturbing communications also fall within the scope of the freedom of expression, just like 'expression that may be regarded as deeply offensive', although these forms of expression can be limited pursuant to Article 10, § 2 ECHR or Article 19, § 3 and Article 20 ICCPR. Article 19 ICCPR and Article 10 ECHR protect the freedom of expression regardless of the means used to express or disseminate opinions, ideas or information: 'Such forms include spoken, written and sign language and such non-verbal expression as images and objects of art. Means of expression include books, newspapers, pamphlets, posters, banners, dress and legal submissions. They include all forms of audio-visual as well as electronic and internet-based modes of expression.'[50] The case law of the Court of Justice has also confirmed that 'officials and other employees of the European Communities enjoy the right of freedom of expression ... even in areas falling within the scope of the activities of the Community institutions. That freedom extends to the expression, orally or in writing, of opinions that dissent from or conflict with those held by the employing institution'.[51]

On the basis of case law of the ECtHR, we will now examine how far this freedom reaches and under which circumstances limitations and sanctions can be justified. The analysis of the case law shows that the ECtHR's focus is on the assessment regarding the 'pressing social need' and on the question as to what is necessary in terms of interference with the right of freedom of expression in the employee–employer relationship in a democratic society—hence, a contextual, substantive and normative debate.

4 EXPRESSING A POLITICAL OPINION

4.1 The Right to Hold an Opinion

Employees can *have or hold* a political conviction. This right is absolute. The employer or public authorities can in no way whatsoever meddle with this freedom. The limitations or restrictions that may apply to the freedom to express, impart or receive ideas and information do not apply to the freedom 'to hold opinions'. General Comment No 34 of the UNHRC clearly states:

9. Paragraph 1 of article 19 [ICCPR] requires protection of the right to hold opinions without interference. This is a right to which the Covenant permits no exception or

---

[50] General Comment No 34 of the UN Human Rights Committee (CCPR/G/GC/34, 12 September 2011), No 12. For the application of Article 10 ECHR, see, eg, Voorhoof (n 41) 15–17. For the application of Article 10 ECHR, specifically for ICT and Internet, see the ECtHR's Factsheet 'New Technologies', www.echr.coe.int/ECHR/EN/Header/Press/Information+sheets/Factsheets.

[51] *Bernard Connolly v Commission of the European Communities* (n 5) at para 43.

restriction. Freedom of opinion extends to the right to change an opinion whenever and for whatever reason a person so freely chooses. No person may be subject to the impairment of any rights under the Covenant on the basis of his or her actual, perceived or supposed opinions. All forms of opinion are protected, including opinions of a political, scientific, historic, moral or religious nature. It is incompatible with paragraph 1 to criminalize the holding of an opinion. The harassment, intimidation or stigmatization of a person, including arrest, detention, trial or imprisonment for reasons of the opinions they may hold, constitutes a violation of article 19, paragraph 1.

Furthermore, the General Comment emphasises:

> 10.   Any form of effort to coerce the holding or not holding of any opinion is prohibited. Freedom to express one's opinion necessarily includes freedom not to express one's opinion.

4.2 The Right to Express Opinions

Pursuant to Articles 19, § 3 and 20 ICCPR and particularly pursuant to Article 10, § 2 ECHR, only the expression, the disclosure of political opinions or actively campaigning for a political party can be subjected to restrictions and, if need be, to sanctions in the context of the employer–employee relationship. In private sector companies the political convictions of employees are not likely to cause many problems, unless the employee chooses to divulge or display these political opinions (buttons, T-shirts and stickers with political or controversial messages, distribution of pamphlets, weblogs, etc), for these actions could disturb the corporate peace or damage the employer's reputation.[52] Sometimes certain forms of expression by the employee may exhibit a certain ideology, certain ethics or attitudes which the employer considers to be irreconcilable with the specific profile of the duties or position of the employee. Quite often this tension is to be found in the domain of religious views, especially in schools. In those cases the restrictions to the freedom of expression, in combination with the employee's freedom of religion and the right to privacy, will usually be considered to be justified, as the ECtHR explained once again in its judgment of 15 May 2012 regarding *Fernández Martínez v Spain*. The Court held the view that terminating the employment of a teacher of religion and Roman Catholic morals can be justified in such a context: 'the competent courts adequately demonstrated that duties of loyalty were acceptable in that their aim was to preserve the sensitivity of the general public and the parents of the school's pupils'.[53] In this judgment the Court emphasises the particular delicacy when the employee/teacher aims his or her messages at young people or children, by stating

---

[52] In Germany this has been the subject of a controversy. See, eg, G Hoyningen-Huene and E Hofmann, 'Politische Plaketten im Betrieb' (1984) *Betriebs Berater* 1050–55; U Zachert, 'Plaketten im Betrieb. Ausdrück von Meinmungsfreiheit oder Störung des Betriebsfriedens' (1984) *Arbeit und Recht* 289–97; U Zachert, 'Ein Stuck Plastik und der provozierte Geist der Obrigkeitsstaates: Zum Anti-Strausz Plakettenurteil des Bundesarbeitsgerichts' (1984) *Demokratie und Recht* 76–80; and R Buschmann and H Grimberg, 'Plaketten als Meinungsaüszerung im Betrieb' (1989) *Arbeit und Recht* 65–77.

[53] *Fernández Martínez v Spain* (n 8) at para 87. See also *Siebenhaar v Germany*, App No 18136/02, 3 February 2011; and *Obst v Germany*, App No 425/03, 23 September 2010. Compare *Schüth v Germany*, App No 1620/03, 23 September 2010.

'that the duty of reserve and discretion was all the more important as the direct recipients of the applicant's teaching were minors, who by nature were vulnerable and open to influence'.[54] Because of the fact that in his private life the teacher showed insufficient respect for Roman Catholic morals, the non-renewal of his appointment as a teacher did not, according to the Court, imply a breach of the right to privacy or to the right to freedom of expression.

Still, it can be stated that in certain circumstances the termination of an employment contract or dismissal does amount to an infringement of the employee's freedom of expression.[55] A remarkable judgment is that in *Lombardi Vallauri v Italy*, a case in which the ECtHR dealt with the complaint of a philosophy of law professor who did not agree with the fact that his application for reappointment at the Catholic University of Milan was rejected with the sole motivation that some of the opinions he defended in public were clearly not in line with the Roman Catholic doctrine. Because this very poorly reasoned decision was still upheld after all legal remedies in Italy had been exhausted, the applicant addressed the ECtHR. The Court held the view that the non-appointment was indeed related to the exercise of freedom of expression. It considered that the applicant did not have sufficient procedural guarantees at his disposal to fight this interference with his (academic) freedom of expression in law, on the one hand because of the inadequate reasoning of the University Board's decision and because of a lack of judicial control on the other. The Court found 'que le manque de connaissance de la part du requérant des raisons à la base de son éloignement a, en lui-même, écarté toute possibilité d'exercice d'un débat contradictoire. Cet aspect non plus n'a fait l'objet d'un examen par les tribunaux internes. De l'avis de la Cour, le contrôle juridictionnel sur l'application de la mesure litigieuse n'a donc pas été pas adéquat en l'espèce. En conclusion, la Cour estime que l'intérêt de l'Université de dispenser un enseignement inspiré de la doctrine catholique ne pouvait pas s'étendre jusqu'à atteindre la substance même des garanties procédurales dont le requérant jouit au sens de l'article 10 de la Convention'.[56]

4.3 *Berufsverbot*

Matters become even more complicated when the government is the employer and the (potential) employee adheres to an ideology which runs counter to the established order. Especially in Germany, this was the subject of a heavy controversy in the 1980s. Extreme left-wing as well as some extreme right-wing activists were given a 'Berufsverbot'. This was contested before the ECtHR in the *Glasenapp*[57] and *Kosiek*[58] cases. Following her application, Ms Glasenapp, a teacher, had signed

---

[54] *Fernández Martínez v Spain*, (n 8) at para 87; and *Dahlab v Switzerland*, App No 42393/98, 15 February 2001. See also *Vejdeland and others v Sweden*, App No 1813/07, 9 February 2012; and *Handyside v UK*, App No 5493/72, 7 December 1976.
[55] *Lombardi Vallauri v Italy* (n 7). See also *Schüth v Germany* (n 53) at paras 73–75.
[56] *Lombardi Vallauri v Italy* (n 7) at paras 54–55.
[57] *Glasenapp v Federal Republic of Germany*, Series A, No 104 (1987).
[58] *Kosiek v Federal Republic of Germany*, Series A, No 105 (1987).

a statement in which she acknowledged the values of democracy A violation of this declaration could be the basis for a termination of the employment. Still, although the person concerned had ties with a Maoist organisation, the KPD, she was not a member. However, in an interview with *die Rote Fahne* she had expressed her sympathy for this organisation. In reaction to this, she was fired. Yet the European Court did not consider this to be an infringement of Article 10 ECHR, but rather considered this to be a discussion about access to a civil service (which is not guaranteed by the ECHR). Since the person concerned did not comply with one of the conditions for appointment (ie, loyalty to the Constitution), she did not have to be appointed.[59] In *Kosiek* (an activist of the neo-Nazi party *Nationaldemokratische Partei Deutschlands* (NPD) and the author of a controversial book), the Court reached a similar conclusion.

About 10 years later, there was the *Vogt*[60] case, which once again concerned a teacher who was a member/activist of a communist organisation (*Deutsche Kommunistische Partei*: DKP) and who had been subjected to disciplinary measures, ultimately followed by dismissal, because of her communist ideology. This time, in its assessment of the interference with Vogt's freedom of expression, the Court took a number of (mitigating) circumstances into account. In the first place the Court commented that the dismissal of a teacher is a rather harsh measure because it is hard for teachers to find a job in another capacity, or in the Court's own words, that 'there are several reasons for considering dismissal of a secondary-school teacher by way of disciplinary sanction for breach of duty to be a very severe measure'.[61] As a French- and German-language teacher, her teaching assignment did not imply any specific security risks either. Moreover, she had not abused her position. She had not attempted to indoctrinate her students and nor was there any indication that she herself had taken up an anti-constitutional stance. The Court stated that 'there is no evidence that Mrs Vogt herself, even outside her work at school, actually made anti-constitutional statements or personally adopted an anti-constitutional stance'. Finally, the Court pointed out that the DKP as a political party was not forbidden in Germany. All this had as a result that the dismissal was qualified as a disproportionate measure from the perspective of Article 10 ECHR.[62] It was also decided that Article 11 ECHR had been violated.[63]

In *Vogt* explicit reference was also made to the ILO, which had examined the *Berufsverbot* because of its inconsistency with ILO Convention No 111 (§ 18), yet it never proceeded beyond a reference. In 1987 the ILO had investigated the *Berufsverbot*. This resulted in a number of recommendations.[64] Later this was also taken up by the Committee of Experts of the Application of Conventions and

---

[59] *Glasenapp v Federal Republic of Germany* (n 57) at para 53.
[60] *Vogt v Germany* (n 4).
[61] Ibid, at para 60. Compare *Schüth v Germany* (n 53) at para 73.
[62] This ruling was not unanimous. A number of judges held that on historical grounds Germany was entitled to bar communists from the civil service. It was also argued that Article 10 ECHR did not apply because the disciplinary sanction did not target an opinion, but membership of an organisation. Nonetheless, this was a minority view within the ECtHR.
[63] *Vogt v Germany* (n 4) at para 68.
[64] Vol LXX, 1987, Series B, Supplement 1. For the text of this very bulky report and a number of comments on this, see K Dammann and E Siemantel (eds), *Berufsverbote und Menschenrechte in der Bundesrepublik* (Cologne, Pahl-Rugenstein, 1987).

Recommendations. After the fall of the Berlin Wall, former GDR citizens instead of radical left-wing teachers were the ones who were castigated. They were mainly targeted because of their actions in East Germany. However, the Committee also looked at the sanctions from the point of view of the freedom of expression.[65] It noted that quite often the dismissal was the consequence of the fact that a person had been a member of a certain political group, and not because of his or her deeds. Figures supplied in 1984 then showed that the number of dismissals was rather small.[66] In 1998 Germany declared that from then on, it would respect the principles put forward in the *Vogt v Germany* jurisprudence. The Committee took cognisance of this and stated: 'Account must also be taken rather of the service record of the dismissed person as well as any possible orientation following the collapse of the Socialist Unity Party, towards the free political order.'[67] In 2000 the Committee declared that Germany was permitted to deal with this matter on a case-by-case basis and also asked to be kept informed.[68] Since 2000, there have not been any more reports on this matter.

Since the *Vogt* judgment, it is clear that measures against civil servants because of certain forms of (political) expression have to be assessed as interference with the freedom of expression, analogous to the situation of employees in the private sector.[69] The starting point is as follows: 'As to the applicability of Article 10 and the existence of an interference, the Court points out that the right of recruitment to the civil service was deliberately omitted from the Convention. Consequently, the refusal to appoint a person as a civil servant cannot as such provide the basis for a complaint under the Convention. This does not mean, however, that a person who has already been appointed as a civil servant cannot complain of not being further promoted if that omission violates one of his or her rights under the Convention. Civil servants do not fall outside the scope of the Convention.'[70]

Despite the application of Article 10 ECHR regarding the freedom of expression of civil servants, the employers/public authorities still have the possibility to take measures against civil servants/employees because of their membership of, cooperation with or manifest sympathy for a political party that is considered to be unconstitutional or undemocratic.[71] In particular, in Germany interference with the freedom of expression is considered to comply with Article 10 ECHR if the public servant, police officer or soldier in question sympathises with the NPD or the *Partei der Republikaner*. Still, it is remarkable that in each of the more recent cases in

---

[65] ILOLEX 061992DEU111.

[66] ILOLEX 061994DEU111.

[67] ILOLEX 061998DEU111, at para 5.

[68] ILOLEX 062000DEU111, at para 3.

[69] See, eg, *De Diego Nafria v Spain* (n 18); *Wojtas-Kaleta v Poland* (n 18); *Lombardi Vallauri v Italy* (n 7); and *Fernández Martínez v Spain* (n 8). See also *Laurence Pay v UK* (n 8).

[70] *D Otto v Germany* (n 13), with reference to *Vogt v Germany* (n 4) at para 43 and *Wille v Liechtenstein* (n 13) at para 41.

[71] See, eg, the ECtHR's consideration in *Vogt v Germany* (n 4) at para 51 and in *D Otto v Germany* (n 13) stating that 'a number of Contracting States impose a duty of discretion on their civil servants, founded on the notion that the civil service is the guarantor of the constitution and democracy. The Court found that this notion has a special importance in Germany because of the country's experience under the Weimar Republic, which, when the Federal Republic was founded after the nightmare of Nazism, led to its constitution being based on the principle of a "democracy capable of defending itself" (wehrhafte Demokratie)'.

which the ECtHR did not find an infringement of Article 10 ECHR, this concerned less far-reaching measures than in the *Vogt* case: no dismissals, but fewer promotion prospects, failure to invite persons for certain assignments, or non-extension of a task.[72] Although, in view of its history, Germany is granted a wide margin of appreciation by the ECtHR in order to protect democracy, according to the case law of the Court's Grand Chamber, great care should nonetheless be taken when membership of or overt sympathy for undemocratic political parties are invoked to legitimise interference with the fundamental rights of the ECHR: 'Every time a State intends to rely on the principle of "a democracy capable of defending itself" in order to justify interference with individual rights, it must carefully evaluate the scope and consequences of the measure under consideration, to ensure that the aforementioned balance is achieved.'[73]

4.4 Consequences of the Exposure of the Employee's Conviction for the Company/Employer

When someone adheres to a political conviction and does not propagate this in the workplace or within the public service, this fact could be considered to be part of the private domain. However, it cannot be ruled out that the political conviction propagated by an employee is harmful to the employer. In *Van Der Heijden v The Netherlands* an employee of the Limburg Immigration Association was fired because he was a member of the 'Centrumpartij', an extremely right-wing and xenophobic party, and campaigned for this party. According to the employer, the party's aim was completely at odds with the values of the organisation in which the employee worked. According to the Commission for Human Rights, the employer was allowed to take into account 'the adverse effects which these political activities might have on the Foundation's reputation, particularly in the eyes of the immigrants whose interests it sought to promote'. Therefore, the dismissal of the employee did not amount to a violation of his freedom of expression or freedom of association.[74]

The more the employee exhibits or advertises his or her political conviction, the more this will be a cause for the employer to take measures.[75] In *Kern v Germany* the Court emphasised that the employee/civil servant in his capacity as a member

---

[72] *D Otto v Germany* (n 13); *E Erdel v Germany* (n 13); and *T Lahr v Germany* (n 13).
[73] *Ždanoka v Latvia*, App No 58278/00, 16 March 2006 at para 100.
[74] *Van Der Heijden v the Nederlands* (ECommHR), App No 11002/84, decision of 8 March 1985.
[75] See also Antwerp Labour Court of Appeal, 17 March 2010, AR 2003/AA/353, www.diversiteit.be/?hide_form=1&action=zoek_advanced&search[woord]=arrest&page=11, in which the Court confirmed an employee's dismissal for serious misconduct. The Court held that a fax sent by the employee from within the company contained a racist message, notably because the fax contained a summons to deny Muslims access to and relief on Belgian territory. Because of the disclosure of this message, the company was right in assuming that the company's reputation had been damaged, all the more so because the company presented itself as a multicultural firm in which people of various nationalities were employed. Because the impression could arise that the racist message came from the company itself, and considering that the procedure for dismissal for misconduct, including the consent of the trade union delegations, had taken place correctly, the Court found that the employee's expression amounted to a serious fault which justified the dismissal for misconduct.

of the extreme right-wing party *Bündnis Rechts* had given extra publicity to a press report dispersed by him in which he voiced his approval of the terrorist attacks of 11 September 2001. According to the ECtHR, the German courts which had confirmed Kern's dismissal were right in referring to both the content of his opinions and to the impact thereof on the public service where he was employed. Express consideration was given to 'the content and the consequences of the applicant's statements which approved the terrorist attacks and assumed the existence of a "Zionist oligarchy" as well as the impact of those statements on the civil service. By addressing the media, he did not sufficiently take into account the adverse effects of such activities on the integrity of the public service.' In this case the dismissal was not a disproportionate measure, even though Kern did not have a position involving politics or security. The fact that he worked 'in a technical sector at municipal level' did not detract from the necessity of the measure, according to the ECtHR, which also had regard 'to the domestic courts' margin of appreciation in the matter'.[76]

Yet for the Court, the nature of the employee's position can be an important, even decisive factor to justify dismissal because of certain statements. Especially for jobs in education and in the context of educational objectives such as tolerance, anti-racism and democracy, employees will have to observe certain restrictions. If they fail to do so, they will have to bear the consequences of overt support for undemocratic or racist opinions. In *Seurot v France* the Court emphasised that 'une telle éducation à la citoyenneté démocratique, indispensable pour lutter contre le racisme et la xénophobie, suppose la mobilisation d'acteurs responsables, notamment des enseignants'. Therefore, the dismissal of a teacher who had propagated racists ideas in the school magazine was not considered to be a violation of Article 10 ECHR.[77]

Also remarkable is the fact that the ECtHR upheld the dismissal of Bruno Gollnisch, a university lecturer, because of his denial of the Holocaust.[78] After an investigation by a parliamentary committee into the functioning of some teachers and students at the Lyon-III University, there was a lot of commotion about racism and denial of the Holocaust. According to the ECtHR, this had created a special situation at the university, which made it clear that there were sufficient and relevant reasons to dismiss Professor Gollnisch for his expression of revisionist ideas during a press conference.[79] The university board, with the approval of the French courts, considered a dismissal to be justified because Gollnisch's words went against academic deontology. Considering university teachers' responsibilities, the ECtHR rejected Gollnisch's complaint on the basis of Article 10 ECHR. It held that 'à l'instar des juridictions internes, que la contribution éventuelle de ses propos aux

---

[76] *Dieter Kern v Germany*, App No 26870/04, decision of 29 May 2007.
[77] *Jacques Seurot v France*, App No 57383/00, decision of 18 May 2004.
[78] *Bruno Gollnisch v France*, App No 48135/08, decision of 7 June 2011.
[79] Yet, during the press conference, Gollnisch had only advocated the right of historians to discuss the extent and characteristics of the Holocaust. Among other things he said: 'Je pense que sur le drame concentrationnaire la discussion doit rester libre. Sur le nombre de morts, sur la façon dont les gens sont morts, les historiens ont le droit d'en discuter. L'existence des chambres à gaz, c'est aux historiens d'en discuter.' And he continued: 'Je ne remets pas en cause l'existence des camps de concentration, il y a eu des déportations pour des raisons raciales sans doute des centaines de milliers ou millions de personnes exterminées. Le nombre effectif des morts, 50 ans après les faits, les historiens pourraient en discuter. Moi je ne nie pas les chambres à gaz homicides mais la discussion doit rester libre. L'existence des chambres à gaz [dans les camps d'extermination], c'est aux historiens d'en discuter.'

thèses négationnistes et le désordre qui pouvait en résulter, et qui en est d'ailleurs résulté, au sein de l'université de Lyon III et, plus généralement de l'université française, était incompatible avec les devoirs et responsabilités qui incombaient au requérant en tant qu'enseignant. Dans ces conditions, le requérant a outrepassé les obligations de réserve et de tolérance auxquelles il était tenu'. According to the Court, the consequences of Gollnisch's dismissal were limited because he still had the possibility to start working at another university.[80]

For that matter, not only the expression of a political conviction, an ideology or religious belief can cause problems in the employe–employee relationship in certain circumstances. Divulging on a website certain sexual 'appetites' can also be deemed to be incompatible with the specific nature of the employee's position, as was demonstrated in Laurence *Pay v UK*. However, given the gravity and conse- quences of such a measure for the employee, a dismissal for these reasons can only be upheld after it has been assessed in the light of Article 10 ECHR. The Court pointed out 'that the dismissal of a specialist public servant, such as the applicant, is a very severe measure, because of the effects on his reputation and on his chances of exercising the profession for which he has been trained and acquired skills and experience'. Here too the special nature of the employee's function played a key role, notably the fact that he worked as a supervisor in probation-period projects with sexual offenders. Finally, the Court held 'that Article 10 applies, in that the applicant was dismissed as a consequence of his expression of aspects of his sexual identity. However, it considers that the interference may be considered "necessary in a democratic society"'.[81]

5 JUDGES AND FREEDOM OF EXPRESSION

It goes without saying that judges are not 'regular' civil servants.[82] They have to be neutral, independent and impartial, which at times is difficult to reconcile with expressing or publicly manifesting a political conviction or membership of a political

---

[80] See however *Lombardi Vallauri v Italy* (n 7), where the emphasis was on the importance of aca- demic freedom (see above), and *Vogt v Germany* (n 4), where the difficulty of finding another job was taken into account. The decision in *Bruno Gollnisch v France* does fit in with the Court's compliance with regard to accepting interference with the freedom of expression when this expression is related to 'hate speech' and especially denial of the Holocaust, as is apparent from other decisions by the ECtHR. See also *Roger Garaudy v France*, App No 65831/01, decision of 24 June 2003; and *Pavel Ivanov v Russia*, App No 35222/04, decision of 20 February 2007.

[81] *Laurence Pay v UK* (n 8). The Court considered that: 'The applicant's job involved, inter alia, work- ing closely with convicted sex offenders who had been released from prison, to ensure that they complied with the conditions of release and did not re-offend. As such, it was important that he maintained the respect of the offenders placed under his supervision and also the confidence of the public in general and victims of sex crime in particular. The applicant may be correct in thinking that consensual BDSM role-play, of the type depicted in the photographs on the BB (Birmingham Bizarre) website, is increas- ingly accepted and understood in mainstream British society. Indeed, the hallmarks of a "democratic society" include pluralism, tolerance and broadmindedness ... Nonetheless, given the sensitive nature of the applicant's work with sex offenders, the Court does not consider that the national authorities exceeded the margin of appreciation available to them in adopting a cautious approach as regards the extent to which public knowledge of the applicant's sexual activities could impair his ability effectively to carry out his duties.'

[82] *Albayrak v Turkey*, App No 38406/97, 31 January 2008 at para 42.

party. The fact that a magistrate follows certain 'coloured' media is in itself not sufficient to impose sanctions on him or her. It has to be established that he or she is not impartial[83] and consequently cannot act as a judge.[84] If a judge expresses his or her philosophical or religious views during the performance of his or her judicial functions, this can be a cause for disciplinary measures and can ultimately even justify the dismissal of a judge, without this amounting to a violation of Article 10 ECHR.[85] In *G Pitkevich v Russia* the ECtHR had to rule on the dismissal of a magistrate 'performing her judicial functions, whereby she expressed her religious views'. The Court pointed out the difference with the judgment in *Vogt v Germany*:

> [W]here the Court found a violation of Article 10 of the Convention because a civil servant had been dismissed on the ground of the mere membership of a communist party, with no account being taken of the context of her breaching the statutory requirements of loyalty, nor a criticism being levelled at the way she had actually performed her duties as a teacher. In the instant case, the context of the applicant's breaching her statutory duties as a judge, namely her specific actions while performing her judicial functions, was precisely defined. The facts adduced by the authorities as warranting her dismissal related exclusively to her official activities, and did not concern an expression of her views in private. The facts found in this respect were therefore 'relevant' to establishing the applicant's suitability as a judge.

In these circumstances, according to the Court, there was no violation of Article 10 ECHR.[86]

---

[83] Ibid, at para 46. In this case a disciplinary sanction was issued against a judge, because he boasted about his Kurdish origins and followed the Kurdish media, from which it was inferred that he supported the PKK. The ECtHR held that the disciplinary measure could be considered as an interference by public authority with the freedom of expression, which indeed also guarantees the right to receive information. The Court formulated this as follows: 'the Court cannot but assume that the authorities attached a considerable weight to the fact that the applicant followed or attempted to follow PKK-associated media. In this connection the Court reiterates that freedom of expression requires that care be taken to dissociate the personal views of a person from received information that others wish or may be willing to impart to him or her'. The Court held the view that insufficient evidence had been produced as to the reason why the disciplinary measure against the magistrate was necessary in a democratic society and therefore found a breach of Article 10 ECHR. The magistrate had also been accused of impairing the dignity of the office because he refused to wear a tie and did not always appear properly shaven in court. But the Court did not consider these reasons severe enough to justify the disciplinary sanction either.

[84] As a matter of fact, having a certain political or religious conviction and even being a member of a Masonic Lodge are not incompatible with the requirements under Article 6 ECHR with regard to the impartiality and independence of judges, considering also the rights guaranteed by Article 8 and 11 ECHR: *Ninn-Hansen v Denmark* (ECommHR), App No 28972/95, decision of 18 May 1999; *Grande Oriente d'Italia di Palazzo Giustiniani v Italy*, App No 35972/97, decision of 21 October 1999; *Salaman v UK*, App No 43505/98, decision of 15 June 2000; *MDU v Italy*, App No 58540/00, decision of 28 January 2003; *Filippini v San Marino*, App No 10526/02, decision of 26 August 2003; *Maestri v Italy*, App No 39748/98, decision of 17 February 2004; and *Grande Oriente d'Italia di Palazzo Giustiniani v Italy (No 2)*, App No 26740/02, decision of 31 May 2007, 2. See also Constitutional Court (Belgium), 13 October 2009, No 157/007, www.const-court.be.

[85] *G Pitkevich v Russia*, App No 47936/99, decision of 8 February 2001.

[86] The Court concluded: 'On the basis of those facts it was concluded that the applicant had intimidated parties to proceedings in court, and that she had promoted the Church in damage of the State interest to protect the rule of law. As a result the applicant called into question her impartiality and impaired the authority of the judiciary. In these circumstances, and allowing for a certain margin of appreciation in this respect, the Court finds that the reasons adduced by the authorities in this case were "sufficient" for the interference with the applicant's rights under Article 10 of the Convention': ibid.

Although in *Wille v Liechtenstein*[87] the Court confirmed that it expects the necessary restraint on the part of magistrates and emphasises that they cannot make statements in public about pending cases,[88] it did however find a violation of Article 10 ECHR. It held the view that the announcement in writing by the appointing authority (in this case the Prince) that because of certain public statements, the magistrate would no longer qualify for a public post was to be considered as an unlawful interference with the freedom of expression: 'The announcement by the Prince of his intention not to reappoint the applicant to a public post constituted a reprimand for the previous exercise by the applicant of his right of freedom of expression and, moreover, had a chilling effect on the exercise by the applicant of his freedom of expression, as it was likely to discourage him from making statements of that kind in the future.' As such, the fact that Wille's points of view had a certain political dimension could not be a reason to justify interference with his freedom of expression:

> The Court accepts that the applicant's lecture, since it dealt with matters of constitutional law and more specifically with the issue of whether one of the sovereigns of the State was subject to the jurisdiction of a constitutional court, inevitably had political implications. It considers that questions of constitutional law, by their very nature, have political implications. It cannot find, however, that this element alone should have prevented the applicant from making any statement on this matter ... Moreover, there is no evidence to conclude that the applicant's lecture contained any remarks on pending cases, severe criticism of persons or public institutions or insults of high officials or the Prince.[89]

In *Kudeshkina v Russia* the ECtHR also found that a magistrate's freedom of expression should not be overly curbed.[90] In 2005 Olga Borisovna Kudeshkina lodged a complaint with the European Court in Strasbourg regarding her dismissal as a judge. After having served as a judge at the Moscow City Court for over 18 years, she was dismissed from her post by a disciplinary council because of a number of statements she had made in the media. In public and in the media, the judge had declared that she had been taken off a case concerning a large-scale affair of corruption and financial fraud. She made these statements in a period in which her mandate as a judge had been suspended, at her own request, because she was a candidate for the parliamentary elections. In several interviews in the context of this campaign, she had referred to manipulations and interventions by high-ranking officials, businesspeople and politicians, who systematically put judges of the Moscow Court under pressure. In her campaign she advocated a thorough judicial reform with a view to a better performing and more independent judiciary. However, she was not elected for the 'Duma'. Shortly after her reinstatement as a judge, she was

---

[87] *Wille v Liechtenstein* (n 13).

[88] 'Since the applicant was a high-ranking judge at that time, the Court must bear in mind that, whenever the right to freedom of expression of persons in such a position is at issue, the "duties and responsibilities" referred to in Article 10 § 2 assume a special significance since it can be expected of public officials serving in the judiciary that they should show restraint in exercising their freedom of expression in all cases where the authority and impartiality of the judiciary are likely to be called in question. Nevertheless the Court finds that an interference with the freedom of expression of a judge in a position such as the applicant's calls for close scrutiny on the part of the Court': ibid, at para 64.

[89] *Wille v Liechtenstein* (n 13) at para 67.

[90] *Kudeshkina v Russia* (n 4).

fired. The ECtHR held the view that her dismissal because of these public statements was a violation of Article 10 ECHR, for this guarantees everyone, including civil servants and magistrates, the right to freedom of expression. The judgment makes it particularly clear that the claim of a breach of professional confidentiality and dissemination of false information as a justification for the judge's dismissal in this case is not convincing. The ECtHR also held that Kudeshkina's allegations could not be considered as personal, unfounded attacks on some judges or on the magistracy, but as relevant and fair comments on a matter of major public interest, without revealing any concrete information about criminal proceedings in progress. The Court pointed out:

> [T]hat the applicant made the public criticism with regard to a highly sensitive matter, notably the conduct of various officials dealing with a large-scale corruption case in which she was sitting as a judge. Indeed, her interviews referred to a disconcerting state of affairs, and alleged that instances of pressure on judges were commonplace and that this problem had to be treated seriously if the judicial system was to maintain its independence and enjoy public confidence. There is no doubt that, in so doing, she raised a very important matter of public interest, which should be open to free debate in a democratic society. Her decision to make this information public was based on her personal experience and was taken only after she had been prevented from participating in the trial in her official capacity.[91]

Although one could take some exception to the fierceness with which Kudeshkina had phrased her points of view, the Court held the view that her well-founded criticism contributed to an important societal debate: 'However, even if the applicant allowed herself a certain degree of exaggeration and generalisation, characteristic of the pre-election agitation, her statements were not entirely devoid of any factual grounds ... and therefore were not to be regarded as a gratuitous personal attack but as a fair comment on a matter of great public importance.'[92]

Furthermore, the Court considered the dismissal of a judge with a track record of 18 years to be a disproportionate sanction, particularly because this would no doubt make other magistrates shrink from expressing critical comments on the functioning of the judiciary and on justice policy in the future. Once again, the Court pointed at the 'chilling effect', as a result of which one may no longer dare to make a public statement for fear of punishment. The Court emphasised that such a 'chilling effect' is detrimental to democracy and that Kudeshkina certainly had the right to raise public awareness for the matters she pointed out. The ECtHR's message is clear: (Russian) magistrates who contribute to the debate about manipulation of the judiciary should be supported instead of being punished with dismissal.

6 FRICTION IN THE EMPLOYER–EMPLOYEE RELATIONSHIP (INDIVIDUALLY)

Employers and employees can have a difference of opinion. It is possible that this would entice the employee to voice criticism on the employer, the company or

---

[91] Ibid, at para 94.
[92] Ibid, at para 95.

the management. This criticism can remain behind closed doors or be expressed outdoors. One of the objectives of external communication could be the signalling of wrongdoings, the so-called *whistle-blowing*.

6.1 Difference of Opinion and/or Criticism

6.1.1 Moderato

The basis of *Wille v Liechtenstein*[93] was a conflict between Prince Hans-Adam II and the President of the Administrative Court, Dr Herbert Wille. During a lecture, Wille had voiced his opinion about a legal problem. In his view the Constitutional Court had the authority to intervene and make a decision in a dispute between the Prince and the Landtag. Later his opinion was published in a newspaper. In a letter to the person concerned, the Prince stated that he would no longer appoint Wille to public office because Wille had expressed an opinion that contravened the Constitution. As a result, Wille entered into correspondence with the Landtag, for which the Prince blamed him. Therefore, the Prince did not honour Wille's request for reinstatement. The case was a matter of difference of opinion, certainly not of harsh criticism. In an academic discussion Wille had taken a stance that went against the interests of the head of state, who was also his employer. In its assessment the Court did take into account that a magistrate may be expected to show some restraint, but it also observed that participation in an academic discussion with a political message may contain some provocation. It emphasised that the measure against Wille 'had a chilling effect on the exercise of the freedom of expression, as it was likely to discourage him from making statements of that kind in the future'.[94] To be able to determine effectively that one is dealing with a violation of Article 10 ECHR, the Court did not confine itself to focusing on the actual expression and the context which was the basis for the interference with Wille's freedom of expression, but also pointed out that future opinions of that nature would be burdened. Therefore, a critical public expression of opinion by an employee, in this case even by a judge, is allowed when it is moderate, ie when it does not include personal criticism or insults and contributes to the public debate.

6.1.2 Internal Discussion

Sometimes, when there is harsh criticism, it takes place behind closed doors. *Raichinov v Bulgaria* relates to the sentencing and cautioning of a civil servant because of disrespect towards a member of the Council for the Prosecution during a meeting of the High Council for Justice in Bulgaria. During this meeting, Raichinov, a departmental head of the Ministry of Justice responsible for the funding and logistics service of the justice system, had cast doubt on the integrity of a Prosecutor-General and implicitly accused him of corruption. The Prosecutor-General lodged

---

[93] *Wille v Liechtenstein* (n 13).
[94] Ibid, at para 50. See also *Kudeshkina v Russia* (n 4).

a complaint against Raichinov, which led to a criminal sentence for insult. The ECtHR found this sentence a breach of Article 10 ECHR. In point of fact it amounts to a disproportionate reaction by a hierarchical superior who should be able to take some criticism: 'Against this background, the reaction of the Prosecutor-General— who was Mr S's hierarchical superior—the resulting criminal proceedings against the applicant, and his conviction seem as a disproportionate response to the incident in issue. In this connection, the Court reiterates that the dominant position which those in power occupy makes it necessary for them to display restraint in resorting to criminal proceedings, particularly where other means are available for replying to the unjustified criticisms of their adversaries.'[95] The Court also drew attention to the fact that the critical statement was uttered during a meeting with a limited number of participants, without any reporting in the media or any other form of publicity: 'The negative impact, if any, of the applicant's words on Mr S's reputation was therefore quite limited.'[96] The contested statement should also be seen in the context of the budgetary talks within the High Council for Justice which the ECtHR considered as 'part of a debate on a matter of general concern, which calls for enhanced protection under Article 10'. Moreover, the criticism was expressed orally, during a meeting, spontaneously and not entirely well-considered: 'It should also be observed that the applicant's remark, while liable to be construed as a serious moral reproach, was apparently made in the course of an oral exchange and not in writing, after careful consideration.'[97] This led the Court to conclude that the inference with Raichinov's freedom of expression 'fails to answer any pressing social need ... and could not be considered necessary in a democratic society. Therefore, it found a breach of Article 10 ECHR.[98]

6.1.3 A Sharp Controversy

So in *Wille v Liechtenstein* the discourse was rather technical, and although outsiders could also take cognisance of this, the discussion was limited to a small circle. *Raichinov v Bulgaria* also concerned a case of criticism within governmental circles and did not go beyond those attending a meeting of the High Council for Justice. In *Fuentes Bobo v Spain*, on the other hand, it was a matter of criticisms with a wide dissemination, which in addition had also been expressed in severe wording.[99]

Fuentes Bobo worked for the Spanish television company TVE. During a period of social tensions, he wrote an article in a Spanish newspaper in which he criticised his employer in no uncertain terms. As a result of his actions, a campaign of harassment was started, to which he responded with pamphlets in which he threatened

---

[95] *Raichinov v Bulgaria*, App No 47579/99, 20 April 2006 at para 51.
[96] Ibid, at para 48.
[97] Ibid, at para 51.
[98] See *Boldea v Romania*, App No 19997/02, 15 February 2007, in which the Court took into account the fact that the allegation of plagiarism was only expressed in the presence of colleagues within a professional context, during an internal meeting, so with a limited degree of publicity and where it moreover concerned an oral exchange: 'il s'agissait d'assertions orales prononcées lors d'une réunion, ce qui a ôté la possibilité au requérant de les reformuler, de les parfaire ou de les retirer'. See also D Voorhoof, 'Onder professoren: plagiaat en kritiek' (2007) 6 *Mediaforum* 196–97.
[99] *Fuentes Bobo v Spain* (n 4). See also *Kudeshkina v Russia* (n 4).

to proceed to protest measures. Thereupon he became the subject of a disciplinary procedure, which he denounced during a radio interview and in which he did not spare his employer. Eventually he was fired. The Court took into account the fact that the employee had expressed his opinion in an offensive way as a consequence of which a sanction was due. However, it also took into account the fact that the criticism was expressed within the context of a conflict with the employer and that, in addition, a public debate had been ongoing about the way in which the company was managed. Another mitigating circumstance was that the gross language had, as it were, been provoked by the interviewing journalist and therefore was more or less a *slip of the tongue*. The Court expressly referred to 'un échange rapide et spontané'. It also remarked that no one had started legal proceedings against him, which rather puts the insulting nature of his statements into perspective.[100] Another important element in this judgment is that the Court held the view that a more lenient sanction could have sufficed. It pointed out that the dismissal of an employee because of criticism on his employer is a sanction indicating 'une sévérité extrême, alors que d'autres sanctions disciplinaires, moins lourdes et plus appropriées, auraient pu être envisagées'. In assessing the gravity of the sanction, the Court also took into account that the dismissal without any compensation had extremely far-reaching consequences for the employee concerned 'eu égard notamment à l'ancienneté du requérant dans l'entreprise et à son âge'.[101]

Sometimes certain circumstances can work out badly for an employee, more specifically when the Court focuses on specific aspects, because of which the interference with the employee's freedom of expression who made the critical statement seems to be justified. The decision in *Predota v Austria* and the judgment in *De Diego Nafria v Spain* illustrate this.

In *Predota v Austria* the ECtHR emphasised that the sharp criticism by the employee did not contribute to any social debate, but was essentially aimed at damaging the employer's reputation:

> The Court is satisfied that Austrian law as interpreted by the Austrian courts, takes account of the necessity to secure an employee's freedom of expression against unreasonable demands of loyalty by his employer ... The Court observes that the applicant did not contribute to a discussion on issues of interest to the general public but harshly and publicly criticised the services and performance of his employer in terms which were likely to harm the latter's reputation in the eyes of its customers. It does not appear that the Austrian courts, refusing in such circumstances to annul the applicant's dismissal, failed to protect him against compulsion in matters of freedom of expression which would strike at the very substance of this freedom. Accordingly, having regard to the circumstances of the case as a whole, the Court finds that the interference with the applicant's freedom of expression under Article 10 § 1 of the Convention was necessary in a democratic society and proportionate to the aim of protecting the reputation or the rights of others, namely those of the applicant's employer.[102]

---

[100] *Fuentes Bobo v Spain* (n 4) at paras 47–48.

[101] Ibid, at para 94.

[102] R *Predota v Austria*, App No 28962/95, decision of 18 January 2000. See also *Stănciulescu v Romania*, App No 14621/06, decision of 22 November 2011, in which the Court stated at para 31: 'The domestic courts established that those statements were made in the context of a conflict which had arisen from the work litigation which had set the applicant against his previous employer, and that they were

The phrasing is remarkable, in that in this case the dismissal apparently was not such that it damaged 'the very substance' of the employee's freedom of expression.

The *De Diego Nafria v Spain*[103] case concerned an official of the Bank of Spain who, after having been posted to private banks for several years, was ordered to return to the state bank. His return was the consequence of a disputed decision prohibiting him from continuing to work as a banker. In his capacity as an employee, he wrote a letter to the assistant manager of the Bank of Spain who was also the head of the inspection department. In his letter he outlined his situation, but also accused some of his colleagues, including the Governor of the Bank of Spain of different kinds of irregularities. He sent copies of the letter to two of his colleagues and distributed photocopies among some of the staff. This resulted in his dismissal. Without referring to *Wille v Liechtenstein*, the Court stated that the employee—especially when it concerns a senior official—should show some restraint in his statements. More specifically, it endorsed the finding of the Spanish courts that this was a matter of serious allegations 'formulées de manière générale, sans apporter aucun élément factuel ou commencement de preuve à leur appui, les accusations proférées par le requérant constituaient, de par leur gravité et leur ton, des attaques personnelles gratuites'.[104] Unlike in *Fuentes Bobo v Spain*, the contested statements were not expressed in an interview or on the spur of the moment. The allegations expressed and circulated by De Diego Nafria were well-considered and the author was fully aware of their scope. Therefore, the dismissal was not considered to be unreasonable.

However, this judgment is unsatisfactory. As the dissenters were right in commenting, the similarities between *Fuentes Bobo v Spain* and *De Diego Nafria v Spain* are striking: both cases concerned a professional conflict in which employees criticised their employer. The employees criticised their respective employers in no uncertain terms because of serious dysfunctions or irregularities on the part of the employers. In both cases a public debate had been ongoing with regard to the controversy and in both cases this led to the employee's dismissal. In the *De Diego Nafria* case there was no *media exposure* whatsoever, in the light of which the sanction could be considered to be even more disproportionate. Furthermore, there was another fundamental aspect which, according to the dissenters, had not sufficiently been taken into account: 'La Banque d'Espagne est un établissement public par excellence et, partant, ses dirigeants sont désignés en tant que gestionnaires d'un service public et non d'une entreprise privée. Cela entraîne ... deux conséquences: la première est que les dirigeants de la Banque d'Espagne doivent accepter des critiques au même titre que d'autres personnalités publiques ou dirigeants d'administrations publiques; la deuxième est que la relation employeur-employé est affaiblie en raison des implications logiques découlant de la relation administration-citoyen.'[105]

---

made with the sole intention of discrediting M.N. and subjecting her to public contempt. The Court is satisfied that the applicant's remarks did not therefore form part of an open discussion of a matter of public concern and that they did not involve the issue of freedom of the press, since the applicant was acting as a private individual.'

[103] *De Diego Nafria v Spain* (n 18).
[104] Ibid, at para 40.
[105] Ibid, at para 42. See also *Bathellier v France*, App No 49001/07, decision of 12 October 2010, in which the Court emphasised the offensive, vicious language in a written document containing sharp

In yet another case the ECtHR held the view that an employee, a school teacher, had gone too far in his criticism of the principal and that his statements could indeed be considered defamatory. Nonetheless, the one-year prison sentence given to him did amount to a violation of Article 10 ECHR. The teacher was also a trade unionist and had openly accused the headmistress of personal enrichment and reprehensible conduct, but it turned out that there was no factual basis for this. However, according to the Court, a one-year prison sentence was too harsh a sanction and it stated that 'the circumstances of the instant case—a classic case of defamation of an individual in the context of a debate on a matter of public interest—presented no justification for the imposition of a prison sentence. Such a sanction, by its very nature, will inevitably have a chilling effect on public discussion, and the notion that the applicant's sentence was in fact suspended does not alter that conclusion particularly as the conviction itself was not expunged'.[106]

In a further case the Court also found that a civil servant had gone too far in his comments in the media. *Poyraz v Turkey* concerned a civil judgment against an inspector of the Ministry of Justice because he had publicly commented and elaborated upon a controversial disciplinary investigation of a magistrate after a report on this matter had been leaked in the media. Emphasising the duty of secrecy and confidentiality on the part of judges and judicial officials carrying out investigations of this kind, the Court considered this to be a necessary interference by the authorities for the protection of the magistrate's honour and good name. The Court underlined that, unlike journalists, 'les personnes investies de responsabilités publiques, tels les magistrats et les fonctionnaires ont une obligation de réserve ... qui impliquerait, en l'espèce, que le requérant se distancie formellement du contenu d'un rapport qui pourrait insulter des tiers, les provoquer ou porter atteinte à leur honneur'.[107] The inspector should indeed have had more regard for his duty of confidentiality concerning the investigation he had carried out: 'Une vigilance accrue doit être observée par les fonctionnaires publiques dans l'exercice de leur droit à la liberté d'expression dans le contexte d'enquêtes en cours et en particulier lorsque ces fonctionnaires sont eux-mêmes chargés de conduire de tels enquêtes qui contiennent des informations couvertes par une clause officielle de secret dans l'intérêt d'une bonne administration de la Justice.' The duty of discretion in these circumstances signifies that officials dealing with confidential information should refrain from expressing their opinions related to their professional activities in the media: 'Dans l'exercice de leur liberté d'expression, les personnes investies de responsabilités publiques doivent faire montre de retenue pour ne pas créer une situation de déséquilibre lorsqu'elles se prononcent publiquement au sujet de citoyens ordinaires qui, eux, ont un accès plus limité à ces mêmes média.'[108]

---

criticism with regard to the management. Also remarkable is that in this decision the Court considered it relevant that 'le requérant n'a pas été puni de la sanction la plus lourde puisque finalement il a été licencié pour faute simple'.

[106] *Marchenko v Ukraine*, App No 4063/04, 19 February 2009 at paras 50–54.
[107] *Poyraz v Turkey*, App No 15966/06, 7 December 2010 at para 76.
[108] Ibid, at paras 78–79.

6.2 Limits of Prohibitions on Publications

In *Cwik*,[109] a case which was dealt with by the Court of First Instance and later by the CJEU, Article 17 of the EU Staff Regulations for Officials was at issue. This article prohibits officials from publishing without prior consent.[110] However, permission can only be denied if this could jeopardise the interests of the EU.

The Court of First Instance started from the principle that an EU official is allowed to disagree with his boss: 'In a democratic society founded on respect for fundamental rights, the fact that an official publicly expresses a point of view different from that of the institution for which he works cannot, in itself, be regarded as liable to prejudice the interests of the Communities.'[111] Therefore, the fact that he or she has an opinion other than the official one is not sufficient to impose a prohibition on making oral or written statements.[112] This means that a prohibition is not permitted if it is sufficiently clear that the opinion of the official in question is not the one held by the EU and that his or her points of view do not harm the EU. Both the fact that a speech or publication is aimed at a specialised public (which is capable of judging in a well-informed way) and the official's position can play a role as well.[113] For instance, it is obvious that the point of view of someone who does not have an executive function and clearly states that he is speaking on his own behalf is less decisive than that of a hierarchically important person. In the *Cwik* case the Court found that there was no genuine risk of the public or readers mistaking the civil servant's opinions for official EU policy, nor was there a risk of his statements being harmful to the EU. On the basis of these considerations, the Court concluded that the employer's interference with the civil servant's freedom of expression was not justified and that in refusing to permit publication of the text at issue on the ground that it was liable to prejudice the interests of the Communities, the European Commission made a manifest error of assessment.[114] This conclusion was upheld by the CJEU, which emphasised that refusal to grant an EU official the use of the freedom of expression can only be justified in very exceptional cases, namely when it can be assumed that these statements can cause serious harm to the EU. The Court states inter alia: 'In so far as the provision [art. 17 § 2 of the Staff Regulations] enables institutions to refuse permission to publish, and thus

---

[109] *Michael Cwik v Commission* (n 5) and Case C-340/00 P, *Commission v Michael Cwik* [2001] ECR I-10269 .

[110] Article 17, § 2 of the Staff Regulations of Officials of the European Communities stipulates: 'An official shall not, whether alone or together with others, publish or cause to be published without the permission of the appointing authority, any matter dealing with the work of the Communities. Permission shall be refused only where the proposed publication is liable to prejudice the interests of the Communities.'

[111] *Michael Cwik v Commission* (n 5) at para 57.

[112] Ibid, at para 58: 'the purpose of freedom of expression is precisely to enable expression to be given to opinions which differ from those held at an official level. To accept that freedom of expression could be restricted merely because the opinion at issue differs from the position adopted by the institutions would be to negate the purpose of that fundamental right'.

[113] See also *Morissens v Belgium*, App No 11389/85, decision of 3 May 1988, where a teacher had publicly declared herself to be homosexual and had been given a sanction for this. The Commission took account of the fact that the person concerned had a responsible function, but also that she had expressed her sexual inclination on TV, as a result of which the message was widely advertised.

[114] *Michael Cwik v Commission* (n 5) at para 69.

potentially interfere to a serious extent with freedom of expression, one of the fundamental pillars of a democratic society, it must be interpreted restrictively, in such a way that permission to publish is refused only where publication is liable to cause serious harm to the Communities' interests.'[115]

In so doing, the Court endorsed the basic principles set out in *Connolly*,[116] although in this case, given the different circumstances, the interference with the EU official's freedom of expression was assessed to be justified, first by the Court of First Instance and subsequently also by the CJEU. In his own time, Connolly, an official working for the DG II Economic and Financial Affairs (monetary policies department), had written a book about the monetary policy of the EU, although earlier requests for permission to write articles about this subject had been rejected.[117] The employer considered the publication of the book as a serious infringement of the Staff Regulations, particularly because the book was very critical of EU policy. Connolly was suspended, removed from his function and ultimately forced to take early retirement. The Court observed that the text had been written in a way that was not in keeping with the dignity of the post he held. A civil servant may be expected to be loyal, which may include that in his statements he is not permitted to go against the objectives of the institution.[118] According to the Court of First Instance, neither the obligation of prior consent nor the series of sanctions imposed on Connolly implied a violation of his freedom of expression as guaranteed by Article 10 ECHR.[119] The CJEU also took the view that the requirement of prior permission does not amount to a form of unwarranted censorship, but, on the contrary, entails a justified restriction of the freedom of expression pursuant to Article 10 ECHR. The Court recognised that civil servants are entitled to freedom of expression, but at the same time it emphasised that 'it is also legitimate in a democratic society to subject public servants, on account of their status, to obligations such as those contained in Articles 11 and 12 of the Staff Regulations. Such obligations are intended primarily to preserve the relationship of trust which must exist between the institution and its officials or other employees. It is settled that the scope of those obligations must vary according to the nature of the duties performed by

---

[115] *Commission v Michael Cwik* (n 109) at para 18. The Court also states at para 19: 'When it applies the second paragraph of Article 17 of the Staff Regulations, the appointing authority must balance the various interests at stake, taking account, first, of the freedom that an official has to express, orally or in writing, opinions that dissent from or conflict with those held by the employing institution—that freedom arising from the fundamental right of the individual to express himself freely—and, second, of the gravity of the potential prejudice to the interests of the Communities to which publication of the relevant text might give rise.'

[116] Case T-34/96 and T-163/96, *Bernard Connolly v Commission* [1999] ECR II-463 and *Bernard Connolly v Commission* (n 5).

[117] The title of the book was *The Rotten Heart of Europe: The Dirty War for Europe's Money.*

[118] *Bernard Connolly* v *Commission* (n 116): 'The duty of loyalty requires not only that the official concerned refrains from conduct which reflects on his position and is detrimental to the respect due to the institution and its authorities ... but also that he must conduct himself, particularly if he is of senior grade, in a manner that is beyond suspicion in order that the relationship of trust between that institution and himself may at all times be maintained ... In the present case, it should be observed that the book at issue, in addition to including statements which in themselves reflected on his position, publicly expressed, as the appointing authority has pointed out, the applicant's fundamental opposition to the Commission's policy, which it was his responsibility to implement, namely bringing about economic and monetary union, an objective which is, moreover, laid down in the Treaty' (§ 128).

[119] *Bernard Connolly* v *Commission* (n 116) at paras 129, 148 and 152.

the person concerned or his place in the hierarchy'.[120] According to the Court, EU officials have to take into account the fact that they are working in an organisation that is responsible for performing duties of public interest.[121] As for the obligation of obtaining prior permission, the Court noted that 'the fact that the restriction at issue takes the form of prior permission cannot render it contrary, as such, to the fundamental right of freedom of expression ... The second paragraph of Article 17 of the Staff Regulations clearly provides that, in principle, permission is to be granted, refusal being possible only in exceptional cases'.[122]

The CJEU, in line with the jurisprudence of the ECtHR, acknowledged the civil servant's freedom of expression, but this freedom is limited essentially by the duty of loyalty. This means that one's freedom of expression is indeed curbed when one enters into the service of an employer.[123] Still, any prohibitions, restrictions and disciplinary sanctions have to be assessed in the light of Article 10 ECHR, clearly restricting the employer's margin to interfere in the right of freedom of expression of the employee or civil servant.

7 ACADEMIC FREEDOM OF EXPRESSION

Academics constitute a very specific group of employees. Quite often they assume a somewhat intractable attitude. In *Sorguç v Turkey*[124] the Court emphasised 'the importance of academic freedom, which comprises the academics' freedom to express freely their opinion about the institution or system in which they work and freedom to distribute knowledge and truth without restriction'. The Court also made it clear that one cannot expect academics to restrict themselves to harmless or innocent statements. In the context of the scientific debate and the academic freedom of expression, no unreasonable restrictions should be imposed: 'it would be particularly unreasonable to restrict freedom of expression only to generally

---

[120] *Bernard Connolly v Commission* (n 5) at paras 44–45.

[121] Ibid, at para 46. An EU official has to fulfil his (or her) obligations with regard to the EU, 'the institution that he is supposed to serve'. An official failing to fulfil these obligations 'would destroy the relationship of trust between himself and that institution and make it thereafter more difficult, if not impossible, for the work of the institution to be carried out in cooperation with that official' (at para 47).

[122] *Bernard Connolly v Commission* (n 5) at paras 52–53.

[123] For instance, people who start working in a Catholic hospital do know that they cannot, either openly or passionately, advocate facilities for abortion: *Rommelfanger v Germany*, App No 12242/86, decision of 6 September 1989. Among other things, the Commission considered: 'If, as in the present case, the employer is an organisation based on certain convictions and value judgments which it considers as essential for the performance of its functions in society, it is in fact in line with the requirements of the Convention to give appropriate scope also to the freedom of expression of the employer. An employer of this kind would not be able to effectively exercise this freedom without imposing certain duties of loyalty on its employees. As regards employers such as the Catholic foundation which employed the applicant in its hospital, the law in any event ensures that there is a reasonable relationship between the measures affecting freedom of expression and the nature of the employment as well as the importance of the issue for the employer. In this way it protects an employee against compulsion in matters of freedom of expression which would strike at the very substance of this freedom.'

[124] *Sorguç v Turkey*, App No 17089/03, 23 June 2009 at para 35.

accepted ideas'.[125] This also applies when academics criticise their employer[126] or colleagues.[127]

The Charter of the Fundamental Rights of the European Union devotes special attention to this specific aspect of the right of freedom of expression. Whereas in Article 11 of the Charter, freedom of expression and information is guaranteed, Article 13 also explicitly protects freedom of the arts and sciences: 'The arts and scientific research are free. Academic freedom is respected.' Scientists and academics can indeed claim a considerable amount of freedom of expression. They are allowed somewhat more than other employees.[128] This is not only apparent from the judgment in *Wille v Liechtenstein* (see above).[129] In *Boldea v Romania* the ECtHR made it clear that it is quite alright for an academic to deliver stinging criticism with regard to the (lack of) scientific level of publications by colleagues. Therefore, the Court held the view that in this case it was better not to sanction the person who, very severely indeed, called a spade a spade and made accusations of plagiarism with regard to the publications of two of his colleagues. The Court's view was that the academic in question was fully entitled to invoke the protection of the freedom of expression. Someone has to be able to tell that the Emperor is naked.[130] In *Sorguç v Turkey* the ECtHR was of the opinion that the Turkish courts and ultimately the Turkish Cour de Cassation had shown too much respect for and set too much store by the protection of the reputation of a person whose name had not even been mentioned, whereas according to the Court more significance should have been given to 'the freedom of expression that should normally be enjoyed by an academic in a public debate'.[131]

In *Lombardi Vallauri v Italy* the ECtHR emphasised that the non-appointment of a philosophy of law professor by the Catholic University of Milan was related to the exercise of the freedom of expression, strengthened by the academic freedom: 'La Cour relève d'emblée l'importance accordée dans sa jurisprudence ainsi que, à un niveau plus général, par l'Assemblée parlementaire du Conseil de l'Europe, à la liberté académique, celle-ci devant garantir la liberté d'expression et d'action, la liberté de communiquer des informations de même que celle de "rechercher et de diffuser sans restriction le savoir et la vérité".'[132] In the event of an interference with the right to freedom of expression of academics, the Court found time and time again a

[125] *Hertel v Switzerland*, App No 25181/94, ECtHR, 25 August 1998. See also *Wille v Liechtenstein*, (n 13).

[126] *Wille v Liechtenstein*, (n 13).

[127] *Boldea v Romania* (n 98).

[128] *See also* J Vrielink, P Lemmens, S Parmentier and the LERU Working Group on Human Rights, *Academic Freedom as a Fundamental Right* (Leuven, League of European Research Universities, 2010), available at: www.leru.org/files/general/AP6_Academic_final_Jan_2011.pdf; D Voorhoof, 'The Legal Framework of Freedom of Academic Expression' in *Third University Foundation Ethical Forum*, Brussels, 25 November 2004, www.google.be/search?hl=en&q=voorhoof+academic+freedom+ethical+forum&rlz=1I7SKPT_enBE430; and J Baert, 'Academische vrijheid, juridisch bekeken' in X, *Ad Amicissimum Amici Scripsimus, Vriendenboek Raf Verstegen* (Bruges, Die Keure, 2004) 18–22.

[129] *Wille v Liechtenstein*, (n 13).

[130] *Boldea v Romania* (n 98). In this case, but also in other judgments, the ECtHR has indicated that academics, when publishing something which produces a societal debate, should be able to withstand criticism, even hard criticism: *Nilsen and Johnsen v Norway* (n 9). See also Voorhoof (n 98).

[131] *Sorguç v Turkey* (n 124) at para 35.

[132] *Lombardi Vallauri v Italy* (n 7) at para 43.

violation of Article 10 ECHR. Only in a number of cases related to hate speech or denial of the Holocaust, like in *Gollnisch v France* (see above), could an interference with the academic freedom of expression be justified.

8 WHISTLE-BLOWING

Whistle-blowing is a very specific form of expression. The employee becomes a moral 'traitor' of the company. In a number of cases dealt with above (*Fuentes Bobo v Spain*, *Raichinov v Bulgaria* and *De Diego Nafria v Spain*) the employee/civil servant exposed wrongdoings or mismanagement, while simultaneously voicing his or her point of view, making it clearly a matter of expression of information, ideas and opinions. In its judgment in *Guja v Moldova* the Grand Chamber of the ECtHR went a step further and also considered the dismissal of a civil servant who had leaked information—more specifically, a letter to the press—to be an unlawful restriction of the right of freedom of expression.[133]

8.1 Guja: Criteria for Whistle-blowing[134]

In 2002 four Moldavian police officers arrested 10 individuals who were suspected of offences related to the parliamentary elections. However, they were all released and the police officers were accused of illegal detention and ill-treatment. An investigation into the conduct of the four police officers was started. The police officers addressed politicians with the request to exert pressure and to have them discharged. Two politicians, the Deputy Speaker of Parliament and the Deputy Minister of Internal Affairs, sent a letter to the Prosecutor-General urging him to discontinue the investigation in this case and to drop all charges. Guja, the head of the press department of the Prosecutor-General's Office, sent a copy of this correspondence to a newspaper, revealing the political pressure on the judiciary in this case. The letters were the basis for an article in which the two politicians were accused of interference with an ongoing criminal investigation. It soon became clear that Guja had leaked the letters to the press, and as a result a disciplinary procedure was started. Guja informed the Prosecutor-General that he had leaked the information because of his belief that such action could help to oppose the unlawful pressure. Despite his noble intentions, he was dismissed.

This case concerned a very specific situation, namely the exercise of the freedom of expression in relation to a case of political corruption. In its judgment the Court took account of the UN treaties ratified by Moldova and the Treaties of the Council of Europe that protect persons (including employees) who expose corruption. It is also interesting that ILO Convention No 158 was quoted in this respect. Article 5

---

[133] *Guja v Moldova*, App No 14277/04, 12 February 2008.
[134] For a commentary, see V Junod, 'La liberté d'expression du *whistleblower*' (2009) *Revue trimestrielle de droits de l'homme* 227–60; and D Voorhoof and T Gombeer, 'Klokkenluiden bij politie en justitie is uitoefening van expressievrijheid' (2008) *Vigiles, Tijdschrift voor politierecht/Revue du droit de police* 245–59.

of this Convention stipulates that 'the filing of a complaint or the participation in proceedings against an employer involving alleged violation of laws or regulations or recourse to competent authorities' is no valid reason for the termination of a contract.

Taking into account the fact that Guja was a civil servant, the principles put forward by the ECtHR in other judgments related to the right of freedom of expression of civil servants were, mutatis mutandis, applicable in this case.[135] The Court did differentiate somewhat because this was a case of whistle-blowing. It noted that 'a civil servant, in the course of his work, may become aware of in-house information, including secret information, whose divulgation or publication corresponds to a strong public interest'.[136] In certain circumstances, exposure of wrongdoings has to be protected. This is, for instance, the case when the civil servant is the only one or one of the few persons who is aware of what happens in the workplace and he or she is the one best placed to reveal this.[137] However, with a view to the duty of discretion, the employee's superiors should be the first ones to be informed of this. Making the information public or imparting it to the press is only permitted as an *ultimum remedium*.[138] Therefore, it was necessary to examine whether or not the information could have been communicated in another way in order to reveal and remedy the wrongdoing at issue. The Court imposed the condition that an internal duty to report also has to be an effective mechanism to remedy the wrongdoing that one wants to uncover: 'In assessing whether the restriction on freedom of expression was proportionate, therefore, the Court must take into account whether there was available to the applicant any other effective means of remedying the wrongdoing which he intended to uncover.' In addition, there are some more factors to take into account:[139] a public interest must be at issue; the information that has been leaked must be accurate; the damage that the information could produce and the public interest will have to be weighed up; the motives for uncovering the information may not be personal or inspired by hard feelings towards a person, or in the hope of a profit (good faith), and the sanction imposed must be proportionate. Moreover, the consequences must be assessed.[140]

Having regard to each of these criteria and factors, the Court concluded that Guja's dismissal amounted to a violation of his right to freedom of expression and especially his right to impart information. It phrased its conclusion as follows: 'Being mindful of the importance of the right to freedom of expression on matters of general interest, of the right of civil servants and other employees to report illegal conduct and wrongdoing at their place of work, the duties and responsibilities of employees towards their employers and the right of employers to manage their staff, and having weighed up the other different interests involved in the present case, the Court comes to the conclusion that the interference with the applicant's

---

[135] *Guja v Moldova* (n 133).
[136] Ibid, at para 72.
[137] See also *Marchenko v Ukraine* (n 106) at para 46. The Court allows for the fact that some individuals have a position of power with regard to the dissemination of information.
[138] *Guja v Moldova* (n 133) at para 73.
[139] Ibid, at paras 74–78.
[140] D Voorhoof, 'Europees Hof neemt klokkenluider in bescherming' (2008) 167 *De Juristenkrant* 3.

right to freedom of expression, in particular his right to impart information, was not "necessary in a democratic society". Accordingly, there has been a violation of Article 10 of the Convention.'[141]

Since the *Guja* judgment, 'whistle-blowing' by civil servants, government officials and even by magistrates is effectively protected pursuant to Article 10 ECHR. The judgment in *Kayasu v Turkey* concerned the disciplinary sanction and criminal conviction of a prosecutor who, as a citizen, had presented a petition to the Public Prosecutor's Office of the State Security Court in which he accused two former high-ranking military officers of involvement in a military coup. The prosecutor had also leaked the text of the petition to the media, which subsequently reported on this. The Turkish authorities considered the text of the petition to be contrary to the pro-fessional duties of the prosecutor, discrediting the state institutions in an insulting way and damaging the reputation of high-ranking military officials. However, the ECtHR pointed out that 'le discours litigieux servait fondamentalement à démontrer un dysfonctionnement du régime démocratique'. Given the gravity of the sanctions, the Court concluded that the interference with the right of freedom of expression of Kayasu was a violation of Article 10 ECHR.[142]

Kudeshkina v Russia also concerned a form of whistle-blowing (see above).[143] During her campaign as a politician in the run-up to the elections, Mrs Kudeshkina criticised the functioning of the Moscow City Court. She ventilated her criticism in a series of interviews on the radio and in the press, and illustrated the mismanagement on the basis of details about a serious criminal case in which she had been involved as a magistrate. She was not elected, but nor could she reassume her mandate as a judge because she herself had become the subject of a disciplinary procedure. According to her superiors, she had behaved in a manner that was not in keeping with the dignity of the profession. Ultimately this led to her dismissal. Although the ECtHR did not disregard the duty of 'loyalty, reserve and discretion', the Court emphasised the context of the public debate in which Kudeshkina's statements took place. According to the Court, generalisations and exaggeration are intrinsic to political speech. It also mattered that the allegations and critical statements were based on fact. Subsequently, just like in *Wille v Liechtenstein* and in *Guja v Moldova*, the Court referred to the 'chilling effect' of the fear for sanctions on the exercise of the freedom of speech.[144]

Other judgments also show that the Court does not want to put an excessive bur-den on the willingness to report (serious) wrongdoings or offences, especially not in situations in which only one or a few employees are informed.[145] In *Marchenko v*

---

[141] *Guja v Moldova* (n 133) at para 97.

[142] *Kayasu v Turkey*, App Nos 64119/00 and 76292/01, 13 November 2008. The Court came to the following conclusion (at para 107): 'Conscient de l'importance de la liberté d'expression sur des ques-tions d'intérêt général, des devoirs et responsabilités des fonctionnaires, et en particulier des magistrats, et après avoir pesé les divers intérêts en jeu, la Cour conclut que l'atteinte portée au droit à la liberté d'expression du requérant, à savoir la sanction infligée pour offense aux forces armées, qui a entraîné sa révocation définitive de la fonction de procureur et l'interdiction d'exercer comme avocat, était dispro-portionnée à tout but légitime poursuivi.'

[143] *Kudeshkina v Russia* (n 4).

[144] *Kudeshkina v Russia* (n 4)

[145] *Juppala v Finland*, App No 18620/03, 2 December 2008; and *Marchenko v Ukraine* (n 106).

Ukraine, just like in *Guja v Moldova*, the Court emphasised that 'the signalling of illegal conduct or wrongdoing in the public sector must be protected, in particular as only a small group of persons was aware of what was happening'.[146] In this judgment the Court concluded that the one-year prison sentence because of defamatory statements amounted to a violation of Article 10 ECHR. A trade unionist, a school teacher, had lodged a complaint with the school inspection (KRU) and with the public prosecutor against the school director, who allegedly had abused her position and used school materials and money for private purposes. When the complaints were not acted upon because of a lack of evidence, the teacher took part in a protest against the school director. The participants in the picket carried placards with various slogans criticising the director and accusing her of abuse of office and the misappropriation of public funds. The director brought a private prosecution against the teacher, who was sentenced to a period of imprisonment of one year, suspended for one year , because of insult. The ECtHR in this case also emphasised the importance of whistle-blowers and found that the criminal conviction because of the letters of complaint to the responsible institutions and the courts was not necessary in a democratic society. However, it did find the slogans during the demonstration expressing sharp criticism and serious accusations insulting and defamatory and in contravention of the presumption of innocence, particularly so because no concrete evidence for the allegations had been produced. But it did consider the one-year prison sentence too harsh a sanction with an obvious 'chilling effect', finding 'that, in convicting the applicant in respect of the letters he sent to KRU and the prosecutor's office, and in imposing a lengthy suspended prison sentence at the end of the proceedings, the domestic courts in the instant case went beyond what would have amounted to a "necessary" interference with the applicant's freedom of expression. There has therefore been a violation of Article 10 of the Convention'.[147] In *Frankovicz v Poland* too, the Court found a violation of Article 10 ECHR, this time following a disciplinary sanction of a doctor who in a medical report for a patient had made negative remarks about the treatment and care of the patient in a certain hospital. According to the Polish disciplinary authorities, this amounted to a form of improper criticism of colleagues, which is contrary to medical deontology. In its response to the Polish government's argument that a disciplinary sanction because of a violation of professional ethics is not a matter that falls within the scope of the ECHR, the Court made it clear that 'matters relating to professional practice are not removed from the protection of Article 10 of the Convention ... The Court thus considers that the applicant's conviction and disciplinary sanction for having expressed a critical opinion on medical treatment received by a patient amounted to an interference with his right to freedom of expression'. The disciplinary sanction was provided for by law, but according to the Court, a general prohibition for doctors with regard to criticising the medical practice of colleagues is too extreme a restriction to the right of freedom of expression of medical staff and to the right to information of patients, who after all may benefit from a 'second opinion'. The Court particularly objected to the fact that the Polish authorities were in no way

---

[146] *Marchenko v Ukraine* (n 106) at para 46.
[147] Ibid, at paras 52–54.

willing to examine the truthfulness of what was described in the report, which implied that any form of criticism of another doctor was forbidden: 'Such a strict interpretation by the disciplinary courts of the domestic law as to ban any critical expression in the medical profession is not consonant with the right to freedom of expression.' This approach 'risks discouraging medical practitioners from providing their patients with an objective view of their state of health and treatment received, which in turn could jeopardise the ultimate goal of the doctor's profession—that is to protect the health and life of patient'.[148] The Court added that the report was not an uncalled-for attack on colleagues, but a report based on medical data regarding the medical treatment of a patient by another doctor, thus indicating that the report was related to a public concern. In these circumstances the disciplinary sanction of a reprimand because of the content of the contested report was not necessary in a democratic society and was to be considered as violating the doctor's right to freedom of expression.[149]

8.2 Whistle-blowers in the Private Sector

Ms Heinisch worked as a geriatric nurse in a home for the elderly. Because of a personnel shortage, the patients could not be given the necessary care, which had also been observed by, inter alia, the inspectorate. Heinisch reported the shortcomings, first to the management of the healthcare institution and later to the justice department, but this was not acted upon. Her trade union became involved as well and distributed leaflets. In response to this, she was brought to account and shortly afterwards she was dismissed.

The ECtHR based itself on the *Guja* case law,[150] with one difference. Heinisch was not employed as a civil servant, but was bound to the employer by an employment contract. Nonetheless, the Court applied, mutatis mutandis, the *Guja* rules[151] and stated:

> While such duty of loyalty may be more pronounced in the event of civil servants and employees in the public sector as compared to employees in private-law employment relationships, the Court finds that it doubtlessly also constitutes a feature of the latter category of employment. It therefore shares the Government's view that the principles and criteria established in the Court's case law with a view to weighing an employee's right to freedom of expression by signalling illegal conduct or wrongdoing on the part of his or her employer against the latter's right to protection of its reputation and commercial interests also apply in the case at hand. The nature and extent of loyalty owed by an employee in a particular case has an impact on the weighing of the employee's rights and the conflicting interests of the employer.[152]

---

[148] *Frankovicz v Poland*, App No 53025/99, 16 December 2008 at para 51.

[149] Ibid. See also *Boldea v Romania* (n 98).

[150] *Heinisch v Germany* (n 4). See also F Dorssement, 'Vrijheid van meningsuiting op de werkplek in twee maten en gewichten. De werknemer mag blaffen, de "watchdog" wordt gemuilkorfd' (2011) 3 *Arbeidsrechtelijke Annotaties* 66–93.

[151] At the time of the *Guja* judgment, it was not completely certain whether those principles would also apply to employees in the private sector. See Junod (n 134) 240 ff.

[152] *Heinisch v Germany* (n 4) at para 64.

There can be no doubt that employees in the private sector too have the right to uncover wrongdoings or reveal illegal conduct on the part of their employer. In such circumstances the right to freedom of expression and the right to impart information must be weighed against the right to a good name and reputation on the part of the employers and their commercial interests. For the rest the *Guja* test must be applied, on the basis of the following criteria and presentation of the questions:

1. Was it not possible for the employee or civil servant to call on his employer, department head or any other authority to disclose the wrongdoings and to remedy these?
2. Does the information relate to serious malpractice or a socially relevant issue?
3. Was the leaked information authentic, reliable and accurate?
4. What harm has been caused to the employer by leaking and making public internal, confidential documents?
5. What motivated the whistle-blower?
6. What kind of sanction was the whistle-blower subjected to and what are the consequences thereof?

In the view of the European Court, the German courts that ruled on Heinisch's complaint about her dismissal did not make a fair assessment in their approval of the dismissal decision. According to the Berlin Labour Tribunal, Heinisch's actions produced a 'compelling reason' for dismissal within the meaning of German labour law, without giving much weight to the aspect of freedom of expression invoked by Heinisch. However, for the European Court 'the criminal complaint lodged by the applicant had to be regarded as whistle-blowing on the alleged unlawful conduct of the employer, which fell within the ambit of Article 10 of the Convention'.[153] According to the Court, the crucial question was whether Germany, on the basis of the positive obligations attached to Article 10 ECHR, sufficiently protected Heinisch's interests vis-a-vis those of her employer. The judgment contains, in succession, an assessment of the general interest regarding the disclosed information, of the alternative ways for disclosure, of the accuracy of the statements, of Heinisch's good faith, of the harm done to the employer and of the gravity of the sanction that was imposed. All things considered, the Court concluded, in an entirely similar fashion to the *Guja* judgment: 'Being mindful of the importance of the right to freedom of expression on matters of general interest, of the right of employees to report illegal conduct and wrongdoing at their place of work, the duties and responsibilities of employees towards their employers and the right of employers to manage their staff, and having weighed up the other various interests involved in the present case, the Court comes to the conclusion that the interference with the applicant's right to freedom of expression, in particular her right to impart information, was not "necessary in a democratic society".'[154] The Court unanimously ruled that Heinisch's dismissal amounted to a violation of Article 10 ECHR.

---

[153] Ibid, at para 43.

[154] *Heinisch v Germany* (n 4) at para 93. Compare *Bathellier v France* (n 105), in which the Court, referring to the *Guja* judgment, emphasised that in this case the employee failed to inform his hierarchical superiors within the company of the alleged problem first, and reported his allegations and personal comments directly to the authorities. This is a remarkable decision because the employee did inform the

8.3 Whistle-blowing and the Future Policy of the Council of Europe

Recently the Parliamentary Assembly of the Council of Europe highlighted the importance of whistle-blowing. Resolution 1729/2010 says: 'The Parliamentary Assembly recognises the importance of whistle-blowers—concerned individuals who sound an alarm in order to stop wrongdoings that place fellow human beings at risk—as their actions provide an opportunity to strengthen accountability and bolster the fight against corruption and mismanagement, both in the public and private sectors. Potential whistle-blowers are often discouraged by the fear of reprisals, or the lack of follow-up given to their warnings, to the detriment of the public interest in effective management and the accountability of public affairs and private business.'[155] The Resolution insists on protective mechanisms for whistle-blowers in accordance with a number of basic principles, clearly in line with the above-analysed case law of the ECtHR. The Resolution aims at 'comprehensive legislation', with a wide scope of application for protected whistle-blowing,[156] and this for civil servants as well as for employees in the private sector.[157] A strong legal foundation for whistle-blowers is insisted upon, inter alia, in labour law, in order to prevent unjustified dismissal or other forms of retaliation in the domain of employment. More specifically, the Resolution is very insistent that the legislation 'should codify relevant issues in the following areas of law ... employment law—in particular protection against unfair dismissals and other forms of employment-related retaliation'. In a Recommendation of 2010 the Member States are invited to guarantee the protection of whistle-blowers and to develop mechanisms to protect them (more) appropriately. The Recommendation also advises taking action with a view to a European Framework Convention for whistle-blowers.[158]

---

management of his company beforehand and did not take his complaints to the media but to the authorities. See also *Stănciulescu v Romania*, App No 14621/06, decision of 22 November 2011 at para 32, in which the Court also referred to this *Guja* principle not being fulfilled: 'Even assuming that the applicant's aim was to inform his employer that M.N. had a previous criminal conviction, in order for his employer to decide whether she had the necessary qualifications to work as a legal advisor, the Court notes that such a disclosure should be made in the first place to the person's superior or other competent authority or body. It is only where this is clearly impracticable that the information could, as a last resort, be disclosed to the public (see *Guja v Moldova* [GC], App No 14277/04, § 73, 12 February 2008). Nevertheless, it appears from the case file that the applicant made those remarks on every available occasion, at the plaintiff's workplace, in front of the courts, in his written submissions to different courts and authorities and that those remarks were neither legal arguments in support of his work litigation nor official notifications signalling a potential professional incompatibility.'

[155] PACE Resolution 1729 (2010) on the protection of 'whistle-blowers', http://assembly.coe.int/Mainf.asp?link=/Documents/AdoptedText/ta10/ERES1729.htm.

[156] Ibid: '6.1.1. the definition of protected disclosures shall include all bona fide warnings against various types of unlawful acts, including all serious human rights violations which affect or threaten the life, health, liberty and any other legitimate interests of individuals as subjects of public administration or taxpayers, or as shareholders, employees or customers of private companies.'

[157] Ibid: '6.1.2. the legislation should therefore cover both public and private sector whistle-blowers, including members of the armed forces and special services.'

[158] PACE Recommendation 1916 (2010) on the protection of 'whistle-blowers', 29 April 2010, http://assembly.coe.int/Main.asp?link=/Documents/AdoptedText/ta10/EREC1916.htm. Whistle-blowing by employees or civil servants is also protected through the recognition of the protection of journalists' sources pursuant to Article 10 ECHR: see, eg, *Goodwin v UK*, App No 17488/90, 27 March 1996; *Voskuil v The Netherlands*, App No 64752/01, 22 November 2007; *Tillack v Belgium*, App No 20477/05, 27 November 2007; and *Financial Times Ltd v UK*, App No 821/03, 15 December 2009.

In a statement of 7 December 2011 the Committee of Ministers of the Council of Europe called for a better legal protection of whistle-blowing, including whistle-blowing through online media and new digital platforms. The Committee of Ministers points out that 'people, notably civil society representatives, whistle-blowers and human rights defenders, increasingly rely on social networks, blogging websites and other means of mass communication in aggregate to access and exchange information, publish content, interact, communicate and associate with each other. These platforms are becoming an integral part of the new media eco-system. Although privately operated, they are a significant part of the public sphere through facilitating debate on issues of public interest; in some cases, they can fulfil, similar to traditional media, the role of a social "watchdog" and have demonstrated their usefulness in bringing positive real-life change'.[159] Therefore, the Committee of Ministers urges that action be taken with a view to effective protection of whistle-blowers pursuant to Articles 10 and 11 ECHR.

9 FREEDOM OF EXPRESSION AND TRADE UNION FREEDOM

The Court has repeatedly referred to the connection between the (individual) free-dom of expression and the collective exercise thereof through protests, pickets, dem-onstrations or associations. When it concerns freedom of expression of employees, this right will be enhanced even more when statements are made in the context of trade union activities as part of the freedom of peaceful assembly and association. As early as 1999 this approach was voiced in *Nilsen and Johnson v Norway*. The Court stated that:

> [A] particular feature of the present case is that the applicants were sanctioned in respect of statements they had made as representatives of police associations in response to certain reports publicising allegations of police misconduct. While there can be no doubt that any restrictions placed on the right to impart and receive information on arguable allegations of police misconduct call for a strict scrutiny on the part of the Court ... the same must apply to speech aimed at countering such allegations since it forms part of the same debate. This is especially the case where, as here, the statements in question have been made by elected representatives of professional associations in response to allegations calling into question the practices and integrity of the profession. Indeed, it should be recalled that the right to freedom of expression under Article 10 is one of the principal means of securing effective enjoyment of the right to freedom of assembly and association as enshrined in Article 11.[160]

See also D Voorhoof, 'The Protection of Journalistic Sources under Fire?' in D Voorhoof, *European Media Law* (Herentals, Knops Publishing 2011) 285–301; and http://europe.ifj.org/assets/docs/053/116/bd24035-fd27774.pdf.

[159] Declaration of the Committee of Ministers on the protection of freedom of expression and freedom of assembly and association with regard to privately operated Internet platforms and online service pro-viders, 7 December 2011, https://wcd.coe.int/ViewDoc.jsp?id=1883671&Site=CM&BackColorInternet=C3C3C3&BackColorIntranet=EDB021&BackColorLogged=F5D383.

[160] *Nilsen and Johnson v Norway* (n 9) at para 44.

A very specific situation is that in which an opinion is expressed as part of trade union action or by a trade union representative. Obviously, in that case, not only is Article 10 ECHR relevant but so are ILO Conventions Nos 87, 98 and 151, which cover various aspects of trade union freedom.

Although the ILO Conventions do not specifically recognise freedom of expression in a trade union context, this can be inferred from the 'jurisprudence' of the Freedom of Association Committee (FAC). In the past this Committee already stated:

> The full exercise of trade union rights calls for a free flow of information, opinions and ideas, and to this end workers, employers and their organizations should enjoy freedom of opinion and expression at their meetings, in their publications and in the course of other trade union activities. Nevertheless, in expressing their opinions, trade union organizations should respect the limits of propriety and refrain from the use of insulting language.[161]

Not just the organisations but also the employees are entitled to express their opinions freely, also through the press, provided that they do not use insulting or defamatory language.[162] This shows that the 'case law' of the FAC is close to the jurisprudence of the ECtHR with regard to Article 10 in this context. In collective disputes however, things can get quite rough, as a result of which activists often use strong language. This can happen orally, for example, chanting slogans, contact with the press or in writing by way of leaflets, posters or articles in the media, including online media.

9.1 Insults by Proxy

Ezelin v France[163] concerned the contestation of a disciplinary sanction against a practising lawyer (avocat),[164] who was also the Vice-Chairman of the trade union of the Guadeloupe Bar. Ezelin had taken part in a demonstration in which insults against the judiciary had been uttered. An infringement of Article 10 was claimed, but the Court held the view that this article constituted a *lex generalis* in relation to Article 11 so that no separate treatment was provided for. The connection between these two articles is very close. Indeed, it is impossible to have a right to association without freedom of expression. In this case the Court considered the disciplinary sanction against Ezelin:

> [I]n the light of the case as a whole in order to determine in particular whether it was proportionate to the legitimate aim pursued, having regard to the special importance of freedom of peaceful assembly and freedom of expression, which are closely linked in this

---

[161] Digest 2006, para 154. See also the 1996 Digest, para 152; 304th Report, Case No 1850, para 210; 306th Report, Case No 1885, para 140; 309th Report, Case No 1945, para 67; 324th Report, Case No 2014, para 925; and 336th Report, Case No 2340, para 652.

[162] Digest 2006, para 155. See also the 1996 Digest, para 153; 299th Report, Case No 1640/1646, para 150; 302nd Report, Case No 1817, para 324; 324th Report, Case No 2065, para 131; 327th Report, Case No 2147, para 865; 328th Report, Case No 1961, para 42; 332nd Report, Case No 2090, para 354; and 333rd Report, Case No 2272, para 539.

[163] *Ezelin v France*, Series A, No 202 (1991).

[164] This does not concern an employee, but still we assume that, mutatis mutandis, the principles in this case also apply in the employer–employee relationship. Indeed, a practising lawyer or a barrister is also subject to a certain hierarchical structure, being also under disciplinary supervision by the Bar.

instance. The proportionality principle demands that a balance be struck between the requirements of the purposes listed in Article 11 § 2 (art. 11-2) and those of the free expression of opinions by word, gesture or even silence by persons assembled on the streets or in other public places. The pursuit of a just balance must not result in avocats being discouraged, for fear of disciplinary sanctions, from making clear their beliefs on such occasions.

On the merits, the sanction in *Ezelin v France* was considered by the Court to be a breach of Article 11 ECHR because 'the freedom to take part in a peaceful assembly—in this instance a demonstration that had not been prohibited—is of such importance that it cannot be restricted in any way, even for an avocat, so long as the person concerned does not himself commit any reprehensible act on such an occasion'. Sanctions for participating in a demonstration may be possible, but only for actions of one's own doing, within the perspective of Article 10 and 11 ECHR.

9.2 Trade Union Press[165]

In *Aguilera Jiménez and others v Spain*[166] the focus was on insults that had been uttered in the trade union press. The cover of a monthly information bulletin showed a drawing depicting a somewhat obscene caricature of a human resources (HR) manager together with a number of employees. In the magazine itself, two articles with a crude and vulgar overtone had been included. The magazine was distributed among the employees and was pinned up on the notice board located inside the company's premises. In a response to this, the members of the trade union's executive committee were dismissed for serious misconduct. The Court sets rather great store by the opinion of the national judges. They confine themselves to stating that, unlike in the case of *Fuentes Bobo*, the drawing and the articles were not made on the spur of the moment, but were well-considered actions. According to the European Court, the Spanish courts had analysed in detail the events complained of, and had concluded that, on account of their seriousness and tone, the drawing and articles amounted to personal attacks that were offensive, intemperate, gratuitous and in no way necessary for the legitimate defence of the applicants' interests. Hence, the applicants had exceeded the acceptable limits of the rights of criticism. Therefore, the Court could find no reason to qualify their dismissal as unjustified.

In a *dissenting opinion* Judge Power commented that the Court jumped to conclusions because the trade union context had not been taken into account:

> One cannot and should not ignore the fact that the applicants were members of a recently formed trade union whose mandate was, presumably, to represent the views and protect the interests of its members. The publications were made within the context of an employment dispute.

---

[165] The increased importance of and the applications through the Internet, including websites and social networks, are true for trade union communication as well. See also K Rosier, 'Liberté d'expression du syndicat sur Internet: l'arrêt de la Cour de cassation française' (2008) 385 *Bulletin social et juridique* 6, www.fundp.ac.be/recherche/publications/page_view/65352.

[166] *Aguilera Jiménez and others v Spain.*, App Nos 28389/06, 28955/06, 28957/06, 28959/06, 28961/06, 28964/06, 8 December 2009.

In academia too, this judgment took a beating[167] and the case was submitted to the Grand Chamber, which expressed itself in a more nuanced manner, recognising explicitly this time the trade union context in this case.[168] The Court in *Palomo Sánchez and others v Spain* indeed emphasised that trade union freedom is only possible if there is freedom of expression:

> The Court takes the view that the members of a trade union must be able to express to their employer their demands by which they seek to improve the situation of workers in their company. In this respect, the Court notes that the Inter-American Court of Human Rights, in its Advisory Opinion OC-5/85193, emphasised that freedom of expression was 'a conditio sine qua non for the development of ... trade unions' ... A trade union that does not have the possibility of expressing its ideas freely in this connection would indeed be deprived of an essential means of action. Consequently, for the purpose of guaranteeing the meaningful and effective nature of trade union rights, the national authorities must ensure that disproportionate penalties do not dissuade trade union representatives from seeking to express and defend their members' interests. Trade-union expression may take the form of news sheets, pamphlets, publications and other documents of the trade union whose distribution by workers' representatives acting on behalf of a trade union must therefore be authorised by the management, as stated by the General Conference of the International Labour Organization in its Recommendation No. 143 of 23 June 1971.[169]

The Grand Chamber also agreed that the cartoon and articles were published in the context of a dispute that was not a private matter, but instead 'a matter of general interest for the workers of the company'.[170]

That being said, the Court stated that the existence of such a matter cannot justify the use of offensive cartoons or expressions, even in the context of labour relations. The Court even emphasised that certain manifestations of the right to freedom of expression that may be legitimate in other contexts are not legitimate in those of labour relations.[171] In this respect the Court referred to the *Digest* of the ILO, which holds that trade unions too 'should respect the limits of propriety and refrain from the use of insulting language'.[172] The Court further considered that 'an attack on the respectability of individuals by using grossly insulting or offensive expressions in the professional environment is, on account of its disruptive effects, a particularly serious form of misconduct capable of justifying severe sanctions'.

The Grand Chamber, leaving a wide margin of appreciation to the domestic authorities in this case, referred to the findings by the Spanish courts that in addition to being insulting, the cartoon and texts in issue were intended more as an

---

[167] See Voorhoof and Englebert (n 19) 733–47; D Voorhoof, 'EHRM laat ontslag van werknemers wegens karikatuur overeind' (2010) 2 *Mediaforum* 57–61; and D Voorhoof and F Dorssemont, 'Vrijheid van meningsuiting en vrijheid van vakvereniging. Noot onder Aguilera Jiménez t. Spanje (EHRM 8 December 2009)' (2010) 2 *European Human Rights Cases* 270–79.

[168] *Palomo Sánchez and others v Spain* (n 4). See also F Dorssemont, 'Vrijheid van meningsuiting op de werkplek in twee maten en gewichten. De werknemer mag blaffen, de "watchdog" wordt gemuil-korfd' (2011) 3 *Arbeidsrechtelijke Annotaties* 66–93.

[169] *Palomo Sánchez and others v Spain* (n 4) at para 56.

[170] Ibid, at para 72. It also recognised at para 71 that 'the cartoon and articles were thus published in the newsletter of the trade-union workplace branch to which the applicants belonged, in the context of a dispute between the applicants and the company P'.

[171] Ibid, at para 76.

[172] Ibid, at paras 67 and 76.

attack on colleagues than as a means of promoting trade union action vis-a-vis the employer. Moreover, the cartoon and the articles did not constitute an instantaneous and ill-considered reaction related to a dispute with the employer, in the context of a rapid and spontaneous oral exchange, as is the case with verbal exaggeration. On the contrary, they were written assertions, published in a quite lucid manner and displayed publicly on the premises of the company.[173] Hence, the Court took particular account of the very offensive character of the cartoon and the wording used in the articles in question, containing personal attacks on other employees and the HR manager. This approach finally led to the finding by the Grand Chamber with a 12:5 majority that there had been no violation of Article 10 in this case, the dismissal of the employees involved being a proportionate interference with their freedom of expression as union labour activists.

The joint dissenting opinion includes some interesting reflections. The dissenters observed that the criticism was not so much aimed at private persons, but rather at persons within the corporate context. The dissenters emphasised that the cartoon, whilst being vulgar and tasteless in nature, should be taken for what it is—a satirical representation. Even it was unquestionably crude and vulgar, the impugned cartoon and articles should have been assessed in relation to the ongoing industrial dispute between the labour union and the employer. The dissenting judges also referredto the 'chilling effect' that the dismissal of all members of the executive committee of a labour union may have on future criticism on the management:

> The imposition of such a harsh sanction on trade union members, who were acting in their own names but also to defend the interests of other workers, is likely to have, generally speaking, a 'chilling effect' on the conduct of trade unionists and to encroach directly upon the raison d'être of a trade union. In this connection it is noteworthy that the mere threat of dismissal, involving loss of livelihood, has been described in the Court's case-law as a very serious form of compulsion striking at the very substance of the freedom of association guaranteed by Article 11.[174]

The dissenters could not agree with the approach by the Court's majority and they criticised the Grand Chamber's judgment for overlooking the social dimension of the situation in this case. They stated that 'the applicants' summary and final dismissal for serious misconduct quite simply deprived them of their livelihood. In terms of proportionality, is it really reasonable today, with the widespread employment crisis affecting numerous countries and in terms of social peace, to compare the potentially disruptive effects of the impugned texts in the workplace with a measure of final dismissal, and thus increased job insecurity for the workers? We do not think so'.[175]

---

[173] Ibid, at para 74. Compare *De Diego Nafria v Spain* (n 18) at para 41.

[174] On the patently dissuasive effect that the fear of sanctions entails for persons exercising their freedom of expression, see also *Goodwin v UK* (n 158); *Wille v Liechtenstein* (n 13); *Fuentes Bobo v Spain* (n 4); *Guja v Moldova* (n 133); and *Kudeshkina v Russia* (n 4).

[175] See the joint dissenting opinion in *Palomo Sánchez and others v Spain* (n 4) at paras 6, 11–12, 17–19.

9.3 The Distribution of Leaflets and Public Defamation

The *Vellutini and Michel v France* case concerned trade unionists who had distributed leaflets with insulting and defamatory content, criticising the mayor of a municipality who had an ongoing dispute with a union member over disciplinary sanctions.[176] Subsequently, the president and the general secretary of the municipal police officers' union published a leaflet, distributed to the residents of the town, containing remarks which, in the mayor's view, were clearly defamatory and were directed against him as an elected official in order to discredit him in the eyes of those residents. The mayor brought proceedings against the trade unionists before the criminal court, which found them guilty of 'public defamation against a citizen holding public office' and imposed fines, after ruling their evidence inadmissible. In addition, they were ordered to pay €2,500 each in damages to the civil party and to publish extracts of the judgment in the local newspaper and the full judgment on the union's website.

Relying on Articles 10 and 11, the applicants complained that they were convicted of public defamation of a person holding public office on the basis of statements made in their capacity as union officials. In the judgment of the ECtHR, account is taken of the fact that the comments were not aimed at the mayor in his personal capacity, but toward his mayoral functions. The mayor had simply been criticised in connection with his duties as head of the municipal police, and no allegations of a private nature had been made against him. The Court also found that the impugned remarks had been made in the context of a debate of general interest and had a sufficient factual basis.[177] Indeed, it emphasised that the applicants' remarks had been made in response to the mayor's accusations about the professional and personal conduct of a member of their union. In that context, as for any individual who took part in a public debate, a degree of exaggeration, or even provocation, with the use of somewhat immoderate language, was permitted. Moreover, the Court took the view that the impugned remarks had not been offensive or hurtful to a degree that went beyond the framework of trade union discourse.[178] It therefore found that the interference with the applicants' right to freedom of expression, in their capacity as trade union officials, had not been necessary in a democratic society.

9.4 Interviews or Statements in the Press or on the Internet

So far only limited jurisprudence of the ECtHR is available on interferences with the freedom of expression of labour unionists because of statements or interviews in the media or for communicating information on the Internet. The communicated

---

[176] *Vellutini and Michel v France* (n 18). See also *Heinisch v Germany* (n 4), a case in which the labour union was involved in the distribution of leaflets reporting and criticising the shortcomings in the management of the healthcare institution in which Heinisch was employed (see above).

[177] *Vellutini and Michel v France* (n 18) at paras 41–42.

[178] The Court also observed that there is a difference between the writings of a journalist and those of a trade unionist. One cannot expect them to have the same accuracy/impartiality (para 41).

cases *Ali Rıza Erdoğan*,[179] *Halil Özbent*,[180] *Satılmış Akkaya* and *Murat İşeri*[181] (all versus Turkey) concern complaints by trade unionists punished in Turkey for making statements to the press.[182] If the Court were to make a link between Article 10 ECHR and the view of the FAC (see above), and following its approach in the jurisprudence in *Wille v Liechenstein, Fuentes Bobo v Spain, Wojtas-Kaleta v Poland, Kudeshkina v Russia, Heinisch v Germany* and *Vellutini and Michel v France* (see above), it goes almost without saying that the ECtHR in these cases would find a violation of Article 10 ECHR.[183]

In another recent case, statements published on a trade union's website were at the heart of the matter. In *Szima v Hungary* the ECtHR concluded that a criminal conviction of a leader of a police trade union for having posted critical and offensive comments on the union's website was to be considered necessary in a democratic society for the prevention of disorder or crime, and more precisely of preserving order in the armed forces. The Military Bench of the Budapest Court of Appeal held that the publication of the posted articles and statements had gone beyond the applicant's freedom of expression, given the particularities of the armed body to which she belonged. In the Budapest court's opinion, the views contained in the documents constituted one-sided criticism whose truthfulness could not and should not be proven. In its judgment of 9 October 2012, the European Court shared the views of the Hungarian courts regarding the nature of the allegations and value judgments expressed by the president of the police trade union, Ms Judit Szima. The Strasbourg Court accepted that the accusations of the senior police management of political bias and agenda, transgressions, unprofessionalism and nepotism were indeed capable of causing insubordination since they might discredit the legitimacy of police actions. It considered that some of the statements could be regarded as value judgments, but that Szima did not provide any clear factual basis for those statements. It also observed that 'it is true that she was barred from submitting evidence in the domestic proceedings—a matter of serious concern—however, in her attacks concerning the activities of police leadership, she failed to relate her offensive value judgments to facts'. The Court was of the opinion that Szima 'has uttered, repeatedly, critical views about the manner in which police leaders managed the force, and accused them of disrespect of citizens and of serving political interests in general' and that these views 'overstepped the mandate of a trade union leader, because they are not at all related to the protection of labour-related interests of trade union members. Therefore, those statements, being made outside the legitimate scope of trade union-related activities, must be considered from the general

---

[179] *Ali Rıza Erdoğan v Turkey*, App No 15520/96 (communicated).

[180] *Halil Özbent v Turkey*, App No 56395/08 (communicated).

[181] *Satılmış Akkaya and Murat İşeri*, App No 29283/07 (communicated).

[182] All three communicated cases are referred to in the factsheet published by the Press Unit of the European Court of Human Rights, 'Factsheet—Trade Union Rights' (February 2012), www.echr.coe.int/NR/rdonlyres/DFF8FD53-E057-4F42-A266-07BC3422A9EF/0/FICHES_Libert%C3%A9_syndicale_EN.pdf.

[183] See also *Karademirci and others v Turkey* (n 47), concerning convictions of plaintiffs because, as members of a medical trade union, they had failed to ask prior permission from the public prosecutor before contacting the press. According to the ECtHR, the trade union members could not have foreseen that their press statements would fall within the scope of a regulation regarding pamphlets, because of which the contested interference by the authorities was provided for by law.

perspective of freedom of expression rather than from the particular aspect of trade union-related expressions'.[184] The European Court considered that the reasons adduced by the national authorities to justify the criminal conviction of Szima were relevant and sufficient, especially in view of the relatively mild sanction imposed on the applicant—demotion and a fine—which could not be regarded disproportionate in the circumstances. On the basis of these considerations, the Court concluded, by six votes to one, that there had been no violation of Article 10 read in the light of Article 11 of the Convention.

As the sole dissent, the president of the Chamber, Judge Tulkens, vehemently disagreed with the reasoning by the Court in *Szima v Hungary*. Tulkens referred to the finding by the Court's majority that Szima's critical remarks had overstepped the mandate of a trade union leader, because some of them were 'not at all related to the protection of labour-related interests of trade union members'. Tulkens wondered whether the Court itself has not overstepped its mandate by casting this judgment on the role of a trade union leader and on the 'legitimate' scope of trade union activities. In finding, without any other explication or justification, that the offending remarks had been made 'outside the legitimate scope of trade union-related activities', the majority dismissed, artificially in Tulkens' view, the trade union dimension of this case to focus purely on the right to freedom of expression. The Court was also satisfied that the sanction was proportionate even though it recognised that several statements made by the applicant benefited from the heightened protection afforded to trade union leaders or were 'pure' value judgments. Furthermore, whilst the fine may be regarded as lenient, the same cannot be said of lowering a police officer in rank. The majority of the Court seemed to neglect the chilling effect that such a sanction may have on trade union expression, as members of police labour unions will be deterred from engaging in legitimate harsh criticism on the management of the police force.

Looking at the final outcome of the judgment in *Szima v Hungary*, it is striking to notice that the Court firmly took as its starting point that 'the members of a trade union must be able to express to their employer their demands by which they seek to improve the situation of workers in their company. A trade union that does not have the possibility of expressing its ideas freely in this connection would indeed be deprived of an essential means of action. Consequently, for the purpose of guaranteeing the meaningful and effective nature of trade union rights, the national authorities must ensure that disproportionate penalties do not dissuade trade union representatives from seeking to express and defend their members' interests' (para 28). However, the reasoning used by the Court, which led to the acceptance of the findings by the domestic courts justifying the applicant's conviction, seems to neglect the important principles the European Court itself said applied. The judgment in *Szima v Hungary* represents a retrograde step in terms of freedom of expression for leaders and members of trade unions.

---

[184] *Szima v Hungary*, App No 29723/11, 9 October 2012, at para 31.

10 CONCLUSION: THE 'CONTEXTUALISATION' OF THE EMPLOYEE'S FREEDOM OF EXPRESSION

The analysis of the case law has made it clear that an employee can assert his or her freedom of expression with regard to the employer, but that in certain circumstances, within a certain context, interference with the employee's freedom of expression can be justified. Within the company, in the workplace, but also outside it and in public, employees can express their opinions regarding all kinds of issues. They can hold political views, criticise the management and even leak internal information, although some restrictions and limits have to be observed if interference or sanctions by the employer are to be avoided.

When assessing the legitimate nature of the employer's interference with the employee's (or trade union's) freedom of expression from the scope of Article 10 ECHR, we consider that the following factors and criteria must be considered:

1. *The content of the opinion or publication, bearing in mind whether or not the opinion contributes to a public debate or relates to a matter of public interest or to workplace or trade union-related activities.*
2. *The medium in which the statements or disclosure were made public.*
3. *The social context of the statements, including the timing.*
4. *The nature of the employee's position.*
5. *The type of company (or department or organisation) the employee is working for.*
6. *The manner in which the criticisms were expressed (language, humour, satire).*
7. *The spontaneous or non-spontaneous nature of the opinions (oral/written).*
8. *The employee's intentions.*
9. *The expression's impact on the company's reputation.*
10. *The impact on the relationship with the employer (a comparative assessment of duty of loyalty and freedom of expression).*
11. *The truthfulness, accuracy or factual basis of the criticism.*
12. *The possibility as a whistle-blower to report internally alleged wrongdoings, fraud or corruption effectively, with sufficient guarantees.*
13. *Previous statements by the employee in response to statements or declarations by the employer.*
14. *Specific characteristics, such as academic freedom, contact with adolescents/children, etc.*
15. *The confidential or non-confidential nature of the disclosed or leaked information.*
16. *The damage to the employer as a result of the publicised or leaked information.*
17. *The nature of the interference (preventive, repressive).*
18. *The procedural guarantees and the type of judicial control regarding the interference or sanction.*
19. *The gravity of the sanction in respect of the (concrete) consequences for the employee.*
20. *The possible 'chilling effect' flowing from an employer's interference with an employee's freedom of expression.*

In his article 'La liberté d'expression syndicale: parent pauvre de la démocratie'[185] Jean-Pierre Marguénaud rightfully questions the ECtHR's attitude in some cases involving trade unionists, especially the Grand Chamber judgment in the case of *Palomo Sánchez and others v Spain*. We on our part too cannot avoid the impression that the Court does not have (enough) regard for the context of collective disputes[186] or for the militant and, at times, sarcastic humour characteristic of trade union militancy and freedom of expression. The flexibility the Court often shows in its line of reasoning in other judgments and the sometimes far-reaching protection of the freedom of expression related to matters of public concern is indeed lacking in this case.[187] In addition, criminal convictions for defamation because employees or trade unionists have criticised or offended the employer are to be considered in most cases, if not in all cases of labour conflicts and social disputes, as disproportionate sanctions. Most recently, by adopting a narrow approach to trade union activities, the Court in *Szima v Hungary* has limited substantially the protection under Article 10 of the European Convention for trade union leaders. Precisely because some of the statements of the president of a police trade union were related to issues of general interest and fell outside the scope of trade union activities or labour-related interests, only a reduced protection under Article 10 was guaranteed, while the public interest aspect in all other circumstances is precisely a decisive element to extend and upgrade the level of protection of freedom of expression.

An additional element of concern is the severe and disproportionate character of a dismissal, of which the impact for the employee or civil servant is not always sufficiently taken into consideration. In *Fuentes Bobo v Spain* the Court rightly held that the dismissal of an employee because of criticism on his employer is a sanction indicating 'une sévérité extrême, alors que d'autres sanctions disciplinaires, moins lourdes et plus appropriées, auraient pu être envisagées'. In assessing the gravity of the sanction, the Court took into account the fact that the dismissal without any compensation had extremely far-reaching consequences for the employee concerned.[188] It is accepted all too easily in other cases that a dismissal of an employee due to the use of his or her right of freedom of expression reflects a pressing social need and is a necessity in a democratic society. Such an excessive interference in the employee's right of freedom of expression, with an obvious 'chilling effect' for others, should only be acceptable in very exceptional cases, obliging employers to react in a more appropriate and less disproportionate way, taking into consideration the far-reaching consequences of a dismissal in today's 'widespread employment crisis affecting numerous countries'. From this perspective, the disruptive character of a text or statement by an employee tarnishing the reputation of the management or

---

[185] *Receuil Dalloz* 2010, 1456; and http://actu.dalloz-etudiant.fr/fileadmin/actualites/pdfs/SEPTEMBRE_2011/D2010-1456.pdf.

[186] See D Voorhoof and J Englebert (n 19) 743 ff.

[187] The dissenting opinions clearly indicate that some judges do have an eye for this. See also R Ó Fathaigh and D Voorhoof, 'Chamber Judgment on Trade Union Freedom of Expression', *Strasbourg Observers Blog*, Human Rights Centre of Ghent University, 14 September 2011, http://strasbourgobservers.com/2011/09/14/grand-chamber-judgment-on-trade-union-freedom-of-expression/#more-1143.

[188] *Fuentes Bobo v Spain (n 4)* at para 94. See also the joint dissenting opinion in *Palomo Sánchez and others v Spain* (n 4) at paras 6, 11–12, 17–19.

the company can be considered to have a far less impact than 'a measure of final dismissal, and increased job insecurity for the workers'.[189] Accepting the legitimate and justified character of a dismissal of an employee as an interference with his or her right of freedom of expression risks curtailing that right itself and stifling freedom of expression in the workplace and in the employment relationship. Such an approach would leave us or bring us back in the situation evocated by the *dissenters* in *Palomo Sánchez and others v Spain*, quoting Glasser: 'Many people ... economically dependent as they are upon their employer, hesitate to speak out not because they are afraid of getting arrested, but because they are afraid of being fired. And they are right.'[190]

---

[189] Quotation from joint dissenting opinion in *Palomo Sánchez and others v Spain* (n 4) at paras 18 and 19.

[190] I Glasser, 'You Can Be Fired for Your Politics' (1979) *Civil Liberties*, no 327, 8.

11

The Right to Form and Join Trade Unions Protected by Article 11 ECHR

ISABELLE VAN HIEL

1 INTRODUCTION

THIS CONTRIBUTION DEALS with freedom of association in the narrow sense of the word, ie, the right to form and join trade unions, and the scope of its protection by the European Convention on Human Rights (ECHR). In the ECHR the right to form and join trade unions is not defined in an extensive way. Article 11 deals with freedom of assembly and freedom of association at the same time, while the right to form and join trade unions is construed as an aspect of the general freedom of association. The UDHR,[1] which inspired the ECHR,[2] contains separate provisions for the freedom of association (Article 20.2) and the right to form and join trade unions (Article 23.4). So do most of the social rights treaties, like the ICESC[3] (Article 8.1), the ESC[4] (Article 5) and, of course, ILO Conventions 87[5] and 98[6]. Only the ICCPR[7] (Article 22.1) and the EU Charter on Fundamental Rights[8] (Article 12.1) use the same terminology as the ECHR. The preparatory works of the Convention explain that the right to form trade unions was inserted in Article 11 'to bring this Article into conformity with the United Nations Universal Declaration',[9] but as the UDHR mentions the right to form trade unions as a right distinct from the right to freedom of association in general, the relation between both rights remains ambiguous.

---

[1] Universal Declaration of Human Rights of 10 December 1948.

[2] D Gomein, D Harris and L Zwaak, *Law and Practice of the European Convention on Human Rights and the European Social Charter* (Strasbourg, Council of Europe Publishing, 1996) 301.

[3] International Covenant on Economic, Social and Cultural Rights of 16 December 1966.

[4] European Social Charter of 18 October 1961 and Revisited European Social Charter of 3 May 1996.

[5] Convention No 87 of 9 July 1948 of the International Labour Organization concerning Freedom of Association and Protection of the Right to Organize.

[6] Convention No 98 of 1 July 1949 of the International Labour Organization concerning the Application of the Principles of the Right to Organize and to Bargain Collectively.

[7] International Covenant on Civil and Political Rights of 16 December 1966.

[8] Charter of Fundamental Rights of the European Union of 7 December 2000, *PB* C 364, 18 December 2000.

[9] Report of 19 June 1950 of the Conference of Senior Officials, Collected Edition of the 'Travaux Préparatoires', 1977, vol IV, pp 242 and 262.

Therefore, in much of the case law of the European Court on Human Rights (ECtHR) and its Commission (EComHR) the relation between the freedom of association and the right to form and join trade unions is discussed, as this relation may affect trade union rights. Since the 1970s, the Court has defined the right to form and join trade unions as 'one form or a special aspect of freedom of association'.[10] The Court's and the Commission's case law on negative trade union freedom reveal that it must be interpreted as an aspect of freedom of association rather than a special aspect, as illustrated by the Commission's statement in *Young, James and Webster* that: 'It therefore follows from the text itself that the right to freedom of association is the overall concept, with the right to form and to join trade unions as an element in that concept, rather than as a separate distinct right for the purposes of this Convention.'[11] At the time, the Commission's statement was not explicitly adopted by the Court.[12] In *Sigurdur A Sigurjónsson*, however, the Court conveyed that 'the right to form and join trade unions in that provision is an aspect of the wider right to freedom of association, rather than a separate right',[13] a statement similar to that of the Commission in *Young, James and Webster*. The Court's approach towards trade union freedom as a derivative of freedom of association and its refusal to recognise the particularity of trade union freedom have been criticised in the legal doctrine.[14] Yet, things may evolve, as a number of post-2006 judgments mention that it is 'a special aspect',[15] while others continue to use the former definition.[16]

Questions of the same kind arise as to the term 'association'. According to the Court, this term possesses an autonomous meaning.[17] Thus, the Court wants to anticipate states avoiding Article 11 by qualifying organisations as 'public' or 'semi-administrative'.[18] The Court itself does not give a definition, but scholars emphasise that the term 'association' pre-supposes a voluntary grouping for a common goal,[19] with a minimum of organisation and stability.[20] Determining whether a specific organisation constitutes an association is important. Organisations governed by public law are not considered to be associations and therefore fall outside the ambit

---

[10] ECtHR, 27 October 1975, App No 4464/70, *National Union of Belgian Police v Belgium*, § 38; ECtHR, 6 February 1976, App No 5614/72, *Swedish Engine Drivers' Union v Sweden*, § 39; ECtHR, 2 July 2002, App Nos 30668/96, 30671/96 and 30678/96, *Wilson, National Union of Journalists and Others v UK*, § 42.

[11] EComHR, Report of 14 December 1979, App Nos 7601/76 and 7806/77, *Young, James and Webster v UK*, § 159.

[12] ECtHR, 13 August 1981, *Young, James and Webster v UK* (n 11).

[13] ECtHR, 30 June 1993, App No 16130/90, *Sigurdur A Sigurjónsson v Iceland*, § 32.

[14] F Sudre, *Droit européen et international des droits de l'homme*, 10th edn (Paris, Presses Universitaires de France, 2011) 620, no 348.

[15] ECtHR, 27 February 2007, App No 11002/05, *Associated Society of Locomotive Engineers and Firemen (ASLEF) v UK*, § 37; ECtHR, 27 April 2010, App No 20161/06, *Ólafsson v Iceland*, § 45.

[16] ECtHR, 30 July 2009, App No 67336/01, *Danilenkov and Others v Russia*, § 121.

[17] ECtHR, 29 April 1999, App Nos 25088/94, 28331/95 and 28443/95, *Chassagnou and Others v France*; ECtHR, 6 November 2003, App Nos 48047/99, 48961/99, 50786/99 and 50792/99, *Popov and Others v Bulgaria*.

[18] Sudre (n 14) 612, no 345.

[19] Gomein, Harris and Zwaak (n 2) 304.

[20] C Tomuschat, 'Freedom of Association' in R St J Macdonald, F Matscher and H Petzold (eds), *The European System for the Protection of Human Rights* (Dordrecht, Martinus Nijhoff Publishers, 1993) 493.

of Article 11. But also for a trade union and its members, it can make a difference whether it is addressed as a trade union or just as an 'ordinary' association. If trade unions are to be qualified as associations of a distinct kind, specific rights may be attributed to them and not to other organisations. Still, in the Court's case law, trade unions are mainly seen as 'plain' associations, so that trade unions and other associations can be treated equally.[21]

Likewise, the horizontal effect of the Convention has been a subject for debate. These days, the Court generally accepts that states are obliged to secure the enjoyment of the Convention rights and freedoms by preventing and remedying any breach thereof, which may involve positive obligations and even the adoption of measures in the sphere of the relations between individuals.[22] In older case law, applications were mostly directed against the state as employer. However, the Court rapidly recognised the obligation for the state to protect individual rights against the action of other individuals or associations, especially in the field of closed-shop agreements.[23] While such agreements constitute in principle an exercise of contractual freedom on both sides, the state may become involved by setting forth in its legislation that dismissals pronounced to enforce a closed-shop system shall be regarded as legitimate and cannot be challenged.[24] By way of the state's positive obligations, industrial relations in the private sector are covered by Article 11.[25]

The closed-shop issue is tightly related to the content of the right to form and join trade unions. Extended to a negative right not to associate, it seems to have been protected earlier on by the Court than the positive right to associate, which was for a long time limited to a right of the individual members that their trade union should be heard.[26] As early case law relates to the negative freedom, this aspect will be examined first. Since the Court links the right of trade unions to choose their members to the negative right of workers not to organise, this subject will be considered subsequently. Finally, the positive freedom is tackled, but only the individual aspect of it—the protection of trade unionists against anti-union discrimination. The other aspects are discussed in other contributions in this volume.

2 THE RIGHT FOR WORKERS NOT TO ORGANISE

Although the text of Article 11 of the Convention only expresses a positive right of freedom of association and none of the other human rights instruments recognises a negative right, the ECtHR quite easily acknowledged a right not to organise. The

---

[21] *Sigurdur A Sigurjónsson v Iceland* (n 13) § 32.

[22] AW Heringa and F Van Hoof, 'Freedom of Association and Assembly (Article 11)', in P Van Dijk, F Van Hoof, A Van Rijn and L Zwaak (eds.), *Theory and Practice of the European Convention on Human Rights*, 4th edn (Antwerp-Oxford, Intersentia, 2006) 836, no 15.5.

[23] ECtHR, 13 August 1981, *Young, James and Webster v UK* (n 11).

[24] Tomuschat (n 20) 503.

[25] A Clapman, 'The "Drittwirkung" of the Convention' in St J Macdonald, Matscher and Petzold (eds) (n 20) 195.

[26] *National Union of Belgian Police v Belgium* (n 10); *Swedish Engine Drivers' Union v Sweden* (n 10).

majority of the decisions relate to closed-shop agreements, in those days a common and lawful practice in the UK and the Scandinavian countries.

2.1 Compulsory Membership

2.1.1 Young, James and Webster—*Post-entry Closed Shop*

In *Young, James and Webster v UK*[27] the ECtHR had to decide on a closed-shop agreement for the first time. It was, however, not the first time an individual invoked the European Convention in protection against a supposedly unlawful trade union practice. In *X v Belgium*[28] a Belgian worker complained about his dismissal, which he attributed to his non-membership of one of the (at that time) two representative workers' organisations. Although the claim was declared inadmissible due to non-exhaustion of all internal procedures and a lack of factual basis, the Commission already clarified its position on the negative aspect of the freedom of association stating that 'it is true that the notion of the freedom of association in itself implies also the freedom not to associate or to affiliate trade unions'.[29] In *Young, James and Webster*, referred by three workers who were fired because of their refusal to join a trade union which signed a closed-shop agreement with their employer after their engagement, the ECtHR—as well as the Commission—proved itself more cautious, only accepting that Article 11 of the Convention implied 'some measure of' negative freedom of association.

After all, the case was without precedent and the Court could not relate to the case law of any other international monitoring body. No international protection of the right not to associate existed.[30] Negative freedom of association was not inserted in ILO Conventions 87 and 98, the UDHR, the ECHR and the original ESC of 1961. Article 20.2 of the UDHR stipulates that 'no one may be compelled to belong to an organisation', but the more specific Article 23.4 only recognises 'the right to form and join trade unions for the protection of his interests'. An amendment introducing the right not to associate into ILO Convention 87 was rejected by the preparatory International Labour Conference.[31] On account of the silence of

---

[27] ECtHR, 13 August 1981, *Young, James and Webster v UK* (n 11). See also PJ Duffy, 'The Closed Shop Case. A Note on *Young, James and Webster v United Kingdom*' (1980) V(3) *Human Rights Review* 205–07; P Lemmens, 'Het "closed shop"-systeem en de vrijheid van vakvereniging (zaak Young, James & Webster)' (1981–82) *Rechtskundig Weekblad* 1701–03; P O'Higgins, 'The Closed Shop and the European Convention on Human Rights' (1981) VI(1) *Human Rights Review* 22–27; AM Dugdale and HF Rawlings, 'The Closed Shop and the European Convention on Human Rights' in MP Furmston, R Kerridge and BE Sufrin (eds), *The Effect on English Domestic Law of Membership of the European Communities and the Ratification of the European Convention on Human Rights* (The Hague, Martinus Nijhoff Publishers, 1983) 283–317.

[28] EComHR, decision of 3 February 1970, App No 4072/69, *X v Belgium*.

[29] The author's translation of 'qu'il est vrai que la notion même de la liberté d'association implique également la liberté de ne pas s'associer ou de ne pas s'affilier à des syndicats'.

[30] G Spiropoulos regretted in 1956 that only a handful of countries protected the negative freedom of association in the same way as the positive freedom of association. See G Spiropoulos, *La liberté syndicale* (Paris, Librairie générale de droit et de jurisprudence, 1956) 214.

[31] Bureau International du Travail, *Etude d'ensemble*, pp 47–49, no 100; and International Labour Office, *Freedom of Association Digest*, p 77, no 364.

the conventions, the monitoring bodies of the ILO concluded that the admissibility of union security clauses was left to the discretion of the states, as long as they were the result of free negotiations between workers' and employers' organisations and were not imposed by law.[32] The Appendix to the ESC even contained an Article 1, § 2 according to which: 'This provision shall not be interpreted as prohibiting or authorising any union security clause or practice.' Pursuant to this provision, the Committee of Independent Experts considered that Article 5 did not provide guidance on the legitimacy of union security clauses or practices. In line with the ILO monitoring bodies, only a form of compulsory unionism imposed by law was incompatible with Article 5 of the Charter.[33]

The ECtHR did not subscribe to the decisions of the ILO and ESC monitoring bodies. Although a general rule protecting negative freedom was also deliberately omitted from Article 11 of the Convention, the Court considered that 'it does not follow [from such an omission] that the negative aspect of a person's freedom of association falls completely outside the ambit of Article 11' (§ 52). Like the Commission,[34] the ECtHR recognised negative freedom of association, despite the fact that the preparatory works explicitly mention that it was 'undesirable' to introduce negative freedom of association into the Convention 'on account to the difficulties raised by the "closed shop system" in certain countries'.[35] In the absence of any defence on § 2 of Article 11 by the British Conservative government, the Court held that there had been a violation as no balance was achieved which ensured the fair and proper treatment of minorities and avoided any abuse of dominant position by the trade unions.

The Court attached high value to the consequences of the closed shop—loss of employment and livelihood—and the political objections of the workers against trade union membership. It regarded the protection of personal opinion afforded by Articles 9 and 10 in the shape of freedom of thought, conscience and religion and of freedom of expression as one of the purposes of freedom of association, guaranteed by Article 11. Scholars agree with the Court that to a great extent, Article 11 represents an extension and expansion of the rights to freedom of thought, conscience and religion under Article 9 and the right to freedom of expression under Article 10.[36] Therefore, the personal autonomy protected by Articles 9 and 10 could only be effectively secured if Article 11 was interpreted so that it also included the negative freedom of association. In this view, to be included in an association against one's real will constitutes a far-reaching interference with personal autonomy.[37] The practical implication is that if the opposition to join a particular trade union is

[32] Bureau International du Travail, *Etude d'ensemble*, pp 47–49, nos 100 and 205; and International Labour Office, *Freedom of Association Digest*, p 77, nos 365 and 366.
[33] CoE, European Social Charter, Committee of Independent Experts, *Conclusions I*, 1970.
[34] EComHR, Report of 14 December 1979, *Young, James and Webster* (n 11).
[35] Report of 19 June 1950 of the Conference of Senior Officials, Collected Edition of the 'Travaux Préparatoires', 1977, vol IV, p 262.
[36] Gomein, Harris and Zwaak (n 2) 301.
[37] Tomuschat (n 20) 502.

connected to the political views of the organisation, this will increase the chances that a closed-shop agreement is contrary to Article 11.[38]

However, the judgment reveals the existence of major differences between the judges of the Court, with 11 of the 22 judges deeming it necessary to formulate a vigorous concurring or dissenting opinion. The three Scandinavian judges[39] wrote a common dissenting opinion in which they, on account of the preparatory works of the ECHR and the ILO practice, denied the existence of a negative freedom of association. In their view, union security arrangements and the practice of the 'closed shop' were neither prohibited nor authorised by Article 11 of the Convention. In their concurring opinion, seven other judges[40] argued that, notwithstanding the preparatory works, the negative aspect of freedom of association was necessarily complementary to, a correlative of and inseparable from its positive aspect. They also regretted that the Court justified the refusal to join an association by considerations, connected with freedom of thought, of conscience or of religion, or with freedom of expression, and took into consideration the consequences of the closed shop to determine the degree of compulsion. One judge,[41] although concurring, observed that the Court's phrasing might give the impression that trade union freedom amounts to no more than a general and individualistic concept of freedom of association, which was in his view not the case.

Due to these differences, the Court did not reject the assumption that 'Article 11 does not guarantee the negative aspect of that freedom on the same footing as the positive aspect' (§ 55). As only a form of such compulsion which, in the circumstances of the case, strikes at the very substance of the freedom of association guaranteed by Article 11 constituted an interference, the option was left open that other forms of compulsion to join a particular trade union could be in line with the Convention. The Court did not elaborate upon the issue, though the Commission did state that: 'The situation might be different where the worker is entering into a contract of employment with an enterprise where a closed shop agreement already exists. In such a case it might perhaps be said that he has consented to join a specific union when taking up employment although there might be elements of compulsion even in those situations' (§ 165). A publication of the Council of Europe of 1996 explains the judgment in the same way: 'As noted above, the Court in the *Young, James and Webster* case did not find it necessary to review the legitimacy of such systems, but limited their review to the narrower issue of continued employment on the introduction of a closed shop system where none had existed before.'[42] As the Court—as well as the European Committee of Social Rights (ECSR)—only distinguishes between closed shops imposed before and during employment, such a closed shop will be regarded as a post-entry closed shop. From a British point of view, however, a pre-entry closed shop would consist of an obligation to become

---

[38] JA Jensen, 'Constitutional Law/Droit Constitutionnel—Denmark/Danemark', (2006) 18(2) *European Review of Public Law / Revue Européenne de Droit Public* 791.

[39] Sørensen, Thór Vilhjálmsson and Lagergren.

[40] Ganshof van der Meersch, Bindschedler-Robert, Liesch, Gölcüklü, Matscher, Pinheiro Farinha and Pettiti.

[41] Evrigenis.

[42] Gomein, Harris and Zwaak (n 2) 306.

a member before being considered for employment, while a post-entry closed shop would contain an obligation to join a specific union shortly after employment.[43]

In the aftermath of *Young, James and Webster*, several complaints were lodged against the UK. In *Reid v UK*[44] a worker was dismissed for failure to comply with a union membership agreement that had entered into force after he had resigned from trade union membership on account of his total dissatisfaction with the union's overall policies. In *Eaton and others v UK*[45] all of the applicants' employment contracts were terminated due to their refusal to join one of the 11 unions, as required by a post-entry union membership agreement, although they indicated that they had no objection to unions as such. In *Conroy v UK*[46] a worker was dismissed on the basis of a closed-shop agreement after his expulsion from the trade union as a result of his accusations against the union (he had distributed pamphlets alleging financial irregularities and breaches of union rules by branch officers of the union). None of these cases resulted in a decision of the Commission or a judgment of the Court, with the UK preferring to negotiate a friendly settlement with the applicants. Only *Sibson v UK*[47] was brought to court. The application of a dismissed worker was denied because he did not oppose trade union membership on account of specific convictions and would have suffered no damage if he agreed to a transfer to a nearby depot. Other distinguishing features that convinced the majority of the Commission as well as the Court to reject the claim were the fact that his livelihood was not at stake, as there was no closed-shop agreement, and that the labour contract provided for his transfer.

2.1.2 Sigurdur A Sigurjónsson—*Membership Imposed by Law*

In *Sigurdur A Sigurjónsson v Iceland*[48] the Court had to decide on the obligation to be member of a professional organisation (Frami) to attain a taxicab licence. Unlike in the previous cases, in this case the organisation was no trade union, but a professional organisation of self-employed drivers, and the mandatory membership was not the result of a collective agreement, but was imposed by law. The organisation also performed certain public functions. Nevertheless, the Court and the Commission judged that it was predominantly a private law organisation and had to be regarded as an 'association' for the purposes of Article 11.

Faced with the Icelandic defence that negative freedom of association had to be interpreted restrictively on account of the preparatory works, the Court noted that 'it did not attach decisive importance to them; rather it used them as a working hypothesis'. It also recalled that 'the Convention is a living instrument which must be interpreted in the light of present-day conditions' and surpassed its previous

---

[43] S Deakin and GS Morris, *Labour Law*, 5th edn (Oxford, Hart Publishing, 2009) 736, no 8.27.
[44] EComHR, Report of 12 October 1983, App No 9520/81, *Reid v UK*.
[45] EComHR, Report of 10 December 1984, App Nos 8476/79–8481/79, *Eaton and Others v UK*.
[46] EComHR, Report of 15 May 1986, App No 10061/82, *Conroy v UK*.
[47] ECtHR, 20 April 1993, App No 14327/88, *Sibson v UK*. See also C Pettiti, 'Le droit de ne pas s'affilier à un syndicat en droit européen' (1993) 12 *Droit Social* 999–1002.
[48] *Sigurdur A Sigurjónsson v Iceland* (n 13). See also F Dorssemont, 'The Right to Form and to Join Trade Unions for the Protection of His Interests under Article 11 ECHR' (2010) 2 *European Labour Law Journal* 191–94 and 198.

Young, James and Webster jurisprudence, now stating that 'Article 11 must be viewed as encompassing a negative right of association' (§ 35). The Court felt that this shift of opinion forced for strong arguments, seeking them, for the first time, outside its own jurisprudence. It noted a 'growing measure of common ground [that] has emerged in this area also at the international level'. Besides Article 20.2 of the UDHR, it referred to other European instruments, like Article 11.2 of the 9 December 1989 Community Charter of the Fundamental Social Rights of Workers, which provides that every employer and every worker shall have the freedom to join or not to join professional organisations or trade unions without any personal or occupational damage being thereby suffered by them, and the 24 September 1991 recommendation of the Parliamentary Assembly of the Council of Europe to insert a similar sentence into Article 5 of the 1961 ESC.[49] The Court also based its judgment on the conclusions of Committee of Independent Experts which, in response to *Young, James and Webster*, already disapproved of some closed-shop practices in certain states, including Iceland,[50] and the practice of the ILO's Freedom of Association Committee, which found union security measures imposed by law incompatible with ILO Conventions 87 and 98.[51]. Nevertheless, the Court refused to determine whether or not this negative right is to be considered on an equal footing with the positive right, arguing that it is not necessary to do so.

No significant weight was attached to the fact that, before being granted the licence, the applicant agreed to become a member. However, the Court did not yet disapprove of pre-entry closed shops, ie, the obligation to join a trade union at the time of taking up a contract of employment as opposed to the situation of a post-entry closed shop in which a similar obligation is imposed after recruitment. Whereas the post-entry closed shop was generally considered as a 'breach of implied conditions',[52] no consensus existed for the pre-entry closed shop. Because the rule that imposed the pre-entry closed shop lacked statutory basis, the applicant found himself in a post-entry closed-shop situation. The Court relied again on the loss of livelihood of the applicant and his ideological objections to membership, although it was clear that the organisation at issue was non-political. The latter makes it less likely to conciliate the closed shop with the Court's case law by the introduction of a non-political membership.[53] All judges agreed with the Court's decision and only one judge[54] repeated his objections. Because the organisation concerned was invested with some public functions, commentaries on the case suggested that the

---

[49] Parliamentary Assembly, Forty-third Ordinary Session (second part), 18–25 September 1991, Official Report of Debates, Vol II, p 502; and Texts adopted by the Assembly, Appendix to Recommendation 1168 (1991), p 5.

[50] *Conclusions XII-1*, 1988–89, pp 112–13; and Governmental Committee's 12th Report to the Committee of Ministers of 22 March 1993, paragraph 113. See also *Conclusions VII*, 1981 and *Conclusions VII*, 1984.

[51] Digest of decisions and principles of the Freedom of Association Committee, 1985, para 248.

[52] Jensen (n 38) 794.

[53] See the proposition by V Mantouvalou, 'Is There a Right Not to Be a Trade Union Member?' in C Fenwick and T Novitz (eds), *Human Rights at Work. Perspectives on Law and Regulation* (Oxford, Hart Publishing, 2010) 460.

[54] Thór Vilhjálmsson.

ban on compulsion may be limited to cases in which the association exceeds its authority to regulate and improve services.[55]

2.1.3 Sørensen and Rasmussen—*Pre-entry Closed Shop*

It was only in *Sørensen and Rasmussen v Denmark*[56] that the Court stopped distinguishing between post-entry and pre-entry closed shops. At the time, pre-entry closed shops were still regarded as lawful in some national legal orders and by the ILO. In the ILO's view, problems related to union security clauses should be resolved at national level, in conformity with national practice and the industrial relations system in each country.

In *Sørensen and Rasmussen* two workers complained about the obligation to become members of a particular trade union set as a condition for employment. They did not share the political opinions of the trade union and wanted to join another trade union. Even though this was already the fourth case on negative freedom of association, the Court introduced a new argument, stating that the notion of personal autonomy is an important principle underlying the interpretation of the Convention guarantees and must therefore be seen as an essential corollary of the individual's freedom of choice implicit in Article 11. Without mentioning it, the Court moved forward in its recognition of the negative aspect of the freedom of association. Whereas 13 years earlier, in *Sigurdur A Sigurjónsson*, the Court had refused to examine this question, it now noted that 'although it has not taken any definite stand on the question whether the negative aspect of the freedom of association should be considered on an equal footing with the positive right, it does not in principle exclude that the negative and the positive aspects should be afforded the same level of protection in certain situations' (§ 56).

According to the Court, the wide margin of appreciation which states enjoy in terms of how to secure the freedom of trade unions to protect the occupational interests of their members must be considered to be reduced where the domestic law of a state permits the conclusion of closed-shop agreements between unions and employers which run counter to the freedom of choice of the individual inherent in Article 11. The Court did acknowledge that individual interests must on occasion be subordinated to those of a group, though the chances that group interests may prevail seem small, as the Court declared that 'a balance must be achieved which ensures the fair and proper treatment of minorities and avoids any abuse of a dominant position'. Therefore, the worker who is aware that trade union membership is a condition for obtaining and retaining his employment must also be protected by Article 11, because 'individuals applying for employment often find themselves in a

---

[55] W Kearns Davis, '*Sigurjónsson v Iceland*: The European Court of Human Rights Expands the Negative Right of Association' (1995) 27(1) *Case Western Reserve Journal of International Law* 317.

[56] ECtHR, 11 January 2006, App Nos 52562/99 and 52620/99, *Sørensen and Rasmussen v Denmark*. See also Jensen (n 38) 789–97; J Cavallini, 'Les accords de monopole syndical (ou clauses de closed shop) sont contraires à la liberté d'association' (2006) 6 *La semaine juridique—Edition sociale* 24–26; N Kang-Riou, 'Vers l'interdiction des accords de monopole syndical en vertu de l'article 11 CEDH' (2006) 20 *L'Europe des Libertés* 20–21; J-P Marguenaud and J Mouly, 'Le modèle syndical danois terrassé par le droit d'association négatif' (2006) 11 *Droit Social* 1022–25; Mantouvalou (n 52) 439–62.

vulnerable situation and are only too eager to comply with the terms of employment offered' (§ 59).

Although the Court's judgment was inspired by the conclusions and decisions of the ECSR, the Court's decision was severely criticised by several of its judges. The Charter had been interpreted more widely as prohibiting without qualification both pre- and post-entry closed shops.[57] Invited by a collective complaint of the Confederation of Swedish Enterprise, the ECSR already stated its disapproval of pre-entry closed shops in 2002, saying on that occasion that clauses set out in the collective agreements which reserve employment for members of a certain union are clearly contrary to the freedom guaranteed by Article 5, as they restrict workers' free choice as to whether or not to join one or other of the existing trade unions or to set up separate organisations.[58] Obviously, not all judges found this practice of the ECSR convincing, as two judges wrote a dissenting opinion.

One of the judges[59] objected to the decision from the perspective of the freedom of contract, while the other[60] found that individual and group interests had not been balanced properly, as the individual worker's interest had been lent too much weight. Other judges emphasised the difference between the two applicants. While the Court held by 15 votes to two that there had been a violation of Article 11 of the Convention in respect of the applicant Rasmussen, only 12 judges thought there was a violation in respect of the applicant Sørensen. Three judges[61] mentioned that they saw a very clear distinction in the degree of compulsion to which the two applicants were subjected, as the applicant Sørensen did not apply for a permanent job but only wanted to be employed as a holiday relief worker and would have had no difficulties in finding another similar job. One judge[62] also refused to accept that the applicant Rasmussen, a gardener, was substantially affected by the closed-shop agreements in part of the gardening sector.

2.2 Other Negative Rights?

2.2.1 Gustafsson—*No Right Not to Enter into a Collective Agreement*

In 1996 the ECtHR had to decide on an alleged violation of an employer's negative freedom of association, when the owner of a restaurant complained about a lack of state protection against the industrial action directed at his restaurant. The collective action aimed at inducing the owner to meet the trade union's demand that he be bound by a collective agreement: either by joining an employers' organisation or by signing a substitute agreement, a common practice in Sweden where no system of universally binding collective agreements exists. The Commission agreed with the

---

[57] Gomein, Harris and Zwaak (n 2) 391.
[58] European Committee of Social Rights, Report Decision on the merits, *The Confederation of Swedish Enterprise v Sweden*, no 12/2002. See also concerning Denmark, *Conclusions XVIII-1 Volume 1*, 2006; Sweden, *Conclusions 2006 Volume 2* and Finland, *Conclusions XIII-5*, 1997.
[59] Lorenzen.
[60] Zupančič.
[61] Rozakis, Bratza and Vajić, as well as Lorenzen.
[62] Lorenzen.

applicant, but the Court did not travel the same road. In *Gustafsson v Sweden*[63] the Court accepted that 'to a degree', the enjoyment of the applicant's freedom of association might be affected by the pressure to join an employers' organisation or to sign a substitute agreement. However, only the first alternative involved membership of an association and no economic disadvantages attached to the substitute agreement compelled the applicant to opt for membership. In reality, the applicant's principal objection to the signing of a collective agreement appeared to be his disagreement with the collective-bargaining system in Sweden.

While the Court considered that Article 11 of the Convention did not guarantee a right not to enter into a collective agreement, it would not go so far as to completely exclude collective agreements from the scope of Article 11. It stated that Article 11 may well extend to treatment connected with the operation of a collective bargaining system, but only where such treatment impinges upon freedom of association. Compulsion which does not significantly affect the enjoyment of that freedom, even if it causes economic damage, cannot give rise to any positive obligation under Article 11. Having regard to the wide margin of appreciation to be accorded to the State in the area under consideration, the Court did not find that Sweden had failed to secure the applicant's rights under Article 11.[64]

On this issue, the Court seemed again divided into two camps. On one side, eight judges[65] wrote a common partly dissenting opinion. They stated that, although they agreed with the decision that there has been no violation of Article 11 of the Convention, they found Article 11 not to be applicable to the complaint made by Gustafsson, as the Court in its *Swedish Engine Drivers' Union v Sweden* judgment had held that the right to collective bargaining was not an inherent component of freedom of association under Article 11. Neither did compulsion aimed at making an employer enter into a collective agreement in itself come within the safeguard afforded by Article 11. Another group of six dissenting judges[66] gave priority to the employer invoking his negative freedom of association against the actions of the trade union to integrate him into the system of collective bargaining and collective labour agreements.

Yet, the Court's decision inspired other courts. Some 10 years later, in *Hans Werhof v Freeway Traffic Systems*,[67] the negative freedom of association was used by the Court of Justice of the European Union to refuse a dynamic interpretation of Article 3, § 1 of the Council Directive on Transfers of Undertakings.[68] The Court decided that, if the collective agreements concluded after the transfer of undertaking would be binding for the transferee, his fundamental right not to join an association

---

[63] ECtHR, 25 April 1996, App No 15573/89, *Gustafsson v Sweden*. See also J-P Marguenaud and J Mouly, 'Comment on *Gustafsson v Sweden*' (1997) 29 *Recueil Dalloz* 365–68; T Novitz, 'Negative Freedom of Association' (1997) 26 *Industrial Law Journal* 79–87.

[64] Some years later, the Swedish courts applied the jurisprudence of the ECtHR in a similar conflict, but the applicant questioned their impartiality on the basis of Article 6 of the ECHR. The ECtHR dismissed the claim in a judgment of 1 July 2003, App No 41579/98, *AB Kurt Kellermann v Sweden*.

[65] Ryssdal, Spielmann, Palm, Foighel, Pekkanen, Loizou, Makarczyk and Repik.

[66] Martens, Matscher, Walsch, Jambrek, Morenilla and Mifsud Bonnici.

[67] CJEU, 9 March 2006, C499/09, *Hans Werhof v Freeway Traffic Systems*.

[68] Council Directive 77/187/EEC of 14 February 1977 on the approximation of the laws of the Member States relating to the safeguarding of employees' rights in the event of transfers of undertakings, businesses or parts of businesses, *PB* L 61, p 26.

could be affected. Though referring to the *Gustafsson* judgment, it may be questionable whether that interpretation is in line with the judgment. The Court of Justice apparently considers the right not to enter into a collective agreement as an aspect of the negative freedom of association, whereas such a right was denied by the ECtHR. It is also worth noting that similar trade union practices as in *Gustafsson* gave rise to the *Laval*[69] decision of the Court of Justice.

However, not only employers contest trade union efforts to enforce collective agreements, although the attempts of workers seem to be even less successful. In *Englund v Sweden*[70] the application of two workers of Gustafsson was declared inadmissible by the Commission, which ruled that the collective actions had no influence on their right not to be a member of a trade union or their working conditions. In *Johansson v Sweden*[71] a worker invoked his negative freedom of association against his compulsory affiliation to a collective home insurance scheme agreed on by his trade union. As the applicant did not dispute his trade union membership, but only the trade union's competence to sign for its members binding agreements on non-work-related issues, the case was decided on the basis of the right of trade unions to draw up their own rules and to administer their own affairs. The Commission observed that when the applicant became a member of the trade union, he thereby entered into a private agreement with the trade union, which, inter alia, implied that he accepted the regulations of the trade union. His application was then declared inadmissible, as there was no indication of an abuse of a dominant position.

2.2.2 Olafsson—*Mandatory Membership Fees Imposed by Law*

In *Olafsson v Iceland*[72] the Court considered the statutory obligation to pay an 'industry charge' to an employers' organisation as a violation of Article 11, due to a lack of transparency and accountability towards non-members. Although the obligation to which the applicant was subject did not involve formal membership, the Court deemed it had an important feature in common with that of joining an association, namely that of contributing financially to the funds of the employers' organisation. Moreover, members who paid the industry charge were entitled to a reduction of their membership fees by an amount equivalent to the charge. To the Court it made no difference that the charge was not paid directly to the employers' organisation, but indirectly through the State Treasury. The amounts were relatively modest and the degree of compulsion to which the applicant was subjected may be regarded as significantly less serious than in other cases, where an applicant's refusal to join a union resulted in the loss of his employment or professional licence and as a consequence his means of livelihood. However, the Court stated that in *Sørensen and Rasmussen* much less serious consequences of a refusal to comply with the requirement to join a union have similarly been found to be capable of striking at

---

[69] HvJ, 18 December 2007, C-341/05, *Laval un Partneri v Svenska Byggnadsarbetareförbundet, Svenska Byggnadsarbetareförbundets avdelning 1, Byggettan and Svenska Elektrikerförbundet*.
[70] ECtHR, 8 April 1994, App No 15533/89, *Englund v Sweden*.
[71] EComHR, Decision of 7 May 1990, App No 13537/88, *Johansson v Sweden*.
[72] ECtHR, 27 April 2010, App No 20161/06, *Olafsson v Iceland*.

the very substance of the freedom of choice and personal autonomy inherent in the right of freedom of association protected by Article 11.

In reality, this was a new reading of *Sørensen and Rasmussen*, as in *Sørensen and Rasmussen* both workers would have lost their jobs, had they refused to be a member of a specific trade union, although one of them was just a seasonal worker. However, in their observations on *Sørensen and Rasmussen*, some scholars have already pointed out that 'the actual consequences of the interference in the interests of (especially) Sørensen is rather small, so that even if such an instance is considered to be a violation of Article 11, it seems difficult to imagine circumstances where closed shop agreements of the traditional kind could be justified'.[73] Others observed that the Court's assumption in *Sigurdur A Sigurjónsson* that 'Article 11 must be viewed as encompassing a negative right of association' could be interpreted as an intention to broaden the effect of that right beyond instances in which compulsion would render the complainant unable to practise her trade.[74]

As in *Sigurdur A Sigurjónsson*, the severity of the Court's approach may be partly explained by the fact that the obligation was imposed by law. Whereas the duty of payment of 'monitoring fees' in the similar *Evaldsson* case,[75] which was surprisingly decided on the basis of Article 1 of the First Additional Protocol to the Convention, had been imposed under a collective labour agreement, the obligation n the present case was imposed by statute, which meant for the Court that the posi- on adopted in the former case could be applied with even greater force. The Court pears to follow the ILO where it objects to mandatory contributions imposed by . However, the position of the Freedom of Association Committee seems to be ·e subtle: when a law imposes a contribution on all workers, members and non- bers, for the benefit of a majority trade union, this is in conformity with the Conventions.[76]

re likely, the Court was inspired by the 2008 *Digest* of the ECSR, which sed the view that 'to secure the negative freedom of association, domestic law learly prohibit all pre-entry or post-entry closed shop clauses and all union clauses (automatic deductions from the wages of all workers, whether embers or not, to finance the trade union acting within the company)'.[77] ly enough, the ECSR had some years earlier tolerated the deduction of tage of each worker's wage to finance the trade union's activity of wage g, the so-called 'monitoring fees', as long as the fees were used for this nd not to finance activities other than wage monitoring. As opposed to R, the Committee stated on that occasion that there was no interference eedom of a worker to join a trade union as the payment of the fee did not lly lead to membership and was not required of members of other trade

ed
X.
tes
tee
by
t a
ade

38) 794.
vis (n 54) 317.
February 2007, App No 75252/01, *Evaldsson and Others v Sweden*. See also the contri-
1 of the First Additional Protocol and the comment on the judgment by F Dorssemont
uropean Human Rights Cases 474–77.
rnational du Travail, *Etude d'ensemble*, pp 47–49, nos 102 and 103; and International
eedom of Association Digest, p 76, no 363.
Europe, *Digest of the Case Law of the European Committee of Social Rights*,
, p 50.

n of
04.

unions. Because the Committee was unable to verify the use of the monitoring fees, it was left to the national courts to decide the matter.[78]

Three decades earlier, the Commission was confronted with a similar case in which it came to an utterly different solution. In *X v The Netherlands*[79] the applicants alleged that the payment of the tax levied by a public law body, the 'Produktschap voor Siergewassen' (PVS), amounted to a compulsory contribution to a private law organisation and implied de facto membership. They maintained that only a small percentage of the proceeds of the tax actually went to the PVS, but that the greater part favoured private law organisations, namely two producers' unions. The solution given to this case by the Commission contrasts with *Olafsson* in two respects. The Commission first observed that, when examining the applicants' complaints, it had to take account of the fact that the PVS and the private law organisations set up around this public law body form part of the economic organisation of the respondent state, whereas in *Olafsson*, like in *Sigurdur A Sigurjónsson*, the public law assignments of the private law association were minimised . Secondly and, more importantly, the Commission considered that it did not follow from the fact that a part of the proceeds of the tax levied by the PVS benefited a given association that there is any de facto obligation to join this association by virtue of the fact that payment of the tax amounts to a contribution to the association. In *Olafsson* the mere payment of a contribution-like charge was considered an essential aspect of membership, so it was not even necessary to analyse whether this charge compelled non-members de facto to join the association.

3 THE RIGHT FOR TRADE UNIONS TO CHOOSE THEIR MEMBERS

When it comes to the internal organisation of the trade unions, Article 11, lik Article 5 of the ESC, is more general than ILO Convention 87. In its case law th ECtHR and the Commission were able to refine and concretise these principle inspired to a large extent by the ILO Convention and the reports of the Freedom Association Committee.

3.1 *Cheall* and *NALGO*—Breach of Trade Union Rules

In *Cheall v UK*[80] the applicant, branch secretary of the trade union ACTS, resig from that trade union and applied for membership of another union, AP Because APEX accepted his membership without observing the 'TUC Disp Principles and Procedures' (the 'Bridlington principles'), the Disputes Comm obliged APEX to exclude the applicant. The applicant challenged his expulsio a civil action, but without success. Before the Commission, he complained abc lack of protection by the British government against the measures taken by the t

[78] European Committee of Social Rights, Report Decision on the merits, *The Confederati Swedish Enterprise v Sweden*, no 12/2002 and with regard to Romania, *Conclusions* 2002 and 2(
[79] EComHR, Decision of 1 March 1983, Application 9926/82, *X v The Netherlands*.
[80] EComHR, Decision of 13 May 1985, App No 10550/83, *Cheal v UK*.

union. The Commission, however, inspired by the ILO Conventions, noted that the right to join a union 'for the protection of his interests' cannot be interpreted as conferring a general right to join the union of one's choice irrespective of the rules of the union, as unions must remain free to decide, in accordance with union rules, questions concerning admission to and expulsion from the union. Indeed, Article 3 of ILO Convention 87 grants workers' and employers' organisations the right to draw up their constitutions and rules, to elect their representatives in full freedom, to organise their administration and activities and to formulate their programmes, while Article 2 makes the right to join an organisation subject only to the rules of the organisation concerned.[81]

For the Freedom of Association Committee, the only limitation on the rights set out in Article 3 of ILO Convention 87 which might possibly be acceptable should aim solely at ensuring respect for democratic rules within the trade union movement.[82] Nonetheless, in order for the right to join a union to be effective, the Commission required the state to protect the individual against any abuse of a dominant position by trade unions. Such abuse might occur, for example, where exclusion or expulsion was not in accordance with union rules or where the rules were wholly unreasonable or arbitrary, or where the consequences of exclusion or expulsion resulted in exceptional hardship such as job loss because of a closed shop, a criterion not used by the ILO. According to Tomuchat, it appears logical to review exclusion or expulsion from a trade union only when the state itself makes membership in such a group a requirement under its legislation—as did the closed-shop system of the UK.[83] In this case the applicant's expulsion was in accordance with the APEX rules, which could not be regarded as unreasonable, and the applicant's expulsion from APEX did not involve the loss of his job because of a closed shop. The Commission concluded that the expulsion of the applicant from APEX was to be seen as the act of a private body in the exercise of its Convention rights under Article 11, which cannot engage the responsibility of the respondent government.

In a second decision, *National and Local Government Officers Association (NALGO) v UK*,[84] the trade union NALGO opposed a prohibition in British law which prevented the expelling of members for crossing picket lines during an official strike. The Commission recalled that trade unions have the right to expel members who do not comply with their rules, but in taking a decision to expel, full weight must be given to the rights of the person whose expulsion is under consideration as well as to those of other members of the association, and the principle of proportionality must be observed. However, the state must protect an individual against abuse of a dominant position by trade unions. The statutory restriction on union freedom in the present case was 'prescribed by law' and had the aim of protecting the 'rights and freedoms of others', namely the individual members. Given the 'margin of appreciation' allowed to states in achieving this, the Commission felt that restriction could be considered 'necessary in a democratic society' within the

reau International du Travail, *Etude d'ensemble*, p 39, no 79.
rnational Labour Office, *Freedom of Association Digest*, no 463.
uschat (n 20) 507.
nHR, Decision of 1 September 1993, App No 21386/93, *National and Local Government sociation (NALGO) v UK*.

meaning of Article 11 of the Convention. The fact that the legislation did not apply to other sectors of society, such as voluntary organisations, can be justified by the particular role played by trade unions in the employment field. Because they are not in the same position as other associations and organisations, there is no discrimination within the meaning of Article 14 of the Convention.

The *NALGO* case was undoubtedly not a shining example, as the ECSR held for years that the restrictions imposed on the right of trade unions to expel members in the UK were not in conformity with the concurrent Article 5 of the Charter. The ECSR emphasised that trade unions are entitled to choose their own members and representatives, and that excessive limits on the reasons for which a trade union may take disciplinary action against a member constitute an unwarranted interference in the autonomy of trade unions inherent in Article 5.[85] Legislation prohibiting a trade union from disciplining members who refuse to take part in lawful strikes or from indemnifying a member for a penalty imposed by law for taking part in a strike is an interference with the autonomy of trade unions in breach of Article 5.[86] Yet, it was only in 2007 that a new case in this field was brought before the ECtHR.

3.2 *Associated Society of Locomotive Engineers and Fireman*—Membership of a Inimical Political Party

In *Associated Society of Locomotive Engineers and Fireman (ASLEF) v UK*[87] British legislation was again contested by a trade union. As British legislation prohibited trade unions from expelling members on the basis of their membership of a political party, it prevented ASLEF from expelling one of its members due to his membership of the British National Party, a political party which advocated views inimical to its own.

The Court referred to Articles 3 and 5 of ILO Convention 87 on the right of trade unions to draw up their own rules and to administer their own affairs. It considered the right to expel members as the counterpart of the negative freedom of association. It stated that as 'an employee or worker should be free to join, or not join a trade union without being sanctioned or subject to, so should the trade union be equally free to choose its members'. As associations are formed by people, who, espousing particular values or ideals, intend to pursue common goals, the right to join a union cannot be interpreted as conferring a general right to join the union of one's choice, irrespective of the rules of the union. It would run counter to the very effectiveness of the freedom at stake if trade unions had no control over their membership. In the

---

[85] Council of Europe (n 76) 49 and 50–51. See also the remarks of the Committee with regard to the application of Article 5 by the UK: European Committee of Social Rights, *Conclusions XIII-3, 1995, Conclusions XIV-1 Vol 2, 1998, Conclusions XV-1 Vol 2, 2000, Conclusions XVI-1 Vol 2, 2003, Conclusions XVII-1, 2004* and *Conclusions XVIII-1 Vol 2, 2006.*

[86] *Conclusions* XII-1, 115.

[87] *Associated Society of Locomotive Engineers and Fireman (ASLEF) v UK* (n 15). See also D Mead 'To BNP or Not to BNP: Union Expulsion on Ground of Political Activity—A Commentary on *ASLEF Lee*' (2004) 33 *Industrial Law Journal* 267–77; J Hendy and KD Ewing, 'Trade Unions, Human Rights and the BNP' (2005) 34 *Industrial Law Journal* 197–216; K Ewing, 'The Implications of the ASLEF Case' (2007) 36(4) *Industrial Law Journal* 425–45.

exercise of their rights under Article 11, § 1, unions must remain free to decide, in accordance with union rules, questions concerning admission and expulsion.

However, the Court added that 'this basic premise only holds good where the association or trade union is a private and independent body, and is not, for example, through receipt of public funds or through the fulfilment of public duties imposed upon it, acting in a wider context, such as assisting the state in securing the enjoyment of rights and freedoms, where other considerations may well come into play or organisational frameworks for trades or professions where membership may well be compulsory or highly regulated, e.g. public law institutions which are not covered by Article 11 § 1 at all' (§ 40). Unfortunately, the significance of this obiter dictum remains uncertain.[88] As the trade union's right to choose its members is considered as the counterpart of the worker's freedom not to join, the Court's statement may be interpreted as an obligation—in certain situations—for trade unions practising closed shops to take up members. Such a requirement would be in line with the opinion of the ILO Freedom of Association Committee that, where union security arrangements require membership of a given organisation as a condition of employment, no unreasonable conditions may be imposed upon persons seeking such membership.[89] The Court, however, only refers to the public duty or role conferred on the trade union or its state funding. The only case law on that issue relates to public law institutions or private organisations performing public duties. While the first are considered not to be covered by Article 11,[90] the latter are generally qualified as 'plain' associations. In *Sigurdur A Sigurjónsson*, although Frami was conferred with certain public duties, no other considerations or requirements to fulfil any other wider purposes were introduced.

Moreover, in its older case law, the Court already applied another criterion to determine the legitimacy of an expulsion. This criterion is still been used. As in the *Cheall* case, the Court stressed that the State must nonetheless protect the individual against any abuse of a dominant position by trade unions. Such abuse might occur, for example, where exclusion or expulsion from a trade union was not in accordance with union rules or where the rules were wholly unreasonable or arbitrary, where the consequences of exclusion or expulsion resulted in exceptional hardship. When there is a conflict between differing Convention rights, the State enjoys a certain margin of appreciation in determining a fair and proper balance. In the absence of any identifiable hardship suffered by the expelled member (no impingement in any significant way on his exercise of freedom of expression or lawful trade union activities, no job lost, no deterioration of his conditions of employment) or abusive and unreasonable conduct by the applicant, the Court concluded that a balance had not been properly struck and that there had been a violation of Article 11 of the Convention.

Paradoxically, until recently, the absence of identifiable hardship was not an element of consideration in the Court's case law relating to dismissal of extreme

interpretation of this obiter dictum, see F Dorssemont, 'Le droit des syndicats d'expulser des adhérents en raison de leurs convictions politiques' (2008) 74 *Revue trimestrielle des droits de l'homme*

International Labour Office, *Freedom of Association Digest*, p 77, nos 365 and 368.

Harris and Zwaak (n 2) 307.

right activists. In *Van der Heijden v The Netherlands*[91] an employee of the Limburg Immigration Foundation was dismissed because of his membership of the 'Centrumpartij', a party with a hostile attitude to the presence of workers from Surinam and other foreign countries in the Netherlands. The Commission accepted that the applicant's political activities were incompatible with the aims of the Foundation and that the employer could reasonably take account of the adverse effects that this political activities might have on the Foundation's reputation, particularly in the eyes of the immigrants whose interests it sought to promote. For these reasons, the Commission considered that the dismissal was a measure necessary in a democratic society to protect the rights of others, although the applicant remained unemployed after his dismissal. However, in a 2012 judgment, *Redfearn v UK*,[92] the Court adopted a more rigorous approach towards unfair dismissal.[93] In the case of a driver dismissed by his employer after his election as a local councillor for the British National Party, the Court took the view that dismissal on the ground of political opinion or affiliation can be allowed, but only if the domestic courts or tribunals are able to assess whether or not, in the circumstances of the particular case, the interests of the employer should prevail over the employee's rights, as the consequences of his dismissal were considered to be serious.

4 THE RIGHT FOR WORKERS TO ORGANISE

Although trade unions and their members brought cases before the ECtHR in the 1970s, such as *National Union of Belgian Police*,[94] *Swedish Engine Drivers' Union*[95] and *Schmidt and Dahlström*,[96] the protection against anti-union discrimination only appears in the Court's jurisprudence in 2002. The Court also ruled on incentives for non-membership, while, with regard to negative freedom of association, the validity of incentives for membership has remained unquestioned.

4.1 *Wilson*—Financial Incentives for Non-membership

It was only in 2002 that the ECtHR pronounced judgment on a case of anti-union discrimination, although this terminology was not yet used by the Court. However, it was not the very first case, as in the past similar cases were handled by the Commission. In the 1 February 1971 decision in *X v Ireland*, the Commission held that anti-trade-union activities in the form of dismissing a shop steward could amount to a breach of Article 11, reversing a decision of 18 September 196 where it drew a distinction between the right to set up an association and the rig to be associated with its administration, management or direction, stating th such supporting rights were not covered by the 'traditional notion of freedom

---

[91] EComHR, Decision of 8 March 1985, App No 11002/84, *Van der Heijden v The Netherlands*
[92] ECtHR, 6 November 2012, App No 47335/06, *Redfearn v UK*.
[93] See section 4.2.
[94] *National Union of Belgian Police v Belgium* (n 10).
[95] *Swedish Engine Drivers' Union v Sweden* (n 10).
[96] ECtHR, 6 February 1976, App No 5589/72, *Schmidt and Dahlström v Sweden*.

association'.[97] Inspired by ILO Convention 87, the Commission recognised that such interference could, in certain circumstances, seriously restrict or impede the lawful exercise of the freedom of association in relation to trade unions which the article aims at securing, and incurs the responsibility of the state for failure to ensure the effective enjoyment of the right protected. In the end, no violation was established, as the applicant could have brought an action against his former employer before the competent courts at the national level. In 2001 an application of a trade union representative was declared inadmissible by the Court,[98] as Article 11 was not securing any particular treatment of trade union members by the State, such as the right to enjoy certain benefits in matters of remuneration. Such benefits were not indispensable to the effective enjoyment of trade union freedom and did not constitute an element necessarily inherent to a right guaranteed by the Convention.

In *Wilson, National Union of Journalists and Others v UK*,[99] British trade unions and their members opposed the British legislation which permitted employers to undermine collective bargaining by offering more favourable conditions of employment to employees agreeing not to be represented by a trade union. Although the Court considered that Article 11 did not imply an obligation to recognise trade unions for collective bargaining purposes, the legislation had to protect the right of workers to be represented by a trade union. The Court emphasised that the freedom of employees to instruct or permit the union to make representations to their employer or to take action on their behalf constitutes an essential feature of union membership. Consequently, the State had to ensure that trade union members were not prevented or restrained from using their union to represent them in their relations with their employers. By permitting employers to use financial incentives to induce employees to surrender important union rights, the UK failed in its positive obligation to secure the enjoyment of the rights under Article 11 of the Convention.

The Court's decision related to the position of the ILO Freedom of Association Committee which had already considered the British legislation incompatible with the provisions of Convention 98.[100] The Committee stated that when, in the course of collective bargaining with the trade union, the employer offers better working conditions to non-unionised workers under individual agreements, there is a serious risk that this might undermine the negotiating capacity of the trade union and give rise to discriminatory situations in favour of the non-unionised staff; furthermore, it might encourage unionised workers to withdraw from the union.[101] The ECSR shared the same views.[102]

---

[97] Tomuschat (n 20) 498.

[98] ECtHR, 21 June 2001, App No 57442/00, *Sanchez Navajas v Spain*.

[99] ECtHR, 2 July 2002, App Nos 30668/96, 30671/96 and 30678/96, *Wilson, National Union of Journalists and Others v UK*.

[100] Committee on Freedom of Association, Case no 1852, *Trade Union Congress v UK*, Report no 309, March 1998; Case no 1730, Report no 294, June 1994; Case no 1618, Report no 287, June 1993.

[101] International Labour Office, *Freedom of Association Digest*, pp 158 and 211, nos 787, 1054 and 1058.

[102] European Committee of Social Rights, *Conclusions XIII-3*, 1996, *Conclusions XVI-1 Vol 2*, 2003, *Conclusions XVII-1*, 2004 and *Conclusions XVIII-1 Vol 2*, 2006.

4.2 *Danilenkov*—Anti-union Discrimination and Sanction

In *Danilenkov and Others v Russia*,[103] the Court had to evaluate a case of anti-union discrimination, also previously submitted to the ILO Freedom of Association Committee.[104] Various techniques had been used by the Kaliningrad seaport company to encourage employees to relinquish their trade union membership, including their reassignment to special work teams with limited opportunities, dismissals subsequently found to be unlawful by the courts, reductions in earnings, disciplinary sanctions and refusals to reinstate employees following court judgments. As a result, membership of the trade union, the Dockers' Union of Russia (DUR), shrank dramatically. DUR instituted both criminal and civil procedures, but the discriminatory acts remained unsanctioned. The Court considered that the Russian State had failed to fulfil its positive obligations to adopt effective and clear judicial protection against discrimination on the ground of trade union membership. The Court found it crucially important that individuals affected by discriminatory treatment should be provided with an opportunity to challenge it and should have the right to take legal action to obtain damages and other relief. Therefore, Russia was required under Articles 11 and 14 of the Convention to set up a judicial system that ensures real and effective protection against anti-union discrimination.

The influence of the precedents of the ILO Freedom of Association Committee and the ECSR can be seen in the Court's decision. For the ILO, anti-union discrimination involves one of the most serious violations of freedom of association, as it may jeopardise the very existence of trade unions.[105] Protection against acts of anti-union discrimination should cover not only hiring and dismissal, but also any discriminatory measures during employment, in particular transfers, downgrading and other acts that are prejudicial to the worker.[106] The *Digest* of the ECSR reflects the same principles, stating that domestic law must guarantee the right of workers to join a trade union and include effective punishments and remedies where this right is not respected. Trade union members must be protected from any harmful consequence that their trade union membership or activities may have on their employment, particularly any form of reprisal or discrimination in the areas of recruitment, dismissal or promotion because they belong to a trade union or engage in trade union activities. Where such discrimination occurs, domestic law must make provision for compensation that is adequate and proportionate to the harm suffered by the victim.[107] Unlike the ECSR, the ILO Freedom of Association

---

[103] ECtHR, 30 July 2009, App No 67336/01, *Danilenkov and Others v Russia*.

[104] Committee on Freedom of Association, Case no 2199, *Russian Labour Confederation (KTR) v Russian Federation*, Report no 331.

[105] International Labour Office, *Freedom of Association Digest*, p 155, no 769.

[106] International Labour Office, *Freedom of Association Digest*, p 157, no 781.

[107] Council of Europe (n 76) 50. See also the remarks of the Committee with regard to the application of Article 5 by the UK: European Committee of Social Rights, *Conclusions XIII-3*, 1996, *Conclusions XVI-1 Vol 2*, 2003, *Conclusions XVII-1*, 2004 and *Conclusions XVIII-1 Vol 2*, 2006; and with regard to Belgium, *Conclusions XVII-1*, 2004.

Committee expresses a clear preference for the reinstatement of the worker in his previous functions.[108]

Though the ECtHR has not yet ruled on the reinstatement of dismissed trade union members, recent case law on 'ordinary' dismissed workers may be offers some guidance. In *Ciocan and Others v Romania*,[109] the Court dealt with the State's responsibility for the non-execution of a final judgment which ordered the employer to reinstate the wrongfully dismissed workers in their previous positions. It considered that the authorities did not take all the measures which could reasonably expected from them. By their passivity, they deprived the applicants' right of access to justice of every useful effect for years, resulting in a violation of Article 6 of the Convention. In *Oleksandr Volkov v Ukraine*,[110] an unlawfully dismissed judge could rely on Article 8 of the Convention to be reinstated. Furthermore, inspired by Article 30 of the European Union Charter of Fundamental Rights and Article 24 of the ESC, the Court gradually extended protection against unfair dismissal. According to *KMC v Hungary*,[111] Article 6 of the Convention also implied a right for the worker to know the reasons for his dismissal, this information being required for a potential claim on account of unfair dismissal.

5 CONCLUSION

Although the ECtHR—as well as the Commission—could only rely on a relatively modest article, over the years a comprehensive case law was developed. However, most of the case law did benefit individuals more than trade unions. The Court's individualist approach has encouraged trade union opponents to bring their cases before the Court, while discouraging trade unions from doing the same. Besides, trade unions could present their cases to specialised international bodies, like the ILO Freedom of Association Committee and the ECSR. The existence of specialised international bodies may explain the Court's reluctance to intervene in trade union rights issues, especially in the earlier years. Scholars disapprove of the Court's only minimal protection of social and labour rights before 2002, as the Court left a wide marge of appreciation to the national governments and obviously considered rights protected by the ESC to fall outside the material scope of the Convention.[112]

The Court's extensive protection of the negative right not to organise while the positive right to organise was limited to a right of the individual members that the trade union should be heard has been severely criticised over the years.[113] The Court has been blamed for misjudging the importance of trade unions and trade union

---

[108] Bureau International du Travail, *Etude d'ensemble*, pp 105–06, nos 219–21; and International Labour Office, *Freedom of Association Digest*, p 167, no 837–53. See also Committee on Freedom of Association in Case no 2265, *Swiss Federation of Trade Unions (USS) v Switzerland*, Rapport nr 335, Vol LXXXVII, 2004, Series B, No 3, Rapport nr 343, Vol LXXXVIX, 2006, Series B, No 3.

[109] ECtHR, 9 December 2008, App No 6580/03, *Ciocan and Others v Romania*.

[110] ECtHR, 9 January 2013, App No 21722/11, *Oleksandr Volkov v Ukraine*.

[111] ECtHR, 10 July 2012, App No 19554/11, *KMC v Hungary*.

[112] Mantouvalou (n 52) 441–43.

[113] Novitz (n 62) 87.

rights at a time in which the influence of trade unions was already decreasing.[114] The real problem, according to the observers, was the protection of the right to organise, not the protection of those who wanted to dissociate from trade union action.[115] A right not to organise would only contribute to the danger of individuals frustrating the action of trade unions designed to protect their interests. Other annotators stress the fact that the Court, like the Court of Justice of the European Union in *Viking* and *Laval*, appears to compare trade unions with states. However, the conflict between the individual and the collective interest is not identical to the individual/state relationship. Trade unions are more vulnerable than states, whose operation cannot be endangered by individuals.[116] Recently, on account of the increase in case law following the expansion of the Council of Europe, the Court has been confronted with more case law on Article 11, resulting in a clearer insight into trade union rights. This evolution goes hand in hand with a more profound interest in the decisions of the other international bodies, and in particular an aspiration to harmonise its view with that of the ECSR.[117] As a consequence, the Court's jurisprudence has become more balanced, which may influence the case law of the Court of Justice of the European Union.

---

[114] IE Koch, *Human Rights as Indivisible Rights. The Protection of Socio-Economic Demands under the European Convention on Human Rights* (Leiden, Martinus Nijhoff Publishers, 2009) 233 and 241.
[115] O'Higgins (n 27) 26.
[116] Clapman (n 25) 197.
[117] Mantouvalou (n 52) 450–52.

12

Article 11 ECHR: The Right to Bargain Collectively under Article 11 ECHR

ANTOINE JACOBS

1 INTRODUCTION

FOR A NUMBER of decades now, the right to bargain collectively has been explicitly recognised as a fundamental right in a number of international documents. It first appeared explicitly in Convention No 98 of the International Labour Organization (ILO), which was adopted in 1949. Article 4 of this Convention sets forth that measures appropriate to national conditions shall be taken, where necessary, to encourage and promote the full development and utilisation of machinery for voluntary negotiation between employers or employers' organisations and workers' organisations with a view to the regulation of terms and conditions of employment by means of collective bargaining.

ILO Convention No 151 extended this right to the public service, with its Article 7 stating that measures appropriate to national conditions shall be taken, where necessary, to encourage and promote the full development and utilisation of machinery for negotiation of terms and conditions of employment between the public authorities concerned and public employees' organisations, or of such other methods as will allow representatives of public employees to participate in the determination of these matters.

ILO Convention No 154 finally gives a definition of collective bargaining (Art 2) and a summary of measures that the States should consider to promote collective bargaining (Art 5).

In Europe it was the 1961 European Social Charter (ESC) of the Council of Europe (CoE) which for the first time explicitly provided that all workers and employers have the right to collective bargaining (Article 6 ESC). It specifies that 'with a view to ensuring the effective exercise of the right to bargain collectively the Contracting Parties undertake (1) to promote joint consultation between workers and employers and (2) to promote, where necessary and appropriately, machinery for voluntary negotiations between employers or employers' organisations and workers' organisations, with a view to the regulation of terms and conditions of employment by means of collective agreements'.

Finally, the beginning of this century saw the right to bargain collectively also being recognised by the European Union (EU) in its Charter of Fundamental Rights.

The explicit mention of the right to bargain collectively in these various sources of international law provokes the question of why such an important document as the CoE's European Convention on Human Rights (ECHR), adopted in 1950, does not explicitly cover the right to bargain collectively, with its Article 11 merely mentioning 'the right to form and join trade unions for the protection of his interests'. However, the scope of this right, as shown in the first decades of European Court of Human Rights (ECtHR) case law, was rather limited, as I shall explain in the next section of this contribution. Then, all of a sudden, the ECtHR in 2008 pronounced its verdict in the *Demir and Baykara* case,[1] declaring that Article 11 included 'the right to bargain collectively'. The intention of this contribution is to research the potential impact of this ruling, highlighting the most important problems of the right to bargain collectively as they have emerged from the national law in this field in the CoE Member States, and taking into account the results of the monitoring activities of the specialised bodies of the ILO and the Council of Europe.

2 HISTORICAL DEVELOPMENT

Does Article 11 ECHR really embrace the right to bargain collectively? If one had asked me this question a few years ago, I would have answered: according to the ECtHR, no. It is clear that the text of Article 11 does not explicitly mention a right to bargain collectively, as emphasised by the ECtHR since the 1970s. The very comparable cases *National Union of Belgian Police*[2] and *Swedish Engine Drivers' Union*[3] were lodged by unions with a substantial membership, but these unions were nevertheless excluded from taking part in the process of collective bargaining in their respective sectors. They considered this as a violation of the collective (human) right of their members under Article 11 ECHR, as it greatly restricted a union's field of action. The ECtHR, however, took the view that paragraph 1 of Article 11 afforded members of a trade union a right to protect their interests and that the trade union should be heard, but left it up to each State to decide on the means to be used to this end. Certainly, a right to bargain collectively and to enter into collective agreements might be one of the ways by which trade unions could be enabled to protect their members' interests. However, this right in no way constituted an inherent element of Article 11 ECHR.

It is clear that, in a free democratic society, unions have various possibilities to make themselves heard. They (themselves or via their members) can issue press releases, stage demonstrations, publish news magazines, petition parliaments, assist their members in court, use the social media, influence elections, and sit on advisory councils, administrative bodies and industrial courts. The right to bargain collectively may be added to this list, though, as according to the ECtHR it was not an indispensable right and was therefore not protected under Article 11 ECHR.

---

[1] ECtHR, 12 November 2008, *Demir and Baykara v Turkey*, App No 34503/97.
[2] *National Union of Belgian Police v Belgium* (1975) 1 EHRR 578.
[3] *Swedish Engine Drivers' Union v Sweden* (1975) 1 EHRR 617.

This line of reasoning was maintained in ECtHR case law until a few years ago. Its decisions in the cases *Gustafsson, Wilson* and *National Union of Journalists and others* were undoubtedly rather positive with regard to trade union involvement in the process of collective bargaining. In *Gustafsson* the ECtHR upheld the Swedish system of unions putting pressure on non-affiliated employers to apply the collective agreement for the sector, if necessary by means of strikes and boycotts.

In *Wilson* (2002) the ECtHR considered the British legal situation of that time, which allowed employers to effectively undermine and frustrate a trade union's ability to protect its members' interests by collective bargaining, as a violation of Article 11 ECHR. In doing so, it recognised the right to bargain collectively as an important but not indispensable right protected by Article 11 ECHR.

However, this line was completely upturned by the decision of the ECtHR Grand Chamber in the *Demir and Baykara* case. In this case a Turkish trade union, active in the civil service, was given access to the bargaining table and had effectively concluded a collective agreement with the municipality of Ganziatep. Since at that time (the mid-1990s) there was no explicit recognition of freedom of association in the Turkish public service and no legal framework for it, the Turkish courts considered the agreement to be null and void. As a consequence of this judicial intervention, public servants had to repay a wage increase granted under the collective agreement.

In this case the ECtHR Grand Chamber reconsidered its earlier jurisprudence, ruling that, having regard to the development of both international and national labour law and to the practice of the Contracting States in such matters, the right to bargain collectively with the employer had, in principle, become one of the essentials of the right to form and join trade unions for the protection of one's interests. In so reasoning, the Court found that there had been a violation of the Convention.

3 SOME REFLECTIONS AND CRITICAL REMARKS ON THE LEGAL FOUNDATIONS OF *DEMIR AND BAYKARA*

Personally I think that the Court is completely right in considering the right to collective bargaining as an indispensable aspect of the right to form and join trade unions. I already held that opinion in 1986 in my PhD, having studied this item notably with regard to the German Constitution (Grundgesetz). The German courts had already recognised such a right under Article 9(3) of the Grundgesetz, which, like Article 11 ECHR, basically only deals with the right to form trade unions. Similarly, the ILO Freedom of Association Committee (FAC) holds that the voluntary negotiation of collective agreements, and therefore the autonomy of the bargaining parties, is a fundamental aspect of the principle of freedom of association.

Mélanie Schmitt, my co-referent at the November 2011 conference which spawned this book, developed some very pertinent thoughts about the nature of the right to collective bargaining, which I include here.

The nature of the right to collective bargaining is determined by the values it embodies.

Looked at from a general perspective, the right to collective bargaining as a human right is part of what it universally means to be a human being and, as a consequence, contributes to preserving human dignity.

Following the traditional distinction, it can be seen as a 'civil and political right' upholding the value of democracy within society. The right to collective bargaining is granted both to workers and to employers and refers to the freedom or 'collective autonomy' of social partners. The State must refrain from interfering in its exercise. This approach also follows the European Social Charter (ESC, Part I, no 6) which states that 'all workers and employers have the right to bargain collectively'. Under ESC Article 6.2 (Part II) 'the Parties undertake ... to promote, where necessary and appropriate, machinery for *voluntary* negotiations between employers or employers' organisations and workers' organisations, with a view to the regulation of terms and conditions of employment by means of collective agreements'.[4]

The right to collective bargaining can also be conceived as a 'social right' providing workers and/or trade unions with a means to constrain an employer's power. In this respect it is a right to be used against an employer and his *unilateral* authority to determine the terms and conditions of employment.

It can therefore be submitted that *Demir and Baykara* reconciles the twin conceptions of the right to collective bargaining being a civil and political right and a social right. An interesting approximation can be made with the approach followed by the Canadian Supreme Court which ruled that 'the right to bargain collectively with an employer enhances the human dignity, liberty and autonomy of workers by giving them the opportunity to influence the establishment of workplace rules'.[5] It also 'permits workers to achieve a form of workplace *democracy* and to ensure the rule of law at the workplace'.[6]

In an international context, the right to collective bargaining is intended more to safeguard domestic labour law and social guarantees against economic values and international competition. The Strasbourg Court implicitly integrates this objective in *Demir and Baykara* by making reference to ILO Conventions. The social and economic objectives embraced by the right to collective bargaining relate both to fair competition between employers and to solidarity between workers, in turn contributing to restoring a certain equality within the employment relationship.

The value of solidarity is, again, incorporated in the Strasbourg Court's reasoning, though in an implicit way by the reference made to Article 28 of the EU Charter.[7]

Thus, one can conclude that *Demir and Baykara*, by reconciling the multiple conceptions of the right to collective bargaining, underlines the convergence of international and European sources. By the comparative method it applies, *Demir and Baykara* also makes it compulsory for the Contracting Parties to comply with the obligations resulting from ILO standards and the European Social Charter, as interpreted by the various committees.

Although there can be no doubt that the right to collective bargaining is an essential aspect of the power of trade unions, in international and domestic law the link between the right to free trade union organisation and the right to bargain collectively is not always established, especially when the parties at the negotiation table

---

[4] Italics by Mélanie Schmitt.
[5] Supreme Court of Canada 8 June 2007, *Health Services and Support Facilities Subsector Bargaining Association v British Columbia*, 2007 SCC 27, § 82.
[6] Ibid, § 85.
[7] Article 28 is part of the fourth chapter of the EU Charter which covers rights based on the value of solidarity. The strong link between solidarity and collective bargaining is also reflected in CJEU case law on collectively agreed pension schemes.

are not necessarily trade unions. In his PhD thesis,[8] Plessen emphasises the structure of ILO standards, cementing the right to organise separately (Convention 87) from that to collective bargaining (Convention 98) and thus demonstrating that the latter is not included in the former. At a national level, the French Constitution similarly makes a clear distinction between the right to free trade union organisation and the right to collective bargaining, as seen in paragraphs 6 and 8 of the preamble of the 1946 Constitution, incorporated in the 1958 Constitution.

The Charter of Fundamental Rights of the European Union (CFREU) distinguishes the right to free trade union organisation (Article 12) and the right to collective bargaining and action (Article 28).

It is therefore submitted that even when one may agree that the right to collective bargaining is included in the right to free trade union organisation, one has to remain humble and recognise that this is a nice outcome, but not an indispensable outcome of interpretation.

The *Demir and Baykara* decision came only a few months after the Court of Justice of the EU (CJEU) ruled on a set of cases (*Viking, Laval, Rüffert, Commission v Luxembourg*), putting severe restrictions on the right to collective bargaining (and strike) by balancing it against the economic freedoms set forth in the EU Treaties. It is thus understandable that many labour lawyers were relieved by the ECtHR's judgment in the *Demir and Baykara* case counterbalancing the CJEU jurisprudence.

The *Demir and Baykara* decision is the fruit of that kind of 'dynamic interpretation' often embraced by constitutional courts in Europe, as it enables them to continually modernise their case law: the ECtHR speaks about the '"living" nature of the Convention'.[9] In the US, many Supreme Court judges like to do the same, although another genus of constitutional lawyers, very loudly represented by Justice Antonin Scalia, abhors it.[10] They defend the hypothesis that by such dynamic interpretation, judges are trespassing upon and impeding the realm of constitutional legislatures. If constitutional texts are not sufficient to establish certain fundamental rights, they must be amended by constitutional legislatures and not by constitutional judges.

For dynamic interpretation, the sky is the limit. In the field of the fundamental right to trade union freedom, the right to collective bargaining in the sense of the rights and obligations concerning collective bargaining (in French: 'le droit de négociation collective') is easily extended to a right to collective bargaining in the sense of the entitlement to sit at the bargaining table (in French: 'le droit à la négociation collective') and to a right to free collective bargaining (free from government intervention). I shall deal with these aspects at the end of this chapter. The next aspect is the right to strike. Just a few months after *Demir and Baykara*, the ECtHR, sitting in a normal chamber and without much reasoning, recognised the right to strike in the *Enerji* case[11] (the following chapter is devoted to this). How long must we wait to see the right to employee involvement in company decision

---

[8] WGM Plessen, *Collectief onderhandelen in de zorgsector* (Deventer, Kluwer, 1996).

[9] *Demir and Baykara v Turkey* (n 1) § 68.

[10] See A Scalia, *A Matter of Interpretation; Federal Courts and the Law* (Princeton, Princeton University Press, 1997).

[11] ECtHR, 21 April 2009, (*Enerji Yapi-Yol Sen v Turkey*), App No 68959/01.

making being recognised as part and parcel of the right to trade union organisation? In his *Habilitationschrift* 'Das Grundrecht auf Mitbestimmung' written back in the 1970s,[12] Wolfgang Daubler already defended the concept that a right to industrial democracy could be derived from the German Constitution. I personally agree with the recognition of such fundamental rights, but have my doubts as to whether it is the task of courts to introduce them.

4 A FIRST EXPLORATION OF THE NEW WORLD, THOUGH NOT *TERRA INCOGNITA*

Now that the ECtHR has recognised the right to collective bargaining as inherent to the right to trade union organisation, we are faced with the task of exploring the various contours and aspects of this newly discovered land. However, unlike the discovery of America by Columbus, we are not mapping *terra incognita*. We have only to look to the national systems of labour law in the various European countries to gain a clear view on a good number of questions that may easily be put to the ECtHR now that it has recognised the right to collective bargaining as falling under Article 11.

We can also see its contours emerging when we look closer at the quasi-case law on the right to collective bargaining developed by the ILO Committee of Experts on the Application of Conventions and Recommendations (CEACR),[13] the FAC[14] and the European Committee of Social Rights (ECSR). Similarly, the decisions in the ESC collective complaints procedures may be consulted.

5 GENERAL OBSERVATION

It is submitted that the ECtHR, in its future case law on the right to collective bargaining under Article 11 ECHR, should not aim at a harmonisation of the national laws on collective bargaining. These laws often have their roots in the historical development of collective bargaining, which differs greatly from one European country to the next.[15] They are the expression of power relations which cannot easily be touched without disturbing the established balances of power in the Member States of the Council of Europe.

The EU, which in general terms is committed to 'rich cultural and linguistic diversity' (Article 3(3) Treaty on European Union (TEU)), more especially must 'take

---

[12] W Daubler, *Das Grundrecht auf Mitbestimmung* (Frankfurt, Duncker & Humblot, 1974).

[13] ILO, CEACR, Giving Globalisation a Human Face. General Survey on the Fundamental Conventions Concerning Rights at Work in the Light of the ILO Declaration on Social Justice for a Fair Globalization, 2008, Geneva, 2012 (further cited as ILO-CEACR); ILO, General Survey on the Freedom of Association and Collective Bargaining, 1994, nr 262 (Document No (ilolex): 251994G10); P Macklem, 'The Right to Bargain Collectively in International Law: Workers' Right, Human Right, International Right?' in P Alston (ed), *Labour Rights as Human Rights* (Oxford, Oxford University Press, 2005).

[14] See ILO, Digest of Decisions and Principles on the Freedom of Association Committee of the Governing Body of the ILO (further cited as: ILO, FAC Digest).

[15] A Jacobs, Collective Self-Regulation, in BA *Hepple, The Making of Labour Law in Europe* (London, Mansell, 1986) 193–241.

into account the diversity of national systems' when recognising and promoting the role of the social partners at its level (Article 152 Treaty on the Functioning of the European Union (TFEU)).

In my view, the ECtHR should therefore, in its future case law on the right to collective bargaining, take reticence as its principal guideline, leaving certain aspects of trade union rights to the discretion of national authorities.

6 THE PUBLIC SERVICE AND STATE ENTERPRISES

Let me start with where it all began in the *Demir and Baykara* case: the right of civil servants to form a trade union and engage in collective bargaining. The *Demir and Baykara* case has confirmed that the right to bargain collectively with the employer has, in principle, become one of the essential elements of the 'right to form and to join trade unions for the protection of (one's) interests', while at the same time recognising that 'lawful restrictions' on this right are allowed with respect to 'members of the administration of the State'.[16] The question arises whether this exception is not too narrow or too wide a restriction and what consequences it has for the bargaining aspirations of the civil servants covered by this restriction. Are they entitled to alternatives?

The ILO has always recognised that Convention No 98 allows exceptions to be made with regard to the armed forces and the police as well as public servants engaged in the administration of the State, ie, not all public servants may be excluded. By contrast, the FAC holds that all public service workers other than those engaged in the administration of the State should enjoy collective bargaining rights.[17] The CEACR has stated that the determination of the excluded categories is to be made on a case-by-case basis in the light of criteria relating to the prerogatives of the public authorities.[18]

Similarly, the ECSR has always recognised that certain restrictions to the right to collective bargaining may be imposed on certain categories of public servants, notably the armed forces[19] and the police.[20] It has, however, often criticised States where the categories of civil servants deprived of this right were too extensive. The same applies to employees in State enterprises. Moreover, the ECSR has for a long time taken the position that *all* public servants are entitled to participate *to a certain extent* in the process determining the regulations applicable to them.[21]

The ECSR is rather lenient towards specific limitations on the freedom of collective bargaining in the public sector, as seen in the following examples.

The Committee accepted the Polish law under which negotiations concerning the remuneration of employees in the nationalised sector have to respect budgetary

---

[16] *Demir and Baykara v Turkey* (n 6) §§ 107 and 154.

[17] ILO, FAC Digest (n 14) §§ 886–87.

[18] ILO, CEACR (n 13) 68–70/85–88/90.

[19] ECSR, *Conclusions* I, p 31; see also the verdicts in collective complaints App Nos 4/1999 (*EUROFEDOP v Italy*) and 5/1999 (*EUROFEDOP v Portugal*).

[20] See also the verdict in collective complaint App No 11/2001 (*European Council of Police Trade Unions v Portugal*) 21 May 2002

[21] ECSR, *Conclusions* III, Germany; see also the verdict in ibid.

thresholds set by law. This means that the content of collective agreements negotiated is subject to preliminary verification by the public authority and the agreements may be registered only if it has been found that the budgetary thresholds have been respected.[22]

The Committee also accepted that in Romania in collective agreements with civil servants not engaged in the administration of the State (eg, school teachers), pay increases, allowances, bonuses and other staff entitlements are fixed by law and therefore excluded from collective bargaining.[23]

In the case of Latvia the ECSR accepted that the State fixes the maximum acceptable amount of allowances and bonuses for civil servants and state officials.[24]

The Committee even accepted that in Germany collective agreements with civil servants ('*Beamte*') may not be concluded on the issue of remuneration, but that these employees are entitled to participate in the bargaining process over all other conditions of employment applicable to them. The ECSR held that this interference with the right to bargain collectively of the employees in question is not disproportionate and satisfies the requirements of Article 6(2) ESC.

Although these verdicts point in the same direction, the precise boundaries and the consequences of the exception made with regard to 'members of the administration of the State' (Article 11, § 2 ECHR) are still far from clear. The ECtHR can therefore expect a wave of applications from this field, forcing it to refine its case law.

7 THE PARTIES TO A COLLECTIVE AGREEMENT

In many European countries, parliaments have clearly established in their laws covering collective bargaining that a collective agreement can only be concluded between—on the employers' side—single employers, ad hoc groups of employers or employer associations, and—on the employees' side—only trade unions. However, in Austria, single employers can only seldom conclude collective agreements[25] and in some European countries, on the employees' side, collective agreements can also be concluded by two or more employees (as in Georgia), works collectives (as in the Ukraine) or works councils. In some countries, like the Netherlands and Germany, works councils may bargain with the employer on specific issues, the competence for which is assigned to them either by law or by a collective agreement with the trade unions.

The CEACR stands out on this point, criticising that in certain countries direct agreements between employers and groups of non-unionised workers are much more numerous than collective agreements concluded with the representative organisations of workers.[26] The Committee called on governments to take measures to prevent direct agreements with non-unionised workers being used for anti-union

---

[22] ECSR, *Conclusions* 2010, Poland.

[23] ECSR, *Conclusions* 2010, Romania.

[24] ECSR, *Conclusions* XIX, Latvia.

[25] See R Rebhahn, 'Collective Labour Law in Europe in a Comparable Perspective' (2003) *The International Journal of Comparative Labour Law and Industrial Relations* 274.

[26] ILO, CEACR (n 13) 82.

purposes.[27] Both this Committee and the FAC[28] consider collective bargaining with representatives of non-unionised workers only to be possible when there are no trade unions at the respective level.

I think the ECtHR in its future case law should not prevent decentralised bargaining by groups other than trade unions when there are no trade unions at the respective level or—when these exist—as long as the minimum level of working conditions laid down in the collective agreement is respected.

In many European countries, parliaments and courts have set certain requirements for associations of employers and employees who want to conclude collective agreements. From a historical perspective, the requirement of a common legal personality has not been a stumbling block in the Netherlands and Denmark, but was refused by German unions. Many countries have formulated specific statutory requirements regarding the legal personality or liability of trade unions. These were acceptable to trade unions in France and the UK, but not in Belgium. Some countries require legal personality of at least two years before their representativeness is recognised[29] or even that of seniority (two years of existence) in the professional and geographical area covered by the collective negotiations.[30]

Besides these more formal criteria, there are the material criteria. Under German and French law as well as in the decisions of the ILO supervisory bodies[31] and of the Council of Europe, a number of material criteria have already been developed, such as independence from employers and the state, effective power to exercise pressure, internal democratic organisation, etc. Obviously 'yellow unions' (unions set up or organised by employers or the State) are considered a threat to a well-functioning system of collective bargaining.

In its quasi-case law the ECSR has accepted that Member States of the Council of Europe may define additional criteria for parties willing to conclude collective agreements. With regard to France, for instance, it has accepted other criteria such as republican values, financial transparency, influence demonstrated by activity and experience, and membership dues.[32] The CEACR holds that the requirement that organisations must be affiliated with a national organisation in order to be able to conclude sectoral and branch-level agreements is incompatible with the autonomy that must be enjoyed by the parties to bargaining.[33]

Such criteria may easily be justified by the ECtHR, but some are not easily applied in practice. In several trade unions in Europe one may question whether the internal organisation functions in a truly democratic way. Official Dutch trade unions receive quite substantial funding from employers, raising the question of whether they are financially independent. A number of official French unions have so few members that they cannot exercise real pressure on the employers. In many Member States new autonomous unions have repeatedly sprung up, often better

---

[27] Ibid, 96–97.
[28] ILO, FAC Digest (n 14) § 944.
[29] ECSR, *Conclusions* 2010, Bulgaria.
[30] ECSR, *Conclusions* 2010, Portugal.
[31] ILO, FAC Digest (n 14) § 966.
[32] ECSR, *Conclusions* XV-1, France.
[33] ILO, CEACR (n 13) 84.

complying with the quantitative criteria than official unions, but have nevertheless been refused a place at the collective bargaining table. Belgium is a prime example of this and, going back to the 1970s, the first case[34] in which the ECtHR had to deal with the right to collective bargaining was in fact caused by this type of policy.

8 THE CONCEPT OF REPRESENTATIVENESS

Legislatures and courts in many European nations require that trade unions (and also employers' associations) should be 'representative' in order to gain the right to collective bargaining. The ILO has long accepted that this concept is not in itself contrary to the principle of freedom of association, provided that the distinction between representative and non-representative unions is limited to the recognition of certain preferential rights, such as the right to engage in collective bargaining.[35] In its *Demir and Baykara* reasoning,[36] the ECtHR wisely recognised that States remain free to organise their system so as, if appropriate, to grant special status to representative trade unions. However, this immediately raises such questions as: what are the criteria for representativeness and can there be more than one organisation considered representative?

The US legislature had already solved this question in 1935 by setting down the rule (in s 9 of the National Labour Relations Act) that only the most representative union in a bargaining unit can exercise the right to collective bargaining and only if it has more than 50 per cent of the cards of the workers in that unit.

In Europe this system is only applied in Malta and Turkey. In several European countries, more than one trade union in the same bargaining unit can be considered representative.

Both the CEACR[37] and the FAC[38] consider both systems of collective bargaining compatible with freedom of association, ie, the system granting exclusive rights to the most representative union, and that under which several unions in an enterprise or a bargaining unit may conclude collective agreements. In cases where no union meets the condition of being the majority union, minority trade unions should at least be able to conclude a collective or direct agreement on behalf of their own members.

The ECSR has also accepted systems in which only trade unions representing an absolute majority of the workforce are granted sole bargaining rights.[39] In such situations the ECSR states that a non-representative trade union nevertheless enjoys certain key prerogatives. It may, for example, approach the authorities in the individual interest of the employee; assist an employee who is required to justify his or her activities to the administrative authorities; and display notices of the services it

---

[34] ECtHR, 27 October 1975, *National Union of Belgian Police*, Series A, No 19.
[35] B Gernigon, *Collective Bargaining: Sixty Years After its International Recognition* (Geneva, ILO, 2009) 4.
[36] *Demir and Baykara v Turkey* (n 6) § 154.
[37] ILO, CEACR (n 13) 92/95.
[38] ILO, FAC Digest (n 14) §§ 950/977.
[39] ECSR, *Conclusions* 2010, Malta; *Conclusions* XV-1, Belgium.

offers on company premises. Moreover, it should receive documentation of a general nature concerning the management of the staff it represents.[40] All this is in line with the opinion of the FAC.[41]

The ECtHR will soon have to pronounce on this issue as there is already a Turkish case pending before the Court in which a question on the calculation of the absolute majority is raised.[42] It is submitted that the ECtHR should, in line with the CEACR, the FAC and the ECSR, also accept the system of a sole bargaining agent.

Nevertheless, many legislatures in Europe, confronted with the harsh reality of a strongly divided trade union movement, have sometimes for political motives (the strongest unions are often the most leftist unions) refused to give a monopoly to the most representative union, instead establishing systems in which more than one trade union can be considered representative and therefore may claim the right to collective bargaining.

Other legislatures have set minimum requirements regarding trade union membership. In this respect, the CEACR has pronounced that the imposition of a high percentage requirement for the recognition of a collective bargaining agent may impair the promotion and development of free and voluntary collective bargaining. Thresholds exist between 10 and 65 per cent (Hungary!). Even a threshold requiring the support of one-third of the workers concerned was considered too high.[43]

The ECSR has only come up with one single criterion, viz that the threshold should be 'reasonable'. It holds that any requirement must not excessively limit the possibility of trade unions to participate effectively in collective bargaining.

In the case of Macedonia, the ECSR has already taken the position that its requirement that at least 33 per cent of the employees at the level at which the agreement is to be concluded must be members of the trade union in order for it to be entitled to enter negotiations is excessive and therefore an infringement of the right to bargain collectively.

In the case of France, the ESCR doubted whether the criteria regarding a trade union's reach were reasonable.[44] In France a trade union must have obtained at least 10 per cent of the votes cast on the first ballot in the latest elections of the staff committee or staff representatives of an enterprise. At the branch, national and cross-sector levels the threshold is eight per cent of the votes cast in all ballots held in the enterprises concerned, and trade unions must also demonstrate that they are geographically evenly represented in the branch of activity concerned. In branches where more than half of the workers are employed in enterprises too small to hold elections (ie, ones with fewer than 10 employees), trade unions belonging to a trade union confederation that is representative at national level, as well as trade unions satisfying the other criteria for representativeness, will be considered representative. Several French trade unions consider the above-mentioned thresholds excessively high.

In Belgium traditionally only organisations belonging to a trade union confederation that is representative at the national cross-sector level are entitled to conclude

---

[40] Ibid.
[41] ILO, FAC Digest, op cit (n 14), § 974.
[42] *Tek Gida Is Sendikasi v Turkey*, App No 35009/05.
[43] ILO, CEACR (n 13) 92–96.
[44] ECSR, *Conclusions* XV-1, France.

collective agreements liable to *erga omnes* extension. The king (ie, the government) used not to be bound by an exhaustive list of criteria for determining representativeness at the national cross-sector level. However, since the adoption of an Act in 2009, such a list now exists and the king has to recognise a confederation meeting these criteria.

In the Netherlands the problem is not so much that employers refuse to negotiate with unions in general. However, it is frequently the case that new unions are established that want to have access to an established collective bargaining system. Courts are disposed to recognise their right to participate in collective bargaining if they can prove relative representativeness (ie, having more members than the unions already at the bargaining table). What also can happen is that employers, unable to reach an agreement with all unions participating in the established collective bargaining system, will bypass one or more of the traditional unions and conclude the collective agreement with one or more of the weaker unions, or even with 'yellow' unions.

What about quantitative criteria applying to employer organisations? The CEACR has considered that the requirement of an employer association representing at least 10 per cent of employers in order to be able to engage in collective bargaining is particularly high, especially for negotiations at the sectoral or national level.[45] In the *UEAPME* case[46] the CJEU avoided a verdict on the question of whether the UEAPME was to be considered a representative employer organisation at the European level, limiting itself to the question of whether the concluded agreement— the European agreement on parental leave—could be considered as sufficiently supported by employers to be representative with regard to implementation by means of a Directive. It confirmed this.

One might expect that, since the ECtHR has recognised the right to collective bargaining within the bounds of representativeness, numerous national trade unions would attempt to use the Court to challenge national criteria. In my view, the ECtHR may soon arrive at a crucial crossroads in its case law on Article 11 ECHR: is it going to respect the various positions of national states on the substantive criteria for representativeness? In my opinion, it should as far as possible—ie, except evidently unreasonable cases—accept the national criteria, as these are intricately interwoven with the national balance of socio-economic power.

9 CRITERIA FOR ESTABLISHING REPRESENTATIVENESS

Within the framework of the ILO, the CEACR requires that determination of the most representative organisation must be based on objective, pre-established criteria, so as to avoid any possibility of bias or abuse.[47] Furthermore, such determination should be carried out in accordance with a procedure that offers every guarantee of impartiality, by an independent body that enjoys the confidence of the parties,

---

[45] ILO, CEACR (n 12) 96.
[46] CJEU (CFI), 17 June 1998, T-135/963.
[47] ILO, CEACR (n 12) 36–37/93.

and without political interference.[48] The CEACR has developed a number of safe-guards when national legislation provides for a compulsory procedure for recognis-ing unions as exclusive bargaining agents: (i) certification to be conducted by an independent body; (ii) the representative organisation to be chosen by a majority of the employees in the unit concerned; (iii) the right of an organisation, which in the previous trade union election failed to secure a sufficiently large number of votes, to request a new election after a stipulated period; (iv) the right of any new organisa-tion other than the certified organisation to demand a new election after a reason-able period has elapsed; and (v) where the legislation provides that only registered trade unions may be recognised as bargaining agents, it should be ensured that the conditions required for registration are not excessive, as otherwise there would be a risk of the development of collective bargaining being seriously impaired.[49]

Similarly, the ECSR requires that the criteria used to determine representativeness must be clear, pre-determined, objective and prescribed by law.[50] France has for years already had such criteria set forth in legislation. The same applies to Belgium, though the criteria have only been exhaustive since 2009. Italy only has them in legislation covering the public sector, whereas they are not enshrined in legislation in the Netherlands at all. The ECSR is prepared to accept that the criteria are not laid down in legislation when the State can show that they are part of established case law.[51] However, even that is not the case in the Netherlands. The ECSR also requires that the application of these criteria be open to judicial review.[52]

Up to now the ECtHR has not explicitly required that the distinction between representative and non-representative trade unions be based on 'pre-established and objective criteria with regard to the organisations' representative character'.[53] In my opinion, the ECtHR should in its future rulings impose on States the obligation to either set forth the criteria for representativeness in legislation or in established case law and to open their application to judicial review, in line with the primacy of the 'rule of law' in Europe.

10 THE PLACE OF A COLLECTIVE AGREEMENT IN THE HIERARCHY OF SOURCES OF LABOUR LAW

The right to bargain collectively also raises the question as to the proper place of a collective agreement (and, where there are several collective agreements concur-rently applicable in a bargaining unit, of each collective agreement) in the hierarchy of sources of labour law.

---

[48] Ibid, 92–93.
[49] Ibid, 93.
[50] ECSR, *Conclusions* 2010, Malta; *Conclusions* XV-1, Belgium.
[51] ECSR, *Conclusions* 2010, Belgium.
[52] ECSR, *Conclusions* XV-1, France.
[53] F Dorssemont, 'The Right to Form and to Join Trade Unions for the Protection of His Interest under Article 11 ECHR' (2010) 2 *European Labour Law Journal* 223.

10.1 The Primacy of a Collective Agreement over Individual Contracts of Employment

The ILO's Collective Agreements Recommendation 1951 (No 91) defines the principle of the binding effect of collective agreements and their primacy over individual contracts of employment, with the exception of provisions in the latter which are more favourable to workers covered by the collective agreement. In this light both the FAC[54] and the CEACR[55] criticise the tendency for the legislature in a number of countries to give precedence to individual rights over collective rights in employment matters.

In most Member States of the Council of Europe the collective agreement still has primacy over individual contracts, though there is at least one important exception: the UK. Here the concept that the collective agreement prevails over the individual contract of employment and internal company regulations is not anchored in law. Explicit provisions in individual contracts which run counter to the collective agreement may thus be binding. The UK situation is to be explained by history. As Kahn-Freund has taught us,[56] British trade unions used to rely on their own strength rather than asking the legislature to give legally binding force to collective agreements, as the latter might also have implied a limitation to their rights to take collective action. This in turn would have given the courts the opportunity to destroy the original content of the collective agreement by their interpretation.

Looked at from today's perspective, Kahn-Freund would not have reiterated his panegyric on the voluntarism of British industrial relations in the light of its implosion as a result of Thatcherism. I nevertheless believe that cases in which individual contracts of employment deliberately violate the collective agreements applicable to them remain a marginal phenomenon in the UK, as in most cases the English courts can derive the binding force of a collective agreement via a range of legal instruments, including contractual clauses specifically referring to collective agreements, the 'implied' term and the agency construction.

On the European continent the primacy of collective agreements over individual employment contracts is well established, though in different forms. There are systems under which collective agreements only apply to the signatories and their members (and not to all workers in the bargaining unit), such as in Germany, and conversely systems under which all workers in a bargaining unit are covered, as is the case in Belgium and France. The CEACR considers both systems to be compatible with the principle of freedom of association.[57]

As each of these different approaches to the mandatory character of the collective agreement has its historic roots and is part and parcel of a domestic balance of powers in a specific country, the ECtHR would be well advised to respect all forms thereof.

---

[54] ILO, FAC Digest (n 14) § 1057.
[55] ILO, CEACR (n 13) 82.
[56] O Kahn-Freund, *Labour and the Law* (London, Stevens & Sons, 1972).
[57] ILO, CEACR (n 12) 92.

10.2 The Position of the Collective Agreement in Relation to Statutory Law and Other Collective Agreements

In all European states the collective agreement is traditionally considered a lower source in respect of the labour law laid down in statutes, ministerial decrees and binding international sources. But here again, this rule of the thumb is undermined by the principle of the most favourable rule: the collective agreement may derogate from the regulations in those higher sources if this is favourable to the workers.

Somewhat more problematic is the situation where a contract of employment is covered by two or more collective agreements. Which collective agreement has priority? These problems, as would also be the case with representativeness problems, could easily be solved, were the principle of the most favourable rule to have universal character and to always be applicable. Then the most advantageous collective agreement would be applicable.[58]

However, in most European countries the principle of the priority of the most favourable rule is not an absolute principle in labour law.[59] Consequently, in situations where the principle of the most favourable source does not apply, collective agreements may deprive workers of more favourable rights, and consequently collective agreements with non-representative unions may become problematic. Let me give some examples.

First example: in a number of countries labour legislation contains provisions allowing collective agreements to deviate from them *in peius*. This has been the case for a number of years in Germany and the Netherlands. In Italy a recent law[60] now allows collective agreements to derogate *in peius* from protective statutory labour law.

French regulations on working hours have in a number of recent cases no longer been construed as mandatory law but as 'default rules', applying only when no collective agreement has been negotiated. Companies are therefore authorised to negotiate the length of the working week, overtime, rest periods and other similar matters in company agreements which take precedence even over collective agreements negotiated at a higher level (even when the latter are more favourable to employees). However, the French legislature has built in a safety provision: the company agreement must be a 'majority agreement', ie, approved by the trade unions which gained the majority of votes in workplace elections.[61]

Such a safety provision is lacking in the Netherlands. The consequence is that collective agreements with unions not representing the majority of workers are sometimes challenged in court by employees unwilling to accept a deterioration in their employment conditions on account of a collective agreement concluded by a 'yellow' union or a union with low membership.

---

[58] Although a collective agreement with minority unions could harm the prestige of the excluded union, this is not too problematic as long as the excluded trade union and its members remain free to take collective action to improve the conditions of employment.

[59] See in France the Cour de Cassation, 17 July 1996; Conseil Constitutionnel, 25 July 1989 and 6 November 1996.

[60] Article 8 of Manovra-bis, Decree number 138, ratified by Legge No 148/2011.

[61] Article L 2253, §§ 1 and 2 of the French Code de Travail.

Second example: in most countries it is a general principle of the law on collective agreements that a collective agreement with a narrower scope must not lay down less favourable rights for workers than those contained in a collective agreement with a broader scope.

However, in a number of countries the collective agreement with the narrower scope may lay down rights and working conditions which are less favourable to employees under conditions determined by the collective agreement with a broader scope. This is the case in the Netherlands, Slovenia and Germany (inter alia in the company agreements referred to as *betriebliche Bündnisse für Arbeit*).

A similar recent provision in France states that cross-sector, sector and company agreements may include provisions which depart wholly or partly *in peius* from rules that apply under an agreement covering a broader geographical area or industrial field, except where they relate to minimum wages, job classifications, collective guarantees on supplementary social insurance or the pooling of funds earmarked for vocational training, unless such departures have been expressly forbidden in an agreement at a higher level. And in Italy recent developments indicate that collective agreements at a company level may depart from collective agreements at a sectoral level on a more general basis (initially in the Fiat-Pomigliano agreement and now sanctioned by law).[62]

The ILO has developed certain norms covering situations in countries where collective bargaining takes place at several levels. The first norm is that the parties should seek to ensure that there is coordination between these levels (Para 4(2) of the Collective Bargaining Recommendation 1981 (No 163)). The FAC considers that, in the event of persistent disagreement concerning the level of bargaining, the best procedure is to provide for a system established by common agreement between the parties so as to take into account the interests and points of view of all concerned, rather than having recourse to a legal ruling to determine a specific level of bargaining. Nevertheless, if it is decided that this issue is to be determined by an independent body, the FAC has considered that in such cases the body should be truly independent.[63]

The CEACR has adopted a somewhat different position, accepting both systems which leave it up to collective agreements to determine the means for their coordination, as well as systems characterised by legal clauses distributing subjects between agreements, giving primacy to a certain level or adopting the criterion of the most favourable provision for workers. The CEACR, however, considers that the interference, as set out in law, of higher-level organisations in the bargaining process undertaken by lower-level organisations is incompatible with the autonomy that must be enjoyed by the parties to bargaining.[64]

Only very few countries have explicitly regulated the hierarchy of labour law sources in their legislation—among them Belgium. In most European countries the place of a collective agreement in this hierarchy still has a number of question marks, many of which have come to the fore now that the recent financial crisis has stimulated many countries to embark on or strengthen the decentralisation of

---

[62] Article 8 of Manovra-bis, Decree number 138, ratified by Legge No 148/2011.
[63] ILO, FAC Digest (n 14) § 991; ILO, FAC, Case No 2375 (Peru), Report No 338, § 1226; and Case 2326 (Australia) Report No 338, § 457.
[64] ILO, CEACR (n 13) 84.

collective bargaining by introducing new possibilities for companies to opt out of collective agreements *in peius* as a way of surviving the crisis.[65]

The ECtHR would be skating on thin ice were it to intervene in these developments. At most, the Court may reserve the power to depart from the principle of the most favourable rule when collective agreements are concluded by a totality of trade unions demonstrating a reasonable degree of representativeness.

11 THE PROMOTION OF COLLECTIVE BARGAINING

In several countries the legislature not only protects the right to collective bargaining, but also promotes the use of collective bargaining through a range of instruments. Within the framework of the Council of Europe, Member States are required to promote, where necessary and appropriate, machinery for voluntary negotiations between employers or employers' organisations, with a view to the regulation of terms and conditions of employment by means of collective agreements (Article 6(2) ESC). The ECSR has consequently always held that, in accordance with Article 6 ESC, if the spontaneous development of collective bargaining is not sufficient, positive measures should be taken to facilitate and encourage the conclusion of collective agreements.

Since the ECtHR has recognised that the right to collective bargaining is inherent to Article 11 ECHR, it may find itself confronted by two questions: (i) at what point is a Member State obliged to effectively engage in positive measures in support of collective bargaining?; and (ii) what are acceptable means to promote collective bargaining? The first question relates to the collective agreement coverage rate. What level must it have attained before the State is obliged to take such measures—20 per cent of the workforce?[66] In the UK the coverage rate is only 30 per cent of the total workforce and in many sectors even less than 10 per cent. Should the ECtHR now oblige the UK to take (more) measures to encourage and facilitate collective bargaining? British unions are already complaining that the British recognition procedure falls short of ILO Convention No 98.[67]

Like many other values that governments may wish to promote, this can be done either by the carrot or the stick.

11.1 The Carrot of Public Procurement

At a global level the ILO has promoted collective bargaining in general by way of Convention No 154. A separate convention (Convention No 94) promotes an instrument traditionally used in many countries, ie, that of linking public procurement to

---

[65] L Laulom, 'How Has the Crisis Affected Social Legislation in Europe?', ETUI Policy Brief, No 2/2012, p 4; S Clauwaert and I Schoemann, *The Crisis and National Labour Law Reforms. A Mapping Exercise* (Brussels, ETUI, 2012) 15–16.

[66] ECSR, *Conclusions* 2010, Latvia.

[67] KD Ewing and J Hendy, 'The Dramatic Implications of *Demir and Baykara*' (2010) 39(1) *Industrial Law Journal* 31.

specific social requirements. By providing that employees performing work under public contracts do not enjoy conditions of labour less favourable than those enjoyed by other workers in the same trade or industry,[68] the States have substantially stimulated the application of sector and cross-sector collective agreements. However, in 2008 the CJEU in the *Rüffert* case[69] considered that this instrument was in breach of EU rules on the free movement of services![70]

11.2 A Stick: Obliging Employers to Bargain

One of the measures with which a State can encourage collective bargaining is to oblige employers to negotiate with unions, as is the case in the US (Article 7 National Labour Relations Act). In Europe some form of compulsion to bargain is applied in France, Luxembourg, the Slovak Republic and Bulgaria.

In the Slovak Republic, failure on the part of the employer to negotiate collectively with the competent trade union is deemed to be a labour law violation and subject to a fine. In Bulgaria employers must pay damages in such cases.

The CEACR does not consider this approach as incompatible with Convention No 98.[71]

Though it is undisputed that the ILO standards do not imply a formal obligation to negotiate and reach agreement, the supervisory bodies of the ILO consider that the parties must respect the principle in good faith and not resort to unfair or abusive practices in this context.[72] The principle of negotiating in good faith, derived from Article 4 ILO Convention No 98, takes the form, in practice, of various obligations for the parties involved, namely: (i) recognising representative organisations; (ii) endeavouring to reach agreement; (iii) engaging in real and constructive negotiations; (iv) avoiding unjustified delays in negotiation; and (v) mutually respecting the commitments made and the results achieved through bargaining.[73]

The obligation to bargain may be seen as a positive measure of the legislature to facilitate and encourage the conclusion of collective agreements. Although employers may oppose such an obligation, arguing that collective bargaining should remain free and voluntary, it is submitted that the ECtHR should respect the decisions of a number of European countries to impose such an obligation on employers.

However, it is questionable whether Article 11 ECHR itself can now be interpreted in such a way that in specific situations the presence of a collective bargaining procedure can be demanded before the ECtHR in cases where national labour law (or even EU labour law) does not oblige employers to bargain with the unions.[74] Personally I am in favour of a general obligation for employers to bargain with the

---

[68] HK Nielsen, 'Public Procurement and International Labour Standards' (1995) 2 *Public Procurement Law Review* 94–101.

[69] CJEU, 3 April 2008, Case C-346/06, *Rueffert*.

[70] N Bruun, A Jacobs and M Schmidt, 'ILO Convention No. 94 in the Aftermath of the *Rüffert* Case' (2010) 16(4) *Transfer* 473–88.

[71] ILO, CEACR (n 13) 85.

[72] Ibid, 82; ILO, FAC Digest (n 14), §§ 933–39.

[73] ILO, CEACR (n 12) 85.

[74] See CJEU (Civil Service Tribunal), 29 September 2011, *Heath v BCE*, F-121/10.

unions in the relevant bargaining unit, even at a European level,[75] though I think that it is up to the legislature and not the courts to make such an inroad into the freedom of contract.

Employers may defend a right to abstain from collective bargaining or from recognising trade unions. In Ireland the Supreme Court has already been confronted with such a demand in a case involving the non-unionised airline Ryanair.[76]

It is submitted that the ECtHR should adopt a balanced position, allowing Member States (against the opposition of employers) to operate an obligation to bargain, provided that national law does not stipulate the mandatory conclusion of an agreement. This would be in line with the position of the CJEU (Civil Service Tribunal) which in the *Heath* case recently refused to derive an obligation to bargain from Article 28 CFREU and Article 11 ECHR.[77]

11.3 Both a Carrot and a Stick: *Erga Omnes* Extension

The possibility of extending a collective agreement *erga omnes* by state decree is certainly a good way of encouraging and promoting collective bargaining. About half of all European countries have such a possibility on their statute books.[78] This possibility is generally considered as compatible with the right to bargain collectively, especially when it ensures the continuing existence of more favourable workers' rights. Both the FAC[79] and the CEACR[80] consider that the extension of collective agreements is not contrary to the principle of voluntary bargaining and is not in violation of ILO Convention No 98.

However, the question may rise as to whether the State can use this instrument of declaring collective agreements binding *erga omnes* to put pressure on the social partners with regard to the content of the collective agreement. Such 'selective' or 'conditional' extension orders have been considered in the Netherlands in a number of cases.

The ECtHR may find itself one day confronted with this question! In ILO circles it is believed (an opinion also shared by Mélanie Schmitt) that this kind of mechanism seems to be more problematic when it limits the right to collective bargaining both in its procedural aspect and in its dimension, especially when the extension can be refused by the State should the content of the collective agreement not correspond to its expectations.

12 THE CONCEPT OF 'FREE COLLECTIVE BARGAINING'

In all these cases the ECtHR may easily become involved in the question of whether the right to bargain collectively also implies the right to *free* collective bargaining,

---

[75] A Jacobs, *Het recht op collectief onderhandelen* (Alphen a/d Rijn, Samson HD Tjeenk Willink, 1986), 407-15.

[76] Irish Supreme Court in *Ryanair Ltd v Labour Court and IMPACT*, Appeal No 377/2005, p 16.

[77] Case F-121/10, Judgment of the Civil Service Tribunal of 29 September 2011 (point no 121).

[78] See F Traxler and M Behrens, *Collective Bargaining Coverage and Extension Procedures* (Brussels, EIRO, 2002).

[79] ILO, FAC Digest (n 14) § 1052.

[80] ILO, CEACR (n 13) 99.

meaning that the government should not interfere in the contractual freedom of the parties. The German idea of *Tarifautonomie*, considered a fundamental right in Germany, is based on the constitutional protection of the freedom of (trade union) association.

The ECtHR should also recognise this freedom in principle, albeit subject to certain limitations. But what limitations are acceptable? Government intervention in wage setting in response to serious economic circumstances? The selective use of tax laws to put pressure on the social partners? What if the contents of a collective agreement conflict with State or EU rules?

12.1 Scrutiny as to Constitutionality/Legality

The CEACR considers that, except where there are instances of serious breaches of constitutional rights in certain clauses of collective agreements (for example, if they establish wage discrimination on the basis of sex), collective bargaining, as an instrument of social peace, cannot be repeatedly subjected to recurrent scrutiny as to constitutionality without losing its credibility and usefulness.[81]

The CEACR also considers that a practice whereby the authorities almost systematically challenge the benefits awarded to public sector workers on the basis of considerations related to 'rationality' or 'proportionality' with a view to their cancellation (by reason, for example, of their cost being deemed to be excessive) would seriously jeopardise the very institution of collective bargaining and would weaken its role in the settlement of collective disputes.[82]

The exception the CEACR makes for discrimination on the basis of sex is easily extended to race. However, we may infer from the CJEU's case law on age-based discrimination that the CJEU allows the social partners a much larger degree of discretion in this field.[83] However, is it large enough, given that other clauses about the same item ('for instance age-related clauses, etc') have already been effectively declared null and void?[84] Will courts respect collective agreements implementing waivers in statutory texts ('opt-out' clauses) in a way that violates EU law? A case is pending before the CJEU about a clause in a national collective agreement pursuant to which a leave entitlement does not accrue in those years in which a certain total gross wage is not earned as a result of illness.[85] The clause is clearly in conflict with CJEU rulings on state laws in this area.[86]

In a recent case (*Commission v Germany*)[87] the CJEU ruled that collective agreements should not violate EU rules on public procurement. It is thus not difficult to see the contours of such 'recurrent scrutiny' already present at the level of the EU authorities.

---

[81] Ibid, 85.
[82] Ibid, 85.
[83] CJEU, 21 July 2011; Cases C159/10 and C-160/10, *Fuchs*.
[84] CJEU, 8 September 2011; Cases C-297/10 and C-298/10, *Hennigs*.
[85] CJEU, Case C-317/11, *Reimann*.
[86] CJEU, 20 January 2009, Cases C-350/06 and C-520/06, *Schultz-Hoff*.
[87] CJEU, 17 July 2010, Case C-271/08, *Commission v Germany*.

The CJEU appeared initially to take a respectful position vis-a-vis the right to collective bargaining. In the 1999 *Albany* case on the conflict between the right to collective bargaining and EU competition law, the CJEU provided collective agreements with a kind of immunity.[88] However, in the 2008 *Laval* case[89] the CJEU concluded that conflicts between fundamental social rights and economic freedoms must be solved along the lines of proportionality.

In my view, the *Commission v Germany* case is of great interest, as the CJEU stated in its ruling that 'the designation of bodies and undertakings in a collective agreement such as that at issue does not affect the essence of the right to bargain collectively'. This phrase reminds us of an old axiom of German constitutional case law, ie, that encroachments on fundamental rights are allowed as long as they do not affect the hard core of a fundamental right ('*Kernbereichsgarantie*'). Is the CJEU considering replacing its proportionality approach by a kind of *Kernbereichsgarantie* approach?

All these examples show that respect of labour and management autonomy (*Tarifautonomie*) has already become a serious issue at the EU level. There is an avalanche of 'recurrent scrutiny' looming in Europe.

The ECtHR was already involved in such scrutiny in the *Swedish Transport Workers Union* case. The Court did not see a violation of Article 11 ECHR in a decision of the Swedish Competition Authority to declare a clause of a collective agreement null and void since it violated free competition rules (the clause prohibited the contracting-out of the distribution of newspapers to contractors who were not covered by a collective agreement).[90] However, this was several years before the *Demir and Baykara* case. The ECtHR now needs to reconsider its case law in the light of its recognition of the right to collective bargaining as inherent in Article 11 ECHR.

12.2 Wage Controls

This brings us to the issue of state intervention in the contents of collective agreements in general out of a concern to promote 'responsible wage increases' or to ride out the storm of economic recession. In the 1980s the repeated wage restraint policies of the Netherlands were criticised by the ILO as an infringement of free collective bargaining.[91] Such interference in free collective bargaining was considered only acceptable under extraordinary circumstances. Yet Belgium still has a law on its statute book requiring the social partners not to deviate *in melius* from the trend of wage increases in its main trade partner countries. The question of wage controls may gain new topicality when national and European authorities find themselves obliged to supervise trends in wage increases or even to impose wage cuts out of a concern to ensure the stability of the euro and to comply with the stability rules

---

[88] CJEU, 21 September 1999, Case C-67/96, *Albany*.
[89] CJEU, 18 December 2007, Case C-341/05, *Laval*.
[90] ECtHR, 30 November 2004, *Swedish Transport Workers' Union v Sweden*, App No 53507/99.
[91] K Boonstra, *The ILO and the Netherlands* (Leiden, NJCM Boekerij, 1996).

regarding national debt.[92] Trade unions in Spain and Greece have already appealed to the ILO and the Council of Europe with regard to such austerity measures, and a Portuguese tribunal has made a reference for a preliminary CJEU ruling.[93]

The FAC holds that if a government wishes the clauses of a collective agreement to be brought into line with the economic policy of the country, it should attempt to persuade the parties to take account voluntarily of such considerations, without imposing on them the renegotiation of the collective agreements in force.[94] If, as part of its stabilisation policy, a government considers that wage rates cannot be set freely through collective bargaining, such a restriction should be imposed as an exceptional measure, only to the extent necessary and limited to a reasonable period of time. It should also be accompanied by adequate safeguards to protect workers' living standards.[95]

The CEACR admits that the public authorities may establish machinery for discussion and the exchange of views to encourage the parties in collective bargaining to take voluntary account of government social and economic policy considerations and the protection of the public interest. In the case of dispute, the issue could, for example, be submitted for advice and recommendation to an appropriate joint body, provided that the final decision rests with the parties.[96]

12.3 Executive Pay and Bonuses for Top Employees

The right to collective bargaining may also become a questionable subject should the State try to get a grip on executive pay and bonuses for specialised employees. Such an Act has recently been adopted by the Dutch Parliament. Could these employees avoid such control by laying down their remuneration in the form of a collective agreement? It is submitted that the high esteem for the instrument of collective bargaining is due to the fact that without the protection of collective agreements, workers are in too weak a position to reach a deal with the employer on fair labour standards. This unequal position is not present with regard to the top jobs on the labour market. Therefore, the right to collective bargaining should not be extended to the upper five per cent of the labour market. This would help to promote the fair distribution of wealth within society.

13 CONCLUSIONS

Dorssemont has written[97] that the proof of the pudding lies not in the recognition of fundamental rights, but in the legitimacy of restrictions to these rights. It remains in the womb of time to see how the ECtHR will inch its way towards adopting a

---

[92] Laulom (n 64) 4; Clauwaert and Schoemann (n 62) 15–16.
[93] Case C-128/12, *Sindicato dos Bancarios*.
[94] ILO, FAC Digest (n 14) § 1008.
[95] Ibid, § 1024.
[96] ILO, CEACR (n 12) 84.
[97] Dorssemont (n 50) 231.

position on statutory or judicial restrictions relating to the right to collective bargaining freshly recognised as inherent to freedom of association.

Through its *Demir and Baykara* decision, the ECtHR has undoubtedly given itself the power to intervene in the collective bargaining laws of the Member States of the Council of Europe. At the same time, it has opened a Pandora's box. It is submitted that this is not problematic as long as the ECtHR limits itself to outlawing extreme cases, such as—as seen is in *Demir and Baykara*—the total impossibility for trade unions to validly conclude collective agreements in a certain sector.

In the same vein the ECtHR may in future rule that other unreasonable aspects of collective bargaining legislation do not stand the test of Article 11 ECHR.

However, it is also argued that the ECtHR should not burn its fingers by getting involved in those typical aspects of national industrial relations which reflect the balance of power in those nations.

I would therefore suggest the following as the main lines for future ECtHR rulings on the right to collective bargaining:

— that the Court accepts national limitations on the right to collective bargaining of civil servants and workers in State enterprises as long as they do not lead to the total exclusion of this right for more than 10 per cent of the workforce in this sector. For the other 90 per cent of the workforce, only the issue of remuneration would be excluded, leaving untouched the right to collective bargaining on all other conditions of employment;

— that the Court respects the differences between the European countries as regards the mandatory character of a collective agreement;

— that the Court honours—apart from evidently unreasonable cases—the national criteria on representativeness, as these criteria are strictly interwoven with the national balance of power in socio-economic matters. It may, however, oblige States to have set forth the criteria for representativeness in either legislation or in established case law and to open their application to judicial review—in accordance with the priority attached to the 'rule of law' in Europe;

— that the Court imposes on States that unions not considered representative may still enjoy certain key prerogatives—as mentioned in ECSR, *Conclusions* XV-1, Belgium;

— that the Court accepts national systems on the place of the various types of collective agreements in the hierarchy of sources of labour law, provided that collective agreements which depart *in peius* from the general standards laid down in legislation or in collective agreements with a broader scope or in the individual contracts of employment enjoy a reasonable degree of representativeness;

— that the Court only imposes on the States an obligation to take measures to encourage and facilitate collective bargaining if the general coverage rate has decreased below 10 per cent of the workers;

— that the Court accepts an obligation to bargain as a useful tool for encouraging and facilitating collective bargaining as long as it does not amount to an obligation to conclude a collective agreement. The Court should not, however, force a Member State without such an obligation on its statute books to establish one;

— that the Court accepts the selective use of the *erga omnes* extension when this is justified by the aim to preclude a collision between collective bargaining results and government socio-economic policies;
— that the Court accepts across-the-board wage cuts or wage-capping measures (temporarily) adopted in response to serious economic or other circumstances;
— that the Court accepts limitations on the right to collective bargaining with regard to the upper five per cent of wage-earners.

13

The Right to Take Collective Action under Article 11 ECHR

FILIP DORSSEMONT

1 INTRODUCTION

THIS CONTRIBUTION SEEKS to analyse the protection of the right to take collective action under Article 11 of the European Convention on Human Rights (ECHR). This Article relates to the right to organise, that is, the right to form and join trade unions. It is mute on the issue of collective action, including strikes and lockouts. Ever since the rise of 'modern trade unions, organised workers have had recourse to collective action, including strikes, in order to promote and defend their interests. Strikes and lockouts should not be seen as a "pathological" moment in a given system of industrial relations. From a legal point of view, they can be seen as lying at the heart of collective labour law, just as dismissal is at the heart of individual employment law, divorce at the heart of family law, and war at the heart of international law'.[1]

For many years, the European Court of Human Rights ('the Court') has been extremely reluctant to accept that the issues of trade union freedom and the right to strike were interwoven. Isolated prohibition or restriction of the right to strike fell outside the ambit of Article 11 ECHR. Only a combined approach against such restrictions and/or prohibitions under both Article 11 and Article 14 ECHR might have offered a prospect of judicial protection. It took until 2002 for the Court to scrutinise restrictions on the right to strike not involving an equality aspect and as late as 2008 to embrace the idea that the right to strike could not be dissociated from the right to organise (*a corrolaire indissociable*). The Court has never qualified the right to strike as more than just 'an important' means to defend workers' interests, as opposed to means considered to be 'essential'.

As might have been the case during the era of the conceptualisation of the right to take collective action in domestic labour law, a lot of attention has been drawn to the issue of whether and how the right to take collective action is indeed 'enshrined' in Article 11 ECHR. The analysis of other issues of the debate is still subject to conjecture. In this chapter, I will analyse ECtHR case law in accordance with the

---

[1] L François, *Théorie des relations collectives du travail en droit belge* (Brussels, Bruylant, 1980) 47–49.

traditional structure of the subject matter as it would be treated in comparative labour law or in contributions on more specialised international labour standards. These contributions focus on restrictions on the right to take collective action as well as on the margin States have to restrict the right to take collective action. The Court's case law will be revisited, that is, confronted with the *Demir and Baykara* canon of intertextual interpretation.

2 FREEDOM OF ASSOCIATION AND COLLECTIVE ACTION

The European Convention on Human Rights (1949) does not pay tribute in any explicit way to the right to strike, let alone to a right to take collective action. In fact, no pre-existing international human rights instrument[2] referred to such a fundamental workers' right. Only *few* Contracting Parties had enshrined a right to strike in their Constitution at the time that the text of the Convention was drafted. The first[3] international instrument to enshrine the right to strike was the European Social Charter (ESC) (1961), with Article 6, § 4 recognising 'the right of workers and employers to collective action in cases of conflicts of interest, including the right to strike, subject to obligations that might arise out of collective agreements previously entered into'. The ESC construes the right to take collective action as intertwined with the right to bargain collectively.[4] It does *not* relate the issue of collective action/strike to freedom of association. Conversely, the specific provision on freedom of association is mute on the issue of strike.[5] In sum, the founding fathers of the ESC deviated from the approach of the ILO's Freedom of Association Committee (FAC). As early as 1952, this supervisory body stated that 'the right to strike and that of organising trade union meetings are essential elements of trade union freedom'.[6]

In view of the absence of any explicit recognition of a right to bargain collectively, the only prospect for *judicial* recognition of a right to strike stems from Article 11 ECHR. This provision starts by guaranteeing freedom of association in a generic way. It continues with the statement that the recognition of the 'freedom of association with others' includes 'the right to form and to join trade unions for the protection of his interests'. The question arises whether the existence of a specific right to 'form and join trade unions' affords latitude for developing a number of corollary rights not regarded as inherent aspects of the more generic freedom of association.[7]

---

[2] The ILO's Declaration of Philadelphia (1944) and the Universal Declaration of Human Rights (1948) are mute on the issue of strikes, lockouts and collective action.

[3] D Harris and J Darcy, *The European Social Charter* (New York, Transnational Publishers, 2001) 104.

[4] See the *rubrica* of Article 6 ESC.

[5] Article 5 ESC (the right to organise).

[6] R Ben-Israel, *International Labour Standards: The Case of Freedom to Strike* (Deventer, Kluwer Law and Taxation, 1988) 64–66; T Novitz, *International and European Protection of the Right to Strike* (Oxford, Oxford University Press, 2003) 192 ; See Case nr 28 (UK-Jamaica), 2nd Report of the Freedom of Association Committee (1952), § 68.

[7] *Per analogiam*: B Creighton, 'Freedom of Association' in R Blanpain (ed), *Comparative Labour Law and Industrial Relations* (Austin, TX, Wolters Kluwer, 2007) 275: 'Whether the latter should be regarded as simply a manifestation of the former, or as a fundamental human right *sui generis*, is a matter of some debate.'

At first glance, the prospects for such a development are bad. 'The right to form and to join *trade unions*' merely paraphrases the basic core of the freedom of association. This basic core relates solely to the *individual* dimension of the right to organise. The provision seems to be addressed solely to individuals in the process of forming or joining a trade union; it does not refer to conduct by trade unions. Hence, the provision is mute about a *collective* dimension. Article 11 does though set forth a criterion for guiding development of the law. The right to organise is recognised for the sake of '*protection of interests*'. Such an objective provides scope for teleological interpretation. Unfortunately, the objective is phrased in a shallow manner. In more specific instruments, the objectives are set forth in a more specific or more ambitious way.[8] Thus, the interests at stake are described explicitly and broadly as 'social and economic interests'. Furthermore, trade unions are presented as being 'in the offensive'. They do not just 'protect' or 'defend', but also 'promote and further' interests.

In the very first case (1975) related to the freedom of trade union association, the ECtHR ruled that the phrase 'for the protection of his interests is not redundant'.[9] The idea that trade unions should have means to protect the interests of their members has been reiterated ever since in constant case law.[10] As a matter of principle, the Court recognised that the *telos* of the right to organise could be used to develop corollary rights which are *essential* or *necessarily* inherent to the right to organise. Restrictions on corollary rights that are essential to the freedom of association need to pass the test of Article 11, § 2.

In this respect, it is crucial to assess whether the legal ability to have recourse to collective action is an *essential* means to protect the interests of trade union members. *A contrario*, the assessment that a specific right does not constitute an essential means to protect those interests would discharge the Court from assessing whether a restriction passes the test of Article 11, § 2. As evidenced by the reasoning in *National Union of Belgian Police*, the only salvation could spring from an assessment of those restrictions in the light of Article 11 combined with Article 14 ECHR.

The approach adopted in *National Union of Belgian Police* proved to be detrimental for trade unions or their members challenging restrictions on the exercise of the right to strike which did not violate the principle of equal treatment. The consequences of this approach became apparent in the *Schmidt and Dahlström*[11] case, in which individual members of a trade union tried to challenge restrictions on the right to strike stemming from the Swedish system of collective bargaining on the basis of Article 11 ECHR. The Court implicitly disagreed with the claim that

---

[8] See Article 5 Revised ESC (RESC) ('for the protection of their economic and social interests'); Article 8 ICESCR ('for the promotion and protection of his economic and social interests'); Article 10 ILO Convention No 87 ('for furthering and defending the interests of workers or employers').

[9] ECtHR, 27 October 1975, *National Union of Belgian Police*, App No 4464/70, Series A, No 19.

[10] See *Wilson and Palmer v UK* , 2 July 2002, App Nos 30668/96, 30671/96 30678/96, ECtHR 2002-V, § 42; *Enerji Yapi-Yol-Sen, v Turkey* § 24; *Demir and Baykara v Turkey* II ECtHR 2008, § 141.

[11] ECtHR, 6 February 1976, *Schmidt and Dahlström v Sweden*, App No 5589/72, Series A, No 21.

the right to strike was an *essential* means to protect the interests of trade union members.[12]

With its *UNISON* (2002) judgment, the Court abandoned this line of reasoning. In *UNISON*, the Court had to assess whether a statutory restriction in the UK to the right to have recourse to strike violated Article 11 ECHR. Despite the fact that the Court repeated that recourse to strike action was merely an important and not an essential means to protect workers' interests, it did assess whether this restriction, when taken separately, contravened Article 11. It adopted a similar approach in subsequent cases related to restrictions on the right to strike (*Dilek, Enerji Yapi Yol Sen*)[13] and in a case related to a restriction to the freedom of collective bargaining (*Demir and Baykara*).[14]

Ewing has rightly pointed out that this shift in case law constituted significant progress.[15] In *Demir and Baykara II*, the Court explained its shift in attitude by stating that 'the evolution of case law as to the substance of the right of association enshrined in Article 11 is marked by the guiding principle to take the totality of measures taken by the State into consideration in order to secure trade union freedom, subject to its margin of appreciation'.[16] Hence, the mere fact that a State recognises the so-called essential means to protect workers' rights is a not sufficient reason to conclude that there is a situation of conformity. Inevitably, the question arises whether the Court will conduct a more stringent scrutiny when prohibitions or restrictions to *essential* means of trade union action are at stake, as opposed to 'mere' important means. In my view, there is no immediate evidence to validate such a hypothesis. However, it might be argued that restrictions, let alone prohibitions, to *essential* means need to be considered less 'necessary' in a democratic society in comparison to restrictions to merely important means. In other words, it might be argued that the margin of appreciation for the Contracting Parties to restrict, let alone prohibit, essential means is smaller.

3 COLLECTIVE ACTION, STRIKE ACTION AND PEACEFUL ASSEMBLY

3.1 The History of Recognition

The issue of whether the ECtHR has indeed 'recognised' the right to strike or the right to take collective action boils down to the question of whether prohibitions or restrictions on the right to strike or the right to take collective action *fall within the ambit* of Article 11 ECHR. Since *UNISON*, this question has ceased to coincide with the assessment of whether the right to take collective action needs to be construed as merely an important or rather as an essential means to protect the interests of trade union members.

---

[12] The applicants phrased it as 'an organic right included in Article 11 of the European Convention': ECtHR, 6 February 1976, *Schmidt and Dahlström v Sweden* (n 11) § 36.
[13] ECtHR, 28 April 2008, *Dilek and others v Turkey*, App Nos 74611/01, 26876/02 and 27628/02.
[14] ECtHR, 21 November 2006, *Demir and Baykara v Turkey*, App No 34503/97.
[15] K Ewing, 'The Implications of Wilson and Palmer' (2003) 32 (1) *Industrial Law Journal* 18.
[16] ECtHR, 12 November 2008, *Demir and Baykara v Turkey*, App No 34503/97, ECtHR, 2008, § 144.

The ECtHR has consistently considered the right to strike as an important means to protect the interests of trade union members. Contrary to the freedom of collective bargaining,[17] recourse to strike was never upgraded from an important to an essential means.

The issue of whether the right to strike is necessarily inherent to Article 11 ECHR came to the forefront in *Schmidt and Dahlström*.[18] Both litigants were members of two 'belligerent' unions which had organised a strike after the expiry of a collective agreement applying to Swedish State employees. The new agreement for the public sector (made universally applicable through a Royal Order) included a 'Strike breaks retroactivity' clause, and the members of the belligerent trade unions were denied certain retroactive benefits. Both applicants argued that the refusal by the employer to retroactively apply certain benefits in a collective bargaining agreement to them as strikers had a chilling effect on the use of the strike threat. The Court unambiguously stated that the right to strike is one of the most important means to protect workers' interests. It considered, however, that a strike was by no means the only way to do so.[19] Indeed, restricting the right to strike did not result in the unions no longer being able to adequately defend the interests of workers. The right to strike was in no way seen as an indispensable tool for defending workers' interests. Contracting Parties have a free choice to regulate the means available to unions and their members to adequately defend members' interests. From that perspective, restrictions on the right to strike never seem to deprive trade unions of means to protect workers' interests.

The case illustrates the high hopes that some academics[20] had placed in the ECHR, despite the sophisticated character of the alleged restrictions deeply rooted in a unique system of industrial relations. The Court proved to be extremely reluctant to tackle legal issues stemming from a system of industrial relations, insisting 'on each State's free choice of the means to be used' [that is, granted] to protect workers' interests through trade union action.[21]

It took nearly a quarter of a century before restrictions on the right to strike were again challenged before the Court on the basis of Article 11 ECHR. On 20 October 1999, the British public sector union UNISON, to which various employees of the University College London Hospital (UCLH) belonged, lodged an application to the Court. As part of the 'Whitley Councils', the union had participated in the discussions on employment conditions in the healthcare sector. The UCLH was considering transferring parts of the hospital from the 'public' to the 'private' sector. The union demanded guarantees that the transferred workers and any new workers to be recruited by the transferee would be assured the same employment

[17] Ibid.

[18] *Schmidt and Dahlström v Sweden* (n 11). See the following passage in § 36: 'their right to strike which is, in their submission, an "organic right" included in Article 11 of the European Convention'.

[19] Ibid, § 36.

[20] One of the applicants was Folke Schmidt, a professor of labour law at Stockholm University.

[21] *Schmidt and Dahlström v Sweden* (n 11) § 36. See also the Court's insistence on the 'sensitive character' of the choices to be made in view of the social and political issues involved in *Gustafsson*: ECtHR, 28 March 1996, *Gustafsson v Sweden, Reports of Judgments and Decisions* 1996-II, App No 15573/89, §§ 45 and 54.

conditions as those set forth in one of the transferor's collective bargaining agreements for more than 30 years. Pressure was put on the transferor to stipulate such guarantees in the acquisition agreements. The transferor refused to include such a clause. After an internal ballot of its members, UNISON gave notice of strike. The UCLH obtained a court injunction prohibiting the strike. A critical factor was the finding that the employer subjected to the strike was considered to be a 'third party' in the conflict. The industrial dispute was conceived as one between the union and the transferee. A provision in the British Trade Union and Labour Relations Consolidation Act 1992 (TULRCA) made the immunity of unions dependent on the requirement that the trade dispute at hand involve a dispute between employees and 'their employer'. UNISON argued that the structural prohibition on strikes impeded it from effectively defending the interests of its workers during the strategically crucial time period of the negotiations regarding the transfer. It claimed that the right to strike was not just one means among others to defend the interests of its workers, instead regarding it as an indispensable means of defending workers' interests. The strike prohibition affected the very heart of the right to organise. The applicant pointed to the close interrelationship between the right to organise and right to collective action in the reports and conclusions of the supervisory bodies of the ILO and the Council of Europe.

The Court decided on 10 January 2002 that this application was inadmissible, on the grounds that it was manifestly ill-founded.[22] At first sight, the judgment appears to confirm *Schmidt and Dahlström*. The Court reiterated its well-known view on the margin of appreciation that States have in regulating trade union freedom. It distanced itself from the proposition that the right to collective action was *indispensable* to defending workers' interests. However, as indicated previously, the Court did assess whether this restriction contravened Article 11 taken separately. In *UNISON*, the Court did not consider that there had been a violation. It adopted a similar approach in two subsequent cases related to the right to strike (*Dilek* and *Enerji Yapi Yol Sen*),[23] sticking to the merely 'important' character of strike action on the one hand, but continuing to assess its restrictions on the basis of Article 11, § 2. The Turkish applicants proved to be more successful on the other hand.

In *Dilek and others*,[24] the Court concluded that there had been a breach of Article 11, § 2. The case was different from *UNISON*, in that it did not relate to a statutory restriction of the right to strike, but to a clear-cut statutory prohibition for civil servants to have recourse to *any kind* of collective action which could suspend, obstruct or slow down the functioning of the public service.

The assessment of the restrictions on the right to have recourse to collective action were considered to be prescribed by law and to pursue a legitimate goal, that is, the proper functioning of the public service. Entailing civil liability of civil servants,

---

[22] ECtHR, 10 January 2002, *UNISON v UK*, App No 53574/99, ECHR 2002-I. See Novitz (n 6) 231–32; and K Ewing, 'Laws against Strikes Revisited' in C Barnard, S Deakin and G Morris (eds), *The Future of Labour Law* (Oxford, Hart Publishing, 2004) 57–58.

[23] *Dilek and others v Turkey* (n 13).

[24] Ibid.

the restriction concerned was considered to be disproportionate in view of the fact that it was imposed on the entire civil service and because the Turkish government was unable to prove how the trade union was able to defend workers' rights in a peaceful way.[25]

In *Enerji Yapi Yol Sen*,[26] the Court had to rule on the legitimacy of a circular recapitulating the prohibition of civil servants having recourse to any kind of collective action based upon the same statutory provisions that had been scrutinised in *Dilek and others*. Despite the fact that the circular had been addressed to civil servants rather than to any trade union likely to organise the strike, this was not a reason for the Court to decide that the application was inadmissible. The Court's judgment was delivered less than seven months after the *Demir and Baykara II* ruling and explicitly refers to the binding methodological tools for interpretation developed by the Grand Chamber. Thus, it examines the relationship between the right to strike and two rights falling within the ECHR ambit: the right to organise and the right to bargain collectively. The specific reference to the right to bargain collectively is natural insofar as this right has been construed as an essential element of the right to join and form trade unions. This relation is examined in the light of two fundamental social rights instruments of international law. The Court primarily refers to ILO Convention No 87. Despite the fact that the provisions of this Convention are mute on the right to strike, the Court takes into account the interpretation given to this instrument by the ILO supervisory bodies. In this respect, it observes that these bodies have considered the right to strike to be interwoven with freedom of association ('un corrolaire indissociable'). Furthermore, the Court observes that Article 6, § 2 ESC establishes a functional link between the right to bargain collectively and the right to strike. Insofar as the right to bargain collectively is necessarily inherent to the freedom of association and insofar as the right to bargain collectively 'without strike' is deprived of its substance, it can be argued[27] that the right to strike does constitute an essential aspect of the right to organise by means of association. In my view, the reference to the ILO case law describing the right to strike as a 'corrolaire indissociable' furthermore warrants the hypothesis that the Court has implicitly recognised the right to strike as an *essential* element of the right to trade union association. The Court therefore did not even examine whether the trade unions had alternative means to 'have their voice heard'.[28]

---

[25] Ibid, § 72.

[26] ECtHR, 21 April 2009, *Enerji Yapi-Yol Sen v Turkey* App No 68959/01.

[27] See F Dorssemont, annotation to *Demir and Baykara*, 12 November 2008, *EHRC* 2009/1, 68–69. See also JP Marguénaud and J Mouly, 'La jurisprudence sociale de la Cour EDH: bilan et perspectives' (2010) *Droit social* 889 (both authors argue that the approach of the Grand Chamber of the Court in *Demir and Baykara* prompted a recognition of the right to strike as an essential means).

[28] In a recent publication, Edström argued that the Court in *Enerji* 'took the position that the right to strike is an independent right, regardless of whether there are other means for taking care of the trade union members' interests': O Edström, 'The Right to Collective Action as a Fundamental Right' in Mia Rönnmar (ed), *Labour Law, Fundamental Rights and Social Europe* (Oxford, Hart Publishing, 2012) 66.

3.2 The Material Scope of 'Collective Action'

As opposed to the British *UNISON* case, one of the Turkish cases provides guidance on the question whether the Court's restriction extends from a right to strike to a more comprehensive right to take collective action. At first sight, the Court did not have to dwell on this question, since under Turkish law, *any* kind of collective action, including strike action, was prohibited for civil servants.

The question whether a prohibition of 'alternative' actions (other than strike action) could pass the test was therefore not the issue. However, the Turkish government did decide to make it an issue in *Dilek and others*.[29] In this case, a number of civil servants had left their post for a couple of hours at a toll plaza on the Bosporus Bridge. They wanted to protest against the working conditions applicable to them. The Turkish government and the applicants disagreed as to whether the action concerned could qualify as strike action. However, the Court felt reluctant to enter into such a semantic debate, considering the question of the definition of strike action to be irrelevant insofar as the action concerned constituted a 'collective action within the context of the exercise of trade union rights' in the generic meaning of the word.[30]

Hence, it seems that the Court wanted to make it clear that the mere fact that a collective action did not constitute a strike action was not as such sufficient to fall outside the ambit of Article 11 ECHR. In sum, in considering that the action fell within the ambit of Article 11 without indicating whether it constituted a strike or not, the Court seems to have recognised a more comprehensive right to take collective action. In my view, the mere fact that the interruption of the toll-collecting activity only lasted a couple of hours does not constitute a reason to disqualify the action as being a strike action. Furthermore, the mere fact that the collective action could only have been welcomed by drivers being allowed to cross the Bosporus for free is in my view immaterial. Despite the Court's language,[31] the collective action does not constitute a go-slow ('action de ralentissement'). Despite the similar effects of the action concerned, it similarly does not constitute a case of free public transport ('grève libéralité'). It is extremely dangerous to assume that *Dilek* allows us to state that actions resulting in 'toll-free' public transport fall within the ambit of Article 11 ECHR. Similarly, they do not constitute strikes, since they require the employees to continue performing their work to some extent, despite its dysfunctional character.[32]

In sum, the Court's reference to such a comprehensive right to take collective action is still unclear. The FAC's case law might help the Court to explore its scope. The FAC has taken a favourable stance vis-a-vis alternative modes of collective action as long as they continue to have a pacific character.[33] Despite the fact that the

---

[29] *Dilek and others v Turkey* (n 13).

[30] Ibid, § 57.

[31] Ibid, § 6.

[32] See the contribution for the AFDTSS colloquium of 21 March 2008: JP Marguénaud and J Mouly, 'Convention européenne des droits de l'homme et droit du travail', http://afdt-asso.fr/fichiers/publications/cedh.pdf.

[33] www.ilo.org/wcmsp5/groups/public/---ed_norm/---normes/documents/publication/wcms_090632.pdf (No 545).

ESC explicitly refers to the notion of 'collective action', the European Committee of Social Rights (ECSR) has until now not given much guidance.[34] The right to take collective action under Article 6 RESC includes an employer's right to have recourse to lockouts. A recent collective complaint procedure introduced by the Belgian trade unions and the European Trade Union Confederation (ETUC) was aimed at clarifying the question to what extent the right to take collective action involves a right to picketing and to what extent this allows trade unions to block the entrance to a plant.[35] The Committee provided some guidance as to the extent of the right to take collective action under Article 6 RESC, holding that 'Article 6 § 4 RESC encompasses not only the right to withholding of work but also other relevant means, inter alia, the right to picketing. Both these components deserve consequently a comparable degree of protection'.[36]

The Committee did not define the precise scope of the right to picketing. It seems to suggest that it cannot be reduced to the mere exercise of freedom of assembly and of expression. However, picket procedures 'operating in such a way as to infringe the rights of non-strikers, through for example the use of intimidation or violence' fall outside the ambit of Article 6 RESC.

This approach did *not* allow considering whether picket actions blocking access to enterprises *without* having recourse to intimidation or violence per se fall outside the scope of the RESC. The French-language version makes clear[37] that collective actions do not just have to infringe the rights of non-strikers, but also have to make use of 'intimidation or violence' in order to fall outside the scope of the RESC. Furthermore, the Committee did not add that such actions need to be 'peaceful in nature', only stating that they should not be based on the use of intimidation or violence.

The Committee gave some guidance on what can be considered as a restriction of a collective action. Such a restriction is at issue whenever the picketing activity does *not* violate the rights of other workers to choose whether or not to take part in the strike action.

---

[34] See F Dorssemont, 'La (non) conformité du droit belge relative à l'action collective par rapport à la Charte sociale européenne', X. *Actualités du dialogue social et du droit de grève* (Kluwer, Waterloo, 2009) 176–82.; and S Evju 'The Right to Collective Action under the European Social Charter' (2011) 3 *European Labour Law Journal*, 201–03.

[35] See the ECSR decision related to Collective Complaint No 59/2009, European Trade Union Confederation (ETUC)/*Centrale Générale des Syndicats Libéraux de Belgique* (CGSLB)/*Confédération des Syndicats chrétiens de Belgique* (CSC)/*Fédération Générale du Travail de Belgique* (FGTB) *v Belgium*: www.coe.int/t/dghl/monitoring/socialcharter/Complaints/CC59Merits_en.pdf. For a comment, see F Dorssemont, 'Libres propos sur la légitimité des requêtes unilatérales *contre* l'exercice du droit à l'action collective à la lumière de la Décision du Comité européen des droits sociaux (Réclamation collective nr. 59/2009)' in PP Vangehuchten and Y Ficher (eds), *Actions orphélines et voies de recours en droit social* (Limal, Anthémis, 2012) 129–48; and P Lyon-Caen, 'La décision du 13 septembre 2011 du Comité européen des droits sociaux à la lumière de la jurisprudence des organes de contrôle de l'O.I.T.' in PP Vangehuchten and Y Ficher (eds), *Actions orphélines et voies de recours en droit social* (Limal, Anthémis, 2012) 121–29.

[36] www.coe.int/t/dghl/monitoring/socialcharter/Complaints/CC59Merits_en.pdf.

[37] Ibid: 'de nature à porter atteinte à la liberté des non-grévistes, par l'utilisation d'intimidations ou de violences, l'interdiction de ces modalités de mise en œuvre ne saurait être considérée comme contraire au droit de grève reconnu à l'article 6§4'. The English-language version states 'through *for example* the use of intimidation or violence'.

The precise scope of the right to choose whether or not to take part in a strike action is a debated issue. The Belgian employers' federation has issued a statement suggesting that picket actions preventing workers from gaining access to the undertaking where they perform their contract of employment falls outside the ambit of Article 6, § 4 ESC. In my view, this interpretation is ill-founded, since the mere fact that an employee willing to work is unable to gain such access by no means forces him to 'take part in the strike action'. A strike is considered to be a voluntary and collective refusal to perform the employment contract. In this respect, the idea that one could be forced to take part in a strike is a *contradictio in terminis*.

A typical example of alternative actions other than strikes are the boycotts to which Swedish trade unions tend to have recourse in order to enforce the conclusion of tie-in agreements. The judgment of the Court of Justice of the European Union (CJEU) in *Laval* has helped spread the reputation of this trade union strategy. Prior to the *Laval case*, this strategy had already been challenged before the ECtHR. Swedish employers claimed that these boycotts challenged their negative freedom of association and violated the protection of their property rights. In *Gustafsson*[38] and *Kellermann*,[39] two employers claimed that they were being pressured through collective action to become parties to a collective agreement.

Neither of these employers was a member of the employer organisation that had signed the industry-wide collective agreement. Becoming a party to the agreement did not imply any obligation to join these organisations. The Court expressly took into account the State's discretionary authority to shape systems of collective bargaining by deciding that this form of pressure did *not* represent a restriction to the *negative* freedom of association. The State's authority to regulate collective actions had the purpose of increasing the 'coverage' of collective agreements. It was deemed a 'social and political issue' with a 'sensitive character'. The employer Gustafsson also claimed that the particular modalities of collective action could be construed as a violation of another human right. He argued that Article 1 of the First Protocol to the European Convention had been violated, claiming that the boycott undertaken by the Swedish unions impaired the peaceful enjoyment of his property. He had been hit by a 'blockade'. The unions were boycotting his company. Because of the transport sector action, his restaurant was no longer being supplied. There was not any physical blockade at the entrance gate. The Court held that such a boycott did *not* impair Gustafsson's property rights, although it was not disputed that the actions hampered the contractual relations between Gustafsson and his suppliers.[40] The boycott in *Kellermann* was directed against a textile company unaffiliated to an employers' organisation and refusing to apply a sectoral collective agreement.

In both cases, the Court shielded boycott actions against ECHR provisions which the applicant considered to be violated. However, neither of these judgments can be used to state that the Court had recognised that boycott actions fell within the ambit of Article 11 ECHR. Hence, no obligation can be deduced from these judgments to recognise boycott actions on the basis of Article 11 ECHR.

---

[38] *Gustafsson v Sweden* (n 21). See L Schut, 'De cao als spin in het web: het recht om geen cao af te sluiten valt niet onder artikel 11 EVRM' (1998) *Nederlands Juristencomité voor de Mensenrechten Bulletin* 18–36.

[39] ECtHR, 1 July 2003, *AB Kurt Kellermann v Sweden*, App No 41579/98.

[40] *Gustafsson v Sweden* (n 21) §§ 56–60.

3.3 Peaceful Assembly and Collective Action

Article 11 guarantees freedom of *peaceful* assembly. There is a difference between *peaceful assembly* and *collective action*. Collective action is intended to exert pressure on an antagonist in order to influence his behaviour. The purpose of *demonstrations* (peaceful assembly) is to make an opinion known. Peaceful assembly and collective action cannot be completely separated. Collective action seeks to enforce union demands. The possibility that peaceful assembly will lead to pressure being exerted cannot in any way be excluded. Insofar as an assembly takes place *during* working hours outside the premises of the employer and insofar as the participants suspend their work to attend a demonstration, it boils down to a strike, which will often entail economic damage.

Certain types of peaceful assembly can take the form of non-violent resistance. A typical example was a sit-in on a public road which interfered with access to an American army base. Such forms of action used to be seen by the European Commission of Human Rights as an expression of freedom of peaceful assembly.[41] The ruling in *Schmidberger*[42] may be pointed to by analogy. In that ruling, the European Court of Justice accepted the Austrian government's reliance on freedom of peaceful assembly as a ground for restricting the free movement of goods. Several environmental activists had blocked the Brenner Pass. A transport company invoked the free movement of goods to hold the Austrian State liable for the damage suffered by it. The more broadly the term 'peaceful' is interpreted, the more the notion of 'peaceful assembly' may be used to exert pressure on employers. In this respect, a sit-in on a public road or in front of a company entrance gate can be considered to fall within the ambit of 'peaceful assembly'.

In *Barraco v France*, the Court similarly ruled that a collective action organised by a drivers' union fell within the ambit of the right to peaceful assembly. In the facts of this case, a truck driver participated in a so-called 'snail operation' (*operation escargot*) completely obstructing traffic on a public highway by driving slowly or even stopping.[43]

In four recent judgments involving Turkey,[44] the Court felt extremely reluctant to address the issue of the right to strike and to assess whether the recognition of

[41] Commission of Human Rights, 6 March 1989, *X v Federal Republic of Germany*, App No 13079/87, Decisions and Reports (DR) 60, p 256.

[42] European Court of Justice, 12 June 2003, *Eugen Schmidberger, Internationale Transporte und Planzüge v Republic of Austria*, C-112/00, Reports of Cases 2003 I-05659. For a comment on this decision, see F Dorssemont, '"Met de vlam in de pijp ...': Vrijheid van vergadering en meningsuiting, recht op collectieve actie versus vrij verkeer: primaat of belangenafweging?' (2004) *Arbeidsrechtelijke annotaties* 77–93.

[43] ECtHR, 5 March 2009, *Barraco v France*, App No 31684/05, ECtHR 2009. The Court assessed that such a criminal prosecution against one of the drivers participating in the operation could be considered to be justified in view of the fact that there was a legitimate goal (the protection of public order and of the rights and freedoms of others) and that the restriction could be considered to be 'necessary in a democratic society'. See also Lörcher, who argues that this judgment amounts to the recognition of strike action in order to participate to a demonstration (*das Recht auf Proteststreik*). See K Lörcher, 'Internationale Rechtsgrundlagen des Streikrechts' in W Däubler (ed), *Arbeitskampfrecht* (Baden-Baden, Nomos, 2011) 178.

[44] ECtHR, 27 March 2007, *Karaçay v Turkey*, App No 6615/03; ECtHR, 17 July 2008, *Urcan and others*, App Nos 23018/04, 23034/04, 23042/04, 23071/04, 23073/04, 23081/04, 23086/04, 23091/04, 23094/04, 23444/04 and 23676/04; ECtHR 15 September 2009, *Saime Özcan v Turkey*, App No

such a right was an essential element of the right to form and join trade unions. In the cases concerned, civil servants had been absent from their work in order to participate in a demonstration in support of a claim for better working conditions. As a result, the civil servants were subjected to criminal sanctions in two cases and to a disciplinary sanction in the two other cases. Though the demonstration had taken place as part of a national civil service strike and was organised by a trade union, the Court refused to address the issue of whether the right to strike was an essential means to protect workers' interests. It did not examine any international law instrument related to the right to strike. Despite stating that the Turkish law constituted a violation of freedom of association, the Court considered the issue of the legitimacy of such a restriction solely in the context of freedom of peaceful assembly. This approach is astonishing, insofar as all applicants explicitly referred to their right to form and join a trade union. In all four cases, the restriction based on the statutory prohibition of civil servants having recourse to collective action was considered to be disproportionate. It also contrasts with a more courageous stance that the Court took in a similar case of disciplinary sanctions against a civil servant for participating in a national strike action.[45]

In sum, the prospect seems to be that the Court will try to avoid the issue of the scope of the right to take collective action. Insofar as certain collective actions can be construed as the exercise of the freedom of peaceful assembly, the Court seems to privilege that avenue. Thus, in *Trofimchuk*, the Court construed a picket action primarily as a *species* of freedom of assembly. This approach may be regretted. The ECSR decision regarding collective complaint 59/2009[46] could be interpreted as criticism of such an approach, with the Committee observing that 'if the right to picketing is linked only to the right to freedom of assembly and freedom of expression, it runs the risk of being restricted more easily than if it were guaranteed as part of the right to collective action'. In view of the fact that the ILO FAC attaches great importance to the peaceful character of alternative actions, the Court might learn from FAC case law in interpreting the scope of what constitutes peaceful assembly.

3.4 The Issue of Personal Scope

3.4.1 Personal Scope

The issue of the personal scope of the right to take collective action seeks to identify the holder of such a right.

The problem is far from academic for a number of reasons. The first concerns the question whether individuals *as well as* associations can invoke violations of such a right before the Court. Two aspects seem to be at the heart of the matter. In

---

2953/04; and ECtHR 15 September 2009, *Kaya and Seyhan v Turkey*, App No 30946/04; *Dilek and others v Turkey* (n 13).

[45] In this case, the Court ruled that the disciplinary sanction violated the right to form and join a trade union: *Karaçay v Turkey* (n 44).

[46] See reference in n 35.

the past, the Court has recognised the *locus standi* of trade unions[47] contesting the violation of the rights of individuals prevented or dissuaded from becoming members of a trade union. The question arises as to what extent individuals have *locus standi* insofar as a trade union is prevented or restricted from organising collective action. A further question is to what extent individuals who are *not* organised as a trade union have a right to take collective action under Article 11 ECHR.

The second reason relates to the question of whether Article 11 guarantees both workers' organisations *and* employers' organisations a right to take collective action. This question is twofold. Insofar as employees can be considered as holders of a right to strike or even a right to take collective action, the question arises as to whether that notion ('employee') needs to be interpreted in an autonomous way. An affirmative answer amounts to a necessity to indicate which elements are essential for such a qualification to be deviated from. Can employers invoke Article 11 to claim a right to have recourse to a lockout?

The third question is somewhat parochial. Under German law, works councils are not authorised to organise collective action.[48] The question is whether such a prohibition, which does not affect the right of individual workers' representatives to participate in a strike, can be challenged on the basis of Article 11 ECHR.

Last but not least, Article 11, § 2 provides leeway for Contracting Parties to restrict the right to organise of specified civil servants. The potential implications of this clause will be examined.

3.4.2 *Individual Employees and Collective Action*

In my view, the individual and collective dimensions of trade union freedom are intertwined. Trade union members have an obvious active and direct interest in contesting violations of the right of trade unions to defend *their* interests. This is particularly true in the case of strike action. Strike action is per se the action of an individual (ie, withholding his labour). The trade union as such cannot go on strike; it can only organise and support strikes. It is not a contracting party of an employment contract and therefore cannot suspend its execution. In fact, a lot of cases related to clear-cut prohibitions or restrictions on the right to strike were driven by individual actors, that is, employees.[49] In many cases, strike action constitutes the exercise of the freedom of assembly by individuals. It is thus perfectly consistent that individuals can challenge restrictions on such a right.

The subsequent issue is more complex. The fact that the Court relates the recognition of the right to strike in respect of freedom of association inevitably raises the question of whether the ECHR guarantees workers a right to have recourse to 'spontaneous' or 'wild-cat' strikes that are neither authorised nor organised by trade

[47] See *Wilson and Palmer*, 2 July 2002, App Nos 30668/96, 30671/96, 30678/96 and 30668/96, ECtHR 2002-V. On this issue, see Ewing (n 15) 13–14.

[48] See § 2 *Betriebsverfassungsgesetz*. The reference to the duty of a works council member to cooperate in good faith with management is interpreted as a prohibition to organise collective actions in their capacity as members of the works council. § 74 specifies this in more detail.

[49] See *Schmidt and Dahlström v Sweden* (n 11); *Karaçay v Turkey* (n 44); *Urcan and others* (n 44); *Saime Özcan v Turkey* (n 44); *Kaya and Seyhan v Turkey* (n 44)

unions. The ILO FAC has been reluctant to recognise such a right, holding that the ILO Conventions do not prevent a State from prohibiting wild-cat strikes.[50] The position of the ECSR is more ambiguous. Though it does seem to construe the right to participate in a strike as an individual right, it does not seem to preclude that Contracting States could construe the right to call a strike as a trade union prerogative.[51] In view of the individualistic stance that the ECtHR has taken in respect of the right *not* to organise, it seems doubtful that it would not be able to recognise that individuals have the right to have recourse to collective action without trade union recognition. In the absence of a provision explicitly recognising the right to strike, such recognition can only be based upon a broad interpretation of either the notion of 'trade union' or the freedom of peaceful assembly. In this respect, it is worthwhile remembering that the Court did (in *Enerji Yapi-Yol Sen*) consider that the circular in question was problematic insofar as it prohibited civil servants from exercising their freedom of peaceful assembly.[52]

In the recent *Sindicatul Pastorul Cel Bun* case,[53] the Court was asked to assess whether the refusal by the Romanian administrative authorities to register an 'alleged trade union' organising priests and employees working for the Romanian Orthodox Church constituted a violation of Article 11 ECHR. It considered *both* categories to perform their functions on the basis of individual employment contracts, even though the contractual nature of the employment relation of priests had been disputed by the Archbishopric of Craiova, stating that the employment relations had a sacramental rather than a contractual character, as priests took a vow rather than signed a contract on their ordination. The Court rightly acknowledged that the remuneration received by both categories was financed by the State. In fact, pursuant to applicable Romanian law, the State paid the remuneration directly to the persons concerned.

In my view, the Court's approach provides evidence of an autonomous approach to the employment relationship, giving the impression that the qualification given under domestic law is immaterial, and distancing itself from a complete 'clericalisation' of the employment relation, excluding such relations from the ambit of the state administration of a Contracting Party.

In my opinion, three elements seem to have been conclusive in the Court's approach of recognising that the citizens concerned fell within the ambit of trade union freedom. These elements are the performance of work, remuneration and the presence of 'authority' or 'subordination'.

The genesis of such a relationship seems to be disregarded, despite the Court's claim that it has a contractual nature. Such an autonomous approach to employment relationships is somewhat reminiscent of that of the CJEU in such matters as the free movement of workers, health and safety, and non-discrimination.

---

[50] International Labour Office, *Freedom of Association, Digest of Decisions and Principles of the Freedom of Association Committee of the Governing Body of the ILO* (Geneva, 2006) No 524.
[51] Evju (n 34) 213–19. See also A Swiatkowski, *Charter of Social Rights of the Council of Europe* (Alphen aan den Rijn, Kluwer Law International, 2007) 233.
[52] *Enerji Yapi-Yol Sen v Turkey* (n 26) § 32.
[53] ECtHR, 31 January 2012, *Sindicatul Pastorul Cel Bun*, App No 2330/09.

3.4.3 Employers and Collective Action

Article 11 ECHR enshrines both a generic freedom of association and a more specific right to form and join trade unions for the protection of his interests. Insofar as individual rights to form, join or not to join an employers' association are concerned, the question whether an association is a trade union or not was considered to be immaterial. The Court adopted such a stance in *Sigurjónsson*.[54] The question arose as to whether an association (Frami) which taxi drivers needed to join to obtain a government licence could be regarded as a 'trade union'. The Icelandic government did not agree with this characterisation. At issue in this case was whether, based on a statutory provision, Iceland could make granting a licence to drive a taxi dependent on prior membership in Frami. The statutory provision created a *pre-entry closed shop* for self-employed people. The government assumed that 'trade unions' concerned worker organisations which defended the interests of their members in conflicts with their employer. Frami, the organisation in dispute, consisted primarily of persons working independently without staff. The Court refused to clarify the definitional scope of the term 'trade union', commenting that Frami could in all respects be characterised as an association. It considered 'that it was not necessary to decide whether Frami' could also be regarded as a trade union, 'since the right to form and join trade unions in that provision is an aspect of a wider right to freedom of association rather than a separate right'.[55] In the same vein, it can be argued that the right of an employer to join or not to join an association is guaranteed by the generic recognition of the freedom of association. Despite the fact that, as such, an association cannot be construed as a 'trade union', it would still fall within the ambit of Article 11.

Since the right to take collective action to defend the rights of members of a trade union is based upon the specific coda (protection of interests), the question to what extent employers' associations can be construed as 'trade unions' or '*syndicats*' cannot be avoided. Indeed, the Court has indicated that the recognition of the right to take collective action is based upon that very coda. Judged otherwise, such a coda would be redundant. The Court has stressed that it is not redundant. If employers' organisations cannot be considered as trade unions, they cannot claim a right to take collective action under Article 11 ECHR.

Article 11 ECHR does *not* provide a definition of the term 'trade union'. Neither does it define 'association'. It does, however, allow the definition of a trade union as an 'association', though without indicating a criterion distinguishing it from associations not considered to be trade unions.

In its case law, the Court has only given guidance on the definition of associations,[56] assessing the issue by examining a set of criteria. It has refused

---

[54] ECtHR, 30 June 1993, *Sigurdur Sigurjónsson v Iceland*, No 16130/90, Series A, No 264.

[55] Ibid, § 32.

[56] See AW Heeringa and F Van Hoof 'Freedom of Association and Assembly' in P van Dijk et al (eds), *Theory and Practice of the European Convention on Human Rights* (Antwerpe, Intersentia, 2006), 826–28; and E Brems and Y Haeck, 'Vrijheid van vreedzame vergadering en vrijheid van vereniging' in Y Haeck and J Vande Lanotte, *Handboek EVRM, v. II* (Antwerp, Intersentia, 2004) 17–20. See especially the following judgments: ECtHR, 23 June 1981, *Le Compte, Van Leuven and De Meyere v Belgium*, App Nos 6878/75 and 7238/75, Series A, No 46, §§ 64–65; *Sigurdur Sigurjónsson v Iceland* (n 54); and

to indicate any decisive criterion, instead attaching importance to the *genesis* (initiative by private individuals or a body established by law) of the entity concerned, its composition and the autonomy granted to set its own objectives and determine its organisation. Other criteria indicate that an organisation under dispute *cannot* be considered to be an association according to the meaning of Article 11 ECHR. In this respect, the Court examines 'the extent to which the entity concerned is being placed under the supervision of public authorities, the extent to which it has been endowed with public law prerogatives of an administrative, rule-making and disciplinary nature or the extent to which the entities concerned employ processes of public authorities'.[57] Since the notion 'association' has an autonomous meaning, the public or private law nature of the structure under the domestic law of a Contracting Party is not relevant. The Court will assess whether a structure can be qualified as an association by weighing these criteria in a given case. Thus, the Court has ruled that a professional organisation established by the government and governed by public law which is basically endowed with surveying public interests does not fall within the scope of Article 11 ECHR.[58] Restrictions on the freedom not to join *such* an organisation are therefore not at issue when examining the (negative) freedom of association, unless an obligation to join these professional organisations excludes the freedom to form and to join a 'genuine' trade union.[59]

At present, the Court's case law does not provide any decisive indication on how to solve the problem of defining the scope of the notion 'trade union'. The use of the terms 'trade union' and '*syndicat*' in the official English and French versions of the ECHR gives rise to the question whether these terms embrace employers' organisations too. If the answer is affirmative, this implies that these terms have an *autonomous* significance. The term '*syndicat*' in the French Waldeck-Rousseau Act covers people engaging in a profession (*une profession libre*).[60] This description makes the use of this legal framework accessible only to those employers who themselves engage in a profession (eg, lawyers or doctors). Traditional employer organisations are not organised in the form of '*syndicats*', but of '*associations*'. An '*association*' is governed by a different legal framework. Employers' organisations cannot in any way be characterised as 'trade unions' within the meaning of Article 1 of the British TULRCA, as they are *not* associations consisting wholly or mainly of workers.

In my view, it is worthwhile interpreting the notion of trade unions under Article 11 ECHR in a way that is consistent with the scope *ratione personae* of the right to organise in more specialised international instruments. Brems and Haeck[61] have suggested that the specific recognition of trade unions should be extended to employers' organisations for reasons of equality of arms.

---

29 April 1999, *Chassagnou v France*, App Nos 25088/94, 28331/95 and 28443/95, ECHR 1999-III, §§ 99–102.

[57] *Chassagnou v France* (n 56) § 101.
[58] *Le Compte, Van Leuven and De Meyere v Belgium* (n 56) § 65.
[59] Ibid.
[60] See Article L 411-2, *Code du Travail*. For a commentary, see R Brichet, *Associations et syndicats* (Paris, Litec, 1992) 444–51.
[61] Brems and Haeck (n 56) 18 (see the use of the Dutch 'evenknie').

ILO Convention No 87 (1948) defines workers' and employers' organisations within the meaning of the Convention as 'any organisation of workers or of employers for furthering and defending the interests of workers or of employers'. Employers are unambiguously included within the scope of the right to organise. Article 5 RESC expressly applies to employers and workers alike. Like the European Convention, Article 8 of the International Covenant on Economic, Social and Cultural Rights (ICESCR) does not make clear who holds the right to organise.

In *Gustafsson*[62] and *Kellermann*,[63] the references to the right to organise were *implicitly* applied to employers arguing that their freedom *not* to join an employers' organisation was being curtailed. It is indeed my view that the Court was aware that it had to deal with an issue of freedom of association in the field of industrial relations. Thus, it acknowledged that the *Gustafsson* case raised sensitive social and political issues 'in achieving a proper balance between the competing interests' and that there was a 'wide degree of divergence between the domestic systems in the particular area under consideration'.[64] Hence, it can be argued that the Court was perfectly aware that it was dealing with the right of employers to join a 'trade union' according to the meaning of Article 11 ECHR. In my view, Article 14 ECHR constitutes a compelling reason to recognise the right to organise for employers and workers alike. In fact, the ECHR does not clarify whether members of a trade union need to be workers. From this perspective, there is no reason why 'members' could not refer to employers. If one takes this interpretation seriously, this means that employers' associations need to have the ability to have recourse to take collective action in order to protect the interests of their members. Unfortunately, however, it seems extremely difficult to construe a right to take *collective* action for an *individual* employer on the basis of Article 11 ECHR. In a scenario related to an industrial dispute at plant level, there is no association on the employer side which can be identified as protecting members' interests.

In a case which has nearly fallen into oblivion, the CJEU opted for an 'autonomous' interpretation of the notion of 'trade union' or '*syndicat*'. In *Asti v Chambre des employés privés*,[65] the CJEU considered that the refusal to allow non-Luxemburg nationals to become members of the Luxemburg *Chambres d'employés* violated Article 8 of EU Regulation 1612/68 on the freedom of movement for workers within the Community. This Article provides that a worker who is a national of a Member State and who is employed in the territory of another Member State shall enjoy equality of treatment as regards membership of trade unions and the exercise of rights attaching thereto. Despite the fact that the Luxemburg chambers did not constitute 'trade unions' under Luxemburg law, it did rule that such a refusal constituted a violation. The judgment is interesting since it would be very doubtful whether these bodies established under public law could qualify as trade unions within the meaning of Article 11 ECHR.[66]

---

[62] *Gustafsson v Sweden* (n 21). See Schut (n 48) 18–36.
[63] *AB Kurt Kellermann v Sweden* (n 39).
[64] *Gustafsson v Sweden* (n 21) § 45.
[65] CJEU, 4 July 1991, Case C-213/90, *Asti v Chambre des employés privés*.
[66] See, in this respect, *Le Compte, Van Leuven and De Meyere v Belgium* (n 56) § 65.

3.4.4 Works Councils and Collective Action

It is obvious that works councils are not trade unions. An application from a Turkish national whose membership in an Austrian works council was retracted on the basis that he did not have Austrian nationality was declared manifestly ill-founded. In *Karakurt*,[67] the Court ruled that works councils were established under Austrian law and that they were not private, voluntary associations within the meaning of Article 11 ECHR. The finding in the dicta that the term 'association' must be given autonomous meaning seems to suggest that the terms 'trade union' or '*syndicat*' within the meaning of Article 11 must likewise be ascribed autonomous significance. This would be a further argument in favour of the notion of trade unions or *syndicats* also covering employers' organisations.

The Court's approach in *Karakurt* deviates from the way in which the Committee of Independent Experts (now the ECSR) addressed the condition of nationality as a pre-requisite for being eligible as a workers' representative on an Austrian works council. The Committee considered this to constitute a violation of the right to organise.[68] According to the Committee: 'This constitutes a restriction on the freedom of trade unions to choose their candidates in such elections.' This approach establishes a link between the issue of eligibility and the collective aspects of trade union freedom.

3.4.5 Members of the Armed Forces, the Police or the Administration of the State and Collective Action

Last but not least, the question arises as to whether the personal scope of the right to take collective actions can be restricted in order to exclude 'civil servants'. The question is relevant insofar as Article 11, § 2 contains a coda allowing restrictions to be imposed on freedom of association with regard to members of the armed forces, the police or the administration of the State. Insofar as the legal construction of the right to take collective action is intertwined with the freedom of trade union association, such restrictions could also extend to the collective dimension of trade union freedom.

The restriction on the freedom of association of members of the armed forces and the police is common to other human rights instruments,[69] though the reference to members of the administration of the State is only found in the ICESCR. It has been argued that the coda does not provide scope for restrictions which cannot be justified by the material (as opposed to personal) grounds mentioned in Article 11, § 2 ECHR.[70] In this respect, the reference to these categories of people

---

[67] ECtHR, 14 September 1999, M *Karakurt v Austria*, App No 32441/96.

[68] Committee of Independent Experts, *Conclusions* XIII-3, p 96; Committee of Independent Experts, *Conclusions* XIV-1, Vol 1, p 74. The criticism was reiterated in the subsequent cycles of control (XV, XVI, XVII and XVIII) See also D Harris and J Darcy, *The European Social Charter* (Ardsley, Transnational Publishers, 2001) 92.

[69] See Article 5 ESC, Article 8 ICESCR, Article 22 ICCPR and Article 9 ILO Convention No 87.

[70] Brems and Haeck (n 56) 35; and A Heringa and F Van Hoof (n 56) 839.

would not constitute a separate ground for restrictions. In an older case[71] relating to the British Government Communication Headquarters (GCHQ), the European Commission on Human Rights adopted an entirely opposite view, stating that 'the second sentence of Article 11 para 2 justifies the imposition of restrictions in the freedom enjoyed by persons in three specified categories which could not be justified under the first sentence'. GCHQ was concerned with national security, providing signals intelligence to the British government. The Commission concluded that the infamous prohibition of civil servants working for GCHQ from becoming a member of a trade union not recognised by the government was legitimate both under the first and the second sentences of Article 11, § 2, disregarding earlier criticism which was expressed by the ILO FAC and the Committee of Experts on the Application of Conventions and Recommendations (CEACR), as well as the Plenary Session of the ILO's Conference. In *Demir and Baykara II*,[72] the Grand Chamber decided to interpret the notion of 'administration of the State' in the light of the interpretation of Article 6 of ILO Convention No 98 given by the ILO CEACR. This Article excludes 'public servants' from the ambit of the Convention on the right to organise and the right to bargain collectively. Since the civil servants concerned worked at the municipal level, the Court ruled that it had not been established that they were 'officials directly employed in the administration of the State'. In other cases involving Turkey[73] and dealing with a general *prohibition* (rather than a mere restriction) on civil servants from organising and/or to having recourse to collective action, the Court ruled that these provisions were disproportionate. The approach adopted in *Demir and Baykara* calls for a restrictive interpretation of the notion of members of the administration. It does not clarify the extent to which Member States can effectively restrict, let alone prohibit the freedom of association of 'genuine' members of the administration. Since the Court disqualified the municipal civil servants as members of the administration within the meaning of Article 11, it remains unclear to what extent Contracting Parties can restrict or prohibit freedom of association in a way that is at odds with the general conditions set forth in Article 11, § 2.[74]

In my view, the mere fact that certain citizens belong to these categories is not sufficient to exclude them from the ambit of Article 11. Though Article 11 states that freedom of association can be restricted, it does not refer to prohibitions suggesting that these could be justified based on the mere fact that the citizens belong to these categories. Conversely, the mere fact that they belong to the categories concerned does not imply that a restriction will need to be considered per se as justified. In the recent *Sindicatul Cel Bun* case, the Court made it abundantly clear that restrictions are possible insofar as the citizens in question belong to the categories concerned and insofar as the restrictions in question are justified. This judgment makes it

---

[71] See European Commission on Human Rights, 20 January 1987, No 11603/85. According to Ewing, the case is a 'classic example of the failure of the Strasbourg system to protect trade union rights': Ewing (n 15) 4.

[72] ECtHR, 12 November 20008, App No 34503/97.

[73] See, inter alia, *Dilek and others v Turkey* (n 13), *Enerji Yapi-Yol Sen v Turkey* (n 26) and the Turkish disciplinary procedures quoted underneath under 3.6 below.

[74] *In extenso*, S van Drooghenbroeck, 'Les frontières du droit et le temps juridique: la cour européenne des droits de l'homme repousse les limites' (2009) 79 *Revue trimestrielle des droits de l'homme* 838–43.

abundantly clear that the mere fact that a workers is being paid by the State is not a sufficient reason to qualify him or her as a civil servant. Two conditions have to be met. It is still unclear in my view *whether* the justified character could be assessed in a way which is essentially different from the classical parameters listed in Article 11, § 2.

3.5 Prohibitions and Restrictions

ECtHR case law on collective action deals with two entirely different situations. The first concerns clear-cut prohibitions of trade unions having recourse to *any* kind of collective action, while the second deals with legal restrictions on the right to take collective action. A distinction can be made here between procedural and more substantive restrictions. The case law does not, however, provide much guidance on the issue of teleological restrictions.

As evidenced by the cases involving Turkey, the Court has adopted a fierce stance against industrial relations systems which completely exclude the ability of workers from having recourse to collective action,[75] construing that such excessive prohibition is disproportionate.

As far as prohibitions are concerned, the prima facie 'shocking'[76] question arises as to whether Member States are *obliged* under Article 11 ECHR to prohibit some collective action when it interferes with rights and freedoms protected under the Convention. This question needs to be distinguished from the *leeway* Contracting Parties might have in prohibiting or restricting collective action in order to safeguard national security or public safety, prevent civil disorder or crime, protect health or morals, or protect the rights and freedoms of others.

Paradoxically, the poor stance on the right to take collective action inspired two Swedish employers to defend the hypothesis that freedom of association under Article 11 ECHR could indeed preclude recourse to collective action. As indicated previously, collective actions were behind the proceedings in *Gustafsson*[77] and *Kellermann*.[78] The Court had to ponder the question whether the fact that employers were pressured through a boycott into becoming parties to a collective agreement limited their right *not* to organise. Though the Court did not follow this line of argument, it did, however, in *Gustafsson* make a reservation in the case of a collective agreement containing clauses restricting the employers' right to organise. Hence, the prospect of a strike cannot be used to compel employers to sign agreements impinging on their freedom of association. In my view, strikes could similarly not be used to force an employer to summarily *dismiss* non-organised workers without a formal commitment to do so enshrined in a collective agreement. Ewing[79] has pointed out

---

[75] *Dilek and others v Turkey* (n 13). See, eg, *Karaçay v Turkey* (n 44); *Urcan and others* (n 44); *Saime Özcan v Turkey* (n 44); and *Kaya and Seyhan v Turkey* (n 44).

[76] However, we are in good company; see Ewing's paragraph entitled 'The right to strike as a threat to human rights' in K Ewing (n 22) 55–57.

[77] *Gustafsson v Sweden* (n 21).

[78] *AB Kurt Kellermann v Sweden* (n 39).

[79] K Ewing (n 22) 58.

that the ECtHR in *Sibson*[80] was not opposed to a prospect of a strike in order to force an employer to transfer an employee to another establishment without any significant change in his economic working conditions.

3.5.1 Teleological Restrictions on the Right to Collective Action

Domestic labour law standards provide evidence of a *teleological* approach of the right to take collective action. Under German labour law, trade unions and workers can only have recourse to collective action insofar as it is related to a collective agreement. The *Tarifvertragsbezogenheit*[81] of the right to strike under German law reveals the restrictive implications of such a teleological approach. Under British law, immunity for trade unions can only be granted insofar as the strike action occurs in the context of a trade (that is, industrial) dispute.[82] The definition of a trade dispute under UK law restricts the number of antagonists against whom industrial action can be directed to one opponent, that is, the current contractual employer of the workers involved in a strike action. The teleological dimension of the right to strike is also at the heart of the debate surrounding the legitimacy of a 'political strike' which tends to be opposed to the non-political strike (in French doctrine, *grève professionnelle*).

It is rather difficult to assess how the Court will deal in the future with the legitimacy of such teleological restrictions. At present, the only attempt to challenge teleological restrictions was the request submitted by UNISON and a number of its members. The strike action which took place in the context of a transfer of undertaking had been disqualified by British judges as an industrial dispute between employees and their current contractual employer. The employees of the transferee had gone on strike in order to safeguard existing rights after the transfer. The British judges considered in a very formalistic manner that the action was not undertaken in the context of an industrial dispute between the employees and their current employer, but that it related to an industrial dispute against a *future* employer. The Court did not validate this reasoning to justify restricting the right to strike. It instead took an alternative avenue, describing the particular economic interest that the business had in the continuity of its services and the exercise of freedom of contract as a legitimate objective for restricting the right to strike. Thus, it did not go along with the British government's assertion that those interests could only be defended within the narrow context of a 'trade dispute'.

The nexus between the right to strike and freedom of association precludes the question of whether workers and trade unions can have recourse to collective action solely in the context of collective bargaining. The ESC inevitably raises such a question due to the functional link between collective action and collective bargaining. The ECSR has avoided the detrimental effect of the link by broadening the notion of collective bargaining to any kind of social dialogue between

---

[80] ECtHR, 20 April 1993, *Sibson v UK*, App No 14327/88, Series A, No 258.
[81] *Tarifvertragsbezogenheit*: the fact that the legitimate character of a strike is dependent on a tight relation with a collective bargaining process in a formal meaning.
[82] See Article 244 TULRCA.

management and labour.[83] Thus, strike action undertaken outside the formal bargaining procedures involving trade unions, though related to a dialogue between management and labour *sensu lato*, falls within the ambit of Article 6 ESC. It is argued that Contracting States do have the possibility to restrict the ability to call a strike to trade unions on condition that forming a trade union is not subject to excessive formalities.[84]

In my view, as a matter of principle, teleological restrictions to collective action cannot narrow the ability of trade unions to 'protect the interests of their members'. Any teleological restriction narrowing down such an objective needs to be justified under Article 11, § 2. Though the wording of the ECHR is somewhat defensive in comparison to other instruments related to the freedom of trade union association,[85] it does not provide any conclusive arguments for restricting the protection of workers' interests to the ambit of the employment contract. Prima facie, these interests should also include the *social* and *economic* interests of workers outside the employment relationship. Moreover, such interpretation is consistent with the nature of an instrument which seeks to defend civil and political rights.

As pointed out by Novitz, the *UNISON* judgment restricts the interests to 'occupational interests',[86] whereby the exact scope of this expression remains unclear. Novitz has expressed a legitimate concern that the notion of occupational interests seems to be narrower than that of 'social and economic interests' upheld by the ILO supervisory bodies. Though the restriction to occupational interests has been used on previous occasions,[87] it is troublesome. It adds a restriction to the interests at stake that is not enshrined at all in the text of the Convention. Furthermore, due to the canon of inter-textual interpretation introduced by *Demir and Baykara*, a broad conception of those interests should prevail. In my view, the notion of 'occupational' can be opposed to 'political' *sensu stricto*. The exclusion of the defence of 'political interests' should not prevent a trade union from defending the socio-economic interests of the working class against governmental institutions.[88]

3.5.2 Procedural Restrictions on the Right to Take Collective Action

Certain Member States of the EU have introduced procedural restrictions on the recourse trade unions can have to strike action. These restrictions range from a mere

---

[83] www.coe.int/t/dghl/monitoring/socialcharter/Digest/DigestSept2008_en.pdf, 56: 'Within those limits, the right to strike should be guaranteed in the context of any negotiation between employers and employees in order to settle an industrial dispute. Consequently prohibiting strikes not aimed at concluding a collective agreement is not in conformity with Article 6 § 4.'

[84] Ibid. On the distinction between the right to participate in a strike and the right to call a strike, see Evju (n 34) 213–16.

[85] In more specific instruments, the objectives are set in a more specific or a more ambitious way. Thus, the nature of the interests at stake is described explicitly and broadly as 'social and economic interests'. Furthermore, trade unions are presented as being 'in the offensive'. They do not just 'protect' or 'defend', they 'promote and further' interests. See Article 10 ILO Convention No 87, Article 8 ICESCR and Article 5 RESC.

[86] T Novitz (n 6) 232–33.

[87] *Schmidt and Dahlström v Sweden* (n 11).

[88] www.ilo.org/wcmsp5/groups/public/---ed_norm/---normes/documents/publication/wcms_090632.pdf, p 529.

information of strike action, with or without a notice or cooling-off period, via an obligation to allow for mediation, conciliation or arbitration, to ballot procedures which submit the legitimacy of strike action to a majority decision of the trade union members concerned. These procedures boil down to preventive restrictions.[89] Both the FAC and the ECSR have severely criticised some of these procedural restrictions.

The FAC has adopted a fierce stance against compulsory arbitration procedures, stating that a procedure ceases to be voluntary when it is not introduced at the request of both parties to the industrial dispute. It has also been very critical about ballot procedures which require trade unions to respect an unreasonably high quorum of participating workers (eg, two-thirds)[90] or which require an absolute majority, let alone a qualified majority.[91]

The ECSR has stated in a more general way that the ballot method, the quorum and the majority required cannot be such that the exercise of the right to strike is excessively limited.[92] It has not made any critical observations as regards other procedural restrictions, such as an obligation to notify collective action to the employer or to respect cooling-off periods.

Both the FAC and the ECSR are more lenient as regards notice or cooling-off periods, and mediation and conciliation procedures.[93]

Two cases of ECtHR case law relate directly to the existence of procedural restrictions under UK and Ukrainian Law. In *National Association of Teachers in Further and Higher Education v UK*, the Court had to deal with the TULRCA provisions regarding the organisation of a ballot in a case of strike. The applicant union alleged that the obligation to provide a list of its members who would have to take part in the ballot to their employer constituted an unjustified restriction of the right to organise. The disclosure of the identity of the unionised workers to their employer was considered to entail a serious *risk* of anti-union discriminatory measures. Despite the union's claim that Article 11 ECHR indeed encompassed a right to strike, it seems likely that the trade union was trying to convince the European Commission of Human Rights to condemn the UK in view of the individual rather than of the collective issues involved. In this respect, it is interesting to observe that the trade union also invoked Articles 8 and 10 ECHR. The Commission recognised that there 'may be specific circumstances in which a legal requirement on an association to reveal the names of its members to a third party could give rise to an unjustified interference with the rights under Article 11'. However, despite a history

---

[89] See also the use of the notion 'preconditions' in Novitz (n 6).

[90] Report No 197 (Vol LXII, 1979, Series B, No 3) 354–55.

[91] Report No 214 (Vol LXV, 1982, Series B, No 1) 266: in the Peruvian case, all workers of the enterprise involved were given a right, irrespective of their membership of the trade union calling for a strike.

[92] See www.coe.int/t/dghl/monitoring/socialcharter/Digest/DigestSept2008_en.pdf, p 57; and Evju (n 34) 217–18.

[93] www.coe.int/t/dghl/monitoring/socialcharter/Digest/DigestSept2008_en.pdf, p 57; www.ilo.org/wcmsp5/groups/public/---ed_norm/---normes/documents/publication/wcms_090632.pdf, p 554.

of anti-union discrimination since time immemorial, it was unable to construe 'that there was something inherently secret about membership of a trade union'.[94]

The facts of the *Trofimchuk*[95] case point to similar procedural restrictions under Ukrainian law. In this case, a worker of a municipal heating provider, Komunenergiya, had been dismissed on the grounds of 'repeated breach of her duties'. One of these breaches related to the fact that she participated in a picketing action on 3 March 1999, taking two hours off work. Ms Trofimchuk was considered to have been absent from work without justification. She argued that she was in fact being victimised for an attempt to establish a trade union and for having participated in a picket against her management. The Court stated that divorcing the applicant's participation in the picket from its consequences, namely her two-hour absence from work, would be too formalistic and 'contrary to practical and effective application'. It ruled that the dismissal insofar as related to such an absence inevitably restricted the right to freedom of peaceful assembly. Though the Court avoided using the term 'participation in a strike', it did not discern sufficient grounds to disagree with the Ukrainian court's application of the relevant domestic law to the circumstances of the applicant's case. The domestic law involved was in fact a strongly procedural regulation of the right to strike, submitting recourse to a ballot procedure. The unjustified character of Ms Trofimchuk's absence reflected the fact that the procedure would have been violated. The procedural rules required the kind of majority vote highly criticised by the FAC and the ECSR. Furthermore, Ukrainian law restricted recourse to collective action to 'trade unions' or 'another association of employees'. *In casu*, the picket action seems to have been organised by a trade union 'still under construction'. In sum, the Court could have taken the opportunity to question the legitimacy of such a restriction regarding the personal scope of the right to strike.

Unfortunately, the Court explicitly refused to dwell on these two crucial questions. Though she had alleged that, given the circumstances of the case, her freedom of association had effectively been violated, the Court stated that Ms Trofimchuk 'did not challenge the conformity of the procedure made available in domestic law to the requirements of Article 11 of the Convention'. In my view, the Court thus completely divorced the issue of the right to freedom of peaceful assembly from the procedural restrictions regarding its exercise. Furthermore, it is astonishing that the Court made no attempt to apply the methodology of inter-textual interpretation developed in the Grand Chamber's *Demir and Baykara* judgment 'to define the meaning of terms and notions in the text of the Convention, taking into account elements of international law other than the Convention, the interpretation of such elements by competent organs, and the practice of European States reflecting their common values'. In fact, the Court provides evidence of a modus operandi which seems to be 'formalistic and contrary to practical and effective application'. It did take into consideration the fact that the notice which Ms Trofimchuk had given to the local authorities *neither* contained an indication of the planned duration of

---

[94] 16 April 1998, *National Association of Teachers in Further and Higher Education*, App No 28910/95, 25 EHRR CD 122. See also Novitz's qualification of the Court's view as 'fairly naïve': Novitz (n 6) 231.

[95] ECtHR, 28 January 2011, *Trofimchuk v Ukraine*, App No 4241/03.

the picket *nor* made it abundantly clear that she would actually participate in the picket. Furthermore, it made an observation related to the fact that she did not give advance notice to her direct supervisor. Given the nature of her responsibilities, which seem to have raised a safety issue, the Court stated that her absence under circumstances provoking a 'serious disruption to the workplace processes' did not provide evidence of 'due respect to the rights and interest of her employer'.

The observations of the Court are in my view not sufficiently conclusive to assess the conformity of the ballot procedure under Ukrainian law with Article 11, § 2 ECHR. It is clear that the Ukrainian judges took the alleged violation of these procedures into consideration to conclude that the absence of Ms Trofimchuk was not justified. However, the Court focused its attention on certain less troublesome procedural restrictions, such as the inaccuracy of the notification. Similarly, the judgment cannot in my view be construed as expressing an approval of the illegitimacy of strikes under Ukrainian law notified by a collective of workers that does not constitute a trade union or a workers' association as such. The Court has built its judgment on a more substantive restriction, stating that the picket action, though only lasting two hours, had led to 'serious disruption to the workplace processes'.

Last but not least, the Court's case law provides no guidance on the legitimacy of compulsory arbitration. In *Federation of Offshore Workers' Trade Unions*,[96] the Court completely disregarded this institutional or procedural dimension of the applicants' request. The applicants had raised the issue that compulsory arbitration was at odds with international standards. The Court instead focused its attention on the balancing of interests, disregarding the non-judicial nature of the procedure under Norwegian law, which allowed administrative authorities to engage in such an exercise.

3.5.3 Substantive Restrictions

The Court's case law relating to mere restrictions (as opposed to prohibitions) of the right to take collective action has not been very beneficial for trade unions. In fact, in several cases pre-dating the *Demir and Baykara* judgment, the Court refused to censure such restrictions, allowing them to easily pass the test of Article 11, § 2 ECHR.

As indicated previously, in *UNISON*, the Court refused to consider the restriction to the right to strike as disproportionate. Despite the fact that the injunction imposed by the British judges seems to have been based on the narrow statutory definition of an industrial dispute, the Court upheld the judgment on the illicit character of the dispute by replacing the former rationale with a distinct one based upon a balance of the rights protected under the Convention and the 'protection of the rights and freedoms of others'.

The Court referred in this context to the particular economic interest that the business had in the continuity of its services and the exercise of freedom of contract as a legitimate objective for restricting the right to strike. The Court did not refer

---

[96] ECtHR, 27 June 2002, *Federation of Offshore Workers' Trade Unions and Others v Norway*, App No 38190/97.

to the issue of public safety which was at the heart of the undertaking concerned: a hospital. It was not an established fact that the strike would endanger public health. The Court seems to have endorsed the view espoused by the British government that these 'interests' fall under the 'rights of others' within the meaning of Article 11, § 2 ECHR.

A few critical remarks can be made with regard to this approach. The Court weighed a right referred to as a 'fundamental freedom' against the employer's purely economic interest. This was not a 'balancing of interests'. The case involved a balancing between a human right and purely private economic interests. It should be recalled that freedom of contract is not mentioned in any human rights instrument whatsoever. UNISON's claim that 'freedom of contract with transferee companies' was hardly a weighty consideration needs to be viewed against this background. The Court was not at all reluctant to view the economic interest of the employer subject to the strike as a ground for curtailing the right to collective action. Collective actions are intended to pressure an employer to accept a particular demand by causing the employer damage. If the damage caused to the employer is automatically considered a proper basis for restricting the right to strike, such restrictions risk depriving a strike of its *effet utile*. The dividing line between collective action and a demonstration will become thinner. In the Dutch *NS* ruling, the Dutch Supreme Court specifically rejected the employer's economic interest as a proper ground for restricting the right to strike.[97] The only exception to this rule is if the employer is a *third party* in the conflict. The British government was convinced that this was the case. The fact remained that the purpose of the strike was to influence the behaviour of the transferor in his negotiations with potential transferees. The French Cour de Cassation and the Italian Corte di Cassazione are not as dogmatic as the Dutch Supreme Court.[98] They are, however, very reluctant to accept the damage to the employer as a proper ground for restricting the right to strike. Unless this damage results in the collapse of the business or impairs productivity (rather than the production), there will be no basis for limiting the right. Mere damage to production is irrelevant. In its monitoring of compliance with the ESC, the ECSR dismisses the idea that the 'proportionality principle' (proportionality of the damage to the demand sought) can be applied as a ground for restriction in accordance with the restriction principles set forth in Article 31 of the Charter.[99]

The Court considered that the strike prohibition pronounced by the English court did not constitute a disproportional restriction of the right to organise. The finding that the prohibition was essentially temporary was an important factor. After the takeover, the union would have more than ample time to negotiate its demands with the transferee. Such reasoning in effect boiled down to the union having the right to lock the stable door after the horse had bolted.

---

[97] Hoge Raad, 30 May 1986, *Nederlandse Jurisprudentie* 1986, 688.

[98] In this connection, see the analysis of French case law in F Dorssemont, *Rechtspositie en actievrijheid van representatieve werknemersorganisaties* (Bruges, Die Keure, 2002) 546–48. For Italy, see G Giugni, *Diritto sindacale* (Bari, Cacucci editore, 2000) 252–53; A Vallebona, *Il diritto sindacale* (Turin, G Giappichelli editore, 2000) 224–25.

[99] See ECSR, XVI-1 (Belgium, 1 February 2002). In this connection, see the analysis in F Dorssemont, 'De prullenbak, een locus naturalis voor het leerstuk van misbruik van stakingsrecht?' (2002) *Nederlands Tijdschrift voor Sociaal Recht* 320–31.

UNISON's infamous course was extended further in *Federation of Offshore Workers' Trade Unions*.[100] At issue in this case was a strike prohibition imposed by an administrative measure. The prohibition was supplemented by a compulsory arbitration procedure to settle a wage-bargaining dispute involving offshore workers. Notwithstanding the fact that such prohibition in a non-essential service was considered irreconcilable with ILO standards by the ILO FAC *and* the fact that the compulsory arbitration procedure had been criticised by the ECSR on the basis of Article 6 (4) in conjunction with Article 31 ESC, the application was deemed manifestly ill-founded by the Court. The gap between the restriction principles of Article 31 of the Charter and Article 11 (2) of the Convention has never been illustrated more pointedly. The Court considered that the *administrative restrictions* which had been challenged in vain before the Norwegian courts did pass the test when balanced against the interests of public safety, 'freedoms and rights of others', and health. Unfortunately, the Court does not clarify at all which freedoms and rights are at stake, let alone how the functioning of the offshore industry raised an issue of public safety and health.

Though the canon of interpretation expressed in the Grand Chamber's *Demir and Baykara* judgment might have prompted the Court to adopt a more cautious approach when scrutinising such restrictions, taking into account more specific international instruments and their interpretation, the first post-*Demir and Baykara* test case (ie, *Trofimchuk*) proved to be extremely disappointing.

In *Trofimchuk,* the Court adopted a dangerous approach by considering the fact that a picket action which only lasted two hours had provoked 'serious disruption to the workplace processes'. Indeed, it is the essence of any collective action that it provokes a serious disruption to the workplace processes. The most current form of collective action, that is, strike action, inevitably leads to serious disruption, since labour is an essential 'resource' in any undertaking. As highlighted before, both the French and the Italian courts have made it abundantly clear that *mere* damage to production needs to be disregarded when imposing restrictions on the right to strike. The question thus arises as to whether this consideration of the Court satisfies the canon of interpretation the Court has developed in *Demir and Baykara*. This canon urges the Court to take into account 'the practice of European States reflecting their common values'. Comparative research would have revealed that the criterion the Court used is at least puzzling. It might be argued that the reference to the disruption of the production processes needs to be understood as a reminder of the goal of the notification procedure. The latter should give the employer fair opportunity to reduce the damage to his enterprise. In this respect, insofar as proper notification has been given, the mere fact that the notified industrial action could provoke serious disruption should be disregarded.

Inevitably, the question arises as to what extent the restrictions on the right to take collective action based on the so-called balancing operation (ie, the proportionality test) that the CJEU undertook in *Viking* and *Laval* could pass the test of Article 11, § 2 ECHR. This question became even more compelling in view of an attempt by the European Commission to fossilise this balancing operation in a

---

[100] *Federation of Offshore Workers' Trade Unions and Others v Norway* (n 96).

draft regulation, which has now been withdrawn.[101] A proper understanding of this balancing operation leads to the conclusion that the CJEU does not just balance interests. It claims to balance fundamental economic freedoms with the right to take collective action. The question of conformity is set to become even more poignant once the EU accedes to the ECHR. Accession would in my view create the right momentum to rebalance fundamental economic freedoms and fundamental rights, such as the right to take collective action and the freedom of collective bargaining. In the landmark judgments of *Demir and Baykara* and *Enerji*, the Court had to assess the conformity of a provision under Turkish law which deprived civil servants of the right to have recourse to any kind of collective action and to constitute trade unions. The judgments do not deal with restrictions based upon conflicting rights and freedoms. These recent judgments do not provide sufficient guidance to predict anything whatsoever. Indeed, in its case law (*UNISON* and *Federation of Offshore Workers' Trade Unions*) preceding these two landmark judgments, the Court adopted a broad interpretation of the conflicting private and public interests which could justify restrictions on the right to take collective actions. Hence, at first sight, the prospects seem bad. However, as indicated earlier on, the Court in *Demir and Baykara* did indicate that it was under an obligation to interpret Article 11 ECHR in the light of 'international law other than the Convention, the interpretation of such elements by competent organs, and the practice of European States reflecting their common values'.[102]

Since *UNISON* and *Federation of Offshore Workers' Trade Unions* disregard the opinions of the ILO's supervisory bodies as well as the case law of the ECSR, the persuasive authority of these 'precedents' is poor. In this respect, it is worthwhile recalling that the ECSR has refused to take into account mere business interests as a justified restriction on the right to take collective action, refuting that a 'proportionality test' was compatible with the exhaustive character of the restrictions under Article 31 ESC.[103] In the same vein, the ILO's Committee of Experts recently considered that 'it has never included the need to assess the proportionality of interests bearing in mind a notion of freedom of establishment or freedom to provide services'.[104] The Committee considered that the 'doctrine articulated in these ECJ judgments was likely to have a significant restrictive effect on the exercise of the right to strike in practice in a manner contrary to the Convention (ie, Convention. 87)'.

---

[101] COM 2012 (130) final, Proposal for a Council Regulation on the exercise of the right to take collective action within the context of the freedom of establishment and the freedom to provide services.

[102] In the same vein, see N Bruun, A Bücker and F Dorssemont, 'Balancing Fundamental Social Rights and Economic Freedoms: Can the Monti II Initiative Solve the EU Dilemma?' (2012/13) *International Journal of Comparative Labour Law and Industrial Relations* 279–306; F Dorssemont, 'How the European Court of Human Rights Gave Us *Enerji* to Cope with *Laval* and *Viking*' in M-A Moreau (ed), *Before and After the Economic Crisis. What Implications for the 'European Social Model'* (Cheltenham, Edward Elgar Publishing, 2011) 225–26; and M Rocca, 'The So-called Monti II Regulation' (2012/13) *European Labour Law Journal* 19–34. See also K Ewing, 'Draft Monti II Regulation: An Inadequate Response to *Viking* and *Laval*', www.lcdtu.org/eu-employment-rights-professor-keith-ewing-on-monti-11%E2%80%B3/.

[103] See, in this respect, ECSR, XVI-1, Conclusion with regard to Belgium. For the situation in Belgium, see Dorssemont (n 34) 167–202.

[104] Report III (1A) Report of the Committee of Experts on the Application of Conventions and Recommendations, International Labour Conference 99th Session 2010, 209.

3.6 Collective Action and Disciplinary Sanctions

The right to take collective action would be deprived of its usefulness *(effet utile)* if employees were not to be protected against disciplinary sanctions,[105] including dismissal for having participated in strike action. The ECSR monitors whether employees on strike are sufficiently protected against dissuasive disciplinary sanctions. With regard to any such dismissal, Member States have a choice between declaring it null and void or imposing an injunction to reinstate the worker. The ECSR does not suggest that pecuniary damages are sufficiently dissuasive. In fact, in the past, it has drawn a negative conclusion as regards Belgium for not offering either of these sanctions.[106]

The *Digest* of the FAC condemns 'sanctions against workers because they attempt to constitute organizations',[107] describing anti-union discrimination as one of the most serious violations of freedom of association. It contains an extensive chapter on 'protection against anti-union discrimination' listing a whole range of sanctions in the field of employment (at the moment of hiring, during employment and at the moment of dismissal).[108]

The issue of disciplinary sanctions following participation in strike action needs to be studied in a wider context. It is just one species of disciplinary sanctions taken against trade union officials or trade union members exercising trade union rights.

The Court's case law relates to 'systematic' union-busting (*Danilenkov*), to disciplinary sanctions subsequent to participation in picketing (*Trofimchuk* and the Turkish cases) or as a result of trade union officials exercising their right to freedom of expression.[109]

In its *Danilenkov* judgment, the Court introduced the notion of anti-union discrimination, stating that 'the totality of the measures implemented to safeguard the guarantees of Article 11 should include protection against discrimination on the ground of trade union membership which, according to the Freedom of Association Committee, constitutes one of the most serious violations of freedom of association capable to jeopardize the very existence of a trade union'.[110]

In casu, the Court had to examine a range of union-busting measures practised by the Kaliningrad Commercia Seaport Co Ltd against dockers affiliated to a trade union called DUR. The latter had organised a strike over pay, better working conditions, and health and life insurance. In retaliation, the employer adopted a series of countermeasures. It decided to assign a number of DUR members to reserve teams not working at full capacity. As a result, the earning time of these dockers was substantially reduced. DUR officials stopped being involved in monitoring the exams

---

[105] In this respect, see also Lörcher (n 43) 185–86.

[106] See ESCR, XVII-1 (Belgium) and XVIII-1 (Belgium).

[107] International Labour Office (n 50) No 338.

[108] Ibid, Nos 769–854.

[109] ECtHR, 8 December 2009, *Aguilera Jiménez and others v Spain*, App Nos 28389/06, 28955/06, 28957/06, 28959/06, 28961/06 and 28964/06; ECtHR, 12 September 2011, *Palomo Sanchez and others v Spain*, App No 28955/06, 28957/06, 28959/06 and 28964/06; and 27 September 2009, *Sisman v Turkey*, App No 1305/05, ECtHR 2011.

[110] ECtHR, 30 July 2009, *Danilenkov and others v Russia*, App No 67336/01, ECtHR 2009, No 123.

related to health and safety regulations. As a result, a disproportionate number of DUR members failed to pass these exams. A number of DUR members became subject to disciplinary sanctions which proved to be unjustified. After an attempt to make certain DUR members collectively redundant had failed, they were transferred to part-time jobs. The trade union had to cope with an alarming drop in membership. A section of the Russian judges refused to acknowledge their competence for the case, holding that the existence of discrimination could be established in criminal proceedings only, due to the existence of a criminal prohibition of anti-union discrimination. The Court observed that this required the victims of any alleged anti-union discrimination to prove a direct intent 'beyond reasonable doubt' on the part of one of the company's key managers to discriminate against trade union members. It also considered that the victims of discrimination only had a minor role in the institution and conduct of criminal proceedings.

This notion provides prospects for more judicial activism in the field of violations against positive freedom of association. Such violations often raise an issue of equal treatment, with other trade unions being treated more favourably than the 'busted' union. More importantly, the concept of discrimination could prompt the Court in the future to accept a reversal of the burden of proof once certain facts allow the strong presumption that the exercise of the managerial prerogative could have been inspired by an intent to discriminate. Such a reversal of the burden of proof would force management to justify the contested practices in more detail. They would have to prove that they were conducting their business in a proper manner and that the choice of workers affected by these practices was *not* related to their affiliation to a trade union. In *Danilenkov*, the Court only indicated that it would be wrong to exclude the enforcement of a prohibition against discrimination through civil procedures and to require proof 'beyond reasonable doubt' of a direct intent to discriminate.[111] It did not state that these civil proceedings ought to allow a *reversal* of the burden of proof.

In the recent *Aguilera Jiménez* case, the Court had to assess whether the *stante pede* dismissal of a number of unionised workers who had published a satirical cartoon in a union magazine featuring a human resources manager and two of their colleagues in a compromising position constituted a violation of freedom of expression and freedom of association. The Court refused to accept that the decision interfered with freedom of association, insofar as the applicants were unable to establish sufficient *indications* that their dismissal was a retaliatory measure (*un acte de représailles*) linked to their trade union membership. Hence, the Court upheld a judgment of the Spanish Constitutional Court in the same dispute. The latter had required the applicants to be able to provide sufficient indications of *direct intent* to restrict the freedom of trade union association.[112] When applied to discrimination disputes, the 'direct intent' requirement is worrying, as it refers to a 'subjective' element that is extremely difficult to prove. In sum, the difference between the *formula* applied by the Court in *Aguilera Jiménez* and the 'proof *beyond reasonable doubt* of direct intent' which the Court disapproved of in *Danilenkov* (stating it

---

[111] Ibid, § 134.
[112] *Aguilera Jiménez and others v Spain* (n 109) §§ 11 and 39.

was deficient) is very shallow. Regretfully, the Court did not examine whether there were sufficient indications that the dismissals in *Aguilera Jiménez* were 'objectively' related to the exercise of trade union freedom. Thus, it was beyond doubt that the cartoon was part of a trade union magazine and that its publication was indeed related to a dispute between the trade union and the employer. When the case was referred, at the request of the applicants, to the Grand Chamber, the latter took an even more formalistic approach by stating that there was no interference with the right to trade union freedom since the dismissals had been the result of the actual content of the offending newsletter and not of the applicants' union membership.[113] The approach has been criticised in an exceptionally harsh dissenting opinion by the judges Tulkens and others as 'artificial' and as revealing 'a certain ignorance, or even suspicion, of trade union action'.

The necessity to introduce such a reversal of the burden of proof also becomes apparent for another reason. Employers do not need to have recourse to formal disciplinary sanctions in order to dissuade workers from forming and/or joining a union. 'Routine' exercise of the managerial prerogative can be sufficient to dissuade workers in this respect. Certain managerial decisions which adversely affect the employment relation of unionised workers or trade union leaders can be presented as falling within the margin of appreciation inherent to the exercise of the managerial prerogatives of managing human resources and conducting the business. In this respect, the *Digest* recalls 'the full importance of Article 3 of Convention 98', which provides that 'machinery appropriate to national conditions shall be established where necessary to ensure respect for the right to organize'. It is unclear to what extent this vague provision warrants a reversal of the burden of proof, once the alleged victim is able to establish facts from which it may be presumed that there has been a case of anti-union discrimination.[114]

The ECtHR does *not* seem to follow this path. In a series of applications involving Turkey,[115] it had to deal with administrative transfers of unionised civil servants, often in association with their appointment as trade union officials. Hence, there were sufficient facts to warrant a presumption of anti-union discrimination. The Court took a very formalistic approach, stating that membership of a trade union did not guarantee special treatment on behalf of the State to be exempted from administrative transfers. It even refused to acknowledge that a transfer could prejudice the exercise of the freedom of trade union association insofar as it did not preclude workers from remaining members of a trade union and engaging in trade union activities 'elsewhere'. The Court considered in all the rulings that administrative decisions fell within the margin of appreciation of the State's freedom to manage its administration (*l'exercice d'une bonne administration du service public de l'Etat*). It was clear that the Court did not want to substitute its appreciation for that of the Turkish administration. Furthermore, it did not modify in any way the burden of proof. In fact, the judgments provide no indication as to why the transfer

---

[113] *Palomo Sanchez and others v Spain* (n 109) § 64.
[114] In this respect, see *per analogiam* Articles of EC Directives 2000/43 and 2000/78.
[115] ECtHR, 20 September 2005, *Bulga and others v Turkey*, App No 42947/98; 20 September 2005, *Ertas Aydin and others v Turkey*, App No 43672/98; 20 September 2005, *Aka v Turkey*, App No 45050/98; and 21 March 2006, *Ademylmaz and others v Turkey*, App No 4146/09.

concerned was justified for reasons related to the proper functioning of the public service.

The Court's approach is disappointing insofar as it amounts to denying any kind of protection to a specific mandate as a workers' representative appointed or presented by a trade union in a specific undertaking. Such protection against anti-union discrimination is necessary to preserve the relationship a union delegate has with the workforce which he is supposed to represent.

An overview of the Court's case law covering more than 20 'transfers' reveals that the latter have affected union officials of only two specific trade unions. Hence, there is some scope to assume that the 'human resources management' provides proof of a systematic policy targeting specific trade unions. The *Digest* construes such policy as a violation of the right to organise.[116]

The *NALGO* case[117] indicates that the ability of trade unions to exercise disciplinary competence can affect the right to efficiently organise collective action. NALGO's application was directed against statutory restrictions to the exercise of disciplinary competences. As indicated earlier, the relevant provisions of the TULRCA precluded disciplinary sanctions against trade union members for crossing picket lines. Though the exercise of disciplinary sanctions facilitates a trade union's capacity to organise a strike in a more effective way, the trade union did not refer to the right to take collective action under Article 11 ECHR, instead building its application on the hypothesis that statutory intervention constituted a restriction of a trade union's autonomy with regard to its internal affairs.

4 PROSPECTS FOR THE FUTURE

It is not crystal clear to what extent the ECtHR will have the courage to adopt a progressive stance on the right to take collective action. The timid recognition of the right to strike as a corollary right not to be dissociated from freedom of association only dates back to the 2009 *Enerji* case[118] contesting a clear-cut *prohibition* of strikes in the Turkish public sector. In two judgments of the Strasbourg Court (*UNISON* and *Federation of Offshore Workers' Trade Unions*) which preceded the *Demir and Baykara* and *Enerji* judgments, the Court adopted a broad interpretation of conflicting private and public interests possibly justifying *restrictions* on the right to take collective action. Hence, at first sight, the prospects do not seem good. In *Demir and Baykara*,[119] the Court indicated that it was under an obligation to interpret Article 11 ECHR in the light of 'international law other than the Convention, the interpretation of such elements by competent organs, and the practice of European States reflecting their common values'. If taken seriously, such an interpretation canon should prompt the Court to examine whether restrictions imposed by the Contracting Parties are in fact consistent with the case law developed by the ILO FAC and that of the Council of Europe's ECSR. Since both previous

---

[116] International Labour Office (n 50) No 802.
[117] ECtHR, 1 September 1993, *National and Local Government Officers v UK*, App No 21386/93.
[118] *Enerji Yapi-Yol Sen* (n 26).
[119] *Demir and Baykara v Turkey* (n 16).

judgments were made in disrespect of the ILO's supervisory bodies as well as of the case law of the ECSR, the persuasive authority of these 'precedents' is poor. In the near future, domestic courts will also be bound to take Article 11 ECHR much more into account, since it has ceased to be 'mute' or 'irrelevant' in the field of strike law.[120] In this respect, it is worthwhile recalling that the ECSR has refused to take into account mere business interests as a justified restriction of the right to take collective action, refuting that a 'proportionality test' is compatible with the exhaustive character of the restrictions under Article 31 ESC.[121]

The posterior *Trofimchuk v Ukraine* judgment[122] relating to the dismissal of a worker for participation in a 'spontaneous' strike is disappointing due to its total lack of any dialogue with the aforementioned committees.

In sum, the prospect that EU accession to the ECHR will provoke a shift in the balance between fundamental economic freedoms and fundamental social rights will depend upon a combination of tools and courage. The method of interpretation introduced in *Demir and Baykara* provides the necessary and indeed sufficient tools to adopt a more progressive attitude, based upon dialogue between the ECtHR and specialised supervisory bodies monitoring fundamental social rights.

---

[120] In this respect, see Lörcher (n 43) 155.
[121] In this respect, see ECSR, XVI-1, Conclusion with regard to Belgium. For the situation in Belgium, see Dorssemont (n 36) 167–202.
[122] *Trofimchuk v Ukraine* (n 95).

14

*Prohibition of Discrimination under Article 14 European Convention on Human Rights**

NIKLAS BRUUN

1 INTRODUCTION

IN THE LAST few decades, regulation of the prohibition of discrimination on different grounds has become increasingly important both generally and within the field of labour law. The reason for and the background to this development have been assessed very differently. Describing this as a mainly positive development, Hepple has tried to periodise the historical development of discrimination law with labour law relevance.[1] He makes a distinction between four periods, the first one of which relates to the situation after the Second World War, when human rights regained importance, with the UN Universal Declaration of Human Rights (UDHR 1949), certain ILO Conventions and of course the European Convention on Human Rights (ECHR) being drafted and adopted. During this period, the distinction between civil and political rights on the one hand and social and cultural rights on the other hand was strictly upheld. The period 1957–75 saw the notion of equality in the context of discrimination law mainly being interpreted as meaning formal equality. During the period 1976–99, the notion of substantive equality gained importance within labour law. EU equality law in particular adopted this approach and it also had a clear impact on such new international instruments as the UN Convention on the Elimination of All Forms of Discrimination against Women (the CEDAW Convention) adopted in 1979.[2] Hepple argues that the concept of substantive

* The author would like to warmly thank Professor Janneke Gerards (Radboud University Nijmegen), who gave important feedback on a preliminary draft of this chapter as well as Klaus Lörcher, with whom I published the article 'Social Innovation: The New ECHR Jurisprudence and its Impact on Fundamental Social Rights in Labour Law' in I Schömann (ed), *Melanges a la memoire de Yota Kravaritou* (Brussels, ETUI, 2011) and which inspired me to further study the ECHR and its Article 14.

[1] See B Hepple 'Equality at Work' in B Hepple and B Veneziani (eds), *The Transformation of European Labour Law* (Oxford, Hart Publishing, 2009) 129–63.

[2] Via the jurisprudence of the CJEU (Case C-43/75, *Gabrielle Defrenne v Société anonyme belge de navigation aérienne Sabena* [1976] ECR 00455, '*Defrenne II*', § 20), ILO Convention No 100 has served to introduce the principle of 'equal pay for work of *equal value*' (emphasis added) in the EU legislation which is now to be found in primary (Article 23 CFREU, Article 157(1) Treaty on the Functioning of the European Union (TFEU)) and secondary law (Article 4 Directive 2006/54/EC).

equality has been further developed from 2000 onwards towards what he calls 'comprehensive and transformative equality'. Alain Supiot shares Hepple's view that discrimination law gained in importance during this period, pointing out that in French law there were 18 amendments between 1985 and 2005 changing and adding items to the list of forbidden grounds for discrimination.[3] He sees this development as part of the privatisation of the welfare state, with an individualisation of rights possibly favouring groups who have always been rather well off, while the weakest groups can only rely on such rights to a very limited extent. In this context it is not necessary to take any viewpoint in the debate concerning the factual effects of discrimination law on the labour market. Nevertheless, we can clearly state that in all Council of Europe (CoE) Member States, discrimination law is an integral part of national labour law and has been strongly promoted by international conventions, their implementation and EU law.

There is a long list of global international instruments (even in the field of labour law) protecting workers in general[4] and female workers in particular against discrimination. Article 2 of the UDHR 1949 prohibits distinctions made on the basis of sex, and in Article 2 of the International Covenant on Civil and Political Rights (ICCPR 1966) each State Party undertakes to respect and to ensure to all individuals within its territory and subject to its jurisdiction the recognised rights, without distinction of any kind, such as race, colour, sex, language, religion, political or other opinion, national or social origin, property, birth or other status. The States Parties to Articles 2 and 3 UN International Covenant on Economic, Social and Cultural Rights (ICESCR) manifestly undertake to guarantee that the rights under the Covenant will be exercised without discrimination of any kind as to race, colour, sex, language, religion, political or other opinion, national or social origin, property, birth or other status, and also to ensure the equal right of men and women to enjoy these rights. Prohibition of wage discrimination based on sex was introduced by the ILO with its Equal Remuneration Convention No 100 (ILO 1958). Similarly, the ILO Discrimination in Employment and Occupation Convention No 111 explicitly prohibits discrimination, ie, any distinction, exclusion or preference made on the basis of race, colour, sex, religion, political opinion, national extraction or social origin, which has the effect of nullifying or impairing equality of opportunity or treatment in the sector of employment or occupation.[5] Article 5(e) of the UN International Convention on the Elimination of All Forms of Racial Discrimination (CERD 1965) addresses employment-related rights, while the CEDAW Convention 1979 specifically addresses the elimination of all forms of discrimination against women generally and in the field of employment (Article 11).

In recent decades a broad international framework has been developed regarding both migrant workers and workers with disabilities. References concerning migrant

---

[3] A Supiot, *The Spirit of Philadelphia. Social Justice vs. the Total Market* (London, Verso 2012) 35.

[4] See also Article E Revised European Social Charter and the relevant case law of the European Committee of Social Rights in this respect.

[5] See International Labour Office, International Labour Conference, 83th Session, 1996, Report of the Committee of Experts on the Application of Conventions and Recommendations, Report III (Part 4B), General Survey concerning the Equality in Employment and Occupation, 1958 (No 111), Geneva, 1996.

workers include the International Convention on the Protection of the Rights of All Migrant Workers and Members of Their Families (ICRMW), ILO Conventions Nos 97[6] and 143[7] and Article 19 of the Revised European Social Charter (R)ESC).[8] Workers with disabilities are covered by the UN Convention on the Rights of Persons with Disabilities (CRPD) adopted in 2006, ILO Convention No 159[9] and, at the European level, Article 15 (R)ESC, as well as Articles 21(1) (non-discrimination) and 25 (integration of persons with disabilities) Charter of Fundamental Rights of the European Union (CFREU).

At the European level, it is interesting to note that the principle of non-discrimination was initially only explicitly recognised in respect of equal pay for work of equal value in Article 4(3) European Social Charter (ESC). It was only through the First Additional Protocol to the ESC that the 'right to equal opportunities and equal treatment in matters of employment and occupation without discrimination on the grounds of sex' was included (as Article 1) in the Social Charter's framework.[10] To some extent in parallel, the EU also started off with Article 119 Treaty on the European Economic Community (TEEC) on equal pay and ended up with the general non-discrimination rights found in Article 21(1) and in particular Article 23 CFREU on equality between men and women.

2 THE CONTENT OF ARTICLE 14 AND THE PURPOSE OF THIS CHAPTER

The numerous international sources prohibiting discrimination on different grounds in employment were adopted after the adoption of the ECHR, the original text of which addressed discrimination in Article 14:

Prohibition of discrimination

The enjoyment of the rights and freedoms set forth in this Convention shall be secured without discrimination on any ground such as sex, race, colour, language, religion, political or other opinion, national or social origin, association with a national minority, property, birth or other status.

---

[6] Migration for Employment Convention (Revised), 1949, in particular Article 6; see, in general, International Labour Office, International Labour Conference, 87th Session, 1999, Report of the Committee of Experts on the Application of Conventions and Recommendations, Report III (Part 1B), General Survey concerning the Migration for Employment Convention (Revised), 1949, (No 97), Migrant Workers (Supplementary Provisions) Convention, 1975 (No 143), Geneva, 1999.

[7] Migrant Workers (Supplementary Provisions) Convention 1975, in particular Article 9(1), even for undocumented workers: 'Without prejudice to measures designed to control movements of migrants for employment by ensuring that migrant workers enter national territory and are admitted to employment in conformity with the relevant laws and regulations, the migrant worker shall, in cases in which these laws and regulations have not been respected and in which his position cannot be regularised, enjoy equality of treatment for himself and his family in respect of rights arising out of past employment as regards remuneration, social security and other benefits.'

[8] EU primary and secondary law is specifically comprehensive in this respect (even for third-country nationals; see Council Directive 2003/109/EC of 25 November 2003 concerning the status of third-country nationals who are long-term residents).

[9] Vocational Rehabilitation and Employment (Disabled Persons) Convention 1983.

[10] In the RESC it has now become Article 20.

The application of this Article by the relevant CoE bodies and especially the practice of the European Court of Huamn Rights (ECtHR) are the focus of this presentation. I want to address the issue of the relevance of this Article for employment-related questions in the light of this practice. I will first look at the structural features related to this prohibition of discrimination, ie, its scope of application. I will then evaluate its potential as a 'labour law' article in the future based primarily on ECtHR case law, but also on the vast existing literature. Finally I will come up with some conclusions and recommendations based on this analysis. The relationship between Article 14 and Article 1 of Protocol No 1 is not analysed here, since the book includes a separate chapter relating to this issue (see chapter 15 by Herzfeld-Olsson).

3 NON-EXHAUSTIVE LIST

The list of discriminatory grounds in Article 14 reflects the values and perceptions current in the late 1940s when the ECHR was drafted. From the point of view of modern discrimination law, one may note that such grounds as disability, age and sexual orientation are not mentioned, as is the case with trade union affiliation or activity. In ECtHR practice the fact that certain grounds are not explicitly mentioned in the Convention has not been a problem. It is very rare for a case to be dismissed on account of it not falling under a relevant or recognised ground. In fact, the list of grounds in Article 14 only gives examples, as seen by the introductory 'such as'.[11] There has naturally been a discussion concerning what limits the wording 'other status' in Article 14 might imply and whether we must require some personal characteristics of innate or inherent character in order to be able to apply Article 14. In the *Clift v UK* case, the Court emphasised its open approach in this regard by stating that: 'The question whether there is a difference of treatment based on a personal or identifiable characteristic in any given case is a matter to be assessed taking into consideration all of the circumstances of the case and bearing in mind that the aim of the Convention is to guarantee not rights that are theoretical or illusory but rights that are practical and effective.'[12]

4 PROTECTED SUBJECT MATTER

The wording of Article 14 includes a significant limitation of the situations to which the Article can be applied, restricting it to the 'enjoyment of rights and freedoms set forth in the Convention'.

The consequence of this is that Article 14 is complementary to the other substantive provisions in the sense that it can be applied only where the facts of the case actually fall under the application of another article of the Convention. In this sense, Article 14 has often been described as being 'parasitic' or having 'no independent

---

[11] S Fredman, *Discrimination Law* (Oxford, Oxford University Press, 2011) 125.
[12] ECtHR (Fourth Section), Judgment of 13 July 2010, *Clift v UK*, App No 7205/07.

existence'.[13] It is not, however, necessary to show that there has been a breach of another provision in the Convention. The Court might find that, though there is no infringement of any ECHR article, discrimination has still occurred:

> Article 14 only complements the other substantive provisions of the Convention and the Protocols. It has no independent existence since it has effect solely in relation to 'the enjoyment of the rights and freedoms' safeguarded by those provisions. Although the application of Article 14 does not presuppose a breach of those provisions—and to that extent is autonomous—there can be no room for its application unless the facts at issue fall within the ambit or one or more of the latter.[14]

It suffices to demonstrate that another provision has been applied in a discriminatory manner, even in situations where the national law implementing an article goes beyond the obligations expressly provided for by the Convention.[15] In the *Okpisz v Germany* case the Court summed up its practice in this respect: 'As the Court has held on many occasions, Article 14 comes into play whenever "the subject matter of the disadvantage ... constitutes one of the modalities of the exercise of a right guaranteed", or the measures complained of are "linked to the exercise of a right guaranteed".'[16]

This approach by the ECtHR has significant implications. It means that although there is no right to housing, education or social security under the ECHR, there is a duty not to discriminate if the State regulates such areas. For example, a State is not obliged to provide parental leave allowances under Article 8. But when it does, its duty not to discriminate under Article 14 is applicable, since parental leave benefits fall under the ambit of Article 8.[17] Although this interpretative approach clearly expands the rather strict wording of Article 14, the restriction is still very significant.

There has also been a debate regarding to what extent the intention or aims of the State Party to regulate a certain area should be taken into account when deciding the scope of application of Article 14. Baker argues that such a criterion should not be regarded as relevant, referring to the *Sidabras and Džiautas v Lithuania* case,[18] where the Court concluded that a ban on admission to civil service positions, dependent on the criterion of former membership in the KGB, fell within the ambit of Article 8's protection of 'private life'.[19] There was no suggestion that the State *sought* to regulate private life and it was well-established case law that the prima facie scope of Article 8(1) alone did not protect the choice of a particular profession. However, Article 14 changed the analysis, focusing on the impact of the ban on the persons concerned as regarding the enjoyment of any right to organise one's private and social life as one sees fit.[20]

---

[13] See Aaron Baker, 'The Enjoyment of Rights and Freedoms: A New Conception of the "Ambit" under Article 14 ECHR' (2006) 69(5) *MLR* 714–37.

[14] ECtHR (Grand Chamber), Judgment of 8 July 2003, *Sommerfeld v Germany*, App No 31871/96.

[15] See T *Makkonen*, Equal in Law, Unequal in Fact (Helsinki University Press 2010) 132–33.

[16] ECtHR (Fourth Section), Judgment of 25 October 2005, *Okpisz v Germany*, App No 59140/00.

[17] See ECtHR (Grand Chamber), Judgment of 12 April 2006, *Stec and others v UK*, App Nos 65731/01 and 65900/01; ECtHR (Grand Chamber), Judgment of 16 March 2010, *Carson and others v UK*, App No 42184/05.

[18] ECtHR (Second Section), Judgment of 27 July 2004, *Sidbras and Džiautas v Lithuania*, App Nos 55480/00 and 59330/00, 42–50.

[19] Baker (n 13) 735.

[20] Ibid.

Looking at ECtHR practice, it is rather difficult to distillate the criteria under which the Court in certain cases considers that, since a violation of a certain article has been established, there is no need to further examine whether Article 14 has also been violated, while in other cases it concludes that there has been a violation of a certain article read in conjunction with Article 14, and yet again in certain cases concludes that only Article 14 has been violated. The last category is easiest to illustrate, as already discussed above: discrimination might occur, although a violation of a substantive article has not taken place, as seen in the example above concerning benefits relating to parental leave. It is more complicated to find criteria explaining why the discrimination aspect is not examined in some cases, though it seems that the Court is gradually beginning to take this aspect more seriously.[21] In this context it is not possible to assess to what extent the authors of complaints are increasingly invoking Article 14 in a well-argued manner. If this is the case, it is of course one factor explaining the development of the Court's jurisprudence.

5 THE CONCEPT OF DISCRIMINATION

Stressing the importance of the prohibition of discrimination, the ECtHR has even proclaimed that 'the prohibition of discrimination in general, and of racial and ethnic discrimination in particular, under Article 14 reflect basic values of the democratic societies that make up the Council of Europe'.[22]

As the concept of discrimination is not defined in the Convention, in several discrimination cases the Court seems to have applied the methodological principles set down in *Demir and Baykara* on how it defines concepts in the text of the Convention,[23] ie, using a consolidated methodology by way of systematic reference to international (labour) standards and the case law of their respective supervisory bodies. This methodology is set out in § 85 of *Demir and Baykara*,[24] where the Court concluded that it 'in defining the meaning and notions in the text of the Convention, can and must take into account elements of international law other than the Convention, the interpretation of such elements by competent organs, and the practice of the European States reflecting their common values'.

The ways in which the concept of *discrimination* is understood in many international instruments have similarly become relevant for the ECtHR. It has adopted a rather broad notion of discrimination where the factual end result seems to be given considerable importance. The Court has held that it is not only differential treatment of similarly situated people that may constitute discrimination, but also that

---

[21] Compare, for instance, the ECtHR (Second Section), Judgment of 2 July 2002, *Wilson, National Union of Journalists and others v UK*, App Nos 30668/96, 30671/96 and 30678/96, where a violation of Article 11 was found, but the discrimination claim was not heard, and on the other hand, the ECtHR (Fifth Section), Judgment of 30 July 2009, *Danilenko and others v Russia*, App No 67336/01.

[22] ECtHR (Grand Chamber), Judgment of 6 July 2005, *Nachova and others v Bulgaria*, App Nos 43577/98 and 43579/98.

[23] ECtHR (Grand Chamber), Judgment of 12 November 2008, *Demir and Baykara v Turkey*, App No 34503/97.

[24] See *Tulkens*, Introduction to the Seminar Dialogue between judges 2009—Fifty Years of the European Court of Human Rights viewed by its fellow International Courts—Strasbourg 2009, p 13.

similar treatment of persons in dissimilar situations might lead to discriminatory results.[25]

The broad notion of discrimination is also applied in the case *Opuz v Turkey*,[26] where the Court accepted the interpretation adopted by the CEDAW Committee[27] in the context of violence in general against women and specifically domestic violence. The CEDAW Committee had earlier considered the duties of the Member States regarding gender-based violence to cover 'all legal and other measures that are necessary to provide effective protection of women against gender-based violence including penal sanctions, civil remedies and compensatory provisions to protect women against all kind of violence', and in *Opuz v Turkey* the Court fully adhered to this position.

Opuz v Turkey dealt not only with Article 14 ECHR but also and primarily with Articles 2 and 3. In this case a husband had continuously used physical violence against his wife and her mother. Ultimately he murdered the mother. The Court further explicitly referred to its above-mentioned methodology in the *Demir and Baykara* case, according to which, in interpreting the provisions of the Convention and the scope of the State's obligation in specific cases, the Court 'will also look for any consensus and common values emerging from the practices of European States and specialized international instruments, such as the CEDAW Convention, as well as giving heed to the evolution of norms and principles in international law through other developments'.[28] Furthermore, the Court referred to the UN Special Rapporteur on violence against women who had considered that there was a rule of customary international law that obliged States to prevent and respond to acts of violence against women with due diligence.[29]

The important conclusion that can be drawn from *Opuz v Turkey* is that the State Party has an obligation to positively prevent discrimination and that breaches of the Convention can occur even in the case of behaviour in the private sphere and by individual actors. This obligation to actively promote prevention and to establish mechanisms for dealing with crisis situations is described by the Court as a general obligation to conduct a kind of *due diligence* regarding these situations. This is an important positive obligation that can also be applied to employment situations. It seems clear that the state has an obligation to prevent work accidents and hazards.[30] A Member State's decision to, for instance, completely close down all authorities dealing with health and safety issues related to preventive safety should actually be regarded as a breach of the Convention.[31]

---

[25] ECtHR (Grand Chamber), Judgment of 6 April 2000, *Thlimmenos v Greece*, App No 34369/97.

[26] ECtHR (Third Section), Judgment of 9 June 2009, *Opuz v Turkey*, App No 33401/02, § 164.

[27] See the CEDAW Convention and General Recommendation 19 issued by the CEDAW Committee, a body established under the Convention and responsible for its supervision.

[28] *Demir and Baykara v Turkey* (n 23). See also ECtHR (Third Section) 28.5.2013, *Eremia v The Republic of Moldovia*, App No3564/11 where the Court explicitly in it reasoning refers to the General Recommendation No 28 on the Core Obligations of State Parties under Article 2 of the CEDAW Convention which was adopted by the CEDAW Committee in 2010 (§ 84).

[29] *Opuz v Turkey* (n 26) § 79.

[30] See ECtHR (Former Section IV), Judgment of 9 May 2006, *Pereira Henriques and others v Luxembourg*, App No 60255/00.

[31] Such measures might not be completely theoretical in times of economic crises and austerity.

From a general point of view, it is not clear how far the positive obligation to prevent different types of discrimination can be interpreted to follow from the Convention, but there is no doubt that such an obligation exists.

The concept of discrimination and 'Article 14 in the Convention does not prohibit Contracting Parties from treating groups differently in order to correct "factual inequalities" between them. Indeed, in certain circumstances a failure to attempt to correct inequality through different treatment may, without an objective and reasonable justification, give rise to a breach of the Convention'.[32]

The interpretation of the scope of the concept of discrimination in the ECHR where prima facie discrimination occurs when different treatment takes place in 'analogous' situations is rather broad. We can therefore usually—in the context of the Convention—avoid discussions on whether a de facto more favourably treated comparable person must exist in the concrete case before discrimination issues can be raised (a hypothetical person is normally enough). On the other hand, the principle of equal treatment is violated only if the distinction (prima facie discrimination) has 'no objective and reasonable justification'.[33] The existence of such justification must be assessed in relation to the aims and effects of the measure under consideration, with regard to the principles which normally prevail in democratic societies.

The Court, however, quite often finds objective and legitimate reasons. In *Kozak v Poland* (2010) the Court accepted 'that protection of the family in the traditional sense is, in principle, a weighty and legitimate reason which might justify a difference in treatment'.[34]

A difference in treatment in the exercise of a right laid down in the Convention must not only pursue a legitimate aim: Article 14 is also violated when it is clearly established that there is no reasonable relationship of proportionality between the means employed and the aims sought to be realised. Moreover, it needs to be emphasised that the States Parties enjoy a certain margin of appreciation in assessing whether and to what extent differences in otherwise similar situations justify a different treatment.

In certain cases where an objection concerning the similarity of the cases is made, the Court might consider the case as prima facie discrimination, but take certain distinctions into account when considering whether the difference in treatment was justified.[35]

6 DISCRIMINATION AND LABOUR LAW

Against the background discussed above, we can conclude that the expansion of the scope of application of Article 11 manifested in the *Demir and Baykara* case will

---

[32] ECtHR (Fourth Section), Judgment of 10 May 2007, *Runkee and White v UK*, App Nos 42949/98 and 53134/99.

[33] ECtHR (Second Section), Judgment of 30 September 2003, *Koua Poirrez v France*, App No 40892/98.

[34] See ECtHR (Fourth Section), Judgment of 2 March 2010, *Kozak v Poland*, App No 13102/02, n 98.

[35] See ECtHR (Fifth Section), Judgment of 3 December 2009, *Zaunegger v Germany*, App No 22028/04.

also bring about an expansion of the potential scope of application of Article 14. Discrimination in situations of collective action and collective bargaining can now be addressed under Article 14. The potential of this new link will be further explored in this chapter, but let us start by saying that there is reason to underline that, since unfavourable treatment of trade union officials and shop stewards who try to defend workers' interests is a common offence (as evidenced by the large number of cases heard by the ILO Freedom of Association Committee), the *Demir and Baykara* case will bring a significant group of cases related to the treatment of trade union officials or representatives during collective bargaining within the scope of application of Article 14. When there is unfavourable treatment due to trade union membership or trade union activity, Article 14 applies.

The case of *Danilenko and others v Russia*[36] forms an excellent example of how Article 11 can be linked to Article 14. In this concrete case a branch of the Dockers Union of Russia (DUR) had been officially registered with the Kaliningrad Justice Department since 3 October 1995. In May 1996 the DUR had taken part in collective bargaining, resulting in a new collective labour agreement being signed. This agreement gave dockers longer annual leave and better pay conditions. As a result, over a period of two years, DUR membership grew from 11 to 275 (on 14 October 1997). According to the applicant's the Kaliningrad seaport employed over 500 dockers at that time. In October 1997 the DUR had started a two-week strike over pay, better working conditions and health and life insurance. The strike failed to achieve its goals and was discontinued. The applicants submitted that since that discontinuation, the management of Kaliningrad seaport had been harassing DUR members, penalising them for the strike and inciting them to relinquish their union membership. This alleged harassment included the following measures: re-assignment of DUR members to special working teams or separate 'reserve teams', resulting in decreased earnings for the targeted workers; allegedly a disproportionally high number of DUR members failed the annual safety regulations test and no DUR representative was allowed on the test committee; and redundancy measures in 1998–99 mainly targeted DUR members (81.8 per cent), although the average rate of DUR membership was 33 per cent. In 1999 some of the disagreements were settled by an agreement between the seaport company management and the DUR, and as a consequence DUR members were transferred to other teams and a uniform system of bonuses was put in place. In August–September 1999 management founded a subsidiary stevedoring company, TPK, which hired 30 new dockers. In December 2000 and January 2001 the seaport offered most dockers lucrative transfers to TPK, though it allegedly excluded all DUR members. Their employment conditions deteriorated in different ways and as a result DUR membership shrank from 290 (in 1999) to only 24 on 6 December 2001. In February 2002 the remaining DUR members were made redundant and dismissed. Court decisions in 2002 found the dismissals to be unlawful and the courts (two instances) ordered the reinstatement of the workers. On 27 May 2002 the managing director annulled the orders for the applicants' dismissal of 20 February 2002 and reinstated them, not however transferring them to TPK. In June the TPK limited company was

---

[36] *Danilenko and others v Russia* (n 21).

reorganised to form the public company Maritime Commercial Port (MTP). On 7 August 2002 all applicants were again dismissed from the seaport company without valid reasons. Based on a court decision, they were again reinstated and after disagreements regarding their position, the Kaliningrad Regional Court confirmed finally that the applicants were to be hired by MTP as dockers (and not as second-category stevedores). The important aspect of the legal procedures that took place in Russia in the referred cases was that all courts dismissed as unsubstantiated the dismissed workers' complaint of discrimination against them and of a violation of their right to freedom of association. The Court therefore assessed the scope of the State Party's obligations under Article 14 of the Convention taken together with Article 11 of the Convention. Referring to the *Demir and Baykara* judgment, the Court argued that an employee or worker:

> [S]hould be free to join or not join a trade union without being sanctioned or subject to disincentives ... The wording of Article 11 explicitly refers to the right of 'everybody', and this provision obviously includes a right not to be discriminated against for choosing to avail oneself of the right to be protected by a trade union, given also that Article 14 forms an integral part of each of the Articles laying down rights and freedoms whatever their nature [see *National Union of Belgian Police*] Thus the totality of the measures implemented to safeguard the guarantees of Article 11 should include protection against discrimination on the ground of trade union membership which, according to the Freedom of Association Committee (ILO, NB), constitutes one of the most serious violations of freedom of association, capable of jeopardising the very existence of a trade union.

The Court therefore unanimously held that there had been a violation of Article 14 of the Convention taken together with Article 11. It referred to the events that had taken place and argued that the clear negative effects of DUR membership on the applicants were sufficient to constitute a prima facie case of discrimination in the enjoyment of the rights guaranteed by Article 11 of the Convention. Furthermore, the State had failed to fulfil its positive obligations to adopt effective and clear judicial protection against discrimination on the ground of trade union membership.

Clearly Article 1, Protocol 1 (protection of property)[37] and Article 2 (protecting the right to life) also have clear links to Article 14, as can be seen by the wide ECtHR practice in these areas. Regarding Article 2, the issue may regard discriminatory measures related to access to healthcare or social services that place an individual's life at risk.[38] Article 3 prohibiting torture, but also inhuman or degrading treatment or punishment, has in several cases been invoked to address racial discrimination that has taken forms of degrading treatment.[39] In addition, Article 4 regarding the prohibition of slavery and forced (or compulsory labour) and Article 8 regarding the

---

[37] ECtHR (Chamber), Judgment of 16 September 1996, *Gaygusuz v Austria*, App No 17371/90 (concerning the refusal of non-contributory unemployment benefit on the grounds that such benefit was reserved to Austrian nationals); ECtHR (Second Section), Judgment of 4 June 2002, *Wessels-Bergervoet v The Netherlands*, App No 34462/97 (the old-age pension of the applicant and her husband had been reduced because the husband had not been insured under Dutch law for a period when he had been working in Germany; the complaint was based on discrimination on the ground of sex). See further Herzfeld-Olsson's chapter in this book.

[38] See ECtHR (Grand Chamber), Judgment of 10 May 2001, *Cyprus v Turkey*, App No 25781/94.

[39] ECtHR (Former Second Section), Judgment of 12 July 2005, *Moldovan and others v Romania*, App Nos 41138/98 and 64320/01.

right to respect for private and family life including sexual orientation and identity, as has already been indicated above, can be linked to Article 14 in a way that constitutes discrimination. The same is certainly true for Article 6 regulating the right to a fair trial and Article 13 regarding the right to an effective remedy.[40]

Protection against discrimination of vulnerable groups of workers, especially migrant or disabled persons, might also in the future be dealt with under Article 14, although we still lack ECtHR case law in this area.[41]

7 FUTURE PROSPECTS

There is huge potential for the ECtHR to become an important final instance in discrimination cases in Europe. On the other hand, there are some important limitations in the Court's practised legal approach as well as in the actual ability of the Court to deal with the flood of cases potentially referred to it in the area of social and labour law if all the new Court opportunities for integrating social rights with civil and political rights are fully utilised and implemented.

As several scholars have pointed out, the primary concern is that the ECtHR seems to have adopted a kind of strange double standard towards discrimination issues, on the one hand being very open to admit and hear these cases, yet on the other hand applying a very strict standard concerning evidence, the burden of proof and also on criteria for indirect discrimination. This has ended in most cases with the ECtHR not establishing that discrimination under Article 14 has taken place. It seems clear that an astonishing discrepancy exists between the standard applied by the Court of Justice of the European Union (CJEU) and that of the ECtHR. I will not examine this discrepancy in depth, as it has been clearly documented by other authors. This conflict is of course of special interest since the integration of EU law with the ECHR is already taking place and the Treaty of Lisbon already states that the EU will join the CoE in order to also become bound by the ECHR. This process should in principle strengthen protection against discrimination since the ECHR is regarded as a minimum and subsidiary regime. Thus, Article 53 ECHR read together with Article 52(3) CFREU enables not only the Member States but also the EU to develop higher protection mechanisms against gender and other types of discrimination.[42]

This development could be a great opportunity to harmonise the practice of both courts (the ECtHR and the CJEU), thereby developing a court practice on discrimination which leaves the adoption of positive temporary special measures to the States Parties and clearly abolishes the formal application of EU equal opportunities law in cases involving the promotion of women's careers (*Kalanke, Badeck,*

---

[40] See especially ECtHR (Second Section), Judgment of 10 July 2012, *KMC v Hungary*, App No 19554/11.

[41] See, however, ECtHR (Third Section), Judgment of 10 July 2001, *Price v UK*, App No 33394/96, where degrading treatment under Article 3 was successfully invoked when a severely disabled person was detained in prison without taking due regard to her special needs. See also R Medda-Windischer, 'The European Court of Human Rights and Minority Rights' (2003) 25(3) *European Integration* 249–71.

[42] See S Besson, 'Gender Discrimination under EU and ECHR Law: Never Shall the Twain Meet?' (2008) 8(4) *Human Rights Law Review* 680.

Abrahamsson, etc).[43] Furthermore, it should make it possible to have EU standards concerning evidence, burden of proof, indirect discrimination, etc also applying as minimum standards in the ECtHR.[44] During this development, the practice of international conventions such as the CEDAW Convention and the ICRMW Convention should be taken into account. Moreover, with regard to sex discrimination, it could for instance limit the broad margin of appreciation left for the nation state, which in many cases has led to a final outcome in favour of the State Party accused of discrimination.

In fact there have recently been some indications that the ECtHR is cautiously reconsidering its jurisprudence concerning the burden of proof and indirect discrimination in cases concerning Article 14. An example of this development is the judgment in the case of *Horvath and Kiss v Hungary*.[45] Here the different treatment of Roma children in the national educational system had been justified by a testing system which had resulted in a large proportion of Roma children being placed in special classes since they were classified as mentally disabled. The case concerned two such pupils who alleged, under Article 2 of Protocol No 1 read in conjunction with Article 14 of the ECHR, that their education in the remedial school had amounted to direct and/or indirect discrimination in their enjoyment of their right to education on the basis of their Roma origin. Without going into the details of the case it is worth noting that the Court here applied a restrictive approach to the possibility of justifying different treatment and a standard similar to the one applied by the CJEU regarding the concept of indirect discrimination and the evidence needed for the burden of proof to be shifted to the respondent State.[46] The Courts justification of such an approach was, however, strongly linked to the specifics of ethnic discrimination and different treatment in the educational sphere.[47]

There is strong criticism against any expansion of the role of the ECtHR. It already has a strong role in Europe due especially to the fact that the Convention has been effectively transposed, even incorporated, into the legislation of most Member States, meaning that ECtHR judgments usually have to be followed and can be enforced. This criticism targets in particular any expansion of the scope of application of Article 14. Marc Bossuyt writes:

> The consequences for the caseload of the Court of its wide interpretations of the scope of the normative provisions of the European Convention are often overlooked or underestimated. Despite the enlargement of the membership of the Council of Europe, the system would probably be able to survive if the Court had limited its jurisdiction to civil rights and

---

[43] See Case C-450/93, *Eckhard Kalanke v Freie Hansestadt Bremen* [1995] ECR I-3051; Case C-409/95, *Helmut Marschall v Land Nordrhein-Westfalen* [1997] ECR I-6363; Case C-158/97, *Georg Badeck and others* [2000] ECR I-1875; and Case C-407/98, *Katarina Abrahamsson and Leif Anderson v Elisabet Fogelqvist* [2000] ECR I-5539.

[44] See Besson (n 42) 676–82.

[45] ECtHR (Second Section), Judgment of 29 January 2013, *Horvath and Kiss v Hungary*, App No 11146/11.

[46] See *Horvath and Kiss v Hungary*, ibid, § 101–108.

[47] In *Horvath and Kiss v Hungary* (n 45) § 106 the ECtHR explicitly states that when indirect discriminatory effect has been shown, it is not necessary in cases in the educational sphere to prove any discriminatory intent on the part of the relevant authorities as it is 'with cases concerning employment or the provision of services'.

fundamental freedoms and to civil and criminal proceedings as envisaged by the founding fathers of the European Convention. By extending, however, its jurisdiction to a great variety of proceedings and to the whole range of social rights, the Court is contributing to an expansion of its caseload which is becoming unmanageable. The future is even less assuring as, till now, only a limited number of States have become parties to the 12th Protocol and as the praetorian extension of the jurisdiction of the Court to social security matters is still very recent. As always, it takes time before the applicants—and their lawyers—discover the full potentiality of those new developments. But once they do, the system runs the risk of collapsing. In order to avoid this prospect, which would be disastrous for the protection of human rights in Europe and for the world at large, hard choices will have to be made. Self-restraint could be one of the options.[48]

Although the interpretative approach by the ECtHR presented above to some extent expands the rather strict wording of Article 14, there have been efforts to open up Article 14 towards a more general prohibition of discrimination.

These efforts resulted in the adoption on 4 November 2000, in Rome, of Protocol No 12 to the European Convention, opening up the content of Article 14 towards a more general application. The wording of the crucial Article 1 of the Protocol reads:

> The enjoyment of any right set forth by law shall be secured without discrimination on any ground such as sex, race, colour, language, religion, political or other opinion, national or social origin, association with a national minority, property, birth or other status.

> No one shall be discriminated against by any public authority on any ground such as those mentioned in paragraph 1.

Ratification of this Protocol has been rather slow. Out of the 18 ratifications so far (July 2013), only seven were by EU Member States.[49] Therefore, there is not much Court practice regarding its interpretation.[50] The slow pace of ratification also shows that Member States have doubts concerning expanding the jurisdiction of the ECtHR to cover general issues of discrimination. A selective approach is therefore to be recommended, under which the Court would avoid becoming a general court in the field of social policy by giving a restrictive interpretation to Protocol 1, Article 1 in relation to social security issues. On the other hand, discrimination in relation to the core articles referred to above (Articles 2–4, 6, 8 and 11) should be dealt with in a way that is consistent with developed discrimination law. This will not only result in a more consistent approach to the burden of proof and indirect discrimination, but will also lead to a more limited approach regarding the national margin of appreciation in discrimination cases.

---

[48] M Bossuyt, 'Should the Strasbourg Court Exercise More Self-restraint? On the Extension of the Jurisdiction of the European Court of Human Rights to Social Security Regulations' (2007) 28 (9–12) *Human Rights Law Journal* 321–32.

[49] Cyprus, Finland, Luxembourg, the Netherlands, Romania, Slovenia and Spain (10 further EU Member States have signed the Protocol).

[50] See, however, ECtHR (Grand Chamber), Judgment of 22 December 2009, *Sejdic and Finci v Bosnia and Herzegovina*, App Nos 27996/06 and 34836/06.

15

Every Natural or Legal Person is Entitled to the Peaceful Enjoyment of His or Her Possessions: Article 1, Protocol 1 to the European Convention on Human Rights

PETRA HERZFELD OLSSON

E VERY NATURAL OR legal person is entitled to the peaceful enjoyment of his or her possessions. No one shall be deprived of his possessions except in the public interest and subject to the conditions provided for by law and by the general principles of international law.

The preceding provisions shall not, however, in any way impair the right of a State to enforce such laws as it deems necessary to control the use of property in accordance with the general interest or to secure the payment of taxes or other contributions or penalties.

1 INTRODUCTION[1]

As T Novitz recently pointed out, discussions on the right to property with regard to employment seldom focus on the worker's perspective.[2] This could be one explanation why it is not apparent what function Article 1, Protocol 1 to the European Convention on Human Rights (hereinafter A1P1) could have in protecting workers' rights. Could A1P1 play any role for workers whatsoever? This question will be addressed in this chapter. As will be seen, the construction of A1P1 does set some clear limits with regard to the potential impact of the right to property in working life. On the other hand, the possibilities that exist are not very widely explored. Wages, pensions and collective agreements can, for example, gain a certain amount of protection through A1P1. These limits and possibilities will be discussed, as will the possible impact of other international human rights and EU law in the development of A1P1.

---

[1] I am very grateful for the invaluable comments I have received on drafts of this chapter from Professor Tonia Novitz and Professor Niklas Bruun. All omissions and faults are of course my own.
[2] T Novitz, 'Labour Rights and Property Rights: Implications for (and Beyond) Redundancy Payments and Pensions?' (2012) 41(2) *Industrial Law Journal* 137.

The chapter is organised as follows: following the introduction, Section 2 explains the position of the right to property as an international human right. Section 3 considers the nature of the right to property and its interrelationship with other human rights. Next, in Section 4, the basic content of A1P1 is reviewed—how is a possession in the meaning of A1P1 established and how can a restriction be justified? The issue of the extent of State responsibility is a crucial aspect of this section. For example, can A1P1 have any implications for private law relationships? A1P1 is a complex human right and this overview is necessary in order to assess the right's potential with regard to aspects of working life. Section 5 offers a somewhat speculative discussion on what may reasonably constitute a work-related possession within the meaning of A1P1. Section 6 includes an overview of some of the cases decided by the ECtHR, illustrating the effects of the right's complexity when applied. Section 7 discusses the interplay between A1P1 and the right to strike and the protection of a collective agreement. Section 8 exemplifies how other international legal sources, including EU law, can be used to promote A1P1. Section 9 includes a few words on the issue of whether EU accession to the ECHR will have any implications for the protection of A1P1 within the EU legal order. The chapter finishes with some concluding remarks.

2 THE RIGHT TO PROPERTY AS A HUMAN RIGHT

While the right to property or the peaceful enjoyment of one's possessions is a right with a strong tradition in many national legal systems, its recognition as an international human right has been controversial.[3] It was included in Article 17 of the Universal Declaration of Human Rights in 1948: 'Everyone has a right to own property alone as well as in association with others and no one shall be arbitrarily deprived of his property.' But when the provisions in the Declaration were to be implemented as judicially binding conventions, the right to property did not achieve the necessary support to be included in any of the UN Conventions on Human Rights adopted in 1966.

Dividing human rights into the different categories—civil, political, economic, cultural and social—can be inaccurate, as one particular human right often pursues several aims.[4] The discussion on the right to property when negotiating the UN Conventions illustrates the difficulties associated with such a division.[5] It was primarily discussed in connection with the International Covenant on Economic,

---

[3] HG Schermers, 'The International Protection of the Right to Property' in F Matscher and H Petzold (eds), *Protecting Human Rights: The European Dimension* (Cologne, Kassel Carl Heymans Verlag KG, 1988) 565–80; Theo RG van Banning, *The Human Right to Property* (Antwerp, Intersentia, 2002) 35 f; A Rosas, 'Property Rights' in A Rosas and J Helgesen (eds), *The Strength of Diversity: Human Rights and Pluralist Democracy* (Dordrecht, Martinus Nijhoff Publishers, 1992) 133 ff; P van Dijk and GJH van Hoof, *Theory and Practice of the European Convention on Human Rights*, 3rd edn (The Hague, Kluwer Law International, 1998) 618.

[4] See the extract in the running text corresponding to note 28 on the *Airey* case and A Eide, 'Economic, Social and Cultural Rights as Human Rights' in A Eide, C Krause and A Rosas (eds), *Economic, Social and Cultural Rights: A Textbook*, 2nd edn (Dordrecht, Martinus Nijhoff Publishers, 2001) 17 f.

[5] Rosas (n 3) 145; C Krause, 'The Right to Property' in Eide, Krause and Rosas (eds) (n 4) 192.

Social and Cultural Rights (ICESCR).[6] But there were differing opinions on how to characterise this right—was it a civil or an economic right and what were the implications of each? Ultimately, the reason for not including the right in the covenants was that the Soviet Union and some of its allies could not accept the inclusion of any provision on compensation related to expropriation.[7] However, even among the non-socialist States, there were hesitations regarding its inclusion.[8]

Some aspects of the right to property, such as intellectual property rights and the right to own property on a non-discriminatory basis, have been given protection in the UN human rights legal framework.[9] It is widely recognised that discriminatory forms of control and/or deprivation of property rights must be terminated.[10]

On a regional basis,[11] particularly in Europe, it has been easier to gain a consensus on a broader right to property. Even though no such right was included in the European Convention on Human Rights (ECHR), it took only two years to decide on an additional protocol to the Convention including, inter alia, *a right to peaceful enjoyment of one's possession*. The debate was, however, intense and many arguments were employed in opposition to this still-controversial inclusion.[12] The Protocol has now been ratified by all 47 Member States of the Council of Europe (CoE), with the exception of Monaco and Switzerland, who are signatories only. The EU Charter of Fundamental Rights also includes, in Article 17, a right to own, use, dispose of and bequeath his or her lawfully acquired possessions. According to this Article, no one may be deprived of his or her possessions, except in the public interest and in the cases and under the conditions provided for by law, subject to fair compensation being paid in good time for their loss. The use of property may also be regulated by law insofar as is necessary for the general interest. A second

---

[6] Van Banning (n 3) 42; Rosas (n 3) 138.

[7] Van Banning (n 3) 45; Krause (n 5) 200 ff.

[8] Van Banning (n 3) 46.

[9] In Article 27.2 of the UN Declaration, the author's right to the protection of the moral and material interests resulting from his or her scientific, literary or artistic production is safeguarded and a corresponding provision is included in Article 15(c) in the legally binding 1966 ICESCR. Other aspects of the general right to property have also been dealt with in the International Convention on the Elimination of All Forms of Racial Discrimination (ICERD 1965) and in the Convention on the Elimination of All Forms of Discrimination Against Women (CEDAW 1979). The starting point in these Conventions is that the States Parties undertake to prohibit and to eliminate discrimination on these grounds and to guarantee the right to everyone, without such distinction, to equality before the law, in the enjoyment among many other things of the right to own property (Articles 5 ICERD and Articles 15.2 and 16.1(h) CEDAW). Prohibiting discriminatory treatment with regard to the right to property is also included in the Convention on the Protection of Refugees in Articles 14–15 (1951) and in the Convention relating to the Stateless Persons (1954) in Articles 13–14, and the International Convention on the Protection of the Rights of All Migrants and Members of their Families (1990) in Article 15.

[10] Van Banning (n 3) 49.

[11] There is also a right to property included in Article 21 American Convention on Human Rights, in Article 14 African Charter on Human and Peoples' Rights and in Article 31 Arab Charter on Human Rights. See more in Krause (n 5) 195; and Rosas (n 3). The Arab Charter on Human Rights was reprinted in 2004 and entered into force in 2008. See more in M Rishmawi, 'A Revised Arab Charter on Human Rights: A Step Forward?' (2005) *Human Rights Law Review* 361–76. An update from 2010 can be found in (2010) *Human Rights Law Review* 169–78.

[12] For example, Schermers (n 3) 580; AR Çoban, *Protection of Property Rights within the European Convention on Human Rights* (Aldershot, Ashgate, 2004) 124 ff; G Gauksdottir, *The Right to Property and the European Convention on Human Rights: A Nordic Approach* (Faculty of Law RWI Lund University, Lund, 2004) 123 f.

paragraph explicitly states that intellectual property shall be protected.[13] This Article is based on A1P1. The meaning and scope of the right are the same as those provided for in the right guaranteed by the ECHR, and the limitations may not exceed those stated there.[14]

Since the fall of the Berlin Wall, more and more States are covered by a human rights system where the right to property is included. However, a common, unified understanding of the right in the global sphere does not seem to exist. It has been argued that the right's connection to the social and economic policies of States makes those States reluctant to agree to international supervision of the right to property.[15] Inspiration for interpreting A1P1 in the ECHR will, however, be taken from articles dealing with issues other than those relating to the application of the right to property in the Conventions. This starting point will be further explained later.

3. A FEW WORDS ON THE NATURE OF THE RIGHT TO PROPERTY

The right to property and the nature thereof have occupied the thinking of many legal philosophers and other scholars throughout history.[16] Though it is not appropriate to refer to that debate here, some thoughts on this issue will be considered below, in order to better understand the right to property in the ECHR context and its possible development.

Sweden, along with the UK, was the most reluctant State to include a right to property in the ECHR. Sweden found it irrational to include the social right to property without including other social rights, such as the right to work and the right to an adequate standard of living.[17] The Swedish and the British governments did not want any restriction put on their potential to nationalise industries for social and political purposes. This point of view reveals a fear of losing the means to strengthen social rights within society and also reflects a complex view on the content of the right to property.

Conflicting views on the meaning and scope of the right to property characterised the negotiations. The property right in the Additional Protocol to the ECHR was intended by the majority of the States to protect *acquired rights* and could therefore run counter to social rights, given that the effective realisation of social rights calls for a redistribution of wealth and resources.[18] Cameron formulates the dilemma elegantly:

> The right to property is controversial, basically because of inequalities in society and finite economic resources. To provide for a strong right to property in such circumstances is to

[13] OJ, C 83/391 30 March 2010.
[14] Explanations relating to the EU Charter of Fundamental Rights, Article 17, OJ C 303/17, 14 December 2007, p 23.
[15] For example, van Banning (n 3) 45; Krause (n 5) 193; K Åhman, *Egendomsskyddet, Äganderätten enligt artikel 1 första tilläggsprotokollet till den europeiska konventionen om de mänskliga rättigheterna* (Uppsala, Iustus Förlag, 2000) 143.
[16] For a general overview, see Coban (n 12) 9 ff. For an overview and analysis of the discussion on work- or employment-related property rights, see Novitz (n 2) 139 ff.
[17] Schermers (n 3) 571; Krause (n 5) 192.
[18] Krause (n 5) 208–09.

run the risk of 'freezing' existing inequitable divisions of property in society and making government redistributive policies more difficult.[19]

Krause points out that if the realisation of property rights entails only a right to own property for those who are in a position to acquire property and a protection against arbitrary interference in these existing property rights, it is difficult, at least morally, to justify the right to property.[20] Schermers argued in 1988 that even if today's right to property is only about enjoying one's property, it is desirable that this right be further developed into a right to possess at least a minimum amount of individual property.[21] According to his point of departure, the right of enjoyment of one's property must be accompanied by a right to acquire a certain amount of property. No real substantial movement in that direction can be detected in the case law of the European Court of Human Rights (ECtHR). This has been explained by the fact that, for a long time, protection has been largely of a negative character, emphasising non-interference by the authorities, rather than of a positive character, emphasising the active measures taken by the State to ensure that everyone in fact enjoys the right to property.[22] A1P1 does not create a positive duty for governments to ensure a minimum level of income or property, instead merely protecting the freedom of individuals to acquire, enjoy and use property.[23] This aspect, according to Coban, distinguishes it from social and economic rights, which vest the right-holder with a claim against public authorities, and reveals the liberal nature of the right to property, associated with a corresponding negative obligation.[24] Frowein, however, states that A1P1 is the only real economic right protected by the Convention.[25] But, as Harris et al explain, the lack of an acquiring perspective confirms that A1P1 is much closer to the notion of property rights as civil rights than it is to modern ideas of property rights as economic rights, even though the provision is now directed towards the defence of economic interests.[26] As will be indicated later in this chapter, the concept of property is rather wide and clearly encompasses rights that could be considered social rights, such as wages and social benefits.[27]

The ECtHR has clarified its view on the applicability of the provisions in the Convention in the social sphere:

> The Court is aware that the further realisation of social and economic rights is largely dependent on the situation—notably financial—reigning in the State in question. On the other hand, the Convention must be interpreted in the light of present-day conditions ... and it is designed to safeguard the individual in a real and practical way as regards those

---

[19] I Cameron, *An Introduction to the European Convention on Human Rights*, 6th edn (Uppsala, Iustus Förlag, 2011) 138.

[20] Krause (n 5) 191.

[21] Schermers (n 3) 570.

[22] Krause (n 5) 191–92. See also Schermers (n 3) 569, who touches upon this issue.

[23] Coban (n 12)157.

[24] Ibid, 164.

[25] JA Frowein, 'The Protection of Property' in R St J Macdonald, F Matscher and H Petzold (eds), *The European System for the Protection of Human Rights* (Dordrecht, Boston, Martinus Nijhoff Publishers, 1993) 515.

[26] DJ Harris, M O'Boyle, C Warbrick and E Bates, *Law of the European Convention on Human Rights* (Oxford, Oxford University Press, 2009), 660.

[27] As early as 1971, the Commission held that contribution to a pension fund could create a property right: *X v Netherlands*, App No 4130/69, Decision of 20 July 1971.

areas with which it deals ... Whilst the Convention sets forth what are essentially civil and political rights, many of them have implications of a social or economic nature. The Court therefore considers, like the Commission, that the mere fact that an interpretation of the Convention may extend into the sphere of social and economic rights should not be a decisive factor against such an interpretation; there is no water-tight division separating that sphere from the field covered by the Convention.[28]

It is up to the Member State to decide what *is to be* protected. A1P1 places no restriction on the Contracting States' freedom to decide whether or not to have any form of social security scheme in place, or to choose the type or amount of benefits to provide under any such scheme. If, however, a State has legislation in force which provides for the payment, as of right, of a welfare benefit—whether conditional or not on the prior payment of contributions—that legislation must be regarded as generating a proprietary interest falling within the ambit of A1P1 for persons satisfying its requirements.[29] Accordingly, the right to property can mean very different things in different countries. The Swedish position during the negotiations on A1P1 implicitly addressed this ambiguity of meaning when referring to the lack of other social rights. If other social rights, such as the right to work and the right to an adequate standard of living, had been included in the Convention, a larger part of the population would have been guaranteed a right to acquire property, which then could be protected by A1P1. The discretion allowed to States in this regard would consequently be less. This starting point is reflected by Eide, who defines the right to property as a purely economic right and, as with all economic rights, one that has a dual function. It serves as a basis for entitlements that can ensure an adequate standard of living, while on the other hand providing a basis for independence and therefore for freedom. As the right to property in the *traditional understanding of the term* cannot be enjoyed on an equal basis by all, it must be supplemented by at least two other rights: the right to work, which can provide an income ensuring an adequate standard of living; and the right to social security, which can supplement and, where necessary, fully substitute insufficient income derived from property or from work.[30] Even if there are signs in the ECtHR's case law that some kind of right to work is implied in Article 8 ECHR, the legal complements to which Eide refers are still far from being included.[31] Since the acquired right perspective in relation to A1P1 seems to be almost carved in stone by the ECtHR, such a development would be important, particularly in countries where the ECHR is directly applicable.

Rosas has observed that from a human rights perspective, property rights are, first, specific human rights; second, may enhance the enjoyment of other human rights; and, third, may, in more generic terms, support a democratic system of government.[32] What is clear is that the social dimension of the right to property

---

[28] *Airey v Ireland*, App No 6289/73, Judgment of 9 October 1979, § 26; *Stec and others v UK*, App Nos 65731/01 and 65900/01, GC Decision of 6 July 2005, § 52.

[29] *Stec and others v UK* (n 28) § 53; *Moskal v Poland*, App No 10373/05, Judgment of 15 September 2009, §§ 30–39.

[30] Eide (n 4) 17–18.

[31] Aspects of the right to work and employment protection have been dealt with in the following judgments: *Sidabras and Dziautas v Lithuania*, App Nos 55480/00 and 59330/00, Judgment of 27 July 2004, §§ 47–50; *Schüth v Germany*, App No 1620/03, Judgment of 23 September 2010, §§ 53–75.

[32] Rosas (n 3) 133.

depends to a large extent on the protection of other social and economic human rights in the Contracting States. Where these have a national legal basis, the right to property can definitely be used to enhance these rights, using Rosas' terminology. As more and more applicants invoke social rights claims related to A1P1, the new case law reveals the potential and limitations in this field. Before discussing the specific implications of A1P1 in employment relations, an overview of the general construction of A1P1 is presented.

4 ARTICLE 1 AP 1: ITS CONSTRUCTION

The Court stated in *Marckx* that, by recognising that everyone has a right to peaceful enjoyment of his or her possessions, A1P1 in substance guarantees a right to property.[33] A1P1 has been described as a wide-ranging fundamental human right to property with only weak protection, permitting many exceptions.[34] It is worth remembering that both legal and natural persons enjoy the right to property. Accordingly, companies fall within the scope of the Article.[35] In this section, some fundamental aspects of the article are reviewed. These have been chosen on the basis of the overall perspective of this chapter.

4.1 Possession

The word 'possession' has been given a broad interpretation. It includes immovable and movable property; tangible and intangible interests such as company shares and intellectual property; judgment debts; contractual rights with economic value; various economic interests and goodwill; as well as pending compensation claims against the State (provided that there is a legitimate expectation for the claims to be decided in the applicant's favour) and public law-related claims, such as pensions.[36] In a nutshell, the concept of possession extends to all manner of things which have an economic value.[37]

Possessions can be 'existing possessions' or claims that are sufficiently established to be regarded as 'assets'. Where a proprietary interest is in the nature of a claim, it may be regarded as an 'asset' only if there is sufficient basis for that interest in national law through a legal provision or a legal act such as a judicial decision—the claim must be sufficiently established in order to be enforceable.[38] In such a case, the issue of whether the applicant had a 'legitimate expectation' of obtaining effective

---

[33] *Marckx v Belgium*, App No 6833/74, (Pl) Judgment of 13 June 1979, § 63.

[34] Schermers (n 3) 571; Coban (n 12) 140.

[35] A Grgić, Z Mataga, M Longar and A Vilfan, 'The Right to Property under the European Convention on Human Rights', Human Rights Handbooks, No 10, *A Guide to the Implementation of the European Convention on Human Rights and its Protocols* (Council of Europe, 2007) 6.

[36] Krause (n 5) 199; Coban (n 12) 170; Harris at al (n 26) 656.

[37] C Ovey and RCA White, *Jacobs and White: The European Convention on Human Rights*, 4th edn (Oxford, Oxford University Press, 2006) 350.

[38] *Lelas v Croatia*, App No 55555/08, Judgment of 20 May 2010, p 56; *Kopecký v Slovakia*, App No 44912/98, Judgment of 28 September 2004, §§ 49 and 52.

enjoyment of a property right can be crucial.[39] By contrast, the hope of recognition of a property right that has been impossible to exercise effectively cannot be considered a 'possession' within the meaning of A1P1, nor can a conditional claim which lapses as a result of the non-fulfilment of the condition.[40] The nature of the condition seems to be irrelevant.[41] Gauksdottir has observed that there is a thin line between potential rights not protected by the Article, and legitimate expectations that a right will materialise, which can be considered to be covered by it. The situation in the State concerned is of paramount importance.[42]

It is not for the ECtHR to decide whether or not a right of property exists under domestic law. An applicant must establish the precise nature of the right in the national law and his or her entitlement to enjoy it.[43] That is the starting point, unless domestic law runs counter to the object and purpose of A1P1.[44] The notion of 'possessions' in the Article, however, has an autonomous meaning independent of the formal classification in domestic law. In each case, the issue that needs to be examined is whether the circumstances of the case, considered as a whole, confer on the applicant title to a substantive interest protected by A1P1.[45]

The property must also be of a certain economic value. A hobby or voting rights connected to shares do not therefore constitute assets in the meaning of the Convention.[46] The demonstration of an established economic interest by an applicant may be sufficient to establish a protected right. The loss of a liquor licence, for example, fulfilled the criteria for possession. The ECtHR explained it in the following way: 'the maintenance of the licence was one of the principal conditions for the carrying on of the applicant company's business, and that its withdrawal had adverse effects on the goodwill and the value of the restaurant'.[47]

Future income could only be considered to constitute a 'possession' if it had already been earned (but not yet paid) or where an enforceable claim existed to it.[48] Fees to notaries which had been statutorily reduced did not constitute a possession. The Commission held that the mere expectation that the regulations on fees would not change could not be considered a possession. The conclusion would have been the opposite if the claim had been based on services already rendered.[49] It can be sufficient for the applicant to show that he or she is entitled to some real, if yet unattributed, economic benefit. As Harris et al point out, this is relevant to

---

[39] An overview of the concept of legitimate expectation is to be found in the ECtHR case *Kopecký v Slovakia* (n 38) §§ 45–52. See also *Vilho Eskelinen and others v Finland*, App No 63235/00, (GC) Judgment of 19 April 2007, § 94.

[40] Gauksdottir (n 12) 137 and the referred case law therein.

[41] Harris et al (n 26) 661.

[42] Gauksdottir (n 12) 141.

[43] Harris et al (n 26) 658.

[44] *Pressos Compania Naviera v Belgium*, App No 17849/91, Judgment of 20 November 1995, § 31.

[45] *Bronowski v Poland*, App No 31443/96, (GC) Judgment of 22 June 2004, § 129. See also Coban (n 12) 148–49; Harris et al (n 26) 658.

[46] Harris et al (n 26) 657; van Dijk and van Hoof (n 3) 620.

[47] Quote from *Tre traktörer aktiebolag v Sweden*, App No 10873/84, Judgment of 7 July 1989, § 53. See also Harris et al (n 26) 658–59.

[48] *HJ Betalaan and J Huiges v The Netherlands*, App No 19438/83, Decision of 3 October 1984; *Denimark Ltd v UK*, App No 37660/97, Decision of 26 December 2000; *Levänen v Finland* App No 34600/03, Decision of 11 April 2006.

[49] *X v Germany*, App No 8410/78, Decision of 13 December 1979.

welfare benefits. The Court has allowed that a welfare right under domestic law is a possession for the purposes of the Article. Moreover, since 2005, no distinction is made between benefits to which the applicant has made contributions and those to which no direct contribution has been made.[50] But it is up to the State to decide whether or not to have in place any form of social security scheme, or to choose the type or amount of benefits to provide under any such scheme.[51] This statement emphasises that A1P1 does not guarantee a right to acquire possessions.[52] The text in the Article is, according to the ECtHR, limited to enshrining the right of everyone to the peaceful enjoyment of his or her possessions.[53]

To conclude, the word 'possession' has been given a broad interpretation. Still, it is worth remembering that the Contracting States enjoy a wide margin of appreciation in legislating which conditions must be fulfilled for the acquisition and the termination of property rights.[54]

4.2 Infringement

According to the ECtHR's case law, the first paragraph of A1P1 comprises three distinct rules. The first, set out in the first sentence of the first paragraph, is of a general nature and lays down the principle of peaceful enjoyment of property. The second rule, in the second sentence of the same paragraph, covers deprivation of possessions and subjects this to certain conditions. The third, contained in the second paragraph, recognises that the Contracting States are entitled, amongst other things, to control the use of property in accordance with the general interest. The second and third rules, which are concerned with particular types of interference with the right to peaceful enjoyment of property, are to be construed in the light of the general principle laid down in the first rule.[55]

The first rule in the Article can be said to be subsidiary to the other two rules. If an infringement dealt with in the second or third rule of the Article, ie, *deprivation* and *control of use*, is not substantiated, the infringement can be dealt with under the first rule—an infringement interfering with one's *peaceful enjoyment* of the possession. The Court has stated that an analysis of the nature of an interference requires a consideration of the first sentence only after it is determined that the second and third sentences do not apply.[56] In order to invoke the first sentence, an interference of the *substance* of property must have taken place.[57] In *Aizpurua Ortiz v Spain*, the modification by the parties to a collective agreement covering supplementary pensions that resulted in a financial loss for retired employees was

---

[50] Harris et al (n 26) 659. The no-distinction principle was established in *Stec and others v UK* (n 28) §§ 47–53.

[51] *Stec and others v UK* (n 28) § 53.

[52] Schermers (n 3) 572.

[53] *Van der Mussele v Belgium*. App No 8919/80, Judgment of 23 November 1983, § 48.

[54] Gauksdottir (n 12) 245.

[55] *Gustafsson v Sweden*, App No 155573/87, Judgment of 28 March 1996, § 59.

[56] *Sporrong and Lönnroth v Sweden*, App Nos 7151/75 and 7152/75, (PC) Judgment of 23 September 1982, § 61.

[57] Ibid, §§ 63–65.

examined under the first sentence of the first paragraph, as the interference did not correspond either to a deprivation or to a regulation of the control of use of the property.[58] A *deprivation* occurs when all the legal rights of the owner are eliminated by operation of law or by the exercise of a legal power to the same effect.[59] Deduction of wages made to cover a monitoring fee laid down in a collective agreement was considered a deprivation of property within the meaning of the second sentence of the first paragraph of the Article.[60] A State may *control the use of property* by requiring positive action by individuals or legal persons, as well as by imposing restrictions upon their activities. Such restrictions might result from planning controls, environmental orders, rent control, import and export laws, forfeiture and confiscation orders, economic regulation of professions, regulation of the use of materials in the course of business, business licences and so forth.[61] An insolvency order can take the form of a *control of the use of property*, as the claimant could, because of the order, no longer obtain the payment of a debt, as the debtor, the private bank, was declared insolvent.[62]

In order to investigate whether an infringement of the first rule has taken place, the Court must determine whether a fair balance has been struck between the demands of the general interest of the community and the requirements for the protection of the individual's fundamental rights. A question that can be asked is whether unjustified differential treatment has occurred.[63] The Court has, however, stated that the search for this balance is inherent to the whole of the Convention and is also reflected in the structure of A1P1. The balance is also applied when the Court deals with the second and third rules in the Article.[64] Harris at al have identified a tendency for the Court to decide cases simply by reference to its 'fair balance' test, irrespective of which sentence, if any, is deemed relevant for that case.[65] It is also clear that it may be difficult to determine which sentence is applicable in a certain case. It seems that the identification of the type of interference is less important to the outcome of a case than is the process involved in the application of the 'fair balance' test.[66]

The balance test involves three important components. First, the infringement must be lawful and pursue a legitimate aim in the public interest.[67] The Court has stated that the most important requirement of the Article is that any interference should be lawful.[68] This means that the interference must be authorised by national law and that the law concerned must be accessible, precise and foreseeable.[69] The 'law' does not have to be enacted by a parliament to fulfil the demand. But an

---

[58] *Aizpurua Ortiz et autres c. Espagne*, requete n 42430/05, arret 2 février 2010, § 48.
[59] Harris et al (n 26) 677 and the referred case law therein.
[60] *Evaldsson and others v Sweden*, App No 75252/01, Judgment of 13 February 2007, § 52.
[61] Harris et al (n 26) 687.
[62] *Kotov v Russia*, App No 54522/00, Judgment of 14 January 2010. Revised by the Grand Chamber on 3 April 2012.
[63] *Kjartan Asmundsson v Iceland*, App No 60669/00, Judgment of 12 October 2004, § 40.
[64] For example *Evaldsson and others v Sweden* (n 60) § 55.
[65] Harris et al (n 26) 667.
[66] Ibid, 668; Gauksdottir (n 12) 248–51.
[67] *Evaldsson and others v Sweden* (n 60) § 53.
[68] *Lelas v Croatia* (n 38) § 71.
[69] Ovey and White (n 37) 361.

individual must be able, perhaps with appropriate advice, to foresee, to a degree that is reasonable in the circumstances, the consequences which a given action may entail. The legal basis for an infringement can accordingly be provided for in a collective agreement. In *Aizpurua Ortiz v Spain*, the Court derived this conclusion from two facts, namely that:

1) collective agreements were legally binding in the Spanish legal system; and

2) the right to bargain collectively with employers has, in principle, become one of the essential elements of the 'right to form and to join trade unions for the protection of one's interest' (Article 11 ECHR), as concluded in *Demir and Baykara v Turkey*.[70]

The principle of lawfulness also requires that the Court verify whether the way in which the domestic law is interpreted and applied by the domestic courts produces consequences that are consistent with the principles of the Convention.[71]

It is quite rare for the lawfulness test to be decisive for the outcome of a case. But there are some examples. In *Lelas*, a case concerning failure to pay additional wages, the Court came to the conclusion that the infringement was incompatible with the principle of lawfulness because the manner in which the national court interpreted and applied the relevant domestic law was not foreseeable for the applicant. The Court therefore found that the impugned interference was incompatible with the principle of lawfulness and therefore contravened A1P1.[72] The starting point for the Court is normally to accept a State's argument that a certain infringement pursues a legitimate aim. The Court is of the opinion that national authorities, because of their direct knowledge of their own society and its needs, are in principle better placed than the international judge to appreciate what is 'in the public interest'. The national authorities accordingly enjoy a *certain* margin of appreciation and the notion of 'public interest' is necessarily extensive.[73] When implementing social and economic policy, the Court finds it natural that the margin of appreciation available to the legislature should be a *wide* one and respects the legislature's judgment as to what is 'in the public interest', unless that judgment is manifestly without reasonable foundation.[74] One reason put forward for this starting point is that opinion within a democratic society may reasonably differ widely on these issues.[75] The Court, even sometimes when the responding State has not put forward any legitimate interest, presumes a plausible interest behind the infringement.[76]

When balancing the opposing interests, the Court examines whether an interference with peaceful enjoyment of possessions strikes a fair balance between the demands of the general interest of the public and the requirements of the protection of the individual's fundamental rights, or whether it imposes a disproportionate

---

[70] *Aizpurua Ortiz et Autres c Espagne* (n 58) § 49.
[71] *Lelas v Croatia* (n 38) § 76; Harris et al (n 26) 669–72.
[72] *Lelas v Croatia* (n 38) § 78.
[73] *James and others v UK*, App No 8793/97, Judgment of 21 February 1986, § 46.
[74] *Moskal v Poland* (n 29) § 61.
[75] *James and others v UK* (n 73) § 46.
[76] *Ambruosi v Italy*, App No 31227/96, Judgment of 19 October 2000, § 28.

and excessive burden on the applicant.[77] In other words, there must be a reasonable relationship of proportionality between the means employed and the aims to be realised.[78] The fair balance test will sometimes require the payment of compensation for the interference with property rights.[79] The reference to general principles of international law in the second sentence of the first paragraph of A1P1 includes protection of aliens' property against arbitrary expropriation without compensation. But nationals can also expect some compensation at least when being deprived of property. The level of compensation depends on the interests at stake, but must be reasonable in relation to the value of the property taken.[80] Krause has pointed out that the proportionality test can lead to a support of social rights, since the elimination of social injustices can justify far-reaching interferences with an individual's property rights. The required compensation for such interference can be lower than the full market value of the property when taken in the context of a social reform. The inherent conflict between the right to property and social rights can be avoided by giving more weight to the social function of property.[81] This is, of course, true, but it also leaves the State wide latitude when balancing the interests of the State and the individual. The margin of appreciation can also be used to justify far-reaching interferences with individuals' economic and social rights.

Moreover, recently the principle of 'good governance' has been referred to by the Court. This requires that where an issue in the general interest is at stake, it is incumbent on the public authorities to act in good time, in an appropriate manner and with utmost consistency.[82] It is desirable that public authorities act with the utmost scrupulousness, in particular when dealing with matters of vital importance to individuals, such as welfare benefits and other property rights.[83] This point is also illustrated by the fact that arbitrariness and lack of legal certainty generated by State action or inaction are circumstances that often lead to a conclusion favouring the position of the individual.[84]

4.3 State Responsibility

An important question in relation to A1P1 when considering employment relations is the extent of the State's responsibility and whether there are any positive obligations on the State to act in this regard. The Court has stated that genuine, effective exercise of the right protected in A1P1 does not depend merely on the State's duty not to interfere, but may require positive measures of protection, particularly where there is a direct link between the measures an applicant may legitimately expect

---

[77] *Moskal v Poland* (n 29) § 64.
[78] *Evaldsson and others v Sweden* (n 60) § 55.
[79] Harris et al (n 26) 677.
[80] Ibid, 680–81.
[81] Krause (n 5) 197–98 and 203.
[82] *Moskal v Poland* (n 29) § 51.
[83] Ibid, § 72.
[84] Gauksdottir (n 12) 280–82; Harris et al (n 26) 676–77.

from the authorities and or her effective enjoyment of his possessions.[85] However, the positive obligations in this context do not mean that a State needs to ensure the existence of a certain distribution of property rights or ensure a certain level of wages or social security. This aspect of property rights, according to Coban, distinguishes property rights from social and economic rights.[86] However, the Court has held that, for example, the authorities should take practical steps to avoid the destruction of an applicant's house situated close to a municipal rubbish tip.[87] The mere award of compensation on generous terms could not remedy this.[88] Positive obligations in this context can be understood as the responsibility of a State to preserve a system of private ownership.[89] The ECtHR has explained that the boundaries between the State's positive and negative obligations do not lend themselves to precise definition and that the applicable principles are similar. In both contexts, the question of whether a fair balance has been struck between the competing interests of the individual and the community as a whole must be taken into consideration.[90] The State's obligation to protect property includes an obligation to prevent private interference. But the Court has held that State responsibility will be engaged only when the private interference with property is an outcome of the exercise of governmental authority, or a failure to exercise governmental authority required by law to uphold private law rights.[91] The legislature or public authorities can, for example, invoke State responsibility, but this is only the case if the legislator in some way infringes on someone's possession through a legal act. This is also relevant when the interference concerns private law relations.[92] On the other hand, a private law that, when applied, leads to unjust results does not invoke the responsibility of the State, irrespective of whether public authorities, such as the courts, can solve disputes connected to them.[93]

The State can also be held responsible when legislative power has been delegated to social partners. In *Evaldsson* and in *Aizpurua Ortiz and Others*, the ECtHR concluded that while the respondent State has to be allowed a wide margin of appreciation in the organisation of its labour market, any system that, in reality, delegates the power to legislate or regulate important labour issues to independent organisations acting in that market requires that these organisations be held accountable for

---

[85] *Öneryildiz v Turkey*, App No 48939/99, (GC) Judgment of 30 November 2004, § 134. See also *Evaldsson and others v Sweden* (n 60) § 63.

[86] Coban (n 12) 164.

[87] *Öneryildiz v Turkey* (n 85) § 136.

[88] Ibid, §§ 135 and 137.

[89] Coban (n 12) 164.

[90] *Broniowski v Poland*, App No 31443/96, Judgment of 22 June 2004, § 144.

[91] Harris et al (n 26) 665.

[92] See, eg, *James and others v UK* (n 73) § 36; *Hiipakka and others v Finland*, App No 29069/95, Decision of 15 May 1996; Coban (n 12) 167.

[93] Coban (n 12) 168 and the referred case law therein. In the earlier *Bramelid and Malmström v Sweden* case, the Commission held that legal provisions governing private law relations between individuals and which compel a person to surrender a possession to another do not interfere with the right to enjoyment of possessions unless these provisions *arbitrarily* and *unjustly deprive* that person of property in favour of another. Subject to the above condition, the legislator can modify these rules of private law as and when necessary: *Bramelid and Malmström v Sweden*, App Nos 8588/79 and 9589/79, Decision of 12 October 1982. It seems that this statement is overruled by the ECtHR: Coban (n 12) 169.

their activities. The infringements in these cases had their legal base in collective agreements. The State therefore had a positive obligation to protect the applicants' interests.[94] The responsibility can be activated if the interference is arbitrary or has imposed a disproportionate burden on the applicants.[95] The general balance test is applied in order to decide if this is the case. In *Evaldsson* and *Aizpurua Ortiz and Others*, the ECtHR came to opposite conclusions in this regard.[96]

In *Gustafsson*, the complaints concerned *exclusively* relationships of a contractual nature between private individuals, namely the applicant and his suppliers. In the Court's opinion, the repercussions of a union boycott, such as the cessation of deliveries, on the applicant's restaurant were not sufficient to bring A1P1 into play.[97] The decisive factor here seemed to be that the authorities had no legal obligation to act to protect the applicant's business from industrial action that interfered with the delivery of supplies as, under Swedish law, the authorities had no legal role to play in upholding relations between the applicant and his suppliers.[98]

The Court has been criticised for not applying a basic fairness test in strict private law disputes, with the result that public bodies can force individuals to bear a loss in favour of other individuals: 'The domestic law's involvement in outcome injustice cannot be denied.'[99] In this respect, the question is whether governmental authority can be invoked in situations where the interference is a result of judicial authority.[100] If this is the case, then civil laws could come under scrutiny. It is, however, now clear that judicial decisions in private law matters can at least be supervised by the ECtHR in order to prevent them from being *arbitrary* or *unjust*. In *Nerva*, a case originating in a dispute between private entities, the Court came to the conclusion that the interpretation of the legal state of play by the national judiciary was not *arbitrary* or *manifestly unreasonable*.[101] In *Transado-Transportes Fluviais do Sado*, the ECtHR stated that it may supervise the decisions of domestic courts, but in cases such as this one, such supervision must be restricted to checking whether the national courts' disputed interpretation was *reasonable* and *not arbitrary*. In this case, the interpretation concerned a private contract between private entities.[102]

There is, however, a difference between scrutiny of the legal basis itself and of the *interpretation* of the legal basis, whether in a contract or in civil law. It seems that only the interpretation can engage the conventional property right.

---

[94] *Evaldsson and others v Sweden* (n 60) § 63; *Aizpurua Ortiz et Autres c Espagne* (n 58) § 49.
[95] *Aizpurua Ortiz et Autres c Espagne* (n 58) § 55.
[96] *Evaldsson and others v Sweden* (n 60) § 64; *Aizpurua Ortiz et Autres c Espagne* (n 58) § 57.
[97] *Gustafsson v Sweden* (n 55) § 60.
[98] Harris et al (n 26) 665; and Coban (n 12) 167.
[99] Coban (n 12) 168–69, commenting on the Court's decision in *ON v Bulgaria*, App No 35221/97, Decision of 6 April 2000.
[100] Coban (n 12) 167.
[101] *Nerva and others v UK*, App No 42295/98, Judgment of 24 September 2002, § 43.
[102] *Transado-Transportes Fluviais do Sado v Portugal*, App No 35943/02, Decision of 16 December 2003.

5 POSSIBLE EMPLOYMENT-RELATED POSSESSIONS

The previous overview indicates that the right to property in A1P1 has limited potential in strictly private employment relations. The State's responsibility is invoked primarily when a public authority acts arbitrarily or unjustly when engaged in a contractual relationship. The applicability is, however, widened by the fact that collective agreements generate State responsibility. A1P1 can also be invoked if it can be shown that the authorities have failed in their duty to uphold a private law right. In public employment relations, applicability is more far-reaching.

Within those limits, it is worth exploring what reasonably constitutes a 'possession' in employment relations. From the previous section, it can be concluded that one starting point when identifying whether an interest constitutes a 'possession' is to clarify whether that individual interest has an acquired economic value. This includes rights arising from both public and private law relationships.[103] The essence of the interest as measured by its nature and importance to the individual should play a role.[104] This aspect has been emphasised when the ECtHR has had to deal with welfare benefits.[105] It could, however, be argued that this aspect should also be taken into account when employment-related interests are discussed:

> The issue that needs to be examined in each case is whether the circumstances of the case, considered as a whole, conferred on the applicant title to a substantive interest protected by Article 1 of Protocol No 1.[106]

Another important aspect is the notion of 'legitimate expectations'. The protection of legitimate expectations comes into play if an enforceable claim to something can be established. This is the case if the claim is earned or is definitely payable.[107] This concept will be further discussed below. But, when considering what can constitute a 'possession' within the employment relationship, it must be emphasised that the basis for establishing a possession is national law. If the possible possessions discussed below have no such basis, then no possession exists. The fact that a possession has no absolute protection must also be taken into account. The protection can be restricted in a number of ways. Finally, as van Dijk and van Hoof put it, A1P1 can come into play where state measures affect economic value.[108]

In the discussion in Section 2 above, Eide argued that the right to property must be complemented by two other rights: the right to work and the right to social security. This implies that the general understanding of the right to property in itself does not include any right to work, as the right to property does not include a right to acquire anything. It also implies that the rights to work and to social security are essential for giving substantial parts of a population the possibility to acquire rights, which can then be protected by a right to property, as only, in one way of the other, acquired rights are protected. This argument is relevant for A1P1. Despite this starting point, it is worth exploring whether any interests connected to work could

---

103 Coban (n 12) 162.
104 Harris et al (n 26) 657 and 659.
105 See, eg, *Moskal v Poland* (n 29) § 39.
106 *Anheuser-Busch Inc v Portugal*, App No 73049/01, (GC) Judgment of 11 January 2007, § 63I
107 Ibid, § 64.
108 Van Dijk and van Hoof (n 3) 620.

constitute a 'possession' within the meaning of A1P1. Even if no general right to work can be detected in A1P1, there is value in discussing whether particular rights connected to work can constitute a possession within the meaning of A1P1. Could it, for example, be argued that a possession is affected if a job applicant is denied a particular employment in violation of applicable prohibitions on discrimination? If such a violation can be remedied by damages based on loss of future income, then this line of argument is possible. Another more far-fetched question is whether the *capacity* to work in itself constitutes 'possession' within the meaning of A1P1. Arguably, the capacity to work has an economic value for the individual. It can be reasonably asserted that this interest is recognised in law when an inability to work, due to sickness or occupational injury, is compensated by public insurance or welfare benefits. Social benefits can in themselves constitute A1P1 possessions.[109] The value of the capacity to work is accordingly dependent on the level of the benefit. However, it would probably be difficult to convince the Court that the capacity, as such, is recognised in law. This can be compared with cases dealing with infringements on the ability of self-employed or professional persons to perform work. One case regarded legislative changes affecting labour consultants: The right to represent clients was restricted, while also being extended to agents other than labour consultants. The applicant alleged that, as a result, his future income would fall. The Commission stated that the profession of a labour consultant was a liberal one, with no fixed income and no guaranteed turnover, and was naturally subject to the hazards of economic life. The Commission also recalled its previous case law that future income constituted a possession within the meaning of A1P1 if the income had been earned or an enforceable claim to it existed.[110] There is, however, case law indicating that a licence to practise certain professions, such as those held by doctors, lawyers and electricians, could amount to a 'possession'. A *beverage licence* could, for example, constitute a 'possession' when it was an important element in the running of the restaurant and the applicant company could legitimately expect to keep the licence as long as it did not infringe the conditions thereof.[111]

If the professional has built up something through his or her own work efforts, a possession could emerge. A *clientele* built up by dint of the applicant's own efforts had, according to the Court, the nature of a private right in many respects and constituted an asset and hence a 'possession' within the meaning of A1P1.[112] The Commission has also held that *goodwill* may be an element in the evaluation of a professional practice.[113] This line of argument could have implications for non-competition clauses. Many aspects of the fruits of one's labour have been considered

---

[109] See running text corresponding to nn 28 and 29 above.
[110] *Casotti et al v Italy*, App No 24877/94, Decision of 16 October 1996.
[111] *Tre traktörer aktiebolag v Sweden* (n 47) § 21.
[112] *Van Marle and others v The Netherlands*, App Nos 8543/79, 8674/79, 8675/79 and 8685/97, Judgment of 26 June 1986.
[113] *HJ Betalaan and J Huiges v The Netherlands* (n 48), repeated in *Pinnacale Meat Processors Company and others v UK*, App No 33298/96, Decision of 21 October 1998.

to be 'possessions' held by companies, such as intellectual property in general[114] and, more specifically, patents[115] and copyrights.[116]

Another question is whether an employment in itself can constitute a 'possession' within the meaning of A1P1. An old Commission decision indicates that this is not the case. The question was whether the conditions leading to the termination of the employment contract, which in turn led to loss of pension rights, could be tried. The Commission argued that those facts fell 'outside the competence of the Commission as the Convention does not guarantee the right of employment in public service'.[117] It has been suggested that there are reasons for interpreting this principle quite narrowly.[118] A number of recent Article 8 ECHR cases have clarified that restrictions to a right to work[119] and that levels of employment protection[120] do not fall outside the competence of the Convention, but that this does not necessarily mean that an employment can constitute an asset in the meaning of A1P1. Coban summarises the situation in the following way: 'Economic interests arising from an employment contract constitute property but not the contract itself.'[121] Arguably, however, an employment contract has an economic value for the worker. It is clear from the case law that the legislator or the parties are free to establish the conditions for termination of employment.[122] If the conditions related to the contract are fulfilled, it can also be assumed that the worker has a legitimate expectation that the contractual agreement will continue and that he or she will continue to earn wages.[123] The right is, however, dependent on the conditions related to, and provided for, in the employment contract and/or in law. This means that if a worker loses the contract in violation of those conditions, an infringement of his or her property rights may have occurred. The fact that future income may only be considered to constitute a possession if it had already been earned or where an enforceable claim to it exists[124] can at least be accommodated in legal systems where unjustified dismissals generate damages based on future earnings or reinstatement. If, for example, a dismissal has to be based on valid reasons and the authorities in a public employment relationship dismiss an employee without such reasons, a violation could have taken place. In a

---

[114] *Aneheuser-Busch Inc v Portugal* (n 106) § 72.

[115] *Smith Kline and French Laboratories Ltd v The Netherlands*, App No 12633/87, Commission Decision of 4 October 1990.

[116] *Melnychuk v Ukraine*, App No 28743/03, Decision of 5 July 2005.

[117] *X v Italy*, App No 7459/76, Decision of 7 October 1977.

[118] P Van den Broek, The Protection of Property Rights under the European Convention on Human Rights, (1986) 1 *Legal Issues of European Integration* 70.

[119] *Sidabras and Dziautas v Lithuania*, §§ 47–50.

[120] *Schüth v Germany* (n 31) §§ 53–75.

[121] Coban (n 12) 155.

[122] This applies in the same way as the legislator is free to set the conditions for a certain wage supplement: see, eg, *Eskelinen and others v Finland* (n 39) § 94.

[123] Such a conclusion is supported by the Commission's way of handling licences to perform a certain work. A licence-holder cannot be considered to have a reasonable and legitimate expectation to continue his or her activities if the conditions attached to the licence are no longer fulfilled or if the licence is withdrawn in accordance with the provisions of the law which was in force when the licence was issued: *HJ Betalaan and J Huiges v The Netherlands* (n 48). See also the discussion on job property in a national context in P Davies and M Freedland, *Labour Law: Texts and Materials* (London, Weidenfeld & Nicolson, 1984) 428.

[124] *Casotti et al v Italy* (n 110).

private employment relationship, this could be the case if, for example, a court acts unreasonably or arbitrarily when deciding on the dispute.

Damages for violations of the employment contract or of the law could also in themselves constitute possession.[125] The circumstances are, however, somewhat unclear as to which legitimate expectation can be considered to have been established in relation to damages.[126]

The loss of the ability to work while in employment due to an occupational injury is also pertinent to this discussion. If the worker is the victim of an occupational injury and it is clear that the employer has not upheld the legal occupational health and safety provisions, and that the national labour inspectorate has not fulfilled its monitoring obligation, it could be argued that the worker has been deprived of his or her 'possession', ie, his or her ability to work, or, at least, the possibility of continuing the employment contract. If the worker is entitled to compensation in such cases, such an argument could be employed. Situations such as this have, however, been dealt with by the Court, but from another perspective. In *Ásmundsson v Iceland*, the issue was the entitlement to a disability pension after a work accident.[127] In this case, the right to receive a pension subject to the fulfilment of certain conditions constituted a possession for the purposes of A1P1.[128] It is clear from the case law that such a right could evolve, irrespective of whether or not the worker has contributed to the fund in question.[129]

It is quite certain that, as Coban and van den Broek suggest, economic interests arising from a contract constitute a 'possession'.[130] Employment-related economic interests based on law can, of course, also be protected. Wages[131] and a number of wage supplements, such as special daily allowances,[132] research allowances[133] and additional payments for children,[134] have been recognised as possessions. There is, however, no right under the Convention to continue to be paid a salary at a certain level.[135] A right to a pension that is based on employment can, in certain circumstances, be deemed to be a property right.[136] This may be the case where the employer has given a more general undertaking to pay a pension under conditions that can be considered to be part of the employment contract.[137] In *Aizpurua Ortiz*

---

[125] *Pressos Compania Naviera v Belgium* (n 44) § 31.
[126] Ovey and White (n 37) 356.
[127] *Kjartan Asmundsson v Iceland* (n 63).
[128] Ibid, § 40.
[129] *Moskal v Poland* (n 29) § 38.
[130] Van den Broek (n 118) 70; Coban (n 12) 155. Van den Broek has suggested a more complex starting point when discussing the different conditions in an employment contract. He argues that some rights, such as working conditions or terms of dismissal, are not, in themselves, of economic value, but that the contract as a whole needs to be considered. This is explained by the fact that each condition is part of a bargain and that it is this bargain as a whole that is of economic value: Van den Broek (n 118) 70.
[131] *Evaldsson and others v Sweden* (n 60) § 52.
[132] *Lelas v Croatia* (n 38) 58.
[133] *Smokovitis and others v Greece*, App No 46356/99, Judgment of 11 April 2002, § 32.
[134] *Zouboulidis v Greece (No 2)*, App No 36963/06, Judgment of 25 June 2009, §§ 28–29.
[135] *Eskelinen and others v Finland* (n 39) § 94.
[136] *Apostolakis v Greece*, App No 39574/07, Judgment of 22 October 2009, § 27.
[137] *Sture Stigson v Sweden*, App No 12264/86, Decision of 13 July 1988; *Klein v Austria*, App No 57028/00, Judgment of 3 March 2011, § 44.

and others v Spain, a supplementary pension under the terms of a collective agreement constituted a possession.[138] For self-employed persons, adjustments of fees based on contracts have been recognised as possessions.[139] Other examples could include overtime compensation and holiday pay, as well as insurance entitlements connected to the employment. In the UK, the issue of whether redundancy payments in the civil service can constitute possession has arisen.[140] It is also reasonable to assume that severance payments based on law or contract could constitute a possession under A1P1.

Liquidation processes have been dealt with by the ECtHR.[141] Rights to preferential treatment of workers' claims after bankruptcy or judicial liquidation should qualify as a possession within the meaning of A1P1.

A general difficulty when discussing whether a work-related right can constitute a 'possession' within the meaning of A1P1 is the unclear division between legitimate expectations and potential rights not protected by A1P1. It has been observed that there is a thin line between potential rights, which are not protected by the Article, and legitimate expectations that a right will materialise, which can be considered to be covered by it.[142] The legislator or the equivalent actors such as parties to a collective agreement have a wide margin of discretion in deciding the conditions for qualifying for a particular social or employment-related right and the scope and amount of this particular right.[143] But there seems to be a difference between rights from which the individual has already started to benefit and future rights that the individual has not yet benefited from. In the first situation, a 'possession' is touched upon and accordingly a balance test must be conducted in cases where State responsibility can be invoked.[144] This implies that if any legislator changes the conditions upholding a particular employment-related right constituting a possession or the amount of such a particular right for employees who have started to benefit from it, a balance test has to be conducted in order to safeguard that such a change is acceptable under A1P1. For employees who have not yet started to benefit from the particular right, the situation is much more unclear. The ECtHR could argue that the conditions giving rise to the future benefit can change and that the legislator has the power to decide on those conditions.[145] This distinction can be quite problematic in cases where part of an employee's pay is, for example, put in a pension fund. The wages are beyond doubt 'earned' and the employee can, depending on the conditions related to the deferment of the payment, be considered to have a legitimate expectation of benefiting from the fund in due time.[146]

---

[138] *Aizpurua Ortiz et Autres c Espagne* (n 58) § 40.

[139] The Commission at least did not exclude that the contractual right to this level of the fee was a possession within the meaning of A1P1, see *Association of General Practitioners v Denmark*, App No 12947/87, Decision of 12 July 1989.

[140] See Novitz (n 2) 154 ff.

[141] *Kotov v Russia* (n 62) (GC) Judgment of 3 April 2012.

[142] Gauksdottir (n 12) 141.

[143] *Moskal v Poland* (n 29) § 38.

[144] See, eg, *Asmundsson v Iceland* (n 63); and *Aizpurua Ortiz et Autres c Espagne* (n 58).

[145] See, eg, *Moskal v Poland* (n 29) § 40.

[146] For a discussion on this problem, see Novitz (n 2) 153 ff.

5.1 Article 14 Taken in Conjunction with A1P1

In this section, a short discussion about the establishment of a possession when dealing with A1P1, taken in conjunction with Article 14 ECHR, the prohibition of discrimination, will be presented. Article 14 is dealt with in chapter 14 of this book. It is, however, worth mentioning that in A1P1 cases taken in conjunction with Article 14, the judgment about whether there is an asset/possession according to the meaning of the Convention is less harsh. The application of Article 14 does not necessarily pre-suppose the violation of one of the substantive rights guaranteed by the Convention. It is sufficient for the facts of the case to *fall within the ambit* of at least one of the provisions.[147] This means that in cases related to A1P1, when a certain group is not entitled to something that is likely to be property for others, Article 14 can come into play. The difference in treatment must be based on an identifiable characteristic or 'status' in order to amount to discrimination within the meaning of Article 14. The Court has made such distinctions when considering possessions related to prisoners and other employees, nationals residing outside and inside a country, one group entitled to disability pension and another group losing that entitlement, former KGB employees and others.[148] The distinctions can accordingly include a wide range of groups not normally covered by provisions on discrimination. Discrimination means being treated differently, without objective and reasonable justification, compared to persons in relevantly similar situations. No objective and reasonable justification means that the distinction does not pursue a legitimate aim or that there is no reasonable relationship of proportionality between the means employed and the aim sought to be realised.[149] The Contracting States also dispose of a margin of appreciation when assessing whether, and to what extent, differences in otherwise similar situations justify a different treatment.[150]

6 THE APPLICATION OF A1P1 IN WORKING LIFE: ECtHR CASE LAW

The previous section discussed what could constitute a possession within the employment relationship. In order to illustrate how property claims with employment connections are handled by the ECtHR, an overview of some cases will be presented that illustrate the complexity associated with applying A1P1.

6.1 Wage-Related Matters

The Convention bodies have consistently held that income that has been earned constitutes a 'possession' within the meaning of the Article.[151] The cases involved

---

[147] *Stummer v Austria*, App No 37452/02, Judgment of 7 July 2011, § 81.
[148] See, eg, *Kjartan Asmundsson v Iceland* (n 63); and *Stummer v Austria* (n 147).
[149] *Stummer v Austria* (n 147) § 87.
[150] Ibid, § 88.
[151] See, eg, *Bahceyaka v Turkey*, App No 74463/01, Judgment of 13 July 2006, § 34: *Erkan v Turkey*, App No 29840/03, Decision of 24 March 2005; *Schettini and others v Italy*, App No 29529/95, Decision of 9 November 2000; *Storksen v Norway*, App No 19819/92; Decision of 5 July 1994; *Evaldsson*

can be divided into two groups: first, cases that deal with income for self-employed workers; and, second, income for employees. In the second group, different aspects of wages are dealt with.

Special daily allowances for employees of the Croatian Army participating in demining operations qualified, in *Lelas*, as an asset constituting a 'possession' within the meaning of the Convention.[152] The Minister of Defence had issued a decision on daily allowances in 1995, but no allowance had yet been paid to the applicant on 21 May 2002. The applicant brought civil action against the State, seeking payment of the allowance. After lengthy proceedings in a number of instances, the final instance came to the conclusion that the wrong person had been acknowledging the debt over several years and therefore no interruption of the statutory three-year limitation period had taken place. The period had thus expired.[153] The ECtHR, however, came to the conclusion that all the conditions of the 1995 decision were fulfilled in this case and accordingly the claim had sufficient basis in national law to qualify as assets protected by A1P1. The decisive element for the final outcome in *Lelas* was that the interference was not considered to have been lawful. The absence of a clear legal provision or publicly accessible document as to who was authorised to acknowledge the debt on behalf of the Ministry of Defence made it quite natural for the applicant to believe that the General Staff of the Croatian Armed Forces, which had continuously acknowledged the debt, was an authority of sufficient rank whose statements could be binding on the Ministry.[154] Accordingly, a violation of the right to property had taken place.

In *Zouboulidis*, the applicant, an official of the Ministry of Foreign Affairs, was refused additional payments to which by law he was entitled. When he brought an action in the civil courts, the Court of Appeal held that he was entitled to the payments, but that the sum must be reduced because of a two-year limitation period which applied to State debts. The applicant claimed that the limitation period reduced the value of his claims without being justified on any public interest grounds. The Court held that in this case, the State had been acting like any other private employer and that privileges or immunities applicable when the State discharged duties governed by public law were not relevant here. In this case, no fair balance was struck between the protection of property and the requirements of the general interest, which was held to be the interest of the State's cash flow, which was in turn held to be very weak.[155]

In *Smokovitis and others*, the question was whether a benefit which the legislator suddenly withdrew for temporary staff could still be a claim creating a legitimate expectation for such staff. As the domestic courts had on several occasions considered that the benefit concerned both permanent and temporary staff, they had created a legitimate expectation and, accordingly, a possession within the meaning of the Convention. In this case, the Court considered that there was nothing in the

---

and others v Sweden (n 60) § 52, implied in *Puzinas v Lithuania*, App No 63767/00, Decision of 18 November 2000.

[152] *Lelas v Croatia* (n 38) § 58.
[153] Ibid, §§ 6 and 24.
[154] Ibid, §§ 77–78.
[155] *Zouboulidis v Greece (No 2)* (n 134) §§ 34–37.

facts of the case to justify legislating with *retrospective* effect, with the aim and consequence of depriving the applicants of their claims for payment of the benefit. The necessary balance between the general interest of the community and the requirements for protecting the individual's fundamental right was not upheld to the detriment of the applicants. There had, accordingly, been a violation of A1P1.[156]

However, it is not possible to conclude that the Convention as a general rule prohibits decisions that retroactively withdraw benefits or pay rises. The outcome will depend on the circumstances of each case. It also seems that a public employer/contractor is free to lower wages/fees, even retroactively, if the decrease is only minor, for employees/self-employed workers who continue to do the same work, if the decision is intended to pursue a legitimate aim. In *Association of General Practitioners v Denmark*, the adjustment of the fees for general practitioners included in a contract between the National Health Service and the Association of General Practitioners was annulled through a legal act, due to the need to reduce the continuing increase in public spending within the sphere of the National Health Service, in particular in light of the country's critical economic situation. Through the legal act, which was adopted two months after an adjustment under the contract should have taken place, the general practitioners were deprived of these two months' salary increases, amounting to approximately 2,000 Danish krone. The Commission held that it would not exclude that the contractual right to this amount was a possession within the meaning of A1P1. The Commission therefore continued, determining whether the deprivation of property was 'in the public interest' and 'subject to the conditions provided for by law'. It found that the State's wish to reduce public spending may, in principle, be considered to be in the public interest. It continued to examine whether there was a reasonable relationship of proportionality between the means employed and the aim sought to be realised. In this respect, the Commission found that the sum of money involved was not disproportionate to the aim.[157]

It is debatable whether this case would lead to the same outcome today. The pay rise was included in an agreement that was at least similar to a collective agreement. The decision by the Minister to repeal the content of that agreement could thus be seen as a violation of the present meaning of Article 11 ECHR, as the right to bargain collectively with employers has, since *Demir and Baykara*, been considered to be an essential element of the right to form and to join trade unions for the protection of one's interests.[158]

There is no right under the Convention to continue to be paid a salary of a particular amount if the conditions for its payment have changed. In *Eskelinen and others*, it followed from an implementing instruction that the applicants did not have a legitimate expectation to receive an individual wage supplement any longer, since the conditions for the entitlement to the wage supplement had ceased to be fulfilled.[159] The wage supplement was connected to a duty station in Sonkajärvi and

---

[156] *Smokovitis and others v Greece* (n 133) § 34.
[157] *Association of General Practitioners v Denmark*, App No 12947/87, Decision of 12 July 1989.
[158] *Demir and Baykara v Turkey*, App No 34503/97, (GC) Judgment of 12 November 2008, §§ 154–55.
[159] *Eskelinen and others v Finland* (n 39) § 94.

could be called a 'remote-area allowance'. The employees had been transferred to another duty station and accordingly lost the remote-area allowance.[160]

Bearing in mind the outcome in *Association of General Practitioners*, it does not seem so surprising that workers cannot successfully claim a certain pay rise through A1P1. In *Schettini and others*, the applicants claimed that the pay rise they were awarded under a collective agreement, whose content they could not influence because they belonged to another trade union, was insufficient. They tried to invoke A1P1 in respect of the financial impact of the collective agreement on their future income, complaining in particular that the salary rises were insufficient. The Court recalled, however, that future income constitutes a 'possession' within the meaning of A1P1 only if the income has been earned or where an enforceable claim to it exists. Furthermore, A1P1 does not guarantee the right to a certain rise in salary.[161]

In *Nerva*, the issue was somewhat different.[162] This case concerned the question of whether a tip left by cheque or credit card should be treated as a separate sum in relation to the minimum wages paid to the waiters or could be part of those wages. The employer did not pay the waiters the total sum (minimum wage plus tip) that such a calculation would produce. The tip was called additional pay on the wage slip. The Court, however, held that the applicants could not maintain that they had a separate right to the tip and a separate right to a minimum remuneration calculated without reference to those tips, as after full consideration of the competing interpretations canvassed for the notion of 'remuneration', the domestic courts ruled that the employer, and not the customer, paid the tips at issue out of its own funds to the applicants and their colleagues. The Court did not consider this conclusion to be *arbitrary or manifestly unreasonable*, having regard to the scope of the expression 'remuneration' and, indeed, to the applicants' acceptance that title to the tips at issue passed to the employer. Moreover, the applicants could not claim that they had a legitimate expectation that the tips at issue would not count towards remuneration. Such a view assumes that the customer intended that this would not be the case. However, this is too imprecise a basis on which to found a legitimate expectation which could give rise to 'possessions' within the meaning of A1P1. In the opinion of the Court, it was for the applicants to come to a contractual arrangement with their employer as to how the tips at issue were to be dealt with from the point of view of their wage entitlement. However, they could not rely on A1P1 to base a claim for a higher level of earnings.

The outcome might seem a bit surprising and it is important to highlight the opinion of the dissenting Judge Loucaides in this case, who came to the conclusion that the tip was a possession in the meaning of A1P1 and that a breach of the applicants' rights had taken place. Judge Loucaides did not think that it could seriously be disputed that in giving the tips, the customers intended that they would be specifically handed over in full to the waiters independently of, and on top of, their salary. It could not reasonably be assumed that when a customer gives a tip in a restaurant in

---

[160] Ibid, §§ 10–11.
[161] *Schettini and others v Italy* (n 151).
[162] *Nerva and others v UK* (n 101).

any form that he or she wants the tip to become the absolute property of the owner of the restaurant. The majority came to this conclusion basically because it followed the interpretation of the national courts. Judge Loucaides underlined the fact that the term 'possession' has an autonomous meaning.

The *Nerva* case illustrates the weakness in relying too intensively on the national court's interpretation of the existence of a property right.[163] The room for manoeuvre for the ECtHR in taking a position other than that of the national court when it comes to establishing a possession is very limited. But there is a small window of opportunity—if the national interpretation is arbitrary or manifestly unreasonable, it can be sidestepped.

Deductions from prisoners' wages have been dealt with rather summarily by the ECtHR. In *Puzinas*, deducting a quarter of the prison salary was deemed to be in accordance with A1P1, as no evidence was shown that such a deduction was arbitrary or incompatible with the general interest. The Court presumed that the deductions were made on account of the fact that the applicant incurred no expenses for board and lodging while in prison.[164] In *Stummer*, not even a 75 per cent deduction was found to be unreasonable, though it appeared rather high to the Court, taking into account the general costs of maintaining prisons and the fact that a prisoner's entire livelihood, including health and accident insurance, is provided for by the State.[165] This can be contrasted with *Evaldsson*. In this case, a 1.5 per cent deduction from the applicant's wages to cover a monitoring fee charged by a trade union for inspection work was considered to deprive the applicants of their possessions.[166] The deductions were, however, lawful (they were stipulated in a collective agreement) and pursued a legitimate aim (the inspection aimed at protecting the interests of workers generally). The deduction constituted payment for a service provided by the trade union. The applicants, who were not members of the trade union, were, according to the Court, entitled to information which was sufficiently exhaustive for them to verify that the fees corresponded to the actual cost of the inspection work and that the amounts paid were not used for other purposes. This was even more important as they had to pay the fees against their will to an organisation with a political agenda that they did not support. The Court found that the monitoring system lacked the necessary transparency. Thus, even having regard to the low amounts of money involved for the applicants, it was not proportionate to the 'public interest' in this case to make deductions to their wages without giving them a proper opportunity to check how the money was spent.[167]

---

[163] For a discussion on *Nerva*, the national legal context and its consequences, see E Albin, 'A Worker-Employer-Customer Triangle: The Case of Tips' (2011) 40(2) *Industrial Law Journal* 196 ff.

[164] *Puzinas v Lithuania* (n 151).

[165] *Stummer v Austria* (n 147) § 103.

[166] *Evaldsson and others v Sweden* (n 60) § 52.

[167] Ibid, §§ 53–64.

7 A1P1 EFFECTS ON THE RIGHT TO STRIKE
AND COLLECTIVE BARGAINING

7.1 The Right to Strike

As was indicated in the introductory sections of this chapter, fears have been raised that the right to property could be used to limit social rights. In this section, the right to property's potential effect on the right to strike and on the protection of collective agreements will be briefly discussed.

The potential effect of A1P1 on the right to strike was at stake in the *Gustafsson* case,[168] in which the applicant submitted that the respondent State's failure to provide protection against the industrial action had caused him pecuniary damage, in violation of A1P1.[169] In this case, the parties to the conflict were private parties. As indicated before, the Court stated that the State may be responsible for interferences with peaceful enjoyment of possessions resulting from transactions between private individuals. The facts complained of must, however, somehow be the product of an exercise of governmental authority, which was not the case here. The Court also stated that the repercussions such actions, ie stopping deliveries, had on the applicant's restaurant were not such as to bring A1P1 into play.[170] The latter statement could indicate that the ECtHR is of the opinion that effects of an industrial action on a particular company in general cannot affect any possession in the meaning of A1P1. But it is somewhat difficult to draw any definite conclusions from this statement. However, it would be in line with the international understanding of the right to industrial action. Restrictions on the right to strike under the European Social Charter and International Labour Organization (ILO) Convention No 87 are in general only permissible if they are intended to uphold a general interest for society as a whole and not the protection of a particular company.[171] The second decisive factor in the *Gustafsson* case was that the authorities had no legal obligation to act to protect the applicant's business from industrial action, which interfered with the delivery of supplies, as under Swedish law, the authorities had no legal role to play in upholding the relations between the applicant and his suppliers.[172]

In many countries, however, national courts can deal with the legality of industrial disputes in a more profound way. A national decision in a private law dispute upholding an industrial dispute between private parties can be tried under the right to property. But the ECtHR can only, at least in private law disputes, assess whether the national decision is arbitrary or manifestly unreasonable. That decision is mainly related to the interpretation of the applicable national law. When the judiciary has interpreted the national law in an arbitrary or manifestly unreasonable fashion, the ECtHR could state that a violation of A1P1 had taken place, provided that any possession in the meaning of A1P1 had been infringed, which, according to the above

---

[168] *Gustafsson v Sweden* (n 55).
[169] Ibid, § 56.
[170] Ibid, § 60.
[171] See www.ilo.org/dyn/normlex/en/f?p=1000:12030:0::NO.
[172] Harris et al (n 26) 665.

discussion, is extremely unlikely. The fact that the right to strike is now interpreted as an important corollary to Article 11 ECHR supports this conclusion.[173]

7.2 Protection of the Collective Agreement

In *Association of General Practitioners*, a legislative interference with a collective agreement was accepted by the ECtHR and in *Evaldsson*, the ECtHR came to the conclusion that a provision in a collective agreement led to violations of the right to property. Is there reason to fear that the social partners' right to freely conclude collective agreements is at risk when confronted with A1P1?

In a recent case, *Aizpurua Ortiz and Others*, on a supplementary pensions scheme included in a collective agreement, the Court came to the opposite conclusion.[174] The circumstances were as follows: a 17-year-old collective agreement was replaced by a new collective agreement under which employees who had been in receipt of a supplementary pension were to be paid a one-off sum equivalent to three monthly payments. The question before the Court was whether the employees had been deprived of their property because of the new terms in the new collective agreement. The Court found that the employees had had a legitimate expectation of continuing to receive payment and that the right to a supplementary pension constituted an asset falling within the scope of the Article.[175] In this case, the Court scrutinised whether the decision of the national court was arbitrary or manifestly unreasonable,[176] observing that the national court had stated that the legislator has chosen a system where the last-concluded collective agreement took precedence over ones previously concluded. Moreover, the relevant provision was not altogether eradicated, but was replaced by a provision according to which the applicants were granted a one-off sum. The interference with the applicants' right to property had, according to the Court, pursued an aim in the general interest, namely to secure the finances of the company and its creditors, and to protect employment and the right to collective bargaining.[177] These motives could not be considered to be arbitrary or having imposed a disproportionate burden on the applicants.[178] With regard to the margin of appreciation enjoyed by States in shaping social and economic policy, the judgment complained of had not amounted to disproportionate interference with the applicants' right to peaceful enjoyment of their possessions.[179]

In *Aizpurua Ortiz and Others*, reference is also made to the outcome in *Demir and Baykara*. *Evaldsson* and *Association of General Practitioners* were decided before that judgment. It is clear that respect for collective bargaining has been strengthened by *Demir and Baykara* and it can be expected to have greater weight when balancing opposing interests in the future. In *Evaldsson*, it seems that the

---

[173] *Enerji Yapi-Yol Sen v Turkey*, App No 68959/01, Judgment of 21 April 2009, § 24.
[174] *Aizpurua Ortiz et Autres c Espagne* (n 58) § 49.
[175] Ibid, § 40.
[176] Ibid, § 51.
[177] Ibid, § 53.
[178] Ibid, § 55.
[179] Ibid, § 57.

collective agreement is assessed along the same lines as a law. In *Aizupurua Ortiz and Others*, the reference to *Demir and Baykara* indicates that the ECtHR will in future take the special protection of collective agreements into account when assessing their impact on a right to property.[180] It does not, however, seem that they are immune from scrutiny.

8 WHAT IMPACT COULD OTHER INTERNATIONAL SOURCES HAVE ON THE INTERPRETATION OF A1P1?

In this section, it will be discussed whether other international sources could have any impact on the application of A1P1. The discussion will first deal with international commitments connected to the ILO and the European Social Charter and the Revised European Social Charter and will then turn to the possible impact of EU law.[181]

There are very few references to other international sources in A1P1 court cases.[182] One explanation is that a possession within the meaning of A1P1 must have a basis in national law. It must be possible to establish the right itself, as well as its economic value, under national law. The Article does not create a right to acquire property.[183] That is the starting point unless domestic law runs counter to the object and purpose of A1P1.[184] This fact is also a challenge for this section. Suggesting possible ways forward that are unlikely to be realised is not constructive.

Many other human rights treaties include different rights to acquire a certain property as welfare rights or prescribe that a particular property should have a certain value. The Revised European Social Charter (RESC) includes, for example, a number of employment-related rights with an economic value: Articles 1 on the right to work, 2(2) on paid public holidays, 2(3) on a minimum of four weeks' annual paid holidays, 4 on the right to fair remuneration, 5 on the right to organise, 6 on the right to bargain collectively, 7(5) on a fair wage or other appropriate allowances to young workers and apprentices, 8(1) on paid leave or benefits for employed women before and after childbirth, 19(4–5) on migrants' rights to remuneration as well as the same level of employment taxes as nationals, and 25 on insolvency. A number of ILO Conventions include similar provisions.[185] Several CoE Member States have also ratified a number of these provisions. But as provisions in

---

[180] A discussion on the representativeness problem connected to this outcome is included in Novitz (n 2) 152.

[181] The European Social Charter was adopted in 1961 and the Revised European Social Charter in 1996. Only 10 of the 43 ratifying States have ratified the European Social Charter.

[182] *Carson and others v UK*, App No 42184/05, (GC) Judgment of 16 March 2010, §§ 49–51. In this case on A1P1, which is dealt with in conjunction with Article 14 on social security issues, the Court—under the headline 'Relevant international law'—refers to ILO Convention No 52 on social security and the ILO Convention of 1982 on the Establishment of an International System for the Maintenance of Rights in Social Security and the 1964 European Code of Social Security, and the 1990 European Code of Social Security (Revised). In the end, because of their limited content, they did not play any role in the outcome.

[183] For example, *Stec and others v UK* (n 28) § 54; *Trakoev and others v Estonia*, App Nos 14480/08 and 47916/08, Judgment of 4 November 2010, § 39.

[184] *Pressos Compania Naviera v Belgium* (n 44) § 31.

[185] See www.ilo.org/dyn/normlex/en/f?p=1000:12030:0::NO.

international conventions, irrespective of whether they are ratified or not, do not in themselves create enforceable rights in many national legal orders, it would be difficult to establish an enforceable possession on that basis.[186]

It is, however, important to emphasise the very strong interplay between the right to property and the protection of other human rights.[187] Effective protection of the right to property requires effective protection of the rights set forth in the RESC and ILO Conventions. These ambitions must therefore go hand in hand. It could also be claimed that a national legal system which does not guarantee these rights runs counter to the object and purpose of A1P1. The wall to be climbed in this regard is, however, high. Yet the concept of property, and the meaning and content of property rights, may be subject to societal and legal change.[188] The ECtHR is developing its case law over time and if this approach is taken on an applicant-by-applicant basis, it is not impossible that the approach will achieve acceptance in the future. The argument must be built up around a very well-established international recognition of the right in question.

The human rights argument can, however, play an important role when the right to property is applied in conjunction with Article 14. If someone is provided with wage levels different from those of the majority, for example, due to his or her status, there must arguably be very special circumstances for accepting a wage level below international standards. It is also easier to fulfil the criteria for an asset in such cases. Another fruitful perspective, in the short run, would be to introduce the international human rights perspective when deciding whether an infringement is justifiable or not. The starting point is that it would be difficult to justify an infringement in violation of other human rights provisions, at least when they are widely accepted among the Contracting States. In *Stummer v Austria*, the ECtHR indicated a possibility in this regard.

In *Stummer*, the applicant, a former convict, complained that the exemption of those engaged in prison work from affiliation to the old-age pension system was discriminatory. The ECtHR stated that a working prisoner was in a relatively similar situation to ordinary employees. It therefore had to examine whether the difference in treatment in respect of affiliation to the old-age pension system under the General Social Security Act was justified. When defining the breadth of the margin of appreciation, it stated that a relevant factor may be the existence or non-existence of common ground between the laws of the Contracting States. It observed that no such consensus existed, but that there was an evolving trend. The CoE's Committee of Ministers had adopted recommendations to the Member States on European prison rules—minimum standards to be applied in prisons. In contrast to the 1987 European Prison Rules, the 2006 European Prison Rules not only contain the principle of normalisation of prison work but also explicitly recommend in Rule 26.17 that 'as far as possible prisoners who work shall be included in national social security systems'.[189] Taking into account the cautious wording in Rule 26.17 and the

---

[186] A Abass, *International Law, Text, Cases and Material* (New York, Oxford University Press, 2012) 160 ff.
[187] See, eg, Rosas (n 3) 133.
[188] Ibid, 133.
[189] *Stummer v Austria* (n 147) §§ 104–05.

fact that only a small majority of States affiliate prisoners to their old-age pension system, the Court came to the conclusion that societies are only gradually moving towards the affiliation of prisoners. At that point in time, there was no common ground for this development. The Court came to the conclusion that the Austrian system was not manifestly without reasonable foundation, but that *the respondent State is required to keep the issue raised under review.*[190]

Decided on 7 July 2011 ie, after *Demir and Baykara*, the *Stummer* case gives us a strong incentive for using other international instruments when assessing interferences with A1P1 cases taken alone, as these can be a valuable tool when establishing whether there is common ground between the laws in the Contracting States.

In the following section, a few examples of how to use other international human rights in strengthening the right to property in A1P1 are explored.

8.1 Wage Deductions

If someone has worked, and thereby earned his or her wages, there is normally a legal right to a particular remuneration under national law. But if the employer then for any reason decides to make deductions from the wages, it would be reasonable to argue that the deductions permissible under national law should fulfil the requirements set forth in Article 4(5) of the European Social Charter (ESC) and the RESC, ILO Convention No 95 and ILO Recommendation No 85 on the protection of wages. The fact that the protection does not fulfil these requirements could be a decisive factor when the proportionality test is made. The European Committee of Social Rights (ECSR) has, for example, concluded that certain legislative frameworks are not in conformity with the obligations emanating from Article 4(5). In Poland, employees must always earn at least 80 per cent of the minimum national wage after deductions. The ECSR considers that for employees on the lowest wages, there will not be enough money left to enable them *to provide properly for themselves or their dependants*. The same applies to the rule that the total amount of deductions may not exceed half the employee's wages or three-fifths in the case of the recovery of maintenance payments. The situation in Poland was therefore not in conformity with the ESC.[191] Domestic law must also contain guarantees to the effect that workers may not waive their right to restrictions with regard to deductions from wages.[192] If such provisions are not prohibited as such, they must be subject to precise statutory provisions, case law, government regulations or collective agreements.[193] All employees must be protected against excessive wage deductions.[194] Assessments of deductions from wages as a result of participation in industrial action should also take into account the obligations in Article 6(4) RESC, which states that any deduction

---

[190] Ibid, §§ 105–10.
[191] ECSR Conclusion XIX-3, Poland, Article 4.5, Slovak Republic, Article 4.5. Poland has only ratified the European Social Charter and has only signed the Revised European Social Charter.
[192] ECSR Conclusion 2010, Lithuania, Article 4.5, Norway, Article 4.5.
[193] ESCR Conclusion 2007, Ireland, Article 4.5.
[194] ESCR Conclusion 2010, Turkey.

from strikers' wages should not exceed the proportion of their wage that would be attributable to the duration of their strike participation.[195]

In Section 6.1 above, two ECtHR cases on deductions of wages from prisoners were mentioned and one on deductions made to trade unions for wage monitoring. In the first two cases, the discussion about the reasonableness of the deductions of 25 and 75 per cent of the wages were very rudimentary. In the third case, on wage monitoring, an in-depth discussion took place. In all three cases, the right to the wages, as well as the deductions, had a legal basis. Even so, the deductions made were treated separately from the establishment of whether there was a property at stake. That separation suggests that it could be possible for the ECtHR to take other international human rights instruments into account when assessing the deductions.

8.2 Pay Intervals

The intervals at which wages are paid are also something dealt with in ILO Recommendation No 85 on the protection of wages. Remuneration fixed on a monthly or annual basis should be paid not less than once a month. It could be argued that failure to pay wages according to the prescribed interval could be a kind of control of property dealt with in the second paragraph of A1P1. The fact that international standards provide for regular payment should be part of the balancing/proportionality test made by the ECtHR. This could be relevant if the deductions are legal according to national law.

8.3 Privileged Claims

According to ILO Convention No 95 on the protection of wages and its Article 11, in the event of the bankruptcy or judicial liquidation of an undertaking, the workers employed therein shall be treated as privileged creditors and paid in full before ordinary creditors. A similar right is to be found in Article 25 RESC. As we have seen, liquidation processes have been dealt with by the Court.[196] Here again we have an earned wage and the question of how to deal with it in an extraordinary situation. The status as a privileged creditor probably has to be based on national law. Any restriction of that right could nevertheless be assessed, taking the ILO and RESC provisions into consideration.

8.4 Differential Treatment

When analysing the right to property in conjunction with Article 14, protection in national law of this particular claim for this particular claimant does not need to

---

[195] ESCR *Digest* 2008, p 58.
[196] *Kotov v Russia* (n 62) GC Judgment of 3 April 2012.

exist. However, other employees must be entitled to a right corresponding to the claim. The challenge is to argue that the differential treatment cannot be justified. In such a claim, other international sources can play a crucial role. With reference to ILO Convention Nos 175 on Part-Time Work, 177 on Home Work and 189 on Domestic Work, differential treatment with regard to different aspects of remuneration can be opposed. The RESC also includes a substantial prohibition of discrimination.

8.5 The EU Impact in this Field

References to EU law, including Court of Justice of the European Union (CJEU) case law and references to the EU Charter of Fundamental Rights, are also made from time to time.[197] Before discussing whether EU law can contribute to the development of A1P1, a few words on the protection of the right to property within the EU legal order are presented.

When the CJEU developed its doctrine that fundamental rights form an integral part of the general principles of EU law, the right to property was in focus early on.[198] In *Hauer*, the Court held that:

> The right to property is guaranteed in the Community legal order in accordance with the ideas common to the constitutions of the Member States, which are also reflected in the First Protocol to the European Convention for the Protection of Human Rights.[199]

As the Court, from its reading of A1P1, could not decide on the matter at hand, it turned to the constitutional rules and practices of the nine Member States in search of guidance.[200] The Court underlined the Community's ability to restrict the exercise of the right to property in the context of a common organisation of the market and for the purpose of structural policy, while at the same time emphasising the need to examine whether the restrictions introduced by the provisions in dispute in fact corresponded to objectives of general interest pursued by the Community or whether, with regard to the aim pursued, they constituted a disproportionate and intolerable interference with the rights of the owner, impinging upon the very substance of the right to property.[201] In *Wachauf*, the question was whether Wachauf was deprived of the fruits of his labour in violation of the fundamental rights doctrine.[202] In *Von Deetzen v Hauptzollamt Oldenburg*, the CJEU held that the Community order does not include the right to dispose, for profit, of an advantage which does not derive from the assets or occupational activity of the person concerned.[203] None of these

---

[197] Eg, *Stec and others v UK* (n 28) §§ 38–41, 58; *Eskelinen and others v Finland* (n 39) §§ 29–30, *Anheuser-Busch Inc v Portugal* (n 106) §§ 35–36; *Aizpurua Ortiz et Autres c Espagne* (n 58) § 24.

[198] Case 4/73, *J Nold v Commission* [1974] ECR 491.

[199] Case 44/79, *Hauer v Land Rheinland-Pfalz* [1979] ECR 3737, § 17.

[200] Ibid, § 20.

[201] Ibid, § 23. Other cases where this formula have been upheld are Case C-177/90, *Kühn* [1992] ECR I-35, § 16; Case C-22/94, *The Irish Farmers' Association and others* [1997] ECR I-1809, § 27; and Cases C-20/00 and C-64/00 *Booker Aquaculture Ltd v The Scottish Ministers* [2003] ECR I-7411, § 68.

[202] Case C-5/88, *Wachauf v Germany* [1989] ECR 2609, §§ 16, 19.

[203] Case C-44/89, *Von Deetzen v Hauptzollamt Oldenburg* [1991] ECR I-5119, § 27.

cases touched directly upon employment-related rights. The notion of the concept of 'possession' seems, however, to be established along the lines defined by the ECtHR. It has now been clarified that the protection of property within the EU legal order is intended to correspond to the protection provided for in A1P1. In the explanations to the EU Charter of Fundamental Rights, where, as mentioned, the right to property is included in Article 17, it is stated that the scope of the right is the same as that provided for in A1P1.[204]

The CJEU has, throughout its history, used different limitation standards when dealing with human rights. It has developed a special Union standard for limitations deviating from the ECHR formula. The differences have been explained in the following way: 'the grounds for interference with rights are more open-ended than provided for under the ECHR, and the threshold which the Community ... must meet to demonstrate justification for limitations is apparently easier to cross'.[205] In cases dealing with the right to property, the CJEU has sometimes used its own limitation formula (*Wachauf* and *Bosphorous*) and at other times has followed the ECHR (*Hauer*). Through the adoption of the EU Charter of Fundamental Rights, however, it seems that the CJEU will in future be obliged to apply the ECHR limitation standard in relation to Article 17 on the right to property. This is provided for both through Article 52.3 and through the explanations related to Article 17.[206]

EU law could have a more direct effect on the interpretation of A1P1 than other international sources. The influence EU law can have on this interpretation is not, however, derived mainly from the interpretation of the right to property in EU law, but from other sources. The EU principles of direct effect,[207] supremacy,[208] State liability in damages[209] and consistent interpretation[210] imply that conclusion. Primary EU law and regulations are directly applicable in national law and the Member States are obliged to achieve the result envisaged by directives. This includes an obligation to take all appropriate measures, whether general or particular, to ensure the fulfilment of that obligation. The obligation is binding on all authorities, including the courts. EU law can in itself establish enforceable rights, including property rights, for individuals. This starting point was confirmed by the ECtHR in *Danegeville*,[211] a case where the Court concluded that France had violated A1P1 by refusing to grant the applicant the benefit of an EU Directive. The applicable provision in this case was considered to be perfectly clear, precise and directly applicable.[212] EU employment law based on primary law such as Article 45 of the Treaty on the Functioning of the European Union (TFEU) on the free movement of workers and the corresponding obligation to abolish discrimination based

---

[204] Explanations relating to the EU Charter of Fundamental Rights, Article 17, OJ C 303/17, 14 December 2007, p 23.

[205] S Peers, 'Taking Rights Away? Limitations and Derogations' in S Peers and A Ward (eds), *The European Union Charter of Fundamental Rights* (Oxford, Hart Publishing, 2004 143.

[206] Ibid, 157.

[207] Case 26/62, *Van Gend en Loos* [1963] ECR 1; Case 43/75, *Defrenne* [1976] ECR 455.

[208] Case 6/64, *Costa v ENEL* [1964] ECR 585.

[209] Joined Cases C-6/90 and C 9/90, *Francovich* [1991] ECR I-5357.

[210] Case 14/83, *Von Colson* [1984] ECR 1891.

[211] *SA Dangeville v France*, App No 36677/97, Judgment of 16 April 2002.

[212] Ibid, §§ 47–48.

on nationality as regards employment, remuneration and other conditions of work and employment, or Article 157 TFEU on equal pay for equal work, both of which are considered to have both vertical and horizontal direct effect,[213] and at least those directives that establish rights with direct vertical effect could be used as a basis for establishing a possession in the meaning of A1P1. Examples are the rights to a maximum of 48 hours' working time per week in Article 6.2[214] and four weeks' paid vacation in Article 7.1 of Directive 2003/88,[215] the right for fixed-term workers not to be discriminated against in respect of employment conditions[216] and the prohibition of discrimination based on sex in employment (2006/54/EC).[217] The same effect can be derived from the application of non-discrimination on the grounds of age in employment and occupation, as it is considered to be a general principle of EU law in that it constitutes a specific application of the general principle of equal treatment given expression in Directive 2000/78.[218] The wide range of rights connected to employee involvement could perhaps be difficult to characterise as possessions within the meaning of A1P1. Voting rights connected to shares have, for example, not been considered to be possessions within the meaning of A1P1.[219] Using EU law in this way would only affect EU Member States and the other CoE Member States would therefore not risk having something imposed on them that they have not agreed to. A1P1 could accordingly be used as an incentive for the effective implementation of EU employment law, including possessions or legitimate expectations within the meaning of A1P1.

EU law could also be one indicator of an accepted practice among the CoE Member States, influencing the balance test as well. It would, however, not be sufficient to base an argument on EU law if no other legal support can be found either in other international law or in national legal contexts.

9 WILL EU ACCESSION TO THE ECHR STRENGTHEN THE RIGHT TO PROPERTY WITHIN THE EU LEGAL ORDER?

CJEU case law has mainly dealt with property other than that connected to the employment relationship. There are no apparent signs that the CJEU has up to now interpreted the right to property within the EU legal order in a more restricted way than is provided for by A1P1. The protection provided through Article 17 of the EU Charter of Fundamental Rights is intended to correspond to the protection provided through A1P1. Nevertheless, the phrasing of the two articles is not identical, with in some instances Article 17 of the EU Charter being slightly more specific. It seems,

---

[213] Case C-281/98, *Angonese* [2000] ECR I-4139, §§ 33–36; Case 43/75, *Defrenne v Sabena (No 2)* [1976] ECR 455, § 24. See also C Barnard, *EU Employment Law*, 4th edn (Oxford, Oxford University Press, 2012) 157–58 and 297.

[214] Cases C-397/01 and C-403/01, *Bernard Pfeiffer at al v Deutsches Rotes Kreuz, Kreisverband Waldshut eV*, judgment 5 October 2004, § 106.

[215] Case C-282/10, *Dominguez v Centre Ouest Atlantique*, 24 January 2012, §§ 32–36.

[216] Case C-268/06, *Impact v Minister for Agriculture and Food and others*, Judgment of 15 April 2008, § 68.

[217] Case C-152/84, *Marshall* [1986] ECR 723, §§ 46 and 49.

[218] Case C-555/07, *Kücükdeveci v Swedex GmbH & Co KG*, §§ 50–51.

[219] See text to n 46.

however, that these textual differences have no correspondence in the interpretation of the respective courts.[220]

The answer to the question in the heading above is likely to be 'yes'. Even though the obligation to safeguard that its activities do not violate any already-existing rights in the ECHR, EU accession would probably strengthen the incentive to make a proper assessment. The far-reaching concept of possession within the meaning of A1P1 has to be taken into account. An EU measure could violate both national and EU employment-related property rights. Through accession, the EU must be aware of the fact that this aspect can come into play. If, for example, certain employees have been entitled to old-age pension benefits and it turns out that they have been gained in violation of an EU economic freedom, it would not be possible, without the application of the balancing test prescribed by A1P1, to withdraw benefits which the workers have already started to profit from. A withdrawal at a point when someone has already gained a legitimate expectation to continue being paid the particular benefit also has to be scrutinised through the lens of A1P1.[221]

10 CONCLUSION

This overview has revealed that A1P1 has a distinct but limited impact on employment-related situations. Its construction makes it to a great extent dependent on national law. There is, nonetheless, an outer limit for the national legislator or judiciary when dealing with a property right. It is also clear that the difference between strictly private relationships and those that also involve a State-related actor is quite wide. The potential for strictly private actors to enforce employment-related property rights is very limited.

A major challenge when dealing with this right is the general understanding of property rights within working life. This aspect is not really explored by actors pursuing employees' rights. This could be changed. The content of A1P1 is, as are all rights in the ECHR, constantly being developed to take societal change into account.

The dependence on national law when establishing a property right within the meaning of A1P1 highlights its reliance on other social and economic human rights. The right to property can promote the application of other human rights when they have been implemented in national law. EU employment law can by itself establish possessions that the Member State must guarantee. In this way, EU law can widen the number of possessions for the individual. The ECtHR can in turn enforce the application of EU law. As such, the systems of the two institutions can mutually enhance each other.

---

[220] The EU Network of Independent Experts on Fundamental Rights, *Commentary of the Charter of Fundamental Rights of the European Union*, June 2006, p 166 f.
[221] See a similar perspective when analysing national law in Novitz (n 2) 153 ff.

Conclusions

16

The European Convention on Human Rights and the Employment Relation

FILIP DORSSEMONT AND KLAUS LÖRCHER

1 THE APPROACH OF THE EUROPEAN COURT OF HUMAN RIGHTS TOWARDS EMPLOYMENT RELATIONS: INTERNATIONAL, INTER-TEXTUAL AND SOCIAL

FUNDAMENTAL SOCIAL RIGHTS are enshrined in specialised international standards. Given the nature of some of these covenants and charters, they can be qualified as genuine human rights. As an international human rights organisation, the Council of Europe (CoE) is committed to the indivisibility and interdependence of human rights. In times which are extremely hazardous for the effective exercise of human rights, the ECtHR is a beacon of light, providing guidance and orientation for those plying troubled waters. Not only all European legal and judicial institutions but also all bodies and persons bearing political responsibility are bound to abide by the letter and spirit of European Court of Human Rights (ECtHR) case law as a European floor for the protection for human rights.

For more than 50 years, in awareness of the important challenges to the exercise of civil and political rights, the Court has stressed how civil, political and also social rights are intertwined. In certain (sometimes extreme) cases, it has recognised that a number of civil rights also have a social dimension, as it so eloquently stated in *Airey v Ireland*:

> Whilst the Convention sets forth what are essentially civil and political rights, many of them have implications of a social or economic nature. The Court therefore considers, like the Commission, that the mere fact that an interpretation of the Convention may extend into the sphere of social and economic rights should not be a decisive factor against such an interpretation; there is no water-tight division separating that sphere from the field covered by the Convention.[1]

Such an approach is mirrored in a reversed way by a famous Resolution of the 1970 International Labour Conference on 'Trade Union Rights and Their Relation

---

[1] ECtHR, 9 October 1979, *Airey v Ireland*, App No 6289/73, § 26. See also *Sidabras and Dziautas v Lithuania*, ECHR 2004-VIII (2004) 42 EHRR 104, § 33 (quoted by Hendrickx and Van Bever in this book) and the Grand Chamber decision: ECtHR, 6 July 2005, *STEC and others v UK*, App Nos 65731/01 and 65900/01, § 52.

to Civil Liberties' stressing how civil rights are crucial for the effective enjoyment of trade union freedom.[2]

Consistent with such an approach, the Court has developed the important method of referring to international standards when interpreting Convention rights. A wide range of sources and standards exists, enabling the Court to establish the current international state of the art regarding a Convention right.

Combining its intertwined rights approach and its method of taking international standards into account in the Grand Chamber's *Demir and Baykara* judgment, the Court has opened the door to a more social dimension, reversing its previous (very restrictive) jurisprudence by recognising the right to collective bargaining as falling within the ambit of the right to form and join trade unions (Article 11 European Convention on Human Rights (ECHR)). More importantly, it has established a new interpretational methodology of inter-textuality, drawing on all relevant international human and social rights standards—whether from the United Nations (UN), the International Labour Organization (ILO), the CoE (in particular the European Social Charter (ESC)) or even the European Union (EU)—and the case law of the competent supervisory bodies in its interpretation of the ECHR. In sum, the ECHR provisions are no longer interpreted in an isolated manner, but in an inter-textual manner. The Court does not operate in a vacuum. The impact of this new interpretational methodology, embodied in the *Demir and Baykara* judgment, constitutes the momentum leading to this book, a book providing the opportunity to revisit the substance of the ECHR relevant to the employment relationship.

This methodology has been criticised for being too activist. It is similarly criticised for interfering with legal niceties particular to Member States, for transgressing the margin of appreciation accorded to the Contracting Parties, etc.[3] This publication departs from a more favourable assessment of the Court's approach, highlighting how it could enhance the protection and enforcement of human rights.

2 THE EUROPEAN CONVENTION ON HUMAN RIGHTS
WITH REFERENCE TO *LABOUR*, THE *WORKER*
AND THE *EMPLOYER*

The ECHR was not adopted as a charter of social rights, let alone workers' rights. Indeed, with the exception of the Declaration of Philadelphia (1944) and the Community Charter of Fundamental Social Rights of Workers (1989), no international instrument relates solely or primarily to workers' rights. However, the

---

[2] This resolution is available in the Proceedings of the International Labour Conference (81st session 1994), which contains a general report by the ILO Committee of Experts on the Application of Conventions and Recommendations (CEACR) (Report III (Part 4B), ILO, Geneva), to which the ECtHR explicitly referred in its judgment (GC) of 12 September 2011, *Palomo Sánchez and others v Spain*, App No 28955/06, §§ 22 and 23.

[3] See recently the inaugural speech of Professor Janneke Gerards, *Het prisma van de grondrechten* (Nijmegen, Radboud Universiteit, 2011); and M Bossuyt, 'Should the Strasbourg Court Exercise More Self-Restraint? On the Extension of the Jurisdiction of the European Court of Human Rights to Social Security Regulations' (2007) 28(9–12) *Human Rights Law Journal* 321–32.

opposite hypothesis deserves credit as well. The Convention similarly does not refer to a distinct category of civil and political rights, referring instead in a very generic way to human rights and fundamental freedoms. The only international instrument to which it pays tribute is in fact the Universal Declaration of Human Rights (UDHR 1948), which is taken 'into consideration' *in its entirety*, despite the fact that the Contracting Parties only seek to 'to take the first steps for the collective enforcement of *certain* of the rights stated in the Universal Declaration'. The UDHR stands as a classical illustration of the indivisibility of civil and political rights and economic, social and cultural rights. This indivisibility was stressed 'avant la lettre', that is, prior to the well-known bifurcation of this set of indivisible rights into civil and political rights on the one hand, and economic, social and cultural rights on the other hand. For this reason, the recitals of the UDHR make no explicit reference to the idea of indivisibility. In its Preamble, the posterior Charter of Fundamental Rights of the European Union (2007) relates the fundamental rights enshrined in the Charter explicitly to the 'indivisible ... values' upon which the EU has been built.

The ECHR is not mute on either the issue of 'labour' or the existence of workers. It explicitly prohibits forced labour in Article 4. It implicitly refers to workers where it recognises the right of 'everyone' to form and join trade unions for the defence of his interests in Article 11. Last but not least, the ECtHR takes the workplace into account in assessing the legitimacy of restrictions to ECHR rights. The Court indeed considers employees to be in a vulnerable position.[4] This vulnerability implies that a restriction generated by an employer's recruitment or dismissal policy might have a 'chilling effect'[5] on the exercise of the Convention rights. However, States, when confronted with applications lodged against them, have also referred to the existence of an employment relationship to justify restrictions of Convention rights by referring to the duty of loyalty, reserve and discretion. The Court has recognised that these obligations can restrict the freedom of expression at work.[6]

The question arises as to whether Article 4 and the related case law provide guidance on the concept of 'labour' which has to be taken into account for the purposes of this provision. The guidance given is indicated in a negative manner. Article 4 delimits the concept of (forced) labour by indicating what does fall outside its ambit. Certain activities are indeed exempted from the ambit of Article 4, meaning that they cannot be construed as 'forced or compulsory labour'. Since it is very difficult to argue that these activities are in fact undertaken on a purely voluntary basis, let

---

[4] See, in this respect above, ECtHR, 11 January 2006, *Sørensen and Rasmussen v Denmark*, App Nos 52562/99 and 52620/99, § 59.

[5] Though restrictions on the Convention right affecting the employment relationship seem to have such a chilling effect, the latter is identified less often in employment cases. The 'chilling effect' was recognised by the Court in ECtHR, 21 July 2011, *Heinisch v Germany*, App No 28274/08, § 91; and in ECtHR, 12 February 2008, *Guja v Moldavia*, App No 14277/04, § 95. Certain judges have criticised the lack of consideration for the issue of the 'chilling effect' in their dissenting opinions in recent employment cases: ECtHR, 12 September 2011, *Palomo Sánchez and others v Spain*, App Nos 28955/06, 28957/06, 28959/06, 28964/06, 28389/063 and 28961/06; and ECtHR, *Trade Union of the Police in the Slovak Republic and others v Slovakia*, App No 11828/08.

[6] See, inter alia, ECtHR, *Heinisch v Germany* (n 5) § 64; and *Trade Union of the Police in the Slovak Republic and others v Slovakia* (n 5) § 57.

alone that a refusal will not be sanctioned by a threat or penalty, it seems likely that these activities cannot be considered to constitute 'labour' as such. In sum, these exemptions might be helpful in defining what constitutes 'labour' for the purpose of Article 4. These exemptions describe activities outside the sphere of a formal economy tying workers to employers. They tend instead to describe obligations not stemming from an employment relationship, let alone an employment contract. Furthermore, they describe a relationship between a citizen and his community at a municipal or even a national level. In a very recent case, *CN and V v France*, the Court has emphasised that for the determination of 'forced or compulsory labour', the nature and volume of the work as such needs to be taken into account.[7] For this reason, it disqualified the activities of a minor assisting her sister (who was subjected to forced labour) with domestic work after attending school and finishing her homework as forced or compulsory *labour*. The Court considered that these were activities which could reasonably be expected from a member of a family or a person belonging to the household ('au titre de l'entraide familiale ou de la cohabitation'). Thus, the Court seems to identify yet another sphere of 'sociabilitas' falling outside the ambit of Article 4 ECHR.

The notion of a 'worker' seems paramount in delimiting the personal scope of the right to organise. Inevitably, the question arises as to which persons can be construed as workers for the sake of delimiting the scope of the right to form and join trade unions.

It could be argued that it is irrelevant whether a 'trade union' is the result of the generic freedom of association or instead of the more specific right to form and join trade unions. A trade union will always fall within the scope of Article 11 ECHR. This definitional issue was first *explicitly* raised in *Sigurjónsson*.[8] In this case, the question arose as to whether an association (Frami) which taxi drivers needed to join to obtain a government licence could be regarded as a trade union. The Icelandic government did not agree with this characterisation. At issue in this case was whether, based on a statutory provision, Iceland could make granting a licence to drive a taxi dependent on prior membership of Frami. The statutory provision created a *pre-entry closed shop*.[9]

The government assumed that 'trade unions' constituted worker organisations defending the interests of their members in conflicts with their employers. Frami, the organisation in question, consisted primarily of *self-employed* persons working without staff. The Court refused to clarify the definitional scope of the term 'trade union', stating that Frami could in all respects be characterised as an association. It considered 'that it was not necessary to decide whether Frami' could also be regarded as a trade union, 'since the right to form and join trade unions in that provision is an aspect of a wider right to freedom of association rather than a separate right'.[10]

This approach is based, however, on the unproven assumption that the protection conferred by the right to organise lacks specificity. Insofar as the ECtHR attaches certain corollary rights to the right to organise not inherent to freedom of

---

[7] ECtHR, 11 October 2012, *CN and V v France*, App No 67724/09, § 74.
[8] ECtHR, 30 June 1993, *Sigurdur Sigurjónsson v Iceland*, App No 16130/90.
[9] See the contribution by Isabelle Van Hiel.
[10] *Sigurdur Sigurjónsson v Iceland* (n 8) § 32.

association, the importance of the definition remains intact. In the case concerned, the Court only had to deal with the *individual* dimension of the right to organise. In our view, the issue of specific corollary rights is more likely to come into play with regard to cases dealing with the collective dimension of the right to organise. In her contribution, Van Hiel actually disqualifies Frami as being a trade union due to the fact that its members were self-employed. If judged otherwise, the association might claim to have a right to bargain and to have recourse to strike, though this runs counter to a classical conception of competition law as we tend to know it. Whether self-employed workers can actually engage in a process of collective bargaining to defend their economic interests remains a debated issue.[11] In sum, the idea that 'everyone' can form and join a trade union should not be taken in a literal sense.

In a subsequent case, *Sindicatul Pastorul Cel Bun v Romania*,[12] the Court did refer to the right to form and join trade unions. The case dealt with an association which organised priests and employees working for the Romanian Orthodox Church for the defence of their professional interests in the Bishopric of Olthania. The Romanian government and the Bishopric challenged the idea that an employment relationship existed between the priests and their bishop, stating that the relationship was based on a religious vow (*serment*) as opposed to a civil law contract. The Court dismissed this argument, ruling that the relationship between the priests and their bishop, let alone between the ordinary workers and their bishop, could not be separated from the rule of contract law, despite the fact that priests took a 'vow' and that all members were financed by the State as opposed to the bishopric. Hence, the Court seems to be moving towards a broader approach to the concept of what constitutes an employment relationship. The mere fact that the alleged 'employer' is not paying the workers or that the origin of the employment relationship with a candidate-priest, being in a state of prosternation as he is on the verge of priesthood, is shrouded in incense seems to be immaterial.

In our view, it is worthwhile interpreting the notion of trade unions under Article 11 ECHR in a way that is consistent with the personal scope of the right to organise in more specialised international instruments. ILO Convention No 87 (1948) defines workers' and employers' organisations within the meaning of the Convention as 'any organisation of workers or of employers for furthering and defending the interests of workers or of employers'. Employers are unambiguously included within the scope of the right to organise. Article 5 of the Revised European Social Charter (RESC) expressly applies to employers and workers alike. Like the Convention, Article 8 of the International Covenant on Economic, Social and Cultural Rights

---

[11] See in this respect the refusal of the Court of Justice of the European Union (CJEU) to apply the Albany immunity to agreements concluded between an association of farmers and slaughterers to fix a slaughterhouse entry price, despite the fact that Article 12 of the Charter of Nice was invoked. (see CJEU, 21 September 1999, *Albany International BV v Stichting Bedrijfspensioenfonds Textielindustrie*, C-67/96, ECR I-05751). The Court ruled that these agreements did not constitute agreements between organisations representing employers and workers: CJEU, 13 December 2006, *Fédération nationale des syndicats d'exploitants agricoles (FNSEA) and Others v Commission of the European Communities*, T-217/03 and T-245/03.

[12] ECtHR, 31 January 2012, *Sindicatul 'Pastorul Cel Bun' v Romania*, App No 2330/09. This case is currently being dealt with by the Grand Chamber following an appeal by the Romanian government which was accepted by the competent panel.

(ICESCR) does not make clear who holds the right to organise. In this respect, it could be argued that the right to form and join trade unions is also applicable to employers. In other words, the notion of 'trade unions' *sensu lato* could refer both to employer associations and to trade unions *sensu stricto*.

In at least two cases, the Court has considered Article 11 ECHR to be applicable to employers who claimed that they had been put under an illegitimate pressure to join an employers' organisation. In *Gustafsson*[13] and *Kellermann*,[14] the references to the right to organise were *implicitly* applied to employers arguing that their freedom *not* to join an employers' organisation was being curtailed. In our view, Article 14 ECHR (prohibiting discrimination) constitutes a compelling reason to accord the right to organise to employers and workers alike.

It is obvious that works councils are not trade unions. An application from a Turkish national whose membership in an Austrian works council was retracted on the basis that he did not have Austrian nationality was declared manifestly ill-founded. In *Karakurt*,[15] the Court found that works councils were established under Austrian law, and were not private, voluntary associations within the meaning of Article 11 ECHR. The finding in the dicta that the term 'association' must be given autonomous meaning seems to suggest that the terms 'trade union' or 'syndicat' within the meaning of Article 11 must likewise be ascribed autonomous significance.

The mere fact that Article 11 authorises Contracting Parties to impose restrictions on the right of freedom of association on members of the armed forces, the police and the administration of the State does not imply that a generic prohibition of their right to organise and defend their interests through trade union action is in conformity with the ECHR. Nor does this formula justify generic restrictions applicable to the 'civil service' as a whole.[16]

The distinction between the private and public sectors does, however, come to the fore in a different context, that is, in the case law related to the freedom of expression of workers and trade union officials. As a general rule, the fact that a worker is working for a public institution or an enterprise offering a 'service of general interest' raises an argument in favour of the protection of workers' statements relating to the functioning of the institution or the enterprise involved. On the other hand, the mere fact that the functioning of these institutions and enterprises affects the 'public interest' necessitates a more cautious attitude on behalf of a public sector worker who, as a public servant, is supposed to provide evidence of a particular form of discretion and reserve. Though employees in the private sector are not exempted from such an obligation, the Court does suggest that there might be a gradual difference.[17]

---

[13] ECtHR, 25 April 1996, *Gustafsson v Sweden*, App No 15573/89. See L Schut, 'De cao als spin in het web: het recht om geen cao af te sluiten valt niet onder artikel 11 EVRM' (1998) *Nederlands Juristencomité voor de Mensenrechten Bulletin* 18–36.
[14] ECtHR, 1 July 2003, *AB Kurt Kellermann v Sweden*, App No 41579/98.
[15] ECtHR, 14 September 1999, *M Karakurt v Austria*, App No 32441/96.
[16] For in-depth analysis, see the contribution by Dorssemont.
[17] See *Heinisch v Germany* (n 5) § 25. On the obligation of reserve and discretion, see the contribution by Voorhoof and Humblet.

In a recent case, *Trade Union of the Police in the Slovak Republic and others v Slovakia*, the 'trust' of the public in the proper functioning has been qualified as a legitimate criterion for restricting freedom of expression.[18] In our view, public trust can only cease to be blind when whistle-blowers are allowed to express their critical views *in foro externo*. In *Heinisch*, the Court ruled in this respect that:

> While the Court accepts that State-owned companies also have an interest in commercial viability, it nevertheless points out that the protection of public confidence in the quality of the provision of vital public service by State-owned or administered companies is decisive for the functioning and economic good of the entire sector. For this reason the public shareholder itself has an interest in investigating and clarifying alleged deficiencies in this respect within the scope of an open public debate.[19]

In sum, the ECHR does not just envisage an abstract citizen. Two provisions are interwoven with the issue of employment relationships. Furthermore, the Court has provided evidence of a growing awareness of the fact that employment relationships generate restrictions to the exercise of Convention rights which need to be justified, given the circumstances of each case and the particular nature of the enterprise or institution concerned. Though it has recognised that these rights can be restricted due to the circumstances involved, it has never ruled that an employment relationship can justify an overall prohibition of the worker exercising or invoking his Convention rights.

3 SUBSTANTIVE ISSUES: INTER-TEXTUALITY AS A HERMENEUTICAL TOOL FOR JUDGES AND PROFESSORS

Inter-textuality has not just been helpful for the ECtHR; it has also been a very helpful tool for scrutinising ECtHR case law in a critical and constructive manner. In their contributions, the authors of this book have pointed out divergences between the approach of the European Court and that adopted by other judicial or quasi-judicial actors. Furthermore, a transversal analysis of the Court's case law with regard to the exercise of Convention rights at the workplace seems to highlight the situation that the issue of contractual waiving of these rights is treated differently depending upon the rights concerned.[20] In some fields, the contractual waiving of these rights is readily accepted on the basis of the idea that a worker can 'restore' his entitlement to exercise those rights by offering dismissal. In other fields, this idea is criticised *in nuce* by challenging the validity of such a legal act, even if undertaken during the recruitment procedure. Last but not least, it is worthwhile comparing cases related solely to the exercise of one single Convention right in order to assess whether the quality of being a worker exercising a right *at the workplace* will be a potential source of restrictions of one's freedom rather than providing an argument in favour of increased protection.

---

[18] *Trade Union of the Police in the Slovak Republic and others v Slovakia* (n 5) § 65.
[19] See *Heinisch v Germany* (n 5) § 89.
[20] On the issue of waiver, see especially the contribution by De Schutter.

A transversal view of the substantive contributions reveals that the Court has taken a very different stance on the issue of waiving rights granted by the ECHR. In *Sorensen and Rasmussen*, the Court sitting as a Grand Chamber ruled in a seemingly general way that it 'can accept that individuals applying for employment often find themselves in a vulnerable situation and are only too eager to comply with the terms of employment offered'.[21] For this reason, the Court did not consider the contractual waiving of the negative freedom of association to be a relevant or valid legal act which could be taken into consideration. In their joint contribution on the right to privacy, Hendrickx and Van Bever have demonstrated that there are limits to the contractual waiving of privacy rights, despite the importance attached to the concept of 'reasonable privacy expectations' in assessing such restrictions. In her contribution in the field of the freedom to manifest religious convictions, Vickers has criticised the reluctant attitude of the Court to recognise the right to *manifest* his religion or belief at work under Article 9 ECHR. The rather illusory or theoretical option an employee has to offer his dismissal is too often treated as a sufficient safeguard. This restrictive approach was finally overruled in *Eweida and Others v UK*.[22]

In his comparison of ECtHR case law in the field of equality and non-discrimination with the *acquis* of the EU, Bruun states that 'it seems clear that there exists an astonishing discrepancy between the standard applied by the CJEU in comparison with the ECtHR'. He argues that the Court has been much more lenient in the absence of a concept of direct discrimination to justify unequal treatment. He is also very critical of the major burden of proof imposed on applicants, as opposed to EU non-discrimination law, which introduces in a number of fields the idea of a reversal of such a burden. Dorssemont's criticism of the Court's case law in the field of anti-union discrimination, forcing applicants to establish an *intention* of the employer, complements this scepticism.

In the contribution by Voorhoof and Humblet, another kind of transversality prompts highly critical comments on the Court's understanding of the right to freedom of expression at the workplace. They compare the freedom of expression of workers *at work* with that of other citizens exercising these rights *outside* the workplace. As a matter of principle, workers are bound by an obligation of loyalty to their employer, irrespective of their status as private sector employees or that of civil servants or employees in the public sector. According to the Court, such an obligation restricts the right to freedom of expression of workers and trade union officials criticising their employer. The difference to the citizenship–State relationship is overwhelming. A State could never invoke the 'loyalty' (patriotic civicism) of its citizens as a way of restricting their freedoms. In fact, citizenship is intertwined with the entitlement to fundamental rights and freedoms, rather than with restrictions thereto. A number of constitutions even grant citizens a right to resist authorities that unduly restrict or violate their freedoms. In the corporate world, the *Diktat* of loyalty is apparently *not* based upon an employer's respect of freedoms. Whereas

---

[21] ECtHR, 11 January 2006, *Sørensen and Rasmussen v Denmark*, App Nos 52562/99 and 52620/99, § 59. See also the contribution by Van Hiel.
[22] ECtHR, 15 January 2013, *Eweida and Others v UK*, App Nos 48420/10, 59842/10, 51671/10 and 36516/10.

the Court has always considered the free speech of journalists to be essential to the proper functioning of democracy, in *Aguilera Jimenez* the Court unfortunately considered that trade union criticism of the work organisation 'did not fall within the context of any public debate on matters of general interest, but related to issues that specifically concerned company P'.[23] This unfortunate qualification was 'overruled' by the Grand Chamber, ruling that the trade union's criticism did concern 'a matter of general interest'.[24] In this respect, the Court seems to suggest that trade union criticism is nearly as worthy of protection as criticism voiced by journalists which is of *public* interest. In *Palomo Sánchez*, the statements expressed transcended a purely individual or private matter, insofar as they related to a collective labour dispute. In *Szima v Hungary*,[25] the Court limited the scope of what a trade union official can publicly state in his capacity as such to criticism regarding labour-related issues. Criticism of the way the Hungarian police functions both internally and externally was not considered to be 'labour related'. In sum, the Court gives the impression that the freedom of expression accorded to trade union officials is of less significance than that accorded to journalists, and even seems to deny the capacity of trade union officials (contrary to ordinary workers) to engage in whistle-blowing.

This differential treatment disadvantaging trade union officials does not stop there. The bounds of loyalty also preclude statements or opinions considered to be 'grossly insulting or offensive'.[26] The question arises as to whether the division between grossly offensive and merely offensive is easy to draw. Furthermore, as indicated in the dissenting opinion in *Palomo Sánchez*, the Court 'gives the curious impression of placing trade union freedom of expression at a lower level than that of artistic freedom and of treating it more restrictively'.[27] In sum, trade union officials do not seem to enjoy the margin of manoeuvre afforded to citizens having recourse to artistic or indeed satirical statements or opinions found in cartoons and caricatures.[28]

In the contribution relating to freedom of religion, Vickers assesses the extent to which the Court's approach in dealing with conflicts between this freedom and other Convention rights deviates from the non-discrimination approach set forth in EU Directive 2000/78 (equal treatment in employment and occupation). Whereas the ECtHR had to assess the collective rights stemming from the freedom of religion to the benefit of the churches and ecclesiastical organisations, the EU Directive adopts a more individualistic stance on the issue, focusing on the individual who argues that he is being discriminated against on the basis of his religion or belief. In the absence of cases brought before the CJEU, it is still hazardous to assess whether the CJEU will deviate in practice from the seemingly more collectivistic stance of the Strasbourg Court. It is even more difficult to assess which of the two approaches can be considered as the most activist. Indeed, the conflict at stake is inherent to

---

[23] See ECtHR, 8 December 2009, *Aguilera Jiménez and others v Spain*, App Nos 28389/06, 28955/06, 28957/06, 28959/06, 28961/06 and 28964/06, § 32.
[24] See *Palomo Sánchez and others v Spain* (n 2) § 72.
[25] ECtHR, 9 October 2012, *Szima v Hungary*, App No 29723/11, § 31.
[26] *Palomo Sánchez and others v Spain* (n 2) § 76.
[27] See the dissenting opinion in ibid.
[28] See also the critique given by Voorhoof and Humblet.

the structure of freedom of religion, a fountain of individual and collective rights. A similar question might arise when assessing ECtHR case law in the field of Article 11 ECHR. As highlighted in the contributions by Van Hiel and De Schutter, the Court has historically had to deal with requests from applicants invoking their negative freedom of association. At the same time, it has also been very reluctant to develop the collective dimension of the right to organise and to recognise rights of trade unions or rights which trade union members could exercise collectively. Since other complaint procedures involving supervisory bodies more specialised in the field of social rights are only accessible to employers and workers' organisations, it is only natural that the Court has become a haven for the individual complaints of people not wishing to become a member of a trade union at all or wishing to belong to a different trade union. Hence, the impression could emerge of a court not very sympathetic or at least empathetic towards trade unions. According to De Schutter, the Court in recent years has somewhat distanced itself from its individualistic stance by ensuring 'that unions can defend the interests of workers by collective bargaining'. The author concluded that in this way 'the "individualist" excursion that started in the early 1990s was closed in 2002 with *Wilson and others* and in 2008 with *Demir and Baykara*'. Van Hiel also stresses that the judgments strengthening trade union rights were pronounced after fierce doctrinal criticism on the rather individualistic and 'negative' approach of the Court towards the right to organise. In line with De Schutter, the author explains that this evolution occurred in an era characterised by a decline in trade union membership. She criticises the assumption underlying the need to protect workers against closed-shop systems (viz against trade unions), stating that it is equivalent to a need to protect the citizen against the State. The implicit analogy between the State and trade unions came once more to the forefront in the *Viking* and *Laval* judgments, with the CJEU putting trade unions on a par with public authorities in deeming them to be actors potentially restricting 'fundamental economic freedoms' through the exercise of their legal autonomy.

Another way to assess the Court's intervention shift from individualistic to collectivist is to compare protection of the right to organise with that of the right *not* to organise. Though both aspects affect the individual dimension of the freedom of association, it is clear that increased protection of the positive freedom of association compared to the negative freedom could be described as favourable to trade unions. In the past, this assumption has been argued on the basis that, whereas the Court protects the positive freedom of associations against sticks (*Danilenkov*) and carrots (*Wilson and Palmer*), it has always demanded that any restriction of the negative freedom of association was operated under the threat of loss of livelihood.[29] The compulsion needed to be operated through the menace of social hardship. Van Hiel's analysis of the *Olafsson v Iceland* case calls for a more mitigated vision. The author rightly points out how the Court construed this case as being very near to the issue of negative freedom of association. In this case, non-affiliated employers were obliged *ex lege* to contribute to the employers' association. Van Hiel points out that 'the amounts were relatively modest and the degree of compulsion to which

---

[29] See F Dorssemont, 'The Right to Form and to Join Trade Unions for the Protection of His Interests under Article 11 ECHR' (2010) 1(2) *European Labour Law Journal* 200–01.

the applicant was subjected could be regarded as significantly less serious than in other cases, where an applicant's refusal to join a union resulted in the loss of his employment or professional licence and as a consequence his means of livelihood'. In sum, though the Court has not yet formally shielded restrictions to the negative freedom of association from financial *incentives* to associate, it has narrowed the gap between the differentiated protection of both positive and negative protection.

In his contribution, Van Drooghenbroeck provides further illustration of the cautious approach the Court adopts to the conflict between individualism versus collectivism. He analyses the so-called 'labourisation of fair trial standards'. The Court does not consider the institution of a collegiate judicature based upon a designation by trade unions of lay judges to be incompatible *in se et per se* with Article 6 ECHR. The Court does not oppose the institutionalisation of the role of trade unions, though it does insist on essential safeguards to uphold fair trial standards.

The divide between individualism and collectivism should not be over-estimated from a procedural point of view. In his contribution, Hendy shows how the Court in some cases has allowed requests to be submitted from individual and collective applicants alike. In *Wilson and Palmer*, where employer practices restricted the individual right of employees to be represented by a trade union and hence the right of the trade union to be heard, according to the author, 'the infringement of an ECHR right impinged directly on the trade union'. The mere fact that in certain cases both individual and collective applicants could submit a request might be a means to overcome the admissibility restriction of Article 35 ECHR, which precludes the admissibility of an application that is 'substantially the same as a matter that has already been submitted to another procedure of international investigation or settlement and contains no relevant new information'. Hendy argues that this obstacle does not preclude preparing the ground for the Strasbourg application through such a procedure of international investigation or settlement. However, solely collective actors should come into play first. The subsequent application solely operated by one or more individual workers could then be distinguished from this collective complaint. A recent judgment of the Court validates another litigation strategy. In *Eğitim Ve Bilim Emekçileri Sendikasi v Turkey*,[30] the Court did not declare an application of a trade union affiliated to a confederation inadmissible, despite the fact that the confederation had previously submitted a substantially identical complaint to the ILO Freedom of Association Committee.

4 PROCEDURAL AND INSTITUTIONAL ISSUES AND CHALLENGES

In addition to all of the substantive issues, the Court faces important procedural and institutional challenges. They can be characterised by two major developments. The first is the EU's accession to the ECHR, which is described in greater detail in Lawson's contribution. This cumbersome and politically difficult negotiation and ratification process—which is still far from achieving its final result—will in the end clarify and enhance the legal status of the ECHR and open up new procedural

---

[30] ECtHR, 25 September 2012, *E itim Ve Bilim Emekçileri Sendikasi v Turkey*, App No 20641/05.

opportunities for citizens under the jurisdiction of EU Member States to challenge EU law directly before the ECtHR.

The second development aims at empowering the Court to cope with the first and probably most acute problem arising inter alia from its own success: the number of applications. Though the 'Brighton Declaration' has concluded to a certain extent the political discussions on the necessary 'Reform of the Court', the practical results remain to be seen.[31] However, the Court is already working on building up its own 'infrastructure', allowing it to deal more effectively with the enormous workload. The well-known backlog of cases is particularly severe in respect of cases assigned to category IV of the Court's own priority policy, ie, the so-called 'non-repetitive and non-priority cases'.[32] However, most of the cases assigned to this category are directly or indirectly linked to issues of social law, in particular all cases dealing with the freedom of association guaranteed under Article 11 ECHR. For the effective exercise of these rights, it is of the utmost importance that these cases do not have to wait years before a final decision is taken, but instead can be decided upon within a 'reasonable time'. One further solution could and probably should be to assign the most important social rights cases to category II, ie, applications raising an important question of general interest (in particular, a serious question capable of having major implications for domestic legal systems or the European system). This would allow the Court to better cope with its own *Demir and Baykara* approach.

In respect of taking into account international standards and their relevant case law, one element could be enhanced dialogue with the supervisory bodies responsible for interpreting and applying the relevant international standards, in particular the European Committee of Social Rights, as well as the ILO CEACR or the UN Committee on Economic, Social and Cultural Rights (CESCR).

5 THE WAY AHEAD

This book wishes to contribute to the debate on human rights approaches in the social field. It aims not only to enrich the academic and jurisdictional discussions, but also addresses trade union legal practitioners who are seeing themselves increasingly confronted with social (human) rights issues.

This publication can help in integrating and indeed strengthening the ECHR dimension in any trade union litigation strategy (at both the national and the European level). Building on arguments derived from the ECHR at the national level will already force the domestic judiciary to take account of and deal with those ECHR provisions which are essentially or nearly exclusively labour related. In this respect, Articles 4 and 11 ECHR are at the heart of forced labour and freedom of association cases. However, this book clearly demonstrates that many other Convention rights can be relevant to labour-related cases.

---

[31] See the contribution by Lörcher.

[32] For the Court's case priority policy and its seven categories (the first three of which are urgent, important (see below in the text) and cases relating to Articles 2–5(1) ECHR), see the contribution by Lörcher.

The exhaustion of domestic remedies and all further steps to be taken to get through the 'admissibility' door for the access to the ECtHR are described in detail by Hendy in his contribution. The experience on which this part of the book is based will be helpful for all trade union and other lawyers engaged in social policy cases in integrating this human rights dimension into their litigation strategies.

This is crucial in an era of seemingly permanent economic crisis, in which the resultant cutbacks in the level of social protection may conflict with Convention requirements on, eg, freedom of association (for deregulating collective bargaining), private life (for termination of employment issues)[33] and property protection (for pensions). Since this is not (yet) the focus of the present publication, the next Transnational Trade Union Rights (TTUR) book will deal with these specific issues in more detail.

However, the approach advocated here transcends the realm of litigation, being beneficial for the system of human rights protection in general. In particular, the different international systems of (social) human rights protection are increasingly under pressure from employers and even from certain governments. Each of the systems (whether UN, ILO or CoE) is worth protecting, and indeed needs to be protected, in order to allow the Court to continue developing its international approach. Trade unions at different levels play an important role in this protection. This publication offers an opportunity to better understand the interaction between the various human rights protection systems.

As such, the publication targets all persons interested in social human rights and in helping to give the ECHR a genuine social dimension.

---

[33] Although not related to the consequences of the crisis, the important judgment in ECtHR (Former Fifth Section), 9 January 2013, *Oleksandr Volkov v Ukraine*, App No 21722/11 recognises in general that termination of employment issues fall within the ambit of Article 8 ECHR (see in particular § 165).

Index

Introductory Note

References such as '178–9' indicate (not necessarily continuous) discussion of a topic across a range of pages. Because the entire work is about the 'European Convention on Human Rights' and the 'employment relation', the use of these terms (and certain others which occur constantly throughout the book) as entry points has been minimised. Information will be found under the corresponding detailed topics.